4c	4d	4e	4f	4g	
Common Words	Superlatives	Present Tense	Triteness	Voice	
4r	4s	4t	4u	4v	
Capitalizing	Abbreviating	Titles	Figures	Miscellaneous Rules	
4j	4k	4l	4m	4n	4q
Identify Persons	Authority Needed	Authority Techniques	Rambling Story	Preparing Copy	What to Quote
5b	5c	5d	5e	5f	5g
Responsibility	Truth and Accuracy	Impartiality	Fairplay	Libel	Invasion of Privacy
					13a
					Newscasts, Preparing Copy
6c	6d		6f	7a	7b
Playing Up a W	Crowding Lead		Interpreting W's	Several Feature Summary	Salient Feature
7e	7f	7g	8a	8b	8c
Interpret. Lead	Identifying Features	Summarizing Features	Variety in Rhetoric	Timeliness	Local Angle (Proximity)
11a	11b	11c	11d		
Rewrites, No Additions	Rewrites, Additions	Follow-ups	Developing Story		
9a	9b	9c	9d	9e	9f
Logical Order	Single Feature Development	Several Feature Development	Lead Feature Abandoned	Summarize Minor Features	Summary Development
9i	9j	9k	9l	9m	9n
Multiple Casualty Story	Chronological Order	Direct Quotations	Transitional Devices	Repetitious Phrases	Block Paragraphs
10b	10c		11a	11b	11c
Human Interest Story	Surprise Climax Story		Rewrites, No Additions	Rewrites, Additions	Follow-ups
12a	12b	12c	13b	13c	13d
Picture with Story	Feature Pictures with Story	Picture, No Story	Newscast Sentences	Newscast Language	Newscast Devices
15c	15d	15e	16a	16b	16c
Eliminate Puffs	Writing Brevities	Better Story Overlooked	Describe Speaker	Describe Audience	Emphasize Speech
16f	16g	16h	16i	16j	16k
Quote Summary-Quote Form	Authority Omitted	Reporting Publications	Personal Interviews	Planning Questions	Describe Interviewee
17c	17d	17e			
Meeting Reports	Convention Features	Special Occasion Features			

Fundamentals of News Gathering, Writing and Editing

Complete with Exercises

Julian Harriss, Kelly Leiter and Stanley Johnson
The University of Tennessee

THE
COMPLETE
REPORTER

FOURTH EDITION

MACMILLAN PUBLISHING CO., INC.
New York

COLLIER MACMILLAN PUBLISHERS
London

Macmillan Publishing Co., Inc.
866 Third Avenue, New York, New York 10022

Collier Macmillan Canada, Ltd.

Library of Congress Cataloging in Publication Data

Harriss, Julian.
   The complete reporter.

   Bibliography: p.
   Includes index.
   1. Reporters and reporting.   2. Journalism—
Handbooks, manuals, etc.   I. Leiter, Kelly, joint
author.   II. Johnson, Stanley P., 1892–1946,
joint author.   III. Title.
PN478.H34   1981   070   80-17714
ISBN 0-02-350600-8

PN478
H34
1981

Printing: 1 2 3 4 5 6 7 8   Year: 1 2 3 4 5 6 7 8

Dedicated to

WILLIS CARLETON TUCKER

"And gladly wolde he lerne,
and gladly teche."

The first Director of the
University of Tennessee School of Journalism.

Good friend and respected colleague of the authors.

This fourth edition of *The Complete Reporter* does not depart radically from the concept and organization of the first three editions, yet there is much that is new about it. A number of chapters have been revised extensively and expanded to reflect the sweeping legal and technological changes in American journalism. Others have been updated to keep pace with new approaches to the news that have been introduced since the last edition. All chapters have been rewritten in part, and there has been considerable editing to improve them. Chapters heavily rewritten and expanded are those dealing with law and ethics and family and lifestyles. Many new examples and illustrations have been introduced to help the student visualize the principles discussed. Exercises in all chapters are new and are the practical type stories reporters have to write for both daily and weekly newspapers.

Although exercises with each chapter have been revised, they still are carefully designed to give the student an opportunity to write stories that relate directly to the material presented in the text. The range of the exercises is broad, and many of them can be used as features or human-interest stories as well as straight news stories. In keeping with the practice established in earlier editions, the exercises are written in telegraphic English, not unlike the notes a reporter would take. This has been done specifically to give the student practice in composing complete sentences from brief notes. The exercises also include libel, unethical statements and trivia to help the instructor make the point that careful reporters do not use such material. Many of the exercises are designed to force the student to use extra thought and effort in writing interpretative stories.

In preparing this edition, we have incorporated many of the suggestions given by teachers who have used the textbook. However, we have retained the many features that have served teachers so well over the first three editions. Those features and the broad scope of *The Complete Reporter* make it ideally suited as a text for institutions offering only one year of journalism or as the beginning text for an institution offering more than one year.

J. H.
K. L.

Disclaimer

The authors want to stipulate at the outset that the use of the masculine gender in referring to both men and women should not be regarded as evidence of sexism on their part.

The use of masculine nouns and pronouns simply makes the writing less awkward. And it is in keeping with the accepted practice of most newspapers at the time this edition was prepared.

PART I
Becoming Acquainted
with Reporting

1. Journalism As a Career   3

Reporting, Doorway to Many Vocations   5
Qualifications of a Reporter   7
A Craft or a Profession?   8
Exercises   12

2. The Reporter in the Newspaper Organization   13

Details of Organization   14
The Morgue   19
New Channels   20
Sources and Beats   21
The Story Process   22
Exercises   24

3. What Is News?   26

News Values   29
Summary: Nature of News and News Value   33
Measuring the Importance of News   34
Story Types   35
News Sources   37
Sample News Analysis   38
Exercises   38

4. Writing in the News Style   42

Newspaper English   43
The Stylebook   48
Preparing Copy   49
Spelling   49
Punctuating   50
Capitalizing   53
Abbreviating   54
Titles   55
Figures   56
Miscellaneous   57
Correcting Copy   57
Exercises   58

5. Ethics and Libel   62

The Pitfalls of Libel   67
Invasion of the Right of Privacy   75

CONTENTS

Other Legal Aspects of Journalism   78
Exercises   81

PART II
Writing the News Lead

6. The Simple (Single-Incident) News Lead   87

The Five W's   89
Playing Up a W   89
Complete Reporting   92
Testing the Lead   93
Exercises   93

7. The Complex (Several-Incident) News Lead   102

The Summary Lead   103
Emphasizing an Outstanding Feature   103
Other Leads   106
Identifying the Features   109
Combining Stories   111
Exercises   112

8. Devices to Polish the Lead   117

Rhetoric   118
Emphasizing News Values   119
Novelty Leads   120
Complete Reporting   124
Exercises   124

PART III
Writing the Complete Story

9. The Body of the Story   135

Developing the Single-Feature Lead   136
Developing the Several-Feature Lead   137
The Chronological Order   144
Direct Quotations   147
Transitional Devices   147
Block Paragraphs   148
Adequacy Versus Trivia   148
Exercises   149

10. Features and Human-Interest Stories   158

    Writing Feature Articles   161
    Writing Human-Interest Stories   163
    Exercises   167

11. Rewrites and Follow-Ups   171

    Rewrites   171
    Follow-Ups   173
    Exercises   176

12. Pictures   179

    Writing Cutlines   181
    Exercises   186

13. News for Radio and Television   189

    Similarities of the Media   189
    Differences in Writing Newscasts   191
    Special Devices in Newscasts   194
    The Extra Job of Television Writers   195
    Exercises   197

14. Policy in the News   204

    Devices to Promote Policies   205
    "Slanting" the Policy Story   207
    Justification of Policies in New Stories   208
    Complete Reporting   210
    Exercises   211

PART IV
Writing the General Story Types

15. Personals and Briefs   215

    Personals   216
    Briefs   218
    Fillers   219
    Exercises   220

16. Speeches, Publications, Interviews   222

    Speeches   222
    The Speech Story Lead   224

The Body of the Speech Story   225
Publications   227
Personal Interviews   228
Exercises   230

17. Meetings and Special Events   235

Types of Meeting Stories   236
Conventions   238
Special Events   240
Exercises   240

PART V
Writing the Simple
Story Types

18. Illnesses, Deaths, Funerals   245

Illnesses   246
Deaths   248
Funerals   252
Exercises   253

19. Fires and Accidents   256

Facts and Sources   257
Complete Reporting   259
Exercises   260

20. Seasons and Weather   264

Weather Stories   266
Exercises   268

21. Crime   274

Crimes   275
Suicides   280
Exercises   281

PART VI
Writing the Complex Story Types

22. Courts, Trials, Lawsuits   289

    The Law and the Courts   293
    Route of a Criminal Case   294
    Route of a Civil Case   297
    Exercises   299

23. Government and Politics   306

    Forms of Government   308
    Specific News Materials   311
    Elections   317
    Exercises   321

24. Business, Industry, Agriculture, Labor   326

    Interpreting the News   330
    The Reporter's Background   331
    Complete Reporting   333
    Exercises   333

25. Education, Research, Science   340

    Covering Education   341
    Covering Research, Science   343
    Exercises   346

26. Religion, Philanthropy, Promotion   353

    Religion   353
    Philanthropy   357
    Exercises   359

PART VII
Writing the Special Story Types

27. Family, Living, Lifestyle Sections   367

    Problems of Social News Sections   371
    Engagements and Weddings   372

Miscellaneous Stories   375
Consumer News   377
Exercises   385

28. Sports   388

Sports Story Leads   392
The Body of the Story   397
Exercises   397

29. Entertainment, Literature, Fine Arts, Criticism   400

Subjects for Criticism   403
Exercises   407

30. Editorials and Columns   409

Editorials   411
Columns   415
Exercises   416

PART VIII
Editing the News

31. Rewriting Faulty Stories   421

Serious Errors   421
Exercises   422

32. Copy Editing   426

Copy Editor's Duties   427
Copyreading Symbols   428
Exercises   434

33. Proofreading   438

Using Proofreader's Symbols   438
Exercises   439

34. Headlines   444

Trends in Headlines   445
Selecting the Headline   450
Principles of Headline Writing   451
Exercises   456

35. Makeup 457

Types of Front-Page Makeup 467
Types of Inside-Page Makeup 469
Exercises 472
General Exercises in Headlining and Makeup 476
Headline Schedule 477
Exercises 480

Appendix: Journalistic Terms 482

Selected Bibliography 488

Index 493

THE COMPLETE REPORTER

BECOMING ACQUAINTED WITH REPORTING

Journalists today are faced with a greater challenge than at any other time in the history of American newspapers. Society is changing dramatically, and a technological explosion has revolutionized the way newspapers are produced. Both are certain to continue, and the successful journalist cannot afford to ignore them. He must continue to broaden his knowledge of society daily, sharpen his ability as a writer and hone his skills to use the constantly changing, sophisticated equipment to produce a newspaper that will meet the needs and demands of the reader.

No longer can a journalist think he has done his job by simply telling the reader "here's what happened." He must also say "here's what it means" and "here's what you can do about it." There is far more to journalism today than learning how to write a basic news story—far more. Nevertheless, it is essential that the reporter first develop a thorough knowledge of the fundamentals of the complete newspaper operation before attempting to gather, write and edit the news. First he must learn the characteristics of journalism as practiced today and be flexible enough to change as the profession and society change. He also should understand the newspaper as an organization and its special role in society. The press is the only private business singled out in the First Amendment. This is both a blessing and a burden, and every journalist should be aware of the unspoken responsibility thrust upon him as a result of the First Amendment.

To attempt news writing without some understanding and appreciation of these basic elements would be as hopeless as trying to write without an ability to use the English language with care and precision.

A FASCINATING QUESTION

"What is news?" is a fascinating question that requires close consideration before any effort is made to write news. It should be established quickly that no wholly satisfactory definition has been found. But that should not discourage the reporter. Like any other professional, a reporter should ground himself in theory to acquire a sense of direction and a facility in handling his subject matter. To attempt to write news with no conception of what news is would be a foolhardy venture.

DEVELOPING NEWS STYLE

News style also must be studied before the reporter attempts to write for the mass media. It differs from other forms of writing in that it involves particular technical problems that require careful study and analysis. To develop a news style to perfection, a reporter must first understand what it is and then practice it.

RESPONSIBILITIES AND RESTRICTIONS

When a reporter sits down to write, he should be influenced by a sense of responsibility to tell his story as accurately, clearly and fairly as possible. But he may be influenced by a number of restrictions. Some of these may be personal, based on his particular knowledge of the details of the story. Others may be placed on him as a result of a particular newspaper policy (there are cases in which publishers have banned from their pages the names of certain political leaders, for example). However, most of the restrictions come under the voluntary classification, recognized in journalism as codes of ethics (see Chapter 5) observed for the welfare of both the press and society. Still other restrictions are imposed by law, and while they are somewhat limited, violation of these may cost a reporter a fine or a term in prison. Observing journalistic ethics and laws is essential to good and responsible reporting.

Journalism As a Career

Philip Graham, the late editor of the Washington Post, once described news as "the first rough draft of history." It certainly is that and more. And the job of gathering and writing that "rough draft" can be exciting, demanding and rewarding for the journalist.

At times, a journalist's life is not unlike the romantic illusion of the hardworking, high-living reporters found in novels, films and popular television series. Reporters with national reputations such as Seymour Hersh, Jack Anderson, Bob Woodward, Carl Bernstein, Tom Wicker, Helen Thomas and a host of others have become media stars. Their presence at a news event can, and sometimes does, distort the real value of the event for the reader. They often become the subjects of news stories and feature articles themselves. No doubt stories reporting Anderson's six-figure annual income from his syndicated column, books and television appearances or Woodward's living in a $250,000 home and commanding a $200,000 advance for an unwritten book, have had some influence on the rush of young men and women seeking careers in the media. Many obviously dream of fame and glory, and the fortune that can come with the power of a journalist to motivate public opinion, help shape foreign and domestic policy and even topple a president from office.

At no time in our history has the impact of the news media on public life been greater. Reliable studies indicate that the public gets most of its information either directly or indirectly from the mass media. And it is equally true that the significance of the reporter as a force in public life has never been greater. But there is far more hard work than glamour and glory involved in being a journalist. Even those who gain some measure of fame and fortune do so with hard work. There is no escaping it—the journalist's work often will be so routine and exacting that it can be boring. But it is this very routine, boring—and extremely vital—groundwork that does lead to the interesting, perhaps exciting, news breaks that just might turn the journalist into a public personality.

The truth of the matter is, however, that the American journalist writes more stories about city council meetings than he does about glamorous film and television stars. He spends more time reporting activities of the police, the fire department and local schools than he does writing about sensational scandals in high office. And, if he does his work with care and accuracy, he is performing a far more vital function for his community on a day-to-day basis than the journalist who spends his hours interviewing vapid movie queens or who devotes his life to muckraking. For, in a democracy, information is vital. And in the information explosion that has marked the last half of the twentieth century, the journalist has a greater influence and responsibility than he has ever had before. He is the one who must not only report this information but also analyze and interpret it for the public. It is through the journalist—and mass media—that most Americans gain most of the information that has an impact on their daily lives. This makes the journalist a vital cog in the democratic system.

A Writer on Current Events. A journalist is a writer who deals chiefly in current events. As contrasted with other types of writers who may employ imagination in their quest for reader appeal, the reporter must deal with facts. He records and sometimes analyzes or interprets what has happened or will happen, and under certain circumstances he is permitted to give his own opinions on the events he reports. The journalist may have vitality and drive, but if he does not have a passion for facts and an ability to write well he probably will not succeed. The two distinctive functions of a journalist are gathering facts—more information than he could possibly use—and composing stories which present this information accurately and interestingly.

The term *journalist* as used above is interchangeable with *newspaper reporter,* for reporting the news is fundamental to virtually all journalistic occupations. While television has challenged newspapers as a principal channel through which news is widely diseeminated (and studies show that the public turns to it for national and international news), newspapers still are the major source of *local* news for most persons. With few exceptions, most television stations provide little more than a headline summary of local news. This is particularly true in the non-metropolitan areas. The typewritten script of most television news shows would fill less than three-fourths of a single page of a standard-sized newspaper. And, despite the rapid increasing technology in the field of electronic communications, data banks and other information storage systems, newspapers remain the chief permanent record of current events. This does not imply, however, that careers in journalism are largely limited to reporting and editing. Many journalism-school graduates find successful and fulfilling careers in newspaper design and production as well as various business functions in the advertising and circulation departments of newspapers. Other communications media offer as many or more journalistic opportunities. But, historically, newspaper reporting is the grandfather of all modern journalistic careers.

REPORTING, DOORWAY TO MANY VOCATIONS

The beginning reporter may launch his career with the reassuring knowledge that opportunities in many different vocations will be open to him in the future. A hurried check of the backgrounds of public persons—living and dead—will produce an impressive list of former newspaper reporters or journalists who became mayors, governors, representatives and senators, ambassadors, actors, corportation presidents, college professors, even a president and a president's wife. Newspaper reporting offers a variety of experiences, particularly in the practice of meeting the public, interviewing and writing, which will equip a person for success in journalistic offshoots as well as nonjournalistic professions.

Intangible Benefits. The common reward of all newspaper men and women is being where the action is. The reporter has a front seat at most public events. He is an ex-officio member of public organizations and committees. Even the beginning reporter carries with him the influence of his newspaper, and doors are opened to him that often are not opened to persons in other professions. The reporter observes events in the making. He is on the "inside" of things in general. The motives, ambitions, cross-currents and cross-purposes of society at large are the plots of his narratives. For a beginner it can be a heady ego trip.

But exposure to the reality of a reporter's life usually ripens his character as perhaps no other schooling can. The true reporter acquires both perspective and insight. He acquires breadth of vision and at the same time a scrupulous regard for detailed fact. His critical faculties are sharpened and his sense of moral values is tempered by daily exercise in judging men and evaluating events. He develops a deep respect for his own personal and professional integrity.

At the same time, the perils and pitfalls of the intangibles should be equally plain to those seeking a career in journalism. The film and novel stereotype of the reporter who takes periodic breaks from his wining and wenching to turn the scoundrels out of office and rescue fair maidens in distress is more fiction than fact. To be sure, some journalists lack manners and morals. Some journalists abuse their rights and privileges. There often will be temptations thrown in the paths of journalists. But a reporter, like any other professional with a job to do, must develop his own code of conduct and personal integrity in keeping with the responsible position he holds in the community.

Opportunities on Newspapers. The future of most reporters is limited only by their talent and their ambition. A talented, self-disciplined, ambitious reporter can become a "big-name" newswriter whose by-line is readily recognized and respected. Or he may become a columnist or commentator who analyzes current events. Newswriting opportunities are available at individual newspapers or with the wire services (the Associated Press or United Press International), syndicated newspaper services and a variety of other organizations dealing in news, including the news magazines.

Another newspaper career open to the reporter is the field of editing. In general, editors supervise the newsgathering activities of reporters, review and copyread their stories, write headlines and arrange placement of stories and pictures in the newspaper. These responsibilities generally do not include gathering and writing news, but some newspapermen who carry the title of editor may have fewer or more duties than those listed under the editing functions. The science editor, sports editor, education editor and other such staff members are generally by-line reporters who specialize in one area of journalism, but some of these editors may also edit copy and write headlines. The editor of a small daily or weekly newspaper usually combines newswriting and editing (and sometimes business management as well). The principal editor (editor-in-chief) of a metropolitan daily commonly limits his duties to writing editorials and general supervision of the entire staff as well as the making of policy decisions.

The editor is sometimes (but not necessarily) the owner or part owner of the newspaper, and as such he is the publisher—another newspaper opportunity open to reporters. The publisher is the chief officer of the newspaper, responsible for its entire operation—editorial, business and mechanical. To be successful as a publisher, one obviously needs management ability in addition to a knowledge of printing processes, and a capital investment to purchase or lease either an existing newspaper or the plant and equipment needed to start one. Ayer's Directory of Publications and the Editor and Publisher Yearbook list more than 10,000 weekly, semiweekly, small and medium-sized dailies and large metropolitan daily newspapers in the United States. Publications serving the newspaper industry frequently have a number of smaller newspapers listed in the "For Sale" columns. Often they may be bought on the installment plan with a reasonable down payment and the balance in periodic payments.

Opportunities in Other Fields. Although the editorial departments of newspapers do not advertise their employment opportunities as training grounds for other vocations, the truth is that some reporters leave after several years of experience to take positions both related and unrelated to newspaper work. Reporting is an invaluable introduction to life at many points. In orienting the young man or woman to the opportunities afforded by the community, it has no equal. The reporter can cultivate contacts and friendships that may enable him to find any type of position that interests him—and the skills that he has developed in gathering facts, interviewing and writing will increase his chances of success. The worlds of commerce and public service are well populated with men and women who got their start on newspapers.

But by far most of the reporters leaving newspaper work find employment in related journalistic areas—press associations, general circulation magazines, trade journals and industrial publications, radio and television stations, publicity and public relations agencies and other publications of business firms, industries, institutions and associations. Advertising is another large field that frequently absorbs individuals with newspaper experience, for journalistic techniques are applied in its various communications efforts.

Finally, the newspaper is a splendid training ground for creative writers. Many successful authors and playwrights of yesterday and today acquired their basic training as newspaper writers. The list is long but a few excellent examples are Ernest Hemingway, Ben Hecht, Charles MacArthur, and more recently Bruce Catton, Tom Wicker, David Halberstam, Tom Wolfe and Gay Talese. The varied experience and constant practice in the careful and precise use of the English language are an excellent basis for literary achievement.

QUALIFICATIONS OF A REPORTER

What makes a good reporter? There probably are as many answers to that as there are reporters, for few agree completely on what makes a good reporter. However, most do acknowledge that, while some persons are better fitted than others to become reporters, it is not true that reporters are born and not made. Given reasonable intelligence, most of the attributes of a successful reporter are acquired, not inherited. Perhaps the best qualifications for a reporter—aside from desire and ability to write for print—are insatiable curiosity (which surely will express itself in part through a strong habit of reading), a flexible and sociable personality, a nature that relishes a variety of experiences, a temperament to work under the pressure of deadlines and a tolerance permitting objective observations of people and events. A successful reporter also needs ambition, drive, determination and, most certainly, self-discipline.

Attributes Desired for Success in Reporting. One who does not have a strong love for and a broad knowledge of the English language is foolhardy to consider a career as a reporter. A desire to express himself in words—an urge to put words on paper—must be part of a reporter's nature. But beyond that desire, the successful reporter must do more than just learn the fundamentals of English composition; he must have mastered them. Without an aggressively inquiring mind the reporter is of little benefit to his newspaper, and his own work would lack any real luster. Unless he is outgoing, the reporter can scarcely enjoy or profit by the numerous personal contacts he must make daily with his news sources and others. While much of the reporter's work is rather routine, it is essential that he never fall into the trap of treating it routinely. Every word a reporter puts on paper should be the best possible one that he can come up with. Fortunately, most of the routine a reporter faces is part of a daily kaleidoscope of events, and his assignment may change rapidly from the commonplace to the exciting. Alertness and quickness of mind are required for a reporter to move smoothly from one assignment to another when the assignments vary greatly in news value. The necessity of working against the clock to meet deadlines, day after day, is a frustrating and often ulcer-producing situation for one who does not have the temperament to work calmly under pressure. Even with all other qualifications, the reporter cannot fulfill his responsibilities unless he can detach his personal life (and biases) from his work and take a position as an unbiased witness in reporting the news and accurately interpreting the facts.

Educational Needs of a Reporter. Although educational training for journalists dates back to the turn of the century, college-educated journalists were not common on most newspapers until well into the 1930s. Today it is very difficult to obtain a position on a newspaper without a college degree—and in many cases a degree in journalism. Accredited colleges and schools of journalism require students to get a broad liberal arts education with a concentration of journalism courses. Because of the vast amount of knowledge needed by a journalist, students in accredited journalism programs take only one-fourth of their work in specific journalism courses; the other three-fourths of their college work is in the arts, sciences and humanities. Those students who hope to specialize in a particular area—politics, science, foreign relations, home economics, agriculture and

7

other fields—are encouraged to bolster their education with additional courses in these specialized areas.

Journalism students generally are required to take courses in English composition and literature, history, political science, economics, psychology, one or more of the natural sciences and one or more of the foreign languages. A foreign language, Spanish, for example, would be a tremendous asset to a reporter working in an area where there is a large Latin American population, such as South Florida or the Southwestern states and Southern California. A course in public speaking often is required. It can prove helpful when covering a speech or when asked to give one, as many reporters and editors are.

The ability to type—with speed and accuracy—is absolutely essential. Even the smallest newspapers are now converting their newsrooms to electronic, computerized operations. And reporters must use electric typewriters or compose their stories on the keyboard of a video-display terminal. In fact, technology is advancing so rapidly that many newspapers are already installing newer, more highly developed automatic systems that require even greater typing skills.

Education is tremendously important for a reporter. However, some persons without a college education have become successful as reporters. Many newspapers in the past have employed high school graduates and "brought them up" in the editorial department. A few still do. But most employers are aware that, in comparison with high school graduates, college-trained reporters generally have a greater capacity for success and thus are worth considerably more to the newspaper. A college-trained reporter brings not only his knowledge of history, psychology, political science and the like but also the ability to use that knowledge to help interpret the events of the day, to put them in their proper perspective so the reader can understand them. Journalism courses are designed to show him how to use the knowledge obtained in other courses for the benefit of his readers.

Advantages of Journalistic Training. Journalistic training is another phase of college education which at first was ridiculed by some newspaper editors (and still is by a few) but today is widely recognized as valuable for the beginning reporter. Many editors, because they were not college graduates, argued that the best education for a reporter was practical experience in the newsroom. In more recent years the same editors admitted, somewhat reluctantly, that while it is good experience it is also limiting. They discovered that college training in journalism not only affords a short-cut to learning the basic journalistic techniques and skills but also gives the beginning reporter a broader understanding of his work. In short, city editors and other staff supervisors have not been as successful in teaching journalistic fundamentals with the trial-and-error method as have instructors with the formal classroom procedure. Hour for hour, the student in the classroom learns these fundamentals in less than one-third the time spent by the beginning reporter taught by the trial-and-error process.

A CRAFT OR A PROFESSION?

The national turmoil of the late 1960s, capped by the Watergate scandal of the early 1970s, and the role the press—particularly newspapers—played during that period, brought unprecedented attention to the men and women who work in the mass media in the United States. Many of them became glamour figures and immediate public personalities. Journalists, especially those reporting from Washington, D.C., had, in the view of several writers, become part of a new society dubbed "mediacracy," described as a public aristocracy of people important in the media and people who gain power through the media.

Enrollments in journalism schools took a dramatic upswing about the same time, and a number of journalists and educators argued that it was a result of the so-called Watergate syndrome. They said young men and women were attracted to journalism because of the so-called glamour and the fame and fortune that came to such reporters as Carl Bernstein and Bob Woodward of the Washington Post as a result of their work on the Watergate scandals of the Nixon administration.

Others disagreed. They argued that the young men and women who were flocking to journalism schools were aware of the declining popularity of the traditional liberal arts degree and were simply seeking an education that would make them more hirable.

But as Watergate faded into the past, enrollments continued to increase. By the mid 1980s enrollment could near the 70,000 mark (this includes all programs—journalism, broadcasting, advertising and public relations). Now some journalists and educators are suggesting that enrollments be limited and more rigid entrance requirements be established.

All this debate has done little to settle the long-standing dispute: Is journalism a craft or a profession? Despite the advancements in education and training and the sophistication in reporting and writing techniques, some insist that newswriters and commentators have no right to place themselves among the professions with such time-honored groups as lawyers, physicians, teachers, ministers and engineers. A penetrating look at the role of the press as well as the work of the journalist should help resolve the debate.

The Press and Society. The press, including the spoken and the written words of journalists, is an important institution in modern society. It is recognized as the principal medium of mass communication, which has become increasingly important because scientific and technological advancements make it more essential to keep the people informed of day-to-day developments. Never before has so much information been available in so short a time. And never before has the task of sorting out this information and passing it along to the public been of greater importance. The mass media, either directly or indirectly, are the chief sources of information for most people.

In a democracy, particularly, the role of the press is of vital importance, as the events surrounding the Watergate scandals attest. The success of a democratic government depends upon the wise decisions of an informed citizenry, for a democracy is ruled by people at the polls. Therefore, the press must be utilized to give the people the information they should have in casting votes on candidates and issues. In this respect the press is a great educational insititution. Its responsibilities in informing the public fairly, accurately and objectively in all matters of public concern are paramount. A responsible newspaper must remove itself from partisan politics in its news columns.

The press as an institution serving the people of a democracy was identified when journalists were designated as the "Fourth Estate." This unofficial title was given to members of the press near the turn of the nineteenth century by the British Parliament in recognition of the fact that the press represents the people and has strong influence upon public opinion. The other three recognized "estates" or classes representing the British people were the clergy, the nobility and the commons. The "Fourth Estate" title is just as applicable today as it was then. For as government grows larger and larger and more complex by the day, it is not humanly possible for a single individual to understand even a small amount of what it does without the aid of the mass media as his source of information and interpretation.

Just as it is used to enlighten the people, the press under the thumb of dictatorial control can be used to enslave a nation. The media of mass communications can be employed to disseminate either truths or falsehoods. Hitler—like other dictators before and after him—gave the world a tragic lesson on a controlled press. The efforts of several presidential administrations in the 1950s, '60s and '70s to control or intimidate the American press provide a frightening lesson on just how fragile the Constitutional guarantee of freedom of the press really is. Fortunately, the press has successfully resisted most overt attempts at control, with the aid of some enlightened public officials. Yet it is a battle the press must continue to fight. Equally important for the press in a free society is its relationship with the people, because they keep the press in business. The readers or subscribers are the life blood of the press. As a member of a free enterprise system open to anyone who cares to venture into competition, a newspaper must maintain the confidence and respect of its readers or its competitors will take over.

The press can be described as a quasi-public agency. It has responsibilities of keeping the public informed, and it is given freedom to do so by the U.S. Constitution. But because the press operates under the private enterprise system, it is divorced from governmental control, and its economic fate is placed directly in the hands of the people.

Journalism and the Professions. While the press is accorded a special place in a democratic society, whether this warrants professional status for journalists can still be debated. Many of the attributes of journalists give them strong claim to this distinction. However, the one basic requirement common to professional status in the United States is missing.

Compared with the accepted professions, journalists have great responsibilities of public service, which demand respect. The journalist is, to a large degree, an educator. He is an architect of public opinion who can influence the enactment or repeal of laws. He is, in a sense, an evangelist who, by factual statements, preaches the virtues of morality. He is guardian for the people of the efficient operation of public offices and institutions. He is entrusted with the power to bring credit or discredit to the names and reputations of his fellow men. What other person provides so many important public services and carries so many responsibilities?

Yet journalism is unlike all the other accepted professions in that it is not—and should never be—a licensed profession. Physicians, lawyers, teachers and others must be licensed (or certified) to practice, and to obtain a license they must complete specific educational programs and in some cases must pass examinations. Further, some of these professional people can lose their licenses if they are found guilty of unethical practices. Such requirements are designed to help maintain standards and to protect the public from damage that could be done by unqualified persons in the professions. (In reality, the licensing and examination system is far from perfect, and the enforcement of standards is highly erratic—resulting often in totally irresponsible delays in the revocation of licenses.)

Licensing journalists, however, would be a form of governmental control of the press. Through license laws, a dictatorial or spiteful government, by hand-picking those who issue the licenses or those who are licensed to write for news-papers and other mediums, could nullify the Constitutional guarantee of a free press. (Some members of the broadcasting industry charge that licensing radio and television stations, which has led to efforts to control content, is indeed a violation of the U.S. Constitution.)

Professional status for journalism cannot be attained by imposing high standards through license laws, but it can be achieved through voluntary efforts of journalists. While no law should require beginning journalists to have a college education, this is a prerequisite which more and more employers are finding much to their advantage. While no law can require that journalists abide by a professional code of ethics, journalists themselves, through organizations such as the Society of Professional Journalists, Sigma Delta Chi, and the American Society of Newspaper Editors, have established voluntary codes. Although journalists with a genuine respect for their responsibilities generally accept these voluntary standards, there are and will continue to be men and women in journalism who violate them for personal gain, without any feeling of guilt or fear of prosecution.

As a result of criticism leveled at the press, from both inside and out, during the period of the war in Vietnam in particular, a number of watchdog publications came into being. They repeatedly called into question the actions and policies of individual newspapers, publishers and the entire mass communications industry. Among the more notable of these were *Columbia Journalism Review*, the *Chicago Journalism Review, More,* and the *St. Louis Journalism Review.* Several other cities had journalism reviews as well and occasionally a new one will crop up. However, most of them have ceased publication and the *Columbia Journalism Review* continues as the chief and most vigorous source of criticism of the media. Several national publications, *Atlantic, Harper's, Saturday Review,* and the Wall Street Journal, report regularly and often critically on the media. And there is an increasing number of books critical of the media published each year by journalists as well as others.

It was during this period of turmoil, also, that a number of press councils were established in several cities and states and the National Press Council was created by the Twentieth Century Fund in the early 1970s. The councils generally investigate complaints against the media but at the same time work to defend freedom of the press. The councils have not had the overwhelming support of some of the nation's newspapers or the broadcasting industry, and most of them have ceased to function. However, the National Press Council continues its work, and a summary of the cases brought before it appears regularly in the *Columbia Journalism Review.*

Several so-called independent organizations were founded to serve as watch-dogs for the media also. The most active has been Accuracy in Media (AIM). In addition, some newspapers have named ombudsmen, in-house critics, to review and critique the performance of the newspaper staff. The Louisville Courier-Journal and the Washington Post both have used this technique for a number of years. In addition to reporting, as it were, their views to the senior editors, they often write a column critical of the way in which a particular story or issue was handled. This in-house critic idea has been praised by many outside the profession but is generally not popular among newspaper staffs.

Even with these watchdogs, the press has its unethical journalists just as medicine still has its quacks, law its shysters, education its tenure-protected inept teachers. Those who faithfully serve the profession of journalism, like those serving other professions, can only hope that the unethical encroachment upon their privileged profession can be kept at a minimum and prosecuted as far as possible through regular legal channels.

EXERCISES

1. Using materials available in your college or local library, write a brief paper on the continuing debate over the meaning of the First Amendment's guarantee of freedom of the press. You might start by checking *Reader's Guide* to *Periodic Literature* for articles published on the First Amendment. Do not overlook such professional publications as *Editor & Publisher, Columbia Journalism Review,* and *Quill* and *Journalism Quarterly,* if they are available. Check the card catalog for any books that have been written on the subject recently that might help you in preparing the paper. Call the editor of the local newspaper and invite him to class for an interview to get his opinion on the subject.

2. Invite several local public officials—mayor, city council members, judge—to class and interview them to find out how much they rely on the local newspaper for information about the community. Ask specifically what kinds of information they seek from the newspaper as opposed to information they obtain from other news sources. Write a brief paper on the results of your interviews.

3. Newspapers are the subject of constant review and criticism in a variety of national magazines and specialized publications such as *Columbia Journalism Review*. Study several issues of *Columbia Journalism Review* and such national magazines as *Atlantic, Harper's, Saturday Review* and the press sections of the national news weeklies.

The Reporter in the Newspaper Organization

The reporter has come a long way in the relatively short history of American journalism. At no time in our history has the significance of the reporter as an extraordinary force in our daily life been more apparent. In a society marked by ever-increasing controls, he enjoys unusual latitude but he also shoulders unusual responsibilities.

Yet in recent years the role of the reporter has from time to time been overshadowed by the news of dramatic advances in the technology of printing and the speed by which news can now be delivered to the public. At times, in the trade press in particular, it has appeared that the technology was more important than the humans involved in the news process. However, like printing technology, the American reporter is better than ever. And without the reporter to gather the news and write it with care and accuracy, all the new technology would be of little use to a newspaper or its readers.

This is not to say that these advances are not significant. Nevertheless, the simple fact is that all others who work for a newspaper are there to make it possible for the reporter's stories to get into print, accurately and attractively presented, for distribution to the reader.

At the same time, reporters cannot afford to be arrogant about their importance—even the media stars—because they would have no newspaper to carry their stories without the very important work of all others in the organization—business and technical as well as editorial. Each of the three major departments of a typical newspaper plays a significant role in the delivery of the news to the readers.

Editorial Department. The function of the newspaper's editorial department is to gather news from various sources as it occurs and to write it into readable, interesting form, edit it and display it in the newspaper. Secondary functions of the newspaper are to instruct or influence the public through editorials and

13

special articles, and to entertain by means of columns, comics and other features. All these materials are processed by the editorial department.

Mechanical Department. News must be transferred from the reporter's typewritten page or the video display terminal screen into type in the composing room and printed on thousands of pages of newsprint in the pressroom. This complicated technical, electronic process is the function of the mechanical department.

Business Department. To finance these two operations, advertising space must be sold, subscriptions must be obtained and the finished product must be delivered to the reader. To handle such operations, most newspapers have separate advertising and circulation divisions. A third division, often in larger newspapers, handles problems of management and business administration. In the smaller newspaper, advertising, circulation and management may be combined as one business department. In the larger newspaper, they may be greatly expanded and sharply differentiated under the direction of the business manager.

DETAILS OF ORGANIZATION

The organization of a newspaper will vary considerably depending upon the size. Metropolitan newspapers frequently have highly developed organizational charts, while a small newspaper may have no formal organization at all. And in rare cases, the organization may even consist of no more than three or four persons. The accompanying diagram (Figure 2-1) would be typical of a newspaper in a city of 100,000 to 200,000.

All papers have a publisher. It often is the title assumed by the owner or the majority stock holder in the corporation, or it can be someone hired to serve in that position. The latter is particularly true at newspapers owned by both large and small chains. The men and women hired as publishers may have no direct ownership in the publication, although some companies do offer such officials opportunity to buy stock in the firm. The degree of involvement in the daily operation by the publisher will vary greatly. If the publisher is closely associated with the operation, he may also be the general manager or editor. He has the power—if he chooses to exercise it—to dictate all policies, editorial as well as business. Generally, that is not the case. A publisher generally delegates authority to others but that does not relieve him of the ultimate—and legal—responsibility for everything that appears in the newspaper. Under the publisher, some major newspapers have a general manager who coordinates the efforts of all departments.

On smaller dailies and weeklies, the publisher may be the owner, editor and even one of the reporters. Horace V. Wells, Jr., publisher, editor and owner of the Clinton Courier-News in Clinton, Tennessee, is highly respected and has been honored repeatedly for his excellence as a newsman. He not only serves as editor and publisher, he covers government for his paper, often sells advertisements and, on Wednesdays, you will find him in the back shop helping to paste up the weekly edition.

The business manager generally has authority over the advertising, circulation and office managers, if a newspaper is large enough to have an office man-

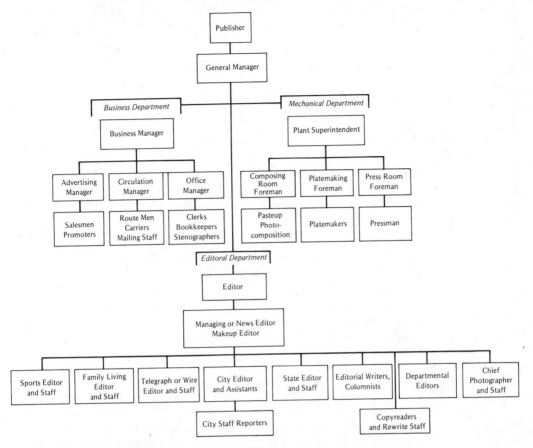

Sample Newspaper Organization

Figure 2-1. This chart shows a typical organization of the three major departments of a medium-sized daily newspaper.

ager. In many instances the business manager also fills that position. In that setup, the advertising and circulation managers report to the business manager, who then reports directly to the general manager or publisher. On much smaller newspapers it is not uncommon for the publisher to also act as his own business manager, and even as an advertising salesman.

The printing process has changed dramatically. Gone from most newspapers is the old letterpress system in which hot metal type was set in reverse line by line. A cardboardlike matrix had to be made from this page form and then a semicyclindrical plate was cast in metal from the matrix and bolted to the rotary press, which produced a direct image on the newsprint from that metal plate. (Only one hot metal operation remained in Tennessee, for example, in the early 1980s.)

In its place, type is prepared on fast photocomposition machines, which produce the finished stories on smooth, flexible photographic paper, which is then waxed or glued to a cardboard page-form and photographed. The image from these negatives is burned onto thin sensitized metal plates that are attached to the press. The image is then produced on the newsprint by the offset method. In the offset process the ink adheres only to the image that has been burned onto

15

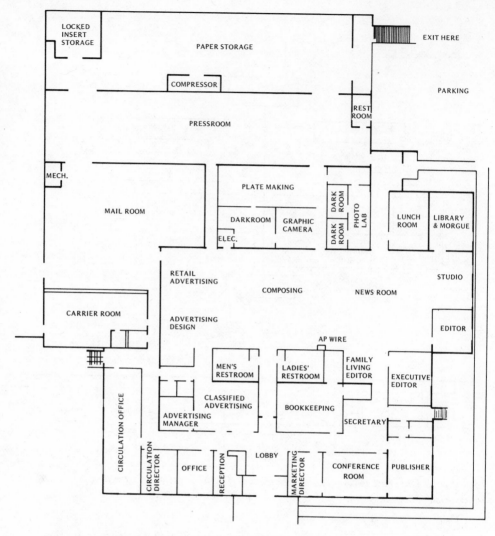

Figure 2-2. This chart shows the floor plan of the Greeneville Sun, Greeneville, Tennessee, one of the most modern community daily newspapers in America. The once-noisy composing room has been replaced by an almost-silent collection of computers and photocomposition machines. Courtesy of the Greeneville Sun.

the plate; it is then imposed on a rubber roller on the press that transfers the image to newsprint. The result is generally a much sharper, cleaner-appearing newspaper.

But even more revolutionary has been the introduction of the computer to the newsroom and the typesetting process. The Age of the Computer is now in full flower in the American newsroom. And many old-timers complain that the once highly romanticized, cluttered, noisy newspaper city room has given way to quiet, carpeted offices not unlike the main office of a large insurance firm.

Certainly not all the old manual typewriters and cluttered desks have disappeared but computerization has swept the nation's newsrooms and printing plants from the mammoth operations such as the Cincinnati Enquirer to the more modest Greeneville Sun in Tennessee. And in the process the editorial and printing processes have been radically altered.

In these advanced, computerized operations, instead of typing a story on a piece of paper, the reporter now writes on the keyboard of a video display terminal (VDT). A keyboard similar to an electric typewriter is attached to a small television screen on which the story appears as it is being written.

By striking the proper keys, the reporter can correct misspellings, eliminate entire words or sentences and move entire paragraphs. When the story is completed to the reporter's satisfaction, he can press another key and the story is automatically filed in a computer memory bank. It remains there until the copy editor, by typing out the correct code number for the story, calls it up on his VDT screen for the editing process.

The copy editor, also working at a VDT, can make further corrections, additions or deletions, edit the story to conform to the newspaper's style and even make it meet exact space limitations. He also can write the headline for the story on the VDT. This edited version can be stored in the computer's memory bank and later fed into the photocomposition machine. In some cases, the story may be sent directly to the photocomposition machine.

In some newsrooms, editors have VDTs with split-screen capability, enabling them to see stories side by side should they care to compare the story written by their own reporter and the story written by the press service that may have covered the same event. These two stories can be edited into a single one on the VDT and the final version stored in the memory bank.

The split screen VDT is particularly useful to newspapers that subscribe to both the Associated Press and United Press International wire services. The wire copy can be stored in the computer memory bank directly from the AP and UPI wire machines and then called up on the VDT screen for editing before being sent on to be set in type.

The computers are programmed so editors can, by typing in the proper codes, set the column width, story length, typeface and headlines. In the early 1980s some newspapers are using still another piece of electronic equipment that permits them to assemble all the material for a single page—story, pictures or illustrations, headlines and advertisements—eliminating the hand-drawn page dummy. This pagination device, originally introduced for making up advertisements, is especially helpful to large metropolitan dailies that have editions running several hundred pages or more. It not only reduces the time required to design each page, it also permits the makeup editor to see what each page will look like before it is set in print.

Many newspapers are equipping their bureaus and reporters sent out of the city on assignment with two-way portable terminals (not unlike a large portable electric typewriter) that are capable of feeding the stories by telephone directly back to the computers in the home office. Those stories then can be called up by the copy editors for processing. This portable terminal eliminates the need to have the reporter on an out-of-town assignment phone the newsroom and dictate his story to another reporter or rewrite man.

A major benefit of computerization has been increased speed and the reduction of personnel, particularly in the printing operation. However, not all editors are in agreement that the end product is as good. A number worry that the editing is not as carefully done, although several studies show that there is little or no difference in the quality of editing, whether it is done on the VDTs or by hand. And some reporters complain they are being turned into typesetters and proofreaders.

Of course, not all newspapers are quite as advanced in the use of electronic technology. Some very small operations do not even own any printing equipment. They contract with a job shop locally or in a nearby city to print the paper.

At newspapers where conversion to electronic production methods is taking place a variety of systems are being used. The type usually depends upon the size of the publication and more often on the amount of money the publisher has to invest.

Some newspapers compose stories at video display terminals and store them in computers until type is needed. The computer can either produce a paper tape of the story, which is fed into a photocomposition machine to produce the type, or it can be connected directly to the typesetting machine, eliminating the paper-tape operation.

Others, most commonly larger newspapers, use scanners (Optical Character Readers) to electronically "read" the reporter's story, which has been typed on a special electric typewriter (generally an IBM) that has special typesetting-instruction symbols added by the reporter and the copy editor. The scanner can "read" copy at a rate of 1,200 words a minute and store it in the newspaper's computer or on discs. From these the story can be called back to the copy editor's VDT in the newsroom for changes if need be, or it can be fed directly into the photocomposition machine that produces the type. (See Chapter 32 for further discussion of the editing process.)

In newspapers that are not so totally automated the reporter's copy is sent to the copy desk, where it is edited to make it conform to the newspaper's style. (This is still done by hand, not on VDTs, at some small newspapers.) The copy editor sends the story to the composing room, where it is set into type, generally on a photocomposition machine. A makeup editor plans which stories, photos and other printed matter go on each page of the news section. Departmental editors often do the makeup of their own sections or assign the task to a staff member. On many newspapers the makeup editor is also the managing editor or the news editor.

All local news stories are written by staff reporters working under the city editor. The stories received from the national news services are handled by the wire editor. Correspondents (out-of-city reporters) work through the state news editor. The family living-lifestyles editor (formerly called women's editors), sports editor and other departmental editors, if a newspaper has them, handle all stories for their pages. However, they usually work closely with the city editor and the news editor, because often a story written by one of their staff rates the front page.

Editorials in newspapers are written by editors and editorial writers. Editors with administrative duties may write few editorials. In some instances, newspapers buy editorials from syndicated services. And the public relations offices of a number of the state and national business and professional organizations and other special-interest groups send materials for editorials to newspapers. Some newspapers use them, but others consider their use unethical and will not print them.

The copy (news stories) written by the staff reporters is carefully corrected and improved by copy editors. Stories received by telephone from reporters or others, and stories not already in proper form for publication, are prepared by rewrite men (usually staff reporters or editors on office duty). On metropolitan newspapers most headlines are written by the copy editors. On smaller publications much of the copyreading and headline writing is done by city, wire and state editors. And on very small publications, the reporter may write his own headlines.

Photographers may serve under a chief photographer but their assignments generally come from the city editor or one of the departmental editors. They may accompany a reporter on an assignment. However, they often cover picture assignments without reporters. And on a number of newspapers reporters serve as their own photographers. The introduction of offset printing has eliminated the need to convert pictures into metal engravings except at those plants still using the hot metal method. In place of metal engravings, the offset process uses a screened photographic negative of the picture.

Departmental editors are in charge of special pages devoted to such areas as business, finance, entertainment (radio, television, motion pictures, the arts, music, books) and the special Sunday sections. On smaller newspapers these departments often are assigned to various staff reports in addition to their regular duties. Departmental editors are usually under the managing editor or city editor.

THE MORGUE

Not shown on the chart but an important tool for all reporters and editors is the newspaper's reference files—traditionally called the "morgue" and sometimes the "library." Most morgues keep rather complete clippings of all previously reported major news stories and of photographs which have been printed by the newspaper. In many cases, they also keep extensive background material gathered by the reporters on various subjects and persons, and clippings from competing newspapers. Pictures, both used and unused, are generally kept in these files. In addition, most morgues keep a wide variety of reference books from world almanacs to the various Who's Who publications along with social and economic data on the city and state. The complete morgue also has on hand biographies of prominent persons—city, state, national and international—ready for instant use. In fact, many newspapers have these stories already written and either ready to set in type or stored in their computer's memory bank. They update them regularly. A newspaper the size of the Chicago Tribune or the Los Angeles Times will have hundreds of them already prepared, and when a famous individual is thrust into the news, the staff has only to write a brief new lead on the story and it is ready for instant printing. Depending upon the size of the newspaper, the morgue may range from a few files to a large reference library. Some papers have converted much of their reference material to microfilm in an effort to save space.

A number of newspapers also have taken advantage of computerization to establish data banks for the complete storage of all information that has been printed in the publication. The New York Times has been a leader in computerized storage of data among newspapers and sells its service to others. The American Newspaper Publishers Association's Research Institute developed a computerized morgue program for small and medium-sized newspapers and is continuing to refine and improve it. Several other electronic data storage firms have also developed systems for storing information normally collected in a newspaper morgue.

A number of libraries are using similar systems. One is called News Bank. It is a collection of news stories by topics from leading American newspapers, which are reproduced on microfiche. A reporter interested in finding out what has been written in other cities about a particular topic, perhaps the problems of nuclear waste, would find this an excellent source.

NEWS CHANNELS

The editorial department of a newspaper receives news through numerous channels and sources:

1. From local sources through the newspaper's own staff of reporters, who gather the news from regular beats, give it background with information from the morgue and do most of their writing in the newspaper office under the direction of the city editor.
2. From national and foreign sources through the news agencies (wire services, bureaus, syndicates)—Associated Press (AP), United Press International (UPI) and others such as Reuters, the New York Times, and the Los Angeles Times-Washington Post news services. In addition, many commercial syndicates provide much of the feature material used. Some of this material is received by teletype and is, except for copyreading and headlining, ready for publication. (Many of the feature services, however, do send material to their client newspapers by mail if it does not fit into the immediate news category.) The wire editor is responsible for handling this material, although he may have the aid of one or more copy editors. Credit is given (by use of name or initial) to the press service on each of its stories used. Usually the initials of a press service are in the *dateline*, which is the line at the beginning of an out-of-city story giving place of origin and sometimes the date. A local story needs no dateline. (Some papers reserve the right to combine stories from various press services to which they subscribe. In those cases the story usually carries a *by-line* saying "Compiled from the press services.")
3. From state and regional sources through correspondents. Much of this material is written and ready for publication, although many state editors often either rewrite the stories or heavily edit them. Such stories often

have "Special to the (name of newspaper)" preceding or in the datelines. In addition, some state editors gather stories by telephone from news sources such as police and city officials in communities within the newspaper's circulation area.

4. From various individuals and organizations, such as chambers of commerce, public information offices of various social, fraternal and educational organizations, public relations agencies, through the mail, by telephone and personal calls. Most of this material is rewritten by the city staff under the direction of the city editor.

Through whatever channel it may subsequently pass, all news must be gathered and written at its source by reporters, and most news is, at its source, local news. An exception is news at state capitals and at the national capital affecting distant communities. In gathering and writing news, a reporter faces substantially similar problems whether he is a staff reporter, a press-service reporter or a correspondent.

SOURCES AND BEATS

A city editor would expect the following sources to yield perhaps 90 per cent of the local news and would assign reporters to gather news from these *beats* or sources daily:

1. The city police station, county jail, fire department, state police and all local hospitals.
2. The city hall (headquarters for city legislative and executive officials).
3. The county courthouse (headquarters for county officials and state courts).
4. The state capitol or state offices (headquarters for state officials).
5. The federal building or offices (headquarters for the post office, federal law-enforcement and other federal agencies such as the Internal Revenue Service, and federal courts), the Weather Service, Border Patrol and Immigration Services.
6. City, county and private schools, colleges and associated organizations.
7. The chamber of commerce, business firms, industries and labor organizations.
8. Civic, fraternal and professional organizations.
9. Churches and associated organizations.
10. Youth organizations and welfare agencies associated with local Community Chests or United Fund and also "health associations" (such as heart, cancer, mental health, alcohol and drug counseling), which might be financed independently.
11. Motion picture theaters, radio and television stations and organizations offering theatrical productions (local symphony orchestras and theatrical groups), athletic events and other forms of entertainment such as promoters of national and internationally famous popular music groups.
12. Funeral homes.

13. Convention centers, hotels, airlines and other firms engaged in accommodating meetings and visitors.
14. Various local news sources, such as ships and shipping, mines and mining, oil, lumber.

It should be apparent from this list of beats that most news is gathered in a regular, formalized, systematic way. A reporter does not stroll about the streets looking for news to happen. Every day the beat reporter is responsible for covering definite offices and organizations where most news originates. Even news of murders, fires and accidents generally comes from regular sources—the police and fire departments, and hospitals.

What beats are listed will be determined by several factors. For example, some newspapers in larger cities have a metropolitan editor who attempts to coordinate all the news in the city and the area immediately surrounding the city. In others, everything beyond the immediate city limits may be the responsibility of the state editor. The physical location and other conditions may result in a reporter's covering parts of several of the beats listed above. Just how the beats are set up, and the number of reporters assigned to each, will be determined on a time-saving and step-saving basis adjusted to the number and ability of reporters on the payroll.

THE STORY PROCESS

The process of getting the story from the event into print and then into the hands of the reader may help clarify the roles of the various departments within the newspaper organization:

1. A reporter sent to cover a newsworthy event gathers the facts by observation, interview and investigation and makes notes for his story.
2. He writes the story, usually returning to the office for this purpose. In critical circumstances, he may have to write the story on the spot and dictate it over the phone to a rewrite man. In most such cases, however, he would give only the facts over the phone and the rewrite man would actually write the story. With computerization, some metropolitan newspapers have installed video display terminals in the pressrooms in such places as the city hall or courthouse; the reporter writes his story on the VDT and it is fed directly into the computer at the newspaper plant by a leased telephone circuit. And, as noted earlier, some newspapers equip reporters with portable VDTs for out-of-town assignments such as major sports events.
3. The typewritten story is delivered to the city editor, who generally reads it and makes whatever changes he feels are necessary. He may even reject it and ask that it be written again. After the city editor passes the story, it then goes to the copy desk, where a copy editor reads it again for such matters as style and checks for factual errors before writing the headline. It is possible that the story could be given a major rewrite at this point, also.

At newspapers using VDTs, the city editor has his own terminal and can "call up" a story on his screen to read it and make changes he feels are necessary. Some city rooms also have equipment that will produce a "paper copy" of a story written on the VDT, and the city editor may use that for making corrections and changes before the story is passed on to the copy desk. However, each newspaper will have its own system, generally depending upon the type of equipment used in the newsroom.

4. The city editor and news editor generally make a record of the story, sometimes indicating its preferred position (for example, "page 1 must" to specify placement on the first page), and send it to the composing room. In newspapers using such electronic devices as video display terminals in their newsrooms, the copy editor may do the editing on the display terminal after the story has been punched into the computer's memory bank and before the story is transferred onto paper tape to be fed into the photocomposition machine in the composing room. On newspapers that have scanners in their composing rooms for punching the story onto the paper tape, reporters and copy editors use electric typewriters and special codes.

5. The installation of computers and electronic typesetting machines has changed the printing operations dramatically. On smaller newspapers produced by the offset method, the stories go directly from the newsroom to the composition room. The foreman distributes them to typesetters, who then produce the justified type on photocomposition machines. The type comes directly from the machine on smooth, flexible photographic paper, which is then pasted on the paperboard page forms (flats) according to a page dummy drawn by the news or departmental editor.

In much larger computerized operations several methods may be used to produce the type. If the newspaper uses the scanner method, the composing-room foreman will receive the edited version of the story, with proper codes for typesetting instructions marked on it by the reporter and copy editor. He will then feed these sheets of paper into the scanner which will "read" them and either punch the story onto a paper tape or record it on a floppy or hard plastic disk for storage. This material is then fed into the photocomposition machine to produce the type on photographic paper. Proofreaders then indicate typographical errors, and the necessary corrections are made before the "type" is pasted onto the page forms. It is also possible to feed the stories directly from the scanner into the photocomposition machine in some operations.

On newspapers where video display terminals are used for writing and editing stories, the corrected story can be stored in the computer and then fed from the computer directly into the photocomposition machine. In some operations after the story has been processed on the VDT and stored in the computer, a paper tape is punched, then fed into the photocomposition machine to produce the type.

The technology of electronically producing tape is advancing so rapidly, some newspapers are already into their "second generation" of computerized equipment. And the day may not be too far away when the entire process from writing and editing the story to creating a plastic or metal printing plate can be controlled directly from the newsroom.

6. From the page forms a photographic negative is made, and this is "burned" onto a thin sensitized metal plate, which is then fitted on the presses in the pressroom, and the newspaper is printed, cut and folded in one operation.

7. The printed newspapers are delivered to the circulation department for mailing, for delivery by routes and for street sales.

Automation has greatly changed the process of producing a newspaper. It has nearly eliminated several departments—the old typesetting room, the stereotype rollers and most of the machines for setting headlines. And the added speed means more late-breaking stories can make the paper if the editors want to use them.

However, the fact that the copy is in its final form when it leaves the VDT means that editors (in some cases reporters) become the typesetters as well as proofreaders. These added duties have caused concern in some newsrooms. Eye strain and fatigue are common complaints. And the concern over possible low-level radiation effects from the VDTs has even been discussed in some union negotiations. Several newspapers have reported that the added duties of the reporter and editor using the VDT have lengthened the editing time, and at least one reported having to add additional persons to its copy-editing staff since computerizing.

Whatever the complaints, it is apparent that no newspaper that has automated will ever go back to the old methods.

EXERCISES

1. Select one day's issue of the daily paper published in your city or a nearby city. Carefully note the local, state, regional, national and international stories printed in that issue. With that issue in hand, watch both a local television newscast and a national newscast the same evening. Check the stories covered in both. Compare the differences in the amount of coverage given each story and also the emphasis placed on a story and the methods of presenting the facts.

2. If possible, tape record a local radio news broadcast and a television newscast the same day and compare them to each other as well as to the issue of the daily paper you generally read.

3. Using the newspapers available in your college or university library, select a major state, national or international news event that has been reported for several consecutive days and compare the way several of these newspapers reported the event. Look for similarities as well as any significant differences in the coverage. Attempt to use a newspaper that is published in or near the city where the event took place and at least one from another state or section of the state should the event you select have taken place in your state.

4. Visit a newspaper plant and tour its complete operation. Before the visit, study the newspaper terminology in the Appendix, the typical organization chart in this chapter and the various steps in the story process from news source to reader so you can identify each during your visit.

A. In the editorial department, note especially the number of reporters and the beats or assignments they cover: rewrite men, copyreaders, editors and so on. Pay particular attention to the types of equipment they use in preparing the news. Learn specifically what each piece of equipment does.

B. In each of the other departments—mechanical, advertising, circulation—follow the processes closely to acquire a clear understanding of the operation and how it relates to all other departments at the paper.

C. In all departments, identify the original source of material that is printed in the newspaper and the actual steps and processes the material must go through before reaching the public.

5. Assuming that you were starting a newspaper in your city, draw up a plan of news coverage for your newspaper. Indicate what other features, such as comics, you would include.

CHAPTER 3

What Is News?

Sweeping social, economic, political and technological changes in American society in the past two decades have had an enormous impact on the content of American newspapers. Yet "news" is just as difficult to define today as it was when the first American newspapers were published.

The problem arises out of the nature of news, which is constantly changing directions and expanding, and the persons who select it for print. An event that would rate the first page in a community of 10,000 might not make the calendar of events in a newspaper in a city of 500,000.

The complexity of trying to pin down a tight description of news can be seen in the following definitions, selected at random:

News is anything printable.

News is an account of an event, or a fact or an opinion that interests people.

A presentation of a report on current events in a newspaper or other periodical or on radio and television.

Anything that enough people want to read is news, provided it does not violate the canons of good taste and the laws of libel.

Anything that is timely that interests a number of readers, and the best news is that which has the greatest interest for the greatest number of people.

News is accurate and timely intelligence of happenings, discoveries, opinions and matters of any sort which affect or interest the readers.

News is everything that happens, the inspiration of happenings and the result of such happenings.

News comprises all current activities of general human interest, and the best news is that which interests the most readers.

It would appear there is no way to cull the common elements in these definitions to reach a general and wholly satisfactory short description of news. Even the vast numbers of communications researchers who have been poking and prodding the psyches of the nation's newspapers and their staffs and readers for the past several decades have been unable to come up with a single, acceptable definition. The simple fact is that there is none. What news is requires a general definition, and the reporter must learn it by practice. It changes constantly and an alert and informed reporter will be conscious of those changes.

Intuition in News Judgment. To some extent the newspaper reporter depends upon his intuition in recognizing news, in distinguishing between news and non-news and in estimating the importance of news to the readers. In his book, *On Press,* Tom Wicker of the New York Times says ". . . instinct, experience, a good memory, a sharp eye, careful attention to surrounding detail, a skeptical sense of the way things work, a wary regard for human nature yield far more useful information and insights than any number of self-serving news sources and official spokesmen." The most respected reporters, Wicker says, and usually the best professionally, are those who most strongly assert their own independence and are willing to rely heavily on their own qualities of intellect and experience.

Certainly newspapermen make important decisions daily that are based on their intuitive news judgment. Nevertheless, practical newspapermen do recognize and apply certain news measurements and definitions when necessary, and a knowledge of these generally accepted rough principles and rules of thumb is essential for the beginning reporter. A serious effort to define news will strengthen his intuitive judgment.

The following discussion is an effort not so much to produce a profound definition of news as to clear the atmosphere for intuitive news perception. It is couched in arbitrary terms to avoid tedious reservations and exceptions. It cuts many corners and begs many questions. It invites criticism and resistance on the part of the reporter, who should improve upon it at all possible points and who ultimately should achieve, if not a generally acceptable definition, at least a reasonably clear perception of news. The generally accepted news values are included in the discussion.

Many commodities obviously are not news, and the newspaper does not deal with them as news. Advertisements, editorials, cartoons, comics, fiction, book reviews, columns of philosophy and personal viewpoints—all appear in the newspaper. All of them may be interesting items, but they are not news. However, news stories may come out of each of these at some point. An advertisement in the classified section of the Kingsport Times-News in Tennessee led to an investigation that resulted in the arrest of two persons who were seeking to lure women into prostitution. Syndicated columnists and cartoonists frequently become the subject of news stories when their work is left out of a newspaper by an editor or editors who found it objectionable.

To simply define news as "whatever appears in the newspaper," or "whatever is interesting to people," or as "interesting items in the newspaper" or as "interesting written or printed materials" is inadequate.

What then, is the essential characteristic of what we recognize instantly and generally as news? The first answer might be that news is "an account of something that has happened"—something that, to distinguish it from fiction, has "actually happened." The non-news items, such as those mentioned earlier, are thus excluded. The definition, however, immediately encounters difficulty.

What should be said of history? Obviously, history is such an account. And, more troublesome still, most things that have actually happened, that do happen every day, are not considered to be newsworthy. An account of routine daily acts—arising, dressing, eating, working—is not news under normal circumstances, although the most trivial event can under certain conditions become newsworthy.

What are these conditions? What is the mix of circumstances or the intrinsic nature of the event that lifts "something that actually happens" into the newsworthy realm where an "account" of it will be interesting to readers?

To state the answer categorically: The newsworthy event is one that affects or changes social, economic, political, physical or other relationships. Or, news is an account of man's changing relationships with his environment. Or, to be even more specific, the newsworthy development is one that disrupts or alters—or shows promise of altering—the status quo, and news is an account of such a development.

Change Essential. These, like many other definitions, suggest change, or potential change, as the essential element in news. Indeed, the same quality is suggested even more directly by the word *news.* At least it is change that has a vital significance for newspaper readers, sometimes affecting them with fear over the loss of jobs, or the promise of prosperity with the opening of a new industry, sometimes stirring their hopes over the new mayor, the new manager, the newlyweds or even the new baby in the house next door. As long as conditions remain the same from day to day, there is nothing to change the pulse of vicarious reader experience on either the up or the down grades of human experience. Let an event disrupt the status quo, however, and its portent, large or small, motivates the hopes or fears of whole neighborhoods of readers. In fact, the individual careless and uninformed about the changing world has little chance to avoid its perils or to take advantage of its opportunities. Whether he is aware of it, the newspaper reader—every individual—is deeply concerned and affected by the changing circumstances in which he is so delicately fixed. Is it not for this reason that he is always interested, and at times vitally interested in news? And is not the news in which he is interested essentially the account of events which do alter, or threaten to alter, the normal arrangements of things and relationships and the routine flow of events?

The objections may be raised that any and all events are disruptions of the status quo. But most individuals are quick to recognize the more obvious events that threaten their security or alter their status. A new tax bill brings a quick response from those who pay taxes and, incidentally, is front-page news. And, if it leads to a taxpayers' revolt, as it has in many instances, it is even more important news.

The difference between routines and disruption of routines is not hard to detect. Nor is there much difficulty in distinguishing between an individual's trifling loss of a handkerchief and a bank failure as disruptions so different in degree that the former could scarcely qualify as a disruption. Certainly the reporter faces a more specific distinction between disruptions and nondisruptions than between news and non-news.

Much news concerns the future and not the past. Many stories deal with councils and conferences and plans. And what about names of persons and places which figure so largely in the news? It seems evident that all of these items are of interest to the reader only if they deal with potential or impending disruptions. Events in themselves are not to be isolated from their context of circumstances, and therefore the circumstances themselves are of interest. Indeed, coming events "cast their shadows," and it is the reporter's special responsibility to warn readers of their coming.

Community Consequence Required. The real difficulty with the definition is that once an event is recognized as a disruption there still remains the problem of whether it is sufficiently disruptive to make an interesting story. The question that must always be asked is: Does it constitute news of sufficient magnitude to be of interest to a sufficient number of readers? If Nancy Parker, age 8, is 30 minutes late coming home from school, it is significant only if she has always been punctual—and then only to her immediate family. It becomes worth publishing only as time elapses and her continued failure to appear leads to the conclusion that she is "missing." Immediately the fact that an 8-year-old girl is missing becomes of major local importance. Why? Is it not because the security of every child in the neighborhood is threatened (actually or potentially)? In the community mind the security of children in general comes to be at stake. It is a matter that everyone needs to know about in order to understand the peril that exists and to take precautionary steps. At just what point a disruptive event breaks into community consequence is impossible to determine by formula. But to think of news as a disruptive event of community consequence certainly does not cloud the intuitive judgment.

The essential nature of news, there is no doubt, can be found in and around the consequential disruption of the status quo and, by the same token, the potential disruption of the status quo. Certainly if everything is the same tomorrow as it is today, tomorrow's newspaper is going to be dull reading. "What happened?" "What's going on?" "Anything new?" These are the questions that should constantly be in a reporter's mind. And if among the activities of a busy mayor's office, or the county jail or the state legislature there is no event or potential in which events may be brewing to disrupt the status quo of routine circumstances, there would seem to be no news that day.

So much for a tentative definition of news. If the definition is sound, disruption (change) or potential disruption is an intrinsic quality of all news events. Disruption separates news events from non-news events. The extent of disruption (community consequence) measures the importance of events and determines their reader appeal.

NEWS VALUES

The qualifications or characteristics of news as commonly recognized are in reality special types of disruption of the status quo. Any newsworthy event will not only disrupt the status quo but will also disrupt it in one or more of the following ways.

Conflict. Most conflicts are newsworthy to some degree. Actual conflict is generally more newsworthy because it is physical and usually leads to injury and damage. Violent in itself, it arouses the emotions of spectators and seems (or may

29

be) of enormous immediate importance. A fist fight between two partisans at a championship football game may rate no more than a single line of type in the game story, if that, because it affords in the editor's eye no important disruption of the status quo. However, let the partisan fans riot after the game, damaging cars, blocking traffic, breaking windows in stores, looting, and it is spread all over page one because the magnitude of the disruption has dramatically changed the status quo. Wars, murders, violent strikes—conflicts of a more disruptive nature—have always received space on the front pages. Some critics say they are given too much space. At the same time, until the past decade, the clash of political, economic and social theories, the debates of scholars and scientists—if measured by the consequence of the issues—probably did not receive enough recognition. One of the major debates of the last half of this century—the safety or danger (depending upon which view you hold) of atomic energy—finally moved out of the academic and scientific halls and onto the front pages of the newspapers. But it took almost 20 years. Today, the debates (conflict) over air and water pollution, nuclear breeder reactors and the hundreds of other issues tied to the quality of life share equal billing with news from the jails and police stations, legislative bodies and divorce courts on the front pages. Tension and suspense are corollary qualities of conflicts and are sometimes considered news values in themselves.

Progress and Disaster. From conflict there follows usually the triumph of one part, the defeat of another. And from the routine struggles of life, not newsworthy in themselves generally, emerge frequently the shining successes. From quiet laboratories come new inventions, new remedies, new devices—progress. And sometimes progress can lead to disaster. Such was the case with DDT, which had been hailed as a major breakthrough in the control of crop-destroying insects. Some 20 years later, it became the subject of major news stories when the federal government finally banned its use after it was linked to cancer in humans. Saccharin was for years a seemingly harmless substitute for sugar welcomed by diabetics and persons with weight problems. But it too became the subject of major news stories when it was linked to cancer and Congress debated banning it. The great promise of nuclear power after the splitting of the atom lost some of its luster more than 30 years later with the accident at the Three Mile Island nuclear plant in Pennsylvania.

Fires and earthquakes may strike suddenly. Jobs are lost. Migrant workers become a regional problem. Sometimes these changes are observed and reported in the making because of the conflicts involved. In other instances only the end result stands out as progress or disaster, emerging from a vague or unknown background. But all are changes, all are newsworthy in greater or lesser degree, for all are disruptions of the status quo.

Consequence. An event that causes or is capable of causing a great sequence of events affecting many persons is obviously newsworthy. It is, in other words, of much consequence. Certain events are of more consequence than others, and those of more consequence will receive more space and larger headlines. Consequence is generally accepted as a news value, and there can be no objections to it as a general measurement of news importance. Its defect as a specific news value is that all newsworthy events have some consequence, for whatever other reason they are newsworthy. Consequence thus tends to be a measurement of all other news measurements rather than an intrinsic characteristic of the news events itself. For example, a football game would not be as great a consequence as a national political campaign, while a war probably would be of greatest consequence of all—especially a nuclear war. Consequence measures conflict. Similarly, consequence may measure disaster or progress. A fire that destroys a private dwelling is of small consequence in comparison to Hurricane David, which killed more than a thousand persons on the Dominican Republic, left additional thousands homeless and destroyed most of the nation's crops.

Eminence and Prominence. It is generally agreed that names make news, and big names make bigger news. Granted that this is true, how is the disruption of the status quo involved in this apparently static news value? If names alone made news, no event would be needed to justify the use of names in a newspaper, and the editor could turn out a fascinating publication by copying pages of the local telephone directory. He would not need reporters, just an accurate typist. Indeed, the "big name," or the "little name" for that matter, must do something to alter the status quo if his name is to go into the newspaper. He may do no more than "stop over" in the city enroute to a national conference. But if he is eminent enough to be attending such a conference, there is sure to be an aura of news potential around him. If he predicts a new Mideast war, the stock market may go down. If he shakes hands with a local political candidate, that candidate's chances for election may be improved greatly. State-level politicians have been known to fly great distances at enormous cost and considerable inconvenience just to be seen and photographed with a president or leading candidate for the presidency. They know it is almost certain to rate space in the newspapers. Big names—prominence—eminence—are newsworthy for the same reason that a political conference or a summit meeting of world leaders is newsworthy. All may be quiet on the surface, but the potentials are there for the significant change that makes news.

Timeliness and Proximity. Two other news values commonly recognized are timeliness and proximity, and both are serviceable in measuring certain qualifications of news. It should be kept in mind that these two elements alone do not make something automatically newsworthy. Rather they are measurements to be applied to all events in distinguishing news from non-news. Timeliness and proximity are measurements to be applied to news after it is recognized, to determine whether it is worth gathering and whether and where it is salable. One of a newspaper's chief assets has to be its freshness—an accident today that tied up local rush-hour traffic for an hour is more timely than one that happened even 48 hours before. It is timely. Similarly, the local accident is more newsworthy than one that tied up rush-hour traffic in the state capital, 200 miles away (proximity).

Novelty. Another news value is novelty. One of the oldest of newspaper clichés is that, if a dog bites a man, it is not news, but if a man bites a dog, it is news. Of course, there are countless stories every year of stray dogs biting individuals who fear they will have to take painful rabies shots unless the dog is found. So the cliché is not fully accurate. But it makes a point. Novelties in the news include two-headed calves, the 250-pound pumpkin, the cat that walks 200 miles to find its owner who moved to another city. Such events are very definite disruptions of the status quo. Some of them are sufficiently novel to bring the laws of nature into question in the popular mind. Coincidences, great contrasts, novel ways of making a living, unusual habits and hobbies, superstitions—anything different—all appeal to many readers. The common element of the appeal appears to be that it is novel—it is unusual. It is a value that is not difficult to recognize.

Human Interest. Many stories appear in newspapers which at first glance do not seem to be news because they do not meet the tests of conflict, consequence, progress and disaster, novelty or any other specific news value. They are called human-interest or feature stories and may be about the woman who claims she can pick up Russian satellites on her hair curlers, a singing dog, the man who claims he has developed a magical potion for growing hair, a 78-year-old man who returns to high school to work for his diploma—there are hundreds of them in newspapers every day. Plainly the reader appeal (news value) of some of these stories can be explained as a combination of the appeals already mentioned—disaster, progress, conflict and so on. Most, perhaps all, are novelties in the sense of being unusual groupings of events. Perhaps they could be called human novelties. Such stories are seldom, if ever, of importance as isolated events. While many events are newsworthy because of their novelty, they may make only a very short news story unless an editor suggests that the reporter turn them into human-interest stories. In that case, the reporter would go beyond the normal practice of just gathering the facts of the event and explore the human element. In short, the reporter amplifies the story by gathering additional material—emotions, biographical facts, dramatic incidents, descriptions, motives, ambitions, yearnings and common likes and dislikes of people. These are not events but the background of events.

Some events lend themselves more readily than others to human-interest treatment. Many events that would not rate publication because of their news values can suggest a sufficient quantity and quality of human background to become the news peg on which the human-interest story can be hung. Sometimes really important events can be so entangled because of the cast of characters and their passions and conflicting interests that a straight news story alone robs the events of much of their significance.

The kidnapping of Patty Hearst by the so-called Symbionese Liberation Army is a classic case. The colorful fabric of the private lives of a rich and influential newspaper publisher and his family was exposed to the public through human-interest stories. And the delusions of a handful of fanatics who hoped to overthrow the government came to light as the newspaper heiress took part in a bank robbery with her captors and became the object of a nationwide police search. The shabby and sometimes shocking details of her life with her captors that came out following her eventual arrest and trial for bank robbery helped give the readers a clearer perspective on the whole story and produced some of the most interesting, if not bizarre, human-interest stories of that period of unrest in our nation's history.

An event acquires significance through its context of circumstances. One cannot measure the news value of a completely isolated event in a human-interest story any more than he can in a news story. Whether a story is treated as straight news or as human interest will be determined by circumstances. Sometimes the event and its consequences stand starkly alone with no visible background. Sometimes the background is aglow with human emotions and contrasts and is more prominent than the events. Other times the distinction is not so clear, and frequently a reporter, recognizing this, presents straight news events with a touch of human interest in the background.

Human interest, then, although not strictly representing a news value measuring an isolated event, is a useful term to characterize those materials that pour through the event to fill the news columns with story materials. Strictly speaking, human interest is a story value and not a news value. The reporter will not need to make this precise distinction. For all practical purposes, human interest can be and is generally accepted along with conflict, consequence, disaster, progress, novelty, eminence, proximity, timeliness and so on as a news value. Any given event may suggest and require some human-interest treatment.

Sex. Sex is generally considered by most editors as a news value. This is especially true when it is coupled with eminence. Readers in the 1930s clamored for every word on the love affair of King Edward VIII of England, who gave up his throne to marry a divorcée, Wallis Warfield Simpson. And as the Duke and Duchess of Windsor they continued to make headline. The multiple marriages of movie star Elizabeth Taylor were reported in detail and read about avidly. The rather casual housekeeping arrangements of actor Lee Marvin, which ended in the courts, the on-again-off-again romances, marriages and friendships of many major rock stars from Mick Jagger to Alice Cooper have definite reader appeal in the news—especially when they contain such other elements as conflict or, perhaps, disaster. The reporter should know—by intuition and instinct—that sex is interesting and frequently in the news.

Miscellaneous Values. Stories of animals are often interesting, but it seems unnecessary to include this interest quality among the news values, as is sometimes done. Usually, the only time animals make news is when they disrupt the status quo: the hero dog, the prizewinning bull, the cat up a tree, the birds nesting in the city hall air-conditioning system. But these are also definite novelties.

Many other types of stories and materials used in the newspaper are interesting. Some are not news from the standpoint of current events, but they are designed to inform or entertain, and often they have elements of timeliness, eminence, sex and so on. Human-interest stories on children, old people, adventure, hobbies—all make news if the events in which they are involved are newsworthy as measured by the general principle of disruption and by specific news values.

SUMMARY: NATURE OF NEWS AND NEWS VALUE

Newspapers deal in a commodity—news. It differs from all other commodities and may be defined as follows:

1. News is an account of man's changing relationships.
2. News is an account of actual events that disrupt the status quo or have the potential to cause such disruption.
3. News is an event of community consequence.

Items of news have intrinsic characteristics known as news values. The presence or absence of news values measures the newsworthiness and reader appeal of an event, thereby determining its worth to the newspaper.

These news values are useful measurements of happenings and, properly applied, will determine whether a given event is news.

Any (newsworthy) disruption or potential disruption of the status quo will be the result of events and potentials characterized by one or more of the following news values:

Intrinsic Characteristics of the Event

1. Conflict (tension, surprise).
2. Progress (triumph, achievement).
3. Disaster (defeat, destruction).
4. Consequence (effects upon community).
5. Eminence (prominence).
6. Novelty (the unusual and even the bizarre).
7. Human interest (emotional background).

Desirable Qualifications
8. Timeliness (freshness and newness).
9. Proximity (local appeal).

General Interests
10. Sex.
11. Animals.

MEASURING THE IMPORTANCE OF NEWS

By intuition or by applying news values, the reporter recognizes news when he sees it. If, however, he should collect all the news that happens in a day in his city, the newspaper obviously would not have space for it. The news that is printed is selected from the mass. The more important is offered to the readers; the less important is left uncollected or goes into the wastebasket to be recycled. And to know what is "more important" a reporter must know his audience—he must know as much about his readers as he possibly can.

News must be measured for its comparative importance to the reader—as when two or more stories compete for space. It must be measured also for its intrinsic importance—to determine the length and the display it should receive.

Several measurements can be helpful in determining reader appeal, in addition to a reporter's intuition or instinct.

Extensity and Intensity. An odor may be strong in one neighborhood, or it may cover a whole community. The scents from a meat-rendering plant, for example, might disturb its neighbors for many blocks. But the stinging and burning smog from an air inversion might stifle the whole city. Both would be news. If the intensity were equal, the citywide smog would make a bigger story. On the other hand, if smell from the meat plant should drive several of the neighbors to take some drastic action—such as seizing the plant and trying to shut it down—and the smog should be merely annoying, the intensity could outweigh the extensity in measuring the importance of the story. The same principle applies to any two stories. The importance of a story is determined by its intensity (the amount of disruption) and by its extensity (the number of persons affected).

Proximity and Timeliness. Discussed as news values, proximity and timeliness are chiefly useful in measuring not the nature of news but its importance for use in a particular newspaper. Since a newspaper sells to a local public, local events are more important than foreign—all other factors being equal. A murder is big news in the city (proximity) where it occurs. A similar murder in a city 500 miles away will receive space in the local newspaper only in proportion to the prominence of the persons involved or to the conflict, novelty, disaster, consequence, human interest or other news values. Otherwise equal, the most recent events will receive most space because of their timeliness.

Relative Consequence. Another news value, consequence, measures the importance of news rather than its essential nature. Community consequence has already been given as a news determinant. Other things being equal, a news event is just as important as results which flow from it. If two men of equal prominence are murdered, one the father of ten children, the other unmarried—and all other values are equal—the murder of the father of ten will be given greater play in the newspaper. If two large groups of citizens are meeting on the same evening, one to celebrate the arrival of spring, the other to demand the resignation of the mayor, the latter is more important because of the consequence that may flow from it.

Variety of Appeal. The more news values in an event, the greater the story interest and the greater its importance. In short, it will have wider reader appeal. A kidnaping is big news in itself; the kidnaping of a prominent person bigger news; conflict and bloodshed make the news still bigger. Each additional element included—human interest, novelty and so on—gives the story even more reader appeal. But it is important to keep in mind that all the values must be of equal importance. Variety of appeal is a measurement of reader appeal only when other values are equal.

Factors of Magnitude. In summary, the following are factors which, as rationalizations, measure the importance of news:

1. The extent of disruption of the status quo (intensity).
2. The number of persons affected by the event (extensity).
3. The nearness of the event (proximity).
4. The recency of the event (timeliness).
5. The extent of results to flow from the event (consequence or significance).
6. The variety of news values in the event (variety).

STORY TYPES

Generally, reporters and editors do not discuss news values or factors of news magnitude, although in some cases they may. They merely apply these values in the writing and editing of news. They do recognize and discuss stories in other terms. They talk in terms of "fire stories" or "accident stories," perhaps, or a "meeting" or a "speech" or a "murder" and traditionally the "weather" story. Most newspaper stories fall into more or less well-defined types which the reporter can study and master without at the same time submitting himself to any rigid rules or formal story outlines. Newspapers generally recognize the following types of news stories and other editorial matter:

General Types

1. Personal and briefs.
2. Speeches, publications, interviews.
3. Meetings and events.

Stories that are classified by the "package" in which they are "wrapped" rather than the contents (or subject matter) of the package. These general types deserve special consideration because they are encountered repeatedly in covering the subject-matter types ("simple," "complex" and "special") which follow.

Simple Types

4. Illness, deaths, funerals.
5. Fires and accidents.
6. Seasons and weather.
7. Crime.

Subject-matter stories that generally require little interpretive writing by the reporter.

Complex Types

8. Courts, trials, lawsuits.
9. Government and politics.
10. Business, industry, agriculture, labor.
11. Education, research, science.
12. Religion, philanthropy, promotion.

Subject-matter stories that generally require interpretation from the reporter's background of specialized information.

Special Types

13. Lifestyles, family living (including engagements, weddings, social events) and consumer news
14. Sports
15. Entertainment (films, television, popular music, theater), literature, fine arts and criticism

Stories and articles which encompass a multiplicity of subjects and which in many cases contain a heavy portion of interpretation requiring a high degree of general and specialized knowledge on the part of the writer.

16. Editorials and editorial
    columns
17. Interpretative and
    investigative

Some story types are more clearly defined than others. Obituaries (deaths and funerals) and weather stories are rather standardized in form and subject matter. On the other hand, business stories range from simple market reports to elaborate accounts of local business developments or world economic conditions. Many of the classifications overlap. Accidents frequently figure in weather stories. A trial may also be a political story. Nevertheless, each type has sufficient distinct problems to be examined independently of the others. The reporter who masters each type will have no trouble with a story in which several types merge.

NEWS SOURCES

Newspaper stories obviously come from many sources. The main beats covered regularly by reporters were noted in the preceding chapter. They include all available offices of the state, county, city and federal government; the headquarters of all civic and professional organizations; churches, schools and charities; and many individuals, public and private, who occupy key positions in business, industry, transportation utilities and other major fields. Increasingly, a number of "events" are purposely staged for the news media, and an editor and the reporter should be skeptical of being "used" by the sponsors of such pseudo-news events.

Many stories may be picked up from a single source. The public relations chairman of a national convention may provide all necessary information for a story on the event. On the other hand, many stories will have to be pieced together from several sources.

However, a careful reporter will always double-check the facts with at least a second source, perhaps the hotel manager where the convention is headquartered. Many reporters have been told by public relations personnel that 1,000 persons were expected when only a couple hundred actually registered. Many stories will have to be pieced together from a half dozen or more sources. A strike may require information from the strikers, their labor union representatives, employers, police, the mayor, the governor, hospitals (if there is violence), charities (if it is a protracted strike) and others—including the President if it is a strike of nationwide significance.

Since all details of news stories are reported, not created, by the reporter, the information in every story should be traceable to its source. The source should be named, and statements should be attributed to the person who made them. A sample news analysis shows how the news in one story was drawn from various sources.

SAMPLE NEWS ANALYSIS

3a

Source of News	News Type: Crime	News Content
Victims, police	Two men, armed with pistols, raced across the Scarritt College campus this morning, attacking and robbing a Methodist bishop, college professor and graduate student.	Kind of crime
Victims, police	The robbery netted the gunmen about $150 in cash and jewelry.	Specific details of amount taken
Victims, police	Bishop Marvin Stuart of San Francisco, Scarritt professor Kebie Hatcher and student Vince Santo were walking to classes about 9:30 a.m., when they were accosted by the gunmen.	Identification of victims
Victim	"I'll put a cap in your a..es if you move," Hatcher said one of the men yelled when he and the bishop were accosted near the college chapel.	More details
Victim	"The little one said that after he pulled an automatic pistol out and cocked it. I could tell he meant what he was saying, so we just stood there. They were both in a big hurry because there were a lot of people moving about on campus."	More details
Victim	Hatcher said the two men "frisked" the bishop and himself, taking the professor's wallet, which contained about $5, and credit cards. The gunmen then twisted the bishop's watch off his arm and demanded he give them his gold wedding band.	
Victim	"Bishop Stuart told them, 'Please no, not my wedding ring,' and pulled away," Hatcher said. "That's when the big guy rared back and whacked the bishop across the face and ran."	
Police	But the robbers did not quit there. Racing across campus, they ran into Santo and stopped him at gunpoint.	More detail
Victim	"Be quiet or we'll kill you," Santo said one of the men yelled. "They asked me for my wallet and money, but I told them I didn't have any with me. I wasn't lying—I didn't."	More detail
	But one of the men noticed a gold coin ring Santo was wearing and demanded he take it off.	
Victim	"The big guy started pulling at it, and my fist naturally tightened," Santo told police. "Then he really couldn't get it off. He hit me	

Source of News	News Type: Crime	News Content
	in the face, and I turned my head down real quick so he couldn't hit my face again.	
Victim	"But he kept on tugging at the ring and hitting me in the side of the head. He was hitting me hard, real hard. He was a big guy—he looked like he played for the Green Bay Packers or something."	
Victims, police	Santo said the next thing he knew someone screamed, and the two men fled on foot. Santo was taken to a doctor, treated and released. He suffered minor bruises. Bishop Stuart did not require medical attention.	More detail
Victim	Stuart, who is the chairman of the Council of Bishops for the entire United Methodist Church, is in Nashville attending a religious workshop.	
Police	Several hours after the robbery, a man was apprehended by police but later released when the victims could not identify him.	Police action

News Values

The outstanding news value of this story is conflict, two robberies on a college campus while students and others are walking nearby. It also contains several other news values—the prominence of one of the victims, the dramatic element of the threats on the lives of the victims—which give it human-interest characteristics. The story is timely because it happened the day of the publication. It was given more length and more detail because of the unusual aspect of a bishop being robbed on a college campus.

EXERCISES

1. Read the front page of your local daily newspaper or the daily that circulates in your area if your city does not have a daily. Classify the stories under local, state, national or international categories. Then classify them by type. Identify the news sources and the news values in each.
2. Most daily newspapers are a combination of local, state, national and international news. However, many smaller daily newspapers tend to emphasize local news. With that in mind, apply the tests of news values to the following items and determine which are worth publishing. Which items deserve placement on the front page with any state, national or international news the editors may select that day? Indicate the sources from which you would expect to obtain enough information to write a complete story.
   A. Local man killed hauling coal in nearby underground mine.

B. Mysterious hairy creature scares residents of rural community nearby, killing dogs and pigs.

C. Late registration ends today at area community college.

D. Local utility granted 10.8 percent power rate increase by Public Service Commission.

E. Business woman establishes scholarship to aid women preparing themselves academically to reenter the job market.

F. Eight-year-old local girl kidnaped, found dead in city park.

G. President of local bank donates $1,000 to local animal shelter.

H. Local student wins prize at state medical school for outstanding performance in bacteriology and pathology.

I. City begins court-ordered busing program today, 1,000 students involved.

J. Fire at Wellington's Restaurant & Lounge caused $2,500 damages.

K. Mechanic arrested for stealing $6,000 worth of diesel engine parts from International Harvester Co., then selling them to a small trucking firm for $750.

L. Three-year-old boy runs into path of car, critically injured.

M. Russian sports exhibit to be displayed locally for two weeks.

N. Lincoln High School students will exhibit paintings in State Student Art Exhibit this month.

O. County Commission approves record budget for next fiscal year.

P. An earth tremor that registered 3.7 on the Richter scale felt by residents of city about 1:23 a.m. No damages reported.

Q. Local carpenter charged with murder of 71-year-old woman and her 42-year-old daughter.

R. Kiwanis Club donated $1,000 to local library building fund.

S. Vandals do estimated $5,000 damage to Madison High School.

T. Community College to offer general education development courses for persons who want to qualify for high school diploma.

U. City manager resigns to take post as regional director of state planning commission.

3. Using daily newspapers available in your college library, compare the coverage of a major national or international news event. Check the papers carefully for the use of sources and compare their use of anonymous sources. Write a brief explanation of which story you found most believable and why.

4. These rough notes are from stories or story leads taken from community newspapers. They are typical of stories you will find in your local newspaper. Classify each under one or more of the story types. Study the importance of each from its news value—consequence, conflict, human interest and so on—and indicate the news value of each. What additional information is needed to expand each story? What sources would you turn to for additional information?

A. The annual membership meeting of the Mt. Juliet Little League will be held at 2 p.m. Sunday in Mt. Juliet Elementary School.

B. For the second time in two weeks, the Monroe County Board of Education has been named as one of three codefendants in a suit over withholding payment for construction of the new Greenback High School gymnasium.

C. David Thomas, 18, fatally injured in a motorcycle accident in Great Smoky Mountains National Park. Second local man to be killed in a traffic accident at the same location.

D. Junior Chamber of Commerce presented its annual Public Service Awards to three students from local high schools. Ceremony and dinner at the Holiday Inn at 7:30 last night. Awards granted to Elsie Embry, senior at West High School;

Joanne Parker, junior at Sara Moore Green High School; and Lavonna Smith, senior at Beardon High School.

E. Bernadine Villanueva, self-proclaimed prophetess, convicted on three counts of fraud for using $43,000 for her personal needs instead of using it to build a spiritual center and metaphysical bookstore. She appealed convictions to State Supreme Court. Today the Supreme Court upheld the convictions.

CHAPTER 4

Writing in the News Style

Style is the sound words make on paper, author E. B. White says. It is basic to good writing. Every piece of effective writing—in a newspaper, magazine, essay, novel—should reflect the writer's commitment to a style that puts life and color into his words.

Some inexperienced writers insist that this is impossible when writing for a newspaper. To see how wrong they are they need only to read some of the stories of reporters ranging from the late Gene Fowler to the current stories of Saul Pett and Jules Loh of the Associated Press or review the newspaper stories written by Tom Wolfe and Gay Talese before they turned to writing books.

Frequently inexperienced reporters complain because they were required to adapt the story (and their personal style) to prescribed newspaper forms. Their creativity is being stifled, they insist, because they must conform to the accepted rules of punctuation and grammar and the principles of rhetoric. A goodly number of English teachers agree. However, in recent years English teachers have come under fire almost as much as newspapers, advertising and television news staffs for the alleged decline and fall of the English language. Yet they still complain that few newspapers adhere to rules of punctuation and grammar and the principles of rhetoric. They point out errors in English grammar that appear in newspapers and crab about the short sentences and short paragraphs that are common to newspaper style.

4a   No newspaper permits its writers to intentionally misuse the English language. And most newspapers spend countless man-hours and amounts of money attempting to make certain that the language is used properly. It is true that newspapers take special liberty in headline writing, and perhaps this practice has given rise to the unfounded belief that newspaper English is a language all its own. However, headline English is not newspaper English; it is not the style observed in the news stories. Headline English is merely a device used in displaying the news stories. News stories should not—indeed, they must not—be written in shoddy English.

While newspaper language follows accepted rules of English, it also strives for certain qualities of style: simplicity, conciseness and vividness; directness, emphasis and originality; clarity, brevity and accuracy. These qualities cannot be sharply defined. They afford no specific rules to follow in achieving excellence and distinction. However, some newspapers, the New York Times, for example, have their own style books, which reporters must memorize and follow when writing stories. Others use the Associated Press Stylebook and require reporters to memorize it. The AP Stylebook is commonly used in writing classes at many journalism schools, and students are tested extensively on its content. Some general principles of news style, most of them conforming with the AP Stylebook, are illustrated as follows:

NEWSPAPER ENGLISH

1. Eliminate Unnecessary Words

4b

   a. Unnecessary articles:

     Weak: The club members attended the meeting.
     Strong: Club members attended the meeting.
     Weak: He returned a part of the money.
     Strong: He returned part of the money.

   (However, only unnecessary articles should be eliminated. For example, the article in "Club members attended *the* meeting" cannot be eliminated. The same applies to "a" and "an.")

   b. Circuitous verb forms:

     Weak: The group will hold a meeting.
     Strong: The group will meet.
     Weak: The judge arrived at a decision.
     Strong: The judge decided.

   c. Adjectives, adverbs, prepositions:

     Weak: Both cars were completely destroyed.
     Strong: Both cars were destroyed.
     Weak: A tall 18-story building.
     Strong: An 18-story building.
     Weak: He stepped off of the train.
     Strong: He stepped off the train.
     Weak: The club will meet on Friday.
     Strong: The club will meet Friday.

   d. Connectives:

     Weak: He said that he would go.
     Strong: He said he would go.

   (However, when two or more *that* clauses follow a verb, the conjunction should be used with all clauses for purposes of clarity.)

e. Well-known place names:

Weak: He came from Chicago, Ill.
Strong: He came from Chicago.

f. Phrases:

Weak: The accident occurred at the corner of Vine and Maple Streets.
Strong: The accident occurred at Vine and Maple.
Weak: The debate lasted for a period of two hours.
Strong: The debate lasted two hours.

g. Clauses:

Weak: All who are interested can vote.
Strong: All can vote.
Weak: The drought that occurred last summer.
Strong: Last summer's drought.

h. Redundancies:

Weak: Past experience had taught him the way.
Strong: Experience had taught him the way.

4c 2. Use Simple, Accurate and Vivid Words

a. Short, common words are usually best. The newspaper is written to be read hurriedly by persons of all levels of intellect.

USE	RATHER THAN
fire	holocaust, conflagration
died	passed away, deceased
man	gentleman
woman	lady
left	departed
body	remains
buried	interred
cancer	carcinoma

4d

b. Superlatives are usually inaccurate. There are a few "catastrophes," "panics" and "fiascos."

MORE ACCURATE	LESS ACCURATE
a beautiful woman	the most beautiful woman
an exciting game	the most exciting game
seldom	never
frequently	always
probably true	absolutely certain
escape	miraculous escape

4e

c. Caution must be taken in the accurate use of present tense:

Wrong: The policeman grabs the prisoner and pushes him into a cell.
Right: The policeman grabbed the prisoner and pushed him into a cell.
Wrong: Smith says he favors the proposal.

Right: Smith said he favors the proposal.
Right: Smith favors the proposal.

d. Tarnished word ornaments (figure of speech) are not vivid:

4f

AVOID

charming hostess	blushing bride
tastefully decorated	host of friends
watery grave	received an ovation
busy as bees	dance divinely
view with alarm	brutally murdered
point with pride	Joe College
stormy session	Mother Earth

e. The active voice is usually more forceful than the passive:

4g

Weak: The man was seen by the students.
Strong: Students saw the man.
Weak: The accident was witnessed by many persons.
Strong: Many persons saw the accident.
Stronger: Eleven persons saw the accident.

But in order to emphasize the proper element, the passive voice must frequently be used:

Weak: The County Election Committee elected W. P. Jones chairman.
Strong: W. P. Jones was elected chairman of the County Election Committee.
Weak: An automobile killed John Brown, county attorney, today.
Strong: John Brown, county attorney, was killed in an automobile accident today.

3. The Reporter Does Not Editorialize (Express His Opinion)

4h

He does not render verdicts or pass judgment, but writes from an objective point of view; consequently, he does not use *I, me, my, we, us* or *our* in a news story except when quoting someone. (Certain types of *by-line* stories are also exceptions to the rule.) Favorable or unfavorable phrases in a news story about a person, place or thing must be factual, not drawn from the opinion of the reporter.

Improper: He is well qualified for the position.
Proper: He is a graduate of Michigan and has 10 years of experience.
Improper: An interesting program has been prepared.
Proper: The program follows.
             (Let the "interesting" things speak for themselves.)
Improper: The decision was unjust.
Proper: The attorney general said the decision was unjust.
Improper: The prisoner lost his temper.
Proper: The prisoner threw his hat on the floor.
Improper: The witness lied.
Proper: The prosecuting attorney said the witness lied.
Improper: He committed suicide by jumping from the window.
Proper: He was killed in a fall from the window, and the coroner ruled it a suicide.

Improper:	Little Johnny Black, 6-year-old darling son of Mr. and Mrs. W. R. Black, died today.
Proper:	Johnny Black, 6, died today. He was the son of Mr. and Mrs. W. R. Black.
Improper:	The attractive young lady will win the hearts of all visitors when she begins serving as hostess at the chamber of commerce next week.
Proper:	The attractive young woman will begin serving as hostess at the chamber of commerce next week. ("Attractive young woman" is permissible in some newspapers if she *is* attractive and young, but many newspapers consider such phrases as puff.)
Improper:	The judge told me (told this reporter) the case was dismissed.
Proper:	The judge said the case was dismissed.
Improper:	The speaker said our city was well planned.
Proper:	The speaker said Blankville was well planned.

4i   4. Sentences and Paragraphs Should Be Short

The news paragraph seldom exceeds 50 words and may be composed of from one to about four sentences. Four lines of typewritten material—about 30 to 40 words—make a well-proportioned paragraph.

In general, the newspaper paragraph is a mechanical and arbitrary—not a logical and essential—group of words. Its chief purpose is to break up the solid column of words to permit easy reading. As fully as its brevity will permit, however, it should achieve the standard qualities of unity, coherence and emphasis. Short, simple sentences are better than long, involved sentences, but the effort to achieve short sentences should not result in a choppy style. Variety in the length and in the opening phrasing of both sentences and paragraphs will avoid monotony.

Involved:	An invitation to new industries to locate in Blankville was issued by the chamber of commerce yesterday at its annual meeting in the dining room of the Hotel Astor, and a new secretary, Henry Ijams, 221 Belmont St., was elected to promote the industrial program, succeeding James Butler, resigned.
Better:	New industries for Blankville will be a goal of the chamber of commerce, and Henry Ijams, former newspaperman, will be the promoter in this effort.
	The chamber adopted its industrial development program and elected Ijams as secretary at its annual meeting yesterday. Ijams, 221 Belmont St., succeeds James Butler, who resigned.

4j   5. Persons Named in News Stories Should Be Identified

The "mayor" in Mayor John Jones is sufficient identification in this and similar cases, of course. If, however, a person named is not so easily pointed out, the reporter must seek other means to identify him.

Numerous types of descriptive facts are used in identifying persons named in the news. The most common include nickname, age, home address, occupation, affiliations with social or religious organizations, public offices held, relationship to local or prominent persons ("nephew of Congressman Jones"), achievements ("city golf champion") and infamy ("ex-convict").

The most commonly used identification is the home address. Some newspapers use both age and home address as a general rule. But the reporter is encouraged to use others in addition to, or in lieu of the home address if better identifications are available. "Trent Street grocer," for example, is a much better identification than the home address of Leonard M. Jones. More persons will know Mr. Jones as a Trent Street grocer than as Leonard M. Jones of 3401 Trent St. To the extent that the purpose of the identification is to point out a particular person—to point him out as he is known by the greatest number of persons— these conventional devices serve well enough.

6. Every News Story Should Reveal or Clearly Imply Its Source or Authority   4k

Unless the reporter is an eyewitness of an event, he gets his facts second hand. To overcome this handicap he must state the authority or source (also called the attribution) for every fact in a news story unless that authority is implied. The reporter usually has three options:

   a. He may explicitly state the source of his information:

> The strike will end at noon Thursday, Mayor Thomas said. (If it is the first reference to the mayor use his complete name.)

   b. Or leave the source implied:

> Ten men escaped from the county jail in the early hours this morning. (The implied source is the sheriff or jailer.)

   c. Or purposely conceal the source to protect some individual or maintain a news advantage:

> A special session of the legislature will be called within 30 days despite the governor's denial of a rumor to that effect, it was learned authoritatively last night.

These options apply to ordinary, day-by-day reporting. Exceptions and qualifications to these general rules of quoting sources are detailed in Chapter 5 which deals with ethics and libel.

Except in unusual cases, editors insist the reporter give the source (authority) of all opinionated items:

> "Mayor Thomas is not qualified for the high office he holds," Councilman John Harkwright said.

Especially is it essential for the reporter to give the source or authority for derogatory statements. In doing so he guards against publishing biased or erroneous statements as his own. As a matter of fact, in some cases he may need to quote several persons in order to avoid presenting one version as the truth. This will alleviate his embarrassment in case he finds that he has been exploited by usually reliable sources that may have ulterior motives in generating certain news stories.

To state his authority throughout a story, the reporter uses both indirect and direct quotations. He employs various devices to alter the "Mr. Blank said" phrase. *This authoritative expression commonly is placed in an unemphatic position, usually at the end of the sentence.* Even in that position, such synonyms as "declared," "insisted" and "pointed out" may be used to avoid monotony. Variety also is achieved in such a sentence as " 'The tax is unfair,' said Tucker," by presenting the authoritative phrase within the sentence:

> Tucker condemned the tax as "unfair."
> The tax is "unfair," Tucker contends.

Words used in the authoritative or attributive expression must be chosen with care. To write that "Tucker pointed out" implies that Tucker stated an indisputable fact with which the writer agrees. In some cases the use of "admitted" is an erroneous connotation of admitting guilt to a wrongdoing. "Whispered," "screamed," "thundered," "declared," "insisted" and other such descriptive words must be used for the sake of accuracy—not for the sake of variety.

4m 7. The Story Itself Should Be Well Organized

The incidents of a story may actually occur in the greatest chaos and confusion. The written story must analyze and relate these incidents one to another and to the central story theme. A speaker may actually ramble in this fashion:

> "Gentlemen, this is a bad bill and ought not to pass. I was talking to Senator Williams last night, and he said the state can't afford all these welfare payments. I'm just as anxious to help the unfortunate as the next man, but I know down in my section we've got more people on welfare than we have people working. Some of them make more money off welfare than they did when they were working. That's why we shouldn't increase payments. This state's practically bankrupt. This bill might just push it over the edge. All we're doing if we pass this bill is paying people to rip off the taxpayer some more. You know it's true."

But the news story probably would read:

> Senator Jones opposed the bill. He argued that the state is nearly broke and cannot afford to increase welfare payments. He warned that this bill might push the state over the edge into bankruptcy.

THE STYLEBOOK

Before attempting to write news stories, the reporter should study thoroughly the stylebook of the publication for which he is working. This guide, which usually is handed a new reporter on his first day, explains the newspaper's style in preparing copy, spelling, punctuating, capitalizing, abbreviating and other such details. The common style is observed by all staff members.

The stylebook does not pretend to be an English grammar or a guide to composition and rhetoric. A reporter is expected to know common grammatical rules before he begins his newspaper career. Also, he should make constant use of a standard handbook of English composition. The stylebook is designed to clarify certain disputed or difficult points and to explain certain accepted usages. One newspaper capitalizes *street* and *avenue* when they are used in placenames (*Fourth Street*), which is called the "up style." Another newspaper uses a lowercase letter (*Fourth street*), the "down style." Some newspapers use a short form for a word such as *through,* making it *thru.* Obviously, not all stylebooks are alike, but the following can be studied as typical:

PREPARING COPY 4n

(*Note:* Newspapers using video display terminals, scanners and other electronic devices will have specific instructions for preparing copy (see Chapter 32). They are quite similar to the instructions below; however, they do include special codes which must be on each piece of copy as well as instructions for making insertions and corrections on electric typewriters.)

1. Prepare all copy with a typewriter.
2. Begin every story on a new sheet of paper (copy paper is generally 8½ × 11 inches in size).
3. Place your name at the upper left-hand corner of every page.
4. Write the "guideline" or "slug" for the story in the same line with your name, or in the line below. This line is a brief identification of the story, such as "fire" for a fire story or "city council" for a report of a city council meeting.
5. Number every page at the top, following the slug.
6. On the first page, leave ample space between the slug and the first paragraph—from one-fourth to one-third of a page.
7. Leave margins of at least one inch on both sides.
8. Double-space all copy.
9. Type on one side of the paper only.
10. Indent five spaces to begin a paragraph.
11. Do not underline.
12. Four-line paragraphs are optimum.
13. Do not split a word at the end of a line.
14. Do not split sentences between pages, and avoid splitting paragraphs between pages.
15. Write "more" or draw a short down-pointed arrow in the center at the end of each page when the story continues on another page.
16. Place an end mark (# or 30) in the center of the page at the end of the story.

SPELLING 4o

Any standard dictionary is the reference for spelling. Also, a city directory, telephone directory, almanac and Bible are useful in checking on the spelling of proper names. The Associated Press stylebook and others also have sections on spelling.

4p PUNCTUATING

Use of the Period:

1. Omit the periods in abbreviations of well-known governmental and other agencies:

   FBI   ROTC   AAA   FCC   ICC   PTA   USDA   US   UN

2. Use three periods (. . .) to indicate quoted matter that has been omitted (four periods if at the end of a sentence and another sentence follows).

3. Use a period to indicate cents only when the figure is more than one dollar and when the dollar mark is used. Otherwise, write the word "cents."

   $1.01   43 cents   nine cents

4. Omit periods in headlines, subheadings, captions, Roman numerals and letters used in formulas.

Use of the Comma:

1. Avoid superfluous use of commas, but do not violate accepted rules as set out in a standard handbook of English composition.

2. Use commas to set off the identification of a person, unless the identification is preceded by "of":

   John Smith, 1012 Towne St.,
   John Smith of 1012 Towne St.

3. Use commas in listing a series (see Semicolon, 1).

4. Do not use a comma between a man's name and "Jr.," and "Sr.," "II":

   John Jones Sr.   James Smith Jr.   George VI

Use of the Colon:

1. Use a colon to introduce a formal series of names or statements:

   The following officers were elected: John Smith, president . . .
   (But "Officers elected are John Smith, president . . .")

2. Use a colon before minutes in writing the time to day, as "3:30 p.m." (But "3 p.m.")

3. Use a colon between chapter and verse in referring to the Bible:

   Luke1:3–5.

Use of the Semicolon:

1. Semicolons should be used to separate a series of names and addresses or similar series containing commas:

Those attending were John Jones, 405 Trace St.; James Smith, 910 Drew Ave.; . . .

Points earned by Joe Jones, 893; James Smith, 745; . . .

2. Semicolons should be used instead of periods in headlines:

Six Convicts Escape;
Prison Guard Wounded

Use of the Dash:

1. Use dashes to indicate unfinished sentences or broken sentence structure.
2. Use dashes to set off highly parenthetical elements and to enclose appositives containing commas.

A crowd assembled in front of the building, but the sheriff—the man for whom they called—was not to be found.

The six students selected—three seniors, two juniors, and one sophomore—will receive . . .

3. Use dashes in Q. and A. quotations, omitting quotation marks:

Q.—How old are you? A.—Fifty-four.

4. Use dashes to indicate omitted letters.
5. Use a dash to separate a dateline from the first word of the lead.
6. Form the dash with two hyphens (--) on the typewriter.

Use of the Hyphen:

1. Use the hyphen in compound adjectives:

coal-black chimney   well-known man
old-fashioned dress   so-called enemy
10-year-old girl   10-yard gain

2. Use a hyphen with prefixes to proper names:

un-American   pre-Christian   anti-Whig

3. Use a hyphen in writing figures or fractions:

sixty-five   two-thirds

4. Use a hyphen between two figures to indicate the inclusion of all intervening figures, as "May 1-5."
5. Use a hyphen instead of "to" in giving scores, as "13-6."

Use of Parentheses:

1. Use parentheses to insert a word within a title:

The Bridgetown (Conn.) Fire Department

51

2. Use parentheses in a direct quotation to insert words that are not the speaker's:

"They (the strikebreakers) shall not pass," said the foreman.

3. Use parentheses to enclose figures or letters that indicate subject divisions within a sentence:

The committee decided (1) to refuse permission . . .
The board voted (a) to build a new athletic field . . .

4. Parentheses are no longer used to indicate the political party or state, or both, of a government official, in abbreviated form. Current style is

Sen. John Smith, D-R.I.

4q   Use of Quotation Marks:

1. Use quotation marks to set off direct quotations.
   Special Note: While most sentences can be written as either direct or indirect quotations, the use of direct quotations in newspaper stories is reserved largely for statements which are best displayed within quotation marks. Examples are highly controversial statements, colorful phrasings, pointed or well-phrased statements, ironical expressions, facts rendered inaccurate by rewording, ideas rendered ineffective by paraphrasing and unusual combinations of words.
2. Use quotation marks to set off titles of speeches, articles, books, poems, plays, operas, paintings, television programs:

"Pride and Prejudice"   "Hamlet"   "Mona Lisa"   "Aida"

(*Note:* Newspapers generally do not use italic body type, and quotation marks are employed as a substitute. However, quotation marks are not used in naming newspapers and magazines.)

3. Use quotation marks to set off coined words, slang and unusual words or expressions the first time such words are used in a story. Do not use quotation marks if the same words are used again.
4. Use quotation marks to set off nicknames when the full name is used but not when the nickname is used instead of the full name:

John "Bud" Smith   Bud Smith

5. In a series of quoted paragraphs, use quotation marks at the beginning of each of these paragraphs and at the end of the last paragraph only.
6. Use single marks for a quotation within a quotation.
7. In headlines use the single quotation mark.
8. Quotation marks should always *follow* adjoining periods and commas:
   "Here," she said.
   His style recalled "Leaves of Grass."

If the punctuation belongs to the quotation, the question mark, the exclamation point, the colon, the semicolon and the dash also are followed by quotation marks:

"What do you want?" she asked.

Otherwise, quotation marks *precede* these punctuation marks:

Have you seen the new motion picture "May Queen"?

Use of the Apostrophe:

1. Use the apostrophe to form the plural of letters but not the plural of figures, as "A's," " '70s."
2. Use the apostrophe to indicate the possessive case:

   New Year's Day   master's degree   children's home

3. Omit the apostrophe in such names as Blank County Farmers League, City Lawyers Association.

CAPITALIZING

4r

Capitalize:

1. Religious demonominations and orders:

   Protestant   Baptist   Jesuit   Franciscan

2. Nationalities, races:

   Germans   Negro   Chinese

3. Names of animals, as Fido or Rover (no quotation marks).
4. Names of political organizations:

   Democratic   Republican   Communist Party

5. National, state and local subdivisions:

   North   South   West Montana   East Blankville

6. Political divisions:

   Blank County   First District   Fifth Ward

7. Words used with numerals to form a proper name:

   Operator 7   Room 32   Lot 21   Journalism 301

8. Titles preceding proper names but not "former" or "ex" preceding such titles:

   President K. L. Burns   Prof. T. M. Smith
   former President K. L. Burns

9. Nicknames, including those of states, cities, schools.
10. *Complete* titles of all public or private organizations:

    General Assembly   City High School
    City School Board   First Baptist Church

City Council   City Department Store
First National Bank   Jones and Company
Southmoor Hotel   Center Country Club

11. Place names:

Lake Michigan   Ohio River   Vatican City
First Creek   Atlantic Ocean
Great Smoky Mountains National Park

12. The first and all principal words in titles of speeches, plays books, poems:

"An Answer to Questions on War"   "The Way of the World"

13. *Complete* titles of streets, avenues, boulevards, roads, as

King Street   Elm Lane   Queen's Way

14. Holidays:

Fourth of July.   Labor Day   Lincoln's Birthday

15. The "Union" in referring to the United States.
16. Abbreviations of college degrees, as "B.A."
17. Abbreviations of "junior" and "senior" to "Jr." and "Sr."
18. Names of legislative acts or sections of documents, as Smith Law, Title D. (A final reminder: If in doubt about capitalizing a word, make it lowercase.)

Do Not Capitalize:

1. Seasons of the year, as "spring," "summer."
2. Points of the compass, as "northeast."
3. The abbreviations "a.m." and "p.m."
4. Titles which follow proper names, as "K. L. Burns, president."
5. Names of studies, except languages, as "mathematics," "French," "literature."
6. Scientific names of plants and animals, except names derived from proper nouns (Hereford cattle).
7. "National," "government," "state," "federal," except in titles.
8. "Association," "club," "army," "navy," "society," except in titles.
9. "Alma mater."

4s ABBREVIATING

Abbreviate:

1. Months of the year of more than five letters when the day of the month is given:

Nov. 24   the last week in January   March 21

2. Times of the day, as 6 p.m.

3. Familiar college degrees, as B.A., Ph.D. M.D..
4. Names of states only when they follow names of cities or countries:

Blankville, Ark.   a town in Arkansas

5. Mr., Mrs., Dr., the Rev., Prof., Gov., Gen., etc., when they precede the name of the person.
6. "Saint" and "mount" only when preceding names:

St. Louis   Mt. McKinley   "Sermon on the Mount"

7. Sr., Jr., II following proper names.
8. Titles of public and private organizations that are well known by the readers *after* such titles have been used once in spelled-out form:

FBI   SEC   CIO   YMCA   UCLA

Do Not Abbreviate:

1. Christmas.
2. "Per cent" as "%," except in tabulation.
3. Names of persons.
4. Points of the compass.
5. Names of cities or counties.
6. Days of the week.
7. Street, avenue, boulevard, etc., when not preceded by both house number and the name.
8. "Company," except when a part of the official name.
9. Association, fraternity, university.
10. "Department" or "building."
11. "And" as "&," except if it is part of a formal name of a firm.
12. Weights or measures, as "pound," "foot."

TITLES   4t

1. Always give a person's first name or initials with the surname the *first* time any name is used. (Use the first name, *not* initials, of unmarried women.) Thereafter, the person may be referred to as

Miss Smith   Dr. Smith
Mrs. Smith   Prof. Smith
Ms. Smith   Gen. Smith
Mr. Smith

2. Some newspapers always use "Mrs." before a married woman's name and "Miss" before an unmarried woman's name, whether the full name or only the last name is used ("Miss Mary E. Smith," "Miss Smith"). Others have adopted the use of "Ms." before the names of all women, married or unmarried. Still others use only the woman's last name with no title after the first reference. Most newspapers do not use "Mr." before a man's name when his full name is given. "John T. Smith"

becomes "Mr. Smith" on further references in some newspapers. However, many simply use the last name "Smith" after the first reference.

3. For most religious denominations, it is correct to refer to the minister *first* as "the Rev. John Smith," and thereafter in a story as "Mr. Smith" ("Dr. Smith" only if he has the doctor's degree). Exceptions: Roman Catholics, "the Rev. John Smith" then "Father Smith." Jewish, "Rabbi John Milton" then "Rabbi Milton." Latter Day Saints (Mormons), "President John Smith" then "Mr. Smith." Christian Scientists have officials with titles of "Practitioner," "Lecturer" and "Reader" instead of "the Rev."

4. Do not use long and cumbersome titles *before* a name. Instead of "Director of Public Parks John Smith" make it "John Smith, director of public parks."

5. Do not refer to a woman as "Mrs. Dr. John Smith" or "Mrs. Prof. John Smith." A wife has no claim on her husband's title.

6. Instead of "Mesdames" or "Messrs." use titles singly.

7. Write it "Mr. and Mrs. John Smith" instead of "John Smith and wife."

8. Do not use "honorable" in a title unless quoting someone else.

9. Do not use double titles such as "President Dr. John Smith." Choose the higher title or the one of greater relevance to the story.

10. Give *exact* titles of faculty members, public officials, business executives. "Professor" and "instructor," for example, are not synonymous for rank.

4u FIGURES

1. Spell out numbers from one through nine, and use digits for all numbers above nine.

Exceptions:

   a. Spell out any number that begins a sentence.
   b. Spell out numbers referring to centuries, as "tenth century."
   c. Spell out ordinal street names, as "Fourth Street" up to 21st.
   d. Instead of "thirty-fifth," "fiftieth," use "35th," "50th," except in referring to centuries.
   e. Spell out numbers in such phrases as "one in a hundred."
   f. Use figures for all sums of money: "$5," "$6.01," "$23."
   g. Use figures for time of day, as "3 p.m.," "8 o'clock."
   i. Use figures in tabulations.
   j. Use figures for any whole and fractional number, as "9½," "4.1."

2. Spell out fractions, except after whole numbers, as "one-third."

3. Do not use 'st," "nd," "rd," "th" after dates. Write "Aug. 10, 1981."

MISCELLANEOUS

Use the Following Style:

all-state	cheerleader	homecoming	reelect
all right	cooperate	Joneses (plural)	somebody
anti-Catholic	everybody	line up	some one
anybody	everyone	newspaper	statewide
anyone	ex-officio	nobody	text book
attorney general	governor-elect	no one	two-thirds
baseball	half dollar	Old Glory	upstate
basketball	half dozen	Post Office	

CORRECTING COPY

The beginning reporter should learn a few of the copyreading marks immediately so that he may know how to make pencil corrections in his typewritten story.

In typing a story it is proper to "x" out words and sentences and to make pencil corrections, but the copy should be clean enough to be readable, and all corrections should be clear beyond a doubt when it leaves the reporter's hands.

An example of how corrections are made with an electric typewriter on copy to be processed by a scanner appears on page 433, in Chapter 32.

Following are the marks used by most reporters:

Delete letters:

    Two men werfe in the car . . .

Delete word or words:

    Two men were were in the car behind us with . . .

Transpose letters or words:

    Twow men in were the car with . . .

Spell out or abbreviate (same symbol in both cases):

    2 men were in the car with Mister Jones.

Insert word or words:

    were
    Two men in the car with Mr. Jones.

Capitalize letter:

    two men were in the car with . . .

Make letter lowercase:

    Two Men were in the car . . .

Period mark (either of two symbols):

Two men were in the car with Mr⊙ Jones ₓ

Separate letters with space:

Two men were/in the car . . .

Bring letters together:

Two men we ͡re in the car . . .

Restore copy that has been marked out:

Two men ~~were in the car~~ with Mr. Jones.
stet

In deleting copy on more than one line, mark out all the deleted material and draw a heavy line directly from the beginning to the end of the deleted material:

Located in the center of the little island is a log cabin,) ~~built perhaps 100 years ago though no one knows for sure and there is no way of finding out,~~ and back of the cabin is the site of the old

Indian village.

In correcting misspelled words that have only one or two letters wrong, mark out each misused letter and place the correct letter above. If a word is badly misspelled, mark out the whole word and write it correctly above:

nonchalantly
The b₀y walked ~~nonchalently~~ into the room.

The reporter should use the symbols whenever possible in correcting his copy because they are time-saving devices. However, if a phrase (or word) is split between two lines, the simplest procedure is to mark through all or part of the phrase and rewrite it correctly between the lines.

EXERCISES

1. Using the daily newspaper that circulates in your area or your hometown weekly, study the first paragraph in each story on the front page. Rank them from good to bad based on their simplicity, conciseness and clarity. Explain your rankings. Select the ones you consider poorly written, explain what is wrong with them and then rewrite them.
2. Select five news stories in which the opening sentences have forty or more words and rewrite them using no more than 25 words.
3. Using any newspaper available to you, select five stories, clip and paste each one on a separate sheet of paper. At the bottom of the sheet list all the errors in style you can find in each one, including errors in spelling, punctuation, grammar and the like. Correct the errors.
4. In the following items you will find numerous examples of faulty newspaper language

or style. Copy the items as given and make the needed corrections using the copyediting marks.

A. The students poured over their books in preparation for the exam which was scheduled to begin at 9:15 a.m. tomorrow morning.

B. Mr. Robert Wiandt, a wealthy merchant, was elected councilman from the Third ward by a narrow margin of only twelve votes.

C. President Dale Burton said the alumnis contribution amounted to 52% of the fund drive.

D. State Senator Don McNeil said he would introduce a bill in the State Legislature this year to set a fifty ton load on all state highway.

E. Johnson admitted that he lived a hand to mouth existance but that he was not guilty of such a lowlife trick of stealing a widow lady's Social Security check.

F. Two men dead; wives injured after collision.

G. A long time Loudon County resident who left to take a corporate position with a Nashville firm, has returned home to supervice the entire operation of the companys Loudon plant.

H. The Reverand Eli Estes morning subject on Sunday, June 4 was You Are A King.

I. There will be a special meeting of the county Republican Party executive committee Tuesday night at 7 o'clock in the courthouse.

J. The race is for three-year-olds only.

K. Students are required to see their academic advisor 1 times each semester.

L. Following her arrest, the unknown woman would not give police her name or her age or where she lived.

M. The distraut mother, weeping profusely, said the missing boy was 5-years-old.

N. Coach Paul Ashdown said the game will effect the standings.

O. The Y.M.C.A.-Martel Ladies Golf Club have announced their winners for last week.

P. The Lake County Criminal court had a busy week with judge Don Hileman dispensing 13 cases.

Q. $5 has been set as the fee for Summer School.

R. The Honorable Sammie Lynn Puett, Commissioner of General Services for the States, will make the formal address to the June graduating class.

S. Police said Summit St. will be closed from 1 P.M. to 5 P.M. tomorrow from Washington Drive to Victory Lane.

T. The woman called long distance to report that somebody in Smithville found her missing purse and mailed it to her, police stated.

U. "Its a wide open race," Lawyer Richard Hollow declared following the announcement by Governor Randolph (Randy) Schults that he would not seek a 2nd term.

V. A worm-eating Bluejay was discovered by Hazel Davidson in Holston Hills, while sitting on the branch of a tree singing.

W. Police stated that the body of a red-headed woman in her late 30's was found in a ditch across from 1901 Hickory Place.

X. The inspirational preaching of the Reverand Billy Joe Gupton is sure to be the highlight of the South Holston Baptist Church's annual homecoming and dinner at 1 in the afternoon next Sunday. The Church is located on Highway 95, just East of Dixie Lee Junction. Everyone is invited.

Y. F.B.I. agents and State troopers are trying to identify the lower half of a decomposed torso found on the Elk River in northern Alabama, a body thought to be that of a Memphis attorney missing since last winter.

Z. Lynwood Dixon, a 25-year-old Brooksville man who gave police a hardtime when they tried to help him from his wrecked car after it had crashed into a telephone pole in Fayetteville Saturday, is in "satisfactory" condition a Huntsville Hospital. He is to be charged with drunken driving.

5. Select a short local news story from a newspaper and retype it to illustrate the correct method of preparing copy. The story should be about a page and a half of typewritten copy. Make any necessary editing corrections before turning in the assignment.

6. A. Clip a story of considerable length from a daily newspaper; underline all words which indicate the source or authority for the facts in the story.

   B. Compile a list of synonyms for the word "said."

   C. The phrase "said Smith" or "Smith said" is commonly used in quoting persons both directly and indirectly in news stories. Select two stories from available newspapers and underline the various devices used by the writer to avoid using the "said Smith" phrase. Do not include synonyms for said.

7. Using the stylebook as your guide, make all the necessary corrections in the following stories to demonstrate your knowledge of copyediting marks.

   (Note: To avoid defacing the text, these exercises should be duplicated on a Xerox or other copying machine by the student.)

A. Smith - commissioners

   A sixty-five dollar a month raise for the Baord of County Commissioners was approved Monday night by and 8 to 5 vote.

   the increase was fifty dollars lower than originalyl proposed. In protesting the pay hike to $200 a month, commissioner Ro bert Jolley said 'now is an un-wise time to vote raises for ours elves.'

   "We have been hard nosed with ohter departments. we can al plead harship, but this should be considered at budget time."

   Commissioner Q. V. Ieinart said a sim ilar reqquest had been ignored during budget deliberati ns. he added that gasolin prices have gone up. "The taxpayers dont expect us to dip into our own pocket to meet expenses."

   "the mileage claim is a specious arguement. We came into office at $118 a month, and this went to one twenty five and then $135," commissioner H. Clyde Claiborne said. "These increases compansate us welll for mileage, and I figure that we can go 340 more miles with the incramentel allowance."

   commisioner Kenneth Wallace siad an increase d number of mettings required more mileage. Commissioner Ja ck Rains said the commissioner's pay did not meet expenses, but this was the wrong time for a riase.

   Voting in favor of the raise were Lenart, Hackworth Shapr, Jack Kenney and Commissioner's Jerry George, Ernest F. Phillips, Helen Norman and Darrell Copeland. Voting no were Jolley, Wallace, Jack Rains, Ada Hayes and Claiborne.

B. Smith - teacher

   A 39-year-old Roosevelt junior high school teachers was arrested today kone charges of distrivuting naroctics,

   Police have char ged Frederick Russel Green, 10201 Grosvenor place, with 6 counts of distributing narcotics. Three of the counts are fro distributing cocaine, 2 for barbiturates, and 1 count each kfor methaqualone and for maintianing a nuisance.

Also arested was Joseph Allen Johnson, 18, of the asme address. Police charge d him with posession of marijuana. He was identified as a maintanence man at the Floro house apartments.

A spokes person for the school superindent siad that Green was place onn administrative leave pending an investigtaion. He has taught a Rosevelt for 3 years.

Police said thier investigation involved salse of drugs at Greens' apartment, not at Roosevlet junior High School.

The investigation by police undercovre drug offficers lasted 2 months.

C. Smith - tax

Sales Tax reciepts for all municipilities in the county were lower last minth, figuers released this week show.

Clinton recieved $23,692.46, compared with $25,02290 last month. Lake Citys' share was $13,470,04 last month and $16,462.17 the mounth before. Norris droped from $1,881.83 to 1,749.48 in the lastest report.

the figures for last month were the Lowest in this fiscul year, except for Clinton, whose reciepts were up $340 over 2 months ago.

CHAPTER 5

Ethics and Libel

American newspapers enjoy a freedom that is unmatched anywhere else in the world.

Yet the press entered the 1980s facing the chilling fact that the courts at all levels—and especially the U.S. Supreme Court—were using their powers to intervene in the editorial freedom of the mass media with ever-increasing frequency.

From the mid-1970s on there has been a growing body of legal decisions to indicate that while the First Amendment says Congress "shall make no law" abridging freedom of the press, it does not prevent the courts from restricting press freedom through interpretation of the law and the Constitution.

The threat of an increasingly hostile judiciary was the central theme of John Hohenberg's book *A Crisis for the American Press,* which was published in 1978. And in 1979, when more than a half dozen Supreme Court decisions placed new restrictions on the press—even permitting closed pretrial hearings—Hohenberg's predictions appeared to be rapidly coming true.

Perhaps a few diehards still hold to the cherished hope that the First Amendment literally means that a newspaper has a right to print anything it wants to print. Most editors know better.

Every responsible editor knows that a newspaper simply cannot—and in a number of cases should not—print anything it wants to, even if the courts permitted. There are numerous reasons—social, economic, ethical—the First Amendment cannot be applied in its broadest, most literal sense to every story.

If a reporting staff is doing its job properly, every newspaper will have in its possession material that is both printable and unprintable—in an ethical sense. Deciding what should and what should not be printed is a constant moral dilemma for the editor and the reporter. Not all stories fit conveniently into a "print" or "do not print" category. In a moral or ethical sense, many fall somewhere in that gray area in between. In such cases most reporters have considerable difficulty in knowing not only what to write but how to write it and when.

It is true that after the Watergate scandal that forced the resignation of President Richard M. Nixon, there seemed to be a headlong rush to get into print with the latest peccadillo of a "fallen" elected official or entertainment superstar. Gossip journalism became a thriving enterprise in the magazine field. And a number of newspapers of national stature established gossip columns whose content raised numerous ethical questions. Chief among these questions certainly would have to be: Does the public really need to know this?

For example: Was it essential for the public to know that the wife of a prominent Senator being considered as a possible vice-presidential candidate was a reformed alcoholic? What did her personal problem really have to do with his qualifications to serve?

On the other hand, if a newspaper learns that a candidate for a local judgeship not only uses alcohol excessively but also uses drugs, should it print that information? And if so, when? After all, if elected he will be passing judgment on persons arrested for driving while intoxicated and certainly will be hearing cases of persons arrested for the use of drugs.

Without attempting to solve these particular problems (and they are not imaginary), one can recognize in them the moral difficulties involved in much news reporting: public interest versus special private interests. Where these two are clearly conceived, the newspaper's policy (discussed in another chapter) may influence its decision and dictate its course of action.

However, where certain larger issues of ethics and policy are concerned, newspapers frequently are influenced by what they consider to be acceptable community standards and by public opinion. For example, how graphic and detailed should a newspaper's description of a murder-rape case be? Should a newspaper publish more, or less, crime news? Under what conditions, if any, should a newspaper report the name of a rape victim? Should the names of juveniles be printed if not forbidden by state law? Most newspapers attempt to be responsible to the opinion of the readers in these areas, although no newspaper can please every reader every day. Even the most well-meaning, carefully reasoned decision dealing with a moral or ethical issue may bring howls of protest, angry letters to the editor and, on occasion, a canceled subscription.

Members of a news staff can and sometimes do influence a newspaper's ethical or moral standards. In one instance, protests by the reporters forced an editor to reverse a decision to print the name of every woman who brought rape charges against a man. Every reporter wants to be proud of the newspaper's general moral or ethical standards. However, the principal concern should be for his own professional code of ethics.

Relation to Public. The reporter cannot ignore the fact that the public welfare may be involved in much that he writes. His writing is addressed to the public. In many cases, his writing is the only—or chief—source that the public (individually or collectively) has for information needed to solve its problems. This responsibility makes careless, slipshod, inaccurate or biased reporting inexcusable. One of the major criticisms of the press—one that often creates a credibility problem—is that "the press is biased." Often what is mistaken as bias on the part of the reader is careless, inaccurate reporting by the writer. Of course, the reporter cannot be expected to be free of mistakes in judgment. He will face situations in which he must make decisions on what, and how, and when and how much of his information he should reveal. His own conscience must guide him. But if he has taken the trouble to develop a sufficient background of information so that his thinking is thoroughly enlightened, he should be able to make sound and unbiased judgments when the public welfare is his objective.

Relation to Newspaper. Most newspapers are genuinely concerned about their reputation for fairness and accuracy. They want the respect of their readers and insist that the reporter perform his duty with truth and the public welfare as his objective. However, some publishers, in pursuit of a policy—frequently social and economic as well as political—may expect much more or much less than the plain unvarnished truth as the reporter sees it. In some instances, too, a change in ownership may cause a newspaper to reverse a policy, political or others. The choice for the reporter will be extremely difficult if he is instructed by his editor to twist the truth in a story. Three possible courses seem to be open to him. He may refuse to alter his own principles and resign. He may accept the assignment and salvage his self-respect as best he can. Or he may attempt to work out with the employer an agreement for his own integrity and independence. There can be no doubt that the first and third choices are strictly ethical—and should be profitable in the long run—in self-respect if not in money.

The problem of ethics was one of the motivating forces behind the establishment of a number of journalism reviews. The major one is the *Columbia Journalism Review,* published at Columbia University in New York City. It evaluates the performance not only of newspapers but all the mass media. And it set an example for many of the reporter-run reviews that were established in the late 1960s and early 1970s.

The *Chicago Journalism Review* was among the first established by staff members of local newspapers. Although it was short-lived, it was a lively and often provocative publication that pointed up what its editors considered the shortcomings of the local media. Lack of financial support forced it to cease publication. Dozens of other local reviews were started but most have disappeared. Two that have weathered all sorts of adversity and still exist are the *St. Louis Journalism Review* and the *Washington Journalism Review.*

In addition, several national organizations were established by individuals or groups to monitor the performance of the mass media. The most prominent of these is AIM—Accuracy in Media, which seems to be conservative in its approach to news.

Relations to News Sources. The reporter's access to news sources is one of his chief professional assets. These sources must be carefully cultivated, and it is obvious that they must be honorably maintained and respected. On the other hand, a reporter must not become a "captive" of his sources and work as their personal spokesman. Sources often attempt to use their close relationship with a reporter to control the news in some fashion. On the basis of self-interest and professional interest, to say nothing of the basis of honor, the reporter cannot divulge secrets or betray confidences. Of course, if ordered to do so by a judge, he may face the dilemma of revealing a confidence or going to jail, for the U.S. Supreme Court has ruled that the First Amendment does not guarantee the right to protect the confidentiality of news sources. A number of states, however, do grant that right. Sometimes it is wise for a reporter not to accept some of these so-called confidences, for the same information may be obtainable from other sources. The intelligent reporter should have little difficulty in managing the ethics of this situation if he is continually aware of the problem. He should have a clear understanding with every person he deals with. When confronted with such common admonitions as "get this on the front page," or "let me check your story," he must explain that his editor, not he, must make these decisions. He can promise not to quote direct language and not to reveal where he obtained the information, but he should be very cautious, indeed, about promising not to use materials in any way. He should respect release dates. He should protect innocent persons from false inference, but he cannot promise to abandon his pursuit of news so long as that news is in the public interest. A reporter should be constantly aware of the fact that many of his sources, particularly in the area of politics, will be attempting to use him to their advantage in their efforts to color the news.

Increasing numbers of persons in public life are resorting to backgrounding sessions or informal conferences at which they will speak to reporters "off the record." Often they are using these sessions to get information out to the public without being identified as the source. A number of reporters willingly cooperate, but the practice is criticized soundly by others. And some newspapers have a policy of not permitting their reporters to remain at such sessions if the source insists on not being identified in the news story that may grow out of the meeting.

Accuracy As a Protection. The best protection against bias in reporting is the indefatigable pursuit of fact and the careful checking of all facts. It has often been said that the three cardinal rules of journalism are accuracy, accuracy, accuracy. As long as the reporter presents the news as it actually occurs, without any ideological shading or emotional coloring, he is performing his duty professionally.

Of course, this will not make the reporter or his newspaper immune to resentment or attack. A large proportion of the news will be injurious to someone or some cause (or will be thought so by the individuals involved). The more important the revelation, the more resistance there is, usually, to the reporting of it. (Certain technical problems of privileged and nonprivileged documents will be examined presently.) Every reporter should remember that in many cases—especially in the area of public affairs—even the most recalcitrant news source often is dependent upon the media for his public image. But a reporter should never use that as a lever in his relationship with news sources. In general, he should depend upon a sound reputation for accurate, professional reporting to overcome resistance, solve problems and open many doors to the sources of news.

Importance of Authoritative News Sources. The careful use of authority in the news is an important means of solving certain ethical problems for the reporter. It is unnecessary and usually unwise for the reporter to assume responsibility for the facts of his story. Occasionally he is an eyewitness. Frequently he is an interpreter. Always he is a reporter, however, and by attributing his materials to their proper sources he clearly reveals the bases for his story. Naturally he should know his sources well enough to know if they are trustworthy as well as authoritative, and he should use extreme caution—make every additional check possible on the information given—when he is dealing with an unfamiliar source. Even if he must conceal the individual whom he would like to quote, he can imply, if not the authority, at least the authenticity of his data. (Some newspapers require reporters to verify information with two or more sources if the original source insists on remaining anonymous.) Despite precautions taken to cite authority and to confirm or verify the information with additional sources, the reporter must occasionally face the ultimate problem that sources will lie.

5a   Codes of Ethics

There are no concrete "rules of honor" for newspapers and their staffs. In fact, each newspaper will have its own "code of ethics," either written or unwritten. Long-time readers of a newspaper easily recognize a newspaper's ethics in the way it presents the news.

However, most newspapers today attempt to follow a set of principles or code of ethics established by such professional groups as the American Society of Newspaper Editors and the Society of Professional Journalists, Sigma Delta Chi.

The American Society of Newspaper Editors adopted a Statement of Principles in 1975 that supplanted the organization's Code of Ethics, originally written in 1922.

The ASNE Statement of Principles follows:

PREAMBLE

The First Amendment, protecting freedom of expression from abridgement by any law, guarantees to the people through their press a constitutional right, and thereby places on newspaper people a particular responsibility.

Thus journalism demands of its practitioners not only industry and knowledge but also the pursuit of a standard of integrity proportionate to the journalist's singular obligation.

To this end the American Society of Newspaper Editors sets forth this Statement of Principles as a standard encouraging the highest ethical and professional performance.

5b   ARTICLE I—RESPONSIBILITY

The primary purpose of gathering and distributing news and opinion is to serve the general welfare by informing the people and enabling them to make judgments on the issues of the time. Newspapermen and women who abuse the power of their professional role for selfish motives or unworthy purposes are faithless to that public trust.

The American press was made free not just to inform or just to serve as a forum for debate but also to bring an independent scrutiny to bear on the forces of power in the society, including the conduct of official power at all levels of government.

ARTICLE II—FREEDOM OF THE PRESS

Freedom of the press belongs to the people. It must be defended against encroachment or assault from any quarter, public or private.

Journalists must be constantly alert to see that the public's business is conducted in public. They must be vigilant against all who would exploit the press for selfish purposes.

ARTICLE III—INDEPENDENCE

Journalists must avoid impropriety and the appearance of impropriety, as well as any conflict of interest or the appearance of conflict. They should neither accept anything nor pursue any activity that might compromise or seem to compromise their integrity.

ARTICLE IV—TRUTH AND ACCURACY

5c

Good faith with the reader is the foundation of good journalism. Every effort must be made to assure that the news content is accurate, free from bias and in context, and that all sides are presented fairly. Editorials, analytical articles and commentary should be held to the same standards of accuracy with respect to facts as news reports.

Significant errors of fact, as well as errors of omission, should be corrected promptly and prominently.

ARTICLE V—IMPARTIALITY

5d

To be impartial does not require the press to be unquestioning or to refrain from editorial expression. Sound practice, however, demands a clear distinction for the reader between news reports and opinion. Articles that contain opinion or personal interpretation should be clearly identified.

ARTICLE VI—FAIR PLAY

5e

Journalists should respect the rights of people involved in the news, observe the common standards of decency and stand accountable to the public for the fairness and accuracy of their news reports.

Persons publicly accused should be given the earliest opportunity to respond.

Pledges of confidentiality to news sources must be honored at all costs, and therefore should not be given lightly. Unless there is clear and pressing need to maintain confidences, sources of information should be identified.

These principles are intended to preserve, protect and strengthen the bond of trust and respect between American journalists and the American people, a bond that is essential to sustain the grant of freedom entrusted to both by the nation's founders.

THE PITFALLS OF LIBEL

5f

Every reporter works with the specter of a libel suit nearby because there simply is no sure-fire method of preventing libelous material from getting into a newspaper story.

In writing news it is not always easy to determine the exact point at which the public's right to know is greater than the individual's right to his good name. A reporter must never forget that every person is protected by law from the publication of libelous or slanderous statements. A person's name—reputation—is of tangible value. And if a reporter damages it, even unintentionally, he could do irreparable harm to a person's position in society, his means of earning a living.

Damage to a person's reputation, if it is beyond the bounds of what a newspaper is legally entitled to print, is called defamation. As a general rule, defamation is divided into two categories—libel and slander. In the view of the courts, libel is written defamation, slander is spoken. Over the years, the courts have expanded the definition of libel, making it include all defamation that offers a greater possibility of harm than does slander because it is written (and is therefore more permanent than slander). As a result, written materials, signs, cartoons, television and even radio broadcasts that have been taped or presented from written scripts have been held by the courts to be libel.

Libel Defined. Libel laws vary in each state. As a result the definition of libel may be slightly different from state to state. However, they all are essentially the same. Libel can be defined as:

> A false statement printed or broadcast about a person that exposes that person to public hatred, ridicule or contempt, lowers him in the esteem of the community, causes him to be shunned or injures him in his business or profession.

It is important to remember that a person may libel another either by outright expressions or by insinuation or innuendo. And a person may be libeled even though he may not actually be named in the offending article.

Elements of Libel. Anyone filing a libel suit, regardless of his status, has to establish these elements:

Publication. That the statement was published (communicated) in some form. In the case of the news media the most common way is either a newspaper article or a radio or television broadcast.

Identification. That the statement was generally understood to refer to the person suing by persons who knew him or members of the general public. The person suing does not have to be specifically named. And members of a group, such as a school board, can be libeled even though they are not individually named.

Injury. That the statement caused actual damages in some tangible manner. This could mean actual loss of money as a result of a lost job or a business contract, for example, or damage to the person's reputation, humiliation or mental anguish and suffering.

Fault. The status of the person suing determines what must be proved. If the person suing is a public person or public figure and the alleged libelous statement concerns his public role, he must prove that the statement was made by the newspaper or broadcast station even though it was known in advance to be false or that there was serious doubt as to its truth.

But if the person suing is a private individual, or a public official or figure suing about a statement concerning a purely private matter not affecting his public role, then he has to prove only that the publisher or broadcaster was negligent in failing to determine that the statement was false and that it defamed him.

Who Can Be Defamed. Any living person can be defamed. A dead person cannot be defamed; however, if the words reflect upon any living person (such as a survivor), the survivor can bring an action in his own right. A corporation or a partnership can be defamed by language that casts aspersions on its honesty, credit, efficiency and other business character. Individual professionals such as doctors and lawyers can be defamed if the language casts aspersions on their honesty or ability to practice their profession. For example, to call a doctor a quack or a lawyer a shyster could be libelous.

Every person instrumental in the publication of a libelous statement is responsible. This usually includes the person making the statement, the reporter, the editor and the newspaper itself, but the newspaper alone is made the defendant in many suits.

Interpretation of Defamatory Words. In all actions for libel and slander, the words alleged to be defamatory must be interpreted as such; they must be understood in the defamatory sense whether or not they are believed by the listeners or readers. If the defamatory meaning arises only from the facts not apparent upon the face of the publication, the plaintiff must establish the defamatory meaning with reference to such facts. If the words are defamatory upon their faces (such as naming the wrong person as a convicted criminal), this is defamatory per se and it does not require proof of the meaning gathered from surrounding events to be adjudged libelous. Such statements as "it is alleged," "it was reported" or "according to police" do not protect a reporter who writes a libelous statement.

Proof Needed. Formerly all libel was actionable without proof of some injury or harm to persons or property. Today, however, many jurisdictions treat libel like slander in that they require proof of damages incurred except in the following cases:

1. The imputation of a serious crime involving moral turpitude.
2. The imputation that the party is infected with a contagious disease.
3. The imputation affecting the plaintiff in his business, trade, profession or office.
4. The imputation reflecting upon the chastity of a woman.

However, all jurisdictions hold that words that are libelous per se are actionable without damage having to be shown, although in most libel cases an effort is made to show damage in order to increase the amount of the judgment.

Intent to Libel. The U.S. Supreme Court, under the late Chief Justice Earl Warren, changed the direction of libel law to favor the news media. In its landmark decision in 1964—*New York Times* v. *Sullivan*—the court ruled that the constitutional guarantees of a free press prohibited a public official from recovering damages for a libelous, false statement relating to his official conduct unless he could prove that the statement was made with actual malice. To prove actual malice, the court said, the public official must prove that the statement was made with deliberate knowledge that it was false or it was made with reckless disregard of whether it was false or not. The burden of proof was on the public official.

The so-called New York Times rule was expanded in the *Butts* v. *Curtis Publishing Co.* case in 1967 to apply not only to public officials but public figures. And in 1971 it was expanded again in the *Rosenbloom* v. *Metromedia Inc.* case to include private individuals involved in matters of general and public interest.

The problem of determining who qualified as a public official frequently plagued the press after the Times ruling. Generally, the press gave the Times rule a broad interpretation. However, in 1974, the Court, under a new chief justice—Warren Burger—took another look at who was public and who was private and came up with a new interpretation in the case of *Gertz* v. *Robert Welch, Inc.*

Gertz, a Chicago lawyer known for his trial work on behalf of civil rights and other causes and the author of several books, charged that he was libeled by the John Birch Society magazine American Opinion. Among other things, the magazine called him a Leninist and a Communist fronter. The magazine article appeared while Gertz was representing a family that had sued the Chicago police department over the death of their son who had been shot and killed by a policeman. The magazine alleged that the suit was part of a plot to destroy the Chicago police department. Throughout the trial against the police department, Gertz kept a low profile, refusing to be interviewed and rejecting efforts of the media to get him to discuss the case publicly.

When he sued the magazine for libel, Gertz was able to find twelve jurors who claimed they had never heard of him despite his local fame. It was a major factor in helping him prove that he was not as well known as the magazine would claim in defending the suit. A jury found that Gertz had been libeled and awarded him $50,000 in damages. In the legal maneuvering that followed, the trial judge threw out the jury's award and said that Gertz was a public figure under the Times rule. Gertz appealed and the District Appeals court upheld the trial judge, ruling that, because the story concerned matters of public interst, Gertz would have to show actual malice on the magazine's part, even though he might be a private citizen. He had failed to do this, the Appeals Court ruled.

Gertz appealed to the Supreme Court which reversed the Appeals Court. The Supreme Court ruled that Gertz was not a public figure in this case and did not have to prove actual malice. In this decision, the Court established that there are two kinds of public figures. One kind is the individual who achieves such pervasive fame or notoriety that he becomes a public figure for all purposes and in all context or the individual who voluntarily injects himself or is drawn into a particular public controversy and thereby becomes a public figure. Gertz did neither, the court ruled. The second kind is the limited public figure. Under this concept, the court said, the nature and extent of an individual's participation in a particular controversy giving rise to the defamation must be considered.

In short, the court was saying that an individual must play a prominent role in a particular controversy before he can be considered a full public figure. And in 1976 the court further narrowed the definition of public figure in Time, Inc. v. Firestone. That case involved a divorce suit and resulted from a blurb in Time magazine that said Russell Firestone had been granted a divorce from his wife, Mary Alice, on grounds of adultery. He had not been. She sued Time, claiming she had been called an adultress. Time claimed she was a prominent socialite and a public figure. It said the 17-month divorce case was well publicized and that she had held several press conferences during the trial. But the court said a divorce suit was not the kind of public controversy referred to in the Gertz decision. It noted that while there was public interest in the case, it was not an important public question.

Under the Times rule, a public official seeking to prove actual malice was barred from inquiring into the state of mind of the reporter and editors when the alleged libelous story was being prepared for publication. Over the years, the Supreme Court has chipped away at that concept. And, finally, in 1979, in the Herbert v. Lando decision, the Court reversed the Times ruling on that point.

In that case, Col. Anthony Herbert, an army officer who gained national recognition for his charges that he reported misconduct of troops and officers in Vietnam but was ignored by his superiors, sued Barry Lando, a television producer for the Columbia Broadcasting System. Herbert charged he had been libeled in a CBS program produced by Lando, which discredited him and his charges against the army. In preparing for the case, Herbert's lawyers sought to ask questions about Lando's state of mind when preparing the telecast. Lando refused to answer their questions. When the case reached the Supreme Court, it ruled that a libel plaintiff, obliged to prove actual malice because he is a public figure, has the right to inquire into a reporter's state of mind.

The decision brought a warning from the Reporters Committee for Freedom of the Press that it "will encourage harassing libel suits and will discourage news about public events."

Late in 1979, the Court acted again to put additional restraints on who might be considered a public person. One case involved U.S. Senator William Proxmire and a scientist. The other involved a former State Department interpreter and *Reader's Digest* magazine.

Proxmire, in a press release, had ridiculed the scientist, Ronald Hutchinson. He awarded Hutchinson his monthly "Golden Fleece" award for wasting taxpayers' dollars with his publicly funded research. Hutchinson had received more than $500,000 to study aggression in monkeys to help the navy and the National Aeronautics and Space Administration better select crews for submarines and space flights. In his press release, Proxmire called the research "monkey business." Hutchinson sued for $8 million.

The other case involved Ilya Wolston, a former State Department interpreter, cited for contempt by a Federal grand jury when he refused to appear during an investigation of Russian spying in the U.S. Wolston later cooperated with Federal officials, and was never indicted for espionage. However, in 1974 he was listed as "among Soviet agents identified in the U.S." in a book called *KGB: The Secret Work of Soviet Agents*. He sued the author, John Barron and the publisher, Reader's Digest Association, Inc.

At the lower court trials, both Hutchinson and Wolston were ruled to be public figures and their libel suits dismissed. When the cases finally came before the U.S. Supreme Court, it reversed those decisions.

In its decisions, the Court said that neither Hutchinson nor Wolston had "thrust" himself into a public controversy in order to affect its outcome. Mere involvement in a newsworthy event, the Court ruled, did not automatically make someone a public figure. (This is a reversal of the Rosenbloom decision and several others of the 1960s.)

The Court also rejected Proxmire's defense that he was immune from libel suits by the Constitution, which states that "for any speech or debate in either House," members of Congress "shall not be questioned in any other place." Proxmire argued that congressmen cannot be held liable for what they say on the floor of Congress. The Court pointed out that what the senator had said was not said on the floor of Congress but in a press release. It ruled that Congressional press releases and newsletters were not immune from libel suits.

Television and Radio—Whether Libel or Slander. Defamation via television is generally considered libel because it is the type of defamation which can be detected by the sense of sight. The vast audience and the ensuing increase in the

71

likelihood of harm are additional reasons given for this interpretation. Radio presents a different problem. Most courts have held that defamation through the medium of radio is slander unless the broadcast is made from a prepared script or from a tape or other recording.

Defenses of Libelous Statements. There are five basic defenses in a libel suit:

The statement is the truth.

The newspaper is "privileged" to print the statement.

The statement is fair comment or criticism.

The statement was made with the consent of the person who claims he was libeled.

The newspaper offered the person the right of reply to the alleged libelous statement.

In general, the first three are the most significant defenses. However, the last two could prove to be of extreme importance to the newspaper's defense in a libel suit. In defending itself against a libel suit, it is the responsibility of the newspaper to prove that one or more of the defenses existed when the story was published.

Truth As a Defense. A newspaper's strongest defense against libel is to be able to prove what it prints is true. A reporter must not rely on hearsay, opinions or rumors if a statement in any way borders on being libelous. A report that "Detective Smith said Tom Johns robbed the store" is libelous unless the reporter can prove Johns actually robbed the store. (Or unless the report is privileged, as explained in the following paragraphs.) Calling a building an "alleged house of ill repute" libels every person living in that house unless the statement can be proved. Fortunately, it is not necessary to prove that a story is meticulously true. Slight inaccuracies of expression are immaterial provided that the defamatory charge is true in substance.

If a statement is true, a libel suit probably will not arise, for truth is generally accepted as a "complete defense." In some states, however, the newspaper's defense must also show justification in printing a derogatory statement that is true. In these states the newspaper must show a good motive for publishing the statement.

A common misconception is that a newspaper or broadcast station is safe so long as it merely repeats or attributes the false and libelous statement to a particular person. This simply is not true. And a newspaper cannot base its defense on the fact that the person it has libeled is guilty of even worse conduct than implied in the libelous statement. If a newspaper falsely publishes that a person is guilty of a robbery, it is no defense to be able to prove that he committed a murder. Likewise, a newspaper cannot imply that a person is guilty of repeated misconduct and then offer as its defense that the person was guilty of such conduct at least one time.

Privilege As a Defense. The reporter is privileged to report derogatory statements that are taken from legislative, judicial or other public and official proceedings and records without fear of successful libel or slander action. Since the meetings and records of such groups as city councils and state legislatures are generally open to the public, the newspaper has a right to step in and represent the public. If a person is defamed in these proceedings, he cannot recover damages. The public's interest, in such cases, outweighs the individual's right to reputation, even though he may suffer real harm. The immunity for the participant in official proceedings is called "absolute" privilege. As long as what is said is relevant to the business of the proceedings it is privileged and not actionable. Anyone reporting such proceedings is given an immunity from successful suit for defamation, also. The protection granted the reporter is somewhat more limited in that it does not protect malice in reports (in most states). As a result, it is known as "qualified" privilege. There are other considerations that must be met by the reporter to enjoy this qualified privilege. The story must be a fair and accurate account of the proceedings. Great caution is necessary in quoting from official proceedings, public records, police reports and other public sources of information.

Some states have laws that spell out in considerable detail the kinds of proceedings and records which are protected as privileged communications. The Proxmire case, cited earlier, is an example of how the concept of privileged material has been narrowed by court decisions.

Fair Comment. Newspapers and other mass media have the right to comment on and criticize the acts of public persons who offer themselves or their particular talent for public approval. But the comment must be:

Fair
Made without malice
Not unjustifiably extended to the private life of the person involved

Actors, artists, authors, composers, speakers and others who offer themselves or their works for public acceptance are subject to comment or criticism by the press. The press also has the right to criticize the public performance of public officials.

However, the defense of fair comment is lost when a newspaper invades the private lives of such persons in most cases. To say that an author is a poor writer because he knows nothing about plotting a novel could be fair comment. To say that he is a poor writer because of his sexual proclivities could bring a libel suit. Writers should be careful to criticize only the substance of an author's book, the caliber of an artist's painting or the quality of an actress's performance.

A classic example on how far a publication can go in commenting upon a matter submitted for public acceptance was illustrated by the "Cherry Sisters Case" (114 Iowa 298). The defendants had published an article in which a reviewer gave the following graphic description of a public performance by three sisters who danced and sang:

> Effie is an old jade of 50 summers, Jessie a frisky filly of 40 and Addie (the plaintiff in the case), the flower of the family, a capering monstrosity of 35. Their long skinny arms, equipped with talons at the extremities, swung mechanically, and anon waved frantically at the suffering audience. The mouths of their rancid features opened like caverns and sounds like the wailing of damned souls issued therefrom. They pranced around the stage with a motion that suggested a cross between the *danse du ventre* and fox trot—strange creatures with painted faces and hideous mien.

That style of criticism is still practiced by some critics today. John Simon, theater critic for *New York* magazine in the late 1970s, gained considerable reputation for his biting, sometimes even savage attacks on performers. In a review of a musical starring actress-singer-dancer Liza Minnelli he wrote:

> . . . I always thought Miss Minnelli's face deserving—of first prize in the beagle category. Less aphoristically speaking it is a face going off in three directions simultaneously: the nose always enroute to becoming a trunk, blubber lips unable to resist the pull of gravity, and a chin trying its damnedest to withdraw into the neck, apparently to avoid responsibility for what goes on above it. It is, like any face, one that could be redeemed by genuine talent, but Miss Minnelli has only brashness, pathos and energy.

Miss Minnelli did not sue despite the fact that Simon's attack was not directly related to her performance in this particular musical. He made no attempt to relate her physical appearance to the role she was playing or the plot of the musical.

In writing about public officials, a newspaper reporter has the right to comment on or criticize that official's performance in his job. The courts have even given the press more latitude in commenting on public officials than they have allowed in criticizing the work of creative artists. Some comment on the private life and personal conduct of the public official is allowed if the official's private conduct has an influence on the way he conducts the public's business.

For example, the late Drew Pearson and Jack Anderson, syndicated columnists, were not sued for libel when they reported in a series of columns that a very influential senior member of the House of Representatives was an alcoholic. He was subject to fair comment—no matter how damaging it might have been—because he was unable to separate his alcoholism from his conduct of his public office.

However, every reporter should be aware that the Supreme Court has continued to narrow the definition of who is a public person or public official. Its recent decisions indicate a growing concern for the privacy of even the most public persons.

Consent. It is not uncommon for a person to give his consent to the publication of material about himself and then change his mind after he sees it in print. On occasion he may even sue because the material is libelous. In most cases, the newspaper is privileged to publish libelous matter if the person libeled consented to it.

The person does have a right, however, to place restrictions on his consent. He may, for example, want to limit publication to a particular time or for a particular purpose. The newspaper loses the defense of consent if it breaks the agreement.

A person may consent to publication of the material either by oral or written authorization. Or it may be implied from the person's words or other conduct. Implied consent may be obtained by requesting and receiving a voluntary acknowledgment and confirmation of the libelous material. But the mere denial of or refusal to answer questions concerning the libelous material does not qualify as consent. A newspaper is on much safer ground if it has written consent when potentially libelous statements are involved.

The Right of Reply. Right of reply is a much stronger defense than consent.

Right of reply simply means that the newspaper gives the person who has been libeled an opportunity to answer the charges or attack made against him. Generally newspapers, simply as a matter of good faith, will not print a libelous attack—even if it is privileged to do so—without giving the person attacked a right to reply in the same article.

It is important to note that the reply cannot exceed the scope of the original attack. The reply must be limited to answering the original attack only. It cannot be expanded to include any other area of concern or to introduce any new material. The chief purpose the right of reply serves is to demonstrate that the newspaper is acting in good faith and is simply not being a party to the original libelous attack. It helps the newspaper prove that it was not acting maliciously.

Statute of Limitations. Most state libel laws set a specific time limit on the filing of libel suits. Generally they range from one to three years after the first publication of the libelous material. A newspaper that circulates in several states should take the precaution of learning the statute of limitations in each of these states.

Criminal Libel. Most libel cases go to civil courts, with the plaintiff suing for damages, but certain cases appear also in criminal courts and may be punishable by fine and imprisonment. Some states hold that criminal prosecution is possible if the statement tends to provoke the person about whom it was printed to wrath, to expose him to public hatred, contempt or ridicule or to deprive him of the benefits of public confidence and social intercourse. Two other special circumstances can be involved. One is libel of the dead, which is presumed to provoke relatives and friends of the deceased to violence, and the other is libel of groups when the libel provokes violence. Both are quite rare, however. Since criminal statutes vary on these points, it is best that the reporter consult his state statutes for the exact rules followed in his state.

Retractions of Libelous Statements. Newspapers attempt to avoid libel suits by publishing retractions of statements which are unquestionably libelous. The retraction should point out and correct the newspaper's errors, and the newspaper should apologize to the person or persons concerned. The retraction notice, in order to be effective, must generally be given space or time that is equivalent to the defamatory matter. For instance, if the defamatory material was printed on the first page of a newspaper, the retraction notice should be published on the first page. (In several states, all retraction notices are required by law to be published on the front page no matter where the original story appeared in the paper.) The retraction does not nullify the claim for damages against the newspaper, though it satisfies many libeled persons and causes them to decide against filing suit. If a libel suit is filed, the retraction may help reduce the damages awarded by indicating lack of actual malice.

INVASION OF THE RIGHT OF PRIVACY 5g

While laws of libel date back almost to the dawn of civilization, the right of privacy—the right to be let alone—is relatively new. The concept was first introduced formally in the 1890s. Originally it related to the use of a person's name or likeness for commercial purposes without the person's consent. However, privacy law has been expanded over the years and has been recognized as a Constitutional right by the U.S. Supreme Court.

Simply stated, the right of privacy is the right of a person to be let alone, to be free from unwarranted publicity and to enjoy life as he wants to without his name, photograph or activities becoming public property unless he waives that right. The right of privacy is a personal one, protecting the feelings and sensibilities of living persons only. Corporations and public institutions, such as a university, have no right of privacy, unless granted by special law. A person's right of privacy ends when he dies and is generally not transferable to his relatives.

A person's privacy can be invaded by newspapers, radio stations, television stations, photographers, motion pictures, books, advertisements and dozens of electronic ways, ranging from wiretapping to supersensitive microphones that can pick up conversations at great distances. However, the extent to which anyone is protected generally depends on his status as a public or private figure. Public officials and public figures generally are more legitimately open to public comment, criticism and scrutiny. However, there are limits on the press even in the case of public officials and public persons.

A person's privacy can be invaded in four ways:

Wrongful Intrusion. This generally involves the invasion of a person's solitude or private affairs without his knowledge or consent. It often involves the use of spying devices such as hidden microphones, wiretaps, hidden tape recorders, high-powered cameras or by obtaining by illegal means a person's private documents. A reporter misrepresenting himself to gain access to a place or a person, especially if he is trespassing on private property, could be subject to an invasion of privacy suit.

Publishing Private Matters. This often results when a newspaper publishes facts about the private life of a person that would offend ordinary sensibilities and that may cause that person mental suffering or embarrassment. Publishing sensational private matters about a person's economic affairs, social or sexual activities, for example, could lead to an invasion of privacy suit.

Placing a Person in a False Light. This can occur when a news story or photograph, for example, implies something other than the facts. The nature of the published material must not lead the public to assume or believe something that is not specifically mentioned or portrayed by the material. This commonly occurs when the writer embellishes the facts for dramatic effect.

Appropriation. A publication is guilty of invading a person's privacy if it uses his name, likeness or personality for advertising or commercial purposes. This should not be confused with the use of a person's name or likeness in connection with a legitimate news story. Most states have laws that grant the mass media the right to use the name or a picture of a person without his consent in connection with a current or even previous news event as long as there is genuine public interest.

On the other hand, the courts have granted entertainers, sports figures and other public persons the "right to publicity." That means they have a right to protect themselves from commercial exploitation. They can "sell" their names and likenesses and profit from it. The press cannot use a name unless it is in connection with a legitimate news event.

Defenses. Truth is normally not a defense in invasion of privacy suits. However, there are three standard defenses:

Newsworthiness. This requires the publication to establish that the information revealed about the person who is suing was newsworthy or in the public interest.

   a. Public Figures: Publications can use the name or photograph or information about a public official, candidate for public office or public figures such as writers, actors, musicians without prior consent as long as they are reporting matters of legitimate public concern about that person's public life. Even the private life of a public person can be made public without his consent as long as it relates legitimately to his public life. The case involving Drew Pearson and Jack Anderson cited earlier is a good example. In addition, the courts have ruled that the public has a continuing interest in a public figure even after his retirement from public life.

   b. Private individuals. If a private individual becomes a party to a public event, even unwillingly, he cannot successfully complain that his privacy has been invaded. A person who happens to be in a crowd watching while police raid a local massage parlor has no legitimate cause for a suit if his picture appears in the newspaper reporting that raid. Any private citizen may become the object of legitimate news interest to the public either as an individual or as part of a group even though it may be unexpected or involuntary.

Consent. This defense requires that the publication show it had the consent of the person who is suing. Consent is not needed for legitimate news events. However, an invasion of privacy suit might grow out of such an event if the reporter obtained information illegally or wrongfully intruded on the private property of a person to collect information for additional stories. Consent, as noted under the section on libel, is not a strong defense.

Constitutional privilege. This privilege provides that a person involved in a matter of public concern cannot recover damages for a story that places him in a "false light" unless he can prove that the newspaper printed the statement knowing that it was false or had serious doubts about its truth.

It should be noted that many persons—scholars, writers, lawyers, journalists and lawmakers alike—believe that the right of privacy is in great peril as a result of sophisticated electronic equipment that permits almost undetectable "spying" on individuals. There also is grave concern about the invasion of privacy as a result of law enforcement agencies, credit bureaus, insurance firms, governmental agencies and a host of others who are collecting dossiers on private citizens for a variety of reasons. Major scandals have developed out of certain governmental agencies' practice of spying on the public, and the federal government as well as many state governments has passed laws seeking to control the collection of evidence on private citizens by federal agencies, credit bureaus and other businesses. Despite these efforts, there is a genuine concern that more and more computer data banks containing all types of information—both true and false—will proliferate and the public's right to privacy will continue to decline or be violated.

OTHER LEGAL ASPECTS OF JOURNALISM

As far as the reporter is concerned, the laws of libel and invasion of privacy in the state where he is working are the most important legal provisions that limit his freedom. However, there are other legal aspects of journalism that restrain the newspaper and reporter alike.

Censorship. The Constitution of the United States guarantees freedom of the press as a fundamental right in a democracy, but the extraordinary power of the federal government during times of national stress (insurrections, wars, threats of war) has resulted in a body of law that encroaches upon this freedom. Throughout our history there have been repeated efforts to censor the press under a variety of disguises. Chief among them have been the various sedition acts that have been passed, restricting publication of information that would "aid and comfort an enemy." The nation does not have an official secrets act; however, official secrets are protected under a variety of other acts, especially since the onset of the atomic age in the mid-1940s. And repeated attempts to revise the U.S. Criminal Code, to include provisions that would essentially be a secrets act, have been made. Official secrets also are protected by the classification system for documents established by presidential executive order. Since government officials and newspapermen have not always agreed on what should be censored, the press continues to fight a battle to protect its right to print.

The press's Constitutional rights were upheld in the famous Pentagon Papers case. The "papers" were classified Department of Defense documents detailing the historical development of the war in Vietnam. They were given to the New York Times by Daniel Ellsberg, a former Pentagon official who was working for the Rand Corporation, a firm that did consulting work for the Department of Defense. The Times began printing excerpts from the papers on June 13, 1971, and four days later Attorney General John Mitchell asked the Times to print no more of the documents "because they would do irreparable injury to the defense interests" of the nation. The newspaper refused and the Department of Justice asked U.S. District Court Judge Murray I. Gurfein to halt publication of the stories. Judge Gurfein, serving his first day as a federal judge, issued a temporary injunction on June 15, preventing the Times from continuing the publication. The Washington Post and other publications began printing parts of the papers. The Justice Department also obtained a temporary injunction against the Post.

The case was rushed to the Supreme Court, and after two weeks the court, in a 6–3 decision, ruled that the government had not shown sufficient justification for imposing prior restraint. Although the press won eventually, many newsmen were gravely concerned that a precedent may have been set when, for perhaps the first time in American history, federal court injunctions imposed prior restraint upon American newspapers.

The media are not free to print everything, of course. The U.S. Criminal Codes and the statutes of all states carry numerous penalties for the publication of pornography and obscenity. Although these may not directly affect a newspaper of general circulation, many newsmen have a genuine concern about them because there is no accepted definition of obscenity and pornography. As a result, they are subject to broad interpretation and certainly might involve a newspaper, especially one that tends to print more explicit material.

Reporters should also be aware of additional Supreme Court decisions that have a direct influence on their work. In 1972 the court ruled in *Brandzburg* v. *Hayes* that a reporter has no right to withhold information about his sources from a grand jury in criminal investigations. Since that case involved the federal courts, a number of states quickly passed laws to permit reporters to keep the names of their news sources confidential in state criminal cases. However, several later Supreme Court decisions have cast a cloud over the validity of the state confidential sources laws.

As a result of the *Zurcher* v. *Stanford Daily* case in 1978, police, with a warrant, are permitted to make a surprise raid on a newsroom to search for evidence of crimes committed by others. In short, police can go into a newsroom and search through the newspaper's files. And in 1979 the court refused to review an appeals court ruling that allowed government investigators access to the telephone company's records of phone numbers called by journalists.

In a series of three cases between 1974 and 1978, the court ruled each time that the press has no more right to access to public institutions than does the general public. These rulings can successfully block reporters from investigating conditions in jails, prisons and mental hospitals, for example.

The court handed the press another setback in 1979, when it refused to hear the appeal of New York Times reporter Myron Farber, who spent 40 days in jail for contempt for refusing to turn over to the defendants his notes at a murder trial. He had claimed protection under the New Jersey state confidential sources act.

A decision that created great concern about court control of the press came in the *Gannett Co.* v. *De Pasquale* case in 1979. The case dated back to 1976, when Judge Daniel DePasquale, at the request of defense lawyers in a murder case, barred the press and the public from a pretrial hearing. The lawyers argued that the adverse publicity would jeopardize their clients' chances for a fair trial. The prosecutor did not object. However, reporters for Gannett's Rochester (N.Y.) Democrat & Chronicle and Times Union challenged the judge's ruling based on the Sixth Amendment's guarantee of a public trial. Judge DePasquale refused to open the pretrial hearing. His decision was first overturned on appeal, and then upheld before it finally reached the Supreme Court in 1979.

In a 5–4 decision, the Supreme Court upheld Judge DePasquale. In the majority opinion, Justice Potter Stewart wrote that the Sixth Amendment's public-trial guarantee belongs only to the criminally accused, not to the public itself. He refused to concede that the press or the public possesses a constitutional right, under the First Amendment, to attend criminal trials. In a separate opinion, Chief Justice Burger stressed that the ruling applies only to pretrial hearings, not to trials themselves. Justice William Rhenquist, who concurred, wrote that defendants, prosecutors and judges should be free to bar press and public from *any* trial for any reason they choose. He wrote that the public had absolutely no right to attend any criminal proceedings. And he said that the First Amendment was not some kind of "constitutional sunshine law."

The decision resulted in so much judicial confusion that Justice Burger and Justice Powell broke a long-standing court tradition and began discussing the case in public. Both of them gave a number of public speeches defending and explaining the decision. They insisted that the court meant only pretrial hearings could be closed. But in the first five weeks after the decision, judges across the nation had closed their courts to the public and the press more than 30 times—at least eight of them involved full trials. Several news organizations—Gannett among them—issued cards to reporters on which was printed a formal protest. The reporters were instructed to read the statement aloud in court if a judge decided to close the court to the public or the press.

The following year the Supreme Court handed down a decision that cleared up much of the confusion created by the Gannett case. In the case *Richmond Newspapers Inc.* v. *Commonwealth of Virginia,* the Court ruled that both the public and the press have a Constitutional right to attend trials.

The case grew out of the murder of a Virginia motel manager in 1975. Three men were charged with the murder and were granted separate trials. One of the defendants was tried three times in secret before charges against him were finally dismissed. The Commonwealth Attorney did not object when the judge closed the court to the public and the press. However, the Richmond Times-Dispatch and the Richmond News-Leader did because their reporters were barred from covering the trials. Their appeal to the Virginia Supreme Court was turned down. That court said the judge had acted with legal authority when he ordered the secret trials. The newspapers pushed the case all the way to the U.S. Supreme Court.

In its 7–1 decision, the Court said: "We hold that the right to attend criminal trials is implicit in the guarantees of the First Amendment: without the freedom to attend such trials, which people have exercised for centuries, an important aspect of freedom of speech and 'of the press could be eviscerated.' "

The decision was hailed as a victory for the public and the press by news executives and First Amendment attorneys.

In addition, there are other legal aspects of journalism that restrain the newspaper and reporter alike.

Copyrights. The U.S. Constitution provides for copyrights just as it does for the freedom of the press, and newspapers must observe the copyright holdings of others. By the same laws, the newspaper can prevent unauthorized use of original materials it publishes by obtaining copyright privileges.

Obtaining a copyright is a relatively simple procedure. Application forms are available from the Register of Copyrights, Library of Congress, Washington, D.C. An author or publisher may secure a copyright by returning this completed application, plus a small fee and the required number of copies of the material, and by carrying a notice of copyright on all copies published.

Written materials may be protected by copyright in the form in which they appear. However, the news facts or the ideas stated in the materials cannot be copyrighted. Copyright is an interest in the way the story is organized and treated. In other words, a newspaper cannot obtain exclusive use of the facts pertaining to a murder story, for example, by copyrighting the initial news break on that story, but it may obtain a copyright to the story as organized and presented.

Even though a newspaper cannot claim exclusive rights to the facts in a news story through the copyright procedure, it can employ other legal methods to protect itself from the wholesale use of its stories by competing news media. Several state courts have ruled that such unauthorized use of news items, taken from a newspaper and not independently gathered, is unfair competition and "violation of a property right."

Reporters may quote copyrighted material verbatim without permission provided such quotations do not exceed a reasonable length and provided the material quoted is properly acknowledged. This privilege protects newspapers in using quotations in book reviews and other types of stories. However, as a common practice most newspapers do seek permission before printing copyrighted material other than news stories. In using copyrighted material from another newspaper, most papers give the other paper credit almost immediately in the story in this fashion: "The Chicago Daily News, in a copyrighted story today, said that . . . ."

For a fuller understanding of copyrights and especially the fair use standards, reporters should read the current copyright law passed by Congress in 1976.

EXERCISES

1. Most if not all of the paragraphs below contain statements that are libelous or unethical. Rewrite those that should be rewritten to eliminate any libelous material. Following each rewritten paragraph, give an explanation of the changes, specifically pointing out the libelous and/or unethical statements. Indicate the paragraphs that are acceptable in editorials or by-lined reviews but not in regular news stories.

    A. Police arrested Paul Pullen, 56, 1028 Main St., two hours after the robbery. They are seeking his brother, Herman, 60, of Elkville, believed to have been his accomplice.

    B. Witnesses say they saw City Councilman John Jackson accepting "a wad of money" from Carpenter's Union President Thomas O'Neal shortly after the council meeting. Jackson cast the winning vote, clearing the way for the union to build its new headquarters in the once all-residential section.

    C. A 60-year-old widow told the state Medical Review Board today that Dr. Elbert Hooker, a Jamestown physician, "turned my husband into a drug addict as sure as I'm sitting here." The board is reviewing Hooker's license to practice following charges by the state Bureau of Criminal Investigation that he had issued more than 10,000 prescriptions for dangerous drugs to known drug users in less than six months last year.

    D. Outside the hearing room, Bo Lolly, a drug addict who agreed to cooperate with the state in its investigation to avoid prosecution, told reporters that Dr. Hooker was "one of the biggest pushers" in the state. "If you have the money, you can get a prescription for anything you want from him," Lolly said.

    E. The school superintendent said the burglary obviously was an "inside job." "Only five people have keys to that storage room, and it is apparent that whoever stole the musical instruments used a key to get in," he said. "There are no signs of forced entry."

    F. In a letter to members of the congregation of the Unified Church of the Gospel, dissident members charged that Pastor Jim Bob Taylor was "guilty of immoral conduct" because he had been "having an illicit sexual affair" with Mrs. Mary Edith Boswick, wife of James Boswick, president of the Board of Deacons.

    G. In a press release issued today from his law office, State Senator Jackson St. John gave his monthly "Cleverest Con" award to Dr. Tilman J. Bradbury, professor of finance at State University. "He has managed to milk the state out of $60,000 in

81

consulting fees during the same nine-month period he was drawing his full-time salary at the University and supposedly teaching a full schedule of classes," St. John said.

H. Actress Mary Lou Thigpen, who married rock star Sunny Day on the stage of the Princess Theater three months ago, gave birth to an eight-pound, nine-ounce daughter today at Westhills Hospital. The baby was named Melodie.

I. City Health Inspector Bennie Cook said he would issue a citation against Jacques, a French restaurant on Cumberland Avenue just off campus, because he had found rat dung in the food on three occasions in the last two weeks. Jack Geiger, owner of the restaurant, could not be reached for comment.

J. Winnie Bowman, lighting specialist for the Public Utilities Board, said in her report that she had refused to issue "Gold Medallion" ratings to the homes in the new Hickory Brook subdivision because carpeting was being installed directly over the electrical wiring in the living rooms and bedrooms of all the homes.

K. Delbert McMillan, candidate for the school board, today accused James Bowman, assistant principal at Roosevelt High School, of permitting students to smoke marijuana while on an out-of-town basketball trip last December. McMillan told the East Side Rotary Club "that is just the tip of the iceberg of what I know about that school."

L. Police said they found a child's brutally beaten body in the blood-stained bathtub. Both arms were fractured several times, his skull was crushed, apparently with a baseball bat found nearby, there were more than 50 cigarette burns all over the body, his front teeth had been knocked out, and his face was a swollen mass of bruises and cuts. "About the only part that wasn't broken or bruised were his toes," Detective James Talley said. "I got sick at my stomach when I walked in there and saw him in that pool of blood."

M. Law enforcement officials believe that through the Alphine Cheese Company, 1421 Cedar St., the Mafia launders millions of dollars in illegal money collected in the area through rackets such as loan-sharking, extortion and traffic in drugs.

N. If music does indeed soothe the savage beast, then it is a good thing the Purple Tornadoes played at the Civic Auditorium last night instead of the City Zoo. At the auditorium they were so bad the audience left in disgust. Had they been at the zoo, the elephants probably would have stampeded and trampled them to death. That might not be such a bad idea.

O. Good Government Inc., a private citizens lobby, today accused Mayor John Elkhorn of "padding his own pockets by forcing political appointees to kick back part of their salaries to him personally in order to hold their jobs." Alva Pierce, president of the group, said "we have some pretty good evidence that's what the mayor is using to live as high as he does. He certainly can't be living that good on the salary the city pays him."

P. Ada Ricks, president of the Rocky Hills Parents Guild, today demanded that Thomas Gillam, coordinator of English at the school, be fired for permitting teachers "to give our children pornography to read." In her letter to County School Superintendent Jason Kirk, she listed five books, including *Catcher in the Rye,* as "the kind of pornography they are making our kids read."

Q. Nurses at Ledford Psychiatric Clinic today walked off their jobs, charging that the chief psychiatrist and owner of the private clinic, Dr. Joseph Ledford, was "practicing witchcraft not psychiatric medicine." They accused him of "cruel and inhuman treatment of the patients" through excessive use of electric-shock therapy.

2. Clip from a newspaper 10 stories containing several types of derogatory statements. Paste them on a blank sheet of paper and explain in the margin if you believe the

statements to be libelous. Indicate what defense you would use if a libel suit resulted from each story.

3. All states have libel laws. Look up your state's libel law in a copy of the *State Code Annotated* in your college library. Write a brief report on its chief provisions such as the definition of libel and defenses permitted.

4. Invite a local editor to class for a discussion of any laws in your state (such as those providing for open public meetings and open public records) that guarantee that reporters can do their work without excessive restraints. Write a short report on the discussion.

5. Newspapers are often accused of violating good taste in reporting some of the more sensational events that happen in their circulation area. Look through several newspapers for examples of stories or parts of stories you consider of questionable taste. Hand in the clippings and your own comments on each of the examples.

6. Interview a local judge about the conflict between the courts and the news media discussed in this chapter. Write a short report on his views.

PART II

WRITING THE NEWS LEAD

Saul Pett, one of the most talented writers for the Associated Press, says, "Writing begins and ends with thinking."

A writer simply must think about what he is going to say before he puts the first word on paper. In fact, putting those first words on paper requires careful, sometimes prolonged, thought, because the most important part of any article is the first sentence—the lead. A reporter's er 're future as an excellent writer hangs on it. His ability to grasp and hold a .der's attention depends on it.

Writing the lead appears to be deceptively simple. Unfortunately it isn't. It is true that a superficial writer may be able to dash off a lead in a hurry, and it may even be readable. But it won't necessarily be good. It is doubtful that many of the leads on important stories in every newspaper really achieve the distinction required for complete, interpretative, penetrating reporting of the news.

The fundamental forms and principles of writing the news lead are presented in the following pages. Forms and principles are extremely helpful, but they are not substitutes for the inward strength and brilliance with which the news lead can and should reflect the vitality of the events reported.

CHAPTER 6

The Simple (Single-Incident) News Lead

Journalistic writing differs from ordinary narrative prose chiefly in form. The same rules of grammar, punctuation and sentence structure apply to both. However, a narrative prose writer places the major emphasis on the end of his story. He generally builds to a climax, telling the most important thing last. The newswriter does the exact opposite. He tells the most important thing first. This example will illustrate the point.

Ordinary narrative style:

> When Jack Norvell returned to his home at 1105 Burchfield Road in Dandridge after a squirrel-hunting trip, he placed his 20-gauge shotgun on the couch in the living room. He asked his mother-in-law, Mrs. Etta Ricks, who was visiting, to watch the gun while he brought in the rest of his hunting gear from his pickup truck. His wife, Mary Kay, had been in the kitchen cooking dinner. She walked into the living room and saw the gun on the couch. She complained to her mother that she had asked her husband not to leave the gun where their three-year-old son, Thomas, might be able to reach it. Mrs. Ricks told her daughter that Jack would be right back. However, Mrs. Norvell picked up the gun to take it into the family den where she said she was going to put it in a gun cabinet. Mrs. Ricks said as her daughter turned to walk out of the room the gun slipped from her hand and discharged when it hit the floor. Mrs. Norvell was struck in the throat by the blast. Norvell said he heard the gun discharge and rushed back into the house, where he found his wife on the living-room floor. He said he attempted to help her while Mrs. Ricks called police. Mrs. Norvell died before police and an ambulance arrived. Norvell told police he forgot to unload the gun.

The news story:

> A 25-year-old Dandridge woman died of an accidental gunshot wound at her home Thursday, police said.
>
> Mrs. Mary Kay Norvell, 1105 Burchfield Rd., was struck in the throat by a

blast from her husband's 20-gauge shotgun. She was carrying the gun from the living room to the den when she dropped it and it discharged, her mother told police.

Jack Norvell, 27, said that he had just returned home from squirrel hunting and had placed the gun on the couch in the living room and asked his mother-in-law, Mrs. Etta Ricks, to watch it while he brought in the rest of his hunting gear from his pickup. He said he had forgotten to unload the gun.

Mrs. Ricks said her daughter, who had been in the kitchen cooking dinner, walked into the living room and complained that she had asked her husband not to leave the gun where their son, Thomas, 3, might reach it.

"I warned her that Jack would be right back," Mrs. Ricks said, "but she picked up the gun and started for the den, where she said she was going to lock it up in a gun cabinet."

Mrs. Ricks said as her daughter turned to walk out of the room, the gun slipped from her hand and discharged when it hit the floor.

Norvell heard the blast, ran into the house and tried to help his wife. Mrs. Ricks called police.

Mrs. Norvell died before police and an ambulance arrived.

Several important differences are immediately apparent in the two stories. The events in the ordinary prose story are in chronological order. Those in the news story are arranged, from beginning to end, in order of their newsworthiness. The climax (most newsworthy event) of the story is, of course, the woman's death. In the first story it is almost the last sentence. In the news story it is placed first.

In ordinary prose the whole story becomes clear *gradually,* building to a climax. In the news story the outstanding fact (most newsworthy) is flashed before the reader in the opening sentence—the *lead.* The object of the lead is to tell the reader as quickly as possible what the story is about. This generally is done in a single sentence or short paragraph. Some newspapers attempt to make each lead a one-sentence paragraph, which is quite desirable if the sentence is not long and involved.

The narrative prose story will include all the minute detail while the news story generally omits details or includes them in the final paragraphs.

This style of writing is usually called the *inverted pyramid* because the "bottom" or end or climax of the chronological story is inverted to the top. It is an outgrowth of the Civil War when correspondents were restricted from sending long stories by telegraph. To make certain all the essential information was sent, the writers told the most important facts first. Although the style has been refined considerably since, most basic news stories still follow this style.

6a *"Logical Order."* The order in which newsworthy facts are organized in a news story will be referred to as the *logical* order. This term is used to distinguish it from the arrangements of events as they actually occur (chronological). *Logical* implies that the events will not be rearranged in a haphazard order but rationally according to their importance. *The order of importance is measured by reader appeal* and the lead is the "showcase" of all, or of the most newsworthy, materials contained in the story. Since the lead reveals either the whole story or its most newsworthy aspects, the subsequent parts of the story should develop in logical order to support the lead. That is, the second most important fact comes second, then the third and so on. This order makes the relationship of a lead to a news story similar to that of a topic sentence to a paragraph.

If news is so written that the story is fully summarized in the lead, what constitutes a "whole story"? What is it that people want to know about a news event? How can one know when he has presented all the essential information? Are there not, for example, many more essential facts in a bank robbery than in an automobile collision? Does not every story differ from every other in the kind of information presented in its lead summary? These questions may be puzzling, but the fact is that, while stories differ in their content, the story lead has a fixed and limited purpose to perform.

THE 5 W'S   6b

Ideally, every news story should answer the questions: Who? What? When? Where? Why? and for good measure How? And they should be answered as quickly as possible for the reader. There was a time when newspapers sought to cram all of these into the opening sentence, which frequently produced 60 and 70 words of almost incomprehensible prose. For example, a lead might have come out like this:

> Mrs. Mary Kay Norvell, 25, 1105 Burchfield Rd., Dandridge, died in her home Thursday after she had been struck in the neck by a blast from her husband's 20-gauge shotgun which she dropped while attempting to put the gun away after he had left it on the living-room couch when he returned home from a squirrel-hunting trip.

The lead certainly answers all the questions:

Who?   Mrs. Mary Kay Norvell
What?   Died of an accidental gunshot wound
When?   Thursday
Where?   In her home
Why?   She was struck in the neck by a shotgun blast
How?   She dropped the gun and it discharged

But it also contains 60 words, is ponderous and is unnecessarily wordy. The sentence would have been even longer had the authority or source—in this case, the police—been included.

As a result of numerous readership studies by such men as Dr. Rudolph Flesch and Robert Gunning, readability formulas were developed. They proved that shorter sentences were more understandable and that it was no longer necessary, for reader interest, to wrap up all the traditional 5 W's in a single sentence or paragraph. Today lead sentences are generally kept to a minimum—no more than 30 to 40 words, depending, of course, on the story. Some newspapers try for even shorter leads.

PLAYING UP A W   6c

The move to simpler, shorter leads has resulted in the practice of featuring one W that is much more important than the others. Often it is difficult to determine which is most important since most news is about individuals and their activities. However, the following examples show how one element can be featured:

The "Who" Lead. If the "Who" is a widely known person (place or thing), it is usually the feature of the lead. The name alone attracts attention. Unless one of the other elements is particularly outstanding, the "big name" comes first.

> Gov. Telford J. Blake announced today that he would not seek reelection to a second term.

A "Who" lead can also be used when a person is not widely known. In such cases, it is usually the person's occupation, sex, age or other distinguishing characteristic that is featured:

> A 19-year-old University sophomore who ran into the side of a moving car was in serious condition today in the intensive care unit at Presbyterian Hospital.

The "What" Lead. If an event is more important than the persons involved, that element should be featured:

> A ban on topless dancing in local taverns was upheld today by a federal judge who said such activity is not protected by the First Amendment.

Many "What" leads start with or include the "Who," as the following example shows:

> Two Roosevelt High School students delivering papers rescued a family of six from their burning home on Glenbrook Drive early today.

In this case, from the standpoint of reader interest the circumstances were considerably more significant than the persons involved.

The "Where" Lead. On occasion the "Where" is significant enough to overshadow the other W's. The following lead is an example:

> In the shadow of a memorial to black Civil War soldiers on historic Boston Commons, religious leaders Monday launched a drive for racial harmony in this troubled city.

Another example:

> Pangnirtung may not be the end of the world but it is in that same general direction. A tiny dot on Canada's northwest . . .

Richard Benedetto of Gannett News Service used the "Where" element effectively in this lead on one of the stories in his series on the quality of education in New York state.

> BROOKLYN—Public School 138, a 75-year-old, four-story brick building, stands in one of New York's poorest black and Hispanic neighborhoods. Many nearby buildings are burned-out shells or trash-strewn hulks.

The "When" Lead. "When" is included in most leads, but it rarely is the most important feature. However, there are some circumstances that may make it significant. For example:

> About 12:20 a.m. today, city firemen plugged a stubborn leak in a propane tanker that had forced the evacuation of more than 3,000 residents in south Pittsburgh.

"When" also is used to show unusual circumstances:

> Less than two months after he had held a City Business College class of students hostage for nine hours, Floyd Geiger did it again.
>
> Geiger, on leave from Lakeside Mental Health Institute, walked into the college yesterday and held another class hostage for 11 hours.

The "When" element can sometimes be used effectively in feature leads. This example by Richard C. Longworth for United Press International illustrates that point:

> LENINGRAD, USSR—It was 3:30 a.m. when the overnight train from Helsinki to Leningrad crossed the Soviet border. The old man woke quickly when the border police flicked on the light.
>
> He was an actor, one of Russia's best, and he managed to . . .

The "Why" Lead. The motive or cause of an event sometimes is the most important feature. Often it is overlooked.

> A shortage of qualified nurses has forced Memorial Hospital to close its maternity center.
>
> Hospital officials said today . . .

Another example:

> To meet increased costs of food and labor, the Maryville School Board voted last night to raise the price of lunch in all school cafeterias.
>
> The increase will range from . . .

The "How" Lead. The "How" also is a potential leading feature which is sometimes overlooked by reporters. It can be an effective device, but care must be exercised not to become wordy in explaining how something happened.

> Using more than 100 phony names, dozens of false Social Security cards and a string of post office boxes all over the state, a Madisonville woman managed to swindle the State Welfare Department out of $1 million in just 18 months.

These examples play up (by placing first) various features of a story. The choice of which element to emphasize is up to the reporter but is usually determined by the material itself. One feature frequently "cries out" its importance and demands to be placed first.

6d *Crowding the Lead.* If, in the simple one-incident story, two or more of the W's seem equally interesting, the reporter will have to choose arbitrarily between them. To try to include them all would simply result in an overcrowded and awkward lead. The accepted practice in the simple news story is to play up only one W in the lead, although some stories emphasize two. If other W's deserve attention, they can be emphasized in the second paragraph of the story.

Generally speaking, the shorter the lead, the better. Newsworthy details held out of the lead will fall properly into the body of the news story. If no single element in the story seems to offer an interesting feature, the routine "Who" lead is generally used:

> A 37-year-old Concord woman was critically injured Thursday night in a two-car accident on Cedar Bluff Road near I-40.

Many stories containing no striking feature must be handled in this way. It is adequate but tends to make dull reading. Many such stories may contain features that the reporter fails to recognize or inquire into.

It is much easier to recognize the story elements (the 5 W's) and the feature after the story is written than it is from the reporter's rough notes. In fact, the reporter himself must determine who is properly "Who" and what is properly "What." If the police chief and a city councilman have a row, the reporter must determine which of the two is to be the "Who" in his lead. In this case, of course, he might evade the issue (as reporters sometimes do) and at the same time acquire a "Who" feature by writing "Two public officials clashed today . . ."—but he does face a problem in determining such story elements and the order in which they should be presented. In the example cited, most reporters would tend to focus on the one who apparently provoked the attack.

6e COMPLETE REPORTING

It is not difficult for the reporter to pick up 5 W's, fling them together and call the result a lead. Much superficial reporting results from this careless approach to writing. The reader is frequently left to wonder what caused the accident or the fire. If he wants to know whether admission is free, whether the public is invited, whether the event will be telecast and when and over what channels—he has to use the telephone. If the event occurred at Sevastopol, do not tell the reader anything about the city—let him look it up in an atlas or a history book. If the injured John Smith lives at 916 Clinton St., what further identification can a reader want? These seem to be the attitudes behind a lot of careless reporting one finds in newspapers. If Congress has just enacted a law, the lead might be

> Price controls were extended for six months by Congress today, and the President immediately announced that he would veto the bill.

Or facts might justify the following lead:

> Price of food, clothing, gasoline and most other products Americans use will skyrocket if the President vetoes the price control extension bill, Congressional leaders predicted today.

In the first lead the reader is given a minimum of information. He is left to figure out the significance of the event for himself. In the second lead the reporter pushed his "What" question below the surface of things and reported an action of extreme significance.

There are strict limits to the amount of material that can be crowded into a lead. There are no limits whatever on the quality of this material. Only by reporting the significance of events instead of their superficial forms can the reporter achieve complete reporting. Whether he achieves this in the lead or later in his story is not wholly important—so long as he does achieve it. The lead, however, is his golden opportunity to present the quality of facts demanded by complete, penetrative use of the 5 W's.

There is no one exact way to write a lead, no one formula that is better than another. But every reporter should develop his own device to test how adequate his lead is after it is written. Following is one such device, which uses the four letters from *news* as keys:

N   for newsworthiness—does the lead say anything worthy of note by readers?

E   for emphasis—does the lead emphasize its most interesting fact?

W   the 5 W's—are all essential W's included in the lead?

S   for source of information—does the lead give (or imply) the source of information, if needed?

EXERCISES

6g

Important: In these and following exercises, notes are written as incomplete sentences resembling telegraphic English. The notes are like those a reporter might jot down in gathering information for his story.

Added to each set of notes, in parentheses, is its source of information unless the notes include or imply this source. In some stories it will not be necessary to state the source, while in other stories it is essential to do so. The student must use judgment in determining which statements require a specific authority.

The student must also show good judgment in the use of direct quotations in completing these assignments. The telegraphic notes within quotation marks indicate direct quotations. If these are used, additional words may have to be added to make them full sentences, of course, but the student should make only obvious additions.

Since these are reporter's notes, they are assumed to be accurate statements from the sources of information. If the instructor permits, the student may convert an unquoted note into a direct quotation. For example, *Jones refused to take part* in the notes may be written *"I will not take part in the meeting," Councilman Jones said.* However, in converting an indirect quotation into a direct quotation, the student should not add imaginary facts.

Students are warned that the exercises contain some notes which, if used as given (and sometimes if used at all), will constitute errors. Such notes include trivia, editorialized matter, statements violating newspaper ethics, libel and misspelled words (and names).

Some instructors may require that their students hand in all completed (and corrected) assignments at the end of a quarter or semester.

1. Write news stories using the following notes:
   A. The Rev. James Franklin Pierce, pastor of the Rocky Road Methodist Church in suburban Beech Grove, and 75 members of his congregation were meeting last night to discuss a proposed new addition to the church's meeting hall to provide space for a new day-care center. Mrs. Ella Albertson, 45, 1221 Fernwood St., who is in charge of the church's day-care program, had just completed a report on the growth of the program and the increased numbers of requests from working

mothers who wanted to bring their children to the center. David Harrall, 51, 3267 Blake St., an accountant for City Power and Light Co., said he heard noises in the hall outside the church meeting room and went to the door. As he opened the door, four men wearing ski masks and carrying guns rushed into the room. Harrall was knocked to the floor. The gunmen forced the men and women to stretch out on the floor. When several members of the group did not move fast enough, one of the gunmen placed a submachine gun to the minister's head and threatened to "blow his head off" if they didn't cooperate. The gunmen forced each person in the room to drop all purses, wallets, jewelry and even the loose change they had in their pockets into plastic garbage bags. They demanded money from the church office but the minister convinced them that he kept no money in the office. Harrall said the gunmen ripped a phone from the wall, threatened to "kill anyone who moves for 15 minutes," shot out several lights in the room and fled. Mrs. Albertson said the men apparently fled in two cars. Donald Scroggins, 33, 12 Middlebrook Pl., the church's choir director, ran a half block to a nearby house and called police. Police Chief Jackson (Bubba) Smith and four other policemen rushed to the scene. Smith said he had put an all-points bulletin out and had asked state troopers for help. He said it would take about 24 hours to get statements from everyone. He declined to speculate on the total amount of money and valuables taken. However, the minister said he had talked to most persons involved, and he estimated the cash taken at more than $600 and "certainly several thousand dollars worth of rings, watches and other jewelry was taken."

(*Sources:* Chief Smith, Rev. Pierce, Harrall, Scroggins, Mrs. Albertson)

B. Linda Bauman, 26, 478 Morgan St., had just arrived home from work late yesterday and was going into her kitchen. She said before she could switch on the lights, a man jumped out of the shadows in the room and grabbed her around the neck. She said she was forced down the steps into the basement. She stumbled and twisted her ankle, and the man dragged her to the center of the basement and began to tie her hands and and feet. She said she screamed and fought with the man, but he slapped her repeatedly in the face and then wrapped plastic duct tape around her head. The burglar went upstairs. Miss Bauman said she could hear him moving around, opening drawers in the kitchen and dumping the contents on the floor. She said she was able to free herself about 30 minutes later. She crawled out of a basement window into the window well, lifted a heavy grate and escaped. She went to the house next door and the neighbor, Dr. Marshall Parker, a dentist, called police. Police arrived in about 10 minutes. They found Sterling Banks, a parolee from the state prison, in the living room. Banks claimed he was checking out the house in his role as an informant for the police. He said he had heard it had just been burglarized. He claims he saw a suitcase on the porch and, discovering the front door was unlocked, was putting the suitcase inside when police arrived and arrested him. Police Chief John F. McAulliffe said Banks was not a paid informant. He said Banks was on parole from an earlier housebreaking conviction. Banks will be charged with housebreaking, robbery and kidnaping, McAulliffe said.

(*Sources:* McAulliffe, Miss Bauman, Dr. Parker)

C. William V. Morris, 75, of 1210 Rudder Rd. had been shopping for groceries yesterday at the Kroger store at 7609 Chapman Highway. He said while he was putting his groceries in the car, two neatly dressed young men walked up and asked him to drive them to a McDonald's Restaurant, about 10 blocks away. They told him that their car had broken down and they would be late for work. Enroute to the restaurant, one of the men took a deck of cards out of his pocket and began playing with them. Morris said he played cards almost every day and considered himself "something of an expert at cards." During the conversation, the man bet Morris that he could not pick a certain card out of the deck. Morris bet he could and a slightly heated discussion followed during which the young men belittled "old folks who think they know everything." Morris said the young man with the cards would not accept his challenge until Morris showed he had money in the event he lost. Morris drove to a bank and withdrew $3900 and returned to the car. The second young man suggested that he lock the money in the trunk for safekeeping. Morris allowed him to lock up the money. Then Morris successfully drew the right card—a king of hearts—from the deck. Morris said the young men said they had the money at the restaurant and would pay him when they reached it. He said he drove up to the back of the restaurant and the two young men walked around to the side of the building and went inside. Morris said he waited in the car for 20 minutes but they did not return. He went inside looking for them but could not find them. He then checked the trunk of his car and found a handkerchief stuffed with tissue. Police said they are investigating. No arrests have been made.

(*Sources:* Morris, Detective Thomas Sweeten)

D. Mrs. Linda Strong, Route 2, Valley Road, Elkville, stood at the window in her living room about 7:30 this morning and watched as her stepdaughter, Teresa, 7, walked about 100 yards to the school bus stop. Mrs. Strong said she was about to turn away from the window when she noticed a cream-colored car driving slowly up to the bus stop. Two other children were at the bus stop talking to Teresa. She said a man jumped out of the car, grabbed Teresa and dragged her into the car. She said Teresa was screaming and the other children started screaming and running away. Mrs. Strong said she ran outside and tried to get the license number but the car sped away before she could see the number. She said she ran back inside and woke up Teresa's brother, Paul Strong Jr., 18, who tried to pursue the car in a pickup truck. He was unable to catch up to it. Mrs. Strong called the Bradley County Sheriff's office and reported the abduction to Dispatcher Ann Cagstain. A bulletin was broadcast to all patrol cars. Lt. Danny Chastin of the Sheriff's office investigated the case. He talked to the two other children who said that there were two men in the car. Mrs. Strong said she thought the car was a late-model Oldsmobile Cutlass. Mrs. Strong told Lt. Chastin that Teresa had lived with her natural mother in Florida until last June when a court awarded custody of the child to her father, Paul, 41, an accountant. Chastin said he had been unable to contact the child's natural mother in Florida. Strong said he thought the abduction might be an effort by his former wife to regain custody of Teresa. "She was very bitter about the court's decision," he told Chastin. Chastin said he would contact authorities in Florida in an effort to locate the child. "We don't want to put all our eggs in one basket yet, but we hope it was an outgrowth of the custody suit and nothing else," Chastin said.

(*Sources:* Mrs. Strong, Strong, Lt. Chastin, Ann Cagstin)

E. Mrs. Mary Horton, 36, 688 Bradford St., and her husband, Joseph, 38, an engineer, went collecting rock samples with another couple, who are also rock hounds. They had heard there were excellent samples at the abandoned Bear T Mine, off Vonore Rd. Horton said his wife was chipping off a rock sample when the boulder on which she was working broke loose, pinning her against another rock. The accident happened about 11:30 a.m. Horton and the other couple, Mr. and Mrs. Jack Lavin, attempted to lift the boulder off Mrs. Horton but were unable to move it. Lavin drove to a nearby gas station and called the Monroe County Sheriff's office. Four deputies and members of the Monroe County Rescue

Squad were sent to the mine. They had to work more than two hours to free Mrs. Horton. She suffered multiple pelvic fractures. She is in serious condition at Sweetwater Valley Hospital.

(*Sources:* Horton, Lavin, Sheriff Buck O'Brien)

2. Clip from a newspaper three short news stories (about three to five paragraphs in length) and rewrite them in chronological order. Include the details you would have reported if you had been the source of the story but which were omitted in the newspaper account.

3. Clip from several newspapers the leads from 10 stories. Paste them on a sheet of paper and identify the W's in each one.

4. Following are rough notes for story leads. For each one list the 5 W's and then write the lead.

A. Elizabeth Diane Knotts, 31
   Comanager, with husband, Holt
   Malabar Motel, 10013 Coast Highway
   Gunman entered motel about 11 p.m. last night
   Demanded money
   Mrs. Knotts refused
   Gunman shot her in the face
   Took all bills from cash register, fled
   Husband checking parking lot at rear
   Heard shot and ran to office
   Found Mrs. Knotts on floor behind the desk
   She was still alive
   She described gunman as tall, thin, about 21
   Mrs. Knotts died on way to Jefferson Memorial Hospital
   Knott declined to estimate how much money taken
   Police still investigating
   (*Sources:* Knotts, Policeman Thomas Chester)

B. State Association of Conservation Districts
   Annual awards dinner last night
   36th annual convention at Hyatt Regency
   Mrs. Grace Riden, Madisonville Junior High, teacher
   Presented annual "Outstanding Teacher" award
   Honored for teaching conservation in classroom
   Praised by Association President William Bell
   She has been teaching 25 years
   Organized conservation club in school
   Author of conservation books for children
   Lectures to student groups on conservation
   Named Woman of the Year last year
   By Business and Professional Women's Club

C. Clyde and Betty Acuff
   Recently bought house at 2312 Vincinda Circle
   Have not moved in
   House outside city limits
   Rural Metro Fire Department
   Called to home at 6 p.m.
   By neighbor who saw fire in basement
   Blaze extinguished. House carefully checked
   At 2:40 a.m. house again burst into flames
   Neighbors saw car speed away

Gas can found near house
Rural Metro Fire Chief Taylor Thompson
Asked state fire marshal
To investigate arson attempts
D. Forrest P. Cawley
Regional Director
U.S. Bureau of Census
Announced plans to open district office
In Fort Hill Building
Will employ 668 temporary workers
Hiring to start next month
Mrs. Betty Connors
Named office manager
Office will serve 13 counties
East of the Big Muddy River
E. County Board of Education representatives
Officials of County Education Association
To meet a 4:15 p.m. tomorrow
City-County Building library
Opening meeting in contract negotiations
Teachers seeking $12,000 minimum annual salary
Current minimum is $9,800
Threaten strike if they don't get it
Board members refuse to comment on demands
Association represents 350 teachers
Last teacher's strike two years ago

5. Using newspapers available in the library, compare the leads on five stories in both a morning and afternoon newspaper in the same city or the same stories which appear in the local newspaper and a newspaper in a neighboring city. Note the difference in these leads.

6. Notes for story leads are given below. List and identify (as "Who," "When" and so on) the fact or facts you think deserve the most conspicuous play in each lead. Then write the lead.

A. Jerri Lynn Whitt, 26, 1507 Woodlawn Ave.
Shot and killed
Paul Thomas Jones last March 1
In an argument at her home
She told police he was beating her
She fired shot in his direction to scare him
She was indicted for involuntary manslaughter
Trial in Criminal Court yesterday
She pleaded guilty
Judge Glenn Ford postponed sentencing
For two weeks to allow
State probation counselor
To make presentencing investigation
B. Tammy Eastbrook, 21
Student at Eastern Community College
Pulling out of Topside Road on to Chapman Highway
Her car hit by another vehicle
Driven by Charles Carpenter, Route 3, Louisville
Rescue Squad had to cut her out of car

97

Takes 30 minutes to get her out of wreckage
Taken to Memorial Hospital at 9:15 p.m.
She dies two hours later
Carpenter treated at hospital, released
No charges filed
State Trooper Pat L. Wilson said
She pulled into path of Carpenter's car
Miss Eastbrook lived at Little River Apartments
On Topside Road in Blount County
Her parents live in Cleveland
Funeral arrangements pending
   (*Source:* Trooper Wilson)
C. Optimist Club area meeting
7:45 p.m. today at Park Plaza Hotel
Members from 150 area clubs expected
Speaker will be
Dr. James E. Creed
International President of Optimist Clubs
He is professor of clinical sciences
College of Veterinary Medicine
Colorado State University, Ft. Collins
D. Patrolman Dennis McGee
Answered disturbance call
At Stop and Go Market, Rocky Hill Center
About 4:30 p.m. yesterday
He arrested Lynwood Dixon, 21, Rocky Hill Apartments
Charged with public indecency, public drunkenness
Dixon was nude
He said he had taken a shower
Discovered he was out of beer
Decided to walk across street
To buy some at the market
Cashier Trudy Weatherwax called police
McGee wrapped him in a blanket
Took him to city jail
   (*Sources:* Patrolman McGee, Mrs. Weatherwax)
E. Sylvester Washington, 89, 305 Council St.
Walking to nearby drugstore
About 6:30 p.m. last night
Crossing College Street at University Avenue
Struck by car, which sped away
Witnesses said it was late-model Buick
Washington taken to University Hospital
Listed in critical condition
F. County Detective George Hipshire
Sent to University Hospital today
After emergency room attendants
Reported a man came in for treatment
For stab wounds in his arms and stomach
Doyle F. Seavers, 43, Shipetown Rd.
Was treated but not admitted to hospital.

Seavers refused to discuss the case
He told Hipshire that the case was
"None of your business. I'll handle it myself"
No arrests have been made
> (*Source:* Detective Hipshire)

G. Mayor Robert Wilson named
Fred Comstock, 49, a labor lawyer
Chairman, City Parking Authority
Authority supervises all city owned
Parking Garages and Parking Lots
Also sets rates for parking
Comstock will serve four-year term
Replaces William Luther, 44,
Retired civil engineer who is leaving the city
City Council must approve appointment
Comes up at meeting next Tuesday

H. Police called to private home
At 505 Clay St., about 4 p.m. today
Found body of Richard Qunsell, 22
Hanging from a tree
Body found by 12-year-old neighbor boy
Police said body was hanging four inches above
A pile of coal in backyard
No note found
Police said Qunsell, who lived alone
Apparently had just lost his job
His nearest relatives live
In Phoenix, Ariz.
> (*Source:* Detective Henry Hansen)

I. American Chemical Corp.
Automotive Products Division here
To lay off 350 hourly workers
At its plant in Meadows Industrial Park
Plant Manager Robert Courtland
Said layoffs to start Friday
Does not anticipate additional layoffs
Blamed reduced orders from major car makers
Hopes to call back employees in a month
Plant employs 2,200 workers
> (*Source:* Courtland)

J. Billy Joe Kratz, 42, Norris
Driving car that ran head on
Into car driven by Elizabeth Cooper
On Norris Freeway last May 22
Mrs. Cooper, 36, Youngstown, Ohio
Fatally injured in crash
Kratz charged with vehicular homicide
Trial in Criminal Court today
Jury found him guilty
Set punishment at 10 years in prison
Judge Steven D. Griffin gave him 30 days

To file motion for a new trial
He is held without bond in County Jail
    (*Source:* Court clerk)

K. Patrolman Rob Goodin answering
Burglar alarm call at 2:15 a.m. today
At Northgate Shopping Center
Turned into center at Broadway and Springs Road
Said brakes on cruiser locked
Cruiser struck a utility pole.
In shopping center parking lot
Goodin treated for cuts and bruises
At St. Mary's Medical Center
Police said the call Goodin was answering
Turned out to be a false alarm
    (*Source:* Police dispatcher)

L. American College of Surgeons
Annual banquet in Chicago tonight
Will present Surgeon of Year award
To local thoracic surgeon
Dr. Jacob Bradshear
Chief of Surgery, St. Mary's Medical Center
For developing new techniques
In pacemaker implants
He is a graduate of State University Medical School
Took advanced training at Duke Medical Center
Has practiced here for 25 years
    (*Source:* ACS press release)

M. Leland Henson, 63, West Jefferson, Ohio
Overnight guest at local motel
Taken to University Hospital.
After being struck on the head
With a gunbutt
Police said Henson stayed overnight
At Prince & Pauper Motel, I-75 and Merchants Drive
Was checking oil in his car about 6:50 a.m.
Man walked up behind him and struck him
Henson grabbed man and tried to take his gun
The assailant fled
Henson said the man apparently was going to rob him
Police said Henson was being held
At the hospital for observation
Henson expects to
Go to Florida tomorrow
    (*Source:* Patrolman David Mould)

N. Three elementary school students
Questioned by juvenile authorities
In connection with $12,000 worth
Of vandalism at Cedar Bluff School
Took place over weekend
Windows smashed, obscenities written
On walls in rooms and halls
With spray paint

Books ripped apart, desks overturned
Lockers broken open, lab equipment destroyed
Juvenile Officer Dottie Sweeten
Said "It must have taken them two days"
Charges will be brought against parents
Under state law making parents
Responsible for acts of their children
Juvenile Court hearing scheduled Friday
Sweeten said boys are 11, 12 and 13 years old
They said they did it because
They hate school
    (*Source:* Officer Sweeten)

CHAPTER 7

The Complex (Several-Incident) News Lead

A reporter's job certainly would be easier if all news events fell into the single-incident story category. It also would not be very challenging.

The test of a reporter's ability to write clearly and coherently comes when he is faced with a story that has several significant angles that must be featured in the lead. This complex type story requires more careful planning and organization to make certain that the separate parts of the story come together coherently.

Suppose a gasoline tanker truck crashed and caused the following damage:

1. The driver was killed.
2. About 100 persons had to be evacuated.
3. Nearly 8000 gallons of gasoline spilled into a river that is the main water supply for the city.

The general rule in writing any news event is to place the most newsworthy thing first. The rule presents no real problem as long as a story has only a single incident to be stressed. However, when the story has more than one significant incident, the reporter's job becomes more complicated. One of two basic methods generally is used in handling a more complex story:

1. Summarize all features—in order of importance—in the first sentence or paragraph.
2. Emphasize the most important or significant incident in the first sentence or paragraph and then quickly summarize all the other important features in logical order in succeeding paragraphs.

In either approach, all the features should be established in the reader's mind before the reporter proceeds very far with developing any one feature.

Here is an example of how the results of the truck crash might be written in a summary lead:

> A tanker truck crashed today on Highway 11-E, five miles east of here, killing the driver, spilling nearly 8,000 gallons of gasoline into the city's water supply and forcing the evacuation of about 100 persons.

The lead is quite long. In fact, that is one of the hazards of a summary lead. And it is a major reason why many editors do not like them.

The following example shows the further development of that lead. At the left is a diagram of the lead and other beginning paragraphs of the story. In this and other diagrams each geometrical shape represents a separate story feature. The diminishing size of the figures signifies the diminishing newsworthiness of the story material:

THE DIAGRAM

Summary of Features

Major Details of Feature No. 1

Major Details of Feature No. 2

Major Details of Feature No. 3

Other Paragraphs in the Complete Story

THE WRITTEN STORY

A tanker truck crashed today on highway 11-E, five miles east of here, killing the driver, spilling nearly 8,000 gallons of gasoline into the city's water supply and forcing the evacuation of about 100 persons.

The driver, Ted E. Brooks, 45, Bristol, apparently underestimated a curve and crashed over an embankment about 9 a.m., State Trooper C. D. Hughes said.

The rig flipped over, and the gasoline drained into the Nolichucky River, the city's main water source. Ronnie Snyder, city water control specialist, said there was no immediate danger of contaminating the water supply.

Civil Defense officials ordered the evacuation of about 100 persons who live in houses across the highway from the accident as a safety measure. They said there was some danger of explosion.

Trooper Hughes said the rig was enroute to Johnson City. It crossed into the opposite lane, ripped up 87 feet of guard rail and plunged over the embankment. When it flipped over, the driver was thrown from the cab. His body was found on the river bank, about 50 feet from the wreck. The truck is owned by the Appalachian Truck Co.

(Further details on all the features would follow in the body of the story.)

EMPHASIZING AN OUTSTANDING FEATURE

If one of the several results of the wreck seems of outstanding importance, then a lead emphasizing that single item might be more effective. Often when a person (or persons) has been killed or critically injured, an editor will want to emphasize that in the lead. In that case, here's how the wreck story might be written:

THE DIAGRAM

Outstanding Feature

Summary of Other Features

Other Paragraphs in the Complete Story

THE WRITTEN STORY

A 45-year-old truck driver was killed today when his gasoline tanker, loaded with 8,000 gallons of fuel, crashed on Highway 11-E, five miles east of here.

The gasoline drained into the Nolichucky River, but officials said there was no immediate danger to the city water supply. Civil Defense officials evacuated about 100 persons who live near the scene of the accident as a safety measure.

The driver, Ted E. Brooks of Bristol, apparently lost control of the rig on a curve, State Trooper C. D. Hughes said. The truck crossed into the opposite lane, ripped up 87 feet of guard rail and plunged over the embankment.

When the tanker flipped over, Brooks was thrown from the cab. His body was found on the river bank, about 50 feet from the wreck.

(Further details on the gasoline spill, the water supply and the evacuation would follow in the body of the story.)

In that example, all the emphasis is placed on the death of the driver. However, because of a possible threat to the water supply an editor may want to stress that in the lead. In that case, here is how the story might be written:

THE DIAGRAM

Outstanding Features

Other Feature

Other Paragraphs in the Complete Story

THE WRITTEN STORY

Nearly 8,000 gallons of gasoline were spilled into the Nolichucky River today when a gasoline tanker crashed on Highway 11-E, five miles east of here today, killing the driver.

The river is the city's chief water source.

However, Ronnie Snyder, city water control specialist, said there was no immediate danger that the city water supply would be contaminated.

State Trooper C. D. Hughes said the driver, Ted Brooks of Bristol, apparently lost control of the rig on a curve. The truck crossed into the opposite lane, ripped up 87 feet of guard rail and plunged over the embankment.

When the tanker flipped over, Brooks was thrown from the cab. His body was found on the river bank, about 50 feet from the wreck.

As a safety measure, Civil Defense officials evacuated about 100 persons who live in houses across the highway from the wreck site. They said there was some danger of explosion.

(Further details would be included in the body of the story.)

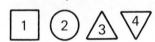

This example features the spilling of the gasoline into the water supply. Then the very important question (Is the water contaminated?) has to be answered. Other features, especially the death of the driver, are presented before going back to elaborate on the lead. A similar lead could be written featuring the evacuation, if the reporter and the editor believe that it is the most significant event. In this particular story it would not be.

Here is a more complicated story. A reporter covering the city school board has the following facts—all of them worth considering for the lead—to work with:

1. Joseph P. Hamilton, city school superintendent, shocked the board members at a meeting today by announcing his immediate resignation.
2. Just a few minutes earlier he had proposed a $70 million cut in the school's $1.4 billion annual budget.
3. He also had proposed cutting about 1,700 jobs from the school systems work force of 48,600 employees, including assistant principals, special education teachers, teachers aides, custodians, tradesmen and other hourly workers.
4. It had been disclosed earlier in the day that school administrators provided misleading information to investors about how the school system would use funds set aside to pay debts. This will have an immediate influence on the city's credit rating.
5. It had been rumored that Mayor Alice Lane had forced Hamilton's resignation. It was also rumored that officials of the city's Education Association, the teacher's union, planned to call for Hamilton's resignation.

Each of these is worth considering for a separate story, but all are related so the reporter has to weave most, if not all, of them into one lead. Here are several examples of how the story might be written:

THE DIAGRAM	THE WRITTEN STORY
Summary of Features	After urging $70 million be slashed from next year's budget and 1,700 jobs be eliminated, School Superintendent Joseph P. Hamilton resigned today amid a growing financial scandal.
	Here is what happened at today's school board meeting:
Feature No. 1	1. Hamilton called for the board to cut the city's $1.4 billion annual budget by some $70 million in an effort to keep the schools from going broke.
Feature No. 2	2. He urged the board to eliminate 1,700 jobs, including assistant principals, special education teachers, teachers aides and a number of hourly paid positions.
Feature No. 3	3. After he had completed his report, he stunned board members by announcing his immediate resignation.
Feature No. 4	4. He denied that his resignation was connected with disclosures earlier today that school officials had given misleading infor-

THE DIAGRAM THE WRITTEN STORY

mation to investors about how the school system would use funds set aside to pay debts.

Feature No. 5

Other Paragraphs in the Complete Story

5. He also denied that Mayor Alice Lane had forced his resignation. And he said he had not heard rumors that the Education Association was going to call for his resignation.

(Further details of these features in following paragraphs. Note: Feature No. 5 was not referred to in the lead but is significant enough to be included in the list of the day's developments.)

This summary type lead tends to run long. In all probability the editor would want to focus directly on the superintendent's resignation. In that case, here is an example of how the story might be written to emphasize that single element:

THE DIAGRAM THE WRITTEN STORY

Outstanding Feature

Feature No. 2

Feature No. 3

City School Superintendent Joseph P. Hamilton stunned school board members today by resigning.

Hamilton told the board members he was leaving "at the end of the work day."

His surprise announcement at the board's regular meeting today came just minutes after he had proposed $70 million in spending cuts and the reduction of the work force by 1,700 to ease the school system's growing financial difficulties.

Hamilton denied his resignation was connected with disclosures earlier today that school officials had given misleading information to investors about how the system would use funds set aside to pay debts.

Other Paragraphs in the Complete Story

(Details of his resignation and all other features in following paragraphs.)

The several-feature lead forms, as illustrated in the preceding examples, go beyond the lead sentence and the lead paragraph. Still, they are leads in the sense that they summarize the various features of the story in showcase fashion before the body developments begin. In the long stories necessary to develop several features, several lead paragraphs are frequently needed and may be thought of as the "lead block."

7c OTHER LEADS

The Combination on Scrambled Lead. There are no hard and fast rules for writing the several-feature lead. The leads illustrated here show two basis methods of "placing first things first." Both of them have variations. The choice of the exact variety usually will be determined by the facts and incidents of the story. Some of the features, for example, may be summarized but not all. Or an outstanding incident may be singled out. It might also be combined with related incidents. And in some cases the reporter may want to take advantage of the drama of an event to depart completely from the hard news lead. Here are several examples: The City Council took the following action at its meeting:

1. Approved a $17,500-a-year pay hike for the mayor, putting his salary at $42,500.
2. Voted to delay starting the salary increase for the mayor until funds are available to give all city workers a merit pay increase, which was promised last year.
3. Turned control of the city's two airports over to the Metropolitan Airport Authority.
4. Approved construction of a union hall in the Fourth and Gill neighborhood for Iron Workers Local No. 384.

THE DIAGRAM

THE WRITTEN STORY
WITH COMBINATION LEAD

Outstanding Features

City Council voted to raise the mayor's salary to $42,500 last night but decided not to start paying him the additional $17,500 until money is available to give all city employees a merit pay increase.

Further Summary of
Other Features

In other action at last night's meeting, the Council also voted to turn the city's two airports over to the Metropolitan Airport Authority and approved construction of a union hall in the Fourth and Gill neighborhood.

Other Paragraphs in the
Complete Story

(Details of story in following paragraphs)

The first paragraph summarizes two of the features by uniting them in dual lead since both deal with pay increases for city employees. The second paragraph adds other features not related to those in the lead but important enough to be placed very high in the story. This method can be called the "scrambled" lead—but a name is unnecessary. If a reporter organizes and relates several features properly and places first things first, he will achieve a proper lead, whatever its name.

Tabulations. Illustrated below is a method of using a tabulation to develop **7d** a summary lead within the story itself. Tabulations may be used either above or within the story—or may be set off by boldface type or by some other device. These devices are used to crowd information into small space, and to flash essential facts before the reader, relieving the lead of cumbersome detail. The lead then can focus on a single fact. Numerals may be used or omitted in listing tabulated items. Note the following illustration:

A One-Column Box (or a Boldface List)

HIGHLIGHTS OF YESTERDAY'S ELECTION

—Guy Randall Schultz elected Governor
—Sally McMillan Stovall elected Lieutenant-Governor

—First Republicans elected to state's two top offices in 100 years

—Property tax referendum defeated by narrow margin

Simplified Lead Made Possible by Preceding Tabulation

For the first time in 100 years Republican candidates have won the two top offices in the state.

Guy Randall Schultz was elected governor and his running-mate, Sally McMillan Stovall, won the lieutenant-governor's post in yesterday's election.

Governor-elect Schultz said . . .

Another type lead used is a variation of the summary lead. Instead of a single sentence (summary leads tend to run long), this style briefly itemizes each feature as in the following example:

The Governor's Tax Revision Study Commission today recommended:

—A graduated state income tax

—Abolishing the state sales tax

—Reducing the gasoline and alcohol tax

—Assessment of all property at 100 per cent of value

"If the state is to avoid financial chaos, it must substitute a reasonable and equitable tax system for the current regressive taxes levied," the Study Commission report said.

The leads discussed so far are the style most commonly used on straight news stories. There are, however, some other variations that are acceptable at a number of newspapers. One of them is discussed in the following paragraph. Others are discussed in Chapter 8, "Devices to Polish the Lead," and Chapter 10, "Features and Human-Interest Stories."

7e   *The Interpretative Lead.* Instead of using one of the various standard news leads discussed so far, the reporter may elect to write an interpretative lead. In this type lead, the reporter, using the facts of the event as his basis, attempts to tell his readers what these facts mean. Interpretation should always be *objective,* based on background knowledge of a situation and an accurate analysis of the facts at hand. If it is the reporter's subjective view, then it becomes editorial opinion. In other words, the standard leads simply report on an event, while the interpretative lead attempts to put the event into perspective for the reader. This type lead is most often used on second-day stories or by newspapers that get second crack at the story. However, it can be and is used more often now in the first telling of a story. For example, if the governor sent a message to the state legislature asking for a state income tax, a standard story might begin:

Gov. Franklin Kamm today asked the state legislature to enact a state income tax to help rescue the state from financial chaos.

In the rest of the story, the reporter gives the details of the governor's proposal, citing figures and so forth. A reporter interpreting the event for the reader might have written:

Gov. Franklin T. Kamm yesterday ignored strong political pressure from his own party and put his own political future on the line when he asked the state legislature to pass a state income tax.

It is almost certain that this session will see some legislative action in this controversial field because of the state's financial crisis, but the governor's political colleagues see the tax issue as an albatross that is certain to ruin their chances in the November elections.

His strong plea for the income tax could hurt the governor's chances in the election when he is expected to be his party's candidate for U.S. senator.

Kamm proposed a tax that would . . .

When use of this type lead (which emphasizes overall meanings and significances) is elected, it is important to include as quickly as possible the facts and events of the story. Some newspapers insist that they be in the second paragraph if not the first. Others include them in the third or fourth paragraph, depending upon the circumstances of the story. In no case should they be ignored or placed much farther down in the story than the fourth paragraph, or the reader simply may be confused.

Considerable debate about interpretative reporting continues among journalists, and many newspapers still approach it with extreme caution. It is, of course, being used increasingly in reporting government and politics and frequently brings cries of "bias" or "inaccurate" from the person whose action is being interpreted. Nevertheless, the increasing complexity of modern society— not just government and politics—seems to require that newsmen explain facts as well as report them. Newspapers, then, have an added responsibility to make certain that the reporter who does the interpretation is a good reporter first and has the necessary background and maturity of judgment to present an accurate and objective analysis of the facts.

Separate Stories. Elections, storms, strikes, wars and frequently large fires and other major events may demand separate stories for the various phases of each, as pointed out earlier. In this case, each story will require either a single-feature or a several-feature lead, developed in the forms already disussed. Many times these sidebar-type stories lend themselves to strong dramatic feature leads. Often these related stories are collected on a single or adjoining pages in a newspaper. However, some newspapers will scatter them throughout the edition.

The manner in which they are displayed will vary. They may all be displayed under a single large headline with each story having its own headline but all stories with the same size headline. Or the paper may elect not to use a single large headline and have various sizes of headlines on the individual stories, depending upon their individual news value.

IDENTIFYING THE FEATURES   7f

The beginning reporter often finds difficulty in distinguishing story features from the mass of story detail. Unless he clearly recognizes the features, he cannot avoid the danger of burying them within the body of the story. Nor can he write the single-feature lead, or any of the several-feature leads, or the body of his story—in other words, he cannot write news stories without definitely identifying the features of his story material.

Simply defined, features are the highlights, the outstanding and most interesting and most significant items, in any given sequence of events or arrangements of materials. The reporter himself must determine what these are. If he can discern the highlight of a previous vacation, the most interesting chapters of a book, the most telling points in an argument or the several outstanding results of a story, he can discern features. No mystery or technicality is involved and yet no rule is available for detecting them.

Ordinarily a speech, for example, contains as features its several main arguments or contentions. Yet, if the speaker suggests in an ad lib that the President should be impeached, or if a fist fight develops in the audience or if a local issue is touched upon, these would seem to be features of the occasion that might rate more attention than the content of the formal speech.

A common fault of the beginner, nevertheless, is to introduce in the body of his story some material that should have been featured in the lead or lead block. When reminded that the body should be used for the development of the lead features, he defends this material as developmental detail of one lead feature. Obviously, a broad lead can bracket almost any number of features. If the reporter should try to get by with a lead that said "Many interesting events occurred in Jackson today," he could conceivably include in the body developments of every unrelated event in the city that day. However, such a lead would conceal and not reveal, as the lead must, the story content. And no editor would accept such a dull, uninteresting lead.

It is the purpose of the lead not to conceal but to give the reader an accurate and complete picture of what is to come later in the story. Even if it is possible to defend buried features (and in most cases it is not), the reporter has violated the basic premise of what a lead should be. If he will keep in mind that he should tell in the lead or lead block the basic elements—the most newsworthy elements—of the story before he begins to explain them with developmental details, he will not bury features. He can display all of them in a summary lead or one of them first in the outstanding-feature lead, but he should be sure to make the display before he begins the development of features.

Perhaps the best guide in recognizing a separate and worthwhile feature of a story is this: any incident or detail that is sufficiently newsworthy in itself to be worth reporting as a single-feature story is a feature of, and can be displayed in, the lead of the several-feature story. At least, all such features must be summarized prior to their full development.

Under this definition, the several and unrelated actions of a city council, if newsworthy at all, are newsworthy separately. In fact, they might—if they are unrelated in substance—be reported as separate stories except for the identity of place and time and method of their occurrence and their author (city council). In other words, they have in common the "Who," "When," "How" and "Where" but they differ as to "What" (happened). A similar identity of some, but not all, of the W's would exist in case of a storm or of any other event presenting several features worth reporting.

It is in the differentiation of the various W's (usually the "What") that the several-feature story is appropriate. In the single-incident story the only features available are the W's themselves, and each W is constant throughout the story. In the several-incident story one or more of the W's will vary. That is, different things happen (different "Whats"), or the same thing happens to different people ("Who") or from different causes ("Why") and so on. Thus, the several-feature story has a specific function to perform—that of highlighting, displaying, featuring the variable W or W's. To bury a feature is to violate the function of this story form.

It should be emphasized that the features presented by a variable W must be newsworthy. They are not to be reported merely because they are variables. For example, if a speech contains four "Whats"—say, four main points or logical divisions—only one or two or three of them may be newsworthy enough to be reported. If a fire destroys a valuable painting, a historical shrine and three chickens, the last item may not be worth reporting—unless, of course, they are very rare and valuable chickens. Any item is a feature only as measured by its newsworthiness—that is, reader appeal. The reporter himself must determine what these features are.

Summarizing the Features. Once the several features have been recognized, the reporter's concern is to summarize them adequately for use in the lead or the lead block. Note the following faulty attempts at summation of several features:

> Four points in favor of consolidating city and country schools were given today by Mrs. Mary Robinson, president of Better Schools Inc., in a speech to the . . .

> Problems of taxation and public health were debated today by the state house of representatives.

> Congress today passed four important pieces of consumer legislation.

Each of these leads recognizes the existence of several features, but the attempt to summarize the features has sacrificed adequacy for brevity. "Four points in favor" has no particular reader appeal and really cannot be classified as a summary of four features. A brief summary of the points themselves is required for an adequate lead or lead block. The features are the meat of the story. An adequate summation of the four features in the "four points" might be:

> The cost of public schools could be reduced sharply by consolidating city and county school systems, Mrs. Mary Robinson, president of Better Schools Inc., told a meeting of the Central Lions Club today.
> Mrs. Robinson said consolidation would also bring about more uniform educational standards, reduce teacher-pupil ratios in the classrooms and greatly reduce the number of students who would have to be bused.

COMBINING STORIES

Separate stories, naturally, will differ in the content of all their W's—except occasionally when several stories may concern the police or the governor or some other functionary, or occur in the same place or even in the same manner and so on. When these accumulate to any noticeable extent, the tendency in newspapers is to combine them. They may be grouped, as separate stories, on the same page with separate headlines or all under a single headline. But as more of the W's become identical, the tendency is to try to put them all into a several-feature story, provided, of course, the combination does not make a very long and rather formidable story for the reader to have to wade through. To avoid long stories some reporters will write the lead story on the major action taken and then separate stories on secondary action.

EXERCISES

1. Clip from any newspaper available to you leads that illustrate three different methods of writing a several-incident lead. Bring them to class and be prepared to discuss their strengths and weaknesses.

2. Below are rough notes for several-incident leads. Follow these instructions in utilizing each set of notes:

First—List the various features in order of their newsworthiness.

Second—Write a lead in summary form, another lead emphasizing an outstanding feature and a third lead in one of the forms explained in this chapter. Diagram each lead in the margin at the left.

Third—Explain which of the three methods you think yields the best lead and why.

A. City School Board meeting last night:

    i. Voted unanimously to break its contract with Stauffer Construction which is handling a $4.1 million renovation project at Franklin Roosevelt High School.

       School Superintendent Edward Andrews said the company is 15 months behind and apparently has 6 more months of work before completing the project.

       Board Member Philip Rohar asked Andrews: "Why haven't you and your people done something about this before now?"

       Andrews said he had personally notified the board's attorney, Benjamin Cardoza, a year ago that the project was "hopelessly behind schedule."

       "What about that, Mr. Cardoza?" Rohar asked.

       Cardoza said he had been "in touch" with the attorney for the construction company but just couldn't seem to "get any action."

       "Well, I move we cancel the contract and sue their bonding company," Rohar said.

       "I second it," Board Member Elizabeth Scull said.

       The motion passed unanimously on a roll call vote.

    ii. Voted to add no more schools to the 12

       Now slated for closing

       Closing proposed after fall enrollment

       Dropped 20 per cent

       Set public hearing on proposed closings

       Third Saturday of next month

       At 10 a.m. in Civic Coliseum

   iii. Accepted new Senior High Policy

       Recommended by Superintendent Andrews

       Referred it to Policy Committee for study

       Policy would crack down on attendance

       Mandate citywide, uniform final exams

       For all subjects taught

       In grades 9 through 12

       Institute a get-tough policy on

       Students caught with drugs at school

       Policy Committee instructed to

Report to Board at next regular meeting

"We will need your recommendations as soon as possible," Board Chairman
Edna Taylor said.

"This will be a hot one and we'll have to hold public hearings on it."

    iv. Named two Minority Affairs Coordinators

For City School System

DeVance Walker, Jr., staffing specialist in Schools' personnel department

Will coordinate activities between

Board and the black community

Ileana Harrell, Spanish teacher at

Roosevelt High School for 10 years,

Will do the same with the Hispanic community

    v. Voted to change time

Of next regular meeting

Will meet at 4:40 p.m.

Instead of 6:30 p.m.

Second Tuesday of next month

B. State University Board of Trustees meeting today:

    i. Rejected proposal by President Alexander Markum

To permit students in dorms

To possess alcoholic beverages

Vote was unanimous

Board President Arthur Williams said:

"You can't believe the heat we have been getting from the public on
this. I just don't think the time is right."

President Markum told the board every comparable

state university in the region permits alcohol in the dorms. "The no-
alcohol rule is extremely difficult to police in a school this size," he said.

Head Resident Les Hyder said his staff expends

thousands of hours annually trying to police the dorms for alcohol. "But
with 20,000 students living in dorms it is simply an impossible rule to
enforce," he said.

    ii. Voted to increase tuition starting next fall

Eight percent over current fee

Which was raised this year by 4 percent

New tuition will be $35

Per·semester hour of course work

Increased cost of "everything"

Blamed for hike by Williams

    iii. Approved a resolution urging State Legislature

To make more scholarship funds available

To needy students to offset

Increase in tuition

Resolution proposed by

Board Member Michael Lollar

    iv. Voted to name the new library

In honor of Mrs. Sandra Hughes Larkin

First woman governor of the state

She served two terms as governor

Then was elected to U.S. Senate

Now serving as Ambassador

To the Court of St. James

C. Stadium roof collapsed today
At least five dead
More than 20 injured
Injured all workmen on the project
>   (*Source:* Police spokesman)

Stadium under construction
Adjacent to city airport
Outer walls and roof completed
Workmen completing insides
The building was four stories high
Designed to seat 19,400 persons
Slated to open early spring
>   (*Source:* Architect Nelson Lipman)

Roof caved in trapping workmen under debris
About 8 a.m.
Approximately 100 workers on the job
Collapse came minutes after
A 747 jet roared by overhead
Plane taking off from airport
Architect and Federal Aviation Aministration
Spokesmen said it is too early
To speculate on whether
The plane had anything to do with collapse
>   (*Source:* Witnesses, Lipman, Thomas Ashe, FAA regional director)

Police, state troopers, firemen from
Three nearby communities dispatched to scene
Civil Defense workers joined them.
Police Chief William Fox said:
>   "Some of the men are digging through the debris with their hands to try to find their friends. We are moving in three cranes to lift the metal framework. It is hampering rescue operations."

An emergency room doctor at St. Mary's
Said they had received 10 injured men
A spokesman for University Hospital said
Police told hospital officials
To expect at least five dead
Police withholding names
Until next of kin notified

D. State University Officials and City Police
Announced the arrest of a
Local accountant who attempted
To take an accounting final exam
For a university student
The man is Stewart V. O'Neill
He received a degree in accounting
Last spring from Whitehall College
He operates his own business here
He is charged with fraud
>   (*Source:* Charles R. Barnard, Dean of Student Conduct, and Detective John Campbell)

Barnard said the man showed up
To take the departmental examination

He was carrying the student's
Identification card
Approximately 400 students taking exam
Teaching assistant checking
Assigned seating remembered the student
When he saw the stranger in his seat
He told the senior professor
Supervising the exam
He called the campus Security Officers
They called city police who
Arrested O'Neill and charged him with fraud
O'Neill admitted that the student
Had paid him $300 to take the exam
Dean Barnard said the student was
Suspended immediately and that
Criminal fraud charges will be
Brought against him also
He said it would be a landmark case
Because fraud charges have never
Been brought against a student
Accused of cheating
He said: "When the word gets out, I don't think we'll have too many hiring
    someone to take their exams."
Barnard refused to identify the student
Because formal charges have not yet
Been brought against him
E. Holdup at newsstand-bookstore last night
Police received call about 8 p.m.
Mary Selph said her husband, Ernest,
Had not returned home from his shop
Police checked The Bookworm
Selph's shop at 1105 Concord St.
Across from south entrance to university
Door was open and signs of a scuffle
About an hour later Selph called home
Said he and clerk, Mellisa Myer, 30,
Had been held up and forced to accompany
Hold up man in Selph's car. He was
Released about 35 miles away
Near rest stop on the interstate
State police and sheriff's deputies
Set up roadblocks on all main highways
Car spotted, got around roadblock
Police chased north at high rate of speed
Trooper Arthur Kozen rammed his car
Into the fleeing auto, forcing it off road
About 60 miles north of here
Kozen said holdup man held gun
To Miss Myer's head and threatened
To kill her if officers came closer
After about an hour of negotiations
SWAT team sharpshooter fired one shot

Bullet struck holdup man in the head
Killed him instantly
Miss Myer was unharmed
Police found bank bag containing $120
In the back seat of the car
The man identified as Dennis Miller
Believed from Des Moines, Iowa
Troopers attempting to confirm
Identity through fingerprints
(*Sources:* Police Chief Marshal Parker, Selph, Trooper Kozen, Miss Myer)

F. Following are highlights of a speech by Joan Horne Dollar, president of No-Nukes Inc., a nationwide citizens group that opposes nuclear power plant construction. Speech given at group's annual meeting at the Civic Coliseum. More than 1,500 delegates from all over the world.

"Lethal radioactive wastes buried or piling up across the nation—from the armed services, nuclear power reactors, hospitals, universities, and industry—could fill 10 million barrels.

"And that amount is increasing by 10 to 30 per cent every year.

"There is enough mildly radioactive waste in the U.S. to cover a small city to a depth of five feet.

"The Atomic Age is almost 37 years old, and the accounting of radioactive debris includes 7,000 tons of burned-out reactor fuel, 70 million gallons of highly radioactive military wastes, 69 million cubic feet of low-level radioactive wastes, and 140 million tons of uranium mine spoils.

"Instead of searching for ways to safely isolate this hazardous material, scientists have been playing around with such crackpot schemes as blasting the wastes into outer space aboard rocket ships. And millions might die if the cargo fell back to earth. They have suggested burying waste deep in ocean sediments millions of years old, but a leak could pollute the oceans. And they have even suggested dropping them into deep holes at least 25,000 feet below the earth's surface but that might trigger earthquakes.

"Because the federal government is not facing up to its responsibility, our organization must take immediate action. With the approval of your board of directors, I have instructed our attorneys to file suit in Federal Court in Washington, D.C., against the Nuclear Regulatory Agency as well as any other government agency or private industry involved with nuclear energy. We will seek an injunction to stop the building and licensing of any new nuclear plants. We will seek the immediate shutdown of all nuclear facilities and we will ask for a permanent ban on the shipping of nuclear wastes from one state to another and from any foreign country into our country."

Devices to Polish the Lead

In his book *On Writing Well* William Zinsser calls the lead the most important sentence in the story. "If it doesn't induce the reader to proceed to the second sentence, your article is dead," he wrote. "And if the second sentence doesn't induce him to continue to the third sentence, it is equally dead."

Reporters and editors agree with Zinsser. They know that the lead is usually the hardest part of a newspaper story to write. Frequently a lead will be good in that it follows all the rules and principles discussed so far. But it may not be the best lead. It may contain all the 5 W's, the proper identification and authority, and emphasize a satisfactory feature. It may, in short, be entirely adequate, but it may also be dull. What is lacking may be vividness, style, class, distinction, attractiveness, brilliance. The reporter's responsibility is to achieve not merely adequacy but vividness. His job is to polish his lead with care. The following lead by Lawrence Knutson of the Associated Press is an example of a well-written, imaginative lead:

> WASHINGTON (AP)—Sen. Lowell P. Weicker, R-Conn., gave a campaign and not enough people came.
>
> So he called a news conference in Hartford, Conn., Wednesday and took himself out of the running . . .

Here is another example of a well-written lead from the Chicago Sun-Times:

> Out in the foothills of the Rockies, the War on Words Committee at the University of Northern Colorado has fired its first salvo against "ya know."

And Henry Hansen wrote this excellent lead in the Chicago Daily News:

> High-fashion photography is a moist lip, a quicksilver mood—and maybe a navel. It is languorous beauty, captured in a flash. And gone.
>
> It is Victor Skrebneski's world. Chicago's most successful . . .

There are a number of devices a reporter can use to polish his lead without sacrificing news interest. In fact, the device might be the thing that would capture a reader's attention when a straight news lead might not.

8a RHETORIC

Good writing demands the use of clear, crisp, colorful, precise language. Another principle of rhetoric is variety of sentence structure. The most usual sentence form is subject-predicate:

> Hospitals serving substantial numbers of Medicare and Medicaid patients must boost rates charged private patients to meet expenses, a study by the state Hospital Association concludes.

This direct form is favored by a number of reporters and editors, especially when dealing with a straight news story. But if the reporter writes all leads that way he stands a good chance of failing to catch the reader's attention. This type lead often is adequate, but it just as often is dull.

Playing up various W's will probably result in the use of a great variety of leads. And if it does not, the reporter can give variety and perhaps some luster to his writing by using one of the following forms:

Phrases

Infinitive: To win back his former wife, Frank Gibson rented a billboard on Interstate 75 and . . .

Participial: Digging his way out of the 24-foot snow drift with his hands, Tom Drake . . .

Prepositional: In an effort to get their names in the *Guinness Book of World Records,* two state university students . . .

Gerund: Filling the university's top post with a football coach is an insult to higher education, in the view of . . .

Clauses

Substantive: That a ban on smoking in all public buildings will be passed by the City Council is the opinion of . . . (Many editors avoid substantive clause leads because they usually are awkward.)

Adverbial: Unless the City Council can come up with a $41 million loan today, the city schools will be broke.

While police and her frantic parents searched the neighborhood, 2-year-old Jane McMillan slept curled up next to the family beagle in the hall closet . . .

EMPHASIZING NEWS VALUES

In the reporter's efforts to place the most newsworthy feature first in the lead, he may fail to study all the features carefully and overlook an angle that might make the difference between a routine or even dull lead and a vivid one. He should always be alert for the use of the various news values (discussed in Chapter 3) as a way of giving his lead some punch.

8b

Timeliness. The words "today" and "tomorrow" characterize most newsworthy leads. Occasionally a story must, however, concern events that happened "last night," "yesterday" or "last week." In this case the reporter should seek a "today" angle.

THE FIRST VERSION OF THE STORY:

> The state legislature's decision in May to trim $40 million from the state budget has resulted in the dismissal of 150 State Highway Department employees. More dismissals are expected in other departments.

SAME STORY, TODAY ANGLE EMPHASIZED:

> The State Highway Department dismissed 150 employees today.
> They were the first victims of the state legislature's decision last May to trim $40 million from the state budget.

8c

Proximity. In addition to striving for a today" angle, the reporter should also look for a "local" angle to his story.

A GENERAL STORY:

> Five young Alabama farmers will be honored as "Outstanding Young Farmers of the Year" at the annual state farm bureau convention Monday.
> They are . . .

SAME STORY, LOCAL ANGLE EMPHASIZED:

> John Crook, 28, who owns a 2,500-acre farm south of the city on Tipton Station Road, will be named an "Outstanding Farmer of the Year" at the annual state farm bureau convention Monday.
> He is one of five young men from across the state who will be honored by . . .

8d

Prominence. Prominent names make eye-catching news.

A GENERAL STORY:

> A $125-a-plate fundraiser to help Sen. Herman Smith's campaign to capture the Republican presidential nomination will be held Saturday night at the Yatt Regency hotel.

SAME STORY, PLUS PROMINENT NAME

> Actress Elizabeth Taylor will be the hostess for a $125-a-plate fundraiser here Saturday to help Sen. Herman Smith's campaign to win the Republican presidential nomination.
> In private life, the actress is married to John W. Warner, a Republican senator for Virginia and a close friend of Smith.
> The dinner at the Hyatt Regency hotel will . . .

8e NOVELTY LEADS

There was a time when most newspaper editors preferred the straight news lead in which the entire story was summarized. Fortunately for the talented writers and, more importantly, for the readers, a variety of types of leads are commonly used. Most of them tend to rely heavily on suspended interest, although the opening paragraph may give one or more of the W's. The other W's usually are conveyed later but still relatively high in the story.

To illustrate all methods of using novelty in the lead would be impossible because there are as many approaches as there are imaginative writers. However, a few of the more common forms are presented below. In these leads the story itself dictates its form, and the reporter should not strain himself to write a novelty lead on a story that does not justify such treatment. Nor does the novelty lead form give the reporter license to practice writing that violates basic rules of simplicity.

The Question Lead. The question lead serves best when a problem with reader appeal or public interest is the central point of the story. Unfortunately, this type lead is used far too often as a crutch by a reporter who will not take the time to work on another more effective approach. Some editors put a limit on the number of question leads that can be used. One of the classic question leads is this one:

O, say can you sing "The Star-Spangled Banner" without mumbling the words and petering out on the high notes?

Here is an excellent question lead by Bill Hance of the Nashville Banner. It helped him share a "Best of Gannett" award for spot news:

Know anybody who needs 59 toilet seat covers? They come in all colors—blue, brown, pink, yellow.

How about 100 units of blood plasma? Or a good glue machine?

Today in East Nashville, you can get . . .

Hance's story was teamed with two others by Larry Brinton and Mike Piggott to detail a six-month police undercover "sting" operation.

Jack Schnedler of the Chicago Daily News produced this outstanding question lead for an interview story on the occasion of the publication of Joseph Heller's second novel, 12 years after his first one was issued.

Tell us, Joe, why do you write so slow?

"Because I can't do it any quicker," says Joseph Heller, in a voice that unmistakably grew up around New York's Coney Island.

"I don't think that slowness in writing is a virtue. I just can't write faster. I'm slow . . ."

The Punch, Capsule or Cartridge Lead. This style lead uses a blunt, explosive statement, short and to the point, which gives the readers the most newsworthy feature.

M. W. Newman was assigned to cover Chicago's worst tornado disaster—54 dead, 1,075 injured and $50 million in property damage. His lead in the Chicago Daily News:

On a perfect day for tornadoes, the sky fell in.

Death came dancing and skipping, whistling and screaming, strangely still one second and whooshing and bouncing the next.

For some in the Chicago area, death was a black cloud . . .

Here is an example that is a bit more direct:

Frazier, the libidinous lion, is dead.

The king of beasts, who fathered 15 offspring after reaching an age comparable to an 85-year-old man, died quietly in his sleep at . . .

The Direct-Quotation Lead. This type lead should feature a short, eye-catching quotation. Far too many direct quotation leads are either too long or so involved the reporter has to go to great lengths to explain them. The keys there are the words "short" and "eye-catching."

Sally Quinn of the Washington Post used the technique skillfully after interviewing Alice Roosevelt Longworth, daughter of President Teddy Roosevelt.

"I still," she muses, rapping her bony fingers against her graying head, "more or less have my, what they call, marbles," and she pulls her flowered shawl around her a little closer, throws her head back and laughs gleefully.

Alice Roosevelt Longworth is 90 years old today.

"I may be an old crone but I can still put on the harness and lumber down the street."

When Mrs. Roosevelt, or Mrs. L. as she prefers to be called . . .

Bob Tamarkin of the Chicago Daily News used the quote lead effectively in this dispatch in the closing days of the war in Vietnam:

ABOARD THE USS OKINAWA—"They lied to us at the very end," said Capt. Stuart Herrington, the tears welling in his eyes. "They promised," he said, biting hard on his lip to hold the tears back.

Shirtless, he sat on the edge of the bunk, shaking his head. He continued:

"I never received an order in my life to do something I was ashamed of. If I would have known how it was going to end, I would have refused the order."

He was speaking of the evacuation of the Americans and Vietnamese during the frantic day last Tuesday when the Americans pulled out of South Vietnam . . .

The Contrast Lead. This style lead reaches for the reader's attention by comparing extremes—the big with the little, comedy with tragedy, age with youth, the past with the present—if such comparison is applicable to the news event.

The following United Press International lead by David Smothers is an example:

WOUNDED KNEE, S.D.—Not so long ago, the old Indians on the Pine Ridge Reservation used to go down to the post office every day. They would stand around in silent groups and wait for the Black Hills to come back to them in the mail.

The rich Black Hills are not coming back to the Oglala Sioux who once ruled them, by Indians or any other device. They are lost to the white man, as are so many things the Indians once called theirs.

The Direct-Address Lead. This type lead speaks directly to the reader, often on a subject of widespread appeal—the weather, for example.

If you plan to go out today, you'd better take along an umbrella. It's going to rain again, the weatherman says.

But the lead can also be used effectively on other stories. Willis David Hoover used it on a story in the Des Moines Sunday Register to tell about a country doctor in Hamburg, Ia.

HAMBURG, IA.—If you thought old-fashioned bedside manner and the personalized touch in doctoring disappeared with the final episode of "Marcus Welby," consider Dr. Roy Wanamaker, M.D.

At a time when the cost of everything else is rising, Wanamaker's fee for an office call starts at a mere $5—but goes all the way up to the astronomical high of $7.50, if things get involved.

Oh yes, no appointment necessary.

But hold on—that's not everything. Wanamaker still indulges in that most forgotten of all medical practices—the house call.

The Descriptive Lead. This type lead tries to paint a word picture of an interesting person, place or thing. It also helps create the mood for the story so it should match the subject carefully.

Here is a descriptive lead by Henry Allen of the Washington Post on a story about the Marine Corps:

PARRIS ISLAND, S.C.—He is seething, he is rabid, he is wound up tight as a golf ball, with more adrenalin surging through his hypothalamus than a cornered slum rat. He is everything these Marine recruits with their heads shaved to dirty nubs have ever feared or even hoped a drill instructor might be.

He is Staff Sgt. Douglas Perry and he is rushing . . .

Wells Twombly described Howard Cosell's voice in a lead this way:

The tones are neither round nor particularly attractive. They don't seduce the eardrums or lull the senses. Quite the contrary. They whistle into the listener's brain and explode like cannon shells. If the victim is the least bit insecure, he has a tendency to panic. Somebody is trying to steal his pablum.

This is no ordinary voice, turned out on an electronic lathe in some third-rate broadcasting school. This voice is violently independent. It throbs with ego. It pulsates with energy. It wants to shock you, amaze you, make you say "wow." It will always irritate you and not just because it comes slamming down from high up inside its owner's nose. It assaults your comfort. It takes the weariest of sporting clichés and makes it sound original. Casual observations are converted into grandiose opinions . . .

The Parody Lead. This type lead attempts to play on words, using widely known proverbs, quotations, song titles, currently popular sayings, book titles and other expressions to help establish an immediate identification with the reader and to bring a bit of sparkle to what otherwise might have been a routine story.

The sentence "Love means never having to say your sorry" was the most famous line in the immensely popular novel *Love Story*. It was the basis for hundreds of jokes and untold numbers of leads, including this one on a story about the tenure system in American universities and colleges:

Tenure means never having to rewrite your lecture notes.

Other examples:

> Silence is golden, but apparently no one ever told Howard Cosell.

> If love is a many splendored thing, Zsa Zsa Gabor's life must be like living in a rainbow.
> Miss Gabor married her sixth husband yesterday . . .

The Historical or Literary-Allusion Lead. This type lead draws on some character or event in history or literature in relation to a current event or a person in the news. The event or literary reference selected should be familiar to the average reader or it loses its impact.

The Bible is frequently used as a reference point by writers. Here are two examples:

> In the beginning, the Southern Appalachians belonged to the Cherokee Indians. They had been here for several centuries when . . .

> A Miami doctor was accused today of taking the Biblical injunction to "love thy neighbor" too seriously.
> Dr. John Jackson was sued for $150,000 by his neighbor, Tod McCaine, who charged that the doctor had "loved Mrs. McCaine so much" she moved out of his home and into the doctor's.
> The alienation of affection suit is the first filed here in 10 years, court officials said . . .

The Staccato Lead. The staccato lead consists of short, clipped words, phrases, sentences, sometimes separated by dashes or dots, to help create a certain mood for the story. It usually is descriptive in nature and should not be used if facts of the story do not justify it.

> The noise begins high. Up in the rafters. It gathers strength. Spills down the aisles. Building relentlessly. It cascades over the railings. It engulfs the expensive box seats. And spills out onto the playing field. A raging torrent of sound. The eardrums vibrate painfully. The heart flutters.
> Pele, the world's greatest soccer player, has just received another message of love from his adoring fans.

Miscellaneous Freak Leads. Freak leads employ a novel approach, often in sentence structure and display, in order to catch the reader's attention. This list can be extended indefinitely, to the extent of the reporter's writing ability and imagination (tempered with accuracy).

> For sale: one town.
> Connie Carpenter, film and television actress who bought a remote hamlet in the Colorado Rockies, today put the town up for sale. Miss Carpenter said she plans to sell Echo Cross Roads and buy an island in the South Pacific . . .

> The Budget
> By Mayor Normal Thomas
> 299 pp.
> City of Jamestown
>   Reviewed by Justin Smith
> What can you say about a book that you can get a copy of free, but is going to

cost you $3.76 for every $100 worth of property you own? Anyone who loves charts and tables and statistics will be fascinated . . .

COMPLETE REPORTING

The best polish a lead can have comes from the inner light shining through essential story elements. If the reporter has chosen the wrong W's or does not see beyond the obvious, no amount of clever language will do more than give the lead a light gloss. There is considerable difference between the following leads:

The Supreme Court this morning affirmed a lower court verdict in the case of R. L. Jameson, operator of Jameson Loan Co.

The "loan-shark business" is outlawed in this state.
The Supreme Court this morning, in affirming the verdict against R. L. Jameson of Jameson Loan Co., upheld the Constitutionality of the recent law requiring
. . .

The first lead is routine and dull—little about it that can be polished. The second one shows that the writer gave some thought and effort to trying to catch the reader's eye and make him want to read on.

The reporter must, however, be careful not to sacrifice fairness and objectivity in order to achieve a polished or colorful lead. Compare the following examples. The first one is fair, the second is almost an editorial:

A third-grade pupil at Lincoln Elementary School was struck and killed by a car about 8:15 this morning while using an unguarded cross walk in front of the school. She was . . .

The city's "rob Peter to pay Paul" mentality caused the death of a third-grade pupil at Lincoln Elementary School today.
Jane Martin, 7, was struck by a car in an unguarded cross walk in front of the school about 8:15 a.m.
Two weeks ago City Council eliminated all school crossing guards in an effort to raise funds to meet pay demands of striking sanitation workers . . .

EXERCISES

1. Rewrite the following leads, striving for variety in sentence structure.
   A. A rural Jamestown man died Friday when the tractor he was driving overturned and he was crushed beneath it.
   B. The university's Old Gold Singers will present their fall show with the theme "Celebration," featuring a group of song medleys and dances spotlighting the music of the past few decades, at 8 p.m. Friday and Saturday in Clapp Recital Hall.
   C. Two Bettendorf teen-agers who received an electric shock when they came in contact with a 8,600-volt power line as they were playing in a treehouse in a huge pine tree in a neighbor's backyard were reported in stable condition Saturday at St. Luke's Hospital.

D. More than 300 conservation officials from 85 counties are expected to attend the 20th annual meeting of the state's County Conservation Board Association at the Five Seasons Center in Falls Creek Falls State Park near Crossville Thursday through Saturday.

E. A 15-year-old Sherwood High School student's parents have sworn out warrants for four 16-year-old youths who they said forced the girl into a corner of an unsupervised classroom at the Sandy Spring-area school Friday and sexually assaulted her.

2. Newspapers are often faced with having to update stories that took place after the previous daily—or weekly—edition. What information would you seek, and from what sources, to make the following leads more "timely"?

A. Eight persons, six of them children, died early Thursday when fire destroyed two frame homes in suburban Chicago Heights.

B. A resident of a senior citizens' home in Fox Lake died Monday in a fall from the window of her fifth-floor apartment, where a fire had broken out.

C. The body of a man, believed to be about 70 years old, was found Saturday by two hunters on Van Deventer Island in northwestern Montgomery County near Seneca State Park.

3. Explain in detail how you would "localize" the following stories.

A. The state Alcoholic Beverages Commission today ruled that male go-go dancers can no longer perform in bars and taverns.

B. A state legislative subcommittee on transportation today recommended that the state sell all its cars and pay state employees mileage to use their own cars on official business.

C. A Federal Aviation Administration spokesman in Washington today defended the U.S. air traffic control system as "the best in the world," despite a rash of charges over the reliability of his agency's radar computers.

4. Prominent names are not given play in the following leads. Write and improve them.

A. A retired political leader and former star quarterback for State College will serve as grand marshal of the annual Homecoming parade at 2 p.m. Oct. 6.

Former Lt. Gov. Henry Hansen, who played football here from 1936 to 1939, will . . .

B A Metropolis man was listed in critical condition Saturday after an explosion and fire in a storage building on his ranch.

Metropolis Fire Chief Bob Gerling identified the man as Kenneth Lundeen, who was district attorney here for five years until he went into private practice in 1980.

5. List the kind of "human interest" data you would seek for a story on each of the following situations.

A. Two sisters in their 60s who had not seen their father since 1940 inherited his half-million-dollar estate. They were not named in his will, but the deceased's sister, who would have inherited the estate, began placing ads in newspapers because she was sure he had two daughters somewhere.

B. State prison inmate Manion Long has gotten a master's degree in guidance and personnel while behind bars and is now permitted to leave prison daily to attend classes at the state university, where he is seeking a degree in criminal justice. He wants to apply for a job as a prison warden when he finishes his current sentence for armed robbery.

6. Clip from any daily or weekly newspapers available to you 10 stories with novelty leads. Label them according to the classification of novelty leads given in this chapter.

7. A. Write question leads from the following notes.
   B. Write another lead on each set of notes, using other novelty forms.
      i. Police called to National Bank and Trust Co.
         Office at Clark and Division streets
         About 5:30 p.m. yesterday
         Bank security guards holding
         Linda Johnson, 27, who gave Los Angeles address
         Bank teller Pam Arnold said
         Miss Johnson tried to cash
         Payroll check for $5,925
         From Nevada Manufacturing Co., 2813 Ashland St.
         Miss Arnold said she became suspicious
         Because amount on check was poorly typed
         She called guards who called police
         While waiting for police to arrive
         Miss Johnson grabbed check
         From security guard
         And ate it
         She was charged with attempted theft,
         Attempted deceptive practices
         Police considering having stomach
         X-rays made for use in court
      ii. Police receive four separate reports
         From motorists near 61st Street and Peoria Avenue
         All reported by phone they had heard
         Screams for help coming
         From trunk of car
         Said car stopped at
         Red light at the intersection
         Voice sounded like that of a woman
         Motorists said they clearly heard
         "Help. For God's sake, help
         "He is going to kill me"
         Told police car sped away
         West on Peoria at about 3:30 p.m.
         One got partial license number
         Police traced car to suburban
         Businessman, who said it had
         Been stolen three nights ago
         Police found the 1970 Lincoln
         Parked in lot at Civic Auditorium
         Across street from Police Headquarters
         About 9:30 p.m.
         "We've checked everything. It
         May have been a hoax," Sgt. Tim Jackson said
8. A. Write punch leads from the following notes.
   B. Write a second lead on each, using another novelty form.
      i. Jackson Browne, owner of "The Stacks"
         Restaurant-bar frequented by university students
         Switched from serving beer in glasses
         To serving it in plastic cups
         From 9 p.m. to closing time

Thursday through Saturday

The busiest nights at the establishment

More than 250 glasses

Stolen or broken each week

Most taken last three days of week

Browne said:

> "One Friday night recently 72 glasses and a pitcher were broken. I just can't afford that kind of loss. Patrons earlier in the week just aren't as wild. I'll continue to serve them in glasses because they rarely break more than one a night."

ii. Lester Gibson, 104, oldest person in state

Seventh oldest Spanish-American War veteran

According to latest Veterans' Administration records

Fought with Teddy Roosevelt

At San Juan hill in Cuba

Enlisted when he was 14

Lied about his age

After war was public school

History teacher in Hamilton County

Went to last Spanish-American War

Veterans encampment two years ago

But confined to nursing home last two years

Died Saturday at Shannondale Nursing Home

Services at 1:30 p.m. Friday

Military honor guard to be

Provided by U.S. Army

He was one of about 225 surviving

Veterans of the 392,000 who fought in

The 1898 conflict with Spain in Cuba

And in Philippine Islands

9. A. Write direct-quotation leads from the following notes.

B. Write a second lead on each, using another novelty form.

i. Excerpts from a speech made by Calvin Sneed, city councilman and candidate for mayor in the city election, to the Downtown Rotary Club yesterday. Sneed is the only Black candidate in the race, and there have been rumors he will withdraw at the last minute and throw his support to Mayor William Hudgens, who is seeking a second term.

"I have no intention of withdrawing from the race for mayor. The rumors floating around the city are quite ridiculous. That speculation is an old-line political trick that my opponents are spreading. I am dead serious about this election, and feel I will be successful in the October primary. And, frankly, I don't think either of the two leading candidates deserve my support. The people know I am running—and running to win. But you wouldn't know that by reading the local paper. The News has actually ignored many of my speeches to area civic groups. I've known from the beginning that they would not support me—even if I were gold. The incumbent mayor has stated that there are no issues in this campaign—only who is best qualified to lead this city. But there are problems, serious problems, facing this city. The city's financial base is being eroded as families and businesses move to the suburbs. We simply must start an orderly plan to annex property—especially in the west. Our bonded indebtedness is almost at a limit, and the mayor wants more bond issues. And our public transportation system has been crippled by the present administration. I don't say I can solve all these problems, but if elected, I'll certainly try."

ii. Following are several direct quotations from an interview with Jump'n'Jack, a male go-go dancer whose real name is Jack Redish, a 35-year-old former truck driver from Chicago. He is in town appearing at the Harbor Inn, the first club in the city to present a male go-go dancer. Appears before women audiences only.

"This business has its highs and lows. And this town has got to be the lowest I've ever seen. I've played in other towns in this state and done quite well. I was a big hit at the Cave in Dallas. But the women in this town aren't ready for male go-go dancers, I guess. Nobody knows I'm here. There weren't more than a dozen women here last night for my opening. I don't know what they are afraid of. It is a clean act. I have lots of fun and usually the women do, too. I don't strip completely. Just down to my gold G-string. You see guys with less on at the beach every day. I can't understand why the women here are so timid. I've been doing this for five years now because I couldn't make a living and support my wife and child as a truck driver. And this is the first time I've had such poor attendance at one of my shows. I'd think I was losing my touch if I hadn't had them standing in line to see me just last week in Lake Charles."

10. A. Write contrast leads from the following notes.

    B. Write a second lead on each, using another novelty form.

       i. Harry Lovejoy, 10905 Concord Hills Lane
        Sitting in his living room
        Watching television news
        About 6:30 p.m. last night
        Wind apparently blew open
        Front door of his house
        He looked up and saw
        Stray dog walking into the house
        He said he tried to grab the dog
        But it bit him and ran
        He called police
        He went to University Hospital
        For emergency treatment
        Humane officer captured
        The dog about a block away
        Dog will be held to determine
        If it has rabies

      ii. The Rev. Martin Taylor, 73,
        Captain of 1929 track team
        Maryville College
        Now lives in Northfield
        About 140 miles away
        Plans to attend his
        50th anniversary reunion
        At Maryville next weekend
        Will leave his home Tuesday
        Will arrive in Maryville Friday
        Plans to make the trip
        On his 10-speed bicycle

11. A. Write direct-address leads from the following notes.
    B. Write a second lead on each, using another novelty form.
        i. Henley Street bridge
           Over Big Muddy River
           Will be closed for repairs
           Starting at midnight Sunday
           Traffic Engineer Darcy Sullivan
           Says repairs will take six weeks
           Traffic will be rerouted
           Over Roosevelt Memorial Bridge
           Sullivan says to expect
           A lot of traffic jams
           Advises drivers to avoid
           Crossing river as much as possible
           Until repairs are completed
       ii. Tomorrow is deadline
           For filing federal income tax
           Must be postmarked by midnight
           Not just in the mailbox by midnight
           IRS District Director Keith Smith said
           Postmaster C. Edwin Graves said
           He will assign extra personnel
           To make pickups at streetboxes
           At 11 p.m. and will have
           Extra crew at main post office
           Canceling mail dropped into
           Boxes there up to midnight
12. A. Attend a campus event such as a parade, an art exhibit, a dance recital, and write a descriptive lead on the event.
    B. Write a second lead on the event, using another novelty form.
13. A. Write novelty leads from the following stories, using any of the forms not mentioned in the above assignments.
    B. Write a second lead on each event, using another novelty form.
        i. Dan Geluso, 14-year-old local youth
           Started collecting rocks seriously
           About three years ago
           Attends meetings of rock collectors
           Goes rock hunting two or three times a week
           Even when family goes on vacation
           Family just returned from Colorado
           Where Dan bought a rock
           For 75 cents in an
           Estes Park gift shop
           He split the rock open
           When he returned home
           And found 2.3 ounces of gold
           Worth more than $800
           Dan plans to save it
           "To see if gold goes any higher"
       ii. Joan Worley, chief librarian
           Wrote Randall Altman, 25,
           A construction worker

Who lives at 33 Riverbend Rd.
Asked him to please return
The 67 overdue books he has
And to include the $500 he owes in fines
Miss Worley said normally
A representative of the library
Would go directly to
The patron's home to collect
But none of her staff is eager in this case
Among the titles Altman has out are
Beginning Kung Fu, Blackbelt
Techniques in the Martial Arts
And the *New Manual of Kung Fu,*
Along with nine other books
On the martial arts

iii. Robert Gates, 41
Owns dairy farm
On Morristown Road
12 miles east of city
Recently went to doctor
Suffering headaches
Nosebleeds, skin blotches
After numerous tests
Doctor suggests he seek
Another line of work
Said he was allergic
To his 60 milk cows
"At first, I laughed
Because I thought it was a joke
It's incredible," Gates said
Gates put his 175-acre farm
And his cows on the market
Will move into the city
As soon as they are sold

iv. Police called to
Kimball's jewelry store
In Westtown shopping mall
Security guard holding
Jerry Dwayne Massey, 19,
A University sophomore
From New York City
Store manager said
Massey had looked at
$10,000 diamond ring
But that the ring was missing
Massey claimed he put it back
And that the clerk put the
Ring tray in the case
Police searched him and
Found nothing but decided
To take him to University Hospital
Because he kept clutching

His throat and asking for water
At hospital he was
Checked with an X-ray scanner
Ring was in Massey's stomach
He was charged with grand Larceny

14. Using newspapers available to you seek out similar stories in each paper and compare how they are handled. For example, seek out a murder story in each of five or six newspapers and compare their leads. In addition to a murder story, compare a fire story, a traffic accident story, and a city council story. Select the ones you think are the most effective and tell why.

WRITING THE COMPLETE STORY

A distinctive and inviting lead may get the reader's attention, but it is the body of the story that holds it. Organizing the body of the story is tremendously important. The body is where the story comes together. If it does not support the lead in a careful and lucid fashion, then the reader may feel cheated—may not even finish the story.

Often organizing and developing the body of a news story can present even greater problems than the lead. Just as there are a number of approaches—styles—in handling leads, the body of a news story can be developed in a variety of ways.

Part Three presents organizational patterns of both the straight news and the feature story. This section also deals with four other areas that present specific problems for which there are specific techniques to use in writing complete stories. These include the organizations of: (1) stories on events about which previous stories have been published; (2) cutlines to go with pictures, which are often important supplements to stories but which sometimes stand alone in the reporting of a news event; (3) news stories for radio and television, and (4) stories which require special treatment if a newspaper's policy is involved.

The chapters in this section have a bearing on the writing of all types of news stories considered in the chapters that follow.

The Body
of the Story

A reporter should not think of his story in isolated parts—the lead, the body, the ending. He must think of it as an integrated piece of writing, with each part carefully tied to the others. In fact, when selecting and writing the lead, the reporter should be conscious of what is to follow. He must know where he is going with the story to make certain what follows the lead merges smoothly and supports the lead.

Here is an example of a rather awkwardly constructed lead that doesn't really fit the story:

> HINCKLEY, Ohio (UPI)—If you can sing "When the buzzards return to Hinckley, Ohio," then you're ready for tomorrow's annual fly-in.
>
> The turkey vultures have been migrating northward and arriving at the same roost on high trees and crags around Hinckley Lake for as long as anyone can remember. For the last 29 years the birds have made it on March 15.
>
> At the arrival of the first turkey vulture, Ranger Lt. Ambrose Berger, of the Cleveland Metropark's Hinckley reservation, and official buzzard spotter for the last 10 years, will be ready . . .

The remainder of the short story goes on to tell how many birds and how many observers usually show up and about the events planned by the Chamber of Commerce.

Nowhere in the story does the writer return to the direct-approach style of the lead. A tortured takeoff on the old song "When the Swallows Come Back to Capistrano," it just does not blend smoothly with the rest of the story.

Whatever form the lead may take, the reporter should exercise both good news judgment and adept writing skills in developing the body of the story. The object is to arrange all the facts and incidents of the complete story in their logical order of importance (or newsworthiness). An incident or parts of it may be retold several times in the story, and in each retelling the additional details should be justified by their newsworthiness, and they should not be obviously repetitious.

9a In telling the story in logical order—arranging facts in the order of descending newsworthiness—the reporter must try to lead the reader carefully from one paragraph to the next. One weak paragraph preceding several interesting ones may mean that the latter paragraphs are not read.

Although editing techniques and the ability to match stories to available space are now more sophisticated than when the inverted pyramid style became common more than 50 years ago, the logical order is still an important aid to the mechanical process of the newspaper. If the copy editor or makeup editor must reduce the length of a story, he cuts paragraphs from the end of the story. He takes for granted that he is eliminating the least important facts. The following rule is an excellent one to follow when writing a standard news story:

Write your story so that, if it is terminated at any point, nothing below this point will be as newsworthy as anything above—at the terminated point the story will be complete, intelligible and effective.

The body of the story serves one or both of two purposes: (1) it explains and elaborates the feature or features in the lead or lead block; (2) it adds and elaborates minor features not summarized in the lead. To achieve these purposes, and at the same time to present facts in a logical order, the beginning reporter should keep the following forms in mind when organizing a story.

9b DEVELOPING THE SINGLE-FEATURE LEAD

If a story contains but one feature, the lead will be built around it. The body of the story will clarify and document the lead by adding the pertinent facts. In this case the problem is to judge the newsworthiness of all facts so that they may be presented in logical order.

Below is an example of this type story.

THE DIAGRAM

Lead: One Feature

| 1 |

Details of the Feature

| 1 |

More Details

| 1 |

THE WRITTEN STORY

Creation of a nonpolitical Civilian Board of Review to investigate all cases of alleged police brutality was recommended in a report sent to Mayor Thomas Swift today.

The report, from a special commission named three months ago by the mayor to study the Police Department, said:

"A Civilian Board of Review is needed because the Police Department is hopelessly politicized and incapable of fairly and impartially investigating itself."

The report noted that the Police Department's division of internal security had not taken disciplinary action against a single police officer although more than 30 persons have charged that they were beaten or manhandled by policemen during questioning and arrest in the past 18 months.

"In two cases where policemen were found guilty in court of assault and battery, the Police Department still failed to take any disciplinary action," the report said.

The proposed Civilian Board of Review would be appointed by the mayor and confirmed by City Council. One member would be selected to represent each of the council districts in the city. They would serve three-year terms.

Mayor Swift named the special commission to study the Police Department in response to dozens of complaints about police brutality. (Any additional paragraphs would give more details of the one feature.)

DEVELOPING THE SEVERAL-FEATURE LEAD   9c

In organizing the several-feature story, the reporter encounters problems not common to single-feature leads. Before studying the various forms that can be used in several-feature development, the beginning reporter should review the purposes of the body of the story and be alert to principal difficulties in organizing a complete news story.

The body of the story should elaborate features presented in the lead or lead 9d block. Any statement in the lead of a news story should be documented in the body of the story. After finding lead features with particular reader appeal, a beginner sometimes will abandon some of them entirely, not mentioning them further in the body of the story or perhaps referring to them again only deep within the story. Such errors violate not only the development purpose of the body of the story but also the principle of logical order. If a feature has enough reader appeal to deserve a place in the lead, it deserves a place in the body of the story—and not a place buried beneath less significant facts.

The body of the story should also add and elaborate other minor features not 9e summarized in the lead. In achieving this purpose, the reporter must be able to distinguish between details of lead features on the one hand and "other minor features" on the other. To make this distinction clearer: Just as major features are summarized in the lead before their details are presented, all minor features should be summarized at their point of introduction before details of them are presented. In other words, the lead paragraph is not the only place in the story where features are summarized. If use of logical order eliminates features from the first part of a story, these features must be summarized at their logical place in the body before details on the added features are presented.

Summary Development. If more than one feature is summarized in the lead, 9f each feature should be elaborated in the order of the presentation in the lead (which is logical order). Note the following example:

THE DIAGRAM

Lead: Summary of
All Features

Details of First Feature

Details of Second Feature

Details of Third Feature

Details of First Feature

All Other Paragraphs in
the Complete Story

THE WRITTEN STORY

Creation of a nonpolitical civilian board to consider cases of alleged police brutality, special human relations training for all policemen and reorganization of the Police Department's Internal Security Bureau were recommended in a report sent to Mayor Thomas Swift today.

The report was prepared by the special commission named by the mayor three months ago to study the city's trouble-plagued Police Department.

The proposed review board would investigate all cases of alleged police brutality because the Police Department is "hopelessly politicized and incapable of fairly and impartially investigating itself," the report said.

Asserting that most instances of alleged manhandling of citizens are unnecessary, members of the commission urged that all policemen be required to take special training in human relations.

"Police are given no courses in human relations during their training period and they obviously do not get any training in it after they are placed on active duty," the report said.

The report pointed out that public dissatisfaction with the department stems from the work of the Internal Security Bureau, which is responsible for investigating civilian complaints against police officers.

"The Internal Security Bureau has not recommended disciplinary action against a single police officer although more than 30 persons in the last 18 months have charged that they were beaten or manhandled by policemen during questioning or while being arrested.

"In two cases where policemen were found guilty in court of assault and battery, the Police Department still did not take any disciplinary action," the report said.

In recommending a Civilian Review Board, the report suggested that members be named by the mayor but confirmed by City Council. Each member would represent one of the city's council districts and would serve for three years.

(Any additional paragraphs would give further details of features summarized in the lead, presenting details in logical order.)

9g   *Outstanding Feature Development.* If one outstanding feature is emphasized in the lead and several minor features are left out, these minor features can be summarized in the second paragraph (see second method of writing several-feature leads). Following this summary paragraph, the story refers to the outstanding feature, giving details. Then, in the logical order, the story considers each of the minor features and the outstanding feature.

The following example clarifies this method:

THE DIAGRAM

Lead: Outstanding Feature

Summary of Other Features

Details of Outstanding
Feature

Details of First Minor
Feature

Details of Second Minor
Feature

Details of Outstanding
Feature

THE WRITTEN STORY

Creation of a nonpolitical Civilian Board of Review to investigate all cases of alleged police brutality was recommended in a report sent to Mayor Thomas Swift today.

The report also urged that all police officers be given intensive training in human relations, and that the Police Department's Internal Security Bureau be reorganized. The report requested a special allocation of $150,000 to begin the training within 30 days.

The mayor received the report from the special commission he appointed three months ago to study the Police Department. He took the action after a rash of reports of alleged police brutality over the past 18 months.

The Civilian Review Board is needed, the report said, because the Police Department is "hopelessly politicized and incapable of fairly and impartially investigating itself."

Asserting that most instances of alleged manhandling of citizens are unnecessary, the report urged that all policemen be required to take intensive training in human relations.

"Police are given no courses in human relations during their training period and they obviously do not get any training in it after they are placed on active duty," the report said.

The report stated that much of the public dissatisfaction with the Police Department stems from the work of the Internal Security Bureau, which is responsible for investigating civilian complaints against policemen.

"The Internal Security Bureau has not recommended disciplinary action against a single police officer although more than 30 persons in the last 18 months have charged that they were beaten or manhandled by policemen during questioning or while being arrested.

"In two cases where policemen were found guilty in court of assault and battery, the Police Department still failed to take any disciplinary action," the report said.

In recommending a Civilian Review Board, the report suggested that members be named by the mayor and confirmed by City Council. One member

139

9. THE BODY OF THE STORY

THE DIAGRAM

THE WRITTEN STORY

would represent each of the city's council districts and would serve for three years.

All Other Paragraphs in the Complete Story ⟱

(Any additional paragraphs would give details of the other features summarized in the lead, presenting details in logical order.)

If the minor features of a story are not as important as some of the details of the outstanding feature, the reporter need not introduce them until he has given the outstanding-feature details. This organization still observes the logical order, as illustrated by the following example:

THE DIAGRAM

THE WRITTEN STORY

Lead: Outstanding Feature

[1]

Creation of a nonpolitical Civilian Board of Review to investigate all cases of alleged police brutality was recommended in a report sent to Mayor Thomas Swift today.

The report, made by a special commission appointed by the mayor three months ago to study the trouble-plagued Police Department, said:

Details of Outstanding Feature

[1]

"A Civilian Board of Review is needed because the Police Department is hopelessly politicized and incapable of fairly and impartially investigating itself."

It pointed out the failure of the Department to take any steps to prevent "the kind of action on the part of policemen that has led to 30 citizens charging that they had been manhandled or beaten."

"An apparent lack of concern for the public welfare pervades the entire Department," the report said.

Details of Outstanding Feature

[1]

A Civilian Review Board would insure the citizens that all complaints against policemen would be fairly and objectively investigated because the board would be nonpolitical, it added.

Members of the board would be appointed by the mayor and confirmed by City Council. One member would be selected to represent each of the council districts in the city. They would serve three-year terms.

Summary of Other Features

② ⚠3

The report also recommended that a special staff be hired for the review committee and it asked for an emergency appropriation of $100,000 to begin the committee operations as soon as possible.

Details of First Minor Feature

②

"A separate staff of investigators and special assistants is absolutely essential to the operation of the proposed committee," the report said. "Without its own staff the committee will have to rely on the Police Department for its investigative work. This obviously would create serious problems for the committee."

THE DIAGRAM

Details of Second Minor
Feature

All Other Paragraphs in
the Complete Story

THE WRITTEN STORY

The need for an independent office staff and
team of investigators makes it essential that approximately $100,000 be appropriated on an emergency
basis to get the committee into operation, the report said.

It pointed out that a regular budget for the
committee would have to be included in the city's
annual budget in all future years, if the committee
is to operate as an effective independent, nonpolitical agent.

(Other details in logical order.)

The Combination Development. 9h

THE DIAGRAM

Lead: Summary or
Two Lead Features

Summary of Other Features

Details Common to
All Features

Details of First Lead
Feature

Details of Second Lead
Feature

THE WRITTEN STORY

Creation of a nonpolitical Civilian Board of Review to consider cases of alleged police brutality,
and special training in human relations for all policemen were recommended in a report sent to
Mayor Thomas Swift today.

The report also recommended that the Police
Department's Internal Security Bureau be reorganized. And it requested an emergency allocation
of $150,000 to begin the human relations training
within 30 days.

The report was made by a special commission
appointed by Mayor Swift three months ago to
study the Police Department. The mayor took the
action after a rash of reports of alleged police brutality over the past 18 months.

In recommending a civilian board, the report
said it is needed because the Police Department is
"hopelessly politicized and incapable of fairly and
impartially investigating itself."

Board members would be appointed by the
mayor and confirmed by City Council. One would
be selected from each of the city's council districts.
They would serve three-year terms.

Asserting that most instances of alleged police
manhandling of citizens are unnecessary, the report
urged that all policemen be required to take intensive training in human relations.

"Police are given no courses in human relations
during their training and they obviously do not get
any training in it after they are placed on active
duty," the report said.

THE DIAGRAM

Details of First Minor
Feature

Details of Second Minor
Feature

All Other Paragraphs in
the Complete Story

THE WRITTEN STORY

The report called the Internal Security Bureau "ineffective" in its present form. It said the bureau took months to conduct the most routine investigation and then rarely came up with any recommendations that "would help relieve some of the intolerable conduct on the part of some policemen."

It noted that the bureau had not recommended disciplinary action against a single police officer although more than 30 persons in the past 18 months have charged that they were beaten or manhandled by policemen during questioning and arrest.

The $150,000 emergency allocation would allow the department to begin an intensive course in human relations on a crash basis within 30 days, the report said. Additional money would have to be allocated in the department's budget to include this kind of training for all new officers in the future and to provide periodic review courses for veterans of the force.

In advocating the Civilian Review Board, the report suggested . . .

(Other details in logical order.)

A combination development with some features buried deep in the story (note the following example) is a common form. This is much like the outstanding feature form illustrated previously in this chapter. In long stories, minor features may be introduced in summary paragraphs at several points in the body of the story.

THE DIAGRAM

Lead: Summary of Two
Main Features

Details of First Lead
Feature

Details of Second Lead
Feature

THE WRITTEN STORY

Creation of a nonpolitical Civilian Board of Review and special training in human relations for all policemen were recommended in a report sent to Mayor Thomas Swift today.

The mayor received the report from the special commission he appointed three months ago to study the Police Department. He took the action after a rash of reports of alleged police brutality over the past 18 months.

The Civilian Review Board is needed to investigate all cases of alleged police brutality because the Police Department is "hopelessly politicized and incapable of fairly and impartially investigating itself," the report said.

Asserting that most instances of alleged manhandling of citizens are unnecessary, the report urged that all policemen be required to take intensive training in human relations immediately.

Summary of Other Features

The report also recommended that the Police Department's Internal Security Bureau be reorganized. And it requested an emergency allocation of $150,000 to begin the human relations training program within 30 days.

Details of First Lead Feature

"The Civilian Review Board would insure the citizens that all complaints against policemen would be fairly and objectively investigated because it would be nonpolitical," the report said. Members would be appointed by the mayor and confirmed by City Council. One would represent each of the city's council districts. They would serve three-year terms.

Details of Second Lead Feature

The report noted that "Police are given no courses in human relations during their training period and they obviously do not get any training in it after they are placed on active duty."

"It is obvious that some policemen prefer to restrain rather than reason with persons they are questioning or arresting," it added.

Details of First Minor Feature

The report stated that much of the public dissatisfaction with the Police Department stems from the work of the Internal Security Bureau, which is responsible for investigating civilian complaints against policemen.

The report pointed out that the Internal Security Bureau "has not recommended disciplinary action against a single police officer although more than 30 persons in the last 18 months have charged that they were beaten or manhandled by policemen during questioning or while being arrested."

All Other Paragraphs in the Complete Story

(Other details in logical order.)

Some newspapers attempt to keep stories reasonably short and, when confronted with handling a report such as the one cited in these examples, elect to make it into several stories. The major story might be a general review of the report, emphasizing the major point and highlighting the minor ones. Then, the editor might have the reporter write three or four more stories, one devoted to each of the recommendations of the report. Generally, the main story would begin on page one, then jump to an inside page, where the other stories would be displayed. A number of papers use the same technique when handling city council and school board stories, for example, if each group takes action on a half dozen or more major issues. This is a graphic device used to attract readers who might not be willing to wade through one very long story.

Multiple-Casualty Story Development. Newspapers have a popular form for stories involving several casualties. An illustration follows:

9i

THE DIAGRAM

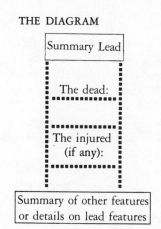

THE WRITTEN STORY

Seven persons, six of them children, died early Thursday when fire, believed set by arsonists, destroyed a frame home at 1529 Wentworth Ave.

Dead are Otis Terry, 39, and his children, Anna Marie, 9; Andrew, 8; Lelia, 4; Letasha, 3; Angela, 1; and Otis Jr., 6 weeks.

All the victims were found in a second-floor bedroom of the house.

Two empty gasoline cans were found at the scene, Raymond Burger, an investigator for the state fire marshal, said.

(More details of the fire in chronological order.)

This form is used when listing casualties who were related. Often, if the casualties are not related and the list is this long, a newspaper will give each name on a separate line immediately following the lead, as in this example.

THE DIAGRAM

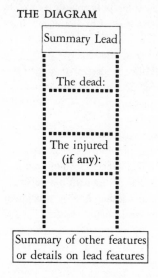

THE WRITTEN STORY

Four Central High School students were killed today in a two-car collision at Central and Vine Avenues.

Dead are:

Janice Knapp, 17, of 1206 Troy St.

James Barker, 18, of 101 King Rd.

Mark Mathews, 17, of 1700 Chestnut Ln.

Debbie Knowles, 17, of 8145 Pine St.

Police said the students were returning to school after a field trip to the County Courthouse when their car was struck from the rear by a car traveling at a high rate of speed.

The driver of the second car . . .

(More details of the accident in chronological order.)

As diagramed in the preceding examples, the stories summarize all features in the lead paragraph. The same form can be used with several features that are not all summarized in the first paragraph. In that type story, paragraphs summarizing other features follow the listing of casualties, in logical order.

9j THE CHRONOLOGICAL ORDER

Stories with strong narrative elements may sometimes best be handled by the chronological order (rather than the logical) in the body of the story. After the lead has summarized outstanding features of the story, the body of the story may be developed narratively. In most cases, however, the narrative paragraphs are interrupted by nonnarrative paragraphs to add additional facts, as in the following example:

THE DIAGRAM	THE WRITTEN STORY
Lead: Summary	

A gunman demanding $1 million and a plane to fly him to Mexico held two employes of the First National Bank hostage for three hours yesterday before surrendering to FBI agents and city police. The hostages were not injured.

FBI Agent Joseph Westfall identified the gunman as Bobby Mack Cable, 41, a former mental patient.

Nonnarrative Details

Becky Barnette, secretary to Jackson McDonald, vice-president and comptroller of the bank, said Cable walked into her second-floor office in the bank building about 12:45 p.m.

Narrative

"When I asked him if I could help him he pulled a gun out of his windbreaker pocket," Miss Barnette said. "I guess I screamed because Mr. McDonald came running out of his office. We were the only two there; all the others were out to lunch."

McDonald said Cable told them: "OK! Keep calm. Just do what I tell you and nothing will happen to you."

Cable ordered McDonald to lock the door from the inside and made the banker push a desk and file cabinet against it as a barricade.

Nonnarrative Details

"Now get on that phone and call the president of this bank and tell him I want $1 million in small bills and an airplane to fly me to Mexico," Cable said. "If I don't get them and get them soon he'll be shopping for two new employes tomorrow."

Narrative

McDonald said he called Harry Jameson, bank president whose office is on the fourth floor. "He wasn't sure that I wasn't just kidding at first, but Cable yanked the phone out of my hand and repeated the demand. He also warned Mr. Jameson not to call police. He wanted Jameson to drive us to the airport in his personal car and then, he said, he would release us just before boarding the plane."

Jameson said he talked to the bank security chief and they decided to call the police and the FBI.

Within 15 minutes, more than 100 city policemen and FBI agents had surrounded the bank. They cleared patrons from the first floor of the building and the parking lots and rerouted traffic.

Miss Barnette said Cable seemed calm and sure of himself. "He talked about the weather and how nice it is in Mexico at this time of year for about 20 minutes. Then he forced Mr. McDonald to call Mr. Jameson again."

Cable grabbed the phone from McDonald and told Jameson: "Listen, turkey, I know you called to the cops. You just bought yourself two dead ones."

THE DIAGRAM THE WRITTEN STORY

Nonnarrative Details

Narrative

Nonnarrative Details

Narrative

Nonnarrative Details

Narrative

Nonnarrative Details

"He was very nervous then and when I started to cry, he told me to 'shut up, them tears ain't going to do you any good where you are going.' "

Westfall said he called McDonald's office in an effort to speak to Cable. At first Cable refused to talk to the FBI agent but then he repeated his demands. He agreed to give Westfall three hours to arrange for the money, the safe trip to the airport and the plane to Mexico.

"That was the longest three hours of my life," McDonald said. "We sat there not knowing what was going to happen next."

Westfall, Jameson and Dr. Robert Marcetti, a psychiatrist, each talked to Cable on the phone during the three hours he held the two hostages.

"When he would talk to Mr. Westfall or Mr. Jameson, he would get angry and scream his demands at them repeatedly," Miss Barnette said. "But when he talked to Dr. Marcetti he was just like a little boy who is ashamed of himself."

McDonald said Cable kept repeating "Yeah, I know, Doc. They ain't harmed me. Yeah, I know, Doc. But I just gotta do it."

"I think my hopes finally began to rise when I heard him talking to the doctor," McDonald said. "Before that I was just plain scared I'd never see sundown."

Dr. Marcetti said he talked to Cable four times, for a total of 45 minutes, before Cable agreed to release the hostages and give himself up.

Westfall said Cable "agreed to send Miss Barnette and McDonald out with his gun, if we would agree to take him out the back way and not parade him in front of the spectators who had gathered outside the building."

Miss Barnette and McDonald were released about 3:45 p.m. McDonald handed Cable's gun to Westfall. Cable waited inside the office for Westfall and Dr. Marcetti. He was led down a flight of stairs and out a rear door to a waiting FBI car.

Cable will be arraigned before U.S. Magistrate Carlos Wilson today.

(Personal details about Cable follow.)

The chronological order in the body of the story is a popular form for many types of stories—accidents, fires, crime, debates, trials, sports, weddings and the like. Most of them are stories with strong narrative elements (fast-moving action or events building up to a climax), lending themselves to the chronological order after summarization of the main feature or features. Use of chronological order does not relieve the reporter of the responsibility for adequate summarization before the chronological order is begun. Care must be taken to avoid jumping into the chronological order too soon. Sometimes only one paragraph of summary is needed; sometimes more than one. A story written in chronological order may be either a single-feature or a several-feature story.

DIRECT QUOTATIONS 9k

In an effort to overcome the problem of monotony in the body of the story, the reporter should use well-attributed indirect and direct quotations. The story should not be a series of direct quotations alone. Neither should most stories be wholly indirect quotations nor summary statements. The "happy medium" is most effective.

Direct quotations aid a story if they are used carefully. Woven in between indirect quotations and summary statements, they breathe life into a story while helping to emphasize certain points. They also are pleasing to the reader's eye because they break the monotony. Some newspapermen frown on a lead that begins with a direct quotation, but this is largely a matter of personal choice, although it may be the result of slipshod writing. Too many reporters are willing to begin a story with a long, lukewarm quotation instead of taxing their mental capacities with the work of composing a crisp, descriptively accurate news lead. If the reporter will remember that the lead is the story's showcase, he will not begin with a direct quotation that does not have strong reader appeal. In most instances, a poorly written summary lead is better than a poor direct quotation lead (see special note on "Use of Quotation Marks," correction key 4q).

Direct quotations may be phrases, clauses or words within a sentence, a sentence within a paragraph or a complete paragraph. Seldom should more than two consecutive paragraphs be direct quotations, for too many quotations can be just as monotonous as too few. In some cases, however, an exceptional quotation may be worthy of several consecutive paragraphs. This rule does not apply, of course, in narrating a conversation between two or more persons, although lengthy discourses of this type are usually interspersed with summary paragraphs.

TRANSITIONAL DEVICES 9l

A news story must have unity, and to achieve this the reporter must weave together the various parts of the story by the use of connective words and phrases. In attempting to achieve brevity, many beginning reporters sacrifice coherence. Unless the sentences within a paragraph or the paragraphs within a story are obviously related, the reporter must indicate the relationship. Sometimes such common connectives or transitions as *also, on the other hand* or *meanwhile* may be sufficient, but in many cases the transition must be clarified by reference to previous subject matter. For example, notice the transition in the fourth paragraph of the sample "combination development" story on page 121:

> *In recommending a civilian board,* the report said it is needed because . . .

The transition (in italics) refers to "Creation of a nonpolitical Civilian Board of Review. . . ." The transition is essential to clarify the relationship of the

9m

fourth paragraph to the lead of the story. Without the transition, the reader might be confused.

In making a transition, the reporter must avoid the verbatim repetition of previous wording in the story. The transition in the above paragraph, for example, should not be worded "Creation of a nonpolitical civilian board. . . ." The transition should be as short as possible, a mere mention of the feature previously summarized.

BLOCK PARAGRAPHS

9n

Standard rules of English composition apply to sentence and paragraph structure, although journalistic style usually calls for shorter sentences and paragraphs.

Each paragraph may have a topic sentence, or several paragraphs may develop different aspects of the same topic. If the topic-sentence principles are observed, most of the paragraphs will be separate units in themselves. They can be shifted to other positions in the story without changes in wording—or they can be eliminated without requiring substantial revisions in remaining paragraphs. These are called block paragraphs. This type paragraph fits ideally into the newspaper pattern because it expedites the editing of a story when the transposition of paragraphs or the shortening of a story becomes necessary either at the copy-editing desk or in the mechanical department.

A paragraph cannot be shifted without editing if a transitional phrase directly connects it with a paragraph that precedes or follows. For example, a paragraph that begins with "on the other hand" could be confusing if it does not immediately follow the appropriate paragraph. In deference to the advantages of block paragraphs, the reporter should avoid transitional phrases which tie consecutive paragraphs together, but he still may employ such phrases from time to time when they are particularly suitable to story construction.

ADEQUACY VERSUS TRIVIA

9o

Every reporter is faced with the question: How much detail should be presented in a story? Some reporters tend to clutter their stories with dull and boring trivia, while others do not include adequate detail to make a complete story. Beyond the point of an adequate development or explanation (with necessary interpretation) of the features in the story, the reporter is guided by reader appeal in selecting details that go into the story. Any and all details of some events are interesting enough to include in the story, but a large part of the details of most events will do no more than waste newspaper space.

Complete Reporting. At this point the opportunities for complete reporting may be suggested.

If all the essential information of the story is crowded into the 5 W's of the lead or lead block, the body of the story can do no more than explore and exploit these same W's. All of them (plus the identification, the authority and the tie-back) are susceptible to endless exploration. Quantity of language is, of course, not the object in a news story. Quality of information is. The problem of complete reporting in body development lies not in writing facility but in research competence. Once the reporter returns from the story scene to the typewriter, the opportunity for complete and competent development of the body of the story must be found in his rough notes, in his memory and in his background of knowledge. Where these fail, competence fails, despite all that logic of language can throw into the breach.

Complete reporting requires competence of research—penetrative curiosity—on the part of the reporter. Lacking this, the reporter will fall into the easy habit of superficial reporting.

EXERCISES

A Reminder: Students should keep in mind the points included in the "Important Note" on page 93 in using story notes in the exercises in this book.

1. Using any daily or weekly newspaper available to you, clip five stories that illustrate forms of body development diagramed in this chapter. Paste them on sheets of paper and draw the proper diagram at the left of each clipping.
2. Using the following notes, write a story illustrating the first form diagramed (the single-feature form.).

Committee to Save Wheaton High School
Met last night in school auditorium
Approximately 500 persons attended
Passed a resolution opposing
School Board plan
To add a vocational-technical center
At the regular high school
Plans call for converting
The 1,327-student school
To 1,000 students and a voc-tech center
Approximately 300 students
Currently headed for Wheaton
Will be forced to attend
Einstein High School instead
Lou Haynes, mother of six sons
Who graduated from Wheaton
And who has a daughter there now
Said the school is the
Most comprehensive in county
More than half its students
Traditionally go on to college
Change would dilute the
Academic program, she feared
Mrs. Haynes, 3267 Belt Parkway,
Will head committee to present
Resolution to the school board
At its next meeting
Others on the committee are
William Muehling, 5 East Circle, and
Vincent Rougeau, 17, vice-president
Of Wheaton's student government

3. Adding these notes to those in Exercise 2, write a story illustrating the second form diagramed (the several-feature summary form).

Group also voted
To hire a lawyer
To sue the School Board
To block the changes at Wheaton
If the board should reject
The group's plea
Group also voted to
Launch petition drive
To get signatures of
Every parent who has
A child enrolled at Wheaton
Mrs. Georgia Forest of 10 Foxhall Dr.
Named head of petition committee
She said the changes were
Proposed by school officials
In an effort to beef up the
Dwindling enrollment at
Einstein High School

4. Adding these notes to those in Exercise 2 and 3, write a story illustrating the third form diagramed (the first outstanding-feature form of several-feature development).

Another resolution
To commission a study
Of the board's plan
By Dr. Gary Minton
Professor of Education
State University and
A specialist in
School administration and population
Mrs. Hayes charged that
The plan was hurriedly drawn up
She said:

"I find myself asking why we in the
Wheaton community have had to defend, even
fight for the existence, of a school and a program
that is working and is considered to be the
best type of delivery of education to a
heterogeneous school population."

5. Adding these notes to those in Exercise 2 and 4, write a story illustrating the fourth form diagramed (the second outstanding-feature form of several-feature development).

Organization also voted
To request School Board
Name committee of parents,
Administrators and
Specialists from State University
To study alternate plans
With idea of leaving
Wheaton as is and to
Locate the voc-tech center
In a more centrally located
Building in the County

Also voted to demand that
Board take no action
On Wheaton plan until
"All other avenues have
Been explored and rejected"

6. Using the notes in Exercises 2, 3 and 5, write a story illustrating the fifth form diagramed (the combination form).

7. Using the multiple-casualty story form diagramed in this chapter, write a story from the following notes.

Two Southern Railway freight trains
Crash about 10 a.m. Saturday
In Glenmary, a small Scott County community
Three locomotives and 49 cars derailed
Scattered over hundreds of yards
Two engineers killed
Brakeman dies hour later of burns
In Scott Community Hospital, Cleveland
Two other brakemen in serious condition
One propane tank car exploded
Sent flames 500 to 600 feet
In the air after the collision
Civil Defense authorities
Evacuated about 100 persons
Who live near the scene
As a precautionary measure
Witnesses said a car
In the middle of one of the trains
Derailed and turned sideways
It was pushed several hundred feet
Down the tracks by following cars
Other cars overturned
Shot up in the air
Fell to the side of the track
Minutes later a second train
Northbound on adjacent track
Hit one of the derailed cars
Spilling its three locomotives
Toward nearby Webb Creek
Its cars tumbled over the tracks
Engineer Doug Brickey, Stanford,
And Brakeman John E. Gronseth, Harland,
In the first train were thrown
From the train by the impact of
Collision of the two trains
Brickey apparently died instantly
Gronseth was seriously injured
Engineer Andrew Lloyd, Huntsville,
In second train
Apparently killed instantly
Brakeman John Sevier, Rugby,
Apparently thrown into
Flames of burning propane tanker

Died hour later of burns

In Scott Community Hospital

Brakeman David Collins, Oneida,

Also on second train

Trapped in wreckage of caboose

In serious condition

At Scott Hospital

Glenmary Volunteer Fire Department

Called to scene but

Fires allowed to burn themselves out

Charles Morgret, Southern spokesman

Said both trains

Headed for St. Louis

Said it was not unusual

For them to be running close

Said it would take a week

To clear the wreckage

> (*Sources:* Morgret, hospital spokesman, Tom Ballard, civil defense director, Herman Jones, 75, who lives about 200 yards away from track.)

8. Write a story using the chronological order from the following notes.

Mayor Robert Walker

Hears noises outside his office

About 10:30 a.m.

Walked out to find

Judith M. Koenick, 28

Who lives at 1012 Washington Ave.

Next to the new Meadbrook subdivision

Which is now under construction

Mayor asked what was wrong

When his secretary started to reply, Mrs. Koenick interrupted:

> "I'm surprised you haven't heard already. I'll tell you what's wrong. I have tried for four months to get someone in the city to force that contractor to do something about the soil erosion and dirt in the streets from that construction site, but all I get is a runaround"

"I don't—" the mayor started to say, but she interrupted

> "I'll spell it out for you. Between the rains washing the dirt into the street and those trucks dropping a ton of it on the street every week, I might as well be living in a mud puddle. I've called everyone I can think of in the city to get something done about it. I talked to the contractor and he told me to get lost. That twit at the construction code enforcement office is afraid of his shadow, the environmental protection people told me the dirt was the price of progress . . ."

"You know, we must all suffer a little inconvenience," the mayor said

But Mrs. Koenick interrupted him

> "I've heard that line so many times I've decided to let you all share that inconvenience with me. I've left a little present at the contractor's office, at the construction code office and with the environmental protection people, and now here's yours"

Mrs. Koenick then dumped a plastic bag of dirt on the carpet in the mayor's outer office

"You can't do that," the mayor shouted

"Looks like I just did," Mrs. Koenick yelled back. "Maybe you can have the contractor clean it up—after he cleans up the street in front of my house."

Mrs. Koenick left the mayor's office

Two hours later she told newsmen by phone that a large sweeper truck was cleaning the street in front of her house

"I know this is just temporary," she said. "It will be just as bad again in about two days. Why should the contractor bother to keep it clean, the city doesn't even make an attempt to enforce the codes. Well I'm prepared to do it all over again. And if that doesn't work, I'm prepared to sue both the city and the contractor"

9. Write stories from the following notes, in each case explain your choice of lead and story form and diagram the story that you write.

A. Police called to investigate
Shooting at Shell Service Station
4525 Rutledge Pike
About 3:15 p.m. yesterday
Found woman with bullet wound
In left temple
Identified as
Mrs. Bertha B. Perkins, 23
Lives at 3916 Titus Way
In critical condition
At University Hospital
Dallas M. Hayes, 38
Station attendant told police
He was handling pistol
When it discharged
Said he didn't know
The gun was loaded
Roger Strong, 14,
A helper at the station
Told police he had loaded
The pistol earlier
Said the shooting was an accident
Mrs. Perkins is
A friend of Hayes
No charges were placed

B. From state highway patrol
A 79-year-old man
Who lives in Burlington
Killed today in
Two-car accident on Highway 534
Five miles east of Burlington
About 9:30 a.m. today
Francis H. Aid
Apparently lost control
Of his Honda
While traveling east
It crossed the median
Collided head-on with
Late model Lincoln
Driven by Larry Kirby Jr., 41
A salesman from Nashville
Aid was dead on arrival
At Burlington Medical Center

153

Kirby listed in
Satisfactory condition
At Medical Center
Trooper Dan White said
Investigation continuing

C. Notes from City Court yesterday
Michael Dwayne Meade, 19
4119 Lewis Road
Charged with obtaining
Drugs under false pretense
David Campbell, druggist
At Safeway Drug Store
1917 Amhurst Road
Testified that Meade
Had prescription filled
Campbell became suspicious
Called the doctor to verify
Found prescription was forged
Called police
Meade arrested about
Three blocks away
Judge Jess H. Ford
Sentenced Meade to
Eleven months and 29 days
On County work farm
Next case
Peter Lomax, 28, 239 Joe Lewis Rd.
Charged with drunken driving
Arrested by Policeman John Vincent
Because car was weaving
Across lanes in 5100 block of Midland
Lomas said he had had only one beer
Said he had been taking medicine
Vincent said he found
Eight empty beer cans
In the Lomax car
Lomax said he collected beer cans
Admitted all the cans in his car
Were from the same brand
Judge Ford sentenced him
Ten days in jail and
Fined him $50
Another case
Winnona L. Stallings, 19
1909 Natchez St.
Charged with receiving and
Concealing stolen property
Policeman Albert Brooks
Said he received tip
Where he could find
Microwave ovens stolen
From Thompson Appliance Co.

Obtained search warrant
Went to Miss Stallings's home
Found 12 microwave ovens
Miss Stallings claimed she
was just holding them
For a friend, who was
Going to give them
As Christmas presents
Judge Ford bound her
To the grand jury
Set bond at $10,000

D. Citizens for Safe Hazardous Waste Control
To meet here Friday and Saturday
At the Hyatt Hotel
Approximately 300 expected

Friday program

8–10 a.m.—Registration

10 a.m.—Opening session. What the state is doing to protect the public from hazardous waste. Speakers: Randall Gibbs, director of the state Board of Solid Waste Control, and Alex B. Shipton, director of Waste Water Control for the state.

Noon luncheon—Speaker: State Rep. William Hart, sponsor of legislation that established strict standards for hazardous waste control for the state.

2 p.m.—Session on dangers of nuclear waste. Speakers: Dr. Milton Bradley, former director of the Oak Ridge Atomic Laboratory who now heads Safety in Science, a group of scientists concerned about protecting the public from hazardous wastes; and Mrs. Alberta Nolan, a former resident of the Love Canal area of Niagara Falls, N.Y., which had to be abandoned because of hazardous waste buried there.

9 p.m.—Banquet, Speaker. Dr. Lynhurst Mumford, professor of nuclear medicine at the State Medical School and a specialist in treating persons who have been exposed to hazardous chemical waste material. Topic: "By 2000 We'll All Glow in the Dark."

Saturday program

10 a.m.—Session on Poisoning of America. Speaker: Michael H. Brown, reporter and author of the best seller *Poisoning of America,* a book that details how industries are lax, not infrequently to the point of criminal negligence, in soiling the land and adulterating the waters with toxic chemical wastes. He will discuss the 34,000 seriously hazardous waste dumps spotted about the country and the threat they pose to public safety and health.

Noon—adjournment

(Note: The fact that the group will meet here has been announced in preceding stories. No news has been printed on the program, however.)

E. U.S. District Court
Leslie M. Philips, 38, of New Orleans
Appeared for hearing on
His request for a new trial
For a previous conviction
On counterfeiting
Brought into court by
U.S. Marshal Walter Green
Philips's wife, Melissa, 18,

Rushed over to hug husband
When Green separated them
Philips was holding pistol
Fired one shot
Wounded Green in right shoulder
Philips and wife fled
Toward back of courtroom
Marshal Bruce Miller
Order them to halt
Philips fired one shot at him
Miller returned the fire
Bullet struck Philips
In stomach, critically wounding him
Mrs. Philips grabbed pistol
Attempted to fire shot
Was overpowered by
Miller and Marshal John Filatreau
Green and Miller taken
To University Hospital
Green in satisfactory condition
Philips in critical condition
Mrs. Philips held in city jail
Charged with helping husband
Attempt an escape and
Assault with deadly weapon
Philips previously sentenced
To 25 years in federal prison
For passing phony $20 bills
When originally arrested
In October of last year
He had $5,000 worth of
Phony $20 bills
Judge James Abramson
Not in court at the time
He said:
> "I heard shots just as I was putting on my robes to go into the courtroom.
> My bailiff wouldn't let me leave my chambers."

Chief Marshal Howard Woodal said
No special security had been taken
"Because it was just a routine hearing for a new trial"
He added that he would review security measures
With Judge Abramson tomorrow
"I hate to have to search everyone," he said
"But if we have to, we will"

F. City's worst snow storm in 10 years
Four feet of snow in 36 hours
Four and a half feet fell 10 years ago
In a 24-hour period
> (*Source:* U.S. Weather Service)

City at a complete standstill
All major streets and highways into city closed
Police and fire service not available

Mayor Keith Smith issues state of emergency
Calls on Governor John Ross
To send National Guard troops
To clear streets for emergency vehicles
To aid rescue of stranded motorists
And families trapped in homes
To haul in emergency food supplies
Gov. Ross said Guard units
Should reach city by sundown
He dispatched two advanced helicopter units
To help with emergency evacuations
> (*Sources:* Mayor Smith, Gov. Ross)

Reports of hundreds of motorists
Stranded in cars on city streets
And on nearby highways
Four unconfirmed deaths
More are expected
> (*Sources:* Police Chief James Grant and State Trooper Warner Sykes)

Emergency shelters to be opened
In public schools
As soon as streets can be cleared
To allow emergency vehicles through
All available Civil Defense personnel
Called to emergency duty
Children, elderly and sick
Will be brought to
Emergency centers as soon as possible
> (*Source:* Civil Defense Director Manard Washington)

Hundreds of persons reported
Stranded in offices and stores
Unable to get home
Mayor urged them to "stay put"
Mayor said: "We are establishing emergency call-in numbers for persons stran-
ded. The numbers will be broadcast repeatedly by local radio sta-
tions. I urge the citizens not to use the police and fire emergency
numbers. And I urge only those persons in dire need of help to call
in."
Mayor added that emergency plan
Will be put into effect
As soon as the Guard units arrive
And as soon as some of the streets are clear
Mayor said: "We will begin a systematic check of every house in the city to
make certain everyone has enough food and the houses are properly
heated. I urge everyone to remain calm and do not panic. I also urge
everyone to stay in their homes."

CHAPTER 10

Features and Human-Interest Stories

In the world of journalism, the word "feature" is applied to a broad range of material. It is one of the most widely used journalistic terms. It may be used to specify some aspect of a straight-news story, such as the W featured in a lead (described previously). Or it may be used to indicate a particular fact in a story. An editor may tell a reporter to feature the heroic rescue in a fire story, for example.

Generally, it is applied to a long list of materials—ranging from comics to columns—that are not considered straight news. And it also is often applied to departments of a newspaper not directly associated with straight news. How it is used depends upon who is using it and what his own frame of reference may be. It is one of those terms for which newsmen have yet to come up with an exact definition.

However, in this chapter, the word "feature" does have a specific meaning. It is used here to apply to a story that is based wholly on human interest—the story that does not quite conform to the rigid standards of hard news. But it should be pointed out that hard news stories can be given a "feature" treatment if the facts are dramatic enough and if the writer is skillful enough to pull it off.

At the heart of a feature or human-interest story are facts representing solid reporting techniques, just as in a straight news story. But the stories differ in style. The news story is timely and written in a straightforward, concise, unemotional style. The feature, on the other hand, may not be particularly timely (though it could be) and it is marked by a blending of imaginative and creative use of the language that can touch a reader's curiosity, amaze him, arouse his skepticism or make him laugh or cry.

To complicate matters in the relationship between features and straight news, it is a rare reporter who can handle human-interest or feature stories well until he knows how to write a compact, coherent straight news story that is packed with names, facts and details.

Human-Interest Stories. One writer summed it up accurately when he said that there is no sharp line of division that runs between straight news and human-interest stories any more than there is an abrupt line between the colors of a rainbow. One hue may shade into the total rainbow and be lost to view just as certain elements of a story that might make it a feature (or straight news) can be lost from the view of a not-too-perceptive writer. Frequently the straight-news account contains strong feature elements, while the human-interest story may owe its very existence to a news event (and in such cases has to be printed along with the news story or lose its impact).

But it should be obvious that as the human-interest values are increased—as the dramatic, emotional and human background materials of the story are played up—they will become, at some point, more important than the news incident itself. When this point is reached, the story becomes primarily a human-interest (feature) story rather than a straight-news story.

Consider, for example, this brief story by Joe Cappo of the Chicago Daily News. It is typical of many that are printed daily:

> Last September, Zoecon Corp. ran a full-page ad in *Scientific American,* asking readers to suggest names for an insect-controlling substance it was researching.
>
> "We're still several years away from developing the product, so we wanted to generate public interest in it," said Daniel Lazare, vice-president of the Palo Alto (Calif.) company that specializes in hormone biology research.
>
> "The product, intended to take the place of insecticide, works on insect reproduction. I guess you would call it birth control for bugs."
>
> Attracted by an offer of $500 for the best entry, "well over 2,000 persons" sent proposed names to Zoecon. The readers outdid themselves, submitting such zingers as: Bugabate, Bugoff, Zu-I-Cide, Harmocide, Celibug, Cella-Bait, Mate-Abate, Catch 284, Contrapestive, Croakaroach, Emascu-Mate, Insectisick, Insexicide, Nile-8, Nitless Wonder, Pest Arrest, Slug-A-Bug, Stalemate, Stud-Dud, Terminit and Zero Bug Growth.
>
> Confronted with an array of sparkling nominations like these, what do you think Zoecon chose? Entocon.
>
> Pfffft.

The news value of the story is of no great significance. And many editors would have rejected it out of hand if it had been written in a straight-news fashion. However, the writer used his imagination and produced an interesting, short human-interest story that drew widespread attention from readers.

A given incident or situation can be handled within the following degrees of human-interest appeal:

1. As straight news with little or no human interest.
2. As straight news plus some or much human-interest treatment.
3. As human interest with little or no hard-news value.

While there is a tendency now, probably as a result of competition from television, to give hard news stories the feature treatment, the incident itself, if properly evaluated, will usually determine what treatment it deserves. In general, human-interest treatment (in the third degree above) is decided upon for those incidents that have slight or nonexistent news value or values but that suggest a rich background of human interest. The human-interest treatment is

159

applied to numerous stories every day that might not otherwise be reported. And they have become an important part of what every newspaper offers its subscribers daily because of their broad reader appeal. In this sense the human-interest story is considered as a separate story type, and it is one form of the more general feature stories.

Other Feature Stories. The news value is also secondary or lacking in much of the material classified as features. Examples would be seasonal stories concerning Christmas, Thanksgiving, Easter and other major (or minor) holidays; articles of advice and guidance; descriptions of hobbies and unusual occupations; informational and background (and human interest) articles on subjects suggested by the news; biographical or historical sketches; sidelights, analysis, instruction and information. This type of writing ranges from narration, related to the news and designed to inform, to descriptive and expository articles independent of the news and intended to instruct or entertain. For purposes of study and class discussion, these stories may be called feature stories or articles to distinguish them from the strictly human-interest stories.

Both the human-interest story and the feature article are (in the typical newspaper office) loosely termed as features or feature stories. (In even a looser and broader sense, newspaper features include columns, cartoons, comic strips and virtually all materials other than advertisements and editorials not considered news.) It could also be a news feature, sometimes called a sidebar, that depends upon a timely news event for its peg (for example, in the newspaper the reaction of the survivors of an airplane crash printed beside the main story about the accident). It could be a color story, such as a description of the crowd the night before the Kentucky Derby or Indianapolis 500. It may be an interpretative piece on the impact of the new tax hike passed by Congress, or an informational piece on the new industries in the city. Whatever the terminology, the human-interest story and the feature article are usually distinct and distinguishable in form and content and purpose. The former is usually a dramatic story proposing to touch the reader's emotions in some way. The latter is usually an expository article, such as those used by magazines, and its major purpose is to inform.

Sources of Features. Today's straight-news stories on the appointment of a new cabinet officer, the firebombing of a public building or the signing of a contract for construction of a new library could be tomorrow's feature presenting a personality sketch of the official, the history of revolutionary activity in the nation or the growth in book publishing, use of libraries or the entire library system of a city. Much feature material is related to the news, as pointed out earlier, and many newspapers, as a result of television and radio's ability to "get there first," are turning more and more to feature treatment of the news. But giving news the feature treatment takes time and the inclination for the necessary research. Of the regular sources, the police beat yields a wealth of tragedy, humor and pathos from which many features may be developed. The most important news stories—murders, airplane crashes, spectacular fires, space shots and hundreds of others—can be highlighted and sidelighted by features: the murderer's life story or the impact of a murder on the victim's family; an eyewitness account of the crash; heroic rescues by firemen; life aboard a space craft. Much of the content of material in magazines or documentaries on television is feature material suggested by the news. In most cases the reporter has to do little research beyond his regular news sources to develop features. He simply must be willing to take the time to dig deeper and be curious enough to ask questions that go far beyond the obvious.

Many features are developed independently of the news, however. The following general classifications of situations and incidents suggest the varied fields in which features may be found:

1. *The Unusual.* Oddities, freaks, coincidences, unusual personalities.
2. *The Usual.* Familiar persons, places, things, landmarks, the handicapped young man who sells newspapers outside city hall, the street-corner minister (the feature writer evokes the reader's "I've always wanted to know about that" response).
3. *Dramatic Situations.* Sudden riches, the prize winner, the abandoned baby, the heroic rescue or nerve-shattering peril, hard luck, animal heroes, the underdog.
4. *Guidance.* Advice to troubled, recipes, health, etiquette, stamp collecting, flower arranging, woodcraft and a host of others—with the more significant, such as advice on how to vote.
5. *Information.* Statistics, studies, records, historical sketches, analogies, comparisons and contrasts of then and now, biographies.

WRITING FEATURE ARTICLES

10a

No standard form or style is used for feature articles. They follow no set rules for leads or the body or the end of the story, as news stories generally do. Some conform to the straight news style with a 5 W's summary lead, but use of the novelty lead (see Chapter 8) is more common. They may be narrative, descriptive or expository. They tell stories, paint pictures, explain conditions—but are fact, not fiction. Features may differ radically from a news story in the matter of style of writing and arrangement of material, but the incidents, facts and persons involved are real, not created. The feature article is generally designed to convey information and not, as in the human-interest story, to dramatize events for the sake of an emotional impact on the reader. Since the feature article cannot rely on news values for reader appeal, it must deal with otherwise interesting and vital subject matter. And it must be written with a flair for words that will turn a somewhat pedestrian topic into an interesting story with high reader appeal. In brief, the chief rule in writing features is "make them interesting from beginning to end."

The following beginnings suggest both the content and the technique of feature articles:

Guidance

Making a will is a sobering act that's easy to put off, which is probably why most people don't have one.

But it's also sobering to realize what can happen if you don't leave a valid document describing how your property should be distributed.

(More details on how to draw up a will)

Are you puzzled—or exasperated—by those funny numbers and letters on the sides of food packages?

Do you know what "86480" on a box of saltines means? Or "004Wl" on grated cheese, or "D 813TB" on a cake mix?

Well, at last, relief is on the way.

(More details on changes in food codes required by a new law)

Information

A feature can be used to provide the reader a variety of information. The following examples show how information about a remote Arctic community was provided by one writer, while another used the feature approach to report a new technological development that could help mankind:

Pangnirtung may not be the end of the world, but it is in the same general direction.

A tiny dot on Canada's northern vastness, that hamlet, just below the Arctic Circle on Baffin Island, is populated by 900 Eskimos, or Inuits, 70 whites, and unspecified numbers of seals. It has a collection of rusting huts, no flush toilets, no bars and a couple of dirt streets. It has an abundance of rocks, cold temperatures, winds and litter.

(Story goes on to describe life in the community and some of the people who live there)

Technology developed to check enemy activity during World War II is being applied by University of Tennessee scientists to help man live in harmony with his environment.

The technique is remote sensing—obtaining information about an object from the air by photographs, infrared imagery, radar and the like. It is being used today to help control corn blight, detect and warn of flooding, aid in combating pollution, assist in the design of efficient transportation systems and improve land-use planning.

(Full explanation of various projects follows.)

Writers frequently used a descriptive lead on their feature stories. Here is an excellent example by John Darnton in the New York Times:

BRAN, Rumania—The castle rises above the misty Transylvanian pine forest like some malevolent specter. A path winds up the craggy promontory, past gnarled pines and sheep grazing beside a murky pond.

At the top is a long stone staircase. It leads to an ancient wooden door, which creaks as it opens, slowly, into a gloomy antechamber. There are cobwebs on the wrought-iron chandelier.

Bran Castle is still the perfect Bela Lugosi setting. But the old place just does not seem the same now that Count Dracula's ghost is no longer around.

The Rumanian Government has officially rehabilitated the Count, whose historical name was Vlad III, or Vlad Tepes—The Impaler. He is now regarded as an early nationalist who fought domination by the Ottoman Empire and espoused a kind of centralization that was a precursor of modern Communist rule . . .

And Maggie Maurice of the Burlington (Vt.) Free Press won first place in a feature competition by simply describing what happened when Poet Archibald MacLeish showed up to read his poems at a gathering one night:

BREAD LOAF—Archibald MacLeish walked in out of the rain the other night and read his poems.

He didn't say much.

Or did he say more than we know?

His words are powerful. And by choosing his poems deliberately, one from this book, one from that, he caught his listeners off guard. They responded just the way he wanted them to . . .

The similarity of feature articles and magazine articles has been pointed out, as has the writer's freedom in selecting the form used in composing his story. While the reporter may abandon the regular news story organization and apply a narrative or expository form in feature articles, he is bound by other general rules of news writing: using short paragraphs, observing the newspaper's style, avoiding monotony in the use of direct quotations and unquoted summary, using transitional phrases to bridge paragraphs and achieve smooth reading and so on. The logical order is used to the extent that the reporter attempts to hold his reader by introducing new features and details in the order of interest or by an interesting narrative. But the general rule of logical order, which permits cutting a story from the end, may be ignored, as it is in the "surprise-climax story form" (illustrated later in this chapter). Many if not most feature articles end with a summary or conclusions, a characteristic of expository writing. This style of writing makes editing a feature story to cut its length a painstaking task.

WRITING HUMAN-INTEREST STORIES 10b

Since most human-interest stories are designed to touch a certain response in the reader, they must rely heavily on the human background of the event, not just the plain unvarnished facts. Even where a newsworthy event is lacking, there exist here and there predicaments and entanglements of human beings—stresses and strains, and dramatic situations with which the human-interest story weaves its patterns. The thoughts, emotions, ambitions—the varied psychological and social data of humanity—are all part of the human background so essential to this type story. They help dramatize the person, place or thing and create an emotional response in the reader.

Saul Pett, one of the Associated Press's top feature writers for many years, put it this way:

We can no longer give the reader the fast brush. We can no longer whiz through the files for 20 minutes, grab a cab, spend 30 minutes interviewing our subject, come back to the office, concoct a clever lead that goes nowhere, drag in 50 or 20 more paragraphs like tired sausage, sprinkle them with four quotes, pepper them with 14 scintillating adjectives, all synonymous, and then draw back and call that an incisive portrait of a human being.

Today the reader wants more . . . he wants to be drawn by substance. He wants meat on his bones and leaves on his trees. He wants dimension and depth and perspective and completeness and insight and, of course, honesty.

After 500 or 1,500 or 2,500 words, the reader wants to know more about a man's personality than that he is "mild-mannered" or "quiet" or "unassuming" . . . Willie Sutton, the bank robber, was mild-mannered, quiet, unassuming. So was Dr. Albert Schweitzer.

163

How can you write about a man without knowing what others have written about him? How can you write about a man without knowing what others think and know of him? How can you write about a man without interviewing him at great length and in great detail and in such a way that he begins to reveal something of himself? How can you interview him that way without planning a good part of your questioning beforehand?

How, when you're collected all you're going to collect, how can you write about a man without thinking long and hard about what you've learned? How can you write about a man without writing about the man, not merely grabbing one thin angle simply because it makes a socko anecdotal lead and leaves the essence a vague blur?

How can you write about a man simply by telling me what he says without telling me how he says it. How can you write about a man simply by telling me what he is without telling me what he is like or what he'd like to be? How can you write about a man without telling me what he is afraid of, what he wishes he could do over again, what pleases him most, what pleases him least, what illusions were broken, what vague yearning remains. How can you write about a successful man without telling me his failures or about any man without somehow indicating his own view of himself? . . .

Give me the extraordinary and give me the ordinary. Does the richest man in the world have everything he wants? Does he bother to look at the prices on a menu at all? That strange, remote, isolated little village way up in the Canadian bush. Don't just tell me about the polar bear and the deer. Tell me, buster, how do they get a suit cleaned there?

Tell me the large by telling me the small. Tell me the small by telling me the large. Identify with me, plug into my circuit, come in loud and clear . . . don't give me high-sounding abstractions . . .

Don't tease me unless you can deliver, baby. Don't tell me the situation was dramatic and expect me to take your word for it. Show me how it was dramatic and I'll supply the adjectives. You say this character is unpredictable? When, where, how? Give me the evidence, not just the chapter headings . . .

Pett's comments help point out an important difference between the art of human-interest writing and the art of writing a play, novel or short story, although the purpose and materials of the reporter are much the same as those of the other writers. The reporter must present life as it is; the dramatist may present it as it ought to be. In the similarity and difference between the two forms of writing a few principles guiding the reporter may be found.

The temptation of the reporter is to improve upon reality in order to make a better story. Pett's warning that the reader wants honesty should be ingrained in every human-interest writer's mind. Of course, the writer has some leeway but it is not easy to define. He is justified in some rearrangement of events as long as he presents the essential truth of the story. But he certainly should not distort for dramatic effect. He should not force a quote upon his subject any more than he should make up a quote out of whole cloth and put it in his subject's mouth. A writer who repeatedly asks a striking miner, "You suffered greatly after the mines closed down, did you not?" to get the striker to repeat the phrase in those words is presenting a false picture.

The reporter is tempted also to adopt emotionalized language to achieve an emotional impact. To do so is to defeat his purpose. The drama and its impact must be inherent in the facts of the story. Simple language is the best medium for transmitting these facts to the reader. Ernie Pyle's famous story on Captain Waskow, which was reprinted in a collection of his war dispatches under the title of *Brave Men,* is an excellent example of how a writer can achieve dramatic impact through the use of simple language.

The human-interest story takes no standard form. Almost any of the rhetorical devices and suspended-interest forms may be appropriate. A novelty lead with the body in logical order is a popular form. The summary lead with the body in chronological order is often used. Following are some samples:

This animal story is from the Associated Press:

> BARDSTOWN, Ky. (AP)—He's heard the gentle voices calling. He's heard do dahs and how the birds make music all the day. And when his 1,000th performance in the Stephen Foster Story is over Sunday night, Herman Durham III will just yawn as usual and hope he can soon go back to sleep.
>
> Herman, a 14-year-old beagle, has appeared in the role of Old Dog Tray in the outdoor musical at the J. Dan Talbott Amphitheater here for 13 years.
>
> A native of Harrisburg, Pa., Herman joined the show shortly after he moved to Bardstown with his owner, Mrs. William C. Durham.
>
> "He's really sleepy, easy going, gentle and lovable," Mrs. Durham said. "He's a fine hunting dog and can still get on the trail of a rabbit, which is pretty good considering his age is the equivalent of a 91-year-old human."
>
> Herman, who has performed before an estimated 600,000 spectators, has goofed only a few times.
>
> "He made his singing debut backstage a few years ago," Mrs. Durham said. "Stephen was singing to Jeannie and right in the best part of the love song somebody stepped on Herman's tail. He let out a terrible howl and the audience roared."
>
> They used to let Herman come on stage for the finale but he kept getting under the large hoopskirts of the women in the cast. The clincher came the night a frog joined the finale.
>
> "That broke the house up," Mrs. Durham said. "That frog would jump and Herman would jump. Then they'd look at each other and jump some more."

During one of the energy crises, Raymond Coffey of the Chicago Daily News used this approach on his interview with a British inventor who ran his car on pollution-free methane gas distilled from manure:

> TOTNES, Devon, England—For Harold Bate this whole noisy business about the energy crisis and automobile pollution is a lot of unnecessary nonsense.
>
> He has been running his car for nearly 17 years now on pollution-free and exceedingly high-octane pig manure.
>
> Furthermore, for $33 including postage he will send you a converter device and full instructions on how you too can run your car on manure—pig, cattle, chicken, dog or almost any other variety.
>
> Bate is not a nut. He is an inventor, and his system works.
>
> He distills methane gas from the manure, puts the gas into small steel cylinders that fit in the trunk of his car and runs a small hose from the cylinder to the engine . . .
>
> (The rest of the story details Bate's work converting manure into power for his car and the way his car performs using the unusual fuel.)

Surprise Climax Form. Still another form often used for human-interest stories is called the surprise climax or "O'Henry ending." The following example is by Eldon Barrett of United Press International:

THE DIAGRAM

Narrative of Details

Surprise Climax

THE WRITTEN STORY

SEATTLE, Wash.—Based on a premise expounded by a psychiatrist, Seattle has just gone through one of the glummest summers on record. It hardly rained at all.

Dr. S. Harvard Kaufman, a resident for 28 years, is convinced that nice weather in Seattle makes most of its residents gloomy.

Why?

"Because they figure it's going to get worse," said Kaufman. "People carry around a lot of guilt. When they are happy, they wonder when the knife is going to fall.

"Good weather in Seattle activates a deepseated sense of guilt in most of the residents.

"From birth they are taught that the weather here is rainy," he said. "They also are taught that because of this the air is clear and the grass is green."

The fact is, there is less annual rainfall in Seattle than in New York, Philadelphia, Washington, Trenton, N.J., and Atlanta, Ga.

But the myth persists that Seattle is the sponge of the United States and Seattleites visiting elsewhere have found it usually expedient to let the legend linger on.

"We are not exactly promoting rain," said Bill Sears, publicist for the Seattle-King County Convention and Visitors Bureau. "But we are promoting its by-products—fresh air, cleanliness and greenery!

"If we can't scrub out the legend that Seattle is in a constant deluge, we might as well put the myth to work," Sears said.

As he spoke, the first downpour of fall was bathing the region, where the worst drought in 33 years had turned the evergreen state into a dusty brown.

And peering out from under umbrellas and foul weather hats were the smiling faces of passersby, obviously delighted that the ordeal of the long, pleasant summer was over.

The object of the surprise climax technique is to hold the reader's attention for an O'Henry type of story ending—a climax with a twist. No rules regarding the logical order or the 5 W's lead apply here; on the contrary, the story builds up as it continues. But the beginning must have an element of suspended interest to attract readers, and its narrative qualities must be strong enough to hold readers to the end.

166   Other sample human-interest stories follow:

MANILA, Philippines (UPI)—A cup of termites a day makes a man "macho" and a good fighter, a government report said Friday.

Feed termites to a gamecock and you will have in your hands a vigorous fighting cock, the report added.

Food connoisseurs, however, are advised to cook their termites first. Two possible dishes offered are termite "burgers" and termite "omelet."

Experts of the Forest Product Research and Industries Development Commission gave the advice at the conclusion of a study into the nutritional potential of termites found in the Philippines.

Commissioner Francisco Tamolang said that the experts found two subterranean termite species to be rich in nutrients needed for the human body.

According to nutrition experts, every 100 grams of edible termites offer 11 different nutrients—chiefly carbohydrates and protein, but also iron, calcium, vitamin A and others.

SOUTHERN PINES, N.C. (UPI)—When the minister asked the father of the bride who was giving her away, the father shook his head, turned around and walked out of the church.

Police said yesterday that when the father, James West McNeill, returned to the church as the ceremony was ending Saturday he brought a 16-gauge shotgun with him.

While McNeill's daughter Joyce and her bridegroom, Lacy Turner, hurried to a reception four blocks away, police say, McNeill fired the shotgun once into the air and then, in a struggle with wedding guests who tried to take the gun away from him, hit guest Ed Quick on the head.

Police quoted McNeill as saying he didn't like the way he was being treated by the bridegroom and his family.

EXERCISES

1. Clip from any newspaper available to you two human-interest stories and rewrite them as straight-news stories.
2. Write a feature story, using the material presented here. It is based on interviews with Bobbie Joe Sallander, a Roosevelt College senior; Sharon Bowman, women's basketball and volleyball coach at the school; and several members of the basketball, volleyball and tennis teams.

   The Roosevelt volleyball team has just won the AIAW State championship and leaves tomorrow for the state capital to compete in the Region II volleyball tournament. Coach Bowman said she believes the team "has a good chance of winning the region and we could go all the way."

   Certainly much of the credit has to go to Bobbie Jo, the coach said. "She is the first triple-threat player we have had at Roosevelt since we have had competitive women's teams."

   In addition to volleyball, Bobbie Jo was a star of the basketball team for three years and a major factor in the tennis teams winning the state championship the last two years in a row.

   "I first saw Bobbie Jo at volleyball practice three years ago," Coach Bowman said. "I knew she was a potentially fine athlete but she seemed so shy. I had to do a lot of talking to convince her to compete. You see, she is deaf."

   Coach Bowman said she explained to Bobbie Jo that the hearing problem wouldn't cause her or the team any problem once they got used to each other.

"After all, she can talk," Coach Bowman said. "She just can't hear." Her teammates learned sign language, and Bobbie Jo listens with her eyes by reading lips and facial expressions. "There isn't much of a communications problem," her teammate Rachel Roberts from Watertown said. "If she's going to get the ball, she'll yell for it. If not, one of us knows to take it."

Bobbie Jo was named all-state in volleyball in both her sophomore and junior years, and the coach expects she will be named again this year. "She is a very fine athlete. Spikes are her strength, and she's also very good on the dink shot, very deceptive," the coach said. The team has a 34–8 record this year.

In addition to her athletic ability, Bobbie Jo is one of the most popular students on campus. This fall she was named homecoming queen, and she has been active in student government on campus.

She enrolled at Roosevelt after graduating from high school in Miami, Fla. Her brother, Gill, is a member of the Roosevelt football team. She has a sister who is a swimming coach in Florida. And Bobbie Jo hopes to be a coach of deaf children when she graduates in June.

"I was on the basketball and swimming teams in high school," she said. "But I like volleyball the most because it is more fun and not so frustrating. My next goal is to go to Chicago next summer to try out for the U.S. Deaf Olympics team."

Bobbie Jo said she did not feel being deaf had hampered her in any way. Most people aren't aware of it. And I don't make a big deal of it. In fact, this is the first time I've ever been interviewed by a newspaper. I hope you won't make a big deal out of it, either. I'm proud of what I've done, but I'm really not all that different."

(Note: You should know that Bobbie Jo can talk, but because she cannot hear, some of her words are not completely clear and she speaks very slowly.)

3. Check with a number of department heads or the director of research on your campus to find out what type research projects are underway. Interview one of the researchers and then write a feature story about his or her project.

4. Using the library as your main source, find a special event or holiday (not Christmas, Easter or July 4th) that is about to be observed—perhaps National Pickle Week or Bachelor's Day—and write a short feature story about it.

5. Write a surprise climax story using the following facts:
Eliza Hermitage, 101, Eastry, England
Lives in nursing home
Celebrated 101st birthday
Sipping brandy and ginger ale
While aboard a hovercraft
Skimming across the English Channel
For about 40 minutes
On her 99th birthday
She took her first airplane ride
On her 100th birthday
She climbed aboard a helicopter
For a one-hour ride over English countryside
Mrs. Hermitage said she is looking forward
To her 102nd birthday next year
"I'd love to try the Concorde next year," she said.

6. Write stories from the following notes
A. Warren Baxter, author of best-selling
   Man As a Sex Object
   On campus to lecture
   In connection with program

He stages a beauty pageant
Contestants wore tight swimsuits
Had to parade on stage
Then walk through audience
Contestants were six male students
Onlookers patted them and occasionally pinched them
Baxter lined them up on stage
Told women in audience to pick
One they would like to date
Based on their physical characteristics only
Men contestants permitted to ask
Women in audience their salaries
And their career goals
Men told to select women
They would date based on salaries and career goals
Baxter said: "For most women, their body is what will determine the financial support they will have for the rest of their lives. For every laugh we have had tonight, there was a serious message."
One male contestant said: "This has been really weird. Now I recognize what women go through."

B. Harold DeWitt, 24, Madisonville
Met the girl of his dreams
When she served him a plate
Of chocolate-chip cookies
In a Madisonville restaurant
Where she worked
He asked for a date, she accepted
They became engaged after six months
They planned to be married in three months
But she had a change of heart
She returned his ring
He asked for a breach-of-promise settlement
4,380 chocolate-chip cookies
"I felt that I should have something for my pain," he said
So he asked for a dozen cookies for each day they had been engaged
The 24-year-old woman, who preferred to remain unidentified
Only missed one deadline
But she caught up the next day
Finally finished the job last week
Her debt was paid and
DeWitt's freezer was full of cookies

C. Security National Bank
Downtown Branch
Police said man walked up to
Unidentified teller about noon yesterday
Teller said: Can I help you?
Man said: This is a robbery. I want the money.
Teller: No
Robber: No? Ok. Call it a loan
Teller: What do you want? A car loan?
Robber: No, I want the money.
Teller: Do you want to see the manager?

Robber: No, he'll probably give me a hard time.

Police said the teller then turned her back on the customer. The man, apparently conceding defeat, walked quickly out of the bank and disappeared in the noon-time crowd.

7. Attend a major campus event, a football game or a major popular concert, for example, and write a feature story—not a straight news story—about it.

8. Locate a fellow student on campus who has an interesting job, hobby, background, or family and write a human-interest story about him or her. Do not pick a well-known student for this assignment.

Rewrites and Follow-Ups

The dwindling number of daily newspapers in the United States has not automatically meant a lack of competition. In many areas where only one daily exists, weekly newspapers have increased their publication to twice, even three times a week, and they have become increasingly aggressive in covering local news. In addition, there appears to be increasing competition from both radio and television news staffs in a number of communities.

A good editor, even when not faced with head-to-head competition of another daily, will know exactly what his competition is doing. If there is a competing daily, he will read it carefully and mark stories to be clipped by a secretary or copy clerk. He will also read and mark for clipping the newspapers from nearby communities in which his newspaper circulates. He also will listen to the news on his car radio and watch local and national news on television.

And if he is doing his job thoroughly, one of the last things he will do before going home is read his own newspaper carefully. He will clip stories from his own paper, just as he does from the competition, make notes in his log regarding each clipping and put some in his file for future use. Many of them, however, will be sent to the various beat reporters, with any special instructions he may have on the story. On a clipping from a competitive newspaper, he may order the facts checked and the story rewritten. On a clipping from his own newspaper, he may write instructions for the reporter to do a follow-up.

REWRITES

In the mind of a journalist, *rewrite* can have several meanings. It may simply mean to rewrite a story from a clipping or press release after all the facts have been verified with the sources. Or it may mean rewriting his own story because the city editor did not like the way he wrote it originally. And on some newspapers, especially afternoon dailies in large metropolitan areas such as Chicago, rewrites may be of an entirely different nature. The city is so large that reporters would risk missing deadlines in taking time to travel from office to story and back to office. So, beat reporters often gather the facts for a story, then telephone the information to a rewrite man in the office who actually writes the story for publication, often with the reporter's by-line. Some long-time beat reporters write very few stories, although their by-lines appear regularly. The rewrite men often are among the best writers and most capable members of the staff. Some papers in smaller cities use this system of rewrite only occasionally, usually for last-minute stories gathered right on deadline.

In rewriting a story from another newspaper, the reporter first verifies the facts in the clipping; then he attempts to get additional facts to use in the rewrite. His object is to have his own story appear to be a new story and not a rewritten one. To accomplish this, he may start the rewrite (1) by playing up any additional newsworthy fact or facts or (2) by reorganizing the story if no new facts are available. In the second case, the story would usually be a shortened version of the original.

11a   Obviously, the first method is preferred, but as pointed out there sometimes are no new facts to add to a story. In any event, the rewritten story, especially the lead, should be as much unlike the original story as possible. The writers of the two leads below did not have much choice—the essential point was the efforts to provide transportation for the handicapped—yet they were able to come up with slightly different leads. The following lead appeared on the story in the morning newspaper:

> Mayor Randy Thompson said Wednesday night he will "figure out some way" for the city to provide transportation service to the handicapped for that which is being discontinued by the Easter Seal Society.
>
> The City Council was told by an Easter Seal official Wednesday night that 500 monthly trips provided the elderly and handicapped will be stopped after Monday due to lack of funds.
>
> "This is obviously an emergency, and I'm not in a position to give absolute assurance, but they're not going to be left without service," the mayor told City Council members.

The afternoon newspaper's coverage of the same meeting used the following lead:

> Knoxville Transportation Authority would probably be able to take over special transportation services from the Easter Seal Society, KTA Chairman W. T. Crutcher told the City Council last night.
>
> "If they are going out of business and there is some way we can take over their vans, we can offer the service cheaper than anyone else," Crutcher said. "We have the personnel, the equipment, and everything."

Often the angle featured in the rewritten lead is taken from the body of the original story as these examples show. The morning newspaper used this lead on its City Council story:

A request to rezone 9.6 acres of land south of Northshore Drive and east of Willman Lane to permit construction of a $3.5 million apartment complex was delayed by the City Council last night.

Councilwoman Brenda Frazier asked for the delay to give the developer and residents of the area, who oppose the development, an "opportunity to work out a compromise."

Earlier the Metropolitan Planning Commission ignored the opposition from the homeowners and recommended rezoning the property from single-family to multi-family to permit construction of the apartments.

If the council gives final approval Tuesday, residents of the area say they will file a suit in Circuit Court to block the rezoning.

(Story goes on to give details of the apartment complex and the dispute between the homeowners and the developer as well as other action taken by the Council at the meeting)

The afternoon newspaper's coverage of the same meeting used the following lead:

If you park illegally and your car is towed in, you'll have to pay $40 instead of $20 to get it out.

The City Council voted last night to double the towing and impoundment fee after police said the problem with illegally parked cars has become "epidemic."

The afternoon newspaper's story did not get to the rezoning until about the eighth paragraph. The morning newspaper's story did not introduce the hike in towing fees until the sixth paragraph.

11b Facts omitted purposely or otherwise by the reporter of the original story are often featured in the rewrite because they give the story a fresh aspect. In striving for a fresh angle, however, a reporter must guard against distorting the essential facts and significance of the story. Sometimes new events occur and give the rewrite man a feature that was not available to the reporter of the original story. In this case, the story is a combination rewrite and follow-up.

Most newspapers receive hundreds of press releases each week and the careful editor has them checked and then rewritten. Sometimes the task of rewriting them can be easy because the real news may be buried in the press release. However, a number of press releases are very well written and the job of rewriting them can be tough. A rewrite man facing a well-written press release needs all the skills and imagination at his command to improve what is basically a good story to start with.

While many reporters object strongly to being assigned rewrites, it is excellent training in the art of writing. Two weeks on rewrite will teach a wordy reporter more about careful, exact writing than any other assignment on the newspaper.

FOLLOW-UPS **11c**

A follow-up is simply an updating of an earlier news story in which the latest developments are reported. The story, naturally, features the new developments, but the reporter must summarize enough of the background of the story

11d

for the benefit of readers who did not see the original—and to refresh the memories of those who did. Because this summary refers to an earlier story, it is called a tie-back.

The tie-back often consists of one paragraph, which immediately follows the lead or second paragraph, but no set rules govern its length or position. One sentence or phrase within a paragraph or within the lead itself may be sufficient to make new developments clear. If the story remains alive for several days, the tie-back becomes shorter and shorter, since the chances decrease daily that a reader has missed all the earlier stories. However, in some stories several paragraphs may be necessary, particularly when the follow-up is published some time after the original story appeared.

The common method of using the tie-back is as follows:

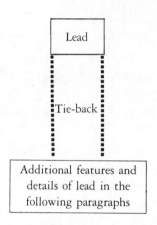

A study to determine the feasibility of growing grapes and fruit trees on strip-mined land is yielding promising but not spectacular results.

The study was initiated three years ago by the Tennessee Valley Authority on a one-acre site in a strip-mined area atop Sand Mountain in Alabama. Results of the project are expected to be of value in reclaiming strip-mined lands throughout the nation.

"Grape production this season was not as good as we were expecting, but our fruit trees did well," said a TVA report.

"Our studies have already determined that there is apparently a micronutrient deficiency in the soil that is affecting grape production, and we are working to correct this. Most strip-mined lands have deficiencies of both nitrogen and phosphorus and we are fertilizing at varying rates to determine how best to overcome the problem," the report said.

The follow-up is handled in the same manner as the rewrite, the reporter using the facts already in hand and diligently seeking new developments. Except for the tie-backs, the follow-ups are written in the same form as the new story.

Most rewrites are brief and rather insignificant items, as a general rule. The pressure on space is so heavy that information previously seen by a large number of readers must be condensed as much as possible. However, if a big story—a natural disaster such as a flood or earthquake, for example—breaks on the competitor's time, the story is not rewritten, in the usual sense of the term. In fact, reporters are sent to cover the story along with the competition, only they have longer to write it. Subsequent stories will be follow-ups—just as they are when the newspaper's own first account deserves later development. Most stories of importance are pursued through later developments for days or weeks and, on rare occasions, even years. Reporting of the Watergate scandals in the federal government covered more than two years. A fire or a storm is followed by accounts of relief and reconstruction. Crime is followed through the trial and sentence.

Gradually, the force of the first explosive event plays out, and the follow-ups dwindle away.

Sometimes the follow-up can develop into a much larger story than the original item. A very small paragraph in a first edition or on a given day is followed by larger accounts until a great story burgeons from insignificant beginnings. Embezzlements, scandals of all sorts, Congressional investigations may come to light, and the story will build slowly. From a seemingly routine break-in at the Democratic National Headquarters in the Watergate Hotel in Washington, D.C., the story built month after month until the ultimate resignation of President Richard M. Nixon.

The Developing Story. Another type of follow-up that offers problems of rewriting is the story requiring "latest developments" changes in several editions of one day's newspaper. If a major court trial is in progress, for instance, the newspaper may want an up-to-the-deadline report of the trial in every edition. A newspaper with three editions (early mail, out-of-city and early street sales; home distribution; and late street sales) will have a different deadline for each edition, and it may require the rewriting of one story (or parts of it) three different times to include the latest newsworthy features in each edition. This type of story is called the developing story, or running story.

It is also a follow-up because it includes developments later than those in the previous story. It is also something of a rewrite. It usually does not entail a rewriting of the bulk of the previous story. A new lead, including latest developments properly linked with previous developments, may be all that is required. Or inserts or adds for the original story may fill the need. As much of the original story as possible is left undisturbed.

While this is not as common as it once was when metropolitan newspapers had seven or eight editions a day (now most metros are down to three or four), it is still used from time to time when a story develops over several editions. For example, a fire is reported at the city jail just before deadline for the first edition and the facts are sketchy. The first-edition story might say:

A fire swept through the jail on the second floor of City Hall shortly before 9 a.m. today, and at least three inmates are known to be dead.

"It could be a lot worse," Police Chief Bill Joe Biggs said. "I just can't tell you anything for sure until the fire is out and we can get in there."

He said he did not know how many prisoners were in the jail, because he had not received the daily head count before the fire started.

"Things have been quiet this week. I think maybe we had 12 or 15 locked up. But I can't really be sure," Biggs said.

He added that he did not have time to identify the dead men.

Heavy black smoke billowed through the 156-year-old building and inmates could be heard screaming for help as firemen pumped thousands of gallons of water through the second-floor windows.

Dozens of policemen joined firemen in trying to reach the prisoners. But most rescue efforts failed because of the intense heat and the heavy black smoke.

"You can't get anywhere near the cell block," Patrolman Ira Bevins said. "If the flames and heat don't stop you, the smoke will."

(To round out the story for the first edition, the writer should include information about evacuating city employees from other offices in the building. He may include some information about the building and the jail, especially if a check of the clipping file shows there have been previous reports about safety conditions at the jail)

Examples of how the story might be changed to include up-to-deadline developments in later editions are the following:

NEW LEAD

At least eight prisoners were killed today when fire swept through the jail on the second floor of City Hall.

The dead were trapped in a large holding cell in the jail. Other prisoners may have died in their locked cells at the rear of the second floor.

INSERT AFTER FIFTH PARAGRAPH OF THE ORIGINAL STORY

Two officers and a trusty who were downstairs smelled smoke and ran to the second floor. They opened one of two doors to the large holding cell, but were unable to open the other door, which may have been blocked by the body of an unconscious inmate, Biggs said.

ADD TO END OF STORY:

Three firemen were hospitalized from smoke inhalation.

Biggs said it was too early to determine how the fire started. He added, however, that it was not uncommon for prisoners to start fires in their cells.

"They set fire to a half dozen mattresses a month," he said.

Of course, if a final death toll is available by the final edition of the day, a new lead should be written. Additional details of the fire may be inserted or added at the end of the story. Because "patching" a story together in this fashion can result in mistakes, many papers will have the story for the final edition completely rewritten.

If time does not permit the revision of a story in an earlier edition, a short (usually one-paragraph) "bulletin" is written to precede the lead of the earlier story. However, this is usually done for the lead story on the front page and only in the event the latest developments are significant enough to warrant this special treatment.

EXERCISES

1. Using only the facts given, rewrite the following story which appeared in a competing newspaper:

A 62-year-old Lonsdale woman was found strangled to death in her apartment about 7 p.m. yesterday.

The victim, Mrs. Emma Truitt Baker, 2251 Western Ave., was face down on the floor in the rear bedroom, police said. A pair of hose and an electric extension cord were wrapped tightly around her neck. Her hands were tied behind her back with a short piece of rope.

Police entered the apartment after the victim's granddaughter, Mrs. Albert L. Griffith, could not reach Mrs. Baker by telephone. The front door was ajar when police arrived at the apartment.

Patrolman Carl McCarter, the first to arrive at the apartment, said a .38 caliber pistol on the headboard of the bed apparently had not been touched and several items of jewelry were in plain sight.

Homicide Detective Ray Price said it appeared that robbery was not the motive in the murder.

He added that he and his partner, Detective Harold Dipper, were working on several leads in the case.

2. Rewrite the following press release to emphasize the real "news" value.

FOR IMMEDIATE RELEASE

Southern Power Co., which supplies electricity to every county in the state, announced today completion of its new $200-million nuclear power plant on the St. John's river, near Townsend.

R. J. Johnson, president of the utility, said the nuclear power plant, which is expected to go on-line by July 1, completes the firm's 10-year construction plan designed to bring "low-cost electricity to every home, farm and business in the state."

"If the plant performs as we expect it to, we may be able to sell excess power to a number of neighboring states as well," Johnson said.

He called the new power plant "a monument to American technical know-how" and predicted that within five years nuclear power will "be a major factor in freeing us from domination by foreign oil producers."

Johnson said the plant was completed despite the efforts of antinuclear groups and skyrocketing construction costs.

In addition to fighting a running battle with the antinuclear forces in and out of court, the company has been faced with staggering increases in construction costs, Johnson said.

"Labor costs have increased 22 per cent in the last two years and the cost of materials have gone up almost 30 per cent," he pointed out.

In spite of all that, Johnson said, the company has kept the project on schedule because "the people of the state need it so desperately."

To offset the enormous increase in costs, Johnson said, the company today filed a request with the Public Service Commission seeking a 12 per cent—across the board—increase in electrical rates to be effective in 30 days.

Johnson said today's request might not have been as high if the Commission had granted the firm its full request 11 months ago. At that time Southern requested a 10 per cent increase but the Commission only allowed a six per cent increase.

3. Rewrite the story in Exercise 1 with the following additional information.

Less than 24 hours after Mrs. Baker was found murdered in her apartment, Detectives Price and Dipper arrested two Kennedy High School students and charged them with the murder. The two 16-year-olds were picked up shortly before noon at the school. The detectives refused to identify them. They said they had received a tip that the two had been seen in the hall of Mrs. Baker's apartment the morning of her murder. Kennedy High School is three blocks from Mrs. Baker's apartment building.

4. The following day Prosecuting Attorney Harold Brown said he planned to try the two juveniles as adults for the murder of Mrs. Baker. He identified them as Adam Brooks, the son of Mr. and Mrs. Dexter Brooks, 45 Woodlawn lane, and Tommy Crater, the son of Mr. and Mrs. Joseph Crater, 1115 Brookside drive. Brown declined to discuss the details of the case. Write a follow-up story.

5. Obtain a press release from the college or university's public relations office or the sports information office and rewrite it.

6. Clip from any daily newspaper available to you three locally written stories you believe will result in follow-up stories. List the possible future developments that should warrant a follow-up for each story.

177

7. Clip from the daily newspaper that circulates in your community three locally written stories several paragraphs in length. Rewrite them without using new facts.

8. Using two daily newspapers published in the same city (which may be available in your library), compare several locally written stories and the rewritten versions that appear in the competing newspaper. Note any new facts appearing in the rewritten version.

9. Clip from any newspaper available to you three stories that demonstrate the use of the tie-back technique.

Pictures

In our visually oriented society, the photograph has become increasingly important in reporting news. As a result, it is essential that the reporter develop his sense of visual perception. To know a good picture when he sees one and to appreciate its importance will certainly be useful to the reporter when he is assigned to write *cutlines* (captions) for a picture or perhaps a textblock for a picture page.

A reporter does not have to be able to take pictures, but he must appreciate what a good picture can do—standing alone or as a way of illustrating his words. Of course, if a reporter can take pictures, he may find it extremely useful, especially on smaller newspapers, where reporters usually double as photographers.

Pictures are a vital part of the modern newspaper. They take the place of many words in portraying the day's news. Pictures speak quickly, vividly, simply, and they give the newspaper a more colorful and more readable typographic appearance. In fact, they are a vital ingredient of modern newspaper design.

In general, pictures will supplement and be used in connection with news and feature stories, on the same page adjoining a story, sometimes on a different page in the same edition (but this should be avoided) or even in subsequent editions with or without follow-up stories. Frequently, however, a picture may tell its own story and stand alone, supported merely by cutlines. These news pictures will, if possible, feature vivid action or a prominent or interesting personality in a new pose, preferably both in a dramatic combination. If a picture of this sort cannot be obtained, the newspaper may use a formal head-and-shoulders photograph of an individual taken from the morgue or shot by the staff photographer. It is also rather common to pull from the morgue a photograph taken on another occasion and to "crop" everything out except the person whose picture is needed. Many papers acknowledge in their cutlines that such photographs were taken earlier.

A creative photographer can make even the oldest situation seem new, just as an outstanding reporter can make the most routine story interesting. It is a matter of thinking, caring and taking pride in one's work. Except for head-and-shoulders photographs (called mug shots), the gifted photographer avoids the stiff "facing the camera" pose and will have the subjects looking toward a focal point for the picture rather than "mugging" or looking straight into the camera.

He will avoid the photographic clichés—the handshakers, the ribbon cutters, the pointers, the check passers—whenever possible. And if he can not avoid such assignments—and most photographers cannot—he will at least approach them from a different angle. Ideally, the photographer should always seek drama, human interest, conflict and other news values in his pictures. All of this is equally important to the reporter because he frequently must aid the photographer on the assignment. In such cases, the reporter records the exact names and initials of persons, "from left to right," while the picture is being taken. And it is the reporter who often must plan the pictures related to his own story. In fact, it is just as essential for a reporter as it is for a photographer to be able to see creatively.

Picture Process. The reporter should be familiar with the picture process:

1. The city editor, or photo editor if the newspaper has one, makes the assignment. It should be as specific as possible. The photographer should be given some idea of the type picture the editor expects.

2. The picture is taken by a photographer; the film is developed and printed. (Some smaller newspapers use Polaroid cameras to eliminate the developing and printing process.) The glossy print is handed to the proper editor—usually the city editor for local pictures. The city editor as well as the Sunday editor, entertainment, sports or women's news editor also will receive many pictures along with the press releases provided by other sources such as public relations persons.

3. The editor determines the news value of the picture, marks the picture where it should be cropped and indicates the size of the cut (or negative, in offset printing) that should be made of it. If the picture has flaws that can be corrected, the editor may give it to a staff artist, who may "retouch" it to strengthen weak lines or "paint out" objectionable features. The artist may also make a layout showing the arrangement of pictures to be used in a picture story.

4. The retouched print goes to the backshop. If the paper is printed by the offset method, a screened negative is made with the offset camera. If the newspaper is still printed by hot metal, an engraver makes a metal "cut" of it.

5. A proof (copy) of the cut is returned to the editor, who may mark it for a special place in the paper.

6. The editor gives the original print or proof to a reporter or copy editor for writing of cutlines. Often, however, the cutlines are written before the picture is sent to the backshop.

7. The print and its cutlines (checked by the editor or a copy editor) are returned to the composing room, where the cutlines are set and assembled with the negative or cut in the page where they will appear.

WRITING CUTLINES

The writing of good cutlines is a fine art. Not everyone does it well. It takes practice, patience and a careful use of words. A good example of cutlines is not one under a photograph of a presidential candidate shaking hands with a voter, and the words "Presidential Candidate John Jones is shown shaking hands with Grocery Clerk Bob Smith." Cutlines should never say "pictured here" or "shown above." It is an insult to the reader. He knows that it is a picture. So why tell him what he already knows.

Cutline styles vary from newspaper to newspaper. Most cutlines are used under pictures. However, some newspapers use them at the side, which is commonly called "magazine style." Readership tests show that overlines or captions should not be used above pictures; readers tend to miss them or ignore them.

The following examples show some of the various styles of cutlines commonly used:

Tribune Photo by James Mavo

The Rev. Patrick Brennan of St. Hubert's Catholic Community in Hoffman Estates and Joanmarie Wermes took an evangelical message door-to-door in the community. "There were a few doors slammed, but a lot of people said, 'Great idea!' " Father Brennan said.

Tribune Photo by Bob Fila

He's back!

The snowman cometh—and it's not the last we'll see of him. This smiling harbinger was created in Rolling Meadows from the Chicago area's first measurable snow of the season, which deposited an average of one inch Tuesday. The National Weather Service is predicting flurries for Wednesday, followed by dry but cold weather through Sunday. More photos and a map of Chicago's snow routes are on the Back Page, Sec. 5.

SCENE EXAMINED—Oak Ridge Police Chief Robert Smith was among several officers who examined the Norris public safety department headquarters, in which two officers were injured in the explosion of a Christmas present delivered to the station Monday morning.—Staff photo by Jim Brent.

Fred Astaire, policeman

New Yorkers actually rushed to greet a policeman Friday, but this cop wasn't on the street to catch criminals, just make a movie. Fred Astaire, 80, donned the costume for the filming of a television movie, "The Man in the Santa Claus Suit," which is scheduled for airing Dec. 23 on NBC.

Blowing In The Wind

Bruce Johnson of Lebanon flings an armload of autumn leaves atop a truck load ready to be hauled away from a local residence. The Cumberland College student discovered that when there's no wind the task is easy, but sudden gusts can make raking or piling leaves as difficult as scooping sand with a fork. (DEMOCRAT photo by Bill Thorup)

Journal Staff Photo by Lon Slepicka

Bedside Wedding

A serious auto accident failed to stop Prince George's County lawyer Fred P. Heyser from showing up at his wedding — despite fractures of the leg and arm, and a dislocated hip. The bride in the Prince George's General Hospital ceremony Wednesday was Joan Strickland, a longtime resident of Glenmont and a graduate of Sherwood High School. A more formal ceremony, with some 200 invited guests, is scheduled a month from now, when the groom is to get out of the hospital. At left is Daniel Van Allen, a friend of the groom's; next to the bride is her sister, Martha, of Chevy Chase; performing the ceremony at right is Pastor Tom White.

Cutlines should be brief. They should tell what the picture is all about and identify people in it. That is all. While the cutlines are much like a story lead, narrating the 5 W's of the picture, they should not repeat the lead of any accompanying story word for word. If it is a straight-news picture, the cutlines should emphasize the most important fact first. Cutlines similar to a feature lead are appropriate with pictures that are not straight news.

While the 5 W's are especially necessary for a picture published without an accompanying story, excessive explanation is a mistake. Remember that the cutlines need not be burdened with excessive details. In fact, when a picture accompanies a story, many newspapers have gone to the briefest possible cutlines because the details are adequately covered in the lead or high up in the story. Under a picture of children being rescued from an overturned bus, which accompanied a story of the bus wreck, the following cutline was used in one newspaper:

Rescuers pull children from a Church of Christ bus after Saturday's wreck

And under a front page of Pope Paul walking down the ramp of his plane after it had landed in Des Moines, Iowa, the Des Moines Register used this brief cutline:

Pope John Paul II is greeted by young
Thomas Anania at Des Moines airport

Here are other examples of the use of pictures:

Straight News Picture Accompanied by a Story. Not all W's are introduced **12a** here, and the cutlines do not repeat the exact wording of the lead. (See Figure 12-1.)

Feature Picture Accompanied by a Story. Cutlines are written in a more col- **12b** loquial tone and contain less detail. They generally emphasize something not mentioned in the lead of the story. (See Figure 12-2.)

Picture Not Accompanied by a Story. Frequently pictures are used as a **12c** follow-up of a story published previously, usually because the pictures were not available at the time the story was used. In this case all 5 W's are adequately presented and explained. Often a picture is used alone simply because it is a good picture, it conveys a certain mood or idea or perhaps the editor just likes it. (See Figure 12-3.)

Picture Stories. Increasingly, newspapers are using picture stories to present information or ideas to the reader. Unfortunately, not all picture stories are carefully conceived and executed. Too often they are thrown together out of what appears to be leftover prints from the day's photo assignments. In rare cases that may work. Most of the time, however, the page will simply look like what it is—a collection of leftover pictures.

To be effective, a picture story must be a well-planned "essay" built around a strong central theme or idea. And all of it should be worked out carefully before the photographer starts shooting. The photographer should return from the assignment with at least one dominant picture that can be used to establish the theme of the photo essay. He should also have a combination of action and reaction shots. And he should provide closeups as well as over-all shots so the page will offer some contrast.

When preparing cutlines (captions) for the photo story, the writer should remember that he must not only describe the picture but also provide some continuity from picture to picture on the page. Captions should be kept to a minimum and they should be stripped of all unnecessary words. They also should be uniform in style.

Many picture pages use a central copy block rather than a complete story. On some picture pages the copy block, a brief summary of the page's theme often set in larger type, supplants cutlines. The text of the copy block, in that

Figure 12-1. Photo courtesy of Joe Stewardson.

THE STORY LEAD
A four-alarm fire heavily damaged the Topside Roofing Company warehouse at 1114 King Road shortly after noon today.

Four-Alarm Blaze

THE CUTLINES
Firemen poured thousands of gallons of water on the Topside Roofing Company warehouse today before extinguishing the four-alarm fire that heavily damaged the building.

184

Figure 12-2. Photo courtesy of the Tennessee Valley Authority.

THE STORY LEAD
If you resent having to answer questions by a census taker—be thankful you aren't a fish.

To study the fish population in area lakes, scientists are setting off underwater blasts . . .

Counting Heads

THE CUTLINES
Scientists separate fish by species during the current study of fish population in area lakes.

case, relates specifically to all of the pictures. On others the copy block is used to tie the pictures together and emphasize the theme of the page. In this case it is important that the copy block simply not repeat information contained in the cutlines.

Figure 12-3. Photo courtesy of the Tennessee Valley Authority.

Rough Riders

Rafting on the Ocee River isn't for the faint of heart. Yet hundreds of adventurers take to the river each week in large inflatable rafts for a bone-jarring—and they insist exhilarating—ride on the river's often turbulent waters.

The following picture page by photographer Jerry Smith for the Morristown Citizen Tribune is a example of a well-executed picture story.

EXERCISES

1. Following are brief notes for cutlines. Explain specifically what kind of picture (closeup, over-all scene and so forth) you would suggest for use in connection with each exercise. Next, write the cutlines for the suggested picture. (Note: These are to be used without accompanying stories.)

   A. Firemen hosing down
      Blazing ruins of home
      At 1914 Elm street

Puppet And Friend

Nancy Higgins and her hand puppet teach the kids about street crossings and traffic lights. The kids really get involved in the story and learn as a result of their involvement. - Staff Photos by Jerry Smith

Nap Time

Rest time is one of the few moments during the day when the children slow down. Willy Fisher is sure he isn't going to miss anything

Students Receive Practical Experience At Early Center

It all looks like fun, but it all has a purpose — learning

That's the Early Learning Center at Walters State Community College, the laboratory pre-school which gives practical experience for child care technology majors.

The pre-school program for 3, 4, and 5 year olds is in its seventh year, under the direction of Roy Clary, area supervisor for child care technology. The youngsters enrolled are children of faculty, staff, and students at the college, and of other community residents.

"We emphasize language development and self-concept enhancement," Clary said. "In other words, we want the child to learn to express himself and to feel good about himself."

Two full-time staff teachers direct the daily program of activities, with at least three students assisting. "Our low pupil-teacher ratio of 5-1 is a real plus for our program," Clary said.

The two full-time teachers are Nancy Haggard and Nancy Higgins, with a combined total of 11 years with the Early Learning Center. Each is a graduate of Walter State's Child Care Technology program. Haggard's B.S. degree in early childhood education is from UT, and Higgins' degree is from Carson-Newman.

"We pull our teaching methods from a variety of approaches," Clary explained.

"We think we select the best ideas from many different curricula."

A study unit is selected for each week, and a wide variety of activities emphasize the subject. The children enjoy films, dramatic play, cooking experiences, art and music activities, and field trips. Learning is geared toward acquiring pre-academic skills.

A newsletter for parents tells the study units for the coming weeks and their objectives, as well as activities planned and their purposes.

The center also is proud of its variety of equipment, such as the Language Master, which plays pre-recorded cards on a variety of subjects such as household objects, money, dangerous things, etc. The child can select his subject, operate the machine himself, and even make his own recording on blank cards.

The center is now accepting applications for Fall Quarter. A maximum of 23 children can be enrolled, and must be three years old by September 17, registration date for Fall Quarter. Each child is grouped by ability rather than age, and each child attends the Center every day. Hours are 8:30 a.m.-12 noon. The Center follows the quarter schedule of the college, and tuition is $90 per quarter.

Clary, 581-2121, ext. 282

Close Times

Close moments are not at all uncommon at the Early Learning Center. Student teacher Suzette Stinson shares a secret with Kyla Foutch.

Here Comes The Bear!

Ashley Clary and Mary Beth Rabon are in the middle of a bear hunt that has just reversed direction. Amber Goldberg seems to be more interested in the excitement than in the fictitious bear

Head Chef

Pudding is on the menu for snack time and it seems to be smooth when Shane Hamilton finishes the mixing. Tammy Ogle, another student teacher, is handy if things should get out of hand

Careful Builders

With a construction project underway, Shane Hamilton and Erik Fleming check box car connectors in order to avoid accidents. The kids have some free play periods that are always put to good use

Figure 12-4. Courtesy of the Citizen Tribune, Morristown, Tennessee.

Fire Captain Barney Ballard
Said hot water heater
Apparently exploded
House completely destroyed
By explosion and fire that followed
No one home at the time
Owner is Jay Collins, 35
Neighbor said he is on vacation in Florida

B. Line of cars and trucks
Four blocks long
Waiting to get into
Phil's Independent Service Station
Located at Walnut and Grand streets
Phil selling gasoline at 50 cents a gallon
For today only
The occasion was 50th birthday
Said about half the motorists
Didn't even wish him
A happy birthday

C. Zoo begins new
Adopt an animal program
Object is for person to
Pledge money to feed
Individual animals for a year
First animal up for adoption
Is Olga, 19-year-old walrus
She eats 60 pounds a fish a day
Costs $13,000 annually to feed her
Zoo Director Telford Chester
He hopes many persons will
Adopt her by contributing $15 each
In return they get
Olga T-shirt with her picture on it
And a color picture of Olga
Wearing red bow
Persons interested in adopting her
Should call Zoo office by noon Friday

2. Clip from any newspaper available to you three local stories that might be improved by the use of pictures. Explain what type pictures you would use with each story. Write cutlines to go with pictures. Hand in clippings with cutlines.

3. Select cutlines from five pictures in any newspaper available to you. Rewrite them and turn them in with the originals.

4. Clip from any newspaper available to you a story that is accompanied by a picture or pictures. Study the cutlines as well as the lead of the story. Rewrite the cutline so it does not sound exactly like the lead of the story.

News for Radio and Television

Radio and television news broadcasts are far more sophisticated today than in their infancy, when they were little more than brief summaries of top stories from daily newspapers and the wire services.

While millions listen to radio newscasts daily, it is television with its satellites, miniature cameras, microwave transmission and other electronic techniques that has captured the attention of the public. Vast audiences tune in each night for the major network news programs, and the weekly news magazine format has become increasingly popular on the local level as well as on the networks.

Despite the demands of time, equipment and the listening and viewing habits of the audience that make them different, the basic ingredient—news—remains pretty much the same for broadcast stations as well as newspapers. What makes an event news for the print media generally makes it news for radio and television as well. The major difference between print and broadcast news is a matter of style. Writing for a newspaper is designed for readers. News presented for broadcast is designed for listeners or both listeners and viewers.

SIMILARITIES OF THE MEDIA

No difference exists in the elements that make something news for print or broadcast. News is a basic commodity. Everything that has been learned (and will be learned) on gathering news, analyzing and selecting newsworthy features, the treatment of stories as straight news versus human interest and so on is vital to news for radio and television. All of these apply to any journalistic medium. In its old *Radio Stylebook,* the Associated Press said: "The first essential of being a good radio news writer is being a good news writer." That statement is as true today as it was when it was written years ago.

The differences between the newspaper and broadcasting media range from the average age of the audience to the details of structuring sentences for listening rather than reading. In between are many other factors that influence the newscast writer in his daily assignments.

The average educational age of the radio-television audience is lower than that of newspaper readers, principally because of the many children (and to a lesser degree, persons who do not read because of lack of education or inclination) who are listeners. Because of the large number of child listeners and viewers, radio and television must go an extra mile in observing good taste and avoiding indecencies, indelicacies and indignities (see Chapter 5 on ethics). Radio and particularly television are under constant pressure from a broad range of pressure groups, about the content of their entertainment shows chiefly but also their news shows and advertisements. Newspapers do get some pressure but not nearly the same amount as does the broadcast medium. In most cases, newspapers and radio and television stations try to reflect what they believe to be contemporary community standards.

The "reception rate" of words per minute is considerably faster for radio and television listeners than it is for newspaper readers. This, of course, means that radio and television can pack more information into the same amount of time. Announcers deliver newscasts at a rate ranging from about 125 to about 150 words per minute.

While newscasts can outstrip newspapers in the reception rate of words per minute, newscasting is at a considerable disadvantage because the listener cannot "rehear" a word, phrase or sentence not fully understood. A newspaper reader, on the other hand, can go over a sentence as many times as desired. Such a disadvantage puts an extra burden on writers for radio and television.

Because a typical 30-minute newscast on television would not fill more than two-thirds of the front page of a standard-size American newspaper, the broadcast news writer has to make every single word count if he is to give his listeners and viewers a complete and well-balanced newscast. The complete job of the radio-television reporter in preparing material for a single newscast (corresponding to a single edition of a newspaper) differs in several respects from that of the newspaper reporter. First, the newscast writer must incorporate a large number of different stories in his assignment, but he does not begin to cover any one of these stories as fully as the newspaper because of limitations on the time allotted for news. Many stories have to be told in the newscast in 30 to 45 seconds. Three minutes devoted to a single news item on a newscast is considered a long story. Consequently, the newscast writer's assignment consists of putting together what amounts to a number of leads and lead blocks—in effect, producing an abbreviated version of the principal news appearing in the entire edition of the newspaper.

Another difference, growing out of the first one, lies in the organizational procedure a newscast writer must follow in preparing his material for the announcer or newscaster. The newspaper writer can devote all of his attention to one story at a time, handing in each story as completed for the editors to take over the responsibility of displaying that story in the newspaper. The newscast writer has to assume the "display" function as well as the writing tasks so he must group and organize the different stories in accordance with their news values and their relationship, and also in an appealing pattern. And in television he must coordinate it with the film, stills or other available visuals.

Newscast reporters may take advantage of a format that is not possible for the newspaper reporter. Both the newscast and the newspaper reporter use the interview process, talking with authoritative sources of information or eyewitnesses. The newspaper reporter can do no more than quote these individuals in print, but the newscast reporter can put them on the air. Obviously, this format requires a different type of writing, including summary statements of the news, introduction of individuals to be interviewed and pertinent questions to ask them. An added hazard for the newscast reporter is that his own interviewing techniques are on display. Any inadequacy is immediately apparent to the viewers or listeners.

13a

In preparing copy to be read on radio and television, the newscast writer does several things that are different from the general practices of newspaper writers. Many of those who read the newscasts prefer that copy be tripled-spaced to facilitate reading, whereas newspaper writers double-space their copy unless their plant is equipped with such electronic devices as a scanner, in which case it is triple-spaced to permit ease in making corrections on an electric typewriter. Newspaper reporters have to pay particular attention to the accurate spelling of names (of persons, places and things). While accuracy is a prime concern of broadcast journalists, the newscast writer is more concerned about transmitting the proper pronunciation of names to the announcers who read the written newscasts. In such transmission, newscast writers use the device of inserting the pronunciation within parentheses immediately following unusual names. The correct pronunciation of questionable names is spelled out in easily recognized syllables, with accented syllables usually indicated by capitals—such as Buehler (BEE-ler), Spivey (SPY-vee), Iglehart (EYE-gull-hart) and Smythe (SMEYE-th). In accord with the preferences of those who announce the newscast, the radio-television newswriter also uses punctuation marks freely in his copy. For example, in some cases an announcer desires three periods (. . .) to indicate pauses.

One other difference in preparing copy—employed by only a minority of radio and television stations—is the use of all-capital letters in typing newscasts. The regular news style of capitals and lowercase has proved to be more easily read than the all-capital style; however, some announcers still prefer the all-capital style because they have become accustomed to it in reading all-capital teletype news. But the practice will vary from station to station.

DIFFERENCES IN WRITING NEWSCASTS

Two important writing techniques mark the difference between news prepared for radio and television and that written for newspapers. One is the construction of sentences and the other is the informal language used. Newscast writers tend to write as people speak—informally and with familiar words. The sentences are short, simple and straight to the point, with emphasis upon the ending. Complex words and phrases are avoided because they are more likely to be misunderstood when heard than when read. But the writing should not be so informal that it fails to win listener respect. These and other differences are outlined and illustrated in the sections that follow:

13b Sentence Structure

1. The inverted sentence structure used in newspaper writing is usually not followed in newscast writing, particularly when the source of authority or the attributive phrase is used at the end of the sentence. The strength of the newscast sentence should be at the end rather than the beginning.

   For example, a newspaper reporter might write:

   Fourteen persons were killed today when a bus carrying senior citizens to a picnic plunged off U.S. 411 and overturned in a stream near Pidgeon Forge, state police said.

   The broadcast newsman probably would write:

   State police say that 14 senior citizens were killed in a bus accident near Pidgeon Forge today. They were on their way to a picnic when the bus plunged off U.S. 411 and overturrned in a stream.

   In radio-television news the source of information should be clearly stated at the start.

2. Sentences are shorter than those generally used in newspaper stories, but variety in sentence length is still a desired quality.

3. Only one principal thought ordinarily is given in each newscast sentence. If longer sentences are used, they tend to be compound rather than complex sentences. (One newspaper sentence will sometimes be divided into two newscast sentences.)

4. Verbs and their subjects are kept reasonably close together. This practice rules out the use of long interrupters between verb and subject. Especially avoided are appositives which introduce a second proper name between the subject and verb. Example: "Mary Ross, secretary to Mayor Jackson Turner, died this morning." A listener may not hear the opening words and will believe that the mayor died.

5. Identification of persons quoted is shortened as much as possible and placed before instead of after the names. Sometimes the identification only is used in one sentence and the name in another to break up extraordinarily long combinations of the two.

6. Incomplete sentences, if used only from time to time, are generally permissible in newscasts.

13c Language

A. The question of tense is heavily debated by radio and television newsmen. Many stations insist that, to give the news a sense of immediacy, the present tense rather than the past should be used all the time. Others consistently use the past tense. And some have adopted a practice of dealing with each individual case separately and using the most logical tense. But generally the present tense is most commonly used.

B. To prevent awkward pronunciations by the announcer, such combinations as alliteration in the sequence of words should be avoided. (*Example:* "the professor protested provisions . . .") Also, the use of too many words starting with "s will result in noticeable hissing. (*Example:* "sister should send some . . .").

C. The overworked "quote" and "unquote" are not used today. Newscasters frequently break down long direct quotes into indirect and direct quotes. They use such terms as "As he put it," "We quote his exact words" and "He said—and we quote him. . . ." If long quotes are used, newscast writers frequently insert qualifiers to let the listener know it is a direct quote. They use such terms as "he continued" and "he went on to say" and "he concluded."

D. If possible, numbers should be rounded off, especially large and detailed numbers. The city budget may be $20,568,987 but the broadcast newswriter will make it "20 million 568 thousand dollars." However, if the number must be specific (like "a new tax rate of 3 dollars and 24 cents") it is not rounded off. Newscasters generally try to use figures sparingly and avoid lists of numbers altogether. They never start a sentence with a figure if they can avoid it.

E. Contractions, generally taboo in newspaper stories except in quotations, are acceptable in newscasts but should not be used to extremes. The use of slang should be avoided unless it is germane to the story. Contractions should not be used if they sound awkward on the air.

F. Newscasts are sparing in the use of adjectives. Often adjectives can be turned into nouns, which are much stronger words from the standpoint of listeners, especially if the adjectival pronunciation has a different sound from that of the noun. (*Example:* "Floridian weather descended upon the city today" could be strengthened by "Florida weather.") Adjectives should be avoided if they fall into the category of being relative words in a newscast that is going to be augmented by film or still photos. The pretty blonde to the news writer may not be pretty to many of the viewers, for example, and may be considered sexist by others.

One of the best illustrations of the difference in writing for newspapers and broadcast stations can be found in stories written by the wire services. Following is an illustration of a story written by United Press International for its newspaper clients and for its broadcast clients. Numbers and letters on the far right refer to paragraphs under 13B and 13c of the correction key.

THE NEWSPAPER VERSION	THE BROADCAST VERSION	SEE UNDER
WASHINGTON (UPI)—The Supreme Court today thwarted efforts by news reporters and historians to obtain transcripts of telephone conversations Henry Kissinger had while he was secretary of state and White House national security adviser.	WASHINGTON (UPI)—The Supreme Court ruled today that Henry Kissinger does not have to make public any transcripts of phone conversations he held while he was secretary of state. A news media group wanted the transcripts on grounds they would provide what the group called "the most complete background on the development of American foreign policy" during Kissinger's term.	13b, 13c 2, 3, A
By a 5–2 vote, the justices ruled that the Freedom of Information Act does not authorize Federal courts to order transfer of the notes from the Library of Congress where		

THE NEWSPAPER VERSION

they are stored, to the State Department for release.

The ruling, however, leaves the State Department free to seek return of the documents. It is likely the department will come under pressure to do so.

Today's decision reversed lower court rulings that had cleared the way for public access to at least a portion of the transcripts of conversations Kissinger had while secretary of state.

Those rulings barred public release of transcripts made for Kissinger in his job as national security adviser for Presidents Richard Nixon and Gerald Ford.

Narrowly interpreting the Freedom of Information Act, a law passed by Congress in 1966 to curtail government secrecy, the court said the State Department had not "improperly withheld" the information because it did not have control of it when the requests for release were made.

Justice John Paul Stevens, in dissenting, said the court was confusing "custody" and "control" with "physical possession."

Kissinger served as national security adviser from 1968 to 1975. In 1972 he was appointed as secretary of state, a post he held until January 1977.

Before he left office, Kissinger donated all the transcripts and other papers to the Library of Congress on the condition that they not be made public for 25 years or until five years after his death, whichever comes later.

13d SPECIAL DEVICES IN NEWSCASTS

Since a newscast is made up of a number of stories, it often must "bridge the gap" from one story to another, particularly when the two have common denominators. Transitional phrases of many types can do this effectively. Some examples: "Meanwhile, at City Hall, Mayor John Smith took action to . . ." (which follows a story that resulted in action at City Hall). "Today's hazardous weather conditions had no effect upon Mayor John Smith, who . . ." (which follows a story on weather conditions). "However," "on the other hand" and other such phrases are applicable at times. The best rule for use of transitions is: use them when they seem helpful or logical; do not use them if they seem forced. And do not use such editorialized transition as "Here's an interesting item" or "You will like this story." Datelines are often used not only to identify where each item originates but also to serve as a transition from one story to another with such lines as "And from Washington comes a report that . . ."

As a teaser to attract listeners, a newscast sometimes begins with a series of three or four rapid-fire, headline-style phrases from leading stories of the day. Often these phrases are flashed on the television screen at the same time the announcer is reading them. This is followed, generally, after a commercial break, with the regular form of newscast. (*Example:* "Fire destroys oil refinery . . . Kidnapped tobacco heir found unharmed . . . Congress takes a vacation. . . . These and other stories in one minute after the following announcement.")

Stories in chronological order can be used in newscasts just as they are in newspapers. However, they should be extremely short, and they usually end with a surprise or a punch line.

THE EXTRA JOB OF TELEVISION WRITERS   13e

In discussing writing for radio and television, the use of the spoken word that will catch and hold the interest of the listener has been stressed. Both types of writing are meant for the ear, but the television newscast writer has an added job of blending his words with the action film, still photographs or other visual materials. While television newscasts show the announcer reading the script for much of the time, the use of film and other visuals to help tell the story is growing daily. Film clips, photographs, artwork and signs of all kinds are used. If sound film is used, the writer has the job of blending the newscaster's comments into what is going to be said on the film so there is not an awkward transition. If silent film is used, the writer must bring alive and complete the story with words. A writer should never attempt to write a script for a piece of film without having first seen what is on the film. If the mood of the words does not match the action on the film, the viewer will notice it quickly.

Visuals are as important to a television newscast as pictures are to newspapers. Visuals add materially to effectiveness in reporting the news and viewer appeal of the news program itself. For the viewer a long sequence of an announcer reading news reports will become monotonous, no matter how well written the report or how handsome the announcer. Moreover, television is wasting its most distinctive feature when it fails to make the best possible use of video in presenting the news. But always the words and pictures must be carefully coordinated so that one will not detract from the other.

Planning and selecting the visuals may be part of the responsibilities of the newscast writer, and in many cases he also gathers them with a motion-picture camera (if he serves as both writer and cameraman). As television equipment becomes more sophisticated and more miniaturized, the men and women gathering and writing news for television have much more flexibility in the type of stories they can cover and in the time it takes. However, to get timely and interesting film on the news of his local community, the newscast writer must keep abreast of and often ahead of news developments to schedule the cameraman at locations where significant news may occur, such as meetings of governmental bodies. For fires, accidents and other unpredictable events, the cameramen are dispatched on an emergency basis. But for most news events cameramen fill specific assignments when they report to work just as photographers for newspapers do.

The quality of judgment used in making assignments will determine the extent to which the finished newscast will have visuals on the principal local news stories of the day. Therefore, the news director or newscast writer must weigh the day's story possibilities carefully and then schedule the filming of only the leading events that are particularly adapted to film. Every television newsman should be aware that some events just do not always produce interesting, let alone dramatic, film. This method of operation will require the writer to decline many requests of publicity chairmen who plan such hackneyed events as the mayor's signing another "special day" proclamation, the election of yet another beauty queen and awarding a "best salesman's cup" to a club member or a good-conduct medal to a member of the military.

Even if the news director or writer does a fine job in scheduling the filming of events, the excellence of the finished visuals depends primarily upon the competence of the cameraman—reinforced by the techniques of the film editor. (At many smaller stations the cameraman may edit his own film.) If good images are on the film, a deft and talented film editor can do wonders with it. If it is just poor photographic work, no one can help it. A cameraman should always be conscious of the artistic aspects of his film. Good filming for television is like taking pictures for newspapers (see Chapter 12)—except that the television cameraman should take advantage of motion instead of still pictures by planning sequences involving movement rather than frozen figures.

For example, in a 45-second film clip of a television star arriving in the city, a cameraman may have to get seven or eight specific scenes: the establishing shot, the greeting at the airport, a shot of the crowd, walking away from the plane, fans seeking autographs as she tries to get into the automobile for the trip downtown, her appearance at the opening of her new movie and a final crowd shot. This takes planning on the part of the cameraman. Of course, some of the shots are taken while the actual event is in progress. But he also must plan other shots to give his film story continuity. The cameraman must study each assignment carefully to arrange an interesting and meaningful sequence of pictures.

The newscast writer selects the film for use from the sequences shot by the cameraman, and to these films the writer may want to add still photographs and other visual materials to complete the video portion of the story. All of these extra duties require precise timing to designate cues for the newscast announcer and others who have a part in putting the visuals on the air. The script for television newscasts must give instructions on synchronizing the video with the audio part of the program. Following is a portion of a television newscast script. It deals with a traffic accident:

(Pix # 1 ls cars, 6 seconds)

. . . . A serious two-car accident
today at the corner of Cumberland and 17th Street

(Pix # 2 2 ms cars, 4 secs)

injured the driver of one of the two cars . . . . .
he was

(Pix # 3 ms and cu man, 5 secs)

thrown against the steering wheel and cracked the
windshield with his head. He is 53-year-old Thomas
Stokes of 1157 Pine Bluff Road.

(Pix # 4 ambulance, 5 secs)

Stokes was taken to University Hospital suffering head
and internal injuries. His condition tonight is
serious. The driver of the other car, Gloria Taylor,
21, of 2027 Audena Street,

(Pix # 5 cop and woman, 5 secs)

was not hurt. She said she tried to stop but her
brakes apparently failed. She was cited for
following too close.

(*Note:* ls means long shot; ms means medium shot; cu means closeup.)

Naturally, each television news operation will have its own way of preparing scripts and giving clues to the announcer. Most stations have their own printed script forms.

EXERCISES

(*Note:* If any name in the following exercises requires a pronunciation insert, the student should determine what that pronunciation will be—except in the cases of names of existing places.)

1. Write a newscast version of each of the following opening paragraphs of newspaper stories.

   A. A city policeman has been arrested on charges of taking $4,000 to serve as a lookout in a burglary.

      The arrest of Patrolman Frank Alberts, 38, of the Fernwood District, was announced today at a press conference held by Police Superintendent Joseph Daniels and Prosecuting Attorney Bernard Cornfield.

   B. Maurice Fisher, a former mental patient once found innocent of murder by reason of insanity, was convicted yesterday of the stabbing murder of a Norwood woman.

      Fisher, 56, had pleaded innocent by reason of insanity but the six-man-six-woman jury rejected his plea.

   C. Leaders of the city's Fire Fighters Union called for a strike authorization vote to be held Friday and Saturday.

      Frank Marconi, firemen's union president, said the city's nearly 150 firemen would postpone the vote if Mayor Wilford Stewart would begin "meaningful negotiations" by Friday morning.

   D. GREENEVILLE (Special)—A 48-year-old Greene County man was killed and his wife seriously injured in a head-on collision on Bailetyton Road, about two miles north of here, last night.

Paul Lutterback, Route 2, Afton, was fatally injured when his car struck another vehicle on a curve about 7 p.m., State Trooper John Clark said. Lutterback's wife, Edna, 48, was listed in serious condition in Greeneville Memorial Hospital.

Lillian A. Johnson, 49, Route 6, Greeneville, driver of the other car, is in fair condition in Morristown Medical Center, Clark said.

E. JACKSON (Special)—Two men were arrested on arson charges shortly after a fire destroyed the Foodtown Supermarket here about 1 a.m. today.

Eddie L. Sisks, 19, Route 1, Jackson, and William F. Bailey, 30, of nearby Martin, are being held in city jail pending a preliminary hearing.

Patrolman Bobby Lewis arrested the men after he noticed them in a parked van in an alley about two blocks from the supermarket.

Lewis said he found four empty five-gallon gasoline cans in the van.

Fire Chief Johnnie M. Banner said the building is a total loss. Paul LaRue, manager of the market, was unable to estimate the value of the building and its contents.

2. Write a one-minute newscast (make it about 150 words) from each of the following groups of newspaper stories.

A.

i. WASHINGTON—The Consumer Product Safety Commission today ordered an immediate ban on the children's underwear product called Snuggies.

The ban came after a group of Congressmen pressured the Safety Commission to make children's underwear subject to the same flame retardant regulations as children's sleepwear.

Jan Pope, a member of the commission, admitted that there had been "at least five reported incidents" of Snuggies catching fire. She said the commission has investigated the product and has ordered it off the market because of the "potential danger" it poses.

A spokesman for Snuggies Inc., the New York City based firm that produces the product, denied that the product was a fire hazard. He said the firm would seek an injunction to keep the commission from enforcing the ban.

ii. A psychological study of smokers and nonsmokers indicates occasional smokers have more problems coping with anxiety than do chain smokers or nonsmokers.

However, Braxton Bragg, a graduate student in psychology at the State University who conducted the two-year study for the Tobacco Institute, said his complete findings will not be ready for at least three months.

iii. MANILA, Philippines—U.S. search planes are flying over mountain villages carrying bags of rice as rewards to inhabitants who can direct them to three missing Air Force jets.

For the 12th day, the planes returned to base without finding a trace of the three Skyhawk jet fighters, which disappeared simultaneously while on a training mission from Clark Field, 50 miles north of Manila.

iv. MAZATLAN, Mexico—An American Express tour bus carrying 24 Americans, most of them elderly, collided Thursday with a vegetable truck and plunged into a ravine, killing seven. Nineteen others were injured.

Six of the dead were from Kansas and Missouri, while the seventh was the Mexican driver of the chartered bus, a United States consular officials said.

Mexican police said the average age of the Americans was well over 60.

The oldest was Wendell Parks, 82, of Wichita, who survived the accident.

The American tourists were traveling from Los Mochis, 250 miles north of Mazatlan, to a resort here when the accident occurred.

v. WHITESBURG—A 5-year-old girl, who had been warned not to cross busy U.S. 11-E, was struck by a pickup truck on the two-lane highway and killed.

Venus Mary Bolt, daughter of Mr. and Mrs. Don Bolt, was killed about 5 p.m. yesterday when struck by a truck driven by Eddie Jack Carey, 45, Route 1, Whitesburg.

Sheriff Jess Hamblen said the girl had been running across 11-E from her home to a neighbor's house "all day." He said she had been warned not to cross the highway.

The Bolts live on 11-E, about five miles west of here.

No charges have been placed in the accident.

vi. Jim Long was robbed of his billfold containing about $6,800 by two masked men who entered Long's Tire and Service Center in the Palm Springs Mall about 5 p.m. yesterday.

Long told police one of the men was armed with a sawed-off shotgun, which police found in Long's pickup truck about 10 blocks from the tire store.

"They apparently fled in his pickup and then ditched it," Detective Bill Box said.

Long said he was alone in the store and was getting ready to close up for the day when the men came in and forced him to lie on the floor. They took only his wallet.

B.

i. LAREDO, Tex.—More than 40 pounds of cocaine worth $10 million, discovered in a secret panel of a station wagon crossing the border from Mexico, exceeds last year's total seizure of the drug in South Texas, authorities say.

Red, a 3-year-old German Shepherd, detected the cache in a car driven by Maria Montez, 32, who police said is seven months pregnant. She was charged with possession and importation of cocaine.

This was the third cache of cocaine Red has sniffed out since being assigned to duty at the border crossing six months ago.

Mrs. Montez, who gave a Brownsville address, insisted that she knew nothing about the cocaine.

ii. Federal Bureau of Investigation agents say 20 military rocket launchers found in a garbage dump just off Highway 411 Sunday were disposable, nonexplosive pieces discarded by a military training unit.

The small metal tubs, similar to spent cartridges, were found by Richard Church, owner of the private dump.

"Some one just dumped them on the ground in front of my main gate when I was closed last Sunday," Richter said.

He turned them over to the Sheriff's Department, who asked the FBI to help with the investigation since the launchers bore government markings.

iii. An unidentified man was found dead in his car shortly before noon today, and police believe the wreck occurred during the night.

The car had plunged down an embankment off Northshore Drive near Westland Lane.

Residents reported hearing a crash about 11 p.m. yesterday, but the wreckage was not found until today.

iv. MURPHYSBORO—Gordon Jack Holler, 21, has been indicted by the Jackson County Grand Jury on charges of raping a woman in the city parking garage June 10.

Holler reportedly exposed himself to a policewoman while being questioned about the alleged rape after his arrest June 11. That same day he suffered minor injuries when he allegedly set fire to his clothing in his city jail cell.

He is allegedly wanted for escaping prison in Indiana, where he was serving time on a burglary conviction, detectives said.

v. JACKSBORO—An unidentified man was found dead Saturday morning in the Stinking Creek area of north Campbell County near I-75, Sheriff Charles Scott said.

A deer hunter, who did not want his name made public, found the body of the man believed to be in his late 20s, in a wooded area about one-half mile from the Stinking Creek interchange on I-75.

Sheriff Scott said the man was fully clothed. There were no marks or wounds on his body.

Scott said he would ask a forensic pathologist at the state Crime Laboratory in Morristown to try to determine the cause of death and to try to determine the man's identity.

3. Write a two-minute newscast (about 300 words) from each of the following groups of newspaper stories:

A.

i. MIAMI—For most of the 17 years of his marriage, Robert Wiandt stayed home and did the cooking, washing, shopping and other housekeeping chores, while his wife taught school and continued her education.

Now, after their divorce, he has been awarded $200 a month in alimony for one year.

Dade Circuit Court Judge Stephen Barnette also ruled that Wiandt, 40, will get to visit his two sons, whose custody was awarded to his former wife.

"My sons were crying. They wanted to stay with me," he said after the decision. "I'm going to appeal the case to try to win custody of my boys."

The alimony will be paid by Wiandt's former wife, Sally, a special education teacher at a high school in North Miami Beach.

ii. CLINTON—Three persons were arrested Wednesday for the shooting death of an Anderson County man, including the victim's former wife, who remarried on Tuesday.

Charged with first-degree murder and conspiracy in the death of Liston Fox are: Peggy E. Fox Russell, Fox's wife at the time of his death; her son and Fox's stepson, Darryl Wilson, 23; and Ronald Wilson (no relation), 31, all of Anderson County.

Fox was shot to death on January 19 in his mobile home, located in the Powell Community in Anderson County. He was the operator of Peggy's Place, a tavern in South Clinton.

The three were arrested within two hours after sealed indictments were returned by the Anderson County Grand Jury Wednesday.

iii. A series of break-ins at six local physicians' offices, all located within two blocks of University Hospital, is being investigated by police.

The break-ins were discovered at 3 a.m. today as police investigated an activated burglar alarm in the office of Dr. Shirley Mathis, 439 Battle St.

Other offices burglarized were those of Dr. Homer Howell, Dr. William

York and Dr. Charles Johnson, all in the building at 439 Battle; and Dr. Ronald Henson and Dr. Elvis T. Brown, in a building at 515 Battle.

Police said drugs were the apparent motive for the break-ins, but they said none of the offices contained any controlled drugs. Damages were limited to shattered glass in the doors at each of the offices.

iv. A Washington Heights man charged with the Saturday shooting death of John B. "Junebug" Allen told police he shot Allen because he thought he was going to be killed.

Detective Bruce Amos said Jack Hollins, 33, of Washington Heights, told him he thought "Junebug had a contract on him." Hollins has been charged with murder in the shooting.

Allen, 43, of 1421 Island St., died in St. Thomas Hospital about three hours after Hollins allegedly pumped four bullets into him with a .38-caliber pistol during a dice game behind a gas station at Willow and Elm streets.

v. MOUNT PLEASANT—City voters here rejected 550 to 348 a proposal to change the present commission-manager form of government to a mayor-councilman system.

The referendum drew 44 per cent of the town's registered voters to the polls, City Manager Jay Johnson said.

"We are pleased with the endorsement," Johnson said. "This was a 63 per cent positive vote."

Yesterday's referendum was called after a number of residents, angered by a sewer rate hike and a proposed property tax increase, complained that city leaders had lost touch with their constituents.

Robert Brown, chairman of a Citizens Committee that circulated petitions for the referendum, said he was disappointed in the outcome.

He charged that Johnson, who became city manager three years ago, is "not responsive to the needs of the people."

vi. MEMPHIS—A tanker truck carrying 8,000 gallons of fuel overturned and exploded yesterday near Memphis International Airport, sending clouds of foul-smelling black smoke billowing over Interstate I-24.

The truck driver, Lela Murphy, 36, of West Memphis, Ark., was able to shove a broken windshield out of the truck cab and crawl to safety before her cargo exploded.

She escaped with only a scratch on her forehead.

B.

i. Jeff E. Price, 20, 3807 Johnson St., was shot in the right side at 5:10 p.m. yesterday, police said.

Price was listed in satisfactory condition today at Presbyterian Hospital. He told police a gun he was handling discharged accidentally.

ii. IRONTON, Ohio.—A Juvenile Court judge said yesterday he has not given up on his plan to sentence a couple found guilty of mistreating their son to seven days in jail on rations of bread and water.

"I'm going to do it if the prosecutor says it's legal," Judge Lloyd Burwell said.

The judge announced his intentions last week, when Joe Ed Morgan and Eva Morgan were found guilty of contributing to the negligence of a child. The couple was accused of putting their 4-year-old adopted son in a wire cage at night so he could not get out of bed and find food.

Burwell said the child was malnourished when taken away from the couple last month and sent to a foster home.

The couple is free on bond, pending an appeal.

iii. GALLAY—A blown tire sent a tanker truck loaded with propane into the path of a gasoline-laden tanker, forcing evacuation of about 800 persons and the closing of a one-mile stretch of U.S. 70 for more than eight hours yesterday.

No serious injuries were reported from the 2:50 p.m. accident, which occurred when a westbound tanker with a blown tire skidded into the path of the other vehicle, Lacy Suiter, state Civil Defense operations officer, said.

About 4,000 gallons of gasoline spilled from the truck, bound for Brownsville, but none of the more explosive propane leaked from the other tanker, which was heading for Bryceville, about 35 miles to the southwest.

Suiter ordered the evacuation of a 1½-mile area around the accident site about 30 minutes after state police reported the collision.

iv. CHICAGO—The Illinois Department of Correction is investigating allegations that the inmate uprising last month in the orientation building at the Stateville Correctional Center was set up by some guards to embarrass the new warden at the prison.

Michael P. Lane, assistant director for adult institutions, said reports that guards set up the disturbance have come "from inmates and other sources."

Four guards and four inmate workers were held hostage for more than three hours during the uprising. They were released without injury after negotiations between the 13 inmates who were involved in the disturbance and the prison chaplain, the Rev. Ronald Stewart.

v. HARLAND, Ky.—Thick smoke from an underground fire has blocked efforts to rescue 127 miners trapped in a coal mine 10 miles southwest of here.

Joseph Margiotta, a spokesman for the Diamond Coal Co., said the miners have been stuck for 12 hours after a fire broke out at the 1,200-foot level of the firm's Mary Kay Mine No. 2.

He said 100 miners were believed to be trapped in fairly safe conditions inside shafts below the 400-foot level. He held out little hope for the others, who were closer to the fire zone, which was engulfed by thick black smoke.

Communications links into the mine apparently have been knocked out by the fire.

vi. Students in an Edison High School government class took to the streets with petitions yesterday urging repeal of laws that they said coddle criminals. To their dismay, they found plenty of supporters.

Most of the adults they approached readily signed the document, apparently not realizing it called for the repeal of the Bill of Rights.

Students in Albert Gore's 11th-grade government class spent two hours in the downtown business district yesterday asking for signatures on mock petitions calling for repeal of the first 10 amendments to the U.S. Constitution, the Bill of Rights. They had deleted the title but retained the text of the amendments.

The students found that 74 per cent of the people who took the time to hear their request signed the petition. About 8 per cent of the people recognized the petition's text as the Bill of Rights, Gore said.

The 30 students talked to nearly 250 persons on the street and in stores.

vii. One secretary in the city law department will be suspended for three days without pay and another will be transferred to the police department following a fight at City Hall.

City Law Director Steve Reese Jr. said his secretary Jamie Overton had accepted the three-day suspension following the fight with Lou Ann Otis, also a legal secretary.

Witnesses said Mrs. Overton struck Miss Otis with her fist after the two argued over the temperature in the office.

Reese said no civil service charges would be filed in the case, since Mrs. Overton accepted her suspension, and Miss Otis agreed to the transfer.

However, Elbert Booker, an attorney hired by Miss Otis, said his client would bring assault and battery charges against Mrs. Overton, because "she is always going around trying to punch out one of the other girls."

4. Complete the following exercises:
   A. If you were limited to five of the stories in Exercise 2 (A and B), select the five you would use and write prenewscast teaser headlines on them. Explain why you selected those over other stories.
5. Complete the following exercises:
   A. List television visuals that you would suggest for the stories in Exercise 1.
   B. List visuals that you would suggest for local stories in Exercises 2 and 3.
6. Buy a copy of the daily newspaper that circulates in your city, and with it in hand, watch a local television newscast that same evening. Compare the stories on the front page of the newspaper with the stories used on the television news program.
7. Make a similar comparison between the newspaper and a local news program on a local radio station.
8. Invite the news director of the leading radio station or television station to class for a discussion of local broadcast news operations.

CHAPTER 14

Policy in the News

Anyone who plans a career as a reporter should be aware of this basic fact of journalistic life: Few reporters have the freedom to "do their own thing." Every newspaper has specific policies—ethical, political, social, economic—that guide what news is reported and how it is presented to the public. Sometimes the policies are vague and change with the circumstances of the story, other times they are blatantly obvious.

An astute reporter will learn them as quickly as possible. That does not mean a reporter should not work to change a policy he believes may be detrimental to the credibility of the newspaper. For example, reporters at one Southern newspaper, aware of public animosity, worked for months to convince the editor to stop using the names of rape victims in news stories.

But reporters should remember that a newspaper is a privately owned business enterprise, and it can be operated as the owner sees fit for any purpose he has in mind, including personal financial, political or social gain. It can promote political or other fortunes of the owner or his friends or any special interests. Unfortunately, some do just that. And this is what has led to considerable wide-spread public criticism of the press. However, responsible owners and editors will avoid any blatant misuse of the newspaper for personal reasons.

The newspaper is also—whether it wishes to be or not—a social instrument. It enters thousands of homes and is read by, or indirectly influences, every member of the family. It offers not merely news but information and entertainment. It promotes—whether it intends to or not—social, economic and political philosophies. The newspaper creates the atmosphere in which character is nourished. It is powerful and influential, and colors and infuses the character, ideals and institutions of the individual, the family and the community.

Because of its power and influence the first duty of a newspaper is to keep the people fully, accurately and truthfully informed. As long as it does, a newspaper can promote its own policies without being accused of perverting the news.

DEVICES TO PROMOTE POLICIES

Editorials. The editorial section is generally recognized and accepted as the editor's (or owner's) platform or soap box. He has the same liberty to voice his opinion as the newspaper reader has to reject it.

It is an open question whether a newspaper should adopt strong policies or pursue a middle-of-the-road course—whether to attempt to shape public opinion or merely to reflect it. Some newspapers assume a strong position on one issue and keep hands off in another. Some newspapers take pride in their fighting qualities, but others boast of detached judgment. The answer is largely to be found in the personality of the editor (or owner if he is active as editor or publisher) and in the newspaper's circulation and advertising accounts. Some editors revel in a good fight. It wins them friends as well as enemies—and perhaps a number of journalism awards for courage. Some even crusade at the risk of physical and financial danger. But, for the most part, a newspaper's editorial policy usually is determined on the basis of profitable reader appeal.

One of the most difficult concepts for the public to accept is that a newspaper has the legal right to pursue any policy it pleases as long as it does not violate libel laws. In expressing editorial opinions, responsible newspapers will label them as such and confine them to the editorial page. In addition, they will publish opposing opinion.

While some newspapers still present only their views and opinions, many seek to balance their editorial pages by selecting columns that reflect a broad range of views. On major local issues, the St. Petersburg Times, for example, often publishes its own editorial and in the next column an opposing point of view on the issue. The New York Times actively solicits diverse points of view for its "Op-Ed" page. Frequently its editors will take a particular stand on an issue in an editorial and print, on the opposite page, an article by someone diametrically opposed to the editors' view. Many other newspapers across the nation follow a similar policy. When the Gatlinburg (Tenn.) Press opposed a plan by the city council to purchase a defunct private golf course, it said so in an editorial. And on the same page it permitted members of the council to tell the readers why they should vote in favor of the purchase at an upcoming city referendum.

In cities and towns served by only one newspaper, editors have a special responsibility to make certain they publish a wide range of opinion, not just their own. Unfortunately, it does not always work that way. Some editors take advantage of their position to force only their views on the public and exclude all others—especially opposing views. In other cases, editors are reluctant to adopt an outspoken editorial policy on controversial issues or political candidates. In some cases it may be because an editor simply does not want to face up to the pressure he will receive from various individuals and groups in the community, including some of his big advertisers. In other cases it may simply be that he believes his publication should be nonpartisan and independent, because it is the city's only newspaper. Rather than taking a stand, he may try to remain neutral by printing all the facts on all sides of public issues or campaigns for public office.

However, this general policy does not prevent the editor from making certain exceptions and giving his opinions, pro and con, on questions and candidates when he feels that the public welfare of the community justifies his taking a stand. In such cases he should keep the columns of his newspaper open to those who disagree with his views. Indeed, even newspapers that admittedly have strong partisan or other unneutral general policies should be willing to print news and public statements detrimental to their policies. To do less would destroy the credibility of the paper.

The Front-Page Editorial. Occasionally, to reinforce the importance of an issue, the newspaper will print an editorial on the front page. The practice is generally accepted despite the criticism that it may be a confession of editorial-page weakness. The column should always be labeled as an editorial to let the reader know that he is reading an editorial opinion, not news.

Other Policy Devices. A newspaper's policy is frequently reflected in cartoons as well as editorials. The "visual editorials" play an important part in political campaigns, in particular, but they also are used most effectively to support other editorial points of view. A cartoon makes no pretense of being unbiased, as a general rule. It is frequently a frank and open criticism of an antagonist and in support of a definite policy. Patrick Oliphant, the Pulitzer Prize-winning cartoonist, told an interviewer that for him there "are no sacred cows . . . no forbidden areas . . . If you are going to be in favor of something, you might as well not be a cartoonist."

Figure 14-1. When President Carter announced plans to draft both men and women, Charles Daniel, prizewinning cartoonist for the Knoxville (Tenn.) Journal, produced this amusing editorial cartoon. He used the classic recruiting poster idea and added a touch of Southern dialect. Courtesy of the Knoxville Journal, Knoxville, Tenn.

Political cartoons were introduced in the American press by Thomas Nast in the mid-1800s and have since developed into a fine art form. Many newspapers that cannot afford their own cartoonists regularly buy the work of major cartoonists, such as Oliphant, from feature syndicates. Lack of a cartoonist to support editorials of a purely local nature can sometimes handicap an editorial campaign. However, many editors employ photographs to help support editorials dealing with numerous local problems ranging from hazardous traffic conditions to slum housing.

In addition, the columnists and other by-line writers may freely express opinions, and local citizens may be invited to contribute letters or articles to strengthen a campaign or crusade. Sometimes a newspaper adopts a slogan that promotes a policy.

The Newspaper Platform. Some of a newspaper's policies may be long-range programs. Others have immediate objectives. The policies of a Democratic, Republican or Labor newspaper at election time may be predictable but their response to other issues will not be. In fact, newspapers that oppose each other politically often may support the same local programs on new schools, more city recreation areas, improved street lights, higher salaries for city policemen and a host of other issues dealing with civic improvement. Many newspapers begin each year with a list of civic goals at the top of their editorial page and then campaign all year long to bring them about. All of its policies taken together, including its more permanent attitudes toward such issues as politics, constitute the newspaper's platform. It has a right to work to achieve that platform. And so long as it is a constructive platform, the newspaper's policy is a powerful influence for the common good. In promoting such policy, the editorial, the cartoon, the signed article and the slogan are legitimate devices beyond question. However, a newspaper that permits its policies to influence the writing and display of the news fails in its responsibility to its community and to the journalism profession as a whole.

"SLANTING" THE POLICY STORY   14a

The temptation is always present for a newspaper engaged in vigorous promotion of a policy to utilize other resources at its command. Its most potent other resource, of course, is the news column.

Several methods have been used to promote a policy through the news:

1. Featuring (and somewhat overplaying) an event in line with the newspaper's policy. This may be done with a large headline, a prominent position in the newspaper and a detailed account of the event. For example, a newspaper campaigning for safe driving may put every accident—major or minor—on the front page with large headlines, saying in substance, "I told you so."

2. Ignoring or "playing down" events opposed to the newspaper's objectives. If mentioned at all, such events may be hidden under small headlines on an inside page or "buried" at the end of a story. If a newspaper opposes a candidate for sheriff, for example, it may give comparatively

little space in which to present his side of the issues. And if he is an incumbent, the newspaper may suddenly discover, about two weeks before election time, that the county is riddled with vice and corruption. Apparently it does not expect its readers to ask why the vice and corruption had not been exposed months or even years before. Such transparent attempts to support a candidate by misleading readers can badly damage a newspaper's credibility.

3. Deliberately writing the news to emphasize certain points in a story while omitting others, thus interpreting an event so that it will best suit the newspaper's policy. Sometimes, unfortunately, facts themselves may be distorted or falsified. For example, suppose a speaker should say: "The working man does not deserve unemployment insurance. He deserves employment insurance, and it is the duty of the employer to see that he gets it." If, to make the speaker look bad, a reporter should play up the first sentence and purposely ignore the second, one would conclude that the speaker is against labor. Good reporting and honest newspaper policy would condemn such a purposely colored account.

4. Editorializing in the news. For example, if a newspaper favors a reduction in the tax rate, it may always refer to the existing *high* tax rate, taking for granted that everyone agrees the rate is high. The newspaper's opinions may be injected throughout the story in this manner. A review of some of the newspaper stories written about the increases in second-class postal rates would serve to illustrate this point extremely well.

5. Writing special stories deliberately designed to support the newspaper's policy. For example, the newspaper can always find prominent local persons or special-interest groups who agree with a given policy. These persons are interviewed, and their statements prominently displayed in the newspaper. Persons against the policy are not usually interviewed. Another example: If a newspaper wants to force an investigation of conditions at the jail, a local mental hospital or a nursing home, it might have a reporter get himself locked up in the jail, committed to the hospital or hired at the nursing home to expose the "disgraceful" conditions that exist.

JUSTIFICATION OF POLICIES IN NEWS STORIES

What are the justifications—if any—for promoting a policy by means of the news? Are all of these and other such devices to be condemned? Obviously so, if their intent is to deceive. Obviously so, if their use prevents the complete, accurate and truthful presentation of the news. Under certain circumstances, however, there is some excuse—if not justification—for the influence of policy on the news.

Subjectivity. Few readers, but all editors, know that the process of gathering and writing news is a subjective one despite all the efforts to make it objective. The selection of assignments, the reporters picked to cover them and their approaches to handling the stories are based on a series of value judgments. It is a cliché in the news business that seven reporters sent to cover the same speech probably will produce seven entirely different interpretations of that speech.

While this may be an overstatement, it is based upon sound observation. Theoretically, a speech has but one interpretation—that is, what the speaker means. Actually, every person in the audience may get a different impression of the speaker's message, including the reporter. The reporter summarizes the speech as it impresses him, using quotations from the speaker to support his interpretation. He may have vast experience covering speeches, but even then he may give a speech a slant quite different from that the speaker had intended. Yet he may be reporting the facts as he sees and hears them.

The complete objectivity necessary to perfect reporting is scarcely to be achieved by the human being. All facts reported to newspaper readers must pass through the minds of the reporter. He observes events and understands facts against the screen of his past experience and through the film of his own emotions. He is not a perfect mirror or a nonrefractory lens. This human frailty plagues every reporter and his newspaper. But a reporter must not use this as an excuse for faulty or dishonest work.

Self-censorship. Most newspapers practice self-censorship. Often this is dictated by what the editor considers good taste and what he believes are the contemporary community standards. While it is true that standards tend to grow more liberal, generally most editors make a serious effort not to offend the sensibilities of their readers. The obscene language of the law court, the gruesome details of a brutal murder, the "inside" story behind a politician's downfall or the "real dope" about the divorce of a prominent citizen may be censored from the story. The reader may not be given either all the information about events reported or reports on all events. The newspaper to this extent fails to report the news fully.

Just how far this censorship in behalf of "decency" should go is debatable. Often, it may not be the public's taste as much as the editor's that generates the censorship. An Ohio editor was dismissed for allowing an infamous four-letter word to remain in a quote by a man known for the use of that type language despite the fact that only a handful of readers complained. The publisher, however, felt the use of the word was bad for the image of his paper and dismissed the editor. In practicing self-censorship, a newspaper must take care that it does not use this power in behalf of a special interest or a special cause. If it does, its policy reporting will be indefensible.

The Moral Purpose. Another excuse for faulty reporting and for allowing policy to influence the news may be the intention to do good. A story may be warped to point a moral—to teach a lesson. Many feature stories become nearly fiction in the process of passing from the scene of action, through the reporter's mind aglow with an honest (or possibly dishonest) emotion, to reach the printed page. Literary license is taken with the facts in many stories to stir readers. Sometimes it may be as "innocent" as the ever-recurring faithful dog story in which a dog allegedly saved his young master from drowning. In actual fact, the dog may have plunged in only when his master staggered into shallow water. Yet many reporters could not resist the temptation to make a hero of the dog. Photographers rush to the home for the traditional boy-dog picture. Is no harm done? And does it make a good story? Maybe. But is it true? After all, the function of the newspaper is to present the news fully, accurately and truthfully, and this type story is neither accurate nor truthful.

There is another hazard in stretching fact for a so-called moral purpose. Sometimes the well-meaning story can backfire. In one case out of the books on libel, a newspaper was found guilty of libeling a family it had tried to help. The father was out of work and the family without much food when the youngest child died. In an effort to help the family, the newspaper printed a sad and touching story of the family's misfortunes, including a statement that the child would have to be buried in a pauper's grave alongside the remains of drunks and derelicts. In the rush of emotion and a desire to move the readers to help the family, the reporter overstated the family's plight. The family sued, charging that it had been held up to ridicule through no fault of its own. The jury agreed and found the paper guilty of libel.

Dilemma in Weighing Stories. Another excuse for playing up a story in behalf of a policy may be found in an occasional dilemma. When two stories are of approximately equal value, it is almost too much to expect a city editor to "bury" the policy story. It is easy for the whole editorial staff to value the policy stories highly. If the newspaper is campaigning for a bond issue, every item bearing upon the need for the bond issue may appear to be important. In weighing stories that have a bearing on newspaper policies, the newspaper cannot recuse itself like a judge whose son is to be tried for murder. Must it not either favor its own child or commit the equal error of "leaning over backward"? Here again the reporter and the staff need almost superhuman objectivity to present the news fully, accurately and truthfully.

A problem sometimes arises when an editor, seeking to please the owner or publisher, gives special treatment to certain stories he thinks will please the publisher. Such a story may not have any real news value that given day, yet it may be prominently displayed, perhaps even on page one. Often organizations deliberately name publishers to their boards in an attempt to gain favorable treatment in the newspaper. And they are quite successful, because many editors would not risk playing down a story they believe might be a "sacred cow" of the publisher.

COMPLETE REPORTING

In pursuing a policy, the newspaper and the reporter have an opportunity to serve the community by placing emphasis on fullness, accuracy and honesty in reporting. A policy to promote worthy causes may indeed be noble. But a newspaper that vigorously promotes the local community chest fund drive year after year but never carefully checks how much of that money goes for campaign overhead and how much to really help the people of the community is not reporting fully, accurately and honestly.

The issues reported in the press are too commonly the plain and unvarnished facts. They lack the intelligible background that an enterprising reporter would gather from library investigations, from studies of experiences of other communities and from other sources of information. Every newsman should remind himself constantly that not all newsworthy material is to be collected on the regular beats. The encyclopedia, librarian, school teacher, scientific laboratories are rich in background material outside the established boundaries of news beats. The reporter can offer a service to his community of a rare order of usefulness if he will utilize the cultural tools his community offers. In many cases the average citizen lacks the time and ability to use these tools, but in the hands of an enterprising reporter they can help him report not only accurately and truthfully but also with the fullness needed by a people trying to manage their own processes of government.

EXERCISES

1. Assume you are working for a newspaper that is supporting a public referendum to increase local sales taxes to raise funds for the public schools. Make a list of the kinds of stories you would write to help convince the public to vote in favor of the tax increase.

2. Search newspapers that are available to you for examples of stories that promote a particular policy of the newspaper (do not include editorials). Clip the examples and paste them on separate sheets of paper. Make marginal notes and point out material in them that specifically relates to the newspaper's policy.

3. Study the locally written editorials in any newspaper available to you the past month to determine if you can identify the newspaper's particular policy on the subjects covered in the editorials.

4. On those same editorial pages count the number of letters to the editor and guest columns that are printed opposing the editorial stand of the newspaper.

5. In every community there are many rumors which the editor does and does not allow to be printed in the newspaper. Collect as many of those rumors as you can. Then interview the local editor and ask his response to those rumors. Also ask him how he goes about supporting the newspaper's policies in the news columns as opposed to editorials. Write a report on that interview.

WRITING THE GENERAL STORY TYPES

PART IV

Reporters and editors have a tendency to label stories by subject—crime, politics, religion, sports and so on. It is a convenient form of internal shorthand for the newspaper's staff, and it generally provides a handy guide to what department will handle a story. However, three types are general in nature because they are not confined to a particular subject.

Personals and briefs; speeches, publications and interviews; and meetings and occasions—all are different types from the standpoint of categories. But all of them are used in connection with every subject covered by a newspaper.

It is important that these general types be considered before the reporter studies the various "simple" and "complex" stories dealing with specific subjects.

Personals and Briefs

The smallest and seemingly least significant of all news stories is the personal item or brief. These short stories, often no more than a sentence or two, can be found in almost every newspaper. As a rule, metropolitan newspapers carry briefs or personal items on only the most prominent persons. In essence, they are nothing more than a glorified personal, not unlike the short stories about the activities of local folks carried by thousands of community newspapers.

Often in the community newspapers the personal items are used as separate stories with individual headlines and may be scattered through the regular news sections of the paper. But they also may be used to fill whole columns, as in the family living or lifestyle sections of many newspapers. Sometimes they are used in the personal column written by the editor or one of the staff members. Their use and placement is unlimited.

They serve several important purposes: They provide information on activities of various citizens as well as social, civic and religious groups in the community, and they can be used to facilitate makeup by filling in small spaces left after longer stories are placed on pages. Even when serving this last purpose, they should be written with the same care and effort that go into the main story each day. A mistake in a name or an address or a fact in a personal item is just as serious as a similar mistake in any page-one story.

Personals and briefs are arbitrarily classified here as a separate story type. Actually, they are a type only in the sense that they emphasize personalities and are short, perhaps relatively unimportant in news value that day in relation to the news value of the page-one stories. In subject matter, they range the entire spectrum of human activity. All of the subject-matter story types discussed more fully in later chapters are represented among them. They are considered to be merely elementary stories, which the beginning reporter is often assigned to write. However, every seasoned reporter knows their value and regularly collects them as he covers his beat or other assignments.

PERSONALS

Names make news—it is a newspaper cliché, but it is also true. And they do not always have to be prominent names. Newspapers have always recognized the news value of names of quite ordinary persons. The names of visitors, guests, committee members, those sponsoring or attending dinners, banquets, conventions and so on are usually listed by newspapers as fully as space permits. Lack of space, not failure to recognize the essential news value of names, excludes many of these smaller items from newspapers in larger cities. However, a number of metropolitan newspapers use them as fillers in place of buying filler material from the news syndicates.

Announcements of trips, visitors, parties, newcomers and a large assortment of relatively minor events that take place in any community are considered personals. The lifestyle pages or family pages (discussed in Chapter 27) often use many such items, but other personals are used throughout the paper as one-two- and three-paragraph stories with headlines.

News Value. It is often difficult to classify personal items by the standard tests for news value—disaster, progress, conflict and so forth. Although a careful study of them will show that in a minor way they may fall into these categories. Mrs. Nancy Parker goes to the hospital, and that might border on disaster for her family. David Thomas is made a first-class petty officer in the navy, and that suggests progress. If these items were of greater consequence, they would be expanded into longer stories—stories to be classified as illness, or death or business. They are very seldom novelties. They contain little human interest of an emotional or dramatic nature. They might represent borderline eminence—that is, if they were about a reasonably well-known local person.

Why run them? Personals, as a class of story, would seem to be a composite of all the news values. Individually, they may be of little consequence except to the persons immediately involved, yet collectively they record the ebb and flow of life in any community on a very fundamental level. They contain virtually all human interests—like gossip—birth, death, illness, conflict and the rest. They give the readers of any newspaper a daily look at the activities of their fellow citizens—not just the prominent ones. And they are extremely well read.

The most common characteristic of most personals is that they are quite local in nature. If a member of a local social club is planning an event—plant sale, card party or fashion show—it is local news of a personal type. A similar event in a community 50 miles away would mean nothing. The personal, then, is a standard item in the columns of newspapers in smaller communities. It is usually unnecessary to belong to an organization or take part in a major news event to be mentioned in the news columns of a small-town newspaper—daily or weekly. A shopping trip to a nearby city or the purchase of a new tractor may be sufficient for one to get his name in the local newspaper in many small communities. In the large city dailies the personal is somewhat confined to the more or less prominent persons and to the activities of local groups and clubs and the personalities of so-called formal society. Rural or urban, however, the newspapers consider the personal items as an important reader-interest and circulation builder.

Sources of Personals. Most personals are telephoned, mailed or brought to the newspaper office by interested persons. Hostesses report their party plans, theme and guest list. Mothers announce the school or vacation plans for their children. Families report on out-of-town visitors. Dinners, parties and other social events are similarly brought to the society or family editor of the paper. And the mail brings a steady stream of press releases from vacation hotels, convention centers and other tourist attractions reporting the local persons who visited there recently. Every regular beat yields personals and briefs to the alert reporter. Public officials and employees go on business trips and vacations. They have children going off to school, babies at home. Behind the public front of every person on every beat are many personal items of interest. Hobbies, along with other recreation and sports activities, are fertile fields for personals. And on a rare occasion a personal item can lead to an even bigger story. The social activities and travels of a Midwestern state official some years ago piqued the interest of a beat reporter, who eventually discovered that the official had stolen $14 million from the state.

Writing the Personals. The personal should be written as a straight-news **15a** story. It should have a well-written lead and contain all the necessary information to make the story complete. The lead requires:

1. The 5 W's. These are essential in all stories, of course, though some of them may be implied only in the lead.
2. Identification of the person or persons mentioned. If a long list of persons is given (for example, the names of new club members) do not try to use them all in the lead. Write a more general lead and include the names in the second paragraph along with their identification. But if the item reports the activities of only one or two individuals, each should be identified. Where possible, a descriptive identity should be included to intensify reader interest. The descriptive identity, lacking in the first of the following personals, is italicized in the second item.

> Mrs. Gaylord Hampton, 1202 Briarcliff Ave., is making a month-long auto trip through the Southwest.

> Mrs. Gaylord Hampton, 1202 Briarcliff Ave., *whose Southern cookbook was published in June,* is making a month-long motor trip through the Southwest. *She will collect recipes for a Chicano cookbook.)*

Here's how to handle a personal with a long list of names:

> Eight members of the Clay County Garden Club will exhibit floral arrangements in the Piedmont Flower Show in Raleigh next month.
> They are: (List the club members and their addresses. If descriptions of the floral arrangements are available, include them. But do not include any if you cannot include all of them.)

Stressing an Interesting Feature. Reporters should always look for interesting **15b** features when writing personals and not be satisfied to use only the basic 5 W's. To say that "The Rev. Thomas O'Neal will leave for Rome Friday" is interesting to friends and members of his church. But what is he planning to do in Rome? Is he just on vacation? Is he attending a church meeting? Will he be going to school there? The minister probably would be willing to answer a few questions and the reporter may find an interesting feature somewhere.

Here is an example of how a personal item might be improved by adding a few details:

Mrs. Ray Rice is recuperating from a broken ankle at her Morgan Street home.

Mrs. Ray Rice, who broke her left ankle in a fall while hiking last week, is completing her new book on "The Big Muddy River" while recuperating. The author, who has written books on four other Illinois rivers, is at her Morgan Street home.

15c   In writing a personal, every effort should be made to avoid referring to persons by such terms as "widely known," "popular" and "beloved." (In newspaper offices, these are called "puffs.") This not only is poor writing but it also is editorializing and should not be permitted in personals or briefs just as it should not be permitted in any straight news story.

BRIEFS

It is often difficult to distinguish between a personal and a brief. Perhaps the best distinction between them is that briefs generally do not pertain to persons. The change in city library hours, the post office's holiday schedule, dates for obtaining new auto licenses, announcements of minor fund-raising events and dozens of other short, but newsworthy, items would be classified as briefs.

15d   Briefs are usually one- or two-paragraph stories dealing with incidents or occasions with broad or limited appeal. Naturally, the wider the appeal —perhaps the closing of public buildings for a holiday—the more prominently they will be displayed in a newspaper. Briefs may be rewrites from other papers or new stories picked up by beat reporters, or phoned in by interested persons. They are used because they are news, and they may be grouped together in a "news briefs" column or used as fillers throughout the paper.

It is difficult to establish a dividing line between a brief and a longer, more important story. An event worthy of no more than two paragraphs in some newspapers may be "blown up," with the inclusion of more details, to five or six paragraphs in other newspapers. The size of the community and its newspaper, the availability of local news and the interest of the readers all are factors which must be considered by the reporter. A story's relative significance—the proportion of readers it will interest—is the major space-measuring device for the reporter.

Like a personal, a brief is obviously a single-feature story—and hardly more than a lead at that. The 5 W's, with the proper play given to the most important W, usually compose the whole story. Further explanation of one or more of the W's may call for a second paragraph.

15e   Careless reporting, notably the lack of an inquiring attitude, sometimes makes long stories into briefs. If the beginning reporter becomes too "brief" conscious, feeling that every story should be told in two paragraphs, he may fail to ask the kinds of questions that could develop a possible page-one story. On the other hand, insignificant news events should not purposely be blown up or overplayed.

FILLERS

Every makeup editor finds himself faced with awkward and often tiny spaces at the ends of columns and over advertisements which must be filled. Even though briefs and personals are often used in these cases, most newspapers have on hand a ready supply of two-, three-, four- or five-line fillers to "plug" these holes. These fillers are usually small bits of information, not necessarily news, and their chief purpose is to fill a small space. Most are used without a headline.

Fillers come from a variety of sources, but most commonly they are purchased from news feature services (syndicates). However, a number of organizations, such as the National Geographic Society, distribute them free to publications. Other special-interest groups also send them along with their press kits or publicity releases. A number of newspapers develop their own from almanacs, government reports and census data, history books and encyclopedias. They are selected with some care to present unusual facts or "fascinating" information or descriptive items highlighting the local scene.

Some examples:

Vassar College for Women opened in Poughkeepsie, N.Y., in 1865.

More than half of all automobile trips in the United States cover five miles or less.

The smallest state in the United States is Rhode Island, which covers only 1,214 square miles.

Mary Queen of Scots took refuge in England on May 16, 1568.

GIVE TO THE MILK FUND

REMEMBER THE NEEDIEST

THE YMCA IS A UNITED WAY AGENCY

Other newspapers use the space at the end of columns to promote the newspaper and some of its services. Some examples:

Subscribe to the Manchester Enterprise—Phone 598-2319

Courier-News Classifieds Pay Off

Your Money
Saturday in Business Day
The New York Times

EXERCISES

1. From any daily or weekly newspaper available to you, clip a dozen personals and briefs and make sample news analyses.

   Note: In making these and other assigned analyses of news-story types, follow the form illustrated in the "sample news analysis," page 38.

2. Clip from any daily or weekly newspaper available to you two or three examples of columns written by country or rural correspondents. Paste them on separate sheets of paper and circle every example of overwriting by the use of such clichés as "beloved" and "a good time was had by all" and so on.

3. The briefs and personals below are faulty. On a separate sheet of paper, answer the following questions about each: (a) What additional questions would you ask in an attempt to get an adequate, interesting story? (b) What statements would you eliminate from the story as it is written, and why?

   A. Dora Doyle gave a farewell dinner party for Thomas and Wanda Martin Thursday night.

   B. Mae Burns spent last week in Indiana with her devoted brother, Jarmon Davidson, who is ill and in a Louisville Hospital. We wish Jarmon a speedy recovery.

   C. Della Gay was in Hyden Wednesday for X-rays.

   D. The Senior Citizens Club of Oakdale will meet at 10 a.m. Tuesday at the Mental Health Center.

   E. The Spanish Fort Estates Garden Club would like to invite all residents of the Estates and Lee Circle to coffee on Thursday from 10 a.m. until noon. Everyone come, join in and bring a neighbor.

4. Write personals or briefs from the following notes:

   A. Descendants of W. C. Jones of Madison County
      Planning first family reunion
      Saturday starting at 11 a.m.
      In Sevierville City Park
      In case of rain
      Will be in City Cultural Center
      All relatives urged to come and bring dinner
      Call 577-8052 or 573-6120
      For more information
      Jones was County Judge for 40 years
         (*Source:* Mrs. Minnie Flynn and Mrs. Luther Jones)

   B. Childbirth Education Association
      To give series of preparation classes
      For expectant couples
      To begin at 7 p.m. Tuesday
      Room 193 at First United Presbyterian Church
      Instructor will be Ann Hensley
      Couples requested to preregister
      Call 974-5155 or 584-5828
         (*Source:* Mrs. Stan Yazdik and Mrs. David Garcia)

   C. Billy Ray Comer
      Spent 10 days with parents
      Mr. and Mrs. John B. Comer
      Who live at 1220 Elm St.
      Returned to Austin, Texas, Sunday
      He is a senior at University of Texas
      On Longhorn football team

Plays tackle
Same position he played
At Jeff Davis High here
He was All-State twice
Father is former "Boomer" Comer
Who led Jeff Davis Rebels
To State Championship in football
Three years in a row

D. Bardstown Jogging Club
To meet at 9:30 a.m. on Wednesday
Courthouse Square
To jog down old road to Oliver Springs
For more information
Call Alice Nuddle, chairperson, 837-9046

E. Athens Recreation Department
Square dancing instructions
8 to 10 p.m. Tuesday and Thursday
In ballroom, Civic Center
No charge for instructions
Teachers will be members of
The Dancing Squares Club
Mike Hoose from Jefferson City
Will be the caller
Sign up at the door
Or call 875-9807

5. Using material available to you in the college or city library or through the local chamber of commerce, write a half dozen fillers containing information about your city.

CHAPTER 16

Speeches, Publications, Interviews

A quick analysis of the news stories in any edition of a newspaper would show that a large number grew out of the spoken or written word. They may have come from a speech, a press conference, an interview or an article in a professional journal or magazine. Even though there may be a vast difference in the subject matter, a careful review of the stories will show that the techniques used in writing them are very much alike.

The principal characteristic common to writing all of them is in the treatment of quotations. Every speech, publication and interview is a collection of direct or indirect quotations from the speaker, writer or the person interviewed. And the work of the reporter is much the same in presenting any of the three in proper news-story form.

SPEECHES

Speech stories are a staple in American newspapers. Yet many of them are poorly written because the reporter does not force himself to be interested in the speech and does not listen carefully. Covering a speech is one of the most exacting assignments a reporter can be given. It is an easy job to paraphrase a speech—many writers do and turn out dull stories. But to report a speech through the use of direct quotations, reducing the speaker's 7,500 words to 300 and still presenting an accurate report of what he said, is much harder. Yet every speech presents a chance to show individuality, resourcefulness and thoroughness.

All speeches—whether formal addresses on special occasions or impromptu remarks during an unstructured gathering—are handled very much alike. Three elements are considered:

1. The speaker.
2. The audience.
3. The speech.

A fourth consideration is the possible interpretation that any of the three elements may need. The proportion of the story to be devoted to each element varies with the comparative importance of each, but no speech story is complete without all three. Generally, in speech stories the emphasis should be put on what is said.

The speaker should be properly identified in the lead. Sometimes this can be **16a** done with a title or a short sentence. If more identification is needed, it can be in the body of the story. This is an amplification of the basic principle of identifying persons named in the news. The reader needs to know who the speaker is and why his statements are worth quoting. Even a description of the speaker, his distinctive characteristics and his manner of emphasizing certain points, is sometimes woven into the story to give it more color. But this type material should not be used in an attempt to hold the speaker up to ridicule.

The audience also should be described. How many were there? Who were **16b** they? Why did they meet? The reporter looks over the crowd, talks with the leaders and reads any available program carefully to help answer these questions. He need not give names of persons present, unless it would be of interest to the reader to know the names of a few of the more prominent ones, but he should tell whether they are bankers, teachers, taxpayers or miners. These facts are, of course, implied at regular meetings of civic clubs and similar organizations, when nothing more than the name of the organization is required. Audience reaction is also frequently worth noting.

The speech is usually the most important of the three elements. "What did **16c** the speaker say?" is logically the first question one asks about a speech. If what is said has interest, the story becomes more than a drab report of another dreary talk.

Some interpretation of one or more of these three elements may be needed. Perhaps the audience is not as representative as it appears for the occasion. Applause may be staged by partisan supporters of the speaker. Perhaps the speaker has affiliations or a record that should be presented to clarify his significance. Perhaps the speech content should be related to larger national movements, editorial campaigns or other programs. Frequently the speech will have significance in local issues. For example, if the speech concerns public recreation and if the community is campaigning for a national park, a story ignoring this relationship would be inadequate and noninterpretative. Interpretation, however, must avoid editorializing. The interpretative reporter is not authorized to express opinion. Interpretation must be merely the presentation of pertinent facts to give the reader a clearer picture.

Getting the Speaker's Words. If the reporter is able to obtain a written copy **16d** of the speech, his job is much easier. Nevertheless, he attends important occasions to gather other facts—audience reaction, ad lib statements, questions from the floor, names of prominent persons in attendance and so forth. Without the advance copy, he must attend and take down a "running story." He does not attempt stenographic notes. He jots down only the important statements and turning points, sometimes summarizing an argument or point made by the speaker, other times quoting directly. He should make every effort to place only the speaker's exact words within quotation marks, particularly in matters that may be controversial. Because direct quotations tend to add emphasis, the reporter should avoid quoting routine, obvious or minor points from speeches. Accurate paraphrasing is usually sufficient to convey the less important elements of a speech. However, a reporter should take care not to paraphrase too much. He should use direct quotes liberally throughout his speech story. Under no circumstances should he turn in a speech story with few or no direct quotes.

In organizing the material of a speech story, the reporter should look for the theme, the logical divisions and unusual or provocative quotes, for a speech may have one or several features just as any other type story. A rambling speech is no excuse for a rambling story. A good speech has a principal theme plus supporting arguments. However, the reporter does not have the responsibility of playing up the theme or of summarizing the entire speech. He is responsible to his readers only for an accurate and newsworthy story. He may play up what he selects as the feature with the most reader appeal, and he may report only the parts of the speech he feels are of interest to the general public. However, in so doing, if he misses newsworthy points and either muffs or garbles the story, this is poor reporting.

16e THE SPEECH STORY LEAD

The lead should feature the most important point the speaker made. Exceptions are (a) if the speaker is very prominent, his name may come first; (b) if the occasion itself is important or embraces several speeches, this may be featured; (c) the entire program may be keynoted or have a central theme. The following examples illustrate these three exceptions:

a. Mother Teresa, Calcutta's "Saint of the Gutters," opened the United Nations' Conference on World Hunger today.

The Nobel Peace Prize winner told delegates from 130 nations . . .

b. Delegates from 130 nations today heard Mother Teresa Calcutta's "Saint of the Gutters," describe how millions of people are starving each year.

The Nobel Peace Prize winner spoke at the opening session of the United Nations' Conference on World Hunger today.

c. The responsibility of the rich nations to help feed the world's starving masses was the theme of the speakers who took part in the opening of the United Nations' Conference on Hunger today.

These exceptions, however, are not strictly speech leads. They are leads for meetings and conventions. They bracket several speeches and lay the groundwork for speeches to follow. They should be used sparingly.

The speech lead and story will be considered here as applying to a single speech as the sole important, or most important, element to be reported. To include this story along with other speeches and debates in a larger convention story will not alter principles in the following paragraphs.

The speech lead will feature the most newsworthy element of the speech. It will do so either by summarizing the entire speech or by presenting the most important single element or statement. In this sense it follows precisely the methods of the several-feature lead. In either the summary or the single-element lead, the reporter can use direct quotations, indirect quotations or interpretation. Following are examples of speech leads:

"Computers have made embezzlement a high stakes crime," Donald Parker, chairman of the State Crime Commission, said today.

"The average embezzler nets $19,000, but those using computers net around $450,000," he told state bankers at a computer crime conference here.

Cigarette smoking may decrease your sexual desire, a University of Louisville researcher told members of the Southern Medical association today.

"Each puff of smoke inhaled into the lungs reduces a person's oxygen supply," Dr. Ibrahim B. Sned said. "And with less oxygen there is less testosterone in the male and less estrogen in the female. That means less sexual desire."

Functional illiteracy is one of the major causes of the staggering youth unemployment problem in the nation, delegates to the State Teachers Association's convention here were told last night.

"The inability to read, write or do simple math . . ."

"Sunday sales have a destructive and demoralizing effect on family life and the home," Joseph Forkshaw III, vice-president of Save Our Sundays, told a conference on Sunday closing laws here last night.

"Everyone should get up in the morning and look in the mirror and say, 'Do I really want Sunday sales?' " Forkshaw said . . .

THE BODY OF THE SPEECH STORY

Throughout the body of the speech story, direct quotations, indirect quotations and interpretative summaries of the speech should be interspersed. (See discussion of "Direct Quotations" in Chapter 9.)

"Quote-Summary-Quote Story." Through years of handling speeches (and publications, interviews and similar assignments), newspapermen have developed a popular form for stories containing a large number of direct quotes. Considered as a "quote-summary-quote" story, it can best be described by an example and a diagram:

16f

THE DIAGRAM	THE WRITTEN STORY
Lead Summarizes All; Features or a Salient Feature; (This example summarizes a salient feature) ⬚1	Gov. Arthur Lane labeled the state's tax structure regressive and unfair Monday, saying it falls most heavily upon the working people, the poor and the old.

THE DIAGRAM

Quote on Feature or
Features in Lead

Summary of Other Features
or Details

Quote: Details

Summary: Details

Quote: Details

Summary: Details
(or new feature)

THE WRITTEN STORY

"State officials need to take a fresh look
at our tax structure with an eye to modernizing it,"
Lane said in a speech to the state's postmasters.

"We need the freedom of an unlimited Constitutional convention so we can examine every possible alternative and find sound, long-range solu-
tions to our revenue problems."

The governor also said the state is operating on the lowest per capita tax basis in the nation, which is threatening state services, and he was
critical of the legislature for this situation.

"Without additional sources of revenue," he
said, "we can expect government services to drop to
levels unacceptable to us as concerned citizens, as
human beings. We just can't allow our state to lose
its place in the national mainstream of progress."

The governor said the current state budget is
inadequate and in his opinion, "is harmful to education, our highway programs, our health programs,
our correctional facilities and other human services."

He told the postmasters the General Assembly
this year "mandated a little more economy than we
had hoped for" and noted legislators declined to
fund an administrative spending program that was
already heavily pared.

"However, my administration will live within
the austerity budget approved by the assembly and
do so in such a way as to allow us to maintain the
highest possible level of services to our citizens."

Lane said tourism has been made a staff division of his office. And, he noted, tourism is boom-
ing.

"It's already apparent that this is going to be
the best year we've ever had."

Notice in the example that a number of references, made throughout the
story, attribute all statements to the speaker. A common error of beginning reporters is the omission of attributions (the source or authority) down in the story,
where they serve to keep reminding the reader that the speaker—not the reporter—is making the statements. Of course, attribution is not needed in every
sentence if the reporter puts the story together so the person being quoted is apparent to the reader. The omission of attribution with a quoted statement is permissible if the source of the quote is clear. Generally speaking, however, every
paragraph containing indirect quotations should include some attribution.

Complete Reporting. The example of the quote-summary-quote story is
straight-news reporting. If the occasion had required it, the following paragraphs
of interpretation might have found a place closely following the lead:

16

The governor's efforts to raise $40 million in new revenue through a proposed severance tax on mining of minerals in the state and a tax on business leases were defeated yesterday in the General Assembly.

A tax review committee has recommended a state income tax to replace the present sales tax. However, it would take at least six years to amend the state constitution, which now forbids an income tax.

The importance of such interpretative reporting—if the occasion requires it—is apparent. Without editorializing, the paragraphs above merely assemble additional pertinent facts to help the reader evaluate the speaker's comments. Nevertheless, it gives the whole story an altered significance and enables the reader to understand the possible motivation involved.

Story Contents. A speech story should include:

Facts	*Sources*
A. Speaker	A. Speaker, various *Who's Who* publications, members of group before whom he speaks, observation of reporter.
1. Present position.	
2. Experience.	
3. Description (if apropos).	
4. Unusual speaking characteristics.	
B. Audience	B. Officials or organization, observation of reporter.
1. Name and type of organization.	
2. Number present.	
3. Purpose of meeting.	
4. Reaction to speech.	
5. Description.	
6. Important persons present.	
C. Speech	C. Speech
1. Theme.	
2. Divisions.	
3. Title.	
4. Quotations.	

PUBLICATIONS

The contents of published articles frequently make news and become the source for straight-news stories. They range often from articles of national or international significance to strictly local. They may be the personal story of a friend of a president or the confessions of a former intelligence agent. But they also might be a national magazine article featuring a local citizen or a scientific journal article written by a local college professor. Hundreds of such publications are checked each year by reporters and turned into news stories. In some cases, the story may be about a publication itself—a new local magazine published by the chamber of commerce, for example. Or a new monthly devoted to sports in the region. Whatever it may be, chances are it deserves a story.

Reporting in this sense is a routine procedure. It is not to be confused with a book review or with "criticism" in the higher brackets. It is not evaluation, and it is not art. The reporter is not supposed to judge the story or publication but to report it. His story will follow the general principles and forms used in reporting speeches.

There is very little difference between a story on a speech and a story on a published article. The author of the article is, in other words, a "speaker," though he uses written words. A news story on an article is, therefore, similar to the report of a written speech. A description of the publication (name, type of publication, frequency of publication) may be necessary, just as a description of the occasion (audience, time of presentation) is necessary in reporting a speech. As in the speech story, the content of the article and not the fact that the article has been written is usually the substance of the lead. The assignment can be handled effectively as a quote-summary-quote story.

PERSONAL INTERVIEWS

Virtually all news stories are results of interviews. The reporter must talk with someone to get facts and quotations for a story, even though he may be an eyewitness of the event. Policemen, hospital officials, eyewitnesses and others are questioned for facts concerning an automobile accident. A club president is interviewed concerning the program of the next meeting. A public official is asked for a statement on charges brought against him. Or a reporter may interview a number of persons to get either a sampling of professional opinion or a "man in the street" poll of opinions on a question of current interest. All such interviews directly related to some news event or public issue are to be called "fact" interviews. They deal with and emphasize the news event or public issue rather than the personalities of the interviewees.

The personal interview is of another type. The subject of such an interview may be a prominent scientist, nationally known professional athlete or leading movie or television performer. Or he may be a bank clerk who made the news because he refused a robber's demand for money. If the story interest and emphasis concern a person's life, mannerisms, personality, achievements, reactions or the like, the story is to be considered a personal interview. The purpose of many of these interviews is to give readers an intimate "closeup" of a famous, infamous or at least notable personality.

Throughout the history of American journalism, a number of writers have made names for themselves as excellent interviewers. They range from Horace Greeley and his interview with Brigham Young to some of the brightest "stars" of the 1960s. Rex Reed became almost as prominent as some of the famous Hollywood stars he interviewed. And Tom Wolfe and Gay Talese developed the basic interview type story into an art form, helping to create the so-called New Journalism of the '60s.

While it is true that Wolfe and Talese frequently wrote about the famous or infamous, they did not start out interviewing only that type person. Each did his share of interviews with persons who were, at best, notable only on a local scale. Yet their interviews—even the early ones in their careers—show that they went

into their assignments prepared. Advance preparation is essential to any successful interview. Without it, a reporter will be hopelessly over his head. One of the
famous stories of interviewing illustrates that point beautifully. Mary Martin, a
major star of the American musical theater, was making one of her rare American
tours in the '60s. At a press conference on one of the first stops on the tour, an
unprepared young reporter asked: "Who are you?" The fact that a newsman did
not know the first lady of the American musical theater made a nationwide story
and caused his publication—and surely the reporter—considerable embarrassment.
Every reporter must know at least some important bits of information about
the person he is going to interview if it is to be a major personality interview.
Various Who's Who publications may give him a brief biography. The newspaper's library or morgue may contain photographs and biographical data in news
clippings or press bureau material. Countless other reference books covering
major personalities in practically every field are available at most libraries. Often
a reference books may be of help. A world almanac or book of facts and a handy
one-volume desk encyclopedia should be a part of every reporter's personal reference library. Often, if no standard reference material includes information on the
person the reporter has to interview, a telephone call to someone in the city may
supply the needed background. With even a slim amount of information, the reporter can begin to formulate a few questions that can be asked in an interview.

Planning Questions. In general, questions should pertain to the work, life or
personal interests of the persons interviewed, but they should be planned to
bring answers that will interest the newspaper reader. Questions should be
timely and, to whatever extent possible, local. Comments of a prominent person
on a current national event (in that person's field) are timely, and on a current
local event both timely and local. Of course, if the subject has absolutely no
knowledge of a local situation, do not waste his or her time by asking a strictly
local question. Obviously, visitors to the city will not feel justified in commenting on most local matters, but sometimes one may be familiar enough with a
local problem to venture a suggestion. Questions should be tailor-made for the
interviewee's profession or background. If a television star is not particularly
known as a political activist, do not spend a great deal of time asking him or her
political questions. Most of the time, the readers could not care less how their favorite television stars vote. Readers usually want to know what the stars are really like. Are they really as nice as they appear on television? Are they really as
tough? Are they like the characters they play?

In preparing questions, the reporter should keep in mind that one question
should lead to another, and the interview should move along in a conversational,
informal manner, the reporter jotting down on paper, tape-recording or committing to memory the answers and attitudes revealed. Constantly taking notes
is inadvisable except for dates, figures and the like, although in some cases it
may be permissible to keep a pencil busy throughout the interview. If a reporter
wants to use a tape recorder during a private interview, he should ask his subject
for permission (some persons do object). However, if it is a mass interview with
the electronic media represented, no special permission is needed since radio and
television reporters will be recording the interview on tape. The reporter should
always be aware whether note-taking or recording makes the person interviewed
self-conscious and "quote timid," and if so the use of pencil or tape recorder

should be avoided. As soon as possible after the interview, however, the reporter should fill out his written notes because the exact responses of the interviewee are then still fresh on the reporter's mind.

The reporter should watch as well as listen. The interviewee's mannerisms, dress, distinctive features and other personal characteristics make copy for the personal interview story. No matter how important the statements, there is always room for a few phrases describing the subject.

Interview Story Forms. In the personal interview, the reporter finds that a variety of approaches will apply—depending upon the person interviewed and what was said. But all interview stories have one thing in common: many direct quotes. A reporter can make use of the quote-summary-quote form in the body of the story, and in that regard the interview story is somewhat similar to the speech story. The lead can be a summary, an outstanding feature, a quote or an anecdote, or simply descriptive to set the scene. The lead, of course, can contain the substance of the interview, but often a striking word picture of the speaker is more desirable if his personal characteristics are particularly impressive. By all means, somewhere early in the story, the importance of the interview must be established, although it does not have to be in the lead or first paragraph.

Another story form that has gained considerable popularity in interviews, especially in some magazines, is the "question and answer" structure. Newspapers, however, use this form sparingly because it generally requires large amounts of space. In this form, the reporter simply writes a short introduction similar to an editor's note, giving a brief biographical sketch of the interviewee, and then reproduces his questions and the interviewee's answers. Often these interviews are done on tape recorders and are simply transcribed and perhaps edited for style and length.

There is a tendency for a reporter to bring himself into the story of a personal interview, but this should not be done. Rarely will the circumstances justify the reporter's including himself in the story.

EXERCISES

1. Using any newspapers available to you as your sources, clip and analyze a story on a speech, a story taken from a publication and an interview.
2. Attend an event in your community or on campus featuring a speaker. Take notes and write a news story on it. (Local service clubs such as Kiwanis and Rotary usually have speakers at their weekly lunches.) Do not use a copy of the speech, even if one is available. Hand in your notes as well as the story.
3. In your college library locate the current issue of the publication *Vital Speeches*. Copy a speech from the publication, and then write a news story based on that speech.
4. Check the radio and television listings for a speech by a major public official. Listen to the speech on radio or watch it on television, take notes and write a news story on it. Hand in your notes with the story.
5. Write a story on the following excerpts from a speech by Dr. James Maxwell, chancellor of the State Medical School, at a meeting of the State Association of Family Physicians here today:

"Health care costs will continue to increase in the next decade and we expect that the No. 1 focus in the coming decade will be how to control those costs.

"Four major factors will continue to cause the increase in health care costs. They are: increased public demand for access to care for certain groups; An increase in the number of physicians and other health-care professionals; lack of competition in the health industry, which would be the best of all cost control mechanisms; and increased knowledge and the cost of applied technology to provide a better quality of life.

"Certainly there will be continued pressure for access to care by a number of special groups, even though that costs money. I think that even those who feel that government responsibility in the health field should be limited will support the demands of increased care for children, the elderly, the handicapped and the catastrophically ill.

"We will even hear cries to limit the number of doctors who go into specializations and other areas of health care but our record shows that this approach does not work. Remember the cry when the space industry peaked and we had graduate engineers pumping gas and selling shoes? Now we don't have enough engineers to go around. They are in demand and are among the highest-paid college graduates.

"There still will be no competition in the health-care field simply because it does not work on the old supply-and-demand system. You don't have competition, because more than 90 per cent of all medical and hospital costs are paid by a third party—the government or insurance companies.

"The increased cost of technology and the public's demand for 'only the best' in medical care will continue to spiral. The so-called miracle drugs and miracle machines cost hundreds of millions annually and will go even higher in the next decade. But we cannot stop research. We cannot halt technological advances. And if we have them, the public has a right to demand they be used.

"Our chief hope for controlling costs will come from careful regional planning of health-care facilities. We certainly will have to put limits on the number of hospital beds. And we must seek ways of sharing expensive equipment. We are doing some of this already through regional hospital and health-care commissions. And doctors are simply going to have to stop ordering costly procedures and tests. There are indications that both the government and insurors are going to place limits on excessive testing.

"And, finally, we are going to see more of an emphasis on what can be done outside the hospital. The more that can be done as an outpatient, the better, because it will help keep down costs."

6. Write a news story on the testimony of Dr. Dorothy Michaels, director of Child and Family Services for the State Human Services Commission, before a committee of the state legislature. The committee is holding a series of state-wide public hearings to determine the need for state-sponsored child-care centers. Today's hearing was in the Community College auditorium.

Dr. Michaels said:

"Social, moral, ethical and economic forces are dramatically altering family life in America. Instead of mom and dad both being in the family picture, there is likely to be only one parent because of divorce. The grandparents and other relatives may live thousands of miles away because our society has become so mobile.

"Economic pressures have changed the role of women. The number of working mothers has increased dramatically. Either women have to work or they want to work to improve the family's lifestyle and they are faced with the dilemma of finding adequate child care. We simply do not have enough day-care centers.

"I know people who are against day-care centers claim that if they are not readily available there will not be as many divorces. Well, I ask you to look at the divorce rate today. We don't have very many centers, and it is as high as it has ever been. And those who claim that increased numbers of day-care centers would Sovietize America simply do not know what they are talking about.

"Do you know what one of the major results of inadequate day-care centers is? I'll tell you. It is an increase in family violence. Homicide is the fifth leading cause of death to infants under one year. We are controlling the number of children in America by killing them.

"We tend to think of the family as a safe, happy network of people who care for each other. On the contrary, it is one of our most violent institutions. It is our nearest and dearest who kill us.

"There isn't an attachment among family members anymore. There is a feeling of helplessness and hopelessness among parents and children. And they are taking out their frustrations in violence on each other.

"Many parents are not concerned with their children, nor are they loving and caring. As a result, children suffer from depression. We see children six, seven, eight and nine years old who are actively suicidal.

"Family life is totally disorganized. In many families no one has the capacity to cope, so we see them turning to violence.

"If the divorced mother of a five-year-old has to be at work at 7:30 in the morning, and the child is sleepy and crying when made to get out of bed, then you can be sure that it won't be long till the mother's frustration turns to violence in many cases.

"There would be less frustration and less violence if that mother knew she could take the child to a day-care center, where it would be fed a hot breakfast and cared for during the day while she worked to support the family.

"I urge this committee to take immediate steps to set up a state-wide network of day-care centers for children. To do less would be criminal."

The committee is to hear tomorrow from Mrs. Ida Dean Serramonte, president of Family Living, a state organization opposed to state-supported day-care centers.

7. Write a news story on the following article by Dr. Osgood Arnsdorf, professor of sociology, University of Leeds in England, appearing in the current issue of the Journal of Contemporary Religious Studies.

Religious cults and sects are rapidly increasing in the United States as replacements for declining traditional denominations, and they are expanding abroad.

While people are not abandoning religion altogether, some 1,000 cults and sects do exist, and many of them are flourishing, especially where conventional churches are the weakest. Those who are drifting away from conventional denominations, in many cases, become members of the unconventional ones.

It should be no surprise that many of these unchurched believers are willing, perhaps eager, to examine new religions, to find a faith that can offer an active and vigorous conception of the supernatural that is compatible with modern culture.

Cults and unconventional sects appeal to many, because they unblushingly promise to give the individual the power to harness supernatural powers to manipulate the natural world.

Other cults have adopted scientific facades to win new converts and evade the law. Actually they are nothing more than a religion posing as science posing as a religion.

Many cults appear to be ill-conceived and implausible. But it only takes a few effective cults to serve as the vehicle for a massive religious renewal. Indeed, it might only take one.

One of the reasons new faiths are attracting so many people is that they have not yet been subjected to the problems of the older faiths, which have suffered defeats at the hands of science.

In the United States, the top 10 cult states, by ratio of cults to million population, are Nevada, New Mexico, California, Colorado, Arizona, Oregon, Hawaii, New York, Missouri and Illinois. However, in total number of individual cults, California leads the list.

The states with the lowest rate of church membership, starting with the lowest, are Washington, Oregon, California, Hawaii, Nevada, West Virginia, Colorado, Maine and Montana.

By contrast, the states with the highest church membership, in order, are Utah, Louisiana, Rhode Island, North Dakota, Mississippi, South Carolina, South Dakota, Wisconsin and Minnesota.

The critics of organized religion have failed to see or appreciate the growing vigor of religion in less "respectable" quarters, just as they have been inclined to dismiss cults as a passing fancy of the young.

What they fail to realize is that cults will continue to proliferate as secularization makes ruins of the dominant churches, and in time some of these cults may become dominant religions.

8. In your college library, or the nearest public library available to you, examine a number of professional journals and publications such as your state's historical journal or a professional journal for political scientists or doctors. Select a by-lined article dealing with an interesting event or study, then write a news story on it.

9. Clip from any newspaper available to you interviews with well-known stage or television personalities written by the wire service Hollywood reporters. With them in hand, read the interviews in the book *Fame and Obscurity* by Gay Talese. Compare the writing style.

10. Interview the most interesting person you know and write a story on him or her.

11. Make a list of questions you would ask your favorite television or sports personality if he or she were visiting your city and you were assigned to interview him or her.

12. Write an interview story from the following notes:

Mary Kathleen Adams, 33, has been named assistant rector of St. Luke's Episcopal Church, which serves the students on the college campus. She is the first woman minister in the community. It is a homecoming for her. She was born here and grew up as a member of the church. She was graduated from high school, studied criminology at the State University, and returned here to become a policewoman. After eight years, she resigned and enrolled at Southwest Theological Seminary.

When you meet her, you notice that she is very relaxed. She is wearing a gray suit and a white blouse. She has brown curly hair and brown eyes. You are a bit surprised because she is not very tall and is not what you expected a former police officer to look like. Here are quotations from the interview:

"I've been a member of this church since the fifth grade. I went to elementary school, junior high and senior high school here in town. In fact, the only time I've been away for extended periods is when I was studying at the university and the seminary.

"My family thought I was crazy when I said I wanted to study criminology. But when I told them I was leaving police work to become a minister, they really thought I had wigged out.

"My first police assignment was as an undercover narcotics investigator. They gave me two weeks of orientation, and then I was out on the street. They took away my police ID, and I was out there on my own. Of course, I was scared. You never get used to that kind of work since you have to rely on your wits. You can never relax.

"But I was determined not to back out. I had several good partners. They

233

taught me a lot. And I guess I convinced the chief of the narcotics bureau that I had something on the ball. A year later he made me the first female narcotics investigator of the department.

"I was taken off the streets—much to the relief of my family—and assigned to investigate drug thefts from hospitals and local pharmacies. It wasn't as dangerous as street work, but there was some danger involved. But I don't like to talk about that.

"About two years later I was promoted to sergeant and assigned to serve as a counselor for families who had a member who was a drug addict. It is really tragic, especially when a young kid gets hooked on drugs. It really tears a family apart.

"Because so many of the young addicts also face their first prison term, I felt I needed some additional training. I took a leave and studied criminal administration for a year.

"As a police officer, you don't see what happens after sentence is pronounced. My classes gave me considerable understanding of the criminal justice system.

"You soon learn that you are dealing with a revolving circle. You see the same people return again and again. You have no idea how frustrating that can be for a police officer.

"I suppose my work in narcotics had something to do with my decision to become a minister. I must admit that I did not think I was doing all I could to help people as a police officer. But I am sure that there were other reasons. It is hard to put my feelings into words. I just knew it was something I had to do.

"My family was surprised—maybe even shocked. But they have come to expect the unusual from me. When I first went to the seminary, I was planning to work as a lay person. I thought I could use my seminary training in some way to help reform the penal system. I had grand ideas.

"But as I got further along in my training, I kept getting this nagging feeling that I was really being called to the ordained ministry. All of a sudden I realized this great calm, that this is what I really was being called to do.

"When I graduated from the seminary, ordained women ministers were not all that unusual. Although I know some people still don't like the idea. Most of the people here have welcomed me and made me feel at home, although some of them still remember me when I was a little girl coming to church with my folks. I know it must be a bit difficult for them to accept my sermons. So I work very hard on my sermons.

"I conduct worship services during the week, also. And I have Bible-study classes, and I am in charge of the youth program. Of course, I instituted a drug-education course. And I teach a Sunday morning class for high school students. I counsel many of the college students who attend our church, also.

"My next project is to develop a program for single parishioners. I want to include widowed and divorced persons as well as those who have never married.

"I hope I get it going before my appointment here ends late this summer. If a reappointment is offered, I'll probably stay. If not, I'll look around.

"I really haven't put away ideas about institutional ministry. Churches are traditionally involved with correctional facilities, although some prison officials are wary of help from churches.

"I'll just have to wait and see. But I have assured my family that I wouldn't switch careers again—at least not right away."

13. Suggest newsworthy pictures and write appropriate cutlines on these preceding assignments in this chapter: Exercise 2, Exercise 6, and Exercise 12.

14. Write a newscast from these preceding assignments in this chapter: Exercise 5, Exercise 6, and Exercise 12.

Meetings and Special Events

Many newspaper reporters dislike covering meetings more than almost any other assignment they are given, unless the story is certain to land on the front page with a by-line. Even the lure of a free lunch or dinner cannot offset the prospects of a dull business session or even duller speech.

Nevertheless, the meeting assignment is standard on every newspaper. Dozens of meetings are held every day in smaller communities and hundreds in big cities. Any edition is almost certain to include stories of civic, fiscal, religious, social, scholastic and professional organizations that are going to meet or have recently met. These are in addition to stories on meetings of governmental bodies that meet regularly to carry on public business.

Almost any group meeting—large or small, organized or unorganized—may deserve a news story, but it is impossible for any newspaper to cover every meeting. For example, in a city of 170,000 in the Southeast there are 465 organized clubs and groups that meet regularly and often seek to have their meetings covered. No one is certain how many groups exist beyond those. So an editor is faced with a problem deciding which ones rate coverage. As a general rule, editors consider the following types most newsworthy:

1. Those with large numbers in attendance.
2. Those which have significant programs or prominent speakers.

Routine meetings generally make routine news (but they can still be well written) and important meetings with real issues involved often make important news. However, in smaller communities almost any organization is newsworthy.

In writing a meeting story, the reporter should keep in mind that there is hardly any news value, after an event is over, to write that "a meeting was held." Tell the reader what happened at the meeting. If a very large number of persons are involved, some editors will permit the reporter to emphasize the number in

17a

attendance: "More than 7,000 persons registered today for the fifth annual convention of . . ." Even at meetings where little or nothing happens, the reporter should look for a fresh angle to his story to keep from having to write "The Tuesday Bridge Club met at the home of Mrs. J. W. Sutherland yesterday." Find out who won or some other angle to feature in the lead. Even when writing an advance story on a meeting, the writer should look for something interesting to put in the lead. He should never settle for "a meeting will be held."

TYPES OF MEETING STORIES

17b

The Advance. Most groups rely on newspapers to publicize their meetings through a preliminary or advance story (or stories). Many groups mail or phone in announcements of their upcoming meetings. A reporter having to prepare a story should check to make certain he has all the information to turn the announcement into a story that would interest many readers—not just the members of the club. He should make certain he has the correct, formal name of the organization (and local chapter if it is a national group), the exact time, date and place, and details on the program such as speakers, entertainment, election or installation of officers and so forth. The more he knows about the program, the easier it will be for him to come up with an interesting lead.

Compare these two meeting leads:

> *Weak:* The Oak Ridge Garden Club will meet in the Valley Unitarian Church at 7:30 p.m. Wednesday to hear a program on conservation education by State Forester A. H. Keally.
>
> *Better:* State Forester A. H. Keally will present a slide show and lecture on conservation education to the Oak Ridge Garden Club at 7:30 p.m. Wednesday in the Valley Unitarian Church.

Every effort should be made to avoid starting stories in the following ways:

> There will be a meeting of Jefferson Junior High School parents at . . .
> Members of the Republican Women's Club will be treated to a delightful . . .
> At 7:30 p.m. Wednesday the auditorium of West High School will become a tropical paradise when members of . . .
> Webb School auditorium will be the scene of . . .

In the body of the story, the reporter should avoid editorial comments on the caliber of the program such as "an excellent talk will be given by" and "a thrilling presentation of operatic excerpts." Such expressions as "All members are urged to attend" and "The public is cordially invited" should be omitted. If the meeting features a speaker or speakers and the club or organization would like others to attend, it is acceptable to use the expression "The meeting is open to the public."

17c

The Follow-up. Most meetings worthy of more than a bare announcement will have produced something of substance on which the reporter can build his story.

It can be

1. A definite action—passage of a law, adoption of resolutions, announcement of plans, endorsement of candidates or issues.
2. One or more speeches.
3. Discussion and debate—conflict, difference of opinion, voicing of views, criticism.
4. Personnel—election of officers, nominations, new members, resignations, membership drives, visitors, prominent members or guests, interesting personalities.
5. Miscellaneous features—music or other entertainment, unexpected interruptions.

The lead on the follow-up story (generally called a folo story) can vary greatly from a summary of the entire meeting to a single outgoing feature followed by a summary of other features. In many cases, reporters attempt to develop a general theme for the entire story if there seems to be a central theme to the meeting:

> An urgent appeal for $2 billion in emergency federal aid to fight recession in the nation's big cities was made at the U.S. Conference of Mayors in Boston yesterday.

The remainder of the story would be built around the central theme of the recession and its effect on the cities and their need for more federal help.

However, a reporter should not try to develop a theme if one does not logically exist. Often some feature that is far from the main purpose of a meeting but is stronger in reader appeal will deserve lead play. The reporter's responsibility is to his readers, not the sponsors of the meeting, and he should select and present the story with the reader in mind. At the same time, he must guard against conveying a distorted view of the meeting. It is important that the story be told in a logical order, with the most important items being told first. The story should not be told in chronological fashion, and it should never sound like the minutes of the club secretary.

Following is an example of a story coming out of a meeting on solar energy. The New York Times writer treated a rather serious subject in a fashion that was certain to attract the reader's attention:

> WASHINGTON, May 31—"Let the Sunshine In," the song from "Hair" advises, and evidently that's what a growing number of Americans want to do.
> In Colorado, ranchers want to use solar heat collectors instead of propane dryers to dry their grain.
> The city of Santa Clara, Calif., plans to heat and cool a few community centers with energy from the sun.
> Solar heating panels have been installed in schools near Washington and elsewhere.
> At Quechee, Vt., construction began this week on sunshine heating for a new colony of vacation and ski homes.
> At a three-day solar conference that ended in Washington today, more than 5,000 persons attended lectures and panel discussions or questioned representatives of several dozen companies—large and infant—that put their wares or systems designs on display in the exhibit hall.
> The conference was organized by . . .

CONVENTIONS

Conventions have always provided newsmen a wide variety of stories and, increasingly, they are becoming the focal point for major news breaks. Planners often schedule a particularly newsworthy speaker to attract the attention of newsmen as well as delegates. And speakers frequently use the convention platform to announce new scientific discoveries, plans for world peace or formation of a new political party or pressure group. Handling the stories generated by a large convention can be a major undertaking for any reporter. A big-scale convention is in reality a series of meetings that offer the reporter a wide variety of features and frequently require him to write multiple news stories. It is not uncommon for several staff members to be assigned to a large convention. And if the convention is a major event—a political party convention or the national meeting of an organization that might attract several thousand delegates—a special convention staff of a dozen or more reporters and photographers under the direction of a special editor might be assigned.

Many newspapers make special effort to "cover all angles" of a large convention held locally, frequently devoting more space to it than the event justifies (in local reader appeal). This type treatment can be justified on several counts: Each of the many delegates is interested in the coverage and is a potential buyer of the newspaper and, furthermore, newspapers generally give broad coverage as a matter of civic spirit. Conventions are important to the economy of any city and the newspaper joins the other organizations of the city in welcoming the visitors and promoting the city as a convention center.

Of course, a large convention also has many angles of local interest. Although they may attract little attention in the largest cities, several hundred visitors in the average city will create news in themselves. Even the smallest of conventions might attract prominent visitors, newsworthy speeches and discussions, resolutions on important issues, unusual persons or incidents and participation of local persons. Any of these should generate considerable local reader interest and make the convention worthy of coverage.

Preliminaries. If the editors of a newspaper decide to give maximum attention to a convention, a reporter may have weeks—perhaps even months—to begin preparing for the event. Long before the date of the meeting, the reporter takes the role of a promoter, writing story after story to feature all phases of the upcoming event. Almost every organization planning a convention has a publicity committee or publicity manager to work with the newsmen, usually providing the reporter with much of the information he needs to write his advance stories. Often the publicity representatives present the reporter with a complete press kit, which includes pictures and biographical sketches of speakers and convention officers, a history of the organization sponsoring the convention, an explanation of important subjects to be discussed and a variety of other material that could be used for human-interest stories about the convention or its delegates. Whenever possible they also provide advance copies of speeches. The reporter cannot reveal the contents of a speech before it is delivered, but he can give an adequate explanation of the speech subject and give the speech the play it deserves if he has an advance copy. And the reporter can ease his job of handling stories during the rush of the convention by writing an advance story on the speech for use after it has been delivered. But he must make certain the speaker actually gave that speech. On some occasions, often with permission of the speaker, a newspaper does publish an advance speech story in all editions on the day the speech is to be delivered. In those cases the lead usually contains the phrase "in a speech prepared for delivery at the (name of) convention today."

All this help from the publicity representatives does not relieve the reporter of his responsibility for gathering material for stories on the convention. If a publicity manager is not available to help him, it is the reporter's job to get this material in advance by writing letters to speakers and officers of the convention or working through the local convention bureau or the hotel or office serving as convention headquarters. Sometimes the number of speakers and the variety of sectional meetings of a convention are so large that the newspaper must omit details of the less important features, so the reporter must be selective in gathering and writing his stories about the convention.

Presenting Convention Features. In preparing a number of advance reports on **17d** a convention, the reporter must plan his stories to avoid repetition of the same features. Each story should have something new in its lead, but the time, date and place of the convention should be repeated somewhere (not necessarily in the lead) every time.

The first story lead generally announces that the convention will be held in the city. Often it emphasizes the approximate number of persons who will attend along with the time, date and place of the convention. Story leads of follow-up stories will highlight different phases of the program (speakers, discussion, officers, entertainment). A summary of other features (minus details) will be included in the body of the story. If a summary of all other features runs the story length beyond the space allotted for it, some of the less important features usually are omitted. It is also acceptable to play up—in the lead—features that have been summarized in the body of the preceding stories even though they are not new developments.

From the day before a convention opens—especially if it is a major one—until the day after it closes, there is a real rush. Often photographers and other reporters team with the reporter in charge to gather speeches, conduct interviews and search out other significant information that was unavailable in advance. In addition to reports on business and the speeches of the convention, many newspapers seek out human-interest stories—on interesting delegates, unusual events in connection with the meeting, comments from delegates on the convention and the city or other material.

All aspects of a convention may be put together in one long story, or they may be divided into a number of stories. The larger the convention, the more stories, generally speaking. If the stories are divided, one main story will be devoted to the major—most newsworthy—event of the convention and include such essential information as number of delegates and other general information. The other stories will present reports from sectional meetings within the convention, interviews and other sidelights. The exact manner in which the convention is covered depends upon its size, overall newsworthiness in relation to all other news that day and the amount of space available in the newspaper.

17e SPECIAL EVENTS

Fairs, festivals, dedications, exhibitions and other large events that attract a great number of persons offer much the same sort of problems as do convention stories. Each presents the possibility of some significant straight-news reports as well as dozens of features. Advance preparation is necessary to obtain details. Several stories, each playing up a different feature, are required before the event takes place, and adequate coverage of all features is necessary while the event is in progress. If the program of the special event is simply substituted for the convention program, the whole assignment involves the same procedure.

EXERCISES

1. Using any newspaper available to you, clip three major meeting stories, including one convention, and analyze them. If local newspapers do not carry such stories at the time of the assignment, locate newspapers from major cities in your college library, Xerox copies of meeting and convention stories from them and then do an analysis of each story.
2. Check the calendar of events for your campus for a meeting. Attend it and write a news story about it. Hand in the notes taken at the meeting along with your story. Coverage of a meeting of a community club or organization would be an acceptable substitute for a campus meeting.
3. Check your campus calendar of events for a current special activity such as a holiday event, film festival or other campus-wide event. Contact the sponsors and obtain enough information to write an advance story. When the event takes place, attend it and write a news story about it.
4. Attend a special event in your community such as a county fair or crafts show and write a human-interest story about it. Turn in your notes along with your story.
5. The annual convention of the State Consumers Counsel will be held on your campus tomorrow and the next day. About 250 persons are expected to attend. The group is a citizens' organization whose chief purpose is to lobby for the interest of the consumer. Theme of the meeting is "Are We Overregulated?" Write an advance story on the convention, including newsworthy facts from the following outline of the program:

   All Sessions in University Center Auditorium

   8:30–9:45 a.m. Registration. University Center Lobby

   10 a.m. Welcome. Dr. Rhonda Barnes, college president

   10:15 a.m. "Looking Out After the Interest of the Consumer." David Calhoun, president of State Consumers' Counsel, reviews the past year's activities of the organization.

   10:45 a.m. "Is Deregulation the Answer?" Counsel Attorney John J. Hamilton discusses what happens when businesses and industries are not accountable to the government.

   2 p.m. "What Are the State Regulatory Agencies Doing for Us?" A panel featuring the chairman of the State Public Service Commission, chairman of the State Banking Commission, and a representative of the state's Consumer Protection Agency.

   3:30 p.m. A film on product safety

   7 p.m. Dinner session

   Address: "Federal and State Governments Must Continue to Protect the Consumer." Rhoda H. Karpatkin, executive director, Consumers Union.

The next day:

9:30 a.m. "New Legislation to Protect the Consumer." State Rep. Jordan Doyle, original sponsor of the bill that created the state's Consumer Protection Agency.

10:45 a.m. "The Myth that Consumer Protection Inflates Prices." A report by Dr. Anna Judson, professor of home economics, University of Clarksdale, who has just completed a 10-year study of industry regulation and its effect on consumer prices.

11:45 a.m. Annual business session of the group.

6. Write a story on the final session of the annual state convention on Women in Law, an organization of women lawyers. The convention lasted two days. Some 100 women lawyers, legal secretaries and para-legal workers attended the meeting at the civic auditorium. At the final session the following occurred:

Nancy Peters, a lawyer from Charlestown, was elected president; Judith Egan, a law professor at the State University, vice-president; Edna Taylor, a lawyer from Louisville, secretary and treasurer (reelected). The new president has been practicing criminal law in the state for 12 years. Recently she has concentrated on cases involving women who have been charged with killing their husbands. Several of her cases have been sensational, because they involved prominent women in the state.

Here are some highlights from the new president's speech to the convention:

"We are gaining clout—politically and economically. There is now a 'fertile climate' for gains, because the women's movement has become a force to be reckoned with. Women will play a large role in public life in the future. That fact has not been lost on astute political and business leaders.

"In this decade we will see the first woman appointed to the Supreme Court. No longer can this country claim it has equal justice under the law. Equal justice means a woman Supreme Court justice. And when a woman is selected, we hope that she will be sensitive to women's rights, that she not be just a token.

"The first woman justice's appointment will be both substantive and symbolic. The appointment will be symbolic. Her services could be substantive. A woman's presence doesn't guarantee any particular impact. Her judicial philosophy is more important. But the symbolism is important also. The first woman on the court definitely will serve as a role model to women in the legal profession and to women in general.

"The first woman selected will have to be exceptional. She will be scrutinized 100 times more carefully than any male candidate has ever been. After all, the selection of justices remains an endeavor dominated by men.

"Remember no woman's group has veto power over the selection. That is a privilege reserved for only one nongovernment organization, the American Bar Association. The group's 14-member judiciary committee has been all male until the late 1970s, when one woman was added.

"It is important to bring to the bench the benefit of women's various experiences representing an important perspective—50 per cent of the nation's population."

WRITING THE SIMPLE STORY TYPES

At most newspapers beginning reporters—no matter how talented—generally have to prove themselves by writing the simpler stories first. The page 1 story does not often go to the novice, simply because the editor would rather trust the story to an experienced reporter.

The classification of stories as simple or complex is a convenient and arbitrary division most editors use when making assignments, even though there is no real technical significance to the classification.

To most editors, single-incident stories—automobile accidents, deaths, illnesses, funerals, minor crimes—would fall in the "simple" classification. Those stories requiring little interpretative writing and little background on the part of the reporter might be added to the editor's list—an award story or public appointment, for example.

The truth is that any single story may turn out to be either simple or complex, regardless of the type. For purposes of proceeding from the less difficult to the more difficult stories, however, the simple or complex classification has proved useful.

Illnesses, Deaths, Funerals

One of the clichés frequently repeated around newspaper offices is that there are three times in everyone's life when his name is reasonably certain to appear in a newspaper: when he is born, when he gets married and when he dies. Another story often told students who want to become reporters is that they will automatically be assigned to write obituaries on their first newspaper job because "obits" are relatively simple to write.

While it may be true that beginning reporters were given obits to write in the past, the practice is not as commonplace today. In fact, more and more editors are aware that the obituary is an important story—one that can make enemies or friends for the paper almost more than any other. If an obituary is accurate and in good taste, the family and friends will never forget it. The article will be read and reread many times, clipped and bound in plastic or pasted in the back of the family Bible. The newspaper will be remembered for the careful, accurate way it reported even the smallest details during the family's time of sorrow. But, let the obituary be inaccurate, a name misspelled, facts inaccurately reported, and the family will never forget it and never forgive the offending newspaper. Everything in the newspaper will be suspect in the eyes of that family—whose members will constantly remind friends and relatives alike that the newspaper had grandpa in the wrong lodge or made some other grievous error and cannot be trusted. Obituaries have grown to such importance that some newspapers have persons who write them almost exclusively.

However, at most newspapers the new reporter will be given the job of writing obits, including those of very prominent residents. How a new reporter handles obits often determines how rapidly he is moved on to other writing assignments. Let him be sloppy and careless and he might be marked as a reporter not to be trusted with important stories. If his work is careful, thoughtful and dignified, he is certain to be noticed and moved on to more pleasing assignments.

News Values. Why are obituaries and stories about illnesses and funerals so important? Evaluating their news value shows they all fall on the disaster side of human experience. They are disruptions of the status quo, and they are of consequence in the community. The removal of almost any human being from the local scene requires social and economic readjustments among relatives and friends. His or her place must be taken; his or her job must be filled by another. The home may be offered for sale; the widow or widower may move to another city; the daughter or son may withdraw from college. All such changes touch the lives of others.

Factors of Magnitude. The importance of the news story is determined by several factors. Illness is measured by its gravity (intensity), approaching death as its climax. And both illness and death are measured by the number of persons affected (extensity) in the community. Thus the prominence of the person and the nature of the illness may determine story importance. A rare disease or accident (even involving someone who is comparatively unknown) is interesting because of its unusualness. Even more important may be stories about the threat of epidemics of quite common diseases. Since prominence usually means being well known, as well as holding a position of importance, the community is more generally affected by matters involving prominent persons. Multiple deaths or cases of illness extend the news importance. Although the story of illness or death (and of the funeral) may frequently stand stripped of its disaster appeal, its news importance may sometimes be heightened by prominence, novelty, consequence, human interest and even conflict.

ILLNESSES

Illness—grave illness—is reported less frequently than its news importance justifies. Patient, family, physician and hospital are often unwilling to have the illness known. Physicians and hospitals usually try to avoid publicity even in the case of very prominent persons. Family and patient may wish to avoid unnecessary alarm to friends, or employer or employees, and sometimes the family wants to hide information from the patient. Often if the person is very prominent—a public official or a major entertainment figure—the illness is not disclosed to assure the person privacy. Illness can affect business matters, contracts, perhaps even diplomatic negotiations as well as various other obligations. Always in the background is the thought that tomorrow or the next day the patient may be well and the less uproar about the matter the better. If the patient's family, physician and hospital all refuse to give a statement on the illness, the reporter should use information available to him with extreme caution.

Illness is not easy to report properly. Highly technical or tenuous conditions may characterize the illness itself. The physician simply may not know the exact nature of the illness. Or the nature of the illness itself may be so technical that it is extremely difficult to translate into layman's language. (However, some medical schools now have special courses to teach medical students how to write and speak in nontechnical language.) The reporter should always keep in mind the emotions and the sensitivities of the patient as well as his family. Once the brief bulletin on the patient's condition is announced, little substance is left for the reporter to take hold of and expand, as a general rule. However, if the person is prominent—a major entertainer or perhaps the governor of the state—frequently the attending physicians will hold a press conference and explain the nature of the illness and the patient's condition. In the prolonged illness of such a prominent person, regular medical bulletins will be issued and the comings and goings of delegations, friends, relatives and others as well as public statements by others may provide copy. The illness story of lesser persons will usually be brief, however, unless they suffer from a rare or unusual ailment.

Although a list of patients admitted to and dismissed from hospitals often is published each day in newspapers in many smaller communities, the reporter gives individual attention to only a few. In addition, sometimes "tips" will lead him to interesting stories about illnesses.

Story Content. Many accounts of illness may contain only one, two or three **18a** paragraphs (most being handled similarly to a personal) and contains the following information:

1. Name and identification.
2. Cause of illness.
3. Condition (fair, serious, critical—an accurate quotation from the doctor or hospital regarding condition).
4. Name of hospital (sometimes "at a local hospital" if person is in a private institution such as a mental hospital).
5. Duration of illness.
6. Members of family at bedside.
7. Effect of illness on person's public position (especially if he is an elected official) or business.

The "Who" is the most important W in most illness stories. It should be in the **18b** lead. For variety, or if the disease or operation is unusual, the cause of the illness or the condition of the patient may be featured. However, if the story is a follow-up, the condition of the patient is usually the feature. Note the examples below:

WHO:

Rachel L. Ralwey, senior home economist for the state Extension Service, is in the intensive care unit of University Hospital today.

CAUSE:

After suffering a heart attack in her office, Rachel L. Ralwey, senior home economist for the state Extension Service, is in the intensive care unit of University Hospital today.

CONDITION (a follow-up):

University Hospital officials report a slight improvement in the condition of Rachel L. Ralwey, senior home economist for the state Extension Service. She suffered a heart attack in her office yesterday.

Hospital Notes. Some newspapers carry regularly a hospital column. It may be merely a list of "Admitted" and "Discharged" with no details given. Some hospitals refuse to make such lists available, while others take a more liberal policy on publicity. It is common practice at many hospitals to ask a patient or his family if there is any objection to being listed as a patient in the daily report to the press. But with or without the cooperation of the hospitals, many personals deal with hospitalization. Following are some common examples:

> Mable Summers, 1244 Savings St., returned to Louisville Thursday for further treatment on her hand. She underwent surgery two months ago and has been undergoing therapy since the cast was removed.

> Martha Belle Colvin of the New Hope Community returned home this week after undergoing open heart surgery in Mary Immaculate Hospital in Lebanon. Her mother, Mrs. Normal Colvin, is employed as a surgical nurse at the hospital.

> Buster Newton, six-year-old son of Mr. and Mrs. Ira Newton, Route 1, Fairfield, was admitted to Community Hospital today suffering from a broken collar bone. Buster rode his tricycle off the front porch of the family home and was injured in the fall.

DEATHS

Death is an important item of news. It may contain all the news values discussed previously. Regardless of news values, death is reported as a public record. No person ever becomes so unimportant that he is not valuable as a vital statistic. The public-health records chart all deaths, and state laws fix standard forms of physicians' reports. Even the nameless drifter found frozen to death under a superhighway overpass is not overlooked. He fits somewhere in a chain of persons and events. While the practice will vary from paper to paper in the treatment of death stories, all newspapers report deaths.

18c   *Obituaries.* The practice of reporting deaths varies just as the terms will vary. At some newspapers, the word *obituary* means a news story written about the death of a person that is published with an individual headline. At others the obituary is the black agate-type alphabetical listing of everyone who has died and has not yet been buried. This list is also called the death notices at some newspapers. All newspapers publish the stories of deaths free if they use them as separate stories. Many newspapers, however, make a per-word charge for death column notices, the same as they do for classified advertisements, and such charges become part of the funeral costs. Whether it is a paid item or not, the form used by the newspaper is standardized to get all essential information. Many newspapers and funeral homes use a standard form as illustrated on the following page.

From this report a rather standard notice is printed in the alphabetical listing. Funeral arrangements usually are included when they are available. Following is an example:

> TOLAND, EMMA R.—Age 64, of 296 E. Shady Side Circle, Crestview, died Monday at Mercy Hospital. She is survived by her husband, George; two sons, Frank B. and Dale; and a sister, Mrs. Margaret Burns, all of Crestview. Funeral services will be at 1 p.m. Thursday at the Crestview Christian Church. Burial will be in Oakmont Cemetery. Friends may call at Northwood Funeral Home, 635 N. Elm St., from 7 to 9 p.m. Wednesday.

This type notice will vary as to the amount of information in it. Since it is paid for by the family, it can include such information as the names of the pall-

```
┌─────────────────────────────────────────────────────────────┐
│                          OBITUARY                            │
│                                                              │
│   Name_____Age_____   │
│   Address_____   │
│   Place of death_____Date_____Time_____   │
│   Cause of death_____   │
│   Date of birth_____Place of birth_____   │
│   Parents_____   │
│   Education_____   │
│   Occupation_____   │
│   Husband or wife (maiden name)_____   │
│   Date of marriage_____Place_____   │
│   Residence here since_____   │
│   Previous residences_____   │
│   Name of present employer_____   │
│   Previous employers_____   │
│   Military record_____   │
│   Church affiliation_____   │
│   Clubs, fraternal organizations, other affiliations_____   │
│   _____    │
│   Special interests or hobbies_____   │
│   Survivors with relationships and addresses_____   │
│   _____    │
│   _____    │
│   Body at_____   │
│   Funeral arrangements_____   │
└─────────────────────────────────────────────────────────────┘
```

bearers, the name of the minister officiating and other material. At some newspapers, these notices are handled by a clerk or a secretary using the information from the funeral home. Others have reporters write the notices from the funeral home reports.

Death Stories. Reporters are called upon to write death stories (or obituaries) that are handled in regular news style. Some newspapers publish these on the same page as the paid notice. Others have separate pages for them. The Indianapolis News, for example, has for years done an excellent job of reporting deaths in that city and surrounding area. Each is handled as a separate news item, and the stories vary in length depending upon the person and the amount of information available. Other newspapers, however, limit these stories to persons who are newsworthy enough to justify this extra attention. In most large cities, the death

18d

of a person who has gained no prominence and who died of natural causes would be reported only in the paid notices column.

While the information in the paid notice or the funeral home's report provides the basic facts for the news story on the death, the reporter often must seek additional information by telephoning or visiting relatives or others mentioned in the notice. If the person is prominent, the reporter frequently checks the newspaper's morgue or library for additional information, and calls friends, business associates and others for material on the deceased. And if the person is exceptionally prominent a reporter should refer to several standard reference books, such as Who's Who, for additional material.

The wire services and most large newspapers maintain rather complete files of hold-for-release obituaries on most of the big names—national and international leaders, for example. Many smaller newspapers maintain similar stories, ready for print, on the most prominent citizens in their communities. These usually are brought up to date at regular intervals.

18e

Story Content. If a newspaper does carry individual stories on deaths, any reporter assigned to write them should keep in mind that the story must provide the following information:

1. Name and identification (address, occupation and affiliations).
2. Age.
3. Day and time of death.
4. Place of death.
5. Cause of death.
6. Duration of illness.
7. Names of members of the immediate family (survivors).
8. Effects of death upon person's public position (if applicable).

While this information is routine, there should be nothing routine about the writing of the story. The reporter should use every journalistic device to show what manner of person the deceased was. This, of course, depends upon details. And the reporter should look for them—colorful incidents, anecdotes, personal traits, personal remembrances of friends and family—to convey exactly why this particular death is news.

Naturally, the first paragraph should sum up the circumstances of the death with name, age, identification by position or profession and time and place of death. The remainder of the story should be a very carefully constructed biographical sketch of the person in an effort to picture for the reader what he or she really was like. It should not be a mere routine summation of the facts of his life and career. While it should contain colorful highlights of the deceased's career, it should not be light or frivolous.

For example, when labor leader George Meany died, the Associated Press story, which appeared on the front page of hundreds of newspapers, began:

WASHINGTON (AP)—George Meany, the gruff former plumber who rose to become the single most powerful force in the American labor movement, died Thursday at age 85.

Meany stepped down in November after 25 years as the only president the AFL-CIO had even known. In December 1977 he had been elected without opposition to a 12th term . . .

The story went on for some 50 paragraphs giving the details of his death from cardiac arrest as well as highlights of his often turbulent career as a powerful labor chief both courted and feared by industrialists and presidents.

When Archbishop Fulton Sheen died, the New York Times began its story under a two-column headline "Archbishop Sheen, Who Preached to Millions Over TV, Is Dead at 84." Writer George Duncan's story began this way:

> Archbishop Fulton J. Sheen, who through his television ministry became one of the best-known figures of the Roman Catholic Church in the United States, died at his home at 500 East 77th Street in Manhattan yesterday after a long battle with heart disease. He was 84 years old.
>
> An ascetic, slender figure with blue eyes so deep-set and piercing that most people thought they were black, Archbishop Sheen was one of the most effective evangelists that the broadcasting era has produced.
>
> From 1930, when he became the first regular preacher on "The Catholic Hour" over national radio, he was the most prominent spokesman of the Catholic Church in the United States and one of the most widely heard clergymen of any denomination.
>
> He was also famous for his conversions, of ordinary folks en masse and of such prominent individuals as . . .

The story continued for another 20 paragraphs and was accompanied by a two-column picture of the Archbishop conducting a church service.

18f

The reporter must write death stories objectively and with dignity. Every effort should be made to resist temptation to make the reader weep. The language of the story should be simple and precise, avoiding saccharine words and phrases such as "he will be missed by all." A person "dies" instead of "passes away"; he is "buried" instead of "interred," no matter what the family and the funeral director say. However, the reporter should learn the practices of the various religions and refer to them properly in his story.

Occasionally the reporter is faced with a problem in writing a death story when he finds that the deceased has a black mark on his past. He might have served time in prison, or been disbarred or his medical license might have been revoked. If the person who was once a convict later became a senator, the story cannot—and should not—avoid mentioning the prison term. If the deceased is a public person, facts of that nature are required for an adequate story. However, if the person is entirely private, many newspapers would elect to leave out such facts, particularly if the person had lived down the incident.

When a death is announced in the afternoon newspaper, the morning newspaper in the same city the next day generally does not repeat the same lead. It usually features a different angle—the announcement of the funeral services, for example. Even if the funeral arrangements were carried in the original obit, they are the feature of the lead for the second-day story. Following are examples:

FIRST STORY:

Vice Admiral Emmett P. Forrestel, 82, a war hero and retired commander of the 9th Naval District, died Friday at Memorial Hospital.

SECOND-DAY STORY:

A military funeral will be held Thursday at the U.S. Naval Academy in Annapolis, Md., for Vice Admiral Emmett P. Forrestel, 82.

The war hero and retired commander of the 9th Naval District, died Friday in Memorial Hospital.

FUNERALS

The funeral announcement is simply the follow-up of a death story, except in the case of more prominent persons whose funerals might attract large numbers of mourners. As in any follow-up, a brief summary of the preceding story must be included, but the lead features the funeral.

18g

Story Contents. The funeral story should provide

1. Time.
2. Place.
3. Whether public or private (open to the public unless otherwise stated).
4. Who will officiate.
5. Place of burial.
6. Active pallbearers.
7. Honorary pallbearers.

Following is a typical funeral announcement:

Funeral services for James Martin Hardin, 86, former Nelson County Sheriff, were held at 11 a.m. Thursday at the First Methodist Church. Burial was in Highland Cemetery.

The Rev. Charles Yankey, pastor of the church, officiated. Members of the Republican Central Committee for Nelson County served as pallbearers.

Mr. Hardin died Tuesday at his home. He had been in failing health for several years.

He served as Nelson County Sheriff for 20 years. He declined to seek reelection for a sixth four-year term after he suffered a heart attack.

Surviving are his wife, Ethel; a son, Joseph; and three grandchildren.

The funeral story of a prominent person would be greatly expanded and reported in the same manner as any other news story of similar importance would be covered. It would include excerpts from the minister's eulogy, description of the service and an account of relatives and prominent friends and members of associations who attended in addition to any other information required to report the funeral adequately to the readers.

The New York Times, for example, reported the funeral of Archbishop Sheen under the headline "Sheen Rites at St. Patrick's." The story was accompanied by two photographs of the funeral services. The story began this way:

Behind the high altar of St. Patrick's Cathedral, the ornate bronze doors of the crypt stood open yesterday as Terrance Cardinal Cooke said the funeral mass for Archbishop Fulton J. Sheen, who died Sunday at the age of 84.

More than 50 ushers dressed in dark suits helped seat the hundreds who attended and then cordoned off the pews as they became full.

Archbishop Edward T. O'Meara delivered the homily, praising Archbishop Sheen for his work in 63 years in the priesthood, during which time he wrote more than 50 books and gained lasting fame and the affection of millions through his radio and television ministry . . .

EXERCISES:

1. Using any newspaper available to you, clip a death story and an illness story and make a news analysis of each.
2. Select a prominent man or woman in your community whose death would be a significant news story. Make a list of the facts about him or her you would seek to write the story. Also list the sources you would use.
3. In your college library locate microfilm copies of a major newspaper such as the Washington Post or the New York Times. Look up how that newspaper handled the death of any major U.S. or world figure. Compare how the story was handled in your local newspaper, which should also be on microfilm.
4. Write stories from the following notes:

    A. Federal Judge William Gordon Thompson, 73
       Putting on robes in chambers
       Before court at 10 a.m. today
       Became violently ill
       Taken to Baptist Hospital by ambulance
       Hospital spokesman reports he is in "critical" condition
       In intensive care unit
       Refused to say what is wrong with him
       Court Clerk David Shapiro said judge
       Became violently ill and passed out
          (*Sources:* Shapiro and Hospital officials)
       Judge Thompson has been on bench here for 31 years
       Known for his strict rules of conduct in his court
          (*Source:* Shapiro)

    B. Billy Gene Yumbert, 17
       Star quarterback for Central High School
       Reported to be patient at University Hospital
       Hospital officials, family members, school officials
       Refuse to confirm the report
       Several students said he was not in classes
       Reporters notice he did not practice with team today
       Unidentified telephone caller
       Tells reporter he saw Yumbert brought in to hospital
       Said Yumbert "was flying higher than the Empire State Building"
       "He was raving and screaming and it took three men to hold him"

    C. Lee Childress, 57
       City Law Director
       Had emergency surgery about 5 p.m. yesterday
       Rushed to hospital from home
       Dr. Marvin Reece, emergency room physician at University Hospital
       Said Childress apparently cut off two toes on his right foot
       While mowing the lawn at his home
       Condition is fair
          (*Source:* Dr. Reece and Childress family)
       Mrs. Childress, Eleanor, said he slipped on the wet grass
       And his right foot went under the power mower
       Mower cut right through his leather shoe

5. Write an obituary using information in the report on the following page.

```
┌─────────────────────────────────────────────────────────────────┐
│                                                                 │
│                    WOODLAWN FUNERAL HOME                        │
│                      Death Report                               │
│                                        Date  March 17           │
│   Name  Joseph W. Anderson                      Age  66         │
│   Address  1980 Winston Rd.                                     │
│   Place of death University Hospital      Date March 17 Time 2:30a.m. │
│   Cause of death  Massive stroke                                │
│   Date of birth  October 25        Place of birth Cleveland, Ohio │
│   Parents  Mr. and Mrs. John A. Anderson (deceased)            │
│   Education  Cleveland Public Schools, AB Case Western Reserve, LLD Harvard │
│   Occupation  Lawyer in private practice                        │
│   Husband or wife (maiden name) Susan Browning (deceased)       │
│   Date of marriage  June 16, 1937         Place Cleveland, Ohio │
│   Residence here since 1946                                     │
│   Previous residences Cleveland, Ohio                           │
│   Name of present employer                                      │
│   Previous employer                                             │
│   Military record Captain, U.S. Army, 1941-1945, in Judge Advocate's office │
│   Church affiliation Western Presbyterian Church               │
│   Clubs, fraternal organizations, other affiliations City Bar  │
│   Association, State Bar Association                            │
│   Special interest or hobbies Grew orchids                      │
│   Survivors with relationships and addresses James W. Anderson, Jr., son, │
│   6519 Mountain View Terr.; one grandson, Joseph W., III       │
│                                                                 │
│   Body at Woodlawn Funeral Home                                 │
│   Funeral arrangements Incomplete                               │
│                                                                 │
└─────────────────────────────────────────────────────────────────┘
```

6. Write a death story using the information in the report in Exercise 5 plus the following information:

He had been a member of the city school board for the last 18 years. He had been chairman of the board until two years ago when he asked his fellow board members to name someone else to the post. Gained widespread local attention for his tough stand during contract negotiations with the teacher's association. He had been in law practice for 43 years. Member of the city and state bar associations as well as the state Trial Lawyers Association. He was president of the Trial Lawyers Association in 1970 and 1971.

7. The next day the funeral home sends you the following report on the funeral arrangements. Write a story.

```
FUNERAL REPORT: Joseph W. Anderson

Time  2 p.m., March 19
_____

Place Western Presbyterian Church
_____

Officiating The Rev. Thomas Samuel Masterson, Pastor
_____

Burial place Lakewiew Cemetery
_____

Active Pallbearers None
_____

Honorary Pallbearers None
_____


_____

Remarks Funeral will be private for family and close friends
_____

Family requests donations to the Cancer Society in place
_____

of flowers
_____


_____
```

8. Write a death story on a prominent individual in your state or at your college or university. Use all available sources in gathering biographical information. Check all information for accuracy. Omit cause of death and funeral details. At the end of your story list the prominent individuals you would get statements from about the "death" of the individual about whom you are writing.

9. Write an advance death story on yourself. Use only the facts of your life as they now exist. Do not embellish them with imaginary detail.

CHAPTER 19

Fires and Accidents

Fires and accidents are standard spot news for almost every newspaper. And the beginning reporter generally spends much of his time writing about them. This type story presents a particular challenge to a reporter since most of the information is gathered after the event and often the details of the event are quite similar. Except in the most spectacular fires or accidents, the facts for the story are obtained from records of the police and fire departments. A careless or bored reporter might turn out a routine and dull story by just using those facts. But an alert reporter will attempt to get additional information from witnesses—policemen, firemen, spectators. Even though most stories of this type are picked up as routine on regular beats—police, fire headquarters and hospitals—or by calls from spectators, the reporter should try to make them interesting.

In some major cities, newspapers are connected with the fire department's alarm system, and the fire bells ring in the city room as well as at fire headquarters. Often newspapers monitor the police radio, also. This gives the newspaper, especially in larger cities, an opportunity to immediately send reporters and photographers to the scene of a major fire or accident to produce dramatic firsthand accounts of the event.

No matter how the information is gathered, certain facts are important. The newspaper reader is eager to know who was injured and the amount of property damage. If, in addition, the drama of major events can be effectively presented, so much the better. But drama should be implicit in the facts (incidents) and not explicit in the language of the story.

OVEREMOTIONALIZED:

Mike Murphy, 16, his eyes glazed with horror, fell to his knees beside the twisted, charred body of his youngest brother, sobbed loudly and thought: "There but for the grace of God, lay I."

That excerpt from a fire story in which 87 children were burned to death in a school fire is a tasteless effort to be dramatic. Even an eyewitness would not know what Murphy was thinking.

FACTS AND SOURCES

Story and Contents. The following formula indicates the facts and sources usually available in a major fire or accident story. Minor stories use fewer details.

Facts

A. Casualties
  1. Name and identification of every person killed and injured.
  2. Manner in which persons killed or injured.
  3. Nature of injuries.
  4. Disposition of dead and injured.
B. Damages
  1. Damages to property.
  2. Description of property.
  3. Owner of property.
  4. Insurance.
  5. Other property threatened.
C. Description
  1. Cause.
  2. Time and duration.
  3. Chronological account of incidents.
  4. Relief work of firemen, police or others.
  5. Spectators.
D. Escapes
  1. Rescues.
  2. Experiences of those escaping.
E. Legal action
  1. Investigations.
  2. Arrests.
  3. Suits
F. Sidelights (human interest, as part of the main story or as separate story).

Sources

A. Police, firemen, hospitals, funeral homes; friends and relatives of dead and injured; witnesses; neighbors

B. Police, firemen and property owners

C. Police, firemen, persons involved, witnesses

D. Police, firemen, persons involved, witnesses

E. Police, firemen, fire marshal, property owners, lawyers employed

19b

In a major fire and accident story the number of persons dead or injured is usually featured. The amount of the property damage is commonly featured if there are no injuries or deaths. But a prominent person involved, an unusual cause, a dramatic rescue or any one of the 5 W's may sometimes be featured in the lead.

Story Forms. Fire and accident stories can range in form and size from a brief to a lengthy several-feature story. The multiple-casualty story form is often used when such treatment is justified. Following are examples of several fire story leads:

An extra-alarm fire on the 80th floor of the Hancock Center Monday night heavily damaged one apartment and sent smoke billowing above Michigan Avenue.

The blaze, which was confined to apartment 8007, forced scores of residents to be stranded in the lobby as firemen commandeered the elevators to haul up hoses and fire axes . . .

[THE CHICAGO TRIBUNE]

VIENNA, Austria (UPI)—A fire swept a Vienna hotel before dawn today, killing 27 people and critically injuring 13 others. Three American tourists were reported among the dead.

Officials said 32 Americans from the Bath, Maine, area were staying at the Hotel am Augarten . . .

JOHNSON CITY (UPI)—Four elderly men were killed Friday evening and five others were injured when fire swept through the upper story of a rooming house in downtown Johnson City.

The fire, whipped by gusty winds, started at 5:45 p.m. in Room 13 of the rooming house atop a restaurant-bookstore called the Sports' News.

A spokesman at Memorial Hospital said the men, all residents of the boarding house, were dead on arrival . . .

Here are some examples of accident story leads:

Edwina E. Holt, 17, 6519 Concord St., was critically injured about 3:30 p.m. yesterday when the car in which she was riding struck a tree on Western Avenue near Keith Street.

She is in intensive care at Presbyterian Hospital.

The driver of the car, Lyndon W. Clevenger, 18, 5708 Wood Rd., told police . . .

A 23-year-old Powell man died today when his car crashed into a creek in Westwood.

William Wayne Price, 23, 2220 Roundtree Dr., apparently died instantly in the 7:30 a.m. crash, police said.

Price's Chevrolet Camaro was southbound on Morrell Road when it crossed railroad tracks and became airborne, police said. The car landed on its side next to a culvert in a small creek . . .

Bronwyn Tuner of the Nashville Banner was an eyewitness to a crash of a church bus on an interstate highway that injured 38 of the 47 passengers aboard. Here's how her story began:

GORDONSVILLE—You could hear the screams 100 yards away.

Through the smoke, from beneath the shambles of bus seats, glass, clothing and torn Bibles, they fought for breath and screamed.

"Get me out, get me out, my God, get me out."

It was a confused, desperate cry heard by motorists who stopped to aid passengers in a church bus which crashed on Interstate 40 Saturday . . .

Vocabulary and Fact Reporting. In reporting accidents—notably automobile accidents, because of their frequency—the reporter must use words carefully, with an eye to precise meaning. Only moving objects collide, strictly speaking. Therefore *"struck* a parked car" is better than *"collided with* a parked car." "The accident occurred *when the car in which they were riding"* is awkward, yet "their car" is usually inaccurate. A number of newspapers, however, have come to accept the latter. Libel actions may grow out of inaccurate phrasing, and the shortcuts of language should be used with care. Except in reports of storms, earthquakes and other "acts of God," colorful language should always yield to fact reporting. The phrase *completely demolished* (or *destroyed*) is redundant. To *demolish* or *destroy* means completely so the word *completely* is unnecessary. A statement that a person is *not expected to live* should be reported as *critically injured* unless a direct quote is available from a physician using those exact words.

Fact reporting and careful language will also help the reporter write without expressing an opinion on the person responsible for a fire or accident. The reporter does not attempt to fix this responsibility. Who the guilty person is may seem apparent from the facts, the arrests and the statements of officials as reported in the case. But the reporter makes no effort to point out the guilty party, for that is the job of the courts. To the contrary, if the reporter has information in his story which he thinks may tend to point a finger of guilt at a person, the ethics of fair play require that he make an effort to get that person's side of the story and report it at the same time. If unable to reach the person, he should indicate that fact in the story.

COMPLETE REPORTING

Generally most disasters are treated adequately when presented as straight news, with little interpretation. However, if they accumulate into a daily threat to the security of life and property, they confront the reporter with a different sort of responsibility. Most communities face the serious continuing problem of automobile accidents. Occasionally there may be a series of fires, and there are epidemics of disease or of crime. What causes these disasters? How do they occur? How could they, how can they, be avoided? Before the community can protect itself or take the proper remedial steps, it must know the facts. The reporter is frequently the only research agent on the job. Only as he can see—or foresee—and report, not merely the surface events but the underlying causes and trends, can the proper programs of reform be undertaken—in some cases, forced upon reluctant or footdragging public officials. Is the electric wiring code so poorly enforced in the community that it represents a serious hazard? Are there danger spots for traffic that result in repeated accidents and perhaps injuries and deaths? Is there a serious threat to community health because of unsanitary handling of waste? Surface reporting of simple events that may grow out of any of the above usually does not reach the heart of the community problem. Complete reporting would in these cases require independent thought, under-the-surface investigation and interpretative analysis. Public service awards are won each year by many newspapers that investigate and report on such community-wide problems.

EXERCISES

1. Using any newspapers available to you, clip a fire story and an accident story and make a news analysis of each.
2. Write stories using the following notes:

A. Tractor-trailer stopped on Bardstown Highway
   Near entrance to Dadeland Industrial Park
   Five miles south of city limits
   Driver Charles G. King, 43, Columbus, Ohio
   Said he had stopped about 1:45 a.m.
   To inspect his rig
   Said he was on right side of the rig
   Near the cab when he looked around
   Saw a car heading toward the rig
   It plowed into the rear of the trailer
   At a high rate of speed
   He called state police on his CB radio
   State Trooper Larry Preston said
   Two young men killed in the car
   Identified as David Pass, 20, Ashland, and
   William Cloud, 19, Bardstown
   Both students at State University
   Preston said there were no skid marks
   To indicate car tried to stop
   Tractor-trailer completely off the highway
      (*Sources:* Preston, King)

B. Rogelio Romero, 4,
   Riding tricycle on sidewalk
   In front of home
   At 1824 Grand Ave.
   About 1:30 p.m. yesterday
   Struck by police car
   Involved in high-speed chase
   Patrolman Robert A. Culver, 36
   Said he was chasing car carrying
   Three teenagers that was speeding
   On Grand Avenue
   Car had neither license plates
   Nor city vehicle sticker
   Culver said third car
   Got in his way
   His cruiser struck third car
   Then jumped the curb
   Struck Rogelio
   Child in critical condition
   In Children's Memorial Hospital
   Mother, Carmen Romero, 25,
   Said she was standing on steps
   Of the apartment building
   Watching her son and two other boys
   Other boys not injured

Police investigation underway
　　(*Sources:* Mrs. Romero, Patrolman Culver, hospital officials, police spokesman)
C. Firemen called to home
　At 210 North Franklin Avenue
　About 12:15 p.m. yesterday
　Building on fire
　Took nearly one hour
　To extinguish the blaze
　House so badly damaged
　Will have to be torn down
　Building owned by John McKinney of Howell Community
　Rented by James Ramsey, 31, accountant
　For city school system
　Lost all personal belongings
　Furniture, clothing, books
　Unable to give estimate
　No estimate on value of building
　Fire Chief Robert Strope said
　Faulty electric wiring
　Appears to be cause of fire
　　　(*Sources:* Strope, Ramsey)
D. Dixon Brooks, 11, 501 N. Lincoln Ave.
　Injured about 9:40 a.m. today
　In car accident
　In his own yard
　Police report he slipped car keys
　Out of mother's purse
　Started family car
　Tried to back it out of drive
　Car knocked over metal lamp post
　Slammed into telephone pole
　Near the driveway
　He suffered cuts and bruises on face and arms
　Being held for observation
　At Lincoln County Hospital
　Mother said Dixon "is nuts about cars"
　Plans serious talk with him
　When he is released from hospital
　About $200 damage to car
　About $50 damage to lamp post
　　　(*Source:* Police, Mrs. James Brooks, boy's mother)
E. State Trooper Tom Spivey
　Reported motorcycle accident
　On Ardmore Highway
　About 10 miles southwest of city
　Marianne Emerson, 14, from nearby Fayetteville
　Killed when thrown from cycle
　As it ran off the road
　Robert L. Emerson, her father
　Was driving motorcycle
　He was thrown off too

Suffered broken left arm, cuts, bruises
In fair condition at Huntsville Hospital
Trooper Spivey said Emerson
Apparently wasn't aware of
Sharp curve in the road
Cycle found about 150 feet
From where it left highway
Accident happened shortly after 11 a.m. today
    (*Source:* Spivey, hospital spokesman)

F. Firemen called to
Concord Professional Building, 10 Concord St.
About 7:05 a.m. today
Fire in office of
Dr. Clyde Lee Bevins, a dentist
On first floor of the building
Fire had burned itself out
When firemen arrived
Extensive damage to furnishings in office
Amount of damage being investigated
Smoke also did heavy damage to
Upstairs office occupied by
Dr. Leo F. Doppleman
Fire Chief Alva Harman said blaze
Apparently the work of arsonists
Evidence of kerosene found in carpet
Of Dr. Bevins's office
Fire marshals Billy Byrd and Bill Kidwell
Are investigating
    (*Source:* Fire Chief Harman)

G. Metro police report
Traffic accident near Blue Grass Airport
About 3 p.m. yesterday
Mrs. William Brown, horse breeder-trainer
Wife of Frankfort attorney and former state senator
Driving car that was towing
A horse trailer
She stopped at traffic light
At Airport Road and U.S. 60
Trailer struck from behind
By City Oil Co. gasoline truck
Truck was empty
Mrs. Brown trapped briefly
under dash of her car
But kicked loose a panel
Crawled to safety
She was treated at St. Joseph's Hospital
Chester Hughes, 56, 1001 W. Broadway,
The truck driver, was unhurt
Mrs. Brown's 11-year-old gelded hunter
Named Crackerjack was killed instantly
It was thrown from trailer
Struck by an airport security vehicle

Killed instantly
Horse was a prize winner
Valued at more than $10,000
Police said no charges would be placed
Until investigation is completed
Hughes said he was looking in
Rearview mirror when the accident occurred
Impact pushed the car several hundred feet
Truck came to rest on the trailer
    (*Sources:* Police, Mrs. Brown, Hughes)

H. City Airport closed briefly yesterday
When private Learjet crashed
About 300 yards from end of main runway
While taking off for Miami
Four persons killed
Two critically injured
Killed were: Anna Stone, 46, president of Stone Interior Designs; Richard Stiles, pilot; Joe Hammond, co-pilot; and Ronald Kramer, attorney for Stone Interior Designs. All four here.
Injured were: Ted Stone, 48, chief designer for the firm, and Lill Peters, 28, also a designer.
FAA has started investigation
Traffic Controller Len Maner
Said he was talking to pilot
Warned him of gusty crosswinds
Apparently winds caught plane
Just as it was lifting off runway
Left wingtip struck the runway
Pilot obviously tried to pull out of
The rolling motion
Plane stalled, flipped over
Crashed upside down in pasture
About 300 yards beyond runway
Maner said:
    "It is a miracle that it didn't explode"
Rescue workers said several might have survived
If they had been wearing safety belts
    (*Sources:* Clifford Hemphill, chief traffic controller, Maner, airport rescue workers, personal observation of wreckage)
Chartered plane was enroute to Miami
Mrs. Stone to sign contract to redecorate
Major hotel on Miami Beach
    (*Source:* Jill Rudd, vice-president of design firm)
Stone and Peters listed
In critical condition at University Hospital
    (*Source:* Hospital public relations spokesman)
Plane owned by Airborne Inc., local charter service
Officials said aircraft was less than year old
Pilot and co-pilot both veteran flyers
    (*Source:* Sid Klein, president of Airborne)

CHAPTER 20

Seasons and Weather

The problem with seasonal stories is they keep coming back year after year. And the reporter is faced with making this year's St. Patrick's Day story different from last year's. Or he must find a new angle to St. Valentine's Day, Mother's Day, the Fourth of July and the dozens of other holidays and anniversaries newspapers dutifully write about each year.

Fortunately most newspapers handle such stories as features, and if a reporter has an active imagination and a flair for words, what might have been a routine story can be turned into a clever, original and highly readable feature.

Chases' *Calendar of Annual Events* and *Appleton's Book of Holidays* are two good guides to seasonal and other special events. And the following chart points out some of the events and dates to receive attention by newspapers. Not all of them are reported by any one newspaper, although all are potential stories. Local interest and available space in the newspaper may be the deciding factors.

To this list may be added many seasonal events of local interest only: anniversaries of Revolutionary or Civil War battles, admission of the state into the Union, anniversary of founding of city and various "weeks" (Book Week, National Newspaper Week and so on) are proclaimed during the year. Once in a while an astronomical phenomenon, such as an eclipse or sun spots, or the arrival of a comet, is also covered in the newspaper.

JANUARY

1—New Year's Day
8—Jackson's Birthday
17—Franklin's Birthday
19—Lee's Birthday

FEBRUARY

2—Groundhog Day
12—Lincoln's Birthday
14—St. Valentine's Day
15—Women's Suffrage Day
22—Washington's Birthday
29—Leap Year Day (every four years)

MARCH

17—St. Patrick's Day

21—Vernal Equinox

Last of month—evidence of spring, first robin, spring fever, outside activities

Between March 22 and April 25—Easter, first Sunday after full moon following equinox. Good Friday, Friday before Easter

APRIL

1—All Fool's Day

13—Jefferson's Birthday

26—Arbor Day (varies in different states)

MAY

1—May Day

Second Sunday—Mother's Day

30—Decoration or Memorial Day

JUNE

First two weeks—school commencements

14—Flag Day

Third Sunday—Father's Day

22—Summer Solstice

During month—many vacations start, trips, picnics

JULY

4—Independence Day

AUGUST

During month—height of "dog days"

SEPTEMBER

First Monday—Labor Day

17—Constitution Day

23—Autumnal Equinox

During month—most schools open, harvest time, fairs held

OCTOBER

12—Columbus Day

Fourth Monday—Veterans Day

30—Hallowe'en

NOVEMBER

First Tuesday after first Monday—Election Day (not every year)

Last Thursday—Thanksgiving

During month—beginning of winter evident, sports, migration of birds

DECEMBER

First of month—Christmas shopping

22—Winter Solstice

25—Christmas

28—Wilson's Birthday

The handling of some seasonal stories was complicated when Congress passed a law making the observance of five federal holidays on Mondays (no matter what day the holiday actually came on) in order to create three-day holidays. They are Washington's Birthday, Memorial Day, Labor Day, Columbus Day and Veterans Day. The matter can get complicated because on some of these holidays, in some states, only the federal offices may be closed. State and local offices may elect to remain open because they observe different dates, so it may not be a holiday for everyone.

20a

Weaving the Story. The key to all seasonal or holiday stories is to combine the present and the past—to tell not only how the holiday will be observed but also why it is being observed. Something is lacking if a feature on Columbus Day fails to recall highlights of the discovery of America. Something is lacking if the story mentions nothing of plans of local residents to observe the anniversary.

The sources for the seasonal story are evident. In developing a feature, the reporter must go to reference books or other sources to obtain facts of the past. He must interview informed persons for facts of the present. He must weave these two together, and to give his story timeliness he usually plays up the present in the lead. Research is a key here. A reporter should not just settle for the quickest, easiest reference work—an encyclopedia. He should check the standard periodical indexes for several years to see what may have been written about the topic. Much historical—and sometimes scientific—research is done annually in many areas that might give a reporter a new approach to a holiday. For example, a check of such indexes turned up a scientist who had made a study of Ireland and produced a theory that it was the Ice Age and not St. Patrick who drove the snakes out of Ireland. The facts gave a fresh touch to a St. Patrick's Day story, and brought dozens of responses by mail and phone from staunch supporters of St. Patrick.

Sometimes the cause of the celebration does not date back to a historical event—for example, the vernal equinox—and the reporter must develop a scientific rather than a historical background. The reporter may assume that many persons will approach a certain "day" with interest, and it is permissible to predict what will be done as an unplanned observance of that day. Depending upon the tenor of the story, the reporter sometimes may make his predictions imaginative as well as factual. However, this approach requires imagination similar to that of an Associated Press reporter who wrote a personality sketch on a turkey as a Thanksgiving feature. Often an offbeat feature can be developed on one of the lesser known "days," such as Bachelor's Day on February 28.

Seeking information on local celebrations, the reporter naturally will question leaders of clubs and organizations. The American Legion and Veterans of Foreign Wars might be the principal sources for a Veterans Day story if there is not a government-sponsored observance planned. The labor unions should provide information for a Labor Day story. Schools observe most of the anniversaries by class programs. Most other organizations will announce such special programs in advance.

20b   *Story Contents.* The formula for a seasonal story:

Facts	*Sources*
A. Explanation of seasonal event	A. Reference books or reliable
1. History or definition.	persons
2. Past observances.	
B. Observance	B. Officials of organizations; reasonable predictions of reporter
1. Formally by organizations.	
2. Informally by whole city.	

20c   WEATHER STORIES

While the weather story is often related to the seasons, it is more important as a news story, usually landing on page one and with surprising frequency becoming the lead story. Farmers, businessmen, factory workers, housewives—all talk about the weather. It is everyday news, whether or not conditions change.

Many newspapers carry a regular front-page news story about the weather, in addition to the reports on an inside page provided by the United States Weather Service. Others carry stories only when there has been a seasonal change—a blizzard, a heat wave, a flood—but will print the daily weather forecast including facts on temperature, precipitation, wind velocity, pressure, humidity, river stage (if a river is near) and clearness of atmosphere. Most papers carry the local forecast on the front page, while more general statistics, and often a weather map, are printed on an inside page.

To avoid writing a routine story based on the day's forecast only, a reporter sometimes searches for human-interest approaches in writing a weather report. In so doing, he must exercise caution to prevent his addition of human-interest and imaginary elements from changing or misinterpreting the forecast. It is a violation of federal law to falsify a weather report.

Special Weather Stories. Often the weather may become the lead story or one **20d** of the major stories of the day. A special story is demanded if:

1. The weather results in disasters—floods, hurricanes, tornadoes, droughts, dust storms, blizzards, lightning and other weather quirks which cause deaths or serious damages.
2. There are sudden changes—cold waves, early snows, heavy rains or other out-of-the-ordinary conditions.
3. Records are approached or broken—highs and lows in monthly and annual temperatures or rainfall.
4. A special event may be affected by the weather—football and baseball games or other major sports events, parades, other outdoor events and even some indoor events. Readers are interested not merely in data but in the social and economic effects of unusual weather. The effects of weather on crops in farming areas can be a major local event and perhaps even have national or international implications. A poor Russian wheat harvest as a result of bad weather eventually affected the price of bread in the American supermarkets, for example.

Such news is obtained from a variety of sources: the hospital, for deaths, injuries and illnesses; the police, for accidents and traffic problems; the fire department, for fires and rescues; the charity agencies, for suffering of the poor; the government buildings, for relief work; the transportation and utility companies, for interruptions in service; and a variety of reports which usually come into the newspaper office from eyewitnesses. All are usually bound together in one weather story.

The multiple-casualty story (page 143) is a popular form to use for weather stories concerning a number of deaths and injuries. Even if there are no casualties, this same form may be used as a convenient method of presenting a wide variety of property damages and other effects, the list of damages taking the place of the list of dead and injured.

Story Contents. Facts sought in getting various weather stories: **20e**

Facts
A. Statistics
   1. Temperature (high and low).
   2. Precipitation.
   3. Visibility.

Sources
A. Weather Service

Facts	*Sources*
4. Humidity.	
5. Wind velocity.	
6. Flood stage (if any).	
B. Forecast warnings	B. Weather Service, police, fire department, relief workers
1. Crop warnings.	
2. Sea or lake warnings.	
C. Casualties	C. Police, fire department, hospitals, friends and relatives, witnesses
1. Names and identification of dead and injured.	
2. Cause of deaths and injuries.	
3. Nature of injuries.	
4. Disposition of dead and injured.	
D. Damages	D. Police, fire department, rescue workers, owners, witnesses
1. Damages to property.	
2. Description of property.	
3. Cause of damage.	
4. Property threatened.	
E. Relief	E. Police, fire department, charitable agencies, city officials, relief workers
1. Relief done.	
2. Relief need.	
F. Escapes	F. Police, fire department, relief workers, witnesses
1. Experiences of those who escaped.	
2. Rescues.	
G. Legal action	G. Police
1. Arrests.	
2. Investigations.	
H. Tie-in or tie-back	H. Newspaper file, reference books

EXERCISES

1. Using any newspaper available to you, clip a seasonal (or holiday) story and a weather story and make a news analysis of each.
2. Check the copy of Chases' *Calendar of Annual Events* in your college library or the local library. Write a story about the unusual holidays and events—not a traditional one such as St. Patrick's Day—scheduled for the coming year.
3. Write stories on the following notes:
   A. Using research material available in library, write a feature story on the first day of spring.
   B. Write a feature on Women's Suffrage Day. Place date as "tomorrow." Research library for background. Check local election officials for statistics on number of registered women voters. Attempt to locate first woman who voted in your community. If she is no longer alive, attempt to locate oldest woman voter. Interview her as part of your story.

C. Write a story for an afternoon newspaper reporting annual Christmas parade that began at 10 a.m. "today." Use following notes.

Parade route from Civic Auditorium
Twenty blocks along Main Street
To Central High School athletic field
10 marching bands from area high schools
Five drum and bugle corps from
Area American Legion posts
10 floats sponsored by local merchants
All in Christmas theme
Depicting scenes of
Christmas around the world
Five Shriner-mounted horse patrols
Riders dressed as Santa's helpers
Salvation Army marching unit
Salvation Army Band
Three special floats
With actors doing scenes
From city's Nativity Pageant
Being presented nightly
Now until Christmas Eve
In Civic Coliseum
Final float features
Santa Claus and reindeer
Mayor Berniece Pizarek
In reviewing stand
In front of City Hall
With family and other city officials

(*Source:* Stephen Lamb, Chamber of Commerce public relations director, and personal observation)

Estimated crowd of 25,000 watched
Only one interruption
Parade had to be halted briefly
So fire engines could cross
Parade route to reach
Scene of fire at downtown gas station
Electrical wiring on car burned
No one injured
Crowd orderly, no arrests
One 78-year-old man
Suffered heart attack
While watching parade
With daughter and grandchildren
Identified as Frederick Welch
Lives with daughter at 1907 Hillcrest St.
Rescue squad rushed him
To St. Mary's Hospital
Listed in stable condition

(*Source:* Police Captain Gordon Loveday, Rescue Squad Chief Jim Bob Locke, Fire Capt. William Fox and hospital officials)

4. Write stories using the following notes:
   A. Weather forecast
      Partly sunny today
      High: 39–41
      Northwesterly winds at 10 to 15 mph
      Chance of showers
      Ten per cent today, 20 per cent tonight
      Mostly cloudy tonight
      Low: 29–31
      Northwesterly winds at 10 to 15 mph
      Mostly cloudy tomorrow
      High: 39–41
      Northeasterly winds at 10 to 20 mph
      Showers clearing
   B. Unseasonably warm weather
      For month of January
      Weather Service reports
      High forecast for today—59
      Low forecast for tonight—38
      Mean temperature today—49
      Pollutants Standards Index: 72 (moderate) at 9 a.m.
      Precipitation for 24 hours
      Ending at midnight: 00
      Hourly temperatures today:

1 a.m.—51	6 a.m.—51	11 a.m.—57
2 a.m.—50	7 a.m.—52	Noon—59
3 a.m.—51	8 a.m.—53	
4 a.m.—49	9 a.m.—54	
5 a.m.—50	10 a.m.—56	

   C. Using the weather forecast for your area for today, write a news story for today's morning newspaper.
   D. City facing third day
      Of rainstorms
      Total rainfall last 36 hours
      Amounts to 5.45 inches
      Rain to continue today
      Decreasing by tomorrow morning
      Expect at least half-inch
      In next 24 hours
           (*Source:* U.S. Weather Service)
      Some mudslides reported
      Canyon Highway blocked
      About 5 miles west of city limits
      One lane opened within hour
      Crews still working to
      Remove mud
           (*Source:* Sheriff's office)
      Residents of foothills communities
      Preparing for worst
      Sandbagging their homes
           (*Source:* Sheriff's office)

One death blamed on storm
Robin Martin, 16, of suburban Crenshaw
Killed when the car she was driving
Spun on rain and mud slicked
Canyon Highway at the city limits
Car smashed into a fence
She was killed instantly
    (*Source:* Sheriff's office, city police)
Rain caused flooding of
Creeks and rivers in area
Flood warnings issued along
White and Russian rivers
Russian reported one foot
Below its banks
Third, Fourth and Gilman creeks
Over their banks and
Flooding residential areas
In suburban Camp Springs
George Henderson, fire chief of Camp Springs, said:
"I've never seen it like this. We are up to our
belly buttons in water."
Henderson said some areas
Were under four feet of water
Civil Defense officials
Considering evacuation of
About 1,000 residents near the creeks
    (*Source:* Henderson, Civil Defense Chief Harry Burton)
Nearly 3,000 customers without electricity
In rural areas south of city
Blamed on rain and flooding
Been out 24 hours
Hope to have it restored
By the end of the day
    (*Source:* Barney Center, manager of Rural Electric Inc.)
Capitola trailer park in
Suburban Beech Grove
Had to be evacuated
When Little Grassy Creek
Went over its banks
About 150 families moved
Most went to stay with
Relatives or friends
    (*Source:* Al Schneider, owner of the trailer park)
Driving rain blamed for
Rash of fender-bender accidents
All over the city
   "There are so many fender-benders we don't have time
to log them all," Traffic Sgt. Ken Miller said.
No major injuries reported
In traffic accidents inside city
    (*Source:* Miller)

271

E. First snow storm of the season
   Six inches of snow fell overnight
   Blowing winds caused drifts
   Two and three feet deep
   Snow to continue today
   Ending by late evening
   Temperature fell below
   Freezing for first time
   This year when it reached 15
   At 3 a.m.
   High today expected to be mid-20s
   Low tonight in the mid-teens
      (*Source:* U.S. Weather Service)
   All city-county schools closed
   Officials will announce late today
   If they will be open tomorrow
   Most side streets and rural roads
   Closed by snow
   School bus drivers say impossible
   To drive on them
      (*Source:* School officials)
   Many businesses closed
   Others opened late
   Manufacturing plants closed
      (*Sources:* Business owners, plant officials)
   Mayor urges everyone
   To stay off streets
   Until street crews clean
   And salt them
   Extra crews assigned to street detail
      (*Source:* Mayor Kenneth H. Boling)
   Most major highways
   Leading to city are
   Clogged with snow and abandoned cars and trucks
   State road crews working to clear highways
   State Police urge emergency travel only
   Report at least 50 cars and trucks abandoned
   Bus schedules disrupted
   About 100 persons delayed at bus station
      (*Source:* State police, bus company officials)
   City bus service almost at standstill
   Some bus lines have no service
   Bus service limited to major streets
   Running infrequently
      (*Source:* City Transit Company spokesman)
   Airport closed for five hours
   During heaviest of snow
   Snowplows cleared runways
   Some service restored
   Airlines reported five flights canceled
   Few passengers in terminal
   Jack Osseo, airport manager, said:

"It is a good thing the snow didn't start falling until about 9 o'clock last night. After that time we don't have too many flights in and out—maybe two. But three of our early morning flights didn't get off the ground."

(*Sources:* Osseo and airlines officials)

City hospitals report
Only two injury cases
Related to snow storm
William Sansom, 65, 1374 Oak St.
Suffered facial cuts when
His car slid on the snow
Going down the Oak Street hill
And struck a tree
Paul LaRue, 18, 2415 Bradford Lane
Fell while shoveling snow
Off his family's drive way
Broke his wrist
Both were treated at University Hospital
(*Source:* Hospital officials)

4. Suggest newsworthy pictures and write appropriate cutlines on the following assignments in this chapter: Exercise 3C, Exercise 4E.
5. Write a 90-second newscast based on Exercise 4E.
6. Invite a representative of the U.S. Weather Service in your area to speak to the class. Write a story about his or her talk.

CHAPTER 21

Crime

Do newspapers devote too much space to crime news? Critics of the press say they do. To counteract their complaints, newspapers in recent years have broadened the coverage of law enforcement, frequently spotlighting the root causes as well as the specific crimes. In addition to reporting muggings, robberies, murders and other so-called violent street crimes, many newspapers now devote considerable space to such crimes as child abuse and neglect and battered wives (and husbands). And considerably more attention is given to the white-collar crimes such as embezzlement, stock manipulation, insurance fraud and the like. In fact, crime stories are no longer the exclusive territory of the police reporter. They turn up on almost every beat. The city police, the county or parish sheriff's office, state police and several other state agencies and numerous federal agencies are involved in various aspects of the fight against crime. Sometimes they enforce identical laws, but each has its separate law-enforcement machinery.

In most cities, the chief source of crime news is the city police station, but in a major city there may be as many as a dozen agencies, all with law enforcement powers. A wide variety of important news is reported to the police—murders, robberies and other criminal acts, accidents, fires, missing persons. City police generally enforce state laws (on murder, larceny and other crimes), in addition to ordinances covering crimes and regulations that apply within the city limits.

The county jail, where the sheriff and his deputies and other county law enforcement officers are headquarterd,is also an important source of crime news. County officers function chiefly outside the city limits to enforce state and county laws, but they also have authority within the city.

Federal officers make few arrests compared with city and county officers, but even this number is increasing as the incidence of crime in general is soaring. Often stories resulting from federal arrests can be of a more spectacular nature than the routine crime story growing out of arrest by a city or county officer. Federal officers enforce laws dealing with kidnaping, counterfeiting, narcotics (smuggling and sale), federal tax evasion, mail fraud, manufacture and sale of illegal beverages, hijacking of airplanes as well as trucks involved in interstate shipment of goods, interference with civil rights and similar matters.

The states generally maintain state police for highway patrol duty, a state bureau of criminal investigation, fire marshals, tax collectors and investigators, game wardens, forest rangers and other units of law enforcement that will produce crime news stories.

Often the first beat assigned to a new reporter is the police beat, which includes some if not all the law enforcement agencies. The police beat is an excellent training ground for beginning reporters because it offers good practice in the fundamentals of reporting, in cultivating news sources, in gathering all the facts needed to write an accurate story (which often requires checking several sources) and in writing under pressure of approaching deadlines. It also presents some serious hazards for the lazy reporter who does not check his facts, or the reporter who gets too close to his police sources and begins to serve as a police spokesman rather than a fair and accurate reporter.

Reporting crime news can be demanding, and at times, if properly done, it is a public service that perhaps can even be a deterrent to certain types of crime. But, badly handled, it can show how to commit crime successfully. It can give a false impression of the amount of crime, or build sympathy for or glorify criminals. Crime news also can help criminals by informing them of police strategy, or hamper justice by "trying the case out of court"—making it impossible to get a fair trial. And, of course, it can turn the spotlight on the law-abiding family of the criminal, adding to their humiliation.

Fortunately, over the years, the leaders in the news media have come to recognize these problems and most newspapers today practice considerable restraint in handling crime news. At the same time the news media continue to fight for their First Amendment rights to report freely and fairly all crime news, despite repeated efforts over the years to force controls upon the media.

CRIMES

Before examining the content of the typical crime story, the reporter should know what is meant by crime. A breach of law is a crime and may be either a felony or a misdemeanor. A felony is one of the more serious crimes, usually carrying a penalty of long imprisonment and sometimes of death. (Although the Supreme Court held in the 1970s that the death penalty was cruel and inhuman punishment, a number of states reenacted their death penalty laws and several executions have been carried out.) A misdemeanor is a minor breach of law, usually resulting in a fine and no imprisonment. A study of most state laws will show that the following crimes are usually regarded as felonies:

Homicide (killing a person)
1. Manslaughter.
   a. Voluntary (intentional, in a fit of passion).
   b. Involuntary (unintentional, through negligence).

275

2. Murder.

    a. First degree (with evident premeditation).

    b. Second degree (no premeditation but intent to kill).

Assault

1. Assault with intent to kill or maim.

2. Felonious assault.

3. Mayhem (maiming).

4. Kidnaping.

Violating property rights

1. Larceny (illegally taking property).

2. Burglary (entering dwelling to take property, housebreaking).

3. Robbery (larceny with assault, threatened or committed).

4. Embezzlement (larceny through trust).

5. Forgery.

6. Arson.

7. Receiving stolen property.

Obstructing justice

1. Interfering with officer.

2. Perjury.

3. Bribery.

4. Contempt of court.

Conspiracy in crime

1. Accessory before fact.

2. Accessory after fact.

Others

1. Gambling.

2. Manufacture, possession or sale of illegal beverages and drugs.

3. Disturbing peace (fight, riot).

4. Sexual crimes.

5. Criminal libel.

Misdemeanors include such violations as public drunkenness, speeding, illegal parking, simple assault and a variety of lesser infractions ranging from littering to public nudity.

21a   In crime stories the reporter must be sure to write only privileged facts gathered from public records, and he must be accurate. Of course, accuracy is important in every news story, but it is vital in crime stories because a libel suit lurks behind every one of them. If a person is arrested and charged with a certain crime, the reporter can say just that. It is a matter of public record. But a detective's chance remark that a certain person committed a crime is not a matter of public record and therefore is not privileged. Its publication may result in a libel suit. Even in cases in which police obtain confessions, the reporter must exercise care. In one case on the records, a man arrested for a crime confessed. During the trial he repudiated his confession and was found not guilty. He then sued the newspaper that had reported his confession and won the libel suit.

A person arrested is not necessarily guilty of a crime. No matter how damaging the evidence, the reporter must not "convict" him in the newspaper story. He can report the evidence that police have against the prisoner, if they will tell him, but he cannot conclude that this evidence shows the person is guilty. A prisoner is always arrested *on charges* of a certain crime, not *for* the crime. In the matter of reporting the evidence police or prosecutors say they have against a prisoner, the reporter should exercise extreme care. At one infamous murder-rape trial in Illinois, a prosecutor claimed he had a pair of the prisoner's blood-stained underwear, which he even showed in court. During the appeal process in the case, it was proved that the underwear did not belong to the prisoner and that the "blood" on them actually was red dye.

If doubt exists that the prisoner gave his right name, the newspapers reports that he "was booked at the city jail as John Smith" or he "gave his name as John Smith." Some newspapers no longer publish the addresses that alleged criminals give to the police because quite often they are fictitious and create certain problems for the legitimate residents at those addresses. Instead, the newspaper may say "John Smith, who lives in the 1200 block of South Park Street, has been charged. . . ." Reporters should use directories and other available sources in checking doubtful information. In fact, it is good practice to check names and addresses automatically, no matter what the arrest record may say. If a prisoner refuses to give his address, the reporter may write "address not given."

Police Records. Two types of records commonly yield local crime news in most localities: (1) city and county jail "blotters" and (2) the complaint sheets or bulletins. The first is an entry book for persons arrested that is maintained at the city and county jails; the second is a record of complaints made to police and of investigations by police. The following illustrations of these records have been condensed to conserve space.

These records give the reporter only a few bare facts about a case. If he wants others, he must interview the officers or the persons involved. Some cases are so trivial that he ignores them altogether.

POLICE BLOTTER

Date	Time	Name	Age	Color	Sex	Occupation	Residence	Offense Charged	Arresting Officers
1/17	9:01 P.M.	John L. Tukes	38	W	M	Mechanic	101 W. Rhodes St.	Larceny	Stamps & Edd.
1/17	10:10 P.M.	Nathan F. Burkhart	27	W	M	Laborer	712 N. 4th St.	Drunk	Jones

COMPLAINT BULLETINS

COMPLAINT	INVESTIGATION
Date 1/17 Time 9:01 AM Taken by Larson	Date 1/17 Time 10:30 A.M.
Complaint: Name: J. D. Hornsby Address: 3102 S. Ailor St. Telephone: 6-2907	Complaint: Home of J. D. Hornsby 3102 S. Ailor St. entered last night
Complaint: Someone entered house: Stole silver, watch, money	Investigation: Following articles missing: Set Rogers Silver Value $40.00. Elgin Watch #6430973, value $25.00 Money $19.07 No suspects
Assigned to: Fox and Knell	By: Fox and Knell

The access to police records and other public records varies from state to state. By the early 1980s, some 30 states had open records laws that require police and almost all other records to be open for inspection by the public as well as the press. The reporter must learn what is the law in his state and, even in the case of states with open records laws, he should not attempt to "throw his weight around." Most police departments cooperate with the press. It is only in extreme cases that newspapers resort to court action to force open public records, as a general rule.

A reporter must use extreme care when copying information from a police blotter and especially from the complaint sheets. Both frequently contain misspellings of names and incorrect addresses. In addition, the complaint sheets often contain misinformation, exaggerations and, from time to time, outright lies. They usually are a form of interoffice correspondence between the complaint desk and the officers. This information has not been verified, so the reporter must check anything he wants to use from the complaint sheet carefully—usually with the investigating officers. Also, the reporter is expected to use good judgment in handling information that he may possess from police sources if publication would aid a suspect in escaping or if there are other justifiable reasons.

While the records illustrated above pertain to city police, records of a similar nature are kept by other types of law enforcement officers—county, state and federal. Every reporter should also know that federal law enforcement agencies, as a general rule, tend to be far less open than city and state officials in revealing information to the press. And while there is a federal freedom of information law, designed to open federal records to the public, certain criminal information is exempt from the law.

The coroner is another public official whose records are often important in crime news, although he does not fit exactly into the law enforcement picture. The coroner makes an inquest into deaths from "unnatural causes"—those in which foul play, violence, suicide or unusual circumstances may be involved. His report, if it shows that the cause of a death points out evidence of crime, may result in arrests by law enforcement officers. However, it must be kept in mind that the coroner's functions are limited to determining cause of death, and he does not "try" a case against persons accused of death. Any legal action arising from his reports must go through the courts in the usual manner.

21b *Story Contents.* The formula of usual information and sources for a crime story might be outlined as follows:

Facts	*Sources*
A. Casualties	A. Police, hospitals, friends and
1. Name and identification of persons.	relatives of dead and injured, witnesses
2. How persons were killed or injured.	
3. Nature of injuries.	
4. Disposition of dead and injured.	
B. Damages	B. Police, property owners
1. Value, property stolen or destroyed.	

Facts	*Sources*
2. Description of property.	
3. Owner.	
4. Insurance.	
5. Other property threatened.	
C. Description	C. Police, persons involved, witnesses
1. Chronological account.	
2. Description of persons involved.	
D. Escapes	D. Police, persons involved, witnesses
1. Rescues.	
2. Experiences of those escaping.	
E. Legal action	E. Police
1. Investigation, clues, evidence.	
2. Arrests.	
F. Tie-backs	F. Morgue-library

21c

The length of a crime story is usually determined by the seriousness of the crime. Other factors that add paragraphs and increase the size of the headline are the prominence of the persons involved, the place of the crime, unusual circumstances and incidents of human interest. Often one of these factors causes a reporter to write a feature story about an incident he might have ignored as "straight news." In selecting facts to go into his stories and in the treatment he gives those facts, the reporter must be careful to observe the ethics of his newspaper with respect to crime news. A review of the ethics of newspapers (Chapter 5) would be appropriate in considering this chapter.

Here are several examples of the leads of crime stories:

DRESDEN, Tenn.—Robert Glenn Coe, 23, of Gleason, was charged Wednesday with the murder, kidnaping and sexual assault of Cary Medlin, an 8-year-old Greenfield girl.

District Attorney David Hayes of Union City said Coe confessed to the murder almost immediately after he was arrested and taken to the Weakley County Jail in Dresden about 8:30 p.m. Tuesday . . .

(The Commercial Appeal, Memphis)

Marcie Davis, 36, of 7517½ S. Coles Ave., was stabbed to death Wednesday night by a woman whose husband she was seeing, Burnside Area homicide investigators said.

Wanda Miller, 40, of 7015 S. East End Ave., drove to Miss Davis's apartment and, while parking, bumped into her husband's car and set off a burglar alarm, investigators reported.

When Miss Davis heard the alarm she went outside and began quarreling with Mrs. Miller, who pulled a knife. Mrs. Miller stabbed Miss Davis seven times in the head, back, shoulders and arms . . .

(The Chicago Tribune)

Sometimes the police can be the victim as this story from the Montgomery Journal, Chevy Chase, Md., shows:

> It is not unusual for a burglar to try to break out of a police station. But one burglar last week broke into one.

> Somebody beat the odds early Saturday morning by breaking into the Gaithersburg City police station and absconding with approximately $10,000 in police radio equipment, police reported . . .

21d SUICIDES

In covering a suicide the reporter must be extremely careful. The official police record, not the reporter's own judgment, determines whether a death is suicide. The record may be established only by action of a coroner.

Even if a man plunges from a 14-story window in front of a large crowd, it may not be suicide. Even if a woman is found dead on a lonely road, a pistol in her hand and a bullet in her head, there may be no definite evidence that she fired the bullet. Until a coroner completes his investigation, the reporter can say only that the person was "found dead," or that he "plunged" or "fell." The reporter should give all the facts surrounding the case, and the reader must draw his own conclusions as to whether it is suicide.

Suicide notes are sometimes found, which may seem to assure the reporter that he may safely call the death a suicide. Nevertheless, it is always best to wait until a public official makes the pronouncement.

It may be possible to discover a motive, after suicide has been clearly established, but again the reporter must be careful. He must not piece together certain facts about the person's ill health, financial difficulties or love affairs, then conclude what he thinks is the motive. If he has a definite, authentic statement of motive, from the suicide note or a close relative, he probably will be safe in using it. If no apparent motive is found, the reporter should say so, and quote those he interviewed to that effect.

Even more caution is necessary in reporting attempted suicides. Unless the suicide attempt is evident and backed up by statements of authorities, or unless the person admits he attempted to end his life, the reporter must give only facts pertaining to the person's actions, rescue and so on. In fact, it is wise to be cautious even in cases where the person admits he attempted suicide. It could be a grandstand play for attention or a fabrication for some other reason.

The method of suicide is usually described in general terms, with few details of methods that might be suggestive for others contemplating suicide. For instance, the name of a poison or drug is seldom used in suicide stories. It is simply called "a poison" or "a drug." Gory details are omitted in suicide accounts, as in most crime stories.

21e Story Contents. A formula for the usual suicide story:

Facts	Sources
A. Name and identification	A. Police, coroner, or coroner's
1. Disposition of body.	report, hospital, relatives,
	friends

Facts	*Sources*
B. Method	B. Police, witnesses
1. Cause of death.	
2. Circumstances surrounding	
death (when and how found).	
C. Motive	C. Police, relatives, friends,
1. Suicide note.	physician
2. Statement from relatives,	
physician, friends, business	
associates.	

Each of the three principal facts named above may be the feature of the **21f** suicide story. An unusual method or motive is usually the feature, unless the person's prominence overshadows that feature. Under no circumstances should the reporter attempt to treat a suicide story in a lighthearted or humorous manner.

EXERCISES

1. Using any newspaper available to you, clip and analyze a robbery or a hold-up story and a suicide story.
2. Following are several crimes reported to police. On a separate sheet of paper explain how you would handle the story on each. For example, tell if you would write a story based only on the information available or if you would call the victim for more information and so forth:
   A. Albert Sidney Johnson, a professor who specialized in teaching criminal law at State University, named police chief yesterday by Mayor Harris B. Leviton. Went to dinner last night to celebrate his appointment. Returned home about 11 p.m., found that his house had been broken into. About $5,000 worth of his wife's jewelry and other personal items, including color television set, clothing, rare coin collection missing.
   B. A 24-year-old woman reported to police that she had been stabbed and raped in a vacant lot in the 7500 block of South Halstead Street at 3:30 a.m. Thursday. She said she left a lounge in the 7400 block and was walking to her apartment about two blocks away when a man grabbed her and forced her into a vacant lot. She said she fought him. But he stabbed her in the left side, raped her and then fled. She went to her apartment and called her parents. They took her to St. Bernard's Hospital. She is listed in good condition.
   C. John Edward Martin, 30, 1445 Hannah St., arrested at his home. Charged with shooting Donald E. King, 18, Raccoon Valley Rd, in the left side. King was walking along Wilson Road when a van with a devil painted on the side approached. A pistol was pointed out the window. One shot was fired, striking King. King was treated at St. Mary's Medical Center. Police broadcast a description of the van. About 9 p.m. Officer Tommy Crook sighted a van matching the description of the vehicle King reported. It was parked behind the Hannah Street address. The steering wheel was missing. Several persons at the house said the van had not been driven for several days. Additional police were sent to the scene. They surrounded the house. A team of five policemen entered the house and made a room-by-room search. They found Martin in the basement hiding behind a furnace duct. He was charged with felonious assault.

D. Floyd E. Geiger, 32, 3267 Schroeder Rd., was arrested yesterday by investigators for the State Public Health Department. He was taken to County Jail and charged with illegally selling contact lenses. He was released under $100 bond. Investigators said he had been operating a mail order contact lens business without being a licensed dispensing optician. The state Attorney General has ruled that persons dispensing optical lenses must have a state license. Smith did not.

E. A 13-month-old boy was shot Friday afternoon by his three-year-old brother. The child, Adam Carrico, son of Mr. and Mrs. Edward Carrico, of suburban Mascot, was struck by a bullet from a rifle when his brother pulled the rifle from a closet and the weapon discharged. The baby is in serious condition at Valley Community Hospital. County deputies said the shooting was accidental. The baby was in a playpen in the family living room when his brother, Robert, pulled the weapon from the closet.

3. Tour the police station or sheriff's department in your community and write a feature story about it.

4. Write stories using the following notes:

A. George Pardoo, 31, 830 Oaklawn Court
Suffered a cut in the chest
During a fight about 10:30 p.m. last night
In Last Lap Tavern, 714 Cumberland Ave.
He was admitted to Presbyterian Hospital
Underwent emergency surgery
Listed in stable condition
Two other men treated
At University Hospital last night
For injuries suffered in the incident
Charged with public drunkenness
Kenneth H. Nathan, 21, Maryville
Treated for sprained wrist
Larry W. Minton, 29, Route 2, Tazwell Pike
Treated for cut head
　　　(*Source:* Detective Herbert Collins)

B. Carol Russell, 20, Route 3, Bean Station
Taken by ambulance
To St. Mary's Medical Center
About 7:30 last night
Had been shot in the abdomen
She died while undergoing
Emergency surgery
Deputy Sheriff Tom Hurst
Said woman locked herself
In bathroom of family home
Shot herself in stomach
With a hunting rifle
Family said she had been despondent
After her engagement
Was broken by boyfriend
　　　(*Sources:* Hurst, family members)

C. Jelly Barn, 28 Westhills Mall
Operated by Sertoma Learning Center
Reported to police
Thieves stole $200

From store cash register
While clerk was in
Rear of the store Saturday .
John Palmer, director of Center
Offered $100 reward
For information leading
To arrest and conviction
Of the thieves

D. David L. Bradley, 33, Apt. 3
1815 Laurel Ave.
In bedroom talking to wife
Heard front door
Of apartment building crash
He grabbed pistol
From under the bed
Went to bedroom door
Which leads to hallway
Saw intruder in hall
Bradley and intruder
Exchanged shots
Bradley struck in chest
Intruder fled
Bradley admitted to
Presbyterian Hospital
About midnight
In intensive care unit
Condition listed as critical
(*Source:* Mrs. Vera Bradley, Detective Buddy Fitzsimmons)

E. Robert Eugene Barnhill, 19
1421 Clinch Ave.
Arrested about 8 p.m. yesterday
Inside Westside Chevrolet, 437 W. Main St.
Police said they were called
By a couple who stopped
At the auto dealer
To look at cars on the lot
Couple said they heard
Loud noise from inside
Closed auto showroom
Said they saw a man
Climbing through a window
Went to nearby pay phone
Called police
Police declined to
Identify the couple
Barnhill charged with burglary
Placed under $10,000 bond
(*Source:* Detective Carles Dragoo)

F. State Highway Department employee
Taking girlfriend home
Found man, shot in head,
Lying beside Riverside Drive

Between Cliftwood and Atlantic roads
About 11:30 p.m. Thursday
County Detectives took victim
To University Hospital
In critical condition
Wound in left side of head
When found he was without
Shirt and shoes
No identification on him
Apparently thrown out of car
Detectives declined to
Identify Highway Department employee
    (*Source:* Detective James Lewis)

G. George S. Roach, 35,
Of 418 Woodlawn Pike
Arrested Sunday
Charged with robbery
Of Paul J. Robinson, 65,
Of 1709 Beaverbrook St.
Ten days ago
Roach charged with
Robbing Robinson of his
Billfold and credit cards
At Robinson's home
Roach placed under $10,000 bond
City Court hearing
Set for next Tuesday

H. Gino's Food Store
At 1701 N. Whipple St.
Robbed about 7:30 p.m. last night
Five persons shot to death
Killed were William Parker, 32, 1758 N. Humboldt Ave., owner; Aida Parker, 38, his wife; Juan Jimenez, 38, 3018 N. Wabash Ave, a patron; Stanley Mirek, 49, 1912 N. Mozart St., a patron; and Mrs. Dorothy Oszakandy, 45, 850 W. Wabasiana St., Mrs. Parker's sister.
One witness to the robbery-murders
Richard Spiegel, 18, 1210 N. Clark St., a clerk
Spiegel told police he was working
In the storeroom at the rear
When he heard shots
He ran to front of store
Found the bodies piled
On top of each other
Each shot in the face
Cash register drawer open
All the money was missing
Said he heard tires screeching
As car pulled away from
Front of the store
Ran outside but could not
See car's license number
Rushed back inside

Called police emergency number
Told police he checked
To see if any of those shot
Were still living
Homicide Commander Rudy Nimocks
Said robbers must have been
Familiar with the store
And perhaps owners and patrons
He said:
    "Looks like they were trying to kill all witnesses. That makes me think they
    were afraid they had been recognized."
Police were swarming
Through the area in minutes
Several "suspect" cars were stopped
But no arrests have been made
Mayor Oakley Leavitt
Said he was shocked by
The viciousness of the killings
Offered a $5,000 reward
For information leading to
Arrest and conviction
Of the murderers
Nimocks said he was
Unable to determine
Amount of money taken
In the robbery
Spiegel said Parker
Rarely kept more than
$100 in the cash register
Parker usually made a
Bank deposit late each day
Some money kept in safe
In rear of the store
Apparently robbers
Did not know about it
Neighbors said Parkers
Only owned store about
Last six months
Previous owner sold out
After being robbed five times
In one year
Nimocks said area stores
Are frequent targets
Of hold-up men
Because most stores are
Mom and Pop operations
In the neighborhood

5. Write a one-minute newscast from the following assignments in this chapter: Exercise
    II A; Exercise II C; Exercise II E; Exercise IV E; and Exercise IV H.

WRITING
THE COMPLEX
STORY TYPES

The growing complexity of modern society has changed the way newspapers report news. No longer can a newspaper simply report what happened. Increasing numbers of stories require interpretation and explanation. Many stories—most generally those involving government and politics, but many others as well—need to be analyzed for the reader if he is to grasp their true significance.

Not all newspapers have accepted this added responsibility, and many editors still prefer to stick to the straight-news account of what happened. There are some risks, of course, because there is an extremely fine line between interpretation or analysis and editorializing. Not every reporter knows the difference, and certainly readers do not always have a clear understanding of the differences between reporting, interpretative reporting and editorializing.

Yet as newsmen grow in education and experience and the practice of interpretation becomes more commonplace, more and more newspapers are using the technique in reporting in the fields of law, business, government, politics and other areas where it is needed to keep readers accurately informed. In these fields the reporter encounters new problems of reporting:

1. Stories often involve a web of conditions and events stretching into the past and into the future and into related fields.
2. The reader must be told not merely the facts but the significance of the facts.
3. Since much interpretation is necessary, the reporter needs a general background of information.
4. And generally he needs a technical vocabulary.

If a reporter is to be successful in his efforts to evaluate, measure and explain the facts of a story, he needs study, practice and experience in fields represented by the complex story types.

Courts, Trials, Lawsuits

Reporters assigned to cover the courts spend far more time going from one clerk's office to another and talking to lawyers than they do in a courtroom covering a trial. Statistical studies show that most newspapers cover only a limited number of trials and lawsuits. The vast majority of criminal cases are settled by plea bargaining and the accused spends only a brief time in court. In civil cases, there is a growing tendency to settle out of court.

Yet court stories—whether the information is gathered outside the courtroom or witnessing the trial—can be among the most difficult and demanding to report because of the complexity of the legal process. There is an added danger, from the newsman's point of view as well as that of the principals involved in the trial: how publicity in the media before and during the trial will affect the outcome. Strong arguments have been made on both sides, but there has been no conclusive evidence to prove that in most instances pretrial publicity prevents a fair trial. The issue arises only in the most spectacular or sensational cases as a general rule.

For the most part, the court story is concerned with events that have appeared previously in the news. Thus, in a sense, it is a follow-up story. The crime, already reported at the time of commission and arrest, will reappear as a trial for murder, or larceny, or arson or embezzlement. Fires and accidents, already reported, may reappear as lawsuits developing from them. Many business conflicts may result in litigation. And, of course, litigation can and does develop from such areas as medical and legal malpractice, violation of civil rights, unfair labor practices and many other alleged violations of both criminal and civil law. After evaluating the importance and newsworthiness of a trial or lawsuit, the reporter may ignore it or write a story summarizing it. Often a reporter may never attend such a trial, obtaining information about it from court officers and documents or the attorneys involved. Usually the trials given lengthy coverage are more controversial or sensational.

In previous chapters, references were made to the freedom of the press and the right of newspapers to publish judicial proceedings as privileged materials. In this chapter, it is necessary to point out that judges have the power to limit those freedoms and rights insofar as the cases in their own courts are concerned. Judges can back up their power by having newspapermen jailed on contempt-of-court charges for refusing to abide by the judge's coverage guidelines. This is not to say that all judges use this power wantonly, although a few have gone beyond the bounds of both reason and law in such matters. The newsman has the right to appeal a judge's restrictions, and a number of them have. For the most part, the higher courts have upheld the rights of the newsmen. The problem from a news point of view is that, if a newspaper elects to obey a judge's gag order and then appeal, the coverage of the trial obviously will be inadequate. Of course, if the newsman disobeys such gag orders, he can be jailed. Reporters involved in such cases generally do not spend long periods in jail. Several, after their release, have appealed in an effort to seek vindication, but that can be a long process.

The conflict here (if any) is between two different provisions of the United States Constitution, one guaranteeing freedom of the press and the other guaranteeing an individual a fair and impartial trial. No ethical journalist would want to deny an individual a fair trial, but newsmen are aware that not all judges are necessarily ethical. In such cases, newsmen frequently feel the only way the defendant will receive a fair trial is with the presence of the media. Other newsmen feel so strongly about their First Amendment rights that they are willing to risk jail by defying judicial gag orders.

Judges and lawyers generally feel otherwise. If a judge thinks the presence of newspaper reporters, photographers or television cameramen in the court will affect court proceedings to the extent that the rights of the individual in receiving a fair trial may be impaired, and justice obstructed, the judge has the power to ban any and all of these communications representatives from the courtroom. In some cases, judges have even banned newsmen and photographers from the courthouse itself. Others have issued extensive rules of coverage for the media, along with stern lists of instructions to all the lawyers and participants as well as court officers in regard to discussing the case with the media. As a general practice, judges—especially federal judges—do not permit photographers for newspapers or television cameramen in their courtrooms. During some major trials, artists are assigned by newspapers and wire services to make sketches of courtroom scenes. However, some lawyers have objected even to this.

Restrictions on a trial coverage naturally will depend upon the individual judge. In most cases such restraints are really unnecessary because newspapers today generally exercise caution in their coverage. They are interested, of course, in seeing that a fair trial is conducted. But they also want to avoid the embarrassment and loss of credibility with their readers that they might suffer if a conviction were reversed upon appeal because of unfair or sensational publicity. Newsmen also would prefer not to be cited for contempt of court by a judge, for that could mean a fine as well as a jail term. The press does have the right of "fair comment and criticism" on the action of a judge or his court, but not while litigation on the case in point is still pending, and caution must be taken even after a decision is reached because of the possibilities of a new trial or an appeal.

A judge does have absolute power in his courtroom (subject to review by a higher court), and, to lessen the animosities between judges and journalists, a number of state press associations and bar associations have worked out sets of guidelines for trial coverage acceptable to both groups. In other states, members of the press have voted against such guidelines, seeing them as an infringement of their First Amendment rights.

Story Forms. For reporting trials and lawsuits no definite forms can be prescribed. The general principles of good news writing should always apply. The lead of a typical trial should either summarize the trial events of the day or emphasize an outstanding feature such as a particular bit of testimony.

SUMMARY:

A defense attorney in the George Paine murder trial used testimony about lost evidence and inadequate photographs, lab reports and fingerprints today in trying to show that authorities bungled the investigation in the death of a jailer.

OUTSTANDING FEATURE:

A deputy sheriff in charge of the investigation into the slaying of jailer Talbert White admitted under cross-examination today that he did not save most of the evidence found in a cell where the jailer's body was discovered.

The body of the story will amplify the lead, as in other types of stories. However, it is essential in a running trial story to include the tie-back in the second paragraph if it is not included in the lead paragraph. Direct quotations, indirect quotations and interpretative summaries will be interspersed, and there will be frequent use of the chronological order. Quotations from the opening and closing arguments of attorneys and from opinions handed down by judges are similar to speech forms and can be handled effectively as quote-summary-quote stories. Quotations from testimony are usually of the short question-and-answer type and can be handled effectively in the chronological order (direct quotations interspersed with indirect quotations or unquoted summaries) after the features are summarized.

The reporter may choose one of two forms in relating the questions and answers. The following narrative style is common for brief excerpts:

"Were you in the cell when Jailer White was stabbed?" Attorney Jones demanded.

"No!" Paine answered in almost a shout. "I had already climbed out the window before he came in. I never saw him."

It is not necessary to use colorful words and descriptions unless needed to convey to the reader some of the sense of drama associated with a key point in the trial. Also, they should not be used if the attorney's voice did not have a demanding tone or if Paine's answer was not a shout. And, if it is evident who is speaking, it may not even be necessary to use their names at all.

The second form is used for extended questions and answers in cases of considerable importance or interest, especially when reporting key testimony:

Q.—Were you in the cell when Jailer White was stabbed?
A.—No! I had already climbed out the window before he came in. I never saw him.

Quotation marks are not necessary in the Q-A form. Before testimony is given in this form, it must be preceded by an explanation such as *Paine's testimony follows.*

In addition to noting feature highlights in court proceedings, the reporter should take notes on the background of court actions—descriptions of the crowd, witnesses, jury. Sometimes a lead feature comes from an event not included in regular court procedure. For example, outside the courtroom the attorney's actions could have a direct bearing on the case and provide a far more significant lead than anything that happened in the courtroom that day. Reporters should be particularly observant during trials, for the courtroom is an excellent source of human-interest stories.

While most court stories are reported as straight news, a considerable amount of interpretation may be necessary to enrich and to make entirely clear the significance of facts and procedures.

22d   *Background and Interpretation.* In addition to having an understanding of the organization of the courts in his state, the reporter assigned to cover any trial must acquire a background of the facts and relationships of the particular case. Is the embezzlement of bank funds related to a previous bank failure, to business conditions or to personal problems of the person charged in the case? Is the case a striking parallel of other cases? When, where and how and by whom was a suit filed, the crime committed? Have there been any previous consequences? Are other suits or indictments pending? What consequences will develop from the case? Is there a particularly interesting problem of law, court jurisdiction, *corpus delicti* or other novel feature involved in the case? Only with such a background can the reporter do full justice to the case and write a clear account for his readers.

A reporter must have a thorough knowledge of legal terms and procedures to write effectively about a case. He must know the difference, for example, between "evidence" and "testimony," and he must use these and other legal terms properly in his stories. He must not only possess a legal vocabulary himself but should also be able to explain legal terminology clearly to his readers. A court story should not sound like a legal brief. The use of many legal terms means nothing to the average reader. No interpretative reporter would leave readers struggling with a sentence like this one:

The state filed nolle prosequi in the first indictment.

The reporter should explain the terms as well as the consequence of legal action. "The grand jury returned a no-true bill against Sidney Westchester . . ." might be understood by a few readers but not the majority; but "The grand jury freed Sidney Westchester of charges . . ." would be clear. If the case involves the Constitutionality or validity of a certain law being tested in the courts, the reporter must explain the consequence of the court ruling. For example, "The State Supreme Court today upheld the Constitutionality of the new open meetings law in the Palm County School Board case" is infinitely more important than "The Palm County School Board was told by the State Supreme Court today that it could not meet behind closed doors anymore." Readers are not expected to be interpreters of court decisions. The newspaper must tell them, in the language of the layman, exactly how a decision affects their routine of life.

Here are several examples of court story leads:

The jury that will decide the 33 murder charges against John Wayne Gacy will be selected from Winnebago County, then transported to Chicago for the trial, Criminal Court Judge Louis B. Garippo ruled Monday.

Garippo made the unusual ruling after Gacy's attorneys requested a change of venue, asserting that there is a "pattern of deep-rooted prejudice" against their client in Cook County.

[THE CHICAGO TRIBUNE]

Paying public officials for favors was nothing new in 1972 to R. Kenneth Vann, president of Browning-Ferris Industries of Knoxville, he testified yesterday in Federal Court.

On the stand for the second day in the retrial of former County Welfare Commissioner John M. Beeler, Vann said he paid a former City Council member, who died 12 to 14 years ago, $1,200 for some favors the councilman did.

[THE KNOXVILLE NEWS-SENTINEL]

A three-year-old provision of state law calling for mandatory 25-year sentences for repeat criminals has been invoked in county court for the first time.

Circuit Court Judge Philip Fairbanks yesterday sentenced a bank robber with at least two earlier convictions to 25 years in prison, without possibility of parole.

[THE MONTGOMERY JOURNAL]

Actual experience and contact with courts may be necessary to acquire an adequate technical background. The following definitions and procedures are more or less uniform in the various states and may be used as a foundation.

THE LAW AND THE COURTS

Two general types of law are recognized: *civil,* under which may be brought suits for damages involving two or more persons, and *criminal,* under which charges of offenses against society may be brought by a governmental officer or a citizen against one or more persons. The authority for enforcing the two types of law comes from the Constitution (Constitutional law), the acts of legislative bodies (statutory law) and customs and judicial precedents (common law). There is still another type law on the federal and state level called administrative law. It generates from the powers granted governmental regulatory bodies such as the Federal Trade Commission or a state Public Utilities Commission to enforce certain rules over particular industries and businesses.

A further classification of the two types is

I. Civil cases
   A. *Cases in law,* which abide closely by the law.
      1. *Contracts*—cases in which the *plaintiff* (the person bringing the suit) claims the *defendant* (the persons against whom the suit is brought) did not follow the terms of an oral or written contract.
      2. *Torts*—cases which treat private injuries not arising from a breach of contract. For example, it is usually a tort for a man to damage someone or his property, purposely or negligently.

293

B. *Cases in equity,* which are distinguished from cases in law in rendering "equitable" judgment by not following definite laws. Persons go to this court when they can get no relief from the definite writs existing in the regular law courts. This relief often is obtained by compulsory or preventive decrees (mandates and injunctions) issued by the judge. Controversies over property ownership are usually brought to this court.

II. Criminal cases

A. *Misdemeanors,* minor criminal cases usually resulting in fines, sometimes in imprisonment.

B. *Felonies,* major criminal cases usually resulting in imprisonment, and until outlawed by the Supreme Court, sometimes death. (See Chapter 21 on Crime.)

State courts—which also include county and city courts serving by authority of the state—and federal courts deal with these types of law. Local affairs and cases concerning state laws are tried by state courts. Cases concerning federal laws and interstate cases are tried by federal courts. The dual system of courts is outlined in the chart on page 295.

To obtain a better understanding of this chart, and at the same time to learn a few of the most common legal terms, it is necessary to trace the route of a criminal case and a civil case in a state court. (Be sure to learn the meaning of each italicized term.)

ROUTE OF A CRIMINAL CASE

I. In the *court of limited jurisdiction* (county or city magistrate)

A. A *warrant* is sworn out, charging person with crime, enabling officers to bring him before magistrate.

    1. If the person has been arrested because he is wanted in another state, an *extradition order* is obtained, which will enable officers in the other state to take the prisoner back.

    2. If the prisoner feels that he is held illegally, he may obtain a *writ of habeas corpus* from a superior court and get an immediate hearing. Then the officers holding him must prove that the prisoner is held for a just cause.

B. The magistrate hears the case.

    1. If it is a *misdemeanor,* he may (within prescriptions of state law) *fine* the prisoner.

        a. *Fines* may be *appealed* from this court to a *court of general jurisdiction,* where such cases are tried anew.

    2. If it is a *felony,* the magistrate may *bind the prisoner over* to the grand jury.

        a. The prisoner may *waive* the preliminary hearing and be bound over to the grand jury.

    3. In binding the prisoner over, the magistrate *sets the bail bond* which the prisoner may post in order to be released until trial.

        a. In some very serious cases, the magistrate may not allow the prisoner freedom from jail but will bind him over *without bond.*

II. In the grand jury

A. Evidence is given to members of the grand jury *ex parte,* or without the presence of the defendant.

    1. Only the evidence against the defendant is heard. This is not a trial body. Cases are not heard in public.

STATE SYSTEM	FEDERAL SYSTEM

State Supreme Court

Appellate Court, usually of last resort for state, though some cases may go from here to U.S. Supreme Court if they involve federal questions.
(Criminal and Civil)

U.S. Supreme Court

Appellate Court of Last Resort in the United States.
(Criminal and Civil)

Court of Appeals

Intermediate Appellate Court, created to relieve Supreme Court.
(Civil only)

Circuit Court of Appeals

Intermediate Appellate Court, created to relieve Supreme Court.
(Criminal and Civil)

Courts of General Jurisdiction

(Where cases are first tried)

In the various states these courts have different names: Circuit, District, Superior, Common Pleas, Chancery. Jurisdiction is in criminal law, law, and equity. Each district court may be divided into units, a separate judge passing on each of the three phases of law named above. Or one judge may have jurisdiction in all three. Petit juries hear many of the cases.

District Court

The Court of Original Jurisdiction in the federal system. One judge hears cases in *law*, in *equity*, and in *criminal* law. This judge also appoints a Bankruptcy Referee who relieves the district judge of these cases.

Grand Jury

This body must hear the prosecutor's evidence against anyone and indict that person before he is to be tried in the district court on a *criminal* charge.

Grand Jury

In many states no person may be tried in a court of general jurisdiction on a criminal charge unless indicted by a grand jury.

U.S. Commissioner's Court

This official is appointed by the district judge to give preliminary hearings on criminal cases.

State Courts of Limited Jurisdiction

These inferior courts handle only petty cases. They enforce local laws in addition to state laws. They serve as courts for *preliminary hearings* in major *criminal* cases, and the *civil* cases they handle are *limited* to *stated amounts* (except in probate courts) by the state code or constitution. The most common inferior courts are shown below.

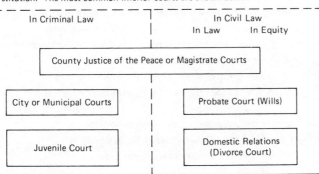

In Criminal Law	In Civil Law
	In Law In Equity

County Justice of the Peace or Magistrate Courts	
City or Municipal Courts	Probate Court (Wills)
Juvenile Court	Domestic Relations (Divorce Court)

B. If the grand jury feels the evidence against the defendant warrants a trial, it may return an *indictment,* or *true bill,* against the defendant, arraigning him for trial in a court of general jurisdiction.

C. If the grand jury feels the evidence is not sufficient or in order, a *no-true bill* is returned, and the defendant is released.

III. In the court of general jurisdiction (officers of this court usually include the judge, clerk, attorney, jury, bailiff)

    A. The trial opens with charges made against the defendant.

    B. Pleas and motions are made by attorneys. Below are some that could be made:

        1. "Guilty" or "not guilty."

        2. Motion for *continuance.*

        3. *Demurrer*—challenges the sufficiency of the indictment.

        4. *Plea in abatement*—contention, among others, that the indictment is illegal.

        5. *Motion to quash indictment*—contention that indictment is unfair or defective.

        6. *Nolo contendere*—defendant does not admit guilt but declares he will not fight case.

        7. *Nolle prosequi*—prosecuting attorney announces he does not wish to prosecute the case, because new evidence has convinced him of the person's innocence or because the attorney does not feel he has a strong case against the defendant.

        8. *Plea of insanity*—claiming defendant is irresponsible.

        9. *Motion for change of venue*—attorney contends he will not get a fair trial in that district and asks to have the case transferred to another district.

    C. The judge acts on pleas or motions.

    D. *Petit* (or *trial*) *jurors* are selected if case continues.

        1. The jurors are selected from a *panel of veniremen,* or a list of persons who have been *summoned* for jury service.

        2. Attorneys on both sides may *challenge* certain veniremen and prevent their serving on the jury.

        3. The judge also excuses from jury service those who show evidence that they may be prejudiced in the case or are disqualified for other reasons.

    E. Opening statements of the prosecutor (in some states) are made to the jury.

        1. He outlines the case and explains what he will attempt to prove.

    F. Testimony is given by witnesses who have been subpoenaed to testify for the prosecution.

        1. Prosecuting attorney questions witnesses—the *direct examination.*

        2. Defense attorney questions same witness—the *cross-examination.*

        3. *Depositions,* usually written sworn statements, are given for witnesses who are forced to be absent or are not present for other reasons.

    G. Opening statements of the defense attorney are made to the jury.

    H. Testimony of witnesses for the defense is heard (same procedure as for prosecution).

    I. The trial is concluded with arguments of attorneys to jury.

        1. The prosecutor speaks first, reviewing what he has proved.

        2. The defense attorney speaks next, reviewing his side.

        3. The prosecutor speaks again.

    J. The judge instructs jury on case.

        1. He explains what decisions it can return.

        2. He explains certain points of law in the case.

    K. The jury deliberates.

        1. If jurors cannot agree unanimously, it is a *mistrial.*

2. If they can agree, they report their *verdict* to the judge.

L. Motions may be made by the attorney of defendant losing case.

    1. He may ask for a *new trial,* claiming errors were made in trial or new evidence has shown up.

    2. He may ask for an *arrest of judgment.*

M. The judge passes sentence if the defendant is found guilty and if the judge rejects motion for new trial.

    1. He may send defendant to prison immediately, issuing a *mittimus,* a court order of commitment to prison.

    2. He may (in some states) declare a *suspended sentence,* holding up imprisonment of the person. He may later put the sentence into effect, placing the person in prison. Or he may keep it suspended indefinitely, so long as the defendant gets in no more trouble.

    3. He may (in some states) place the defendant on *probation,* which might be called a suspended sentence on good behavior for a certain period of time.

    4. He may fine the person.

IV. In the *appellate courts* (appeal made on errors, with a *transcript* or *record* of trial sent to appellate court)

A. The decision may be *reversed.*

B. The decision may be *affirmed.*

C. The case may be *remanded* (and reversed or affirmed) or returned to the court in which it originated and a new trial ordered.

V. After the appellate courts

A. The governor may *commute* (or decrease) the sentence.

B. The governor may issue a *reprieve,* staying for a time the execution of the sentence.

C. The governor may *pardon* the prisoner outright.

D. The prisoner may be put on *parole* and allowed his freedom after he has served part of the sentence. But he has to report to parole officers periodically.

ROUTE OF A CIVIL CASE

(Similar in some respects to a criminal case. Explanations of similar steps and terms are not repeated.)

I. In the court of limited jurisdiction (the case may be heard here if the amount involved is lower than the maximum fixed by law for such courts)

A. The plaintiff submits his *declaration* or *complaint* that he is due relief or compensation.

    1. If the case involves recovery of property, the magistrate may issue a *replevin,* which is a court order enabling officers to take the property.

    2. The magistrate may also issue a writ of *attachment,* usually when the plaintiff convinces him that the defendant may dispose of certain property involved in the suit. By that writ, the court takes charge of the property until the case is settled.

B. The defendant is summoned to answer the complaint.

C. The magistrate hears the case and passes judgment.

    1. Either party may appeal the case to higher court, where it is tried anew (*de novo*).

D. The magistrate may attach the funds of the defendant (if he loses) to carry out the judgment. This order may be served on a third party, who may owe or will owe money to the losing party. In other words, the magistrate may *garnishee* the losing party's income if the court's judgment is not paid.

II. In the court of general jurisdiction (cases may originate here, or they may come up from courts of limited jurisdiction; in either case, they are handled similarly)
   A. The plaintiff submits declaration, which is recorded with the clerk (the declaration sometimes is not necessary in appeals from courts of limited jurisdiction).
   B. The defendant is summoned.
   C. The defendant may submit motions and demurrers attacking the complaint.
   D. The defendant submits his *answer* or *plea,* which is recorded with the clerk.
   E. The plaintiff submits motions and demurrers attacking the answer.
   F. The case is set for trial.
      1. Trial may be held by judge without a jury.
   G. If the trial is by jury, the jury is selected.
   H. The attorney for plaintiff makes an opening statement (in some states).
      1. The plaintiff's attorney explains case and outlines arguments.
   I. The attorney for defendant makes an opening statement.
   J. The plaintiff presents evidence.
   K. The defendant presents evidence.
   L. The plaintiff may present more evidence in rebuttal.
   M. The defendant may also present more evidence in rebuttal.
   N. The plaintiff's attorney makes his closing argument.
   O. The defendant's attorney makes closing argument.
   P. The plaintiff's attorney makes his rebuttal.
   Q. The judge renders a decision in the case (if tried without jury) or he instructs the jury.
   R. The jury deliberates and returns verdict if agreed upon unanimously.
   S. Motions may be made by the attorney on either side.
      1. He may ask for a new trial or arrest of judgment.
   T. The judge renders his judgment on any motions.
   U. The judge acts on the verdict.
III. In the appellate courts
   A. The decision may be reversed.
   B. The decision may be affirmed.
   C. The decision may be remanded (and reversed or affirmed) to the lower court and a new trial ordered.

Cases in equity are usually not tried before a jury. The judge (sometimes called a *chancellor* when there is a separate court of equity) hears cases and renders verdicts and judgments.

The *probate court,* named in the chart above, has a limited jurisdiction in the disposition of a deceased person's property. If the person dies *testate* (having written a will), the probabe judge has the *executor* named in the will carry out its provisions. If the person dies *intestate* (without a will), the judge appoints an *administrator* for the property.

Only a small portion of cases will be followed through the full routine outlined above. Still, nearly every step may result in a separate news story if the case is important enough. The outline should be checked against local variations because each state determines its own court procedure.

EXERCISES

1. Using any newspaper available to you, clip a one-day trial story and a trial story that extends over several days and make a news analysis of each.
2. Invite the reporter who covers courts for the local newspaper, the local prosecuting attorney and a local judge to class for a panel discussion of the courts and the press.
3. Attend the court in your city where such cases as traffic violations are tried, observe a number of cases before the court. Write a feature story on your "day" in court.
4. Arrange to visit a criminal court in your area on a day a major case is underway. Write a news story on the events that occur in court that day.
5. Write brief news stories from the following notes:
   A. Case decided today
      In Circuit Court
      Judge Billy Joe White
      Awarded $1,900 in damages
      To Dr. John Sevier
      Former English professor
      At Fillmore College
      Who was dismissed
      Eighteen months ago
      For using profanity
      Abusing university dress code
      Improper general attitude
      Toward the university
      Sevier had sued
      For $50,000 damages
      Included University President
      Dr. Frank Welch as defendant
      Judge White ruled
      Welch was within
      Scope of his authority
      Dismissed the suit against him
      But assessed the $1,900 damages
      Against the university
   B. Three persons bound
      To County Grand Jury today
      By City Court Judge
      Carmen Townsend
      Kathleen Lanier, 22, Chicago
      Accused of selling 2 ounces
      Of cocaine for $3,100
      To undercover narcotics agents
      On three occasions last fall
      Bond set at $2,000
      Garrison Lee, 18, Newark, N.J.
      Charged with burglary
      Arrested inside home
      Of Jack Mayfield, 3301 Woodbine Ct.
      Police answered silent alarm call
      Found Lee dismantling
      Stereo set worth $1,500
      Also had garbage bag full

Of silverware, coins, other items
Bond set at $3,000
Mayfield owns leading
Insurance firm in city
Said home had been
Broken into four times
Before he installed alarm
Roger S. Clark, 42,
Brother of County Sheriff
Lamar (Bubba) Clark
Charged with receiving
And concealing stolen property
Arrested by police investigating
Stolen car ring
Police found dismantled
Remains of two stolen cars
Hidden behind giant stacks
Of old auto and truck tires
In the rear of the junkyard
Owned by Roger Clark
On Mt. Vernon Highway
Three miles east of city limits
Bond was set at $5,000

C. In Circuit Court today
Mrs. Walker (Sally E.) Elkins
Filed $4 million damage suit
Against Tyler Oil Co. of Madison
Publix Transport Co. of Madison
And Burton Hall, Maryville,
A driver for Publix
She charged that her husband
Walker Elkins, 78
Was fatally burned
In a gasoline explosion
At a Maryville gas station
Where Elkins was getting
Gasoline for his car
Suit says Hall was
Delivering gasoline to the station
Gasoline was leaking onto the ground
More than 100 gallons on ground
As Hall pumped gas from
The tanker into holding tanks
Spilled fuel ignited
Flames engulfed Elkins
In his car
Car's gasoline tank exploded
Elkins died few hours
Later in Maryville hospital
Suit charges negligence
Said there had been
Previously reported complaints

About leaking gas when
Tankers were unloading
At the station

D. In County Criminal Court today
Willie S. Boykins, 72
Found guilty of first-degree murder
In the slaying of his
Neighbor during an argument
Over a loud stereo
Clarence Buchanan, 33,
West Stevenston Street
Was killed with a
Single 25-caliber bullet
In the living room
Of his home
Boykins called police
After the shooting
Under state's "Class-X" crime law
Boykins sentenced to
Life in prison
He will not be
Eligible for parole

E. In County Criminal Court today
Lyndon W. Clever, 24,
Of rural Newport
Was found not guilty
Of the shotgun slaying
Of Rufus Grooms, 32,
410 Western Ave.
His attorneys argued
He shot Grooms in self-defense
Witnesses testified Grooms
Wanted to kill Clever
Because he was to
Testify against Grooms
In an earlier shooting case
Grooms confronted Clever
In the parking lot of
Barney's Chevron Station
1510 Main St.
Clever testified that
He shot Grooms with
A shotgun he had in his pickup
Because he thought Grooms
Had a pistol in his jacket pocket
As he approached the pickup
The jury deliberated
About four hours before
Finding Clever not guilty

6. Write a story from the following notes:

This assignment deals with a trial that was held in Criminal Court. Bernadette Villalobo, 42, a self-styled holy woman and prophetess, has been charged with four counts of fraud and indicated by the County Grand Jury. Three local women claim they gave her nearly $45,000 to establish a spiritual consciousness center and bookstore here. The money was supposed to be used to buy a house for the center and a former church building for the bookstore. The center and bookstore never opened. The three women first sued Villalobo in Circuit Court and won a judgment against her. Then criminal charges of fraud were brought against her. The district attorney handling the case for the state is James McCartney. The defense attorney is Martin Block. The state's case was presented first. McCartney called Mrs. Margaret C. Downs, one of the alleged victims, as his first witness. Excerpts from transcript of the trial follow:

McCARTNEY: Please give the court your name and occupation.

DOWNS: Mrs. Margaret C. Downs, a retired school teacher.

McCARTNEY: Do you know the defendant, Bernadette Villalobo?

DOWNS: Yes, sir.

McCARTNEY: When and under what circumstances did you meet?

DOWNS: I am interested in reincarnation, and I met her when I was invited by my friend, Mary Alice Sweets, to attend a lecture in a motel room here.

McCARTNEY: Was the proposed spiritual center discussed that night?

DOWNS: Yes, sir. At the end of the lecture we were told of her plans to come here and set up a special center and a bookstore.

McCARTNEY: Were you asked at that time to contribute to the center or bookstore?

DOWNS: No, sir. We were told that she had set up about 30 centers in other cities and would finance the one here herself. We were told she was a very wealthy woman because people came to her for advice all the time.

McCARTNEY: When were you first asked to contribute money to the center?

DOWNS: Well, let's see. I think it was on her third visit here. On the second one she took Mary Alice and I for a ride and pointed out a house on Chapman Highway and said: "That's the house where we will set up our center." When she came back the third time, we attended her lecture one night and the following day she called and said she needed $10,000 immediately to close the deal on the house.

McCARTNEY: Did you give it to her?

DOWNS: I went directly to the bank and arranged to borrow $8,546 and gave the cash to Bernadette. We went in her Cadillac to a lawyer's office to close the deal. But she made me wait outside in the car.

McCARTNEY: Why did you give her the money?

DOWNS: From the very first time I met her I didn't have control of my actions . . .

BLOCK: Objection, your honor. The witness . . .

JUDGE JOHN IVEY: Objection overruled. The witness may complete her answer.

DOWNS: Mrs. Villalobo is a very charismatic person. She told us she was a holy woman and a prophetess. At times when I was with her I felt I was in a trance. It was a feeling I had never experienced before.

McCARTNEY: Did you ever give her any more money?

DOWNS: Several months later I borrowed another $5,000 to buy books and supplies for the store.

McCARTNEY: Did she promise to repay you?

DOWNS: Oh, yes. She gave me a note and promised to repay me within a month.

McCARTNEY: Did she?

DOWNS: No. I never saw any of the money. And I got some books from the Southland News Co., but they came COD.

After a series of other questions, McCartney finished his direct examination and Block began his cross examination. Excerpts follow:

BLOCK: Mrs. Downs, do you really expect this court to believe that an intelligent woman—a school teacher—could really be taken in this way? Come now, Mrs. Downs.

MCCARTNEY: Mr. Block is badgering this witness.

JUDGE IVEY: He just began asking questions. Go ahead, Mr. Block.

BLOCK: What about it, Mrs. Downs. How could you be taken in so by Mrs. Villalobo?

DOWNS: Well . . . Well, there was just something about her. I had this feeling that I knew her from somewhere else.

BLOCK: Where? Had you met in another city at an earlier time?

DOWNS: No. Not another city. I seem to recall her from another life.

BLOCK: Another life? What do you mean? Explain to the court, please.

DOWNS: Yes. Well, you see, reincarnation is a part of the concept we have been studying. I have done a lot of reading on the subject and Bernadette lectured on the . . .

BLOCK: No further questions.

MCCARTNEY: Let her finish.

JUDGE IVEY: Gentlemen. We'll have none of that in my court. Finish your answer, please, Mrs. Downs.

DOWNS: Bernadette lectured on reincarnation often and we talked about it often in our private sessions. We talked about it a lot. She helped me recall what it was like over there, on the other side. I came to trust her. I came to feel sure that I had known her before. In another life.

At this point, Judge Ivey recessed the court. He explained that he had to attend the funeral that afternoon of a personal friend and former law partner in another city. The case will resume at 10 a.m. the following day.

7. Testimony in the trial continued for several days. Among the other witnesses for the state were Mary Alice Sweets, a retired music teacher, and Mrs. Evelyn B. Sloan, widow of a minister. Miss Sweets and Mrs. Sloan testified that they had joined Mrs. Downs in giving Mrs. Villalobo money for the center and bookstore. Other state witnesses included a real estate broker, a lawyer and several city detectives who investigated the case. The state rested its case and Block began his defense by calling several witnesses including a yoga teacher who said Mrs. Villalobo was indeed a holy woman. She testified that she had seen Mrs. Villalobo's palms bleed and had witnessed her cure the sick through the power of her hands. Then Block called Mrs. Villalobo to the stand. Excerpts from her testimony follow:

BLOCK: Mrs. Villalobo, did you tell any of these women that you would finance the spiritual center?

VILLALOBO: Certainly not. It was to be their center. I made that very clear.

BLOCK: Did you accept money from them for the center?

VILLALOBO: Yes. I accepted $1,000 to be used as a down payment on the house from Mrs. Downs. But I did it because it was their center. Why should I pay down on it?

BLOCK: Did you accept other funds from them?

VILLALOBO: Yes.

BLOCK: How much?

VILLALOBO: I can't be certain. Perhaps $40,000 or so. But it was secured with notes. I promised them they'd receive it all. I explained that some of the delay in starting the center and bookstore here was because of my busy schedule. I have five other centers and bookstores in three states and I keep a busy travel schedule.

BLOCK: Did you intend to cheat these women?

VILLALOBO: No. It was just a matter of lack of communications. I was so busy I just couldn't handle everything at once and they were impatient.

Block followed with a series of other questions in which she described difficulties she had with book publishers and other suppliers of her bookstores and unavoidable delays with lawyers and real estate agents that led to the misunderstanding with the three women. She even testified that she had money and could repay the women. When Block completed his direct examination, McCartney began the cross examination. Excerpts follow:

McCARTNEY: Mrs. Villalobo, will you tell the court, please, the number of spiritual centers you have established or helped to establish?

VILLALOBO: In all, 31, I believe.

McCARTNEY: Will you tell the court the names of the cities in which they were established?

VILLALOBO: Well, let's see. There was one in San Francisco, and one in Tampa, and one in Franklin, and the one here . . .

McCARTNEY: There never was one here . . . but do go on.

VILLALOBO: I'm trying to, but you won't let me. You are trying to confuse me. You are like the newspapers and television stations; you are trying to destroy me.

JUDGE IVEY: Mrs. Villalobo, control yourself. I will not tolerate such outbursts in my court.

McCARTNEY: Are you a prophetess? Can you see in the future . . . into the past?

VILLALOBO: Yes, I am.

McCARTNEY: And yet you can't remember the names of the centers you established?

BLOCK: Your honor, he is badgering the witness.

McCARTNEY: How much property did you own when you first came here?

VILLALOBO: Well, I paid $17,500 on property near Franklin, where I planned to open a center.

McCARTNEY: Do you have any documentary evidence of this?

VILLALOBO: Not with me. The receipts are at home.

McCARTNEY: You could not remember to bring with you a receipt for $17,500 for a down payment on property; an item that might be important in this trial?

There was no audible reply.

McCartney then questioned her at length about a number of property deals she had been engaged in in other states. In each case he got from her the admission that she either had to forfeit the money or that the deals did not go through. He also questioned her at length about her alleged association with King Hussein of Jordan and other prominent persons. Then he questioned her about her visit to his office after her indictment.

McCARTNEY: Why did you visit my office although your attorney advised you not to?

VILLALOBO: I couldn't help myself.

McCARTNEY: Do you recall while sitting in a chair in my office placing your folded hands to your forehead to contact your attorney?

VILLALOBO: No, I do not.

McCARTNEY: Come now. Remember I told you that you had better use the telephone. And you replied: "I do not need a phone, I CAN contact people."

VILLALOBO: No. I do not. Why are you doing this to me? Why are you doing . . .

JUDGE IVEY: Mrs. Villalobo. I warned you. No more of that.

MCCARTNEY: No further questions.

Write a story for the next morning's edition of your newspaper.

8. The next day both the prosecution and the defense gave their final arguments. McCartney told the 10 man and two women on the jury that they had witnessed a classic case of fraud during the eight-day trial. "Her scheme needs to be stopped now because she refuses to acknowledge what she has done. She has powers. She can look you in the eye and define your weaknesses and your vulnerabilities and she is able to convert that vulnerability into cash." Block told the jury the only reason the case came to trial was because the alleged victims had turned against Mrs. Villalobo. They loaned her money in good faith when she tried to help them, and then they turned on her, he said. He also told the jury that the state had tried to belittle her "gifts and talents. She is being tried as a saint or a god, I'm surprised the state has not tried to burn her at the stake."

After the final arguments were presented, Judge Ivey instructed the jury about the laws governing the case. The jury retired to deliberate. Three hours later the jury returned with its verdict—guilty on all four counts. She faces 15 to 26 years in prison. She would serve, at the most, five to 10 years before parole.

Judge Ivey gave her attorney 30 days to file for a new trial. He set her bond at $90,000. She was returned to County Jail because she could not post bond.

She stood quietly when the verdict was read. She did not cry. Later in an interview at the jail she said her problems stemmed from a lack of communications with the three women. She did not deny owing the money but insisted that it was a civil not a criminal matter.

She vowed to continue her counseling and spiritual work from behind prison walls.

"I counseled while I was in jail here after my arrest last year with many prisoners as well as with many who came to visit me," she said. "I will continue my work."

She expressed concern because her psychic powers were stressed in the trial and not her healing powers. "My healing has not been emphasized at all, and that is the most important part of my work."

Write a story for the next morning's edition of your newspaper.

9. Write a newscast using the following assignments in this chapter: Exercise 5A, Exercise 5B, Exercise 8.

CHAPTER 23

Government and Politics

News is a fundamental force in the struggle to govern, Douglass Cater wrote in his book, *Power in Washington*. The veteran Washington reporter and author was, in a manner of speaking, restating Thomas Jefferson's views on the role of the press in a free society.

The free press is an essential ingredient in a democracy. Whether it is the fourth branch of government (Fourth Estate), as it has been called, is debatable. But there can be no doubt that the major role it plays in providing the public information about government is one of the chief reasons democracy works. James Madison's statement, "A popular government without a popular information or means of acquiring it, is but a prologue to a farce, or a tragedy or perhaps both," is as true today as when he made it in the late 1700s.

There have always been people in government who have sought to subvert the press. Certainly the infamous Watergate scandals of the 1970s were not something new in our history. Every era has had its Watergate. And the outcome was almost always the same. Public reaction, based on information supplied by the press, proved that Jefferson was correct when he wrote that "the way to prevent . . . irregular interpositions of the people is to give them full information of their affairs through the channels of the public papers . . ."

Although government is the public's business and public officials frequently are in conflict with the mass media, most recognize that the media perform a significant role in our society. Yet there has never been a time since the adoption of the First Amendment to the Constitution that there have not been efforts on every level of government to restrict and control the mass media. This makes the task of telling the people about their own business often difficult and occasionally hazardous.

But the people must be informed if democracy is to work. They provide the money and select the managerial personnel to run the government. Properly financed and managed, government seeks to insure the various benefits of "life, liberty and the pursuit of happiness" through private initiative. Improperly operated, it may mean insecurity of life and property. At thousands of points, day in and year out, the complex machinery of democracy touches and influences the daily lives of citizens. There is no way of escaping it—even in death. It affects jobs, business, education, health, safety, transportation—all aspects of public welfare.

A function of the newspaper is, or should be, to keep the people informed about all of the affairs of government. Without complete reporting, the stockholders in this enormous business are without knowledge to select proper representatives in government or to judge their acts thereafter. The press not only informs the public, it also is an important source of information for the nation's leaders as well. Every day the president gets a news summary culled from dozens of newspapers, television news shows and news magazines. In every Congressional office, staff aides clip newspapers from the home district to keep the representative or senator informed of current events "at home." Governmental agencies at both a federal and state level frequently subscribe to the wire services in an effort to keep informed. The mass media provide the foundation on which most public officials base their knowledge. Naturally, it is supplemented with other information.

Government News. What do people want to know and need to know about government? What is meant by government news and by political reporting? Much news that comes from government offices is of the various types discussed in other chapters. Some of these stories include:

Type of Story	*Sources*
Crimes and accidents, suicides	Police, sheriff, state police
Illness, deaths, accidents	Public hospitals
Fires and accidents	Fire departments
Trials and lawsuits	Courts
Weather	U.S. Weather Service
Meetings	Legislative bodies and boards

In other words, government is the source of virtually all types of news. And in reporting these matters the reporter is giving an account to the public of governmental activities. Over and beyond these reports of daily activities are ill-defined but important materials that need reporting as government news by a political reporter. They do not constitute a story type, perhaps, nor are they easily defined. Nevertheless, they can be illustrated and studied, and they must be written if the public is to have a complete report of its government.

The Political Reporter. A political reporter does not cover a political campaign or political personality only. It is true that he may spend a good deal of time on the campaign trail, listening to the same speech over and over again. But much of his time is spent—or should be spent—looking at the purely political aspects of government. A political reporter—or any journalist covering government—should center his attention on the politically appointed—the safety director, not the policeman. He may not visit the state hospital but he would talk to the health commissioner. He may be only mildly interested in the construction of a particular superhighway but very much interested in the statewide

23a

307

highway program and what firms are getting the contracts. Along the way the good reporter will collect personals and briefs and pass along tips for other stories to the city editor, but as a political reporter his chief job is to look for attitudes and theories and plans and programs. He would, in short, be interested in going beneath the surface of routine government news, coming up with stories on issues and policies and the broad aspects of government. It should be his chief role to interpret government actions and policies for the readers of his newspaper.

There are specific matters—and others not so specific—that the political reporter should look for and report. The specific items include:

> Legislative actions (whether of the state legislature, the city council, the governing body of the county, or Congress).
> Executive branch actions (whether of the governor or mayor, or department heads).
> Judicial decisions (of the supreme court usually—not trials and lawsuits but precedent-making decisions).
> Financial and budgeting matters (including bond issues, debt reductions, taxes and tax delinquencies).

The less specific items would include any of the following matters pertaining to any governmental office—whenever they are of sufficient importance to affect policies and trends:

1. Daily records.	7. New laws.
2. Periodic reports.	8. Enforcement of laws.
3. Changes in personnel.	9. Taxes imposed and paid.
4. New projects and programs.	10. Publications.
5. Speeches.	11. Changes in policies.
6. Discussions.	12. Interviews and features.

Just what the substance of these items would be can only be determined by the reporter in contact with, and thoroughly informed about, a specific officer or official over a period of time. The political reporter should be so well informed about the activities of a governmental office and its officials that he can detect any significant changes which should be reported to the public. He certainly should not have to wait for the changes to be announced by the officials. Often the unannounced changes involve political developments that should be exposed.

A reporter's duties (as both a government news and political news reporter) require a thorough knowledge of government itself. The following brief analysis of governmental forms and their news potential should prove helpful.

FORMS OF GOVERNMENT

In general, there are four levels of government: city, county, state and federal. Each provides the citizen certain services, paid for ultimately by taxes. Each has a legislative, an executive and a judicial branch. The legislative branch, composed of representatives elected by the voters, enacts the laws that make possible those services and imposes the taxes that bring in revenue to support the services. The executive branch, composed of persons elected and appointed, carries out the laws of the legislative branch, performs the services and collects the taxes to pay the bill. The judicial branch, composed of persons either elected or appointed, administers justice, interpreting laws enacted by the legislative branch as well as common laws and Constitutional laws. In addition to these four levels of government, there may be others, such as special districts created by legislative act to perform and charge for special services (such as water and sanitation). And on a state and federal level there may be regulatory agencies empowered to enforce administrative law governing numerous state and federal agencies such as public utilities commissions and the Federal Trade Commission.

City Government. The accompanying charts show sample forms of city government. The specific form of any particular city can be found in its charter, which is granted (enacted like any other bill) by the state legislature. The charter will define the duties and powers of city officials and otherwise outline the corporate structure of the city. Cities can change their form of government, but it usually requires a popular election and in some cases approval of the new charter by the state legislature. No reporter should attempt to cover city hall or report any aspect of city government or political affairs without a complete understanding of the city charter. He will find that no one else (probably including the mayor and the city law director) is thoroughly acquainted with it, and his particular knowledge will lend strength and authority to his reporting.

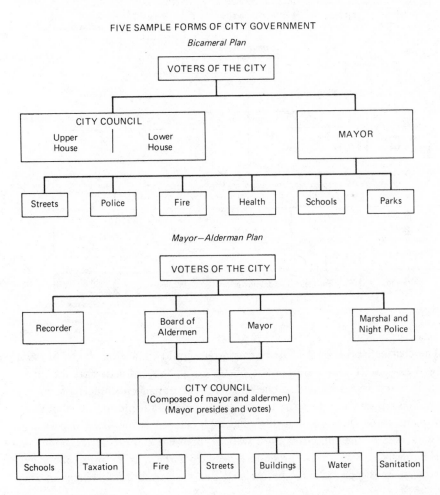

FIVE SAMPLE FORMS OF CITY GOVERNMENT

Bicameral Plan

Mayor–Alderman Plan

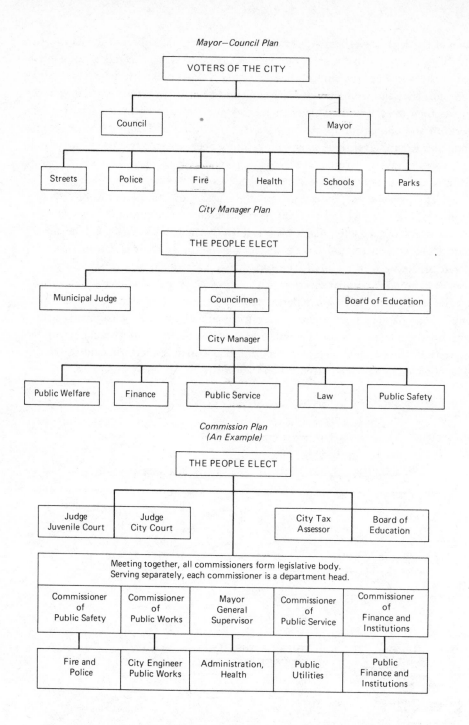

Mayor—Council Plan

VOTERS OF THE CITY

Council

Mayor

Streets | Police | Fire | Health | Schools | Parks

City Manager Plan

THE PEOPLE ELECT

Municipal Judge | Councilmen | Board of Education

City Manager

Public Welfare | Finance | Public Service | Law | Public Safety

Commission Plan
(An Example)

THE PEOPLE ELECT

Judge Juvenile Court | Judge City Court | City Tax Assessor | Board of Education

Meeting together, all commissioners form legislative body.
Serving separately, each commissioner is a department head.

Commissioner of Public Safety | Commissioner of Public Works | Mayor General Supervisor | Commissioner of Public Service | Commissioner of Finance and Institutions

Fire and Police | City Engineer Public Works | Administration, Health | Public Utilities | Public Finance and Institutions

The charter (and even a chart the reporter should draw from it for his own use) will suggest the many important phases of city government that should be reported. Major issues should be checked with the proper city officials from day to day. The reporter should resist the tendency to have all information about city government come from the mayor's office. He should know every department head and most of the subordinates as well as the office staffs, and he should see them regularly. Every official pronouncement from the mayor's office about any

department in the city should be checked out with additional sources in that department. It is important to keep in close contact with department sources, for current problems change from time to time. One month may find the live public issue to be teachers' salaries. The next month it may be the traffic plan, or zoning irregularities or garbage collection. In most cities today, most problems tend to fluctuate in importance. So none should be overlooked or ignored. Knowledge and background and personal acquaintance with city officials and employes are paramount for success in reporting city affairs. But a reporter must not let himself become a captive to his sources. He must have independent sources of information to insure that he does not become simply a public relations tool for the current administration.

County Government. Forms of county government (see sample charts) vary from state to state and in some cases even between counties within a state. It is important that the reporter covering county government have a complete knowledge of the local county government structure. Unlike the city, the county has no charter. It derives its forms and powers from acts of the state legislature and from the state constitution and perhaps from precedent. This often makes the task of learning about government structure difficult, and it may force the reporter to spend a lot of time reading old legislative acts in the state code. But it is essential that he know the facts about how his county's government evolved. Without that knowledge he may be unable to recognize the special political interests that will attempt to control government and perhaps bias the news by the information given to him. He should draw a chart of his county's government, list officials and their duties and become familiar with the enabling acts under which the county operates. It is also essential to check any new enabling acts passed by each successive state legislature that can influence county government.

State Government. A sample state government is shown in the accompanying chart. The reporter must, however, master his own state government. Knowledge of the state constitution should be the reporter's most important tool. But there will be many reorganization bills (statutes) that have altered the basic pattern established by the constitution, setting up the current form. Every state publishes regularly, as a "Blue Book," a reference volume on state government which includes the constitution as well as descriptive material on all other branches of government. Any reporter covering state government should have his own personal copy.

SPECIFIC NEWS MATERIALS   23b

All of the story forms previously discussed and diagramed are employed in reporting government and politics. They are used to present the following types of specific story materials.

Legislative. No aspect of the state legislature, city council and governing body of the county should be ignored. Frequently what happens behind the scenes, at committee meetings, occasionally secret sessions of public officials and lobbyists and seemingly routine staff conferences, can be more important and significant than what happens at the public sessions of these legislative bodies. It is at these private sessions where much of the groundwork is done, decisions are made and even deals are struck.

THREE FORMS OF COUNTY GOVERNMENT
"Long Ballot" Plan Used by Some Counties

THE VOTERS ELECT

By Several Counties	By Whole County	By Districts in Each County

By Several Counties
- Chancellor
- Clerk and Master
- Circuit Judge
- Attorney General
- Circuit Court Clerk

By Whole County
- County Court Clerk
- Superintendent of Education
- Sheriff
- Tax Assessor
- Health Officer

By Districts in Each County
- Register
- Trustee or Financial Officer
- Board of Education
- Road Commissioner
- Justices of the Peace
- Quarterly County Court
- Constable
- Coroner

County Manager Plan

COUNTY VOTERS
- Probate Judge
- Board of County Commissioners
- Common Pleas Court
- Manager
  - Director of Finance
  - Director of Public Works
  - Director of Public Welfare
  - Director of Recording

Limited Executive Plan

COUNTY VOTERS
- Common Pleas Court
- Board of County Commissioners
- Probate Judge
- Executive
  - Director of Finance
  - Director of Public Works
  - Director of Public Welfare
  - Director of Recording

312

ORGANIZATION OF A SAMPLE STATE GOVERNMENT

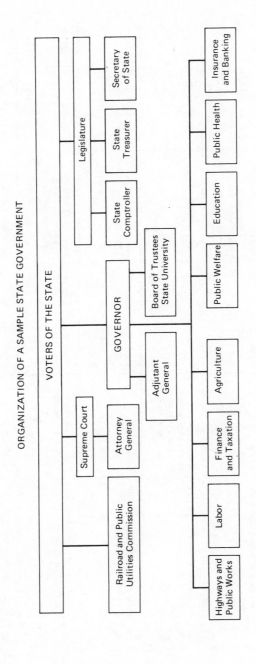

A SUMMARY OF GOVERNMENTAL SERVICES
PROVIDING SOURCES OF NEWS

Services and Activities	City	County	State	Federal*
Protection of person and property	Police Fire Courts Building inspectors	Sheriff Magistrates Deputies Constables Courts	State police, courts, fire marshals, rangers, game wardens, National Guard	Army Navy and Marines Air Force Coast Guard FBI inspectors
Promotion of health	Water supply Health Department Garbage and sewage disposal, Hospitals	Health Department	Health Department	Public health service
Regulation and promotion of agriculture	None	Agricultureal agents and departments	Department of Agriculture	Department of Agriculture and other agencies
Regulation and promotion of business of industry	City ordinances enforced by inspectors	Licensing	Department of Commerce (may have another name)	Department of Commerce and other agencies
Regulation of working conditions	Usually none	Usually none	Department of Labor	Department of Labor and other agencies
Construction and maintenance of public roads	Department of Public Works, Streets	Department of Highways	Department of Highways and Public Works	Bureau of Public Roads and other agencies

Education	School boards Superintendents Libraries	School boards Superintendents Libraries	Department of Education and state institutions	Office of Education and other agencies
Conservation of natural resources	Parks Planning agencies	Agricultural agents Planning agencies	Department of Conservation	Department of Interior, Regional agencies
Regulation, control, and operation of public utilities	City water Power Light	Rural electrification corporations	Utilities and Railroad Commissions	Interstate Commerce Commission
Promotion of general welfare Social Security	Department of Welfare, almshouses Hospitals	Almshouses Hospitals	Department of Welfare, mental hospitals Special schools	Social Security and programs of many other agencies
Other major services		Property and other records	Regulations and controls	Post Office, Department of State (foreign relations)
Administration	Taxes Budgets Regulations Routines	Taxes Budgets Regulations Routines	Taxes Budgets Regulations Routines	Taxes Budgets Regulations Routines

* Federal agencies form too vast a network to permit detailed analysis here. Only standard services are suggested.

A governmental reporter has to be alert. New laws are important news, but even more important are proposed laws, or proposed changes in zoning or plans for projects that would commit the taxpayers to enormous public debt. The public record is replete with examples of public officials who, by behind the scenes maneuvering, have cost taxpayers countless billions of dollars through unneeded and occasionally foolhardy projects. The public depends upon the reporter for advance information that will help prevent this type abuse of public office. Citizens frequently want the opportunity to be heard. Once alerted, citizens can act to arouse public opinion against unnecessary waste of the tax dollar. Carefully observing and reporting the trends in legislation, the reporter is the watchdog of the public welfare. He will not only cover the legislative session but also follow the bills into committee rooms. He will poll authoritative opinion. He may canvass similar legislation in other states or communities to determine whether it has been successful or constructive. And he will seek to tell his readers what it will cost them.

Executive. An alert governmental reporter will be aware of the relationship between the executive branch and many new laws. While the executive officials may insist that they are only the executors of the law, they in fact often are the sponsors for reasons that may not always be the most honorable. A good reporter will know what government official is behind a law and why. And once a law has been passed, a reporter must be aware of its permanent news potential. If it is a tax law, for example, the reporter should follow its effects, checking with the proper executive official, perhaps the commissioner of finance, or city financial director. What is its yield? Is it easily enforced? And, naturally, he should check with the public to see whether it is popular and how it directly affects taxpayers.

Aside from its function in the execution and enforcement of new legislative measures, the executive branch of government (governor, mayor, county judge or manager and chief department heads) is a permanent news source. Are the laws being enforced? Too strictly? Not strictly enough? What specific problems arise from day to day? What new policies are in effect? The reporter also must make certain that the executive branch (through the specific departments of government) is providing the proper services to the public as required by laws and paid for by tax dollars.

The reporter not only keeps the public informed; he also provides an important function in aiding the executive branch to educate the public about matters of government. But the reporter must be careful not to become just an unquestioning mouthpiece for the executive. The governmental reporter plays a key role. Without him as a news channel the interaction of government and the people would be difficult.

Judicial. A political reporter must also watch the courts closely. Here the same laws that he saw enacted and put into operation may come up for adjudication. The trials and lawsuits will usually be covered by other reporters, but sessions of the Supreme Court or any court in which decisions are fraught with economic and social consequences—in which the Constitutionality of laws is involved—will find the political reporter present.

Fiscal. The revenues and expenditures—the budget of state, county and city—demand careful attention from the political reporter. Bond issues, taxes, delinquent taxes, special assessments and the entire financial structure, fixed and current, need adequate interpretation to the people. The cost of government increases every day while the quality of governmental services sometimes declines. The reporter must tell the public why and what it can do about it. Government officials may tell why costs are going up, but usually the explanation is wrapped in technical terms and governmental double-talk. The reporter is responsible for equipping himself thoroughly for the task of translating all of this into plain language the public can understand.

Public Records and Meetings. To cover government effectively, a reporter must have access to public records and the right to attend meetings. Even in states that have open meetings and open records laws, questions arise over what is and what is not a "public record" or a "public meeting." National and state journalistic organizations continue to conduct crusades charging officials with too much secrecy in government, demanding that all public records and meetings be open to the public (open to the press, for the press must base its claim for access upon the public's right of access). The Tennessee Press Association, for example, sponsored such a campaign with a slogan, "What the People Don't Know WILL Hurt Them," and was able to obtain a state law requiring that all public records be open to the public—and the press. It followed with campaigns to protect the confidentiality of news sources and to open all public meetings. Although all three laws have been tested in the courts and upheld, public officials still seek ways to circumvent them and conduct public business in secret.

Of course, there is no quarrel over certain types of public records and meetings, such as property transfers, delinquent tax notices, arrests, periodic fiscal reports, city council meetings and sessions of the state legislature. The disputes have been over certain types of records that officials claim are not open to public inspection, despite the wording in the laws that says "all," and certain types of meetings (special sessions of the city school board, for example, when personnel matters are being discussed) that officials do not want the press or public to attend even though public business is being conducted. Newspapers have had varying success in opening records and meetings that have been closed for unjustified reasons. In any event, if there is not an open record or open meeting law in a state, the press can demand the right to see records and to attend meetings that are accessible to anyone other than specified government officials and employes. And the press can insist that final action on a legislative or governing matter (such as action taken by a school board) be taken in open session. In states where open meeting laws exist, the press has successfully sued public bodies, forcing them to rescind action taken in secret meetings. In states where such laws do not exist, the press should bring the pressure of public opinion, legislative actions and the courts to force governmental bodies to conduct the public's business in the open.

ELECTIONS

23c

Despite the efforts of the press to inform the public of the issues and the candidates, public apathy is not uncommon in most elections. Increasing numbers of citizens simply are not voting at all levels of government. A reporter assigned to election coverage has a special responsibility to write accurately and fairly so the voters can be fully informed. The complexity of the nation's various election laws complicates the reporter's job. The nation's system of political parties and elections practices has grown up by trial and error. And while various state laws have stabilized them somewhat, the primary and general election practices require a broad knowledge and considerable political acumen if they are to be properly interpreted for the public.

The following charts are simplified pictures of party organizations. The national party system is basically a two-party system with third-party efforts emerging in response to the intensity of the issues before the public at a given time. The states, however, show considerable variations in their forms and practices. The political reporter will need to make the same serious investigation of his state's election laws as of his state and local government to report political campaigns adequately.

The reporter is also expected to evaluate candidates for office. He must understand not only machinery but also personalities and issues. Without editorializing—unless he is conducting a signed column—he must, as a reporter, present these subtleties to his readers in factual accounts. Obviously he can do this only after careful study or long experience and close contact with the politics of his community, state or nation. He may interview candidates, write biographical sketches, develop questionnaires. He must report adequately from day to day the reactions of candidates to issues. Finally he will perhaps accompany the candidate through the campaign, reporting speeches and audience reaction, and end by tabulating the results precinct by precinct on election night.

PARTY ORGANIZATION AND METHODS OF CALLING CONVENTIONS
(Democratic and Republican Parties)

National Executive Committee

Composed of representatives from each state and territory chosen by the national convention. In general, manages the national party affairs and issues the call for the national convention.

State Executive Committee

Composed of representatives from each congressional district chosen at biennial primary elections. In general, manages state party affairs and, in response to call of National Executive Committee, issues call to County Executive Committees for the election of delegates to the State Convention.

Congressional District Executive Committee

Composed of the chairman of, or other delegates from, the County Executive Committees of the particular district. Frequently inactive.

County Executive Committee

Created usually by party usage. Its organization is different in each of the political parties and is not uniform in the counties, even in the same party. The committee issues call for county convention or primary election to nominate party's candidates.

STATE PRIMARY ELECTION MACHINERY
(Democratic and Republican Parties)

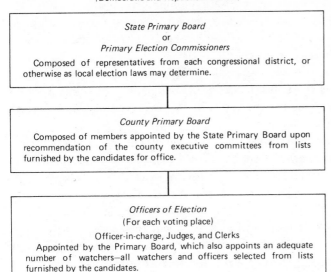

State Primary Board
or
Primary Election Commissioners
Composed of representatives from each congressional district, or otherwise as local election laws may determine.

County Primary Board
Composed of members appointed by the State Primary Board upon recommendation of the county executive committees from lists furnished by the candidates for office.

Officers of Election
(For each voting place)
Officer-in-charge, Judges, and Clerks
Appointed by the Primary Board, which also appoints an adequate number of watchers—all watchers and officers selected from lists furnished by the candidates.

STATE GENERAL ELECTION MACHINERY

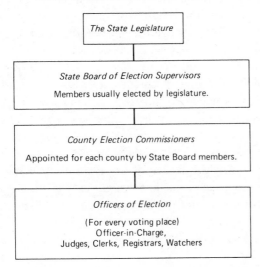

The State Legislature

State Board of Election Supervisors
Members usually elected by legislature.

County Election Commissioners
Appointed for each county by State Board members.

Officers of Election
(For every voting place)
Officer-in-Charge,
Judges, Clerks, Registrars, Watchers

Interpretation of Politics. Covering politics offers endless pitfalls for a reporter. If he is not careful and alert, he may find himself being "used" by one candidate or the other. Even the most routine handout from a candidate must be carefully interpreted or the reporter may find himself innocently advancing the cause of one candidate over another. A reporter simply must "know his politics." He must see the facts behind the news in the handout, the motives of governmental actions, the underlying party machinery as it grinds meal for its supporters, mud for its opponents. The public more or less depends upon him to expose the bad and commend the good deeds of public officials. In response to everything a candidate for office says or does, the reporter should look for motives. And he should exlain those motives to the reader.

23d

To represent his readers faithfully, the reporter of governmental news must be a student of public opinion and political philosophy. He also must work his way to the "inside" with many politicians and with political organizations in order to keep a finger on the pulse of action. In short, he should know as much as anyone else about the local political organizations and their candidates. This does not mean, however, that he bargains his rights as a reporter to obtain an inside seat. In many cases the political reporter is one of the oldest and best reporters on the staff—one who has the ability and personality to be an important figure in the political life of the city.

Reporting politics and government is a year-round job, but at election time most newspapers devote special attention to the campaign and the candidates. The public turns to the newspapers for information about the candidates for office, the issues at stake, the political alignments and maneuvers. The reporter must wade through the propaganda being dished out by the candidates and their staffs to tell the voters what they need to know about the issues as well as the men and women seeking office. And, when the votes are counted, he must analyze election statistics so that they mean something to the reader.

Frequently newspaper policy (see Chapter 14) is involved in reporting politics and government. This will arise if the newspaper has partisan views on those holding or running for office or if it has a policy relating to government affairs. Such policies may range all the way from efforts to consolidate the city and county school systems to a campaign to change the entire form of city government. More than all other communications media, newspapers have taken the lead in crusading for governmental reforms. The public has come to expect the newspaper to be not only a guardian of governmental conduct but also an adviser on progressive steps needed in governmental organizations. Newspapers rejecting their responsibilities and conducting unreasonable partisan coverage of election campaigns (and some still do) are doing a disservice to the public and their communities. Obviously, candidates seeking endorsement of newspapers may be swayed by the opinions of the press when they set their platforms. It is essential that a reporter recognize this. With such great responsibilities, the reporter who covers government and politics must be one of the most competent members on the staff.

Here are some examples of leads on stories about government and politics:

Maryville City Council unanimously approved on final reading a $13.6 million budget for the next fiscal year Tuesday night, and left unchanged the city's $3.17 property tax rate for the seventh consecutive year.

[THE MARYVILLE-ALCOA DAILY TIMES]

City officials, digging their heels in for some hard economic times, this week cut back on plans for more than a dozen construction projects including the proposed $4.5 million aquatic center, new parking lots and a horse center in Potomac.

[THE MONTGOMERY JOURNAL]

Athena Cablevision was awarded its long-sought $2-a-month rate increase by City Council last night but only because Councilman Casey Jones had a change of heart late in the meeting.

[THE KNOXVILLE NEWS-SENTINEL]

CEDAR RAPIDS, Ia.—Huddled under a yellow blanket, Gov. Edmund "Jerry" Brown sat in a chilly DC-3 for 45 minutes Monday flying here to try to convince the students at Thomas Jefferson High School to tell their parents that he should be President.

But the moment he got off the plane, he learned it was all for naught. He was late, the students had to go to lunch, and the speech had been canceled.

[THE CHICAGO TRIBUNE]

EXERCISES

1. Using any newspaper available to you, clip three political stories and analyze each one.
2. Draw an organization chart for your city, county and state governments, using the charts in this chapter as guides.
3. Using the state *Blue Book* (available in your college library) as your guide, enter the names of all top state government officials on your state chart. Obtain the names of all city and county officials and department heads from the mayor and county commission offices and enter them on your other charts.
4. Write a news story based on each of the following sets of notes:
   A. City government today
      Questioned by investigator
      From Federal Office of Revenue Sharing
      About number of minority employes
      In several city departments
      Investigator for ORS civil rights division
      Expressed unhappiness with
      Imbalance in number
      Of minority employees
      In seven city departments
      Police, Fire, Service, Finance
      Waste Water Control, Recreation and Airport
      Investigator ordered city
      To "set up realistic goals"
      To hire more women and blacks
      In those departments
      City Law Director Ashton Gill
      Said Investigator Jackson Lawlson
      Ordered him to project number
      Of new employes needed
      In the next two years
      And to establish goals
      For hiring women and blacks
      To fill adequate number
      Of those positions
      Gill said order follows
      Letter last month
      From ORS officials
      Threatening to withhold federal funds
      From the city
      If more women and blacks

Are not hired
Mayor Thomas Blackburn said
He did not think money
Will be withheld
If city acts in good faith
Gilbert Sanderson, city's Equal
Employment Opportunity officer
Said he set goal
For 14 per cent of new
Policemen to be women and blacks
City is seeking to hire
Forty new policemen
Gill said he was given
A 90-day deadline
To complete his projections

B. Police Chief Amos Jackson
Said today he would ask
City Law Office to prepare
An ordinance to double
City towing fee
From $20 to $40
Said other cities this size
Have $40 fee
Said cost of towing
Has almost doubled
Also number of
Illegally parked cars
Has quadrupled in last two years
Problem especially bad
Around the University
City tows cars
Left in tow-away zones
And no-parking areas
Also cars that have
Delinquent parking tickets
Accumulated on them
Jackson said he couldn't
Give figure on amount
Towing fees bring city
No records kept on total
Number of cars towed
Asked how he knew
Total number had quadrupled
He said he was going by
"What my men tell me"
City Finance Director Ken Johnson
Said he could get the total
"But it will take a day or so"
Councilman Carl Jones
Said he would oppose
The ordinance when it

Comes before City Council

Jones said: "I don't think the city should be able to arbitrarily jump towing fees 100 per cent. I think some city officials are trying to take advantage of the public by raising the rates without justification. I will want—in fact, I'll demand a thorough study of the problem before the council takes any action on the proposal."

Ordinance to come before

City Council Tuesday night

5. Write a story using the following notes:

City seeks to sell

General obligation bonds

In amount of $9.8 million

To finance Main Street

Reconstruction project

And modernization of

Traffic signals throughout city

Bond Consultant John Cole

Of Best and Co., bond consultants,

Said city probably would have

To pay six per cent interest

On the bonds over

A 20-year period

He said the city would

Have to pay $588,000 in interest

And $50,000 in principal

During the next fiscal year

City officials said they

Estimated a 6.25 per cent rate

When they prepared the

New city budget

Cole said bond market

Has been favorable

And stable on municipal bonds

Advised city to sell

Bonds now rather than wait

If bonds are sold

At six per cent interest

The city's interest on its bonds for

Coming fiscal year

Will amount to $7,299,000

Compared to $6,699,000 this year

The new bond issue

Will cover city's share

Of federally funded traffic

Improvement projects

Mayor Thomas Coleman said

It is important to sell

As soon as possible

Because federal funds will not be

Made available until the

City has raised its share

For the projects

Members of the City Council

Approved increasing the bond issue
From $8 million to $9.8 million
To cover cost overruns on
The first phase of the project

6. Write a news story using the following notes:
State Senator Carlton Towers, D-Troy
Introduced bill yesterday
Setting strict penalties
For selling beer
And alcoholic beverages
To anyone under 18
The bill calls for revocation
Of beer and liquor licenses
For anyone convicted
Of knowingly selling intoxicants
To persons under 18
Present law says beer sales
To minors can result
In license suspension
Up to 10 days
Towers said alcoholism
Among high school age youth
Is rampant and even
Elementary school officials
Are reporting grade school pupils
Showing up at school
Under the influence of alcohol
Companion bill introduced
By Sen. Burton Creech, R-Athens
Would make it a felony
To sell beer and liquor
To minors
On the second conviction
First conviction under this bill
Would still be considered
A misdemeanor
With penalties of
A $500 to $1,000 fine
And 30 days to six months in jail
On second offense
Fines could go
As high as $3,000
Under the new bill
With a prison term
Of one to three years
Creech said he realized
That under Towers's bill
There should be no second offenses
Creech said: "Unfortunately, not all our operators are licensed."

7. Attend a meeting of the city council or its equivalent in your community and write a news story on the meeting. Turn the story in, with your notes, the following morning.

8. Invite the mayor of your city to class for an interview. Question him about current problems facing city government. Write a news story based on the interview.

9. Suggest newsworthy pictures and write appropriate cutlines on the following assignments: Exercise 4B, Exercise 5.

10. The mayor presented his recommendations for the city budget for the next fiscal year to the City Council last night. Public hearings on the budget will be conducted by the council's finance committee next week. Analyze the table below and write an interpretative news story from it.

	Appropriations for Present Fiscal Year	Appropriations Recommended for Next Fiscal Year
Debt Service	$ 6,989,155	$ 7,336,582
Administration	2,231,173	1,421,173
Finance	885,823	890,338
Law Department	403,883	402,288
Information Systems	483,419	506,483
Police	8,425,365	8,921,838
Fire	9,995,247	10,036,520
Public Service	1,016,348	985,517
Traffic Engineering	2,119,311	2,365,485
Recreation	2,589,671	2,524,906
Libraries	897,022	924,000
City Schools	4,809,523	4,884,523*
Public Transportation Services	810,000	864,026
Totals	41,655,940	42,036,679

*The bulk of the city school budget comes from state funds. The city has assigned $4 million in Revenue Sharing Funds to city schools. The remaining $884,523 comes for other revenue sources such as taxes.

CHAPTER 24

Business, Industry, Agriculture, Labor

The increased importance of the economy has brought about a demand for reporters who have training in economics and finance as well as journalism. And at the same time there has been a renaissance in the coverage of economic news in most newspapers. Stories about business and the economy are no longer automatically relegated to the business pages. They regularly make the front page of every newspaper in the nation.

In fact, there may be a business or economic angle to any story. The football game that brings 85,000 persons to a city on a Saturday afternoon certainly has an economic impact. A prolonged and harsh winter, normally just a weather story, will have an impact in increased home and industrial heating costs, perhaps closed plants, delayed spring planting and the like. Editors expect reporters to be able to gather the facts and write coherent economic stories—often for the front page.

Perhaps the greatest impact has been on the business pages. Once many editors were content to reprint the publicity releases (perhaps rewritten) from local industries or their parent companies along with the wire service stock quotations. Being a business-page reporter then was not a particularly demanding job. However, today's business or financial page reporter must have more than just a passing knowledge of economics and finance. He must be able to understand what is going on and to explain it to his readers in a language they will understand. Several trends have brought this about. Probably the most significant is the changing nature of ownership of American business and industries. Millions of small investors now own stock in major corporations and have an interest in their success. They keep up by reading the financial pages. In addition, the nation experienced unprecedented economic expansion in the three decades after World War II. To report and interpret these developments, the business or financial page reporter has had to become something of a specialist in economics and finance. National and international economic events and trends often have direct influences on local business, industry, agriculture and labor. A depression, major unemployment, inflation, a poor wheat crop in Russia, frost damage to the coffee trees in Brazil—all can have a direct influence on the economic life of a community.

It should also be pointed out that the economic health of a community will have an effect on the newspaper. Being a business, the newspaper derives its financial support as an advertising medium for the establishments that compose the economic structure of the community. As a general rule, newspapers do not open their news columns to free advertising space just to please advertisers. At the same time, most editors realize that there are many legitimate news items developing within the business community that have strong reader interest.

Even the routine business stories are usually of much local consequence, affecting the pocketbooks, jobs, household budgets and in general the plans of local citizens. The stereotyped real estate transfers reported in a "column" without benefit of lead will be read by many adult readers. The price paid for the corner building lot may reflect the value of every piece of property in the block. Will a service station be located there? Or perhaps an all-night market or a laundromat? If so, it may be the first sign of decay of a substantial residential neighborhood. Progress or disaster thus may move below the surface of a routine as well as a major business story. The announcement of the consolidation of two major steel firms in other cities might have a direct bearing on a local steel plant which is a subsidiary of one of the merged firms. Will they phase out the local operation? Or perhaps they may expand it, bring new money into the community, creating new jobs.

While it is true that handouts, publicity releases and promotional stories may save the business reporter a lot of leg work, a reporter must always question their news value. Is a fashion show or a Santa Claus parade or a Washington's Birthday sale legitimate news or free advertising? The news policy of the individual newspaper will determine how much and in what manner such material will be accepted. Many newspapers join with local merchants in promoting some events. Some national "weeks" and "days" with a commercial tinge may be publicized. Mother's Day, Father's Day, Harvest Moon Sale Days (with special entertainment features provided by the stores) and other worthy though special-interest occasions may find the reporter writing not news but promotion and publicity. In all such cases the safeguard of honest reporting is the ability to distinguish the wolf in sheep's clothing. A Washington Day sale, for example, can be a legitimate news story if traditionally thousands of people start lining up outside stores at midnight to get first crack at the bargains when the doors open in the morning.

Types of Establishments. Establishments and organizations that come within a community's economic complex include:

Retail stores
Wholesale distributors
Banks and finance firms
Real estate agencies
Insurance agencies

24a

Transportation firms—passenger and freight—both surface and air

Industries

Communications—telephone, telegraph

Business and industrial organizations—chamber of commerce, Better Business Bureau, various trade associations, automobile club

Farms

Agricultural markets

Agricultural organizations and agencies—state, county and federal

Labor—organized and unorganized

Plus various types of service establishments, some indigenous to the locality

The extent to which a newspaper will cover each of these activities may depend upon local characteristics. If a sizable number of the newspaper's subscribers are engaged in one of the activities, special sections of the newspaper may periodically be devoted to news and timely information published for the benefit of those subscribers and other interested readers. Such sections range from the fairly common farm page used in regions that have substantial agricultural interests to a special section on a new airport, for example. Many newspapers put out annual business and industry editions or so-called progress editions devoted to the economic growth of the community over the previous year. Whether or not any special sections or pages are printed on a regular basis, stories from all of these economic activities are published as the news becomes available. And frequently the story may appear on the front page if it is of major significance. A prolonged drought in an agricultural region is sure to make page one, just as a strike that idles a large number of the city's work force may be the main story of the day.

Types of Stories. The great variety of stories from business, industry, agriculture and labor will not conform to any simple general type. Some will be reported as meetings, speeches, interviews and publications. Some will appear as trials and lawsuits. Even crime, accidents, fire, illnesses, deaths and funerals may affect the economic life of the community and require an interpretation of this influence.

Following are some general varieties (rather than special types) of news on economic developments which appear from day to day in the newspapers:

1. *Markets.* Stocks and bonds, livestock and commodities—mostly tabulations and stereotyped reports, national and local, but accompanied by interpretative stories.
2. *Real estate.* Routine transfers, new additions, large sales, improvements and expansions of buildings. Building permits issued.
3. *Merchandizing.* Retail and wholesale stores—expansions and improvements, new corporations and partnerships, mergers, bankruptcies, prices, cost of living.
4. *Finance and banking.* Stockholders' and board meetings, dividends, bond issues, discounts and interest rates, the money market in general, refunding, trends.
5. *Industry.* New industries, new products, improved processes or methods, expansions, removals, bond issues, mergers.

6. *Transportation.* Changes in schedules, rights of way, board meetings, stocks and bonds, refunding, rates.

7. *Labor.* Wages and hours, unemployment, strikes, lockouts, relief, policies.

8. *Business and government.* Taxes, legislative acts and court decisions affecting business, regulations and enforcement.

9. *Agriculture.* Crops, sales, droughts, new methods of farming, regulation by government, new varieties.

For all of these varieties, stories on personnel changes (including human-interest stories on retirements) are available along with a countless supply of features to the imaginative reporter.

Story Forms. Just as these story varieties run the gamut of different story types, so also will the story forms vary. Straight-news stories, simple and complex; human-interest stories; feature articles—all will be used in presenting the news on business, industry, agriculture and labor.

To report on the economic life of his community, a reporter will need an adequate background and an ability to interpret—both of which he can gain from experience and study.

Here are some examples of stories dealing with business, industry, agriculture and labor:

> If you are among those who grumble about how much you have to pay the tax collector in April, it's partially your fault.
>
> With a little advance planning, you can shave your annual income tax bill. You have a little more than a month to work at it. If you wait until April—even if you wait until January 1—you'll miss some tax-saving opportunities . . .

> Marketers everywhere are familiar with our old friend the Working Woman. They know her average age, spending habits, consumption patterns.
>
> Her demographic profile is etched into the minds of canny ad people everywhere, because her dollars suddenly became one of the hottest forces on the U.S. consumer scene . . .

> About 2,400 employees and former employees of Allied Chemical Co. who have been laid off at any time during the last 18 months will share in $5 million in trade readjustment allowances, a spokesman for the Amalgamated Clothing Workers Union said today.
>
> The allowances are paid from federal taxes on imports. Workers who were laid off from companies adversely affected by imports are eligible for the payments. Allied Chemical makes seat belts.
>
> Some local workers will get as much as $5,000 . . .

> Organized labor is expected to step up its campaign early this year for congressional investigations into what it considers "union busting" law firms, consultants and trade associations.
>
> "Union busting is now a major American industry, with sales of well over a half a billion dollars a year," Robert A. Georgino, president of the AFL-CIO Building and Construction Trades Department, charged today . . .

> Speculators aren't the only ones who profit from high gold prices. The U.S. Government, which owns 262 million ounces of gold, is about $40 billion richer than it was 10 days ago.

The profit is all on paper, though, and that's where most of it is likely to stay. Were the government to sell large amounts of gold, the price would drop sharply . . .

INTERPRETING THE NEWS

24c   Interpretation is the key to most stories on business, industry, agriculture and labor—even most of the routine stories. The reader usually wants to know why something happened and what it means to him. And he wants it told in a language he can understand. The worlds of business, industry, agriculture and labor have languages—jargon—all their own, and the reporter must not fall into the trap of thinking the reader will understand them because he (the reporter) understands them. Statistics seems to be a common language to business and industry, so a reporter should learn to simplify statistics for his reader without distorting them. For example, the average reader probably would not take the trouble to analyze "A total of 60,612 of the 147,604 persons in Thomasville own automobiles, according to. . . ." The figures probably will slip right past him. But he may be interested in "Two out of every five Thomasville residents own an automobile. . . ." The significance of statistics should be made clear. Usually a comparison is needed. How do the figures compare with other figures? Are they high or low? How do they compare with figures of past years and other sections of the nation? Most figures are meaningless unless comparisons are given. When the reporter writes that local automobile sales increased 50 per cent last month, he should tell the reader how many automobiles were sold last month and the month before if the percentage is to have any meaning.

24d   The following list of technical terms used by business, industry, agriculture and labor will emphasize the need for interpretation: *partnership, corporation, articles of incorporation, charter, bonds, refunding bonds, serial bonds, sinking-fund bonds, common stock, preferred stock, bankruptcy, referee in bankruptcy, "bull" and "bear" markets, collateral, call loans, strikes and lockouts, clearinghouse, assets and liabilities, discounts, interest, dividends, premiums, exchange, liquidation, credit, trusts, monopolies, receiver, Federal Reserve, surplus, socialism, communism, state capitalism, contracts, overhead, trustees, directors, interlocking boards, pyramiding, holding companies, public utilities, municipality, debt and deficit, "blue sky" laws, audits, balance sheet, tariff, parity, balance of payments, gold reserve.* In using such terms the reporter should either translate them or use them within a context that enables the reader to understand their meaning.

Some economic terms may require only simple definitions, but others require analyses that are possible only if the reporter knows the language of business and industry. Such documents as an auditor's report, a profit and loss statement or a market report require special knowledge in economics to read and translate accurately.

THE REPORTER'S BACKGROUND

A reporter needs an academic foundation in economics, sociology, economic history, economic geography and political economy to cover business, industry, agriculture and labor with any degree of success. These subjects generally are studied by journalism students at college, but one should never make the assumption that those few required courses dealing with economics give a reporter a sufficient background for depth reporting in the economic structure of the community. They help, but the college graduate stands at the entrance—not at the exit—of his economic education.

The college courses will give a reporter the general theories, principles and history of economics, but a successful business or financial page reporter needs more than that. He must learn the specifics of economic activities in the locality where he works and be able to tell his readers how national and international events and trends influence the local economic community. He should have ready answers, in a notebook if not in his head, to basic questions on the area—population, wealth, chief sources of income, chief occupations, tax rates, school enrollment, bank deposits, labor force, value of properties and other vital facts about the community and the people whose economic life he will attempt to interpret. Most of this information is available in standard reference works such as an atlas or a state statistical survey. However, the local chamber of commerce will have more up-to-date statistics on the community as a general rule.

With all of this, the reporter is just starting. To establish himself as a competent journalist on economic affairs, a reporter needs to acquire additional expertise in each of the four areas of economic coverage.

24e *Business.* A thorough knowledge of the business houses and a more than passing acquaintance with the business executives of the city are a major requirement for a business page reporter. Retail and wholesale stores, finance houses, transportation agencies and other firms, and particularly the principal officers of these firms, are news sources for the business reporter. He must know about these businesses to get the real news. He must be able to separate the free advertising and publicity from legitimate news in order to present an accurate picture of the city's economic progress or decline.

The reporter should develop a relationship with the major business executives in the city. If the reporter is respected, the business executives will be willing to answer penetrating (and sometimes distasteful) questions, and a number of them will volunteer tips that can lead to important stories. Since business firms are private enterprises and a reporter has no legal right to see their records (in most cases), it is essential that he cultivate contacts. An alert reporter with good contacts should be able to anticipate most stories that will develop on the business beat.

24f *Industry.* Most industries have their sales sights on regional or national rather than a local market. Nevertheless, the people employed by a local industry are local citizens, and their activities as well as the industry's well-being are of interest to all the people of the community. They are vital to the local economy, especially if there are only a limited number of industries in the community. The reporter covering industries should know them well—the products they manufacture, the number of persons they employ, the distribution of their products, the sources of their raw materials and the people who manage and operate them. As in the case of covering local businesses, the reporter must cultivate and keep alive his news sources in industry.

24g

Agriculture. One does not have to be a farmer to be interested in agricultural news. In fact, what happens on the farms of the nation can and does have a day-to-day influence on the life of everyone. A prolonged drought that wipes out the corn crop is reflected in the prices of the supermarket shelves. Freezing weather that damages the truck crops can send prices of fresh vegetables skyrocketing. And an extended farm laborer strike may cut the supply of some products completely. In dozens of ways every day the news emanating from the nation's farms influences our lives. Well-written, informative farm news should hold the interest of most readers. The local agricultural community can be an important source of news. The county agricultural and home demonstration agents, farm bureaus and other offices of agricultural agencies and associations have long-standing affiliations with hundreds or thousands of individual farm operators, and these offices generally are the primary sources of agricultural news. The reporter must know the officials and the scope of services of these organizations if he is to be effective.

Knowledge of agriculture is also required of the reporter if he is to explain accurately the how and why of farming to the reader. It is all too easy for a "dude" reporter to make a screamingly funny mistake in writing about planting peas or milking cows. A few such errors will cost a reporter the confidence of both his news sources and his readers. A reporter from a nonfarm background can educate himself through reading and regular visits to farms. A reporter who does not know should not be afraid to ask questions or to look up information. Even reporters with farm experience should refer to books and other publications regularly to keep abreast of the latest developments in the field.

24h

Labor. The labor beat can be one of the most significant on a newspaper, especially in a highly industrialized and unionized area. A community's labor force, which constitutes much of the total population, cuts across the areas of business, industry and agriculture. This makes the job of the labor reporter particularly sensitive, especially in times of labor disputes. A strike against a major advertiser, for example, might present serious financial problems for the newspaper if the advertiser did not like the tone of the stories. He might seek to influence the coverage by threatening to withdraw his advertising from the newspaper. That does happen but it is the exception rather than the rule.

The labor force can be organized by crafts or industries or not at all. As a result, covering the labor beat involves developing many sources of news. The general run of labor news offers no more than briefs on elections, routine meetings, social events and the like. But when strikes are threatened or in progress, or contracts are up for renewal, it may become front-page news. A labor reporter should make every effort to report the labor-management affairs that are settled without any strife just as vigorously as he does those that threaten or result in conflict. News sources cultivated by the handling of routine stories often become quite valuable during periods of labor strife. Moreover, to develop latent interest in labor news, the reporter needs to search for stories and features that are not centered on conflict.

A labor reporter should not be a crusader for labor or a spy for management.

He is a reporter and no more. However, he should be well versed in the advantages and disadvantages of organized labor, in the structure of labor organizations, in the extra benefits of labor membership (such as welfare funds), in the salary scale of laborers and in other data important to his locality. He should also have a working knowledge of the major labor laws that affect all workers as well as those that have a direct bearing on the industries in his community. This knowledge will enable him to enrich his labor stories with accurate interpretation.

Labor stories demand a careful balance. A reporter should never take sides. When he is writing of strikes and lockouts, for example, he should make his interpretation an objective one—giving the facts but not stacking the deck for one side or the other. On the other hand, his knowledge of strikes will lead him to treat them as a result of disagreements between management and labor rather than as military warfare (which sometimes happens when a police reporter is assigned to cover a strike).

COMPLETE REPORTING

24i

The most important form of interpretation in reporting the economic life of a community is that which reaches below the surface of events and brings forth significances and trends. The stockmarket figures, commodity prices, car loadings and other financial data are usually not significant in themselves. Compared with what they were a year ago or last month, they may have a meaning and be a prophecy of the future. This does not mean that the reporter should become a forecaster; on the contrary, he must be cautious about making forecasts on business conditions because serious consequences may result—stock shifts, sales slumps and the like. Nevertheless, the reporter can point up the trends of the past. Although analyses of business conditions may be the prerogative of "business analysts" or special columnists, the reporter himself cannot afford to restrict his questions to the obvious facts.

Is a factory to be established in the community? What, then, will be its effect upon the labor situation, unemployment, housing, taxes, the demands on city utilities and services? No columnist or analyst writing for a feature syndicate can interpret this sort of local story to the citizens. Only the reporter can provide this service. Complete reporting is a public service expected of him. Concerning a new city auditorium, a new freeway through the city, a strike at a major industry or the status of retail sales during a recession, the question is not just "What is happening?" but also "What does it mean in the lives of local people?"

EXERCISES

1. Using any newspaper available to you, clip and make a news analysis of a business, labor and agriculture story.
2. Invite a local stock broker to class to discuss various aspects of the stock market. Write a news story based on that interview.

3. Write stories using the following notes:
  A. Officials of City Corp.
       New York-based department store chain
       And parent company of
       Robert's stores
       A state-wide chain of
       Twenty department stores
       Said today City Corp. plans
       To make public its
       Reorganization plan for
       The Robert's chain
       Next Tuesday at the
       Downtown Robert's store
       Creditors notified by mail
       Of the meeting
       The company filed for protection
       Under federal bankruptcy law
       Six months ago
       Company expected to ask creditors
       For more time to look for
       A buyer for the money-losing chain
       If time isn't granted
       Company expected to close
       All 20 stores
  B. Drs. Lincoln Jones and Hepburn T. Armstrong
       Two local veterinarians who
       Specialize in orthopedic surgery
       For domestic animals
       Have formed company
       To start producing
       Special cartlike unit
       To support hind legs
       For paralyzed dogs
       Device looks like sulky
       Used in harness racing
       Made of lightweight aluminum alloy
       And stainless steel
       With foam padding to prevent abrasion
       First one developed 16 years ago
       Provides new freedom for paralyzed dogs
       Will be manufactured locally
       Expect to hire 100 persons within a year
       Prices range from $49.95 for small breeds
       To $140 for large dogs
  C. New driving school opened today
       Owned by Bronco Gervits
       Former world-champion race driver
       Has been tutoring other race drivers
       Since his retirement two years ago
       New school designed for
       Average commuter to help
       Typical driver survive

Daily trip to and from work
Called School of Advanced Driving Techniques
Located at Sundown Raceway
Two miles east of Walker Springs exit
On Harbor Freeway
Gervits said one-day course
In advanced highway driving
Covers basic vehicle dynamics
Skid control, evasive maneuvers,
Emergency braking, weight control
And how to control a car in tight quarters
And around obstacles
Cost is $150
Gervits said: "Freeway driving is like war. It is a mixture of long periods of
    boredom interspersed by short bursts of terror. Our course isn't for those just
    learning to drive. It is for those who wish to improve their skills above the
    average level"

D. Jackson Foam and Fiber
Local industry in Riverbend Industrial Park
Notified 100 employes today
They would be furloughed
At the end of the month
Jacob Bailey, industrial relations manager
Said a slump in contracts
Is forcing the firm
To reduce its workforce
"We hope it will be temporary," he said
Firm employes 225
It manufactures foam stuffing
For furniture and auto seats
Bailey said firm negotiating
With major aircraft manufacturer
For "an important contract"
Said employes would be
Called back as soon as
Firm signs that contract
Said he hoped it would be
Six weeks to two months

E. Goldman's Department Stores Inc.
Chicago-based firm
Announced plans today
To build new store here
First store outside Chicago area
Will be built in
Old Hickory Shopping Mall
Frank Stillwell, company president
Said market studies prove
This is one of the most
Dynamic and growing trade areas
In the entire nation
Stillwell said company had considered
A store here 10 years ago

But held off until about two years ago
When firm began planning store here
Because of the improved economic outlook
Of this entire area
Ground will be broken
Next Monday for the $6 million building
H. & M. Construction Co. is the general contractor
Stillwell said to open the store
"By the end of the year"

F. Second National Bank
Board of Directors
Voted today to increase
Quarterly dividend 2 cents per share
To 30 cents for the fourth quarter
Also announced that
This is the last dividend
Which will be paid
Under Second National name
Bank will become
Roosevelt National Bank
The first on next month

G. The governor of Cairo
And six Egyptian business leaders
Will visit here for a week
Of trade talks next month
James C. Clark, mayor's
Economic and community development adviser
Said they also will explore
Education and cultural exchanges
With officials at State University
Clark said Gov. Beatrice Madison
And other state officials
Have been invited to a dinner
Mayor Richard Bodkin will give
For the Egyptians at
The Executive Dining Room
In the University Center
First trade mission here
By anyone from Egypt
Clark said

4. Write a feature story based on the following notes:

C.C. Simpson and his son, Gary, own a 1,00-acre farm in nearby Crossville. They raise pigs for the area market. They fatten 15,000 pigs each year at a rate of 3,500 every three-and-a-half months. All are sold to Star Packing Co. here. They have been raising hogs for five years. Used to raise Black Angus cattle but changed because Gary got interested in hogs while a member of the Future Farmers of America in high school.

Simpson farm considered a model of efficiency, County Agent Roger Miller said. Nothing is wasted. Even the hog manure is used to fertilize the corn the Simpsons grow to feed the hogs.

"We got out of the cattle business five years ago," C. C. Simpson said, "and we've sunk $500,000 in equipment and facilities for hogs. We're completely automated—push-button style—and now are raising corn to feed them."

By touching one button on a control panel in his feed mill, Simpson mixes grain for feed. Another button releases water to flush the concrete stalls. Another sends feed forced by air through underground pipes into any stall desired. And a dryer processes corn grains before it is mixed in the feed mill.

The home-grown corn is the talk of the county. The elder Simpson said: "My farmer friends don't believe me, but we produced 192 bushels of corn per acre by using manure instead of costly conventional fertilizer."

The cost of heating the sheds and pens in the winter is practically nothing. Gary Simpson explained that each pen will hold 350 to 600 hogs. The hogs produce their own warmth in winter. He said 350 of them emit enough body heat to warm a five-room house. "Sometimes it get so warm in the sheds in the winter that we have to lower canvas flaps on the sheds to allow the heat to escape."

Automation has made the Simpsons' job a 40-hour week affair, unlike most farmers who work 60 to 80 hours a week, County Agent Miller said.

"We work from 7 a.m. until 4 p.m. Monday through Friday," Gary said. "The weekend is for rest and recreation. And we have been able to cut our farm work force drastically because of the automation. Now all the work associated with the hogs is handled by my dad, one hand and me. Of course, we add extra hands at corn planting and harvesting time, but that's for the fields not the hogs."

One reason it takes so few is that the hog farm is designed so the hogs are never more than a snout away from a trough, filled with a strictly balanced diet and a fresh-water tap. The hogs eat and sleep and get fat.

In an effort to keep ahead of high feed prices, the Simpsons are clearing woodland on their farm at a rate of 100 acres a year so they can plant more corn. "We are looking forward to the day when we do not have to buy any feed on the market," C. C. Simpson said.

He said he acquired the farm 18 years ago and founded a cheese firm but sold that and went into the cattle business. But now he is sold on hogs.

"They are the smartest animals around," Gary Simpson said. "They really are sharp. Within five minutes after transfer to our hog sheds, they learn to squeeze a faucet and suck water from the fountain."

5. Following are items from news releases sent to the business editor by local firms. Combine them in a "Business Briefs" column made up of one- and two-paragraph items:

    i.   Rasmussens, Inc., announced today that its downtown store will be given a new $100,000 aluminum coat.

        Albert Sharon, president, said work will begin Monday on the installation of the new, two-toned bronze covering. It will take approximately six weeks to cover all exterior walls, he added.

        "The new covering will not only give our store a fresh look, it also will provide additional insulation, which is an important factor in these energy-conscious times," Sharon said. "By reducing our energy bills we can continue to keep our prices at a level that is favorable to our customers."

    ii.   Sunshine Mining Co., the state's largest phosphate producers, announced today that its stockholders have approved the acquisition of Key Oil Co.

        Key Oil, based in Orlando, owns 150 service stations in three southeastern states.

        The stockholders of Sunshine also voted to change the firm's name to Sunshine Energy Enterprises.

W. O. Davenport Jr., formerly chairman of the board and chief executive officer of Key Oil, will assume the same duties at Sunshine Energy. Rockwell Swanson, president of Sunshine Mining, had announced his retirement last month.

iii.   Dixie Lee Insurance Co. has completed installation of a fully electronic telephone switchboard system at its national headquarters in suburban Glen Park.

Warren Bestos, president of the firm, said the 450-telephone system replaced the insurance company's old cord-type switchboard.

Called the Dimension 2,000 system, it is the largest to be installed in the state by the Bell Telephone System, Bestos said.

"This new switchboard system will greatly improve our overall communications capabilities," Bestos said. "It certainly is the finest in the state and perhaps even the nation."

iv.   Health-Care, Inc. has signed agreements to manage five more hospitals, Dr. Derry Hall, the firm's president, announced today.

Health-Care, a hospital management firm, founded here 10 years ago by Dr. Hall and six other local physicians, now manages 150 hospitals across the nation.

The new hospitals to be managed by Health-Care are in Clermont, Fla.; St. Paul, Minn.; Tacoma, Wash.; Missoula, Mont.; and New Orleans, La.

The firm now manages 150 hospitals with 20,000 beds in 28 states.

v.   Revitalization of the downtown business sections is "something you can bet on," Alvah H. Wingfield, chairman of the New World Center Action Committee of the Chamber of Commerce, said today.

In a speech prepared for delivery at the Chamber's annual Progress Luncheon, Wingfield said the recent announcement that the Hilton chain planned a 300-room hotel and two private investors were planning a new office tower "virtually assures us a new and revitalized business district."

"Interest in the downtown business district has never been as high in my memory. There is more interest on the part of significant and qualified developers and financial institutions than in any period of the 20 years I have been active in the Chamber.

"Within three years we will have reversed the trend of businesses moving to the suburbs," Wingfield said.

He predicted that the demand for business and office space in the central business district will quadruple within three years.

"Within three years we will have them standing in line to get space in a downtown building," he said.

Wingfield is president of Lennar Corp., one of the community's largest construction firms.

6. Write a story on the following notes:

Guards at the State Prison, located just outside the city, have been negotiating with prison officials over a new contract for three months. Their current two-year contract expires in two weeks.

Rumor has it that they are threatening to "call in sick" Sunday to press their demands for higher pay. Source is one of the negotiators for the guards but he asks not to be identified.

Lt. Adolphus L. Bailey, president of the state-wide union that represents the guards at all state prison facilities, said he had heard the rumor also. "I understand they will be calling in sick with the flu."

The guards are paid $1,105 to $2,109 a month. They are demanding to be placed on a par with members of the state highway patrol, who are paid $1,299 to

$3,319 a month. They also are demanding more vacation time, dental insurance and provisions to accumulate more sick leave.

George W. Dunne, state corrections commissioner, who is the state's chief negotiator, said he had not heard of the "job action."

"I have promised them I will do what I can to get them a raise, but their demands amount to 20 to 24 per cent, which is absolutely unthinkable. And if they do not show up for work, it will make it all the more difficult to convince everyone that their demands are fair."

He added that any guard who calls in sick and does not have sick leave coming will be "docked for every minute he is off."

There are some 250 guards employed at the local prison. More than 1,400 are employed at all of the state's prison facilities.

Dunne said the department might have to ask for a special session of the state legislature if the guards do not back off from their demands.

"The legislators are the ones who appropriate the money," Dunne said. "And as you know, they only voted an 11 per cent pay increase for all state employes this year."

CHAPTER 25

Education, Research, Science

Teacher walkouts, rejected bond issues for new schools, declining enrollments in inner-city schools, busing, increased student violence, rapidly declining educational achievement, lack of funds to meet payrolls and a host of other problems beset American schools today. The once-quiet school beat has become a major one, producing important stories at most newspapers today.

The cost of education still ranks as the biggest item in the budget of most cities. And it is of special concern because everyone helps pay for it whether or not he or she attends school or has children who attend. In addition to their educational roles, schools also frequently play a major role in the social life of a community. The press has a particular interest in schools, for in addition to being a source of news, the schools are producing tomorrow's consumers of newspapers.

As educational institutions continue to grow as an important source of news, newspapers are making an effort to report more than just the routine items such as enrollment figures, bond issues and faculty changes. These are extremely important, of course, and form the backbone of most school coverage. But today's newspapers are devoting increasing amounts of space to try to help the taxpayer understand what is happening not only in local schools but also across the nation. Problems in school financing, trends in classroom teaching, labor negotiations with teachers and dozens of other significant problems are being reported as never before. Newspapers also are showing increased interest in church-related and private schools as well as the trade schools that have developed in many areas.

Research and education go together. Those in the field of education, especially those on the upper levels, seek not only to teach but also—through research—to add new knowledge. Research, of course, is by no means confined to educational institutions. Government agencies, industries, hospitals and clinics and private laboratories sponsor many research programs. However, a large percentage of those programs are linked to educational institutions, either through special contracts or through the services of educators as consultants. In any event, educational institutions must train most if not all of the personnel qualified to operate research programs.

The word *science* has not been used so far in the discussion of research. This word was purposely avoided because science and research are too often considered as synonymous. Research in the basic sciences, medical sciences and engineering has become tremendously important, dramatically so. In fact, major "scientific" developments have become a staple of news, so much so that many newspapers have science editors. This is especially true in major educational and scientific centers where extensive research is always under way. While science deserves this recognition, research in other fields of knowledge should not be excluded. Studies in the humanities and the social sciences deserve—and generally get—almost equal attention.

COVERING EDUCATION 25a

Coverage of education today is a major challenge to the media. The editor who assigns just any reporter to cover the beat is shirking his responsibility to the newspaper and the community. A reporter does not have to be a former school teacher or to have taken education courses in college to cover the field effectively. But he certainly must have an understanding of the educational system. And he must keep informed about what is happening in education generally and on the local scene specifically.

To cover the education beat effectively, the reporter must know the organizational structure of the public and private school systems in his community. Whether it is a single school or a large educational system, the organizational pattern of each will be much the same. At the top is some type of board, elected or appointed, on which membership is considered a public service. The board is generally composed of prominent individuals who serve without compensation. Members of the board meet regularly and are responsible for the total operation of the school or the school system. The voters elect or empower the board to employ an individual, usually a professional educator, who serves as the chief administrator (superintendent, president, chancellor, headmaster) of the school or system. From that point on, the functions of the board and the administrator usually are clearly defined.

The board, after consultation with the administrator, should set the basic policies for the operations of the school or the system. It should decide on capital-outlay measures, and should formalize appointments, retirements, leaves of absence and terminations of faculty and staff. For his part, the administrator should be in complete charge of operating the school or system within the policies set forth by the board, and he should also make recommendations on the appointments, terminations and other matters requiring formal school board action.

Board members are not expected to move into the professionalized area of administration, nor should the administrator extend his authority beyond the policies fixed by the board. In actual practice, it does not work that way. Board members often get involved in such matters as teacher assignment, new curriculums, student disciplinary matters and other areas on a day-to-day or individual basis. And many superintendents have been known to "dictate" to boards on a variety of policy issues. The latter is especially true in cities and counties where the superintendent is an elected official. The operation of school systems in such major cities as Baltimore, Boston, Chicago, Minneapolis, Philadelphia, St. Louis, Washington, D.C., and San Francisco and of those in dozens of smaller cities has been jeopardized because of disputes between board members and superintendents that have grown out of the wide range of difficulties facing the schools—squeezed budgets, rising teacher militancy, increased crime in the schools and, in some areas, race problems.

The top organizational officials, as well as the subordinate ones (supervisors, principals, deans, directors, department heads), are vitally important to the operation of a school or an educational system, but the most important function is the teacher-student relationship. Everything else should be done for the purpose of getting the teacher and the student together, giving them adequate facilities for the learning process, hoping that the student will absorb the desire for learning as well as the knowledge that the teacher can transmit. Presumably, if the organization is efficient and effective at the top levels, it will achieve these goals at the teacher-student level. It does not always work that way, however, and it is essential that the education reporter be aware of that fact.

Scope of Coverage. The education reporter usually is expected to cover the activities of all levels of the school systems in his city, from the policy-making boards to the teachers in the classrooms. Large or small, the education beat offers many routine stories as well as major news breaks, features and interpretative pieces. Some of the routine stories:

1. Scheduled dates—opening and closing, holidays.
2. Enrollments—statistics, comparisons, trends.
3. Honors—citations of students and faculty.
4. Changes in curricula—courses added and dropped.
5. Commencements—speakers, graduating students.
6. Personnel changes—appointments, resignations, retirements.
7. Board meetings—policies, budgets, capital-outlay plans.
8. Activities of affiliated organizations—education associations, parent-teacher chapters, "booster" groups, alumni.

Major stories develop in such areas as teacher strikes, academic freedom of teachers, racial strife, crime in the schools, rejection of bond issues by taxpayers and a long list of other troubles that often beset school systems. While these are important stories, and generally rate the front page, there are numerous other major interpretative and feature articles that can come out of the schools. The alert reporter will be looking for them constantly.

Following is an example of a school story from the New York Times that goes beyond routine coverage:

> The rigid chronological barrier that has long existed between high schools and colleges is being increasingly breached by tens of thousands of restless American teenagers who are performing college-level work before they get their high school diplomas.

A movement that began with a trickle is growing larger each year and hastening the time when educators will have to reassess the wide overlap that has developed between the last year of high school and the first year of college.

Arthur Lilling, a senior at Midwood High School in Brooklyn, is taking an entire schedule of college offerings in English, calculus, French and biology taught by faculty members in his own school through the nationally sponsored Advanced Placement Program.

Maxine Medaglia is dividing each day between courses at Suffern High School and nearby Rockland County Community College in suburban New York.

Beth Silverman, who would have graduated this month from high school in Dayton, Ohio, is instead completing her second year at Simon's Rock College in Great Barrington, Mass., and . . .

A problem facing all education reporters involves the cooperation of board members and the school officials with the press. School board members and officials are extremely sensitive to criticism from the media or the community. They are equally as sensitive when the press reports (as it should) on major problems, such as student unrest. Boards frequently meet in private to conduct "public" business, and school officials decline to provide information needed for a reporter to write a balanced story. However, as noted earlier, in some 30 states there are open meetings laws and open records laws which reporters can rely upon to obtain their information if officials are uncooperative and if the newspaper elects to follow that course. Ideally, school officials and the press should cooperate in an effort to inform the public and improve the cause of education.

25b

Story Forms. Education stories range from the one-feature brief to the multifeature report of a significant board meeting. In between can be found all story forms, including human-interest stories on students and teachers and feature articles on school activities.

COVERING RESEARCH, SCIENCE

25c

So much new knowledge is pouring out of the millions of research projects and studies being conducted by scientists and other scholars that newspapers simply cannot keep up with it. These studies push the boundaries of man's knowledge to new heights almost daily and the public is not aware of the advancements because the changes are frequently so specialized it is difficult if not completely impossible for a layman to understand them. As long as science or scholarship remains enshrined in technical language, society cannot understand it fully. It must be interpreted to the people, reduced to terms laymen and legislators can comprehend. Newspapers have become increasingly aware of their responsibility not only to keep the public informed about scientific developments but also to interpret their implications for the public. That is why a number of newspapers have employed reporters specially trained in science and medicine, who can communicate with the scientists almost as equals and can then translate new developments accurately and clearly for the reader.

The science editor or any other reporter covering research has problems and responsibilities he must understand and master to do a creditable job. Reporting a research project—giving the public an understandable explanation of research

343

findings—is quite often an assignment unlike any other given a journalist. He faces three challenges; first, the researcher (or researchers); second, the research project; third, the accurate and interesting interpretation of that project to the public. Any one of those three can give the journalist a very difficult experience.

The Researcher. In interviewing a researcher, the reporter must keep in mind that the subject of the interview may not be eager for, or even mildly interested in, newspaper publicity. Often a researcher prefers to write his research findings himself for a scientific publication or for presentation at a scientific gathering. Because scientific news has been poorly handled in the past, he may be afraid of both inaccuracies and sensationalism in the newspaper account. Having spent days or months on a carefully worded paragraph, he usually is averse to having his composition slashed to bits in a three-minute effort by a reporter on the excuse of emphasizing an "interesting" feature. Dullness, often attached to preciseness, is a researcher's prerogative. Frequently, he does not see—and may be indifferent to—the utility or human-interest aspects of his work. Consequently he may have no sympathy whatever with the reporter's problems in writing the story for the general public.

A researcher may even be antagonistic toward publicity because reporters have been guilty of mishandling research stories. A newspaper article on his project will mean little if anything to his professional career. In fact, it might have a negative effect. He might be branded by his colleagues as a publicity hound—especially by a fellow scientist who might be nearing a breakthrough in the same area. Or he might be hounded by well-meaning people—as well as kooks—who phone, write or even come in person to his home or laboratory seeking his help. Medical researchers generally are extremely cautious about announcing breakthroughs in the mass media for that reason. Fortunately, as newspapers have made a serious effort to improve science writing, many leading scientists have become more willing to share their findings with the public. They realize that they have an obligation to do so just as a newspaper has a responsibility to report scientific discoveries carefully and accurately.

Obviously, then, the reporter's opening task is to establish himself with the researcher, winning enough confidence for at least a chance to show a sincere desire for accurate interpretation. An explanation of the need for public appreciation of research is the reporter's main approach. Most researchers would agree. Although they may be publicity-shy individuals, uncomfortable outside their laboratories and libraries, researchers are generally understanding people who will respond to sincere expressions of interest and cooperation. Some of them need more persuading than others. While the reporter must admit that local newspaper publicity may not add to a researcher's professional stature, the points can be discreetly made that such publicity does enhance the prestige of the researcher's institution or organization and that it will attract favorable attention to him (and his family) in the community and perhaps even additional financing for other projects. Most major institutions and organizations have men and women on their public relations staff to assist reporters in their efforts to work with scientists and researchers. They can be a valuable asset but the reporter should not rely on them alone for his information.

The Research Project. A reporter must recognize the two broad types of research: (1) basic or fundamental research and (2) practical or utilitarian research. Further, he must understand that a basic research project, even though it may make little sense to him, is the predecessor of practical research, the value of which is evident. The atom was not split until numerous basic research projects uncovered fundamental secrets of the atom. A project that may appear on the surface to be pointless, even frivolous, may prove to have enormous consequences. Sir Alexander Fleming's early experiments with molds eventually led to the wonder drug penicillin. If the reporter does not understand the value of a basic research project, that does not make the project any less justified. Neither the average reporter nor the general public is competent to judge its value.

Many thousands of research projects, basic and practical, are being conducted at considerable cost to the people of the nation through the National Science Foundation and other federal and state agencies. Some will turn out as failures, but others will pay spectacular practical dividends that make the total cost of research look small indeed.

It is fairly easy to report a project dealing with an improvement in the rate of emission of pollutants from automobiles by the use of a new catalytic converter. But what can be done, for example, with a project "concerned with the synthesis and biochemical evaluation of drugs which influence psychological processes through their effects upon the central nervous system"? The answer calls for interpretative skill.

Interpretation of the Research Project. While dullness is the researcher's prerogative, it is the reporter's enemy. Given a task of writing an interesting story, the reporter seeks to humanize the research project, spelling out what it means to the public in clear, careful and accurate words. If the reporter can find what the discovery or theory means to the average person, he has the key to the story—the lead feature. The rest of the story provides the details necessary to give the layman a clear picture. Early in his career as a science writer, a reporter should begin to develop a dictionary of the scientific or professional words used by the researchers in the various fields he may be covering. And he should work with the researchers to develop acceptable definitions or synonyms that the layman can understand. Far too many reporters—not only those covering science but also those covering other professional fields—fall into the trap of writing in professional jargon and not in language the general reader can understand.

The keys to research projects that are designed to fill specific practical needs are ready-made, but the secrets of many basic projects are not easily unlocked. For basic research the reporter must interpret the nature and findings of the project without stretching facts in an attempt to indicate practical value. The interpretation can perhaps explain that a project reveals knowledge that may contribute to the solution of practical problems, but this must be done with extreme caution. Between the following two paragraphs, for example, is a world of difference:

> The reaction of cells to certain acids manufactured by the human body is being studied by Dr. A. B. Count, Southeastern University zoology professor, who hopes his findings will contribute basic knowledge to science's fight against cancer.

> A cure for cancer is being sought by Dr. A. B. Count, Southeastern University zoology professor, in studying the reaction of cells to certain acids manufactured by the human body.

25d

If the first paragraph is accurate, no one can blame Dr. Count for becoming furious with the reporter who takes the liberty of "interpreting" the basic research project as is done in the second paragraph. As a researcher who demands facts and accuracy, he cannot shrug off such "sensationalizing" reporting. He considers such extravagant claims as damaging to his professional career, and he remembers this the next time a reporter approaches him for a story.

Every effort should be made—with the researcher's help—to tell the readers of any practical use of a research project. However, the reporter must recognize that there are times when no practical angle is available. These are cases of pure basic research being performed solely for the purpose of finding new knowledge. Sometimes that new knowledge (or the search for it) is itself interesting enough to give the reporter the key to his story. Other times it may be so complicated and so far from public interest that the reporter must abandon the story.

In gathering information to interpret a research story, the reporter must ask many questions. He must convert technical terms into common language, and this requires many questions. He must be sure the possible lead angles that he detects are accurate, requiring more questions. In other words, the reporter should have a clear understanding of what he is attempting to explain or he may garble the whole story in pursuit of an erroneous idea. A reporter doing a story on a scientific development or a research project simply must allow himself the amount of time needed to conduct a thorough and careful interview so there can be no misunderstanding of the information he has collected. Careful, thoughtful, accurate research stories cannot be written in a few minutes. They may require hours—even days—and multiple interviews.

25e   *Story Forms.* All forms can be used in writing research stories, which could range in length from one paragraph to several columns. If the research has significant practical value, the straight news format is generally used. As the practical value diminishes, there is a rise in the use of the feature story form to achieve a more interesting presentation.

EXERCISES

1. Using any newspaper available to you, clip four stories for each of the categories covered in this chapter—education, research and science—and analyze each one.
2. Compile a list of the various public and private elementary and secondary schools, the technical and trade schools, college and universities and any state or federal agencies from which school, research and science stories would be available in your area.
3. Write stories using the following notes:
   A. Riverbend Military School
      Three miles east of city
      On Wild River Road
      Will mark its 100th birthday
      On July 4
      Boarding School
      About 250 students
      Faculty of 30
      Staff of 100
      Lt. Col. Gilbert Sitwell

Announced today
That beginning this summer
School will enroll
Female students
For first time
In its history
One dorm has been
Converted for female students
School takes students
From grades 6 through 12
But will accept females
For grades 10 through 12 only
Females will receive
Military training
Similar to that
Given male students
Sitwell said the change
In enrollment policy
Follows numerous requests
From parents of female students
Who desire the type
Education and training
Riverbend can offer
Sitwell said the faculty
And Board of Trustees
Approved the policy
After a survey of
Current students and alumni
Showed they had no objections
B. County School Superintendent
Branden A. Roop said today
A check of chemistry labs
Turned up small amounts of
Picic acid, highly explosive chemical
Used in manufacture of
Explosives and dyes
Hazardous materials teams
Will visit schools
Starting Monday
To remove the acid
It was discovered
In storage rooms
At Hester, Madison, Roosevelt
Blue Grass and Grant high schools
Rural Metro Fire Department
Will handle removal
Schools will not be evacuated
But students in classes next
To storage areas will be moved
To other classrooms temporarily
While acid is being removed
Each school has only small amount

No one knows how long
It has been in schools, Roop said

C. Federal grand jury here
Conducting investigation
Into alleged overpurchasing
Of materials by city school system
Ten persons called
To testify Thursday and Friday
FBI, U.S. Attorney's office staff
Collected information
For three months
Before material was presented
To the grand jury
Deals with purchases of
Maintenance materials and
Labor such as painting
And plumbing contracts
Informed sources said
Grand Jury looked at
Records of former school maintenance
Director John Yarnell
Who resigned six months ago
And purchased a motel
A state audit was made
At that time
But results not released
Grand Jury also looked at
Records of two local hardware firms
Sources said
U.S Attorney John Preston
Refused to release names
Of the firms or persons
Who were called before
The Grand Jury
Informed sources said
Most were former employees
Of school maintenance department
And employees of suppliers
School Superintendent Bonita Green
Who won the post
In last November's election
Said something "stinks" in the department
And this is the best way
To find out what it is all about

D. City School Board
Held first meeting
Since the recent election
At Board of Education offices
At 7:30 p.m. yesterday
Elected officers
First time in board's history
A woman was elected president

Mrs. Jane McMillan
Who had been vice-president
Was elected new president
She has served four terms
On the board
Was not up for reelection to board this year
Mrs. McMillan is a lawyer
In private practice
Has three children
Who attended public schools
Now all are in college
Her husband, Dr. Dan McMillan
Is a psychiatrist
On the staff of
Morningside State Hospital here
Other new officers are
Dr. Raymond Griffin, vice-president
Mrs. Sara Coleman, secretary
Paul Bell, treasurer
All elections by acclamation
E. National studies show
High blood pressure increasing
Dramatically among teen-agers
And young adults
City school system
In cooperation with
State Heart Association
State Department of Nutrition Services
And Physical Education Department
At State University
Will begin new
Fitness awareness program
In eight area schools
Involving 250 students
Who volunteered for program
Program to determine effects
Of increased physical activity
On heart disease risk factors
Such as obesity, high blood pressure
Students will be evaluated
At the beginning of the program
To determine their condition
During the fitness program
They will be monitored
Students in special program
Will supplement regular PE activities
With jogging 12 minutes
Each class period
When six-month program
Is over schools will study
Data and determine
If changes in PE program

In all schools are needed
Carole Cole, PE teacher
At West High School
Is program coordinator
F. City school officials concerned
About increased absenteeism
More than 2,700 pupils absent
On any given day
Figures do not include
Students who cut classes
Or who attend classes
For just part of day
Absentee rate is about 5 percent
Low by national standards
But officials are concerned
One major reason is money
State funds given schools
On basis of average daily attendance
Theoretically, it costs schools
About $3.50 in state funds
Each day a student is absent
System lost about $1.8 million
In state funds last year
System must provide teachers
And classrooms whether students
Attend or not
Also concerned because truancy
Is illegal in this state
Parents can be prosecuted
For not seeing that children
Are in school
To help fight absenteeism
Schools opened a new
Attendance Referral Center
At the start of last school year
With $40,000 grant from
State Law Enforcement Planning Agency
Center focuses on children
At junior high level
Where absenteeism is most prevalant
Deborah Jones, center director, said
Studies show major cause
Of cutting school is academic problems
Students make low grades
Get turned off
Start skipping school, she said
Center provides counseling
For child and parents
So far Center has counseled
About 90 students
"We are candid with them. We let them know
We will turn them over to juvenile court," Jones said.

4. Write a story on the following notes dealing with a County School Board meeting:

Special session called by County Board of Education to discuss financing of building program and improvements for Jonesboro Middle School. At 7 p.m. at Board of Education offices in County Courthouse.

Conrad Schumpert, county schools business manager, told the board that there is about $8.5 million in available revenue for construction and renovation of school buildings this year. But he said the school system has about $13 million of top-priority improvements officials want to make. In addition to Jonesboro, other priority schools are Calhoun Intermediate School, Bessie Love Elementary School and Henderson Middle School. Schumpert said the first priority is Jonesboro Middle School. "There are 14 portable classrooms at the school, more than at any other school in the county," he said. He told the board if all the work is done on the other schools there will not be enough money left to do the work at Jonesboro Middle School. Or if Jonesboro is completed at least one of the other projects would have to be dropped. He said it would take about $5.6 million to complete the first phase at Jonesboro. Calhoun's renovation will cost $4.7 million, Bessie Love's improvements will cost $1.9 million and renovations at Henderson will cost $700,000. Members of the board voted to ask the County Commission for an additional $4.5 million for the building program, with the money earmarked for Jonesboro. The board also approved asking the Commission to authorize bidding on the first two phases of the Calhoun project. They agreed to delay the third phase, which will cost an estimated $975,000. Schumpert urged the board to "press on with the building program. The longer we wait, the more expensive the building program becomes."

5. Attend a meeting of your local city or county school board. Write a story about the meeting and turn it in the next morning along with your notes.

6. Dr. Vincent Campbell, professor of zoology at the State University, has been doing research on the impact of coal production on streams and rivers in the New River Drainage Basin on the eastern side of the state. The four-year study is financed by a $1.5 million grant from the U.S. Department of Energy. Dr. Campbell grants you an interview. Write a story from the following notes taken at the interview:

Many streams in the coal-producing region of the state seem to be recovering from the effects of strip mining much faster than scientists believed possible. Two-thirds of the streams under study in the New River Drainage Basin have returned to near normal levels some 20 years after mining activities ceased. The streams we have been studying were not polluted by acid from the mines, which is a very serious problem in most strip-mining areas. The streams we have been studying are rather tiny, and most are located near strip mines and they feed into other streams that feed into the major rivers in the area. We aren't far enough along on our study to make any statement about the rivers yet. But most of the tiny streams were heavily polluted by excess soil sediment. We feared these streams might never recover, and if they did, it could take hundreds of years. But we were wrong. One of the biggest surprises was that the streams that recovered so rapidly were near strip mines where no reclamation was carried on.

Let me hasten to point out that this shouldn't be interpreted to mean reclamation efforts or regulations should be relaxed. They do indicate environmental concerns, and the need for coal might be more easily balanced.

We also found out that the diversity and number of fish and insects in 16 of 24 streams under study here in the eastern part of the state have returned to levels that existed prior to mining. A creek unaffected by surface mining was used for comparison with the 24 polluted streams. As you may know, sediment, eroded from the mines into the streams, is the major enemy of animal life. Silt covers their breeding grounds, their eggs, and even buries some fish and insects.

In order to survive and eventually return to the stream from which they came, fish must have a way to find refuge in another body of water. In every case where fish normally are found in small streams in the basin, but the number drops to one or zero when mining begins. This research says two things to me: that these streams are perhaps more resilient than we first thought, and that the impact of mining on the entire water system be considered before strip mining begins. Now we consider only the individual streams. It also tells me that with proper restoration techniques the amount of time a stream would be affected by surface mining can be reduced considerably from the 20 years it took for the test streams.

Dr. Vaughan pointed out that this is only a preliminary report and that more detailed reports would be issued as he completes more work on the study.

7. Interview a faculty member on your campus who is engaged in research and write a story about his or her work.

8. Suggest newsworthy pictures and write appropriate cutlines on the following assignments in this chapter: Exercise 3D, Exercise 6.

9. Write a 90-second newscast using the following assignments in this chapter: Exercise 3B, Exercise 3C, Exercise 3F, Exercise 4 and Exercise 6.

CHAPTER 26

Religion, Philanthropy, Promotion

Newspapers are often criticized for carrying too much "bad" news. Generally that criticism comes from persons who have not studied a newspaper—any newspaper—carefully. A systematic check of the news in almost every newspaper would show that a majority of it is "good," in the sense that it reports on the accomplishments of people and organizations. Every newspaper devotes thousands of column inches annually to what can be classified as "good" news. Certainly much of that news falls in the category of religion, philanthropy and promotion.

Man's subordination of his own interests to those of serving his fellow man involves both religion and philanthropy. Religion preaches this philosophy; philanthropy practices it. The two are intertwined insofar as service to mankind is concerned, but from the newspaper's standpoint the expression of such service desires is made through a variety of news sources which are not closely related. In this respect, religious institutions form a large category of similar news sources; philanthropic movements involve many different news sources. Promotion deals with the newspaper's editorial support of these efforts in behalf of public welfare.

RELIGION

While the vital force of spiritual life in a civilized society leaves no question of the newspaper's responsbility to report religious activities and developments, the press has not always done an effective job. For many years the news of religion in most newspapers was relegated to a single page on Friday or Saturday. And that was devoted largely to sermon titles or announcements of guest pastors; except, of course, during a major religious holiday such as Easter or Christmas. These so-called religion pages still exist today but they cover a broad range of topics dealing with religion as well as the local church announcements. Equally

353

important is the effort of most editors to evaluate news of religion along with all other news that comes in daily. So now newsworthy events involving religious movements and trends as well as churches and ministers are regularly reported throughout the newspaper and not just on a weekly church or religion page. In fact, a number of religious leaders have become frequent front-page news. And a variety of trends in religion such as the rise in popularity of Eastern religions in the West and the battle over women becoming priests frequently rate as much or more space in the news sections of most newspapers as they do on the religion pages.

Of course, a general circulation newspaper should advocate no religion but should be a channel of communications for all religions. Freedom of religion, like freedom of the press, is protected by the Bill of Rights of the United States Constitution, and the press must recognize both the place of religion and the right of religious choice in its columns.

The proportion will vary from community to community, but a conservative estimate is that substantially more than half the people served by a newspaper are members of a church or synagogue. News of religion, then, should have many potential readers. While religious institutions have a large total membership, the news interest of an individual member is, first, in his own church; second, in his denomination; then, to a milder degree, in other churches. Sometimes the churches are competitive to the point that publicity given to one may stir up envies of the members of others—even of the same denomination. Religion news must therefore be broad enough in denominations, diverse enough in the same denominations and selective enough in the newsworthiness of materials used that readers will recognize the stories on religious activities as solid news rather than puffery or press agentry in favor of a particular minister, church or denomination.

As noted earlier, many newspapers publish a weekly page or special section devoted largely to news of religion in the community, appearing generally on Friday or Saturday. A member of the staff may hold the title of religion editor or church editor (often in addition to other duties), and it is his or her job to gather and write the material for this page or section. Much of the material comes by way of press releases or telephone calls from ministers or persons acting in a public relations capacity for a church or religious organization. As a general rule, the news appearing on this page or in this section would not be classified as major news stories dealing with religion.

A hotly contested pastor-versus-a-faction-of-the-congregation controversy, however, may be reported on the front page. A split in a major congregation, especially if it lands in the courts, or the filing for divorce by a popular minister or the leaving of the church by a local priest or nun to get married is a story that almost surely will get front-page play. News sources cultivated by the religion editor in handling routine stories often prove valuable in gathering information when such special stories develop.

The religion reporter must learn the organizational patterns of the churches he writes about, for the sources of news on religion include church-governing officials as well as local churches. But he must have outside sources as well, for church leaders frequently are unwilling to discuss controversial issues with the press. Church organization varies widely among the different denominations. Some are completely independent, and they select their ministers and set up their own programs. At the other extreme, some local churches are under the strong control of a central governing body, which assigns the ministers to the various churches and also has a strong influence on the local program of each church.

The program of a church encompasses many activities in addition to worship services and Sunday schools. It may also include the sponsorship of such projects as foreign or domestic missionary work, local relief projects, kindergartens, grade and high schools and colleges and universities. It is not uncommon for religious leaders and their congregations to be involved in very controversial moral, social and political issues in a planned and organized way. All of these activities make news, in the religion section, in the education section or on the front page or other sections when there are special news stories.

The Religion Section or Church Page. Newspapers that carry a regular page or section on religion should use a systematic plan of compiling news for that section. Church officials should be informed that they must submit materials for the section by a specific deadline, which puts the burden of getting publicity upon the churches and at the same time protects the religion editor from the criticism of members whose churches are not mentioned in the news.

Some highly newsworthy stories can often be developed from the materials submitted by the churches, but for the most part these handouts must be condensed into one- or two-paragraph stories if used at all. On the other hand, the reporter may have to get additional information to develop the better stories that are submitted.

A religion editor or reporter—a good one—must take pride in his assignment, for he can make the news on religion as important as much of the other news in a given edition. If he looks upon his work as a chore, news on religion will be no more than a compilation of brief rewrites of handouts. If he wants his section to be a strong influence on the life of the community—spiritual or otherwise—he can make it reflect accurately the community's religious or moral tone. The religion reporter who depends wholly upon church handouts for his news suffers from one of three (or a combination of three) serious faults: (1) lazy habits, (2) little interest in writing religion news or (3) poor newspapermanship. To do an acceptable job, the reporter must plan his section in advance, scheduling significant stories and features on the most important trends in the religious life of the community, on the most newsworthy developments and on timely or seasonal events. Such stories as these require that the reporter seek out his information. In some of these cases the church handouts can give him ideas and can be incorporated in the stories, but in all cases the reporter must do some interviewing, analyzing and writing.

It is important that the religion reporter, like the reporter in any other specialized field, be constantly aware of what is happening in the field of religion nationally and internationally as well. Current trends or controversies frequently can be localized, resulting in significant stories.

Following are some subjects and types of stories that the reporter may develop from materials submitted by the churches and from his own effort:

1. Regular worship services (some newspapers publish a weekly listing of church services).
2. Sermons—if unusual.
3. New buildings or other facilities.
4. Changes in church personnel.
5. Special events and campaigns—evangelistic efforts, fund-raising drives for worthy causes, attendance promotions.
6. New policies of local church or denominational groups.
7. Meetings of denominational groups, ministerial associations and lay groups.
8. Human-interest and feature stories—on unusual church members, historical anniversaries, retiring pastors, interesting projects of Sunday school classes, work of missionaries.

The following story from the Chicago Tribune is an example of a story that does not fit into the routine church story category:

> Sunday School students across American are being exposed to stories referring to rats, roaches, crap shooters, and numbers players.
>
> It's part of a special approach to religious education prepared by blacks for blacks.
>
> The church school materials utilize street level experiences of some blacks—employing in part a black lingo and ghetto setting—to impart religious values.
>
> The black-oriented curriculum materials for youth and adults go mainly to black churches, but now also are being circulated among Presbyterian, Roman Catholic, Baptist, and Mathodist churches—traditionally white-dominated faiths.
>
> Produced by Chicago-based Urban Ministries, Inc. (UMI), an independent publisher, the materials are full of street language—"dudes" being "ripped-off," "grooving," "splitting," "digging it," and finally "getting it together."
>
> "Our whole thrust is to be relevant to the black experience and also be professional about it," said Henry Soles, Jr., UMI's director of publications . . ."

26b   *Interpreting Religious Terminology.* It is essential that any reporter writing about religion make a serious effort to learn the technical words and phrases commonly used by the various denominations. One denomination's language is often another's jargon. What is called the *pastor* in one story may be the *father, rabbi, elder* in other stories. These and other religious terms—especially those associated directly with the worship service—must be understood by the reporter. He should use them correctly or not at all, and from time to time he must interpret them for his readers.

Here are some examples of church-story leads:

> Although the current gold and silver rush has meant instant cash to many people, it's been one big headache for most church administrators.
>
> The problem for the churches is that among the thousands of people who've been selling gold and silver trinkets and keepsakes, some have been cashing in on stolen church property . . .

> Inflation not only has begun pinching the pockets of Americans, but it's started to take its toll on the foreign missions of at least one denomination.
>
> The Southern Baptist Convention reported this week that overseas inflation plus

the devaluation of the dollar is threatening to "squeeze the financial life blood out of Southern Baptist foreign missions . . .

PHILANTHROPY

The basic meaning of philanthropy is "love of mankind." However, a secondary and more general meaning has developed that entails the expression of such love and concern for others in terms of hard cash. Fund raising is the objective of drives, campaigns, civic projects and numerous other efforts in behalf of philanthropic movements to contribute to the health, welfare and betterment of individuals as well as the community as a whole.

Philanthropy includes a wide diversity of activities. Among them are projects designed to promote and support religious and educational institutions and programs, the cultural arts (music, drama, art), character-building youth groups, welfare agencies, senior citizens organizations, Christmas charities, disaster relief, hospitals, community civic projects, historical observances, recreational facilities, the treatment of and research for the cure of diseases and disabilities and other promotions which require funds to be raised. Not all philanthropic movements ask for money, however. Some solicit a person's time; others a pint of blood; or housing accommodations for visitors or the needy in an emergency; or old clothes and newspapers; or a pledge to drive safely or to eliminate fire hazards. Whether for money or for time or blood, all these movements are in the public interest—the service of mankind—and, as such, are associated with philanthropy. All of them can generate not only promotional stories but also special stories of major significance to the community.

Sponsors of philanthropic movements are many times more numerous than the types of movements. Included are the Community Chest or United Fund organizations; Red Cross; Salvation Army; the YMCA and YWCA along with their youth counterparts in other religions such as the YHMA; Boy Scouts and Girl Scouts; all types of civic and service clubs and fraternal groups; drama, music and art societies; recreation organizations; health associations, such as those serving in the areas of tuberculosis and heart disease; societies to assist the blind, deaf and physically handicapped; and churches, schools, colleges, hospitals and similar institutions. Newspapers also sponsor their own philanthropic promotions. Some of the various philanthropic movements are short-term drives; others are long-term continuing efforts, generally on an annual basis.

The newspaper, a public service institution itself, is by its very nature interested in philanthropic programs and promotions. Much space and the time of reporters and editors will be contributed to the success of worthy causes. In these cases the newspaper often will make an exception to its regular demands for stories based strictly on newsworthiness, and it will accept material that is more promotional than informative.

It is one of the paradoxes of the newspaper profession that the critics are always citing the "negative" or allegedly "sensational" content of newspapers but rarely mention the thousands of column inches of free space given to the promotion of the community and especially to the many philanthropic drives. A study

357

might reveal that there is indeed a much better balance of "good" news and "bad" news than critics would have the public believe.

Problems in Publicizing Philanthropy. Handling news of philanthropy poses some special problems for a newspaper. Often an editor must take the responsibility of deciding whether the publicity being sought is intended to promote the self-interest of an individual or organization rather than a charitable or other social goal. If a newspaper uses all of the publicity that certain groups wish, it risks loss of reader interest and consequently of circulation. On the other hand, if it restricts such publicity sharply, the newspaper risks loss of the good will of the groups involved.

The number of different philanthropies has increased to the point that the public has insisted upon the consolidation of many of the fund-raising campaigns under a Community Chest or United Fund plan. Even though such plans have combined many campaigns—in some cities 50 or more charitable or welfare-type agencies receive funds from such plans—many social service and charitable groups still elect to carry on their own local and national campaigns with special weeks or months set aside for fund drives. Newspapers generally bear a heavy portion of the promotional work for such plans as United Fund and Community Chest. Occasionally an editor may decline to support a campaign that he believes should be part of a united drive. However, most editors find it difficult not to give space to any legitimate cause. As a result, most newspapers spend considerable time and money in writing about these various public service activities.

26c   *Promoting Philanthropic Movements and Civic Projects.* Newspapers serve as the principal channel of communications for most of the promotional efforts. However, various media are used in the campaigns and drives—letters, brochures, meetings, radio, television, billboards.

Despite all the publicity in newspapers and other news media, the most effective method of soliciting funds is the person-to-person approach—the volunteer worker visiting the prospective donors. Many employers arrange for a monthly deduction plan from the donor's paycheck, which has contributed greatly to the success of such fund drives. Solicitation by mail and other means is used when the number of prospective donors is so great that direct contact is impractical. Numerous professional fund-raising organizations have come into existence to conduct local as well as nationwide campaigns for a fee. And, like the amateur fund raiser, they rely on the newspaper for publicity.

How does the newspaper fit into these approaches? Publicity given a project in the press will "set the stage" and help develop a climate of generosity among prospective donors. And, of course, the recognition afforded by the publicity stories is important in obtaining and encouraging volunteer workers. However, the sponsors of the project will be greatly disappointed in expecting such publicity to do the whole job. While many people may be inclined to give to a worthy cause publicized in the press, very few remember to respond to their inclinations unless a solicitor visits them or a letter reminds them. These are things that the reporter and the campaign sponsor should keep in mind, or they may expect too much from newspaper publicity.

A newspaper can publish many promotional stories for philanthropic movements and projects. Following is a listing of some of the developments that could be reported:

1. Initial announcement of campaign or project.
2. Appointment of persons in charge of project.
3. Appointment of personnel or committees who will assist.
4. Various meetings of campaign workers—goals set, campaign plans, time schedules.
5. Series of straight-news stories, features and human-interest stories reporting recent benefits of the project.
6. Special stories on large donations.
7. Progress reports on campaign.
8. Stories on conclusion of campaign and its achievements.

EXERCISES

1. Using any newspaper available to you, clip four different stories on religion and philanthropy and make a news analysis of each.
2. Using any newspaper available to you, study the stories on the religion or church page. List the various religious terms used in the stories. Define the terms and make a note of those that are used exclusively by what denomination. For example, *monsignor* is a title used only by certain Roman Catholic priests.
3. Attend a church service and write a story on the sermon.
4. Write stories using the following notes:
   A. Hamilton County Baptist Association
      Annual evangelism conference
      Rev. Charlie Hyder, chairman
      Of Evangelism Committee
      In charge of conference
      Hyder said conference
      Will be Monday and Tuesday
      Next week at the
      East Ridge Baptist Church
      Speakers will be
      Dr. James E. Coffin, pastor
      Community Baptist Church
      Santa Rosa, Calif.
      Past moderator, Redwood Empire
      Baptist Association of California
      Evangelist James Robinson
      Southern Baptist evangelist
      And television minister
      From Hurst, Texas
      Services begin at 10:30 a.m. both days
      Afternoon sessions at 1:30 p.m.
      Evening sessions at 7 o'clock
      Dr. Coffin will speak at all sessions
      Robinson will speak at 8:15 p.m. Monday only
      Local pastors also on program
   B. Write photo caption on picture showing teen-agers John Siter and Charlene Andres from the Beth Sholom Congregation planting a tree on synagogue property in observance of Arbor Day in Israel. Arbor Day has been observed on the Jewish calendar for centuries, Rabbi Yitzochok Adler said.

C. Signal Mountain Presbyterian Church
   Will present a special program
   Called "A Night in Brazil"
   As part of its 7 p.m. services Sunday
   Featured will be
   Mr. and Mrs. Harvey J. Musser
   Missionaries in Brazil since 1969
   Mussers from Lewisburg, W. Va.
   He has been director of
   Banderirante School, boarding school
   For children of missionaries
   Who are stationed in Brazil
   She is a registered nurse
   Also teaches music, directs choir
   And helps care for children at school
   Both have been very active
   In Presbyterian Church in Brazil
D. Executive Board of the
   Holston Methodist Conference
   Held quarterly meeting
   Last Tuesday and Wednesday
   At Louisville Methodist Church
   Voted to sell its
   Bankson Memorial Mission Center
   At 2009 Ruby St.
   To the Miracle Baptist Church
   Mission Center began in 1957
   Held regular Sunday services
   Bible school, other church activities
   Such as school clubs
   Combination church and social center
   For low-income families
   Changing population patterns
   Reduced number of persons
   Who used the center
   Conference plans to
   Develop similar programs
   At several inner-city churches
   Before end of the year
   Duane Highlander, director
   Of special ministries, said
   Miracle Baptist to pay
   $125,000 for the building
   Its congregation will
   Use building as a church
   And will open a day-care center
   Have 36 children already enrolled
   Miracle congregation now meets
   At Mary Ann Garber School
   Rev. Archie Stewart said
E. First-Centenary Players
   New drama group

Formed by Nancy Lane Wright
Former college drama professor
And ten other members
Of First-Centenary United Methodist Church
Group open to anyone
Interested in performing in dramas or musicals
Not limited to church members only
Mrs. Jeanne Lane
Ten years experience as director
With "Up With People"
Will be assistant director
First meeting of group
Will be at 4 p.m. Sunday
At the church

F. Union Hill Baptist Church
Plans special services
At 6 p.m. Sunday
For the ordination of
Rev. George Williams
To the ministry
And Lamont Ervin and Gus Winston
As deacons in church
Rev. John Ryan
Uncle of Rev. Williams
Will speak at the services
A baptismal service
Will follow at 7 p.m.
Church at 1900 N. Chamberlain Ave.

5. Write a news story for the church page using the following notes:

Volunteer Mission Committee of the state Conference Work Area on Missions announced that 20 persons from United Methodist churches in the state are going to take part in a special evangelical mission starting the first of next month. They will fly to Jamaica and spend 12 days doing construction work and providing medical and dental services to Jamaicans. State group will include two physicians, three dentists, two ministers, 10 construction workers and three support personnel.

They will rebuild a community building and fellowship hall at Trinity Methodist Church in the village of Anchovy, nine miles from Montego Bay. The building was destroyed by fire. The doctors and dentists will work with Jamaican medical officials treating patients at several locations in the Methodist district in Jamaica.

The project was organized in cooperation with the Mamaican Methodist district superintendent, who supervises 11 churches with the help of one other minister and one deaconess. Each Methodist district in the state is being asked to contribute $1,500 for supplies and materials, including tools and medicines. The state group will carry such tools as electric hand saws and drills, hand tools for carpentry and masonry work and a rotary lawn mower. The tools will be left for the Jamaicans to use.

Each person on the team will pay his or her own fare, and churches will contribute to the cost of the mission. The missionaries will live with members of the St. John's Methodist Church in Montego Bay.

The Rev. Willard Bradford, Calvary United Methodist Church here, is in charge. He said the complete list of the persons in the group will be announced within 10 days.

6. Write stories from the following notes:

   A. Volunteer Rescue Squad
      Members to be collecting
      This Saturday and Sunday
      At major intersections
      Throughout the city
      Given special approval
      By City Council to
      Collect from cars
      Stopped for traffic
      At city intersections
      This type collection
      Banned by City Council last year
      Rescue Squad given approval
      Because all members are adults
      No teen-agers or children collecting
      This is only means
      Squad has of raising funds
      To support its work
      It operates emergency ambulances
      Assists police and firemen
      In rescue work such as
      Dragging river and lakes
      For victims of boating accidents
      Assisting police in cutting
      Wrecked car apart
      To free trapped victims
      Capt. Leo Plant, Chief of Squad, said:

        "This once a year collection is our only means of support. We deeply appreciate the City Council lifting its ban for us. Without the contributions we collect this one weekend we would have to close down our four centers."

   B. Suggest a suitable picture for Exercise A and write cutlines for it.

   C. League of Women Voters
      Announced new program today
      Called "Adult Aid"
      Program is to teach
      Adults to read and write
      Mrs. Lydia Mapes Williams
      League president
      Said many adults cannot
      Take part in the
      Democratic process
      Because they cannot
      Read and write
      One hundred league members
      Will conduct classes
      Two nights a week
      At city schools and civic centers
      She said League has contacted
      Dozens of organizations

To help spread the word

"We have 15 students signed up already. And we expect three times that many by the end of the month. Many of them have been referred to us by their friends and ministers," Mrs. Williams said. "We are even prepared to do home tutoring for persons who can't come to group lessons. All they need to do is contact us, or have a friend contact us, at 974-4561."

Mrs. Williams said

First class will be held

At 3 p.m. Monday

At West Hills Recreation Center

D. Suggest a suitable promotion picture for Exercise C and write cutlines for it.

E. City-County Medical Society

City Teachers Association

Joined forces to open

A counseling center

For teen-agers with alcohol problems

First of its kind in state

Located in converted store

At 542 W. Chicago Ave.

Center to be manned by

Volunteer doctors, school teachers

School counselors and nurses

New center has lounge area

Six private counseling rooms

Helen Beakerman, president of CTA, said: "We asked the medical society for help in setting up this center because the problems of teen-agers abusing alcohol has increased so rapidly in the past three years. It is not uncommon to have a drunk student show up for your class almost daily. The problem is widespread. It knows no social or economic barriers"

More than 100 volunteer counselors

Have been given special training

First teen-agers will be referred

From the public and private schools

Mrs. Beakerman also expects referrals

From juvenile authorities

"We are working on a plan to have juvenile authorities refer first offenders to us," Beakerman said

Center will be open seven days a week

From 10 a.m. until 9 p.m.

After hours there will be

A telephone hotline service

F. Suggest a promotion picture for Exercise E and write cutlines for it.

7. Assume that your newspaper decided to conduct a campaign to raise funds to pay for medical expenses and living expenses for an out-of-state family who had been involved in a major traffic accident in your city. The father is critically injured and will require extensive surgery. The mother and two children suffered extensive injuries and will be hospitalized for at least a month. Grandmother and two other children suffered only minor injuries. Must stay here because they have no where to go. Family had sold home. Moving to Florida to resettle. They need money for food and a place to live. Social service agencies can only offer limited aid. Outline the number and type stories and photographs you would want to develop for your campaign to help raise public funds for the family.

WRITING THE SPECIAL STORY TYPES

Straight-news stories on current events of a general nature are the foundation of any good newspaper. But no newspaper publishes only straight news. Readers demand more. And every newspaper devotes large amounts of space daily to specialized types of writing that, when done well, can be among the most exciting material it publishes. Such materials include the sports page, the editorial page, the section devoted to family, foods, fashions and social events and the reviews or criticisms of television, movies, music, books and the fine arts. These are usually considered to be newspaper departments with special problems of their own.

Even though the departments are specialized, the principles of straight news reporting apply in these specialized areas when the news intention is paramount. Both the sports page and the page covering social events tend to be news departments primarily. However, both also cover a broad range of extracurricular activities that have led to the development of certain writing devices not commonly applied to straight news. Editorials and criticism, while they may be based on news events, require a style of writing somewhat different from the standard news approach most of the time.

It is essential that every reporter learn the techniques needed for handling these specialized stories, for, sooner or later, most reporters are required to handle assignments for one or more of these special departments.

Family, Living, Lifestyle Sections

The drastic and dramatic changes that began taking place in the so-called society or women's sections of newspapers 10 years ago continues unabated today. No section of the American newspaper has changed so much—for the better. To be sure, this section still covers the social activities of the community (but not just of the elite), and there is the ever-present parade of engagements, weddings, teas, garden parties, receptions and occasionally lavish spreads for debutantes. But these no longer dominate. Today's pages frequently are not even called society or women's pages. In an effort to have the title reflect the broad scope of news on these pages, such titles as "Family, Foods and Fashions," "People's Page," "Focus," "Tempo," "Poster," "Style," "Family Page" and just plain "People" have been introduced. Even those that have retained such titles as "For and About Women," "Women's World" and "Society" have dramatically broadened their coverage.

Besides devoting attention to the entire social life of the community and providing an assortment of stories and columns on every topic from how to make better biscuits to how to handle an overly amorous husband, these pages offer the reader an impressive variety of subjects of major concern not just to women but rather to all readers. Stories on such issues as the woman alcoholic, the woman shoplifter, the unwed mother, the problems of a divorced woman in today's society, the runaway mother and increasing crime among women are almost standard fare now. Part of the change in coverage was an outgrowth of the blossoming out of women in the business and professional worlds during and after World War II. No doubt the women's equality movement of the late 1960s and '70s influenced the content of the pages somewhat. And certainly the development of more accurate readership studies has proved to editors that the woman reader is not content with social notes alone. There can be little doubt that this broadening of coverage of the so-called women's pages has increased readership to include many men who before might have ignored those pages as being too "light" or "fluffy" or "unimportant."

Except on the smallest newspapers the family section is under supervision of a special editor, and on the larger newspapers this editor has one or more assistants. The writers of this section usually operate independently of the city editor, and they may be responsible only for the gathering and writing of news or also for the editing—copyreading, rewriting, headline writing and makeup.

The staff of this section is generally a "woman's world" both figuratively and literally. In a few cases, however, men serve as competent members of the staff. In fact, several large newspapers have had men as their family section editor, in particular when the section has been broadened. And in a number of cases, columns by men—both locally written and syndicated—appear in these sections.

It is also true that a number of social news writers—especially in major cities such as Washington, D.C., New York and Chicago—have produced front-page stories of considerable importance as a result of their coverage of social events or through their social contacts.

News Values. Most pages still carry a large number of personal items. They may be collected in a column or they may be used as individual stories with headlines of their own. Their reader appeal may be measured by the various news values in miniature (see Chapter 15), but their largest single value still is prominence. The prominence of persons involved measures the importance and therefore the length of society stories. Prominence in this sense must be understood as local and relative rather than national or absolute. The smallest and most unpretentious town or community will have its relatively important social persons, usually based on wealth or professional position. It was to report the nonessential and purely social activities of these persons and groups that the society page was created by New York City newspapers in the last half of the nineteenth century. Initially only the social activities of the so-called elite were reported. However, this began to change gradually and in the period immediately following World War II most newspapers broadened their concept of "society" and began to cover the social activities of the entire community. Although the banker's daughter generally got the biggest picture and story when she announced her engagement, no longer was the engagement of the baker's daughter ignored. In more recent years, many newspapers have sought to standardize the coverage of engagements and weddings by using the same-size picture and story for everyone regardless of social standing in the community. Nevertheless, prominence is still a major news value. Most newspapers still base their general policy on the principle that names, especially the widely known names, make news. But they recognize that all names make news if they are involved in certain types of activities suitable for the section.

Basic Types of Social News. Engagements and weddings are reported in greater or less detail as measured by the prominence of the persons involved except at newspapers which have a policy of printing all such stories and pictures exactly the same size. Indeed, engagements and weddings have more content and substance than most other social events. They are news in the sense of having economic and social consequence aside from highlighting a social "season," if a city still has a formal social season. Engagements and weddings are a multibillion-dollar-a-year business in the United States and support a vast array of businesses with thousands of employees.

Other kinds of news found on these pages include:

1. Personals and briefs not carried elsewhere in the newspaper.
2. Births (if not published elsewhere).
3. Entertainments: receptions, teas, parties, dances, luncheons, showers, dinners.
4. Women's clubs and organizations: routine meetings, programs, speeches and special activities such as benefits, bazaars, recitals and various charity events.
5. The society column or social notes (sometimes "gossip" or editorialized comment by a writer about the local scene).
6. Stories and columns on fashions, recipes, child care, interior decorating, family relationships, home and beauty tips.
7. Stories and columns on local women in the business and professional world.

Other Types of Stories. While the types listed above frequently dominate the family section of newspapers, especially in smaller communities, a vast range of stories dealing with significant social, political and moral issues also appear regularly in these sections. Many of these stories come from the wire services or feature syndicates, of course. In some cases, a writer may seek to localize such a story by getting local persons to comment on the story content. In others the writer may compose a full-blown local story on the same topic. A survey of these sections of a dozen newspapers will reveal a broad range of stories on important issues: "What to Expect When You go to a Marriage Counselor," "How to Protect Your Child from a Molester," "Problems Confronting a New Divorcee," "Prejudices Against Women Doctors and Women Ministers," "How to Survive the First Year of Marriage," "What You Should Tell Your Child About Sex," "How to Tell If You Are Becoming an Alcoholic," "The Extramarital Affair" and dozens of other topics that 20 years before might not have even made the newspaper.

Frequently these stories dominate the page as the lead items, with the traditional social news being given secondary play. However, some newspapers do reserve special days for prominent display of engagements and weddings, just as they have special days when food or fashions or home decorating may be the major stories.

In displaying these nontraditional stories, many editors combine them with dramatic photographs to give them added visual impact.

In addition, many newspapers have developed specialists in consumer news who write stories designed to help the reader cope with the problems often associated with making major or even minor purchases of every possible product or service. It might be something as relatively simple as how to tell you are not getting cheated by your butcher to how to cope with a doctor who will not give you adequate time to discuss your medical problems.

Often these stories have enough dramatic appeal that an editor will give them front-page display. But for the most part they tend to be included in what

369

is generally known as the family pages no matter what those pages may otherwise be called.

Here are some leads from nontraditional type stories that have become almost standard fare in the family or lifestyle sections of many newspapers:

Elizabeth and George had celebrated 50 wedding anniversaries when George had a stroke and died 14 days later.

Katie and Paul were still newlyweds when Paul died unexpectedly in a car accident.

Elizabeth, 68, and Katie, 27, weren't ready to bury their husbands and their futures together. But they did, and it still hurts sometimes.

Three of four women in the United States will become widows. One of six women older than 21 is already a widow. Those who don't remarry and die natural deaths will spend 18 years alone.

These statistics are based on the 1970 U.S. Census. Current statistics are probably much higher, said Nanetta Walls, a clinical psychology graduate student at Memphis State University.

Ms. Walls wrote her doctoral dissertation about widows and recently began a program for widows. Three groups of Memphis widows meet 90 minutes each week to discuss their grief, problems and search for happiness and peace . . .

[THE JACKSON SUN]

Valary Marks of the Nashville Banner detailed for her readers what life will be like when the home computer becomes as commonplace as the television set in this story that began:

It's a world where ROMs, RAMs, Apples, TRS-80s and strange creatures called floppy disks abound, and we're racing headlong into it.

The world of home computers.

"In probably five years, every house built will have a computer system built-in," said Charles Bradshaw, director of the computer center at Vanderbilt University.

Nearly any manual chore around the house that can be rigged to a system of pulleys and gears can be timed, activated, regulated, gauged, adjusted—in a word, controlled—by a computer . . .

In this story about a lawyer who took her new baby to the office with her daily, Marlene Cimons of the Los Angeles Times reported on a growing trend among private companies, government agencies, churches and other groups to adjust to new demands on the American family:

WASHINGTON—In the six months after the birth of attorney Lynda Zengerle's second child, visitors to her office might have encountered a curious sight: paper diapers, a wind-up swing and a tiny basket containing a sleeping baby.

"When I wanted to nurse him, I just closed my office door and did it," she said. "The phone never bothered him. He slept most of the day. And when he woke up, the secretaries would fight over who was going to play with him. I would meet my clients in a conference room most of the time and not let them into my office."

News Sources. The editor who handles social news generally becomes personally acquainted with the prominent women and others of the community who are principal news sources. Weddings and many social events are planned with the cooperation of the reporter and with adequate publicity arrangements. Clubs and organizations usually have publicity officials to cooperate in promoting major social events. If tips are required, the country clubs, hotels, florists, caterers and others generally supply them with abundance. Far from having to seek news, the editor is generally under pressure for more and more space. In fact, it is not uncommon for prospective brides or their mothers to attempt to arrange the engagement announcement (or even the date of the wedding) on a day when they feel their story will be given the largest amount of space in a newspaper. Despite the great amount of news that comes in unsolicited, to have a well-rounded section the editor does have to seek other timely stories and features.

Another valuable asset for a writer assigned to the family section could be specialized knowledge in such fields as foods and nutrition, family relations, child development, textiles and clothing, interior decorating, fashions, beauty and the many subjects that fit under the general classification of home economics. The college student who is looking forward to the prospect of serving on such a staff will do well to select courses that may be available in the fields listed above. A vigorous program of independent reading will help fill the gap if no such courses are offered. A writer for the family section should be as familiar with the subject matter in her field as the political writer is with the field of government. Writers highly qualified in certain special fields such as foods or clothing generally are assigned to write by-line columns.

While it is important to be versatile and to want to write about something besides engagements, weddings and social events, it is essential that the writer for this section recognize that "social" news is important and should not be ignored. The same care and effort should go into a purely social item as goes into preparing an obituary.

PROBLEMS OF SOCIAL NEWS SECTIONS 27a

One of the most serious problems facing a reporter handling social news is the lack of story substance—in events, formal speeches, business conducted and real consequence of any sort. Social events not only are typed but also tend to be stereotyped. Yet the reporter must strive for freshness and variety. The monotonous, stereotyped story forms must be avoided. A second and very definite responsibility is that all names must be spelled correctly. To misspell a name or use the wrong initial of a person is to strike at the heart of social or any other kind of news. There can be no acceptable excuse for carelessness. Also, great care must be exercised by the reporter and editor to check the source of announcements of engagements and weddings to assure validity. Many a practical joker has sent a phony engagement announcement to the newspaper "to get a laugh on a friend," and some of these announcements have unfortunately been printed.

Lead Features. One of the most critical problems for the reporter, in avoiding stereotyped forms and writing more effectively, is the selection of the proper feature or features for the story lead. Any social function or "occasion" will produce the following subject matter, within which the feature may be sought. **27b**

1. The occasion itself may be defined. Perhaps it is an anniversary or perhaps the hundredth anniversary of an event. Perhaps it is devoted to a "cause" or it may have other special features or a theme.

371

2. The place itself may be significant—an ancestral home, a national shrine or the site of a local historical event.

3. In general, the persons present offer the most obvious feature. Hosts and guests, honorees, distinguished visitors, those in the receiving line, those who "poured," committee members, names—all are available features.

4. Decorations and color schemes may be featured—or costumes, or gowns or jewelry.

5. Refreshments and music or other forms of entertainment may also be featured.

The following are typical examples of leads on social event stories:

Mr. and Mrs. Bert J. Luce will have an informal picnic from 1 to 4 p.m. Sunday at their home, 318 Lynwood Ln., to celebrate their golden wedding anniversary.

Pink and green—the bride-elect's favorite colors—will highlight the table decorations at a tea honoring Alice Jeanette Tidwell from 2 to 5 this afternoon.

A covered dish supper was the feature of the monthly meeting of the Get Up and Go Club at 7 p.m. Thursday in the club's recreation center at Orlinda.

A birthday cake in the shape of a butterfly was served with ice cream and yellow punch at a party given Margaret Heart on May 31.

The Zucchini Parfait, a rock band from Southeastern University, will play for the Kappa Kapers at Riverside Country Club Saturday.

Willie V. Hooker, author of "Big River," a novel about life on the Mississippi River, will be honored at a party given by her niece, Mrs. Ellie Bradley, at the Hillside Inn Thursday evening.

27c   *Writing Style.* Not only must the writer of social news overcome the stereotyped story form wherever this can be done without straining for effect, but also every effort should be made to add variety and freshness to each story. "Mr. and Mrs. L. B. Brooks of Tracy City announced the marriage . . ." may become monotonous except in standardized columns of announcements. In describing events of social importance, the writer has the privilege of going into detail, including a measure of freedom in using adjectives. However, this freedom is limited by accuracy, and it does not permit the use of puffs or gushy language. All luncheons are not necessarily "delicious," nor are all brides automatically "pretty" or "lovely." And certainly not all parties and entertainments can be "the biggest social event of the season." Superlatives should be used with great care, if at all. Such expressions as "everyone is cordially invited" and "a good time was had by all" are as out of place in the women's section as in any other part of the newspaper. Accurate language, reporting the facts of the occasion with restraint and adequacy, will lend strength to the page.

ENGAGEMENTS AND WEDDINGS

The wedding story of socially prominent persons is still perhaps the most important social story in many newspapers, especially in smaller communities. (As noted earlier, some larger newspapers do tend to play down weddings or standardize them.) While the engagement is played up by means of pictures and stories about entertainments preceding the wedding, the wedding story tends to be the most demanding. To insure accurate information, most newspapers have elaborate questionnaires for the prospective bride to complete. It calls for all names and addresses of those participating, for descriptions of gowns, flowers, ribbons, types of ceremony and for all other essential information about the bride and bridegroom and their families, backgrounds and plans. With such adequate preliminary information, the reporter needs to take few notes on the actual occasion of the wedding, if the reporter attends. In most cases, the story is written directly from the form, with calls made to the prospective bride or her mother for verification.

The following illustrations will make clear the technique of these stories:

A Wedding Story Lead

Miss Susan Lee Frazier became the bride of Thomas Frank Smith III at 7:30 p.m. yesterday at Memorial United Methodist Church. The Rev. Dr. Frank Settle read the vows.

An Engagement Story Lead

Miss Katherine Ann Collins and William Baker Turner will be married in a 10:30 a.m. ceremony on September 30 at Eastminster Presbyterian Church.

Another version of an engagement lead:

Mr. and Mrs. Harold R. Collins of Brownsville announce the engagement of their daughter, Katherine Ann, to William Baker Turner, son of Mr. and Mrs. Thomas Walker Turner of Mill Valley.

A September 30 wedding is planned at . . .

A Complete Wedding Story

Wayside Chapel in Cades Cove was the setting Friday for the marriage of Carol Elaine Good to Ralph James Simpson. The 7:30 p.m. double-ring ceremony was performed by the Rev. Thomas Coleman, minister of youth and education, All Souls Episcopal Church.

The bride is the daughter of Mr. and Mrs. James P. Good, 517 Bryant Ave. She is the granddaughter of Mrs. Pearl Good, Rt. 7, Martin Mill Pike. The bridegroom's parents are Mr. and Mrs. Ray Simpson, Rt. 19, Old Kingston Pike. He is the grandson of Mr. and Mrs. Carmack Quillen, Goodletsville.

A program of nuptial music was presented by Mrs. Patty Ray, soloist, and Richard Smuthers, classical guitarist.

The bride, given in marriage by her father, wore a gown of silk organza and lace over taffeta accented with seed pearls, long sheer sleeves with lace cuffs and a chapel train. Her two-tiered bouffant veil was attached to an open camelot headpiece and she carried a cascade of ice blue poms and baby's breath centered with a white orchid atop a white Bible, a gift from an aunt. She also carried an heirloom handmade handkerchief belonging to her great-grandmother, Mrs. Lena Morrell Dobbins.

Barbara Good, sister of the bride, was maid of honor. She was attired in a princess style gown of blue flocked nylon over blue taffeta with a large blue picture hat trimmed in white daisies, and carried a long-stemmed white rose.

Bridesmaids were Mrs. Susan January and Sharon Hastings. They wore gown and hats identical to those of the maid of honor. Each carried a colonial nosegay of blue and green daisies and baby's breath.

Wendy Heller was flower girl, and David Good, brother of the bride, was ring bearer.

Serving the bridegroom as best man was his brother, Albert John Simpson. Ushers were Randy Good, brother of the bride, and George Browne.

The chapel, nestled in a lovely green valley, was decorated with wild flowers picked by the bride and bridegroom on his uncle's mountain ranch. Candelabra with burning tapers provided the only light for the early evening ceremony. The couple repeated vows which they wrote themselves in addition to the traditional Episcopalian wedding service.

Immediately following the ceremony an informal reception was held on the lawn of the chapel.

After a wedding trip to the Gulf Coast, the couple will make their home in Westel, where he will open a law practice.

The bride was graduated from the junior college department of Belmont School and from Union University, where she was a member of Delta Delta Delta sorority. She majored in library science.

Mr. Simpson was graduated from Georgia Military College and Southeastern University School of Law. He was a member of the Alpha Tau Omega fraternity and editor of the Law Review.

Here is an example of an unusual wedding story from the *Knoxville News-Sentinel:*

Miss Terry Nell Morris, artist and illustrator, hand-lettered the invitations for her wedding to David Allan Quimby, which took place at 2 p.m. Sunday at the home of the bride's parents, Dr. and Mrs. Robert W. Morris Jr., Duncan Road.

Parents of the bridegroom are Mr. and Mrs. Henry H. Quimby, 944 Brantley Drive.

Dr. R. Frank Porter, retired Methodist minister, officiated at the ceremony.

The bride chose a gown of ivory lace and cotton trimmed in ivory satin ribbon and pearl buttons. She made her veil of rose-patterned lace and carried a bouquet of white roses with baby's breath.

Roxanne Morris, sister of the bride, was maid of honor, and LeAnne Quimby, sister of the groom, was bridesmaid. They wore ivory lace Gibson Girl dresses and carried long-stemmed roses with baby's breath.

The bridegroom had his father as best man. Robert W. Morris III, brother of the bride, Steven K. Minor and Michael Tuller were ushers.

Ring bearer was the bride's black Labrador retriever, whose full name is Barney DeWitt Morris. Barney's wedding attire was an old-fashioned white collar with white tie.

The bride made the wedding cake and her mother catered the other refreshments for the reception at the Morris home.

After a trip to Disney World, the newlyweds will be at home on Canberra Drive. The bride, a graduate of Webb School and the University of Tennessee, attended Parsons School of Design, New York. Two of her books for children are soon to be published by Random House.

The groom is resident maintenance engineer for West Town Garden Apartments.

MISCELLANEOUS STORIES

The largest group of strictly social stories is provided by entertainments. Receptions, teas, parties, dances, luncheons and dinners are all reported as fully as the prominence of the persons and the magnitude of the occasion require. Another large group includes the reports of churches and club activities which may be largely social yet may also have significant program substance. They present no special difficulties or peculiar problems other than those already mentioned. The following are some examples:

Entertainments

In honor of Cherokee deb Cathy Hayes, Dr. and Mrs. Oliver Cunningham and Mr. and Mrs. Eldon Bright will be hosts at a cocktail-buffet from 7 to 9 Tuesday evening. The party will be at the Bright home, 2619 Tawanda Dr.

The poolside party will have a Hawaiian motif with special music by the Surfers, a Hawaiian musical group from Miami.

Guests will include the deb's sorority sisters and their escorts.

Clubs and Organizations

The first of three artistic workshops of the Flower Lovers Club will begin at 10 a.m. Friday at the Senior Citizens Center. The workshops will continue on consecutive Fridays from 10 to noon.

Mrs. J. L. Wilburn Jr., president-elect of the State Federation of Garden Clubs and an accredited judge, will be the instructor.

Arrangements will be based on the 48 artistic design entries in the schedule of the Valley Fair's flower competition which is entitled "A Star Spangled A-Fair." The flower competition is following the patriotic theme of this year's fair.

Flower Lovers Club members will compete in general horticulture, rose and artistic classes this year.

Trips

Announcements of the comings and goings of local people generally fill many columns on most pages devoted to social news. Prominent within the group are vacation trips, sons and daughters going to and from college and visits to friends and relatives. Of course, most metropolitan papers do not use such items unless they have a specific society column in which the travels of some of the city's more famous—or infamous—personalities may be included. Following are common examples which perhaps could have been enriched with feature materials:

Cathy Foster is coming in this afternoon from Mexico City for a brief visit with her parents, Mr. and Mrs. Lester Foster.

Cathy has been doing graduate work in art at the University of Mexico City since last fall.

Roger Vaughn and his mother, Mrs. Edwin B. Vaughn, went to Halls Crossroads for a dinner party given for Roger and his bride-to-be, Melba Ricks. Mr.

and Mrs. Carl Pouncey of Halls Crossroads were hosts at the dinner-shower at Lehigh Country Club.

Mrs. Leonard Goodman and her daughter, Missy, of 2 Timbergrove Ln., will leave Thursday for Asheville, N.C., where they will visit Mrs. Goodman's mother, Mrs. Alberta Jackson.

Mrs. C. G. Greenville of Rushville and her sister, Mrs. I. M. Stone, of Iron Mountain, will leave tomorrow to take Mrs. Greenville's son, St. Clair, to South Bend, Ind., where he will enter Notre Dame University.

Guests

Hosts and hostesses with out-of-town guests frequently ask newspapers to announce the fact not only to honor the visitor but also to inform other friends who might wish to entertain them. So numerous are personals about visits that they might well be labeled "Arrivals" and "Departures." Following are examples:

Mr. and Mrs. Jay Wilson, and their new son, Eddie, spent several days with Mr. and Mrs. Edward Wilson, 36 Mockingbird Ln. Eddie, who is just 6 weeks old, is the first grandchild of the Edward Wilsons.

The George Turner family are the houseguests of Mrs. Mabel Stone at her summer cottage on Melton Hill Lake. Ellie Turner is the former Ellie Stone.

Mr. and Mrs. Tom Midget and daughter Tina are visiting Mrs. Midget's mother, Mrs. Val Keely, 903 Linwood Dr., for a week.

Births

New York and Hollywood columnists elevated personals to a level of national interest. Their gossip columns concern persons so prominent that proximity is not a consideration. Prenatal announcements first became common in these columns, where mention of pregnancy was softened by the use of such euphemisms as "anticipating," "blessed-eventing," "three-ing" and "infanticipating." That style of writing has all but disappeared but certainly not the interest in births, especially on a local level. The birth notice remains a major personal item in many newspapers, especially in the smaller cities and towns. The birth notice will usually give the names and addresses of the parents, the time and place of birth, weight and sex of the infant and the name, if it has been chosen. Following are some examples:

Mr. and Mrs. James E. East, 809 Scott Dr., are the parents of a daughter born June 4 at St. Joseph's Hospital. The baby has been named Robbie Elizabeth.

James Robert Sprainer, born yesterday at University Hospital, is the namesake of both his grandfathers. The baby is the first child of Mr. and Mrs. Donald Sprainer (Betty Brock) of Corbin, Ky., formerly of Johnson City.

CONSUMER NEWS

The consumer movement of the 1960s and 1970s generated considerable debate among newspaper staffs on the role of the reporter as an advocate. A number of papers quickly established a consumer-news beat and urged the reporter assigned to it to help consumers fight the battle with big business and government. Other newspapers argued that they already were carrying consumer news and that it should not be singled out for special treatment. They were opposed to reporters playing the role of advocate.

Many papers established so called Action-Line type columns to help the average citizen who might be having difficulty with a local store or perhaps a government agency. This type column is still very popular today and some newspapers carry it on the front page because of the high reader interest. Reporters assigned to write this type column now have their own professional organization.

The more aggressive consumer reporters launched a wide range of investigations that produced front-page news stories and often brought about reform or spurred legislation to protect the consumer. Dozens of reporters investigated such things as the shabby workmanship and exorbitant prices of local television and auto repair shops or the unsavory practices of used car dealers. Others tested the often exaggerated claims of advertisements. Banks, funeral homes and other institutions that had been considered untouchable were being investigated in the name of consumer advocacy.

Several newspapers established buyer panels of citizens who tested products and reported their findings to the readers. And the comparison-shopping story in which a reporter compared the price of the same brand-name product at a number of retail outlets and reported the findings became commonplace.

Although there has been considerable business backlash, most papers who established consumer reporting continue to engage in some form of it. They cover newsworthy consumer events, write about product safety, cover changes in laws affecting consumers, provide shopping guides from products and services and make critical assessments of everything from food to colleges.

Those newspapers without consumer reporters of their own often run consumer-oriented stories from the wire services or buy a syndicated consumer column. Consumers Union now syndicates material from its magazine *Consumer Reports,* for example. And many newspaper chains have a consumer reporter whose work appears in all the papers in the chain. Ann McFetters, the consumer reporter for Scripps-Howard newspapers, does a consistently good job of reporting consumer affairs from Washington. Louise Cook does a similar job for the Associated Press.

After an initial flurry of consumer news reporters and even some consumer newspapers, a number of dailies began incorporating consumer news in the family living and lifestyle sections. The rationale behind this decision was that consumer news was not unlike the reports on foods, fashions, home furnishings and other family and home-oriented articles that have become the staple of this type section.

The New York Times, for example, has a Living Section on Wednesdays. It reports on weddings and engagements separately in its Sunday edition. The St. Louis Post-Dispatch combined fashions, decor, wine and food in its Lifestyle section on Sunday. The Washington Post mixes fashions, food, culture, entertainment and even books and health in its Style section.

And many smaller dailies and weeklies also have developed family and living sections that includes social news as well as consumer-oriented stories, food, fashions and entertainment. The Montgomery Journal, an award-winning weekly from Chevy Chase, Md., calls its section Tempo. The Jackson Sun in west Tennessee includes a broad range of consumer stories in its Living section and tends to downplay the traditional engagement, wedding and social-event type stories.

No matter where the consumer story appears it requires particular care. It is a form of business reporting but the emphasis is placed on the role of the buyer or user rather than the producer. As such it is frequently critical of the producer or seller. This type story can damage a person or a business and can bring a libel suit.

Here are some leads from consumer-news stories:

WASHINGTON—Motorcycle deaths are skyrocketing and the Federal Government is getting concerned.

The average motorcycle rider, says the National Highway Traffic Safety Administration, has up to a five times greater change of getting killed than the driver of a car . . .

Are your children among the 20 million in this country under 14 who aren't fully immunized against polio, measles, rubella, mumps, diphtheria, whooping cough and tetanus?

Too many parents fail to get their children immunized because they think these diseases are threats of the past and no longer pose a problem, doctors at the Center for Disease Control in Atlanta say.

"There is a whole generation of parents who never have seen a polio victim and who are unaware of the iron lung," Dr. Alan Hinman . . .

Car shoppers should beware of "bargain cars" offered for super low prices this spring.

The Automobile Owners Action Council warned today that each spring the market is gutted with cars that have been soaked with water—especially salt water—in winter storms.

Salt water corrodes electrical systems and can turn these bargains into rusting hulks within months . . .

Here is a question from the Action Line column in the Miami Herald:

My daughter is a nurse. I would like to have her nurse's cap bronzed. Is there any place locally that does that kind of work? —Mrs. CTK, Miami Shores.

Sure. Take the cap to Artistic Bronze Inc., 13867 N.W. 19th Ave., Opa-Locka. It's the only local firm that does that type bronzing. Owner Les Garthwaite says he has bronzed baby shoes, briefcases and pilot's caps, among other things. "You name it, we'll do it," says Garthwaite. He has only turned down one job. That happened the day a lady brought in the body of her pet cat and asked if it could be bronze-plated.

today's living

THE LENOIR CITY NEWS, THURSDAY, JUNE 8 1978—PAGE 1B

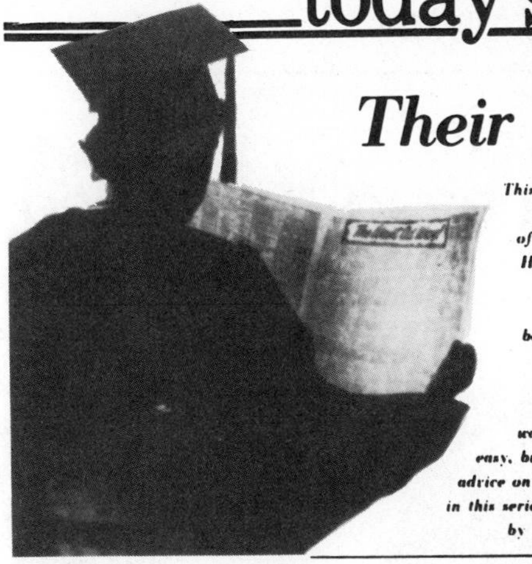

Their first job is getting one

This week more than a third of Lenoir City High School's graduating class will begin looking for jobs. The experts say finding work won't be easy, but they offer advice on job hunting in this series of articles by Lisa Akchin.

THIS WEEK, after their caps and gowns are packed away and the last graduation celebration has been held, about 68 of Lenoir City High School's graduating seniors will be knocking on employer's doors in search of full-time work.

This group of young people — more than a third of the senior class — doesn't plan to go to college or get further training, says Leona Saidak, a guidance counselor at the high school.

And, she said, many of them haven't realized that it may be difficult to get a job.

It's about to hit them that after school is out they'll have no place to go, she said. East Tennessee is not a hot bed of jobs. It's hard for people just coming out of school.

Lynn Russell of the Loudon County Employment and Training Office says jobs in the county are "few and far between."

Both Saidak and Russell put partial blame for the job shortage on the lack of mobility in Loudon County.

Everyone wants to stay here and work in Loudon County, said Russell. Some people don't even want to drive to west Knox County for a job even though the salaries are higher there.

Saidak said most students seeking work right after high school will end up with "blue collar" jobs.

We don't have a lot of students that work for the shops on Broadway, she said.

Production line or factory work is a good choice for people without special skills, said Russell.

Opportunities for unskilled and semi-skilled workers are fairly good in Loudon County, she said, because the area has a number of large factories and a lot of construction.

Saidak says she suggests students look for work in Oak Ridge or with TVA, because these jobs usually offer good salaries and fringe benefits.

Other large employers she suggests students check with are Eaton Corporation, Maremont and the Ralston Purina Mushroom Farm.

Many of Lenoir City's high school graduates will find job hunting a frustrating, time-consuming experience, said Saidak, but they are not alone.

Jobs are scarce, she said, "whether you're coming out of high school, a Ph.D. program or the 10th grade."

Playing the game

JOB HUNTING is a game, says employment counselor Nancy Petty. And, as in all games, it helps to play by the rules and make the right moves.

"The employer is carrying the ball, and you don't get anything unless you play with him," said Petty, who works in the Loudon County Employment and Training Office. "It's on the applicant to prove to the employer that he's what the employer is looking for."

Playing by the rules means job hunters should dress neatly and project a pleasant, cooperative attitude when meeting with employers.

The right moves center around communicating. Get the word out that you want a job. Prepare a resume. Meet the people who can help you most. And talk intelligently about your abilities and the job in question during interviews.

Looking neat for interviews is important, said Petty. Even if the normal working dress at a company is blue jeans, it is best to dress up a little for a job interview, she said.

Women should wear dresses to interviews, because pants are still not accepted everywhere. Revealing clothing and heavy make-up are also inappropriate for interviews.

Men looking for jobs should have moderate length, neatly-combed hair. Many men say they'll cut their hair if they get the job, said Petty. But that's not the right approach.

"Job hunters have to make a decision to conform to the employer's expectations before they go into that office the first time," she said. "The second time it may be too late."

Attitude is as important as appearance. The right attitude for job seekers is pleasant and cooperative, said Petty.

People should give the impression that they will work hard and be open-minded about taking on assignments, she said.

Some job hunters get discouraged about not finding work and have a hostile attitude toward employers, said Petty.

Too many people come in here with a chip on their shoulders, said her co-worker Lynn Russell.

Young people are particularly prone to attitude problems, said Petty.

Sometimes with youth, there's this arrogance that nobody can tell you anything," she said. "It's best to put that aside when looking for a job."

Playing by the rules puts you in the game. Making the right moves wins the game.

"One of the best ways to learn about job openings is through word-of-mouth.

Move around town, talk with people," says high school guidance counselor Leona Saidak. "It's a communication thing. Job hunters have to make it known they want a job."

Preparing a resume or personal data sheet is another good strategy.

A personal data sheet listing things like age, address, abilities, school participation and awards really makes a big impression on an employer," said Betty Wilcox, an office education teacher at Loudon County Vocational School.

First, a resume shows you've put some effort into the job hunt. Second, it gives a busy employer the chance to look you over at a glance. Finally, it advertises your achievements and abilities.

One woman was hired as an executive secretary right out of high school because the list of awards on her resume was so impressive, said Wilcox.

Before contacting companies, it is good to find out something about each business so you can talk intelligently about it. This will tell the employer you're really interested in the job.

With resume in hand, job hunters should visit companies and fill out job applications, said Wilcox. Be sure to complete them neatly and according to the directions. This shows you are careful and can follow instructions.

Another good strategy is talking to the person who can do the most for you — the person in charge of hiring.

After filling out an application, ask to speak to the personnel director or whoever is in charge of hiring," said Wilcox. "Sometimes this is possible."

During an interview, she said, speak clearly and use the best possible grammar. Don't be timid. Employers look for enthusiastic, outgoing people.

After an interview, job hunters should write a letter thanking the employer for the time spent with them, said Wilcox.

Because so few people take time for this courtesy, those who do will stand out in employer's minds.

The people who get ahead in the job game are those who communicate their abilities to employers and make the effort to be neat and cooperative.

Making the right moves and playing by the rules is important because a lot of people are competing for a small number of jobs.

"Because the job market is limited," said Wilcox, "they're only going to take the very best ones."

The job people

THE LOUDON COUNTY Employment and Training Office offers a variety of services to job hunters, but it is often the last place they turn.

Nancy Petty, an employment counselor with the agency, says a lot of people don't understand what the employment agency can do for them.

Many job hunters avoid the office, located in the Bacon Building in Loudon, because they think it serves only low-income people, she said.

Petty and her co-worker, Lynn Russell, do have special job placement programs for low-income people. But that's only half the story.

They also maintain job listings for the general public and will work to place all job hunters, regardless of income, in jobs that meet their needs.

When people first come to the employment office, they are asked to fill out an application listing their work history and basic information such as age and address.

The application tells very little about the job hunter, said Petty. To find out more, individuals may be given aptitude tests to reveal their interests and talents.

In some cases, Petty talks to job hunters in counseling sessions to find out more about them.

"It's not psychoanalysis," she said. "We just want to make some plans for the future. We try to pin down what they're interested in and see if it's realistic for this area."

Once job hunters define their goals and interests, the employment office tries to place them in either a federally-funded job program or a regular, unsubsidized job.

Petty and Russell monitor the employment situation in Loudon County and try to steer job hunters into satisfying work.

The employment office has extensive job listings on microfilm, said Petty. The listings, for jobs all over East Tennessee, are updated twice a week. Positions listed range from waitress to psychiatrist.

The employment office also keeps in close touch with employers such as Maremont and Union Carbide.

Frequently Petty and Russell are able to place their clients with one of these companies when openings occur.

"We can help people," said Petty, "because we have more pull with the factories and other employers than somebody just walking in off the street."

The employment office can also place people in federally-funded job and training programs. All but one of these programs is restricted to low-income people.

The income guidelines are not disclosed because people might distort their income to get a job, said Petty. But she did say the guidelines rule out all but those with "very low" incomes.

The federal programs include vocational training, public service employment, part-time work and the Job Corps.

Six to eight Loudon Countians attend school as part of the vocational training program, said Petty. The federal government foots the bill for their training.

The public service employment program provides about 50 jobs in government and non-profit organizations for Loudon Countians, said Petty. The jobs range from carpentry to clerical work. Individuals must be unemployed at least 15 weeks to be eligible for public service employment, she said.

Low-income status is not required for participation in the part-time work program. There are nine part-time positions in the Loudon County area. The employment office tries to match the job to the applicant's interests and needs. Possibilities include maintenance, clerical and construction work.

The Job Corps is a national work training program for 16 to 24-year-olds. Participants attend camps throughout the country, with their training, room, board and a small salary paid for by the government.

The federally subsidized jobs are filled now, said Petty, but many will turn over between now and fall. She suggests job hunters interested in both federal positions and unsubsidized positions contact the employment office now.

JOB HUNTER'S DICTIONARY

There may be more to the salary an employer offers you than meets the eye.

Many companies give their employees a financial boost by supplementing their salary with fringe benefits such as insurance and pension funds.

These benefits can be worth about 25 per cent of an employee's base salary, says Bill Hildreth, president of First National Bank of Loudon County. So it pays to check out the extras offered by employers.

Hildreth recently gave NEWS reporter Lisa Akchin basic information on various fringe benefits. This information appears below.

pen•sion fund

A stated amount of money set aside for an employee's retirement through employer contributions, paycheck deduction or both. After retirement, the employee can collect his pension in a variety of ways, such as monthly or annually. Pension checks generally amount to about 50 per cent of an employee's salary.

in•sur•ance

Many employers offer group insurance plans at lower rates than individuals can get on their own. These group insurance packages can include health, life and disability insurance. The amount of coverage offered varies, as does the portion of the coverage paid for by the employer. A number of group insurance plans also cover spouses and children, but again, the portion of the coverage paid for by the employer varies.

pro•fit shar•ing

Some companies put aside part of their annual profits for employees. A percentage of the company's profits is divided among employees, usually in proportion to their salaries. This money is invested, and when employees retire or leave the company they get their share of the profits plus interest.

cre•dit un•ion

A non-financial institution in which employees can save money. The credit union has a board that invests the money deposited, mainly in loans to credit union members.

Continued on page 5B

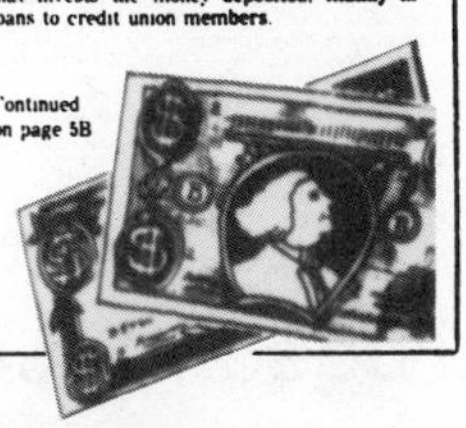

The number one thing I look for is . . .

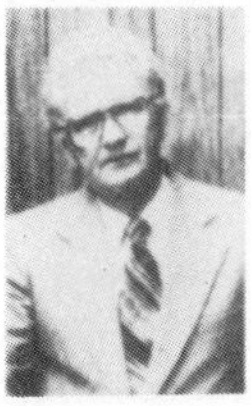

"The first thing I look at is their grades, because the biggest problem we have with high school students is they can't count money. I usually ask them if I came in and bought a $3.01 item and gave them a $10 bill, how would they give me my change."

H. H. "Mac" McIntosh
Penney's Manager

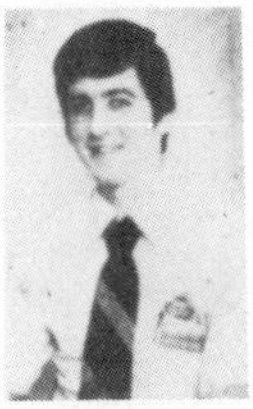

"Anyone who can just open up to me in the interview and smile and be an outgoing person is what I look for. Smiling is big in this business."

Steve Larrabee
Burger Queen Manager

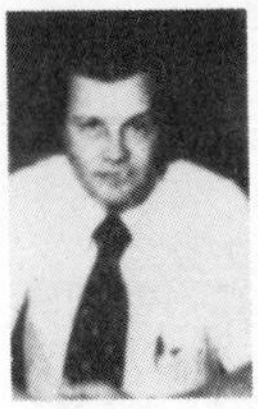

After making a thorough check of each applicant's background and qualifications, "appearance is the number one thing I look for. I look for neatness. Do they have all their clothes buttoned up? Is their hair combed and clean? Do they have shoes and socks on?"

Robert "Buster" Custead
Personnel Department
Maremont Corporation

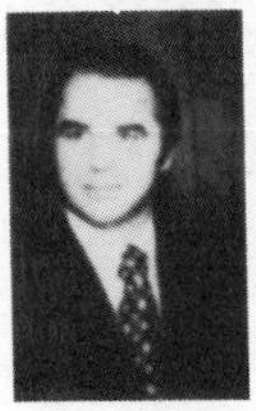

"Number one, I look to see if they are residents of Lenoir City or the particular area they want to work in. We try to pick people from that vicinity because they know the people from that area and they know them."

Ed Bell
President
Bank of Loudon County

Figure 27-1. *The Lenoir City News, an East Tennessee weekly, devoted its "today's living" section to the problems of finding a job the week after high school graduation. The section has won numerous prizes in state-wide competition.* Courtesy of The Lenoir City News, Lenoir City, Tenn.

Cosmetics: putting out money to look good

By MARY S. REED
Features Editor

If beauty truly is in the eyes of the beholder, then Americans are spending billions of dollars each year to make sure lookers get a good impression.

Sales of cosmetics — from mascara to lipstick, from shaving cream to mustache wax — are higher than ever as consumers resort to bottles, tubes and jars to make themselves beautiful, sexy or just confident about their appearance.

ADRIFT IN A sea of advertising promises and hundreds of products, the consumer often has a hard time selecting the best product for his needs.

Most people just aren't that informed about cosmetics or how to use them, said Debbie Traugott, manager of the local Merle Norman Cosmetic Studio. That's why her studio — like many other cosmetic dealers — gives lessons on how to apply the makeup. Merle Norman just sells its own brand, but the customer still has hundreds of products from which to choose, said Mrs. Traugott.

A department store like a Parks-Belk or Kisber's will carry several major brands, with trained beauty consultants — as they are called — who specialize in particular brands.

At Parks-Belk, for example, Karen Patterson has been trained by Estee Lauder to promote that brand. Across at another of the numerous cosmetic counters, Mary Williams displays her Elizabeth Arden wares.

The Food and Drug Administration has tried to help consumers by mandating the listing of ingredients, in order of amount contained, on all cosmetic products. Persons with allergies for a particular ingredient can check the listing to decide whether to avoid the product.

THE LABELING has helped some, but "it's not a universal cure-all to give the consumer everything she needs to make value comparisons," said Martin Greif, assistant to the director of FDA's division of cosmetics technology.

Take the cost of the product, for example.

In cosmetics, expensive does not necessarily mean better. A $5 product and a $25 product may list similar ingredients. The higher-priced brand usually contains a higher grade of the ingredients, but usually the cheaper product will work just as well, explained Joan Boaz, part owner of Patricia Stevens in Memphis and a professional makeup artist.

Cost for makeup basics can range from below $50 to hundreds of dollars — depending on the brand.

FDA's Greif said he sees "no rationale" for the wide price discrepancies found in the cosmetic industry.

Consumers should know they're paying for more than ingredients in the bottle or tube, he said. They pay for packaging, the firm's overhead, research and advertising and the prestige attached to a particular brand, he explained.

"They're very often paying for hope" — hope that the product will make them look or feel better, he said. "Maybe it's worth the price, but it's not inherent in the product."

A COSMETIC is like food, explained Margaret Morrison, a writer-editor in FDA's office of public affairs who wrote a pamphlet on cosmetics. "If it's served in a nice room on a pretty plate, it's more appealing."

It's hard to put a price tag on psychological aspects of makeup, said Irene Williamson, director of consumer and media affairs for Avon Products Inc.

There's a benefit to the makeup if it makes you feel good, agreed a representative from Revlon Inc.

That aspect of makeup is definitely not overlooked by the cosmetic industry. Whole lines are created with the right price tag and image to appeal to a particular audience.

Revlon, for example, manufactures Formula II for the working woman and then Charlie to appeal to the young audience. Formula II features unbreakable makeup and long-wearing cosmetics, whereas Charlie products have a 20's attitude in color and packaging.

If you're confused by the plethora of cosmetics available, here are some more suggestions to help make intelligent decisions:

• Know your skin type — whether it's dry, normal or oily, said Ms. Williamson. Different types require different products and treatments.

Know other things about yourself: How much makeup do you feel comfortable with? Do you have

This illustration from Germaine Monteil depicts the 'fashionable' way to wear makeup this fall.

any brand preferences? Where will you wear the makeup?

• If you have no particular preference, pick out a cosmetic line that is readily available and that appeals to you, advised Helen Rader, a leader with the University of Tennessee Agricultural Extension Service. Talk to the beauty consultant; she'll help you choose what's best for your skin type. If you don't like the way she treats you, go to another consultant, she added.

• Buy the smallest size available until you find what you like, said Ms. Rader. Buy just the basics.

• Play around with various products, said Ms. Williamson. Being happy with makeup involves a lot of trial and error, she added.

• Read labels. If prices differ, but ingredients look the same, try the lower-priced product.

• If you have allergies, read labels and avoid products that have lots of perfume because perfume is a major cause of allergies, said Ms. Boaz.

• Do not share another person's cosmetics and keep the lids on products to avoid contaminants.

• Do not use makeup on irritated or injured skin. Applying more makeup to cover up a problem possibly caused by the makeup is a viscous cycle, and it heals no better.

• If your skin breaks out, stop using the product, it the problem persists, see a physician. Dismissed by the myriad of cosmetic-related skin problems he treats, the dermatologist said he tells patients with skin problems not to use cosmetics. He said he goes by a general rule: The cause of acne in a woman over 25 who is not on birth control pills is her makeup — until proven otherwise.

• Report adverse reactions or problems to the manufacturer (the address is required on the label) and the FDA (5600 Fishers Lane, Rockville, Md. 20852).

Unlike additives and drugs, cosmetics do not have to be proven safe and effective before they're put on the shelves. Relatively few cosmetic products, however, are hazardous, Greif said. But FDA does rely on complaints to help it decide whether a product should be removed from the market.

Deep, rich colors highlight today's makeup styles

Makeup styles, like those of clothing and hair, have their ins and outs.

If you prefer the natural look — using makeup so people can't really tell you're using makeup — you're out.

IF YOU'RE still using pastel pink lipstick, frosted nail polish, eyeshadow to match the color of your eyes and and painted on eyeliner, you're even further out of it.

Color — intense shades of blues, greens, browns and reds — is the key of today's look in makeup, say the beauty consultants.

Instead of using an eyeshadow to match the color of your eyes, for example, the shadow should coordinate with what you're wearing, explained Debbie Traugott, manager of the local Merle Norman Cosmetic Studio.

Lip pencils are popular to line the lips. Women still use eye pencils for liner, but now they're smudging the liner to create a soft effect, added Mrs. Traugott.

Cheek color is redder, says a brochure by Elizabeth Arden. It's "worn higher on the cheekbones and encircling the eyes and hairline, almost a part of eye makeup."

Although color is an important part of makeup this year, it can be overdone.

Jan Boaz, part owner of Patricia Stevens Career College and Finishing School, has taught others how to apply makeup for 15 years and she urges people to limit their makeup to the workplace. A working woman would look out of place wearing high fashion makeup to the office, she said.

A FOUNDATION should be neutral, not rose or orange on your face, she added. Makeup involves more than blushers, lipsticks and eye shadows. It also involves a twice-daily routine of cleansing, toning and moisturizing, said Ms. Boaz and other makeup specialists.

Foundation and other makeup can't hide bad skin, said Irene Williamson, director of consumer and media affairs for Avon Products Inc.

To be neat means lifting the oils and dirt from the face. A toner, often with an alcohol base, tightens the pores and cleans out bacteria. A moisturizer returns moisture to the skin. Even if your skin is oily, you should put the moisturizer under the eyes because that area has no oil glands, said Ms. Boaz.

For makeup application that allows two weeks to a month to move dead skin cells and oils, to dirt.

If there are some more tips from Avon's "Beauty Guide":

• Apply makeup in the right light.

• Blend your foundation, powder, blush and blusher so all the hard edges disappear. Use your middle and ring fingers for the lightest touch.

• Use color to your advantage by concentrating on your good features instead of trying to cover up the bad. Keep in mind the basic color principle of light and dark: Light, bright or shiny color makes an area seem to come forward. Dark or matte color makes it seem to recede.

When applying makeup, advised Ms. Boaz, remember to work in upward, outward motions with a light finger. Avoid circular, or down strokes.

Pageants lure many seeking 'discovery'

By The Associated Press

Some girls enter beauty pageants for the prize money, some just for fun, but for many it's a calculated career step. Too often, they miscalculate.

"They spend their money and what do they get for it? Blue ribbons and tin cups," says a modeling agent who declined to be named.

BUT SOMETIMES it works. Take the case of 18-year-old Julie Floyd, who won a New York modeling job along with a crown.

As long as there are stories like Julie's, beauty contests will be big business. In order to flourish — and it does flourish — pageantry needs contestants. For now the supply seems infinite: uncounted thousands of girls compete each year in pageants.

Many contestants hope to be "discovered." But Sid Sussman, a Silver Spring, Md. pageant producer who runs 90 contests in 40 states annually, says some pageants lure girls with little hope.

"These teen pageants that find lists of girls and invite them to enter — of course they enter," he says. "The only criteria to be a finalist is whether you can come up with $200. They go after people who are below average, paths to characters and say 'We want you.'"

Last of three-part series

You're outstanding.' You'd steal to get the money."

Hopes of "discovery" endure, says Sussman because "if you look at glamour superstars like Linda Carter and Farrah Fawcett, you'll find most were in pageants. They were wandering around some rinkydink little town with no hope of being noticed and a pageant did the trick."

EACH YEAR, four modeling school associations run meetings that are a combination of seminars and pageant-like contests. Aspiring models pay entry fees, travel and hotel costs to attend. Two years ago, Julie entered the International Fashion Modeling Association pageant.

When the honey-blonde Phoenix teenage r won, the grande dame of New York modeling was watching. Today Julie is modeling in New York for Eileen Ford.

But there's a cloud over Julie's success. Both Mrs. Ford and Julie's teacher, Helen Rogers of Phoenix's Plaza 3 school, say Julie never got the $2,000 cash prize that was promised to the winner.

Horvath of Johnstown, Pa., thinks many girls leap into pageantry without looking first.

"A lot of girls see a program like Junior Miss and realize what a good opportunity it can be. Then they enter a contest without knowing if it's a good program. I was lucky," she says.

Susan entered Junior Miss after a friend who competed told her about the scholarship money at stake. Along with her crown, Susan won a full four-year college scholarship and $25,000.

Susan thinks some girls enter pageants because they're hungry for recognition. "If it's the only way you can't don't see anything wrong with wanting to be recognized for that. If you have high cheek bones, more power to you."

YES, SAYS Sussman. "Most people are never in the spotlight and all want to be. But he says greed is a key motive. "Affluent kids don't enter pageants. They've got a car, a closet full of clothes. Their daddy sends them to Europe. Pageants can't offer them anything."

Sometimes it's more complicated than that. Sometimes it's simpler. Ask the contestant.

When pert, Josephine Simard of North Brunswick, N.J. was asked to enter the state Miss Teen USA pageant, "I wasn't going to do it, but my school counselor said go ahead and

The reigning Junior Miss, Susan, try it. She wanted me to have the experience." Afterward, Josephine pronounced it "fun."

Mothers have another perspective. Consider Pat White of tiny Celina, Tenn, whose 17-year-old daughter Donna was named Miss Teen USA's Miss Hospitality-Tennessee for selling the most advertising for the pageant program.

After the Tennessee contest, Mrs. White and Donna — who wants to camp le someday for the Miss America crown — tagged along to the North Carolina, West Virginia and New Jersey Miss Teen USA pageants.

Mrs. White was useful to pageant director Gloria Wooding as a gofer and sometime judge. Donna helped tutor the contestants in the Miss Teen USA song and dance routine and in return, promenaded with them in each pageant, wearing her Miss Hospitality sash.

"THERE'S NO way I could have paid any amount of money for the experience Donna has had," Mrs. White commented. "Prices can't be placed on that."

Figure 27-2. The billion-dollar cosmetics industry was the focus of this "living" section front page in The Jackson Sun. It combined important consumer information about purchasing with a story on current makeup styles. The section has won dozens of state and national prizes for its content and design. Courtesy of The Jackson Sun, Jackson, Tenn.

Janet Smith isn't her real name. She doesn't want her identity revealed. She's afraid the company she works for now wouldn't approve of her radical student days.

'I was truly a social anarchist,' she says. 'I wouldn't belong to any of the social organizations. We thought SDS (Students for a Democratic Society, a protest group) was too organized.

The university brought charges against Janet in connection with her protest activities.

Now, she works in a big office building for a major Southeastern industrial firm. She is its ranking woman executive.

Her clothes are conservative and businesslike.

And, she admits, she is part of the Establishment.

Life has changed, but student radical remembers

Students rampaged and tangled with lawmen at many colleges Tuesday but classes were boycotted peacefully as hundreds of campuses.

Anger over the fatal shooting of four students at Kent State University by National Guardsmen kept demonstrations, memorial services and vigils going through the night in college towns.

Some of the demonstrations erupted into rock throwing, window-smashing confrontations with local police, state police and Guardsmen.

— The Associated Press, Wednesday, May 6, 1970

TUSCALOOSA — Gov. Albert Brewer today warned protesters at the University of Alabama he would tolerate no violence. He spoke after a night of disorder at the sprawling Tuscaloosa campus.

— The Birmingham News, Thursday, May 7, 1970

BY BRETT GUGE, News staff writer

It was this nation's finest hour. It was its darkest hour.

Americans will not soon forget the days that followed the deaths of four Kent State University students, gunned down during a demonstration against the Vietnam War.

Before the end of that fateful week in May 1970 nearly 230 colleges and universities were closed down by a wave of student outrage.

VIRTUALLY NO campus was left untouched by the emotionalism that swept across the land. Even in the tradition-bound South, the winds of change grew to gale force.

Ex-activist: Not again, but no regrets

Hank Hawkins today at 36.

Inside

Bridge Col.	2-B
Classified	4-B
Culp	2-B
Features	3-B
Garden Col.	27-B
House Plan	28-B
Rafferty	2-B
Real Estate	27-B
Supermarket	2-B

Figure 27-3. The Birmingham (Ala.) News combines interesting graphic display with in-depth reports on the front page of its Pace feature section. Courtesy of The Birmingham News.

381

Taste

Chicago Tribune Monday, November 26, 1979 Section 6 Classified inside

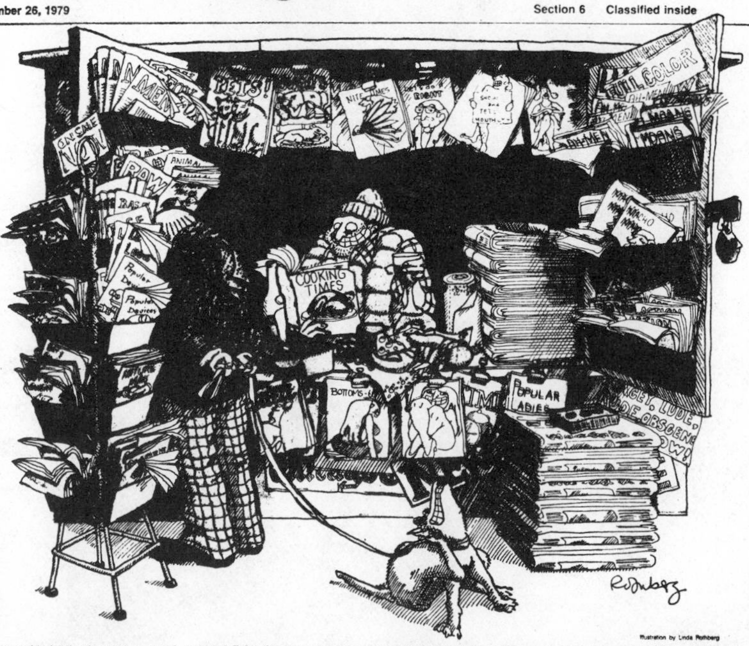

Illustration by Linda Rothberg

A critical eye on hot food magazines

By Cheryl Lavin

In the beginning there was Gourmet. The year was 1941, and while most Americans' culinary concerns centered on K-Rations, ersatz coffee, Spam, and Hershey bars, Earle R. MacAusland had a taste for something finer. To satisfy his craving, he introduced a magazine devoted to good food and gracious living. And when Johnny came marching home — after an introduction to beaujolais, french bread with a little pate or a bit of *fromage*, some *coq au vin* and *boeuf bourguignonne*, he realized that MacAusland had something.

But the new magazine's circulation grew slowly. For 20 years MacAusland was the only person publishing a magazine that treated food as an end in and of itself — something beautiful to look at and interesting to read about.

Then in 1961 Bon Appetit appeared. It was really a monthly listing of wholesale and retail wine prices filled out with recipes donated by the Doughnut-Makers Association and Cranberry Growers Institute.

Today, food magazines are a hot number. There are easily a dozen on the market, all the way from Weight Watchers to Wok Talk. When the new issues come out, the city's gourmet shops stock up on the featured bundt pans or duck presses or ice-cream makers because they know that when the magazines hit the mailboxes, the local cooks and bakers will rush in, their ovens already warming.

Each magazine has fabulous recipes that make you salivate while reading them. (The art of food photography is so advanced that merely flipping through the slickly designed, color laden pages is fattening.) The magazines publish the same food writers and follow the same calendar. When one magazine is doing sorbets, the others are doing sorbets. The same is true for fish mousses, puff pastry, and Morrocan cuisine.

In the final analysis there are only 101 ways to cook hamburger. Some of the magazines take hamburger seriously. Some romance it to death, with the history of the first hamburger ever cooked and a personal memory of "The first time I ever ate a hamburger in a little bistro in Paris off the Rue Bonaparte." Some will survey the 10 top hamburger cookers. Some will tell you who was seen eating a hamburger, where, and with whom. But each magazine has its own way to cook that hamburger. The difference is in the approach, not in the table of contents.

GOURMET, $1, SUBSCRIPTION, $12:

If Gourmet were a woman, she would have blue hair, shop at Lord & Taylor, take tea at the Walnut Room, wear sensible shoes, and vote a straight Republican ticket. It is that kind of magazine — good, gray, dependable.

The magazine is timeless. There is no news in it, nothing even as topical as a book review. The pictures are deliberately static: Nothing in them moves. An Easter table appears as lifeless as something unearthed at Pompeii. And the pictures are almost devoid of people, except for a nameless peasant huddled over his tortilla. Food usually is shot from a high angle or against a monochromatic background that makes it look like a study in color and texture rather than anything edible.

MacAusland began the magazine in 1941 with a circulation of 30,000. Today there are 650,000 loyal readers who pass on bound copies to their children and grandchildren. From the beginning, Gourmet devoted as much space to travel as to food.

The text is as frozen — cans are "tins" — as the pictures. With its huge editorial staff, everyone — readers as well as writers — comes out sounding like Henry James.

In the Sugar and Spice column where readers send in their favorite recipes, one typical reader writes: "Sirs: Having subscribed for many years to your delightful magazine, I feel remiss in not having written you long ago . . ." A review of a New York restaurant reads: "The main dining room is commodious and well laid out. A rather low ceiling makes up in acoustic efficiency for what it lacks in architectural felicity . . ." A travel story on an English country house rhapsodizes: "What a delight it is to come back to the warmth that is Chewton Glenn, with its comfortable elegance . . . an elusive serenity that is interwoven with sheer spiffiness."

Gourmet views both cooking and travel as armchair sports. Though it has two test kitchens and four full-time helpers, not many readers can take all of the 50 monthly recipes seriously — like the one for noodles in broth with seafood and broccoli that begins "Clean 8 ounces of squid and chop the tentacles and the flaps finely."

It is a magazine to read slowly, while sipping a sherry, away from the cares of the world. It is not one to slop up with splatters of cooking grease from a bubbling pot of spaghetti sauce. The very layout of the recipes, with the ingredients scattered throughout the instructions, makes for interesting reading rather than practical advice.

Gourmet's world is a timeless one where nobody mentions calories or cholesterol or is ever in a hurry. The only nod they give to reality is a monthly feature called *Gastronomie sans argent* that tells you what to do with two leftover loaves of french bread. But it is a world that such advertisers as Godiva chocolates, Rolls-Royce, Steinway pianos, Porsche, and Gorham silver are willing to enter for $12,500 per four-color, full-page ad.

Monthly departments include restaurant reviews from New York and California and a restaurant listing that states: "Because of limited space, we are obliged to restrict our . . . listings primarily to those fine restaurants . . . that have indicated a desire to reach Gourmet's readers by becoming advertisers." In Chicago, those restaurants include the Magic Pan and the Walnut Room.

BON APPETIT, $1.25, SUBSCRIPTION, $9.95.

If Bon Appetit tried any harder, it would burst its staples. You want food processor recipes? It has food processor recipes. You want microwave recipes? It has microwave recipes. You want natural food recipes, fast recipes, recipes for two? It has them — along with restaurant recipes, basic recipes, wine news, a wine quiz, news items, restaurant reviews, and cookbook reviews, and that's just in the monthly departments.

But it wasn't always this way. Bon Appetit began almost 20 years ago as a liquor store giveaway. One typical recipe from the old days for lemon-pepper dip called for one pint of sour cream and one tablespoon lemon-pepper marinade and had the following directions: "Blend." Ingredients were heavy on canned corn, envelopes of seasoned coating mix, packages of pie crust mix, envelopes of whipped topping mix, hot roll mix, canned chicken broth, canned fruit cocktail, packages of Jell-o, and the ever-popular onion soup mix.

All that changed when Knapp Communications bought the magazine in 1975 and told editor Paige Rense to do with it what she would (see story on page 3). In four years she has increased the circulation from 250,000 to 1.1 million, making it the No. 1 magazine in terms of growth of advertising in the country according to the Publishers' Information Bureau. Those advertisers, as varied as Pillsbury Plus Cake Mix and Erno Lazlo skin preparations, pay $14,155 for a full-page, four-color ad.

Today the magazine takes a something-for-everyone approach to food. It is the most practical of the food magazines, doing diet stories from time to time, including a gorgeous feature called "Where have all the calories gone?" that highlighted a lavish low-cal buffet. A recipe for truffle soup thoughtfully gave a mushroom alternative. But BA cannot compete with some of the more sophisticated food magazines in terms of sheer beauty. Side-by-side with such visuals as a nearly pornographic peaches and crab salad on a moonlit beach, BA's deep-dish chicken and corn pie and berries and cream seem almost Girl Scoutish.

The emphasis is on real people, and the magazine recently dropped its celebrity cook feature.

One monthly section, "Too Busy to Cook?" tells how just plain folk cope with a busy schedule and a love for good food. One typical subject was a "fashion model and executive secretary, studying for a master's degree in a family counseling . . . also the mother of three school-age children who works as a volunteer in a computer math program . . . and finds that six is just the right number for a sitdown dinner."

But the magazine by no means talks down to its readers. A recent monthly cooking class with Jacques Pepin introduced them to *fruits de mer boudin*, stuffed pigeons, eggplant custard, and a chocolate truffle cake made with four separate recipes. Each dish was accompanied by pictures and precise text that practically insure success.

INTERNATIONAL REVIEW OF FOOD AND WINE, $1.50, SUBSCRIPTION $9.95.

Food and Wine is People magazine with a wooden spoon and a wicked way with a *pate brisee*. It is breathless, chatty, witty, gossipy, trendy, and fun with French puns (the monthly entertaining feature is called "fete accomplie") and the last word on Chilean wines.

Michael and Ariane Batterberry, authors of a dozen books including Bloomingdale's Book of Entertaining, began the magazine in May, 1978, as one of Playboy Enterprises' new publications. They have been on their own for a year, attracting 250,000 readers; advertisers pay $4,200 for a full-page, four-color ad to hawk such items as French-cut T-shirts with wine labels on the front.

"We want the magazine to be like somebody's witty, well-informed friend who comes to your house every month, says Michael Batterberry, whose magazine covers the widest scope of any. In any issue there might be an article on equipment, food news (such as the latest in the Otto affair, the country inn discovered by the New Yorker and almost destroyed by the New York Times), humor, economics (Nicholas von Hoffman on moola — or milk as crude, white oil), and even sex (the wonderfully raunchy tale by Lesley Blanch, author of "The Wilder Shores of Love," that ends with a recipe for a "roll in bed with honey").

BUT THE MAGAZINE doesn't slight the more traditional areas, namely recipes, restaurants, and travel. F and W can romance a food story with the best of them (an article on ice-cream making, quotes Laura Ingalls Wilder: "Let's make ice cream! Royal shouted."). But what they do best is drop you in the midst of a chi-chi world so delicious you hunger for the company as well as the food.

For instance, "The triumphant return of the

Continued on page 3

Here's to J.D. Cox, tin cans, and yet other unsung forces

By Karen De Witt

When you pop the next can of cold beer, offer a toast to J. D. Cox, who in 1887 introduced the capping machine that broke the hold of skilled craftsmen on the can industry and opened the field to mechanization.

If milk is your preference, take a moment to consider a frustrated, fiftyish Gail Borden Jr., burning up milk and money to produce condensed milk and eventually an empire.

Then give a cheer for the British West Indians who, in protecting the price of their molasses, killed the American rum industry and set the stage for the American Revolution.

This is history seen through the evolution of American food technology.

Recently, 15 scholars gathered for three days at the Smithsonian Museum of History and Technology to discuss how the 19th-Century effort to give Americans more variety and better quality in food resulted in the giant food conglomerates of today.

The theme, according to Dr. Terry Sharrer, conference organizer and a museum curator, was adopted from Arthur Schlesinger's "Food in the Making of America," an essay in a book he published in 1949, "Path to the Present." In it Schlesinger noted that "food is a want which precedes and conditions all other hopes, aims, and achievements."

IN PAPERS ON a variety of topics, participants traced food technology to such major national trends as urbanization, population growth, the westward movement, and industrial expansion.

"We want to know how we got to where we are today," Sharrer said.

The group agreed that technology had done it. The accumulation of agricultural surpluses and new methodologies in southern Ohio, for example, led to the breweries and meat packing industries that made Cincinnati a great urban center in the mid-1800s.

In 1914, J. L. Kraft's process for "hermetically sealed, completely sterilized" containers for cheese radically altered the variety and availability of cheese for consumers.

Such small advances in technology took food preservation from the rather primitive home products of a century ago to the cornucopia of products on supermarket shelves today.

Something as simple and common as the tin can is "a technological *tour de force*" that brings us peaches out of season, oysters in August, almost anything anytime, according to Eugene S. Ferguson, a symposium participant and senior resident scholar at the Hagley Museum outside Wilmington, Del.

Ferguson charted the course of the tin can from the early 1800s, when a skilled tinsmith could make 100 cans a day, to the 100 billion cans — half of which are used for beer and soft drinks — being made and thrown away today.

GETTING FROM THEN to now involved machines and a turn from skill to dexterity. It started in the 1870s with the introduction of stamp

Continued on page 6

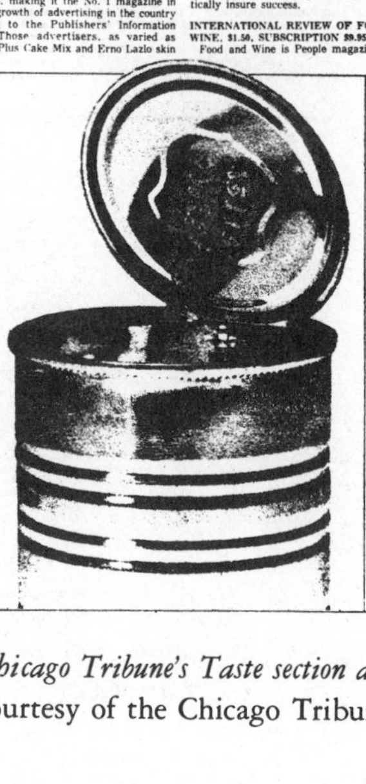

Du Jour

Restaurants slow down, cut prices

By Fran Zell

McDonald's had been telling us for a long time that we deserved a break. But it wasn't until last August that the country's largest fast food hamburger chain gave the slogan a more palatable economic twist. It rolled back prices on hamburgers and cheeseburgers at 1,225 company owned stores. (It turned out to be mostly a symbolic break, since last week McDonald's raised prices on just about everything else.)

Other restaurants, from plain to posh, from corporate-owned to independent, have followed suit in cutting prices with everything from straightforward slashes to "let's make a deal" promotional gimmicks.

The Marriott-owned Roy Rogers chain cut its burger prices. Denny's and Sambo's introduced special $1.99 breakfasts. Golden Bear and company-owned Victoria Stations lowered prices as much as 20 per cent.

At the Cook Shanty, a touristy lumberjack theme restaurant in Hayward, Wis., owner Anthony Wise installed a potato scale — for children, not vegetables. Those who weigh in under 85 pounds can indulge in the restaurant's all-you-can-eat menu for $1, the same price

Continued on page 6

***Figure 27-4.** The front page of the Chicago Tribune's Taste section always features strong graphic design to support the stories.* Courtesy of the Chicago Tribune.

Figure 27-5. *Many newspapers are emphasizing special food sections one or more times a week. The Montgomery Journal, Chevy Chase, Md., always uses dramatic color photography to highlight its lead story on its "tempo" section.* Courtesy of The Montgomery Journal, Chevy Chase, Md.

Buffets to eat with only a fork

By Carol Haddix

IMAGINE THE SCENE of the party: A lovely home, large and comfortable. A long table set with flowers, stacks of plates, and rows of silverware, followed with myriad pots, platters, and pans of heady food combinations and beautiful stemware filled with bubbly champagne. The hostess tells you to help yourself to the buffet and find a seat.

You are tempted by all the food and heap your plate high with salads, relishes, and entrees. The plate becomes heavy and unwieldy. Your left hand holds the napkin, spoon, fork, and knife while your thumb and forefinger precariously balance the plate. Your right hand successfully grasps the bubbly as you look for a place to land. You find it. Bending your knees slowly so not to upset the balance of things, you aim for the seat, but the plate wins — the once-molded gelatin salad slowly slips off the edge and the deviled egg rolls threateningly in the same direction, while the knife dangles briefly from under the clutched napkin, then crashes to the floor, following the gelatin in its embarrassing descent.

It's another one of those awful buffets.

EVERYONE HAS HIS tales of horror when it comes to eating at buffet parties. But buffets needn't have such a grim reputation. "Simplify" is the code word many hostesses need to program a nonstress dinner buffet. Simplify the food and the implements and guests will find it easier to cope.

That's why we've planned three buffet menus to serve 10 or 20 for which the only implement you need is a fork. "Fork only" buffets solve that problem of where to put the knife and spoon when you're squeezed between the heavyset insurance salesman and the matronly librarian and with no table in sight.

"Fork only" buffets mean that the food on the plate is manageable — no tricky drumsticks to carve with a knife, no slippery or juicy steaks to tangle with, and no soupy, cream-sauced vegetables that inevitably intermingle with all the food on your plate.

"Fork only" buffets offer only two or three dishes for the dinner plate, so the "piling high and wide" syndrome won't happen to guests, yet the food is so good that they won't miss the usual overabundance of dishes. Our buffet menus stress many room temperature foods that can be done ahead, and a few that can be reheated quickly just before serving and placed in a chafing dish. This means less work for the hostess, and easy self-service for the guests.

THE EMPHASIS ON forks is only natural. After all, though it was the last eating implement to be invented (sometime in the 18th Century in Italy), it's a dandy, all-purpose utensil, filling in the gap left by the uncouth knife and the awkward spoon. As food writer Raymond Sokolov put it in a recent article for "Natural History" magazine, "Now it would be unthinkable to dispense with forks at any normal meal; one can imagine making do without a knife or a spoon, but a fork, never."

Today's "fork only" buffets probably would have had our prefork ancestors laughing at the awkwardness of the affair, for they were accustomed to the ancient practice of merely dipping the fingers into a common pot of stew, then to their mouths, and back again. But, according to Sokolov and food historians, the phenomenon of the fork seems to parallel the changes in Western manners and civilization after the Reformation (luckily for us).

Here then, are three civilized menus for carefree fork buffets. The American gothic menu is a hearty, winter buffet featuring a beef stew so thick a fork can easily handle it, easy-to-eat cheese biscuits, and a tossed salad with a creamy, nonrunnable homemade thousand island dressing. Use separate dessert plates, of course, for the apple pie.

A more elegant buffet includes a do-ahead fish terrine, layered with pureed vegetables in the nouvelle cuisine style, a salad of marinated vegetables, herb bread, and a hazelnut chocolate torte.

Finally, there's a trip to the Middle East with a buffet of eggplant dip and pita bread, meat and cheese-filled boreks, or turnovers, a spinach salad, and a rich nut dessert drizzled with sugar syrup. Recipes serve 10, but can be doubled, with pan size adjustments, to serve 20.

American gothic buffet

Hearty beef stew
Poppyseed cheese biscuits
Tossed lettuce and tomato salad
Homemade thousand island dressing
Apple streusel pie with whipped rum topping
Hearty red wine   Coffee

Elegant fork buffet

Layered fish and vegetable terrine
Zucchini and broccoli vinaigrette in lettuce cups
Herbed french bread
Hazelnut mocha torte
Dry white wine   Espresso

Middle Eastern buffet

Eggplant-onion dip
Pita bread
Meat and cheese borek
Spinach-sesame seed salad
Kandopita (walnut cake)
Beer   Turkish coffee

Hearty beef stew
10 servings

3½ pounds boneless beef chuck
⅓ cup flour
Oil
4 cups beef broth
1 can (15 ounces) tomato sauce
1 tablespoon worcestershire
1 teaspoon salt
½ pound green beans, cut in 2-inch pieces
3 carrots, cut in 1-inch pieces
3 red potatoes, cut in 1-inch cubes
2 medium onions, coarsely chopped
2 stalks celery, sliced

Trim fat from beef; cut into 1-inch cubes. Dust with flour. Heat 3 tablespoons oil in dutch oven; brown beef in small batches, adding more oil as needed. Add broth, tomato sauce, worcestershire, salt, marjoram, thyme, and pepper. Heat to boil; cover and simmer 1 hour. Add 2 cups water, beans, carrots, potatoes, onions, and celery. Heat to boil; reduce heat and simmer, covered, 45 minutes. Stew may be cooled and refrigerated overnight. Reheat slowly; adjust seasonings before serving.

Recipes continued on page 3

Tribune photo by Lee Locke; food styling by Donna Meyers

Figure 27-6. *Graphic artists at the Chicago Tribune turned to the Grant Wood classic painting for their inspiration when planning this clever cover for one of the newspaper's food sections.* Courtesy of the Chicago Tribune.

EXERCISES

1. Using any newspaper available to you, clip five traditioal and nontraditional type stories from a family or living section and analyze them.
2. Check businesses, industries, educational institutions and government agencies in your area for women holding nontraditional positions—such as women construction workers, coal miners, bank presidents—and interview them for a story on how they were accepted by their coworkers or persons they supervise.
3. Select several products that do not normally fluctuate in price—perhaps a standard brand of tooth paste, deodorant, aspirin or cough medicine—and make a price-comparison survey at major supermarkets and independent stores in your community. (Make certain the products are not being offered as a leader item that week or are not on sale.) Write a story about your findings.
4. Assume you had been assigned to write an Action-Line type column for your local newspaper. Ask six persons for questions then contact local sources to obtain answers. Write a column based on the questions and the answers you have obtained.
5. Interview a local person who may be well-known among friends and relatives as an outstanding cook. Write a feature story about that person and include the recipes for several of his or her favorite dishes.
6. Write stories using the following notes:
   A. Elizabeth Wellington Wright
      Graduate of McMinn County High School
      And State University
      Security analyst for Thompson-McKinnon Securities Inc.
      Member of Cleveland-Athens Cotillion
      Presented at the club's Holly Ball
      Also the city's Cotton Ball
      Engagement announced by Mrs. Junius Greenwood Wright
      Her late father, Junius Wright, was an attorney
      Marriage will be in the fall
      Date to be announced
      Raymond Clay Speckman is to be the bridegroom
      He was graduated from John Overton High School
      And Harvard Law School
      He is in private law practice here
      His parents are Mr. and Mrs. Grover T. Speckman, Hillsdale
      He is a communicant of St. Bartholomew's Episcopal Church, Hillsdale
   B. Sheila Darlene Forshee
      Daughter of Mr. and Mrs. Errol J. Forshee
      Of Atlanta and granddaughter of
      Mr. and Mrs. Edgar T. Forshee of this city
      And Gorden C. Whitener
      Son of Mr. and Mrs. John A. Whitener
      Of 1410 Maloney Road
      Married Saturday in Tremont Baptist Church
      The Rev. Gene Varner officiated
      Miss Kathy Forshee was sister's maid of honor
      Joyce Greeson and Sandi Strunk were bridesmaids
      Dawn Eldridge, niece of bride, was flower girl
      Gilbert C. Whitener was his twin brother's best man
      Groomsmen were Lloyd and Marion Whitener
      Brothers of the bridegroom

Serving at the church reception were
Miss Marion Whitener, Miss Lloyd Whitener, Mrs. Wayne Escoe,
Sisters of the bridegroom, and Mrs. George Kesller, bride's aunt
Wedding trip to Puerto Rico
Couple will reside at 11 Daisy Lane
He is a consulting engineer
For state highway department
She is employed by First National Bank
As a trust officer

7. Write news stories from the following notes:

A. A to Z Women's Service Award Banquet
Scheduled for Saturday
At 7:30 p.m. at Greenhills Country Club
Sponsored by four women's service clubs
Altrusa, Pilot, Quota, Zonta
To honor outstanding women in community
Winners must have made outstanding contribution
To community life in three of five categories
Civic, social, religious, cultural, educational
Member of sponsoring clubs not eligible
Tickets are $8 a person
Available from Mrs. Mary Nell Johnson
Telephone 821-5187
Speaker will be Mrs. Janet Elkhart
Candidate for U.S. Senate
In last national election
And chairman of board of
First Federal Savings Association

B. Arrowhead Garden Club
Members will present fashion show
Of clothing they made
At monthly meeting
Thursday at 10 a.m.
At home of Mrs. John Campbell, Tipton Station Road
Mrs. Jack White will be cohostess
Mrs. Christian Davis, president, will conduct
Election of officers

C. Mr. and Mrs. Ronald Mason
Of Jefferson City
Announce birth of a son, Justin Andrew
Born at Jefferson City Memorial Hospital
At 10:32 p.m. last Thursday
Couple has another child
Leslie, a 2-year-old daughter
Grandparents are Mrs. Irene Mason of Locust Street here
And Mr. and Mrs. C. W. Ford of Madisonville

D. New home demonstration club formed
Named "The Better Ideas Club"
Members voted to meet
Second Wednesday of each month
At 10 a.m. at a member's home
Mrs. James Burn, extension agent, presided

Mrs. Bryant McDaniel elected president
Other officers are Mrs. Theodore Brown, vice-president
Mrs. Clyde Swartout, recording secretary
Mrs. Ed Ingram, treasurer
Next month's meeting will be at
Home of Mrs. Lewis Johnson

CHAPTER 28

Sports

The range of stories on many sports pages has broadened considerably in the last 10 years. The most obvious change has been in the amount of space given to coverage of women's athletic teams at colleges and universities. However, there has not been quite the dramatic change in the sports pages overall as there has been in such sections as business and family living.

Part of this might be because readers of sports pages want to know the score of last night's game and enjoy reading about the key plays—even when they have watched them on television or in person. But much of it certainly has to stem from the reluctance on the part of a number of sports writers to undertake investigations into the seamier side of sports such as the grade scandals that often rock the college athletic world.

A classic example of this can been seen in the grade scandal that developed at a Pacific Coast Athletic Conference university. An athlete signed an affidavit that he had not taken courses in which he had been given grades. The sports pages of the daily newspaper in that city declined to investigate the charges and print stories about them. And when the newspaper's investigative team undertook the assignment, the sports editor tried to pressure the city editor to drop the investigation and not run any stories on the grounds that it would hurt the team's recruiting. He ran the stories anyway.

Interest in sports remains high. And sports stories are some of the best-read—but frequently the worst-written—articles in American newspapers. To the talented writer the sports page offers an unlimited challenge, for sports reporting allows far greater freedom of expression than does writing straight news. A number of writers—Grantland Rice, Damon Runyon, Paul Gallico, Red Smith, Jim Murray and others—made sports writing an art form. All, of course, had several things in common—discipline, a thorough knowledge of sports, imagination and, most important, a command of the language. Unfortunately, too many persons writing sports have more of a command of clichés than of the language and little technical knowledge of the sports they cover. A sports writer who turns in a lead saying "Southeastern's swimmers ran roughshod over the Tryon State Tigers yesterday" needs as much help as the reporter who wrote a 17-inch story on a basketball game and never used the term *basketball* a single time, opting in favor of every known cliché from "round-ballers" to "hoopsters."

The sports reporter's field is broad enough and interesting enough to challenge the finest talent. Every sport has rules and records. It has its gallery of personalities and hall of fame. Psychological factors deserve exploration, in the Grantland Rice fashion. Sports ethics and aesthetics and larger aspects of recreation and the social good are involved. There are abuses to be corrected, campaigns to be waged, promotion and education to be designed. And when writers and readers alike begin to take it all too seriously it is helpful for a writer to take a lighthearted look at what it all means in the manner of Jim Murray. Perhaps in no other field of reporting is the opportunity greater for mastery of background and for application of standards of judgment. And perhaps in no other field of reporting does the reporter have quite the freedom of self expression.

The World of Sports. The sports section is a world unto itself. Generally, on larger newspapers, it is operated as an independent department, with the sports editor and his staff responsible for all phases of gathering, writing and editing. Having this freedom, the sports staff often leans toward a flamboyant display of its stories, producing pages that are heavy with large headlines and illustrations plus detailed treatment of sports developments. Some readers may see a curious misconception of news values in a newspaper's having a three-paragraph story with a small headline telling about a $1 million cancer research grant on a page in the general news section, then a 20-paragraph article with an eight-column headline and three photographs on the sports page of the same newspaper presenting the news about a race horse that shattered a leg and had to be destroyed. A journalistic truism that the sports pages constitute an isolated special section, its stories not to be weighed with the scales used for other news columns, has brought about the apparent anomaly. If anyone doubts this reasoning, the newspaper can support its contention by pointing to the high readership of the sports section. The fears that television, which devotes countless hours to the coverage of sports, would detract from readership of newspaper sports pages has proved unfounded. If anything, it simply has whetted the appetite for more reading. It also in turn has forced many sports writers to use greater care and accuracy in reporting. The reader who has seen a game on television before reading his newspaper will not accept the sports writer's account if the writer takes too much literary license with what happened on the field.

News Values of Sports. The whole scale of news values characterizes sports news. Clustered around conflict as the pivotal appeal are prominence, progress, disaster, human interest and—in the sports sense—consequence. Moreover, the reader is a "fan," highly conditioned for ready response, at once appreciative and critical. The sports reporter—usually a by-line writer—acquires "a public," which may become a valuable career asset. Thus there is something over and beyond the news values—something of camaraderie and clan *esprit* which enhances reader interest in the sports page. Men particularly, but also women and children, look at the sports section for news on their favorite teams, and frequently to see what their favorite writer had to say about a game or a team.

28a

Qualifications of the Sports Writer. In his work the sports reporter has certain responsibilities which are perhaps not different from, but merely more obvious than, those in less specialized reporting. Two of these have been mentioned—background and judgment either by experience or extensive reading.

Background can be acquired. One does not have to be a former football player to write about football. But a detailed knowledge of the fine points of the game is certainly essential. Many sports reporters are "addicted" to one or more sports and have been since childhood. This can be a help but it also can be a hindrance, especially if their "addiction" clouds their judgment. Other sports they may have to master somewhat vicariously. The background should be historical as well as technical. A fire, an accident or an occasion may be reported adequately from within the event. Too frequently, also, sports reporting confines itself in the same manner. But the richness of reporting from a full background outside the event is self-evident. The Kentucky Derby winner is related to Derby winners of all time, and of all tracks and of the current season, and is the "foal" of "sire" and "dam" of distinguished ancestry, with various records and winnings scattered along the way. Many—perhaps even most—readers will have a partial knowledge of this background. They not only want to be told what they already know (and it had better be correct) but they also want their knowledge expanded. They want the whole significance of the event, and they look to the sports reporter as interpreter and final authority. They demand that he have background. If the background of the reader is deeper than that of the writer, the writer is faced with a serious credibility gap.

To some extent, also, the sports reporter can acquire good judgment if aided by adequate knowledge. Familiarity and experience with various sports will acquaint the reporter with the standards used to measure the merits and demerits of play and players. Ultimately, though, the reporter will succeed or fail because of the accuracy or inaccuracy of his independent judgment. A reporter's ability to see beyond the surface and the statistics is a tremendous asset. It is insight, too, and not background, that must detect the cause of weakness or the source of strength of a team or of an individual player. (Some call it a "gut" feeling.) Nor can a sports reporter take comfort in the thought that, if he fails to detect and report an error or an achievement, no one will be the wiser. Unlike other reporters, he writes for a public, some (or much) of which has observed the same event—in person or on television—with a highly critical eye. A positive mandate for his success is sound judgment.

A third desirable qualification is perspective, or detachment—which should be the result of sufficient knowledge plus good judgment. Being a fan of a particular game or a team does not always make one the best of sports reporters. Thumping the drums for the local team with brass and bias is not detached reporting. The reporter's responsibility is to the public and not to the local team. Although the fans are quick to resent any lack of unrestrained support for the local heroes, they will in the long run, respect the sports reporter's honesty, accuracy and detachment. The sports reporter is not merely a reporter; he is a judge and must conduct himself accordingly. With these special prerogatives, he must avoid arrogance, for this violates detachment and honesty. The sports writer cannot take over and run a team through the newspaper columns, and he is usurping the coach's authority when he attempts to do so. There is a difference between good critical judgment and second-guessing—and every sports reporter should learn it early in his career.

Scope of Sports Writing. Sports writing ranges from straight news reporting through all degrees of interpretative and feature writing and the editorialized column. A sports event may be treated in any one of these degrees or in all of them combined. The general practice is to treat the important event as straight news (utilizing any of the lead and story forms already discussed) with sufficient interpretation to enrich the report with its background. Separate stories, features and columns devoted to all the necessary sidelights supplement the straight-news account. Many newspapers permit sports writers to use a highly informal style, often with few restrictions on editorializing even in the story handled as straight news. Careful reporters keep their editorial comments to a minimum in their straight-news account of a sports event.

For important sports events, "buildup," or advance, stories and articles sometimes are used for days, even weeks, before the event. Then the event is thoroughly covered when it occurs, and "post-mortem" stories may be used for days afterward in commenting on what took place.

News Sources. Local and regional schools and colleges, recreation departments, professional teams of all types, sponsors of all kinds of sport leagues (such as Little League groups, bowling leagues and country clubs) and other local organizations which promote or conduct events belonging in the sports world are all covered by the sports staff. The editor has, on the one hand, a problem to keep from overlooking some activities deserving space and, on the other, to avoid giving too much space to some teams and groups which have very active publicity directors or chairmen. A sports staff could not begin to cover all events deserving space, but with the proper encouragement and instructions the sports writers can get valuable assistance in gathering news from many of the people engaged in the various sports. Many newspapers arrange with high school and even junior high students to phone in results of games the newspapers are unable to staff. Little League coaches or their wives, interested parents, bowling lane owners, tennis and golf club professionals generally are willing to call in the results of an event.

28b A word of caution is needed on sports news sources. Gambling on sporting events seems to be a national pastime, but the sports staff should be cautious about quoting gambling odds on sports events. Although the practice is more commonplace today in reporting on upcoming professional events, most newspapers avoid reference to gambling odds on amateur events such as college football and basketball.

28c *Style in Sports Writing.* Good sports writing will be vigorous, virile, audacious. It should not be hackneyed or so exaggerated that it strains the boundaries of believability. Somewhere between standard English rhetoric and the bizarre patterns into which the language can be bent, the reporter must find his own style. This does not mean that he is relieved of responsibilities of observing basic rules of English grammar. In fact, because of the freedom of expression given most sports writers, it is essential that he have an even greater command of the language than other reporters. A sports reporter's objective is to bring the event to the reader with all the impact that event had upon the spectators. He cannot achieve this effect through twisting and straining and mangling the language. Nor can he obtain a quick passport to success by imitating a style that another reporter has made effective. Perhaps the only possible advice is "Be yourself, but be your best self through constant practice, continuing education and self-criticism."

The informality of writing used on most sports pages permits the sports reporter to use colloquialisms, metaphors, similes and other figures of speech which other reporters avoid. He achieves brevity and vividness with active rather than passive verbs and precise adjectives. There is a great difference between carefully selected, precise verbs and adjectives and the worn-out cliché such as "banged the apple" and "smacked the pill." Since the reporter does have so much freedom, he should try to be original but must temper his language with sound judgment and good taste. By all means, he must remember that he is writing for the spectator rather than the athlete, and his language must not be so technical that the general public will not understand it. At the same time, however, he must be aware that the coach and the athlete will be reading his story. If he displays an ignorance of techniques and the language of the sport, they are not likely to respect him as a writer and may not cooperate with him willingly in interviews.

28d SPORTS STORY LEADS

The sports page contains stories of a wide variety of events. Most space is devoted to such major sports as football, baseball, basketball, golf and tennis, but other sports include swimming, hunting, fishing, automobile and horse racing, track, volleyball, trapshooting, bowling, boxing, wrestling and gymnastics. Depending upon the season, and perhaps the section of the country, skiing, hockey, soccer, polo, rowing, rodeos, hiking and a variety of other sports might even get more space than some of the major spectator sports. In an effort to be complete, most sports pages try to carry stories on all major events in all sports. In many cases these include horse shows, dog shows and other events that might not be classified as a true sport.

The sports reporter usually reports these events in a news fashion. Although allowed more freedom in the use of language, he usually follows the regular news principles in building the story. The 5 W's are generally in the lead of the straight-news account of the event, and the features usually are summarized at the beginning and elaborated as in the body of the story. The general principles of the single-feature and the several-feature leads also apply to straight sports writing. However, many sports stories, particularly the second-day story on an event or a sidebar story, take a strong feature approach.

No matter what type of sports event he covers, the reporter may look for one or more of the following elements to provide him with features for the story:

1. The score of the game or the outcome of the event (the final score may be subordinate to other features but it certainly should be in the lead or no later than the opening sentence of the second paragraph).
2. Spectacular plays.
3. Scoring plays or sequence of plays.

4. Individual stars.
5. The significance of the game—championship or effect on record.
6. General comparison of teams or opponents.
7. Background of game—weather, crowd, special occasion.

The following leads illustrate the use of the various features available to the sports reporter:

The Score or Outcome

BLOOMINGTON, Ind.—Butch Carter fought off the pressure Sunday to lead Indiana to a 76-73 overtime victory over Ohio State and the undisputed Big 10 championship.

Or

Piling up a score of 40-0 in the first half, the Baylor Bobcats won an easy victory over South Texas State yesterday afternoon.

Individual Stars

Quarterback Matthew Reed scored two touchdowns in the final quarter to carry Birmingham to a 23-17 World Football League victory over Philadelphia Saturday night.

Or here is a more featurized lead emphasizing an individual player:

The consummate baseball pitcher works in this town. His name is Jim Palmer and today he showed just how overpowering a big-league hurler can be when he has velocity, variety, control, maturity and a strong wind blowing in behind him.

Palmer pitched the third one-hitter of his career today, a 1-0 victory over Kansas City before 11,610 at Memorial Stadium.

Significance of the Game

Len Randle's 17th-inning single carried Texas to a 7-6 victory over the Cleveland Indians today in the longest game of the baseball season and virtually assured the Rangers a shot at the pennant.

Comparison of Teams

The sluggish Boston Celtics came to life in the opening minutes of the second half to whip the slow-moving New Orleans Jazz 113-100 in a National Basketball Association game Wednesday night.

Background of Game

A crowd of 72,434 watched the Houston Oilers defeat the New Orleans Saints 13-7 in the first paid event ever played in the $163 million Louisiana Superdome in New Orleans.

Optional Leads

Sam Boyle, deputy sports editor of the Associated Press, told readers of the AP Log that there is a growing use of the optional lead on sports pages.

This type lead may be based on a quote, an after-the-game visit to the locker room or perhaps an analysis of a player's or team's style.

Boyle said their use is partly in response to television. Readers already know the score in the morning; now they want something else to read. Readership surveys have shown that more people reading the sports pages look to them for that extra dimension.

Sometimes a good quote tells the story of a sports event better than the score alone would. It is after a game that the material for a good optional lead is gathered. The kind of copy that makes for a good optional approach is generated as often off the field as on. And that is the material that television misses, either because of the limitations of the camera or because the camera goes elsewhere when the final score is in.

Here are some examples of optional leads:

PEBBLE BEACH—A man standing near the first green at Pebble Beach Saturday morning failed to recognize the faces in the approaching foursome and turned to his pairing sheet.

"Edwards? David Edwards?" he said quizzically, reading from the sheet. "One of the leaders, wasn't he?"

Was and is.

Tied with Tom Kite entering the third round of the 39th Bing Crosby National Pro-Amateur, the anonymous Edwards emerged alone, shooting par 72 for an eight-under 208 total and a two-stroke lead over . . .

MIAMI—Before the game, the public address system in the Orange Bowl malfunctioned as the Miami Dolphins were being introduced, lending credence to their "No-Name" reputation.

But by the time it was over, two of the oldest, most familiar names to a decade of football fans reintroduced themselves to the nation. Bob Griese and Larry Csonka are alive and well and living in the New England Patriots' end zone. Together, they destroyed the Patriots 39-24 on Thursday night's version of Monday night football . . .

Randy Schultz of the Palm Beach Post used this optional lead on his story of the opening day of the National Slow Pitch Softball Championship:

The mid-70s have been hard times. In the past three years, Al White has driven a forklift in Jacksonville, helped drill an Oklahoma oil well and dispensed airline meals in Miami.

Yet White is no drifter blown about by unemployment; his job reference is the talent to hit a softball, and that is more seductive in the right circles than a college degree.

Once the sport was nothing more than First Methodist vs. First Baptist with everybody heading out to Flo's afterwards for fried chicken. Now softball has become a corporate vehicle in the land of tax write offs and market analysis. Sponsors offer company jobs to players like White as inducement to relocate and play for the team.

White is now employed by Jerry Pendergast, who sponsors Jerry's Catering, a fine team that at 10:15 this morning in Jacksonville plays the Starke Green Machine in the first round of the National Slow Pitch Softball Championship . . .

Franco Harris, the key ingredient

By Don Pierson
Chicago Tribune Press Service

LOS ANGELES—The eyes that sparkle in the expressive face of Franco Harris looked startled when he was told this week that one football publication called him the "Player of the Decade."

"That's quite surprising," he said. "I feel very honored."

Two minutes later, someone asked his reaction to comments by Oakland safety Jack Tatum, who called him a sideline-to-sideline runner who isn't tough when it's third and one.

"We know that by pounding him hard and often Franco Harris will in turn is going to be warped," wrote Tatum.

"I didn't give it much thought. My record against Oakland speaks for itself," he said. Harris' record always has to do the talking, because Harris doesn't. He is polite, but private, the mystery man of the Pittsburgh Steelers.

Franco doesn't like to be bundled. He doesn't care a lot," says defensive tackle Joe Greene.

WITH THE RETIREMENT of O.J. Simpson, Harris is the No. 1 active runner in football. He trails only Jim Brown, Simpson, and Jim Taylor on the all-time list.

He is the all-time leading rusher in postseason games, rising to the occasion so consistently that he is known as one of the sport's best "money players."

Until his arrival in 1972, the Steelers had never made the playoffs. They have not missed them in Harris' eight seasons.

He has been the leading rusher in 13 of the 16 postseason games he has played. When the Steelers won their first Super Bowl after the 1974 season, Harris set a record of 158 yards rushing.

When the Steelers were knocked out of the playoffs by Oakland in 1976, Harris did not play in the game.

ASKED ABOUT the rise of the Steelers from 5-9 to 6-8 to 11-3 in Terry Bradshaw's first three seasons, Bradshaw told Playboy magazine: "We drafted Franco Harris and had an outstanding offensive line. We started running the

football and making things happen. We were a very young and very exciting football team. But Franco was really the key to our offense.

"We had some key personnel at that time, and our football team was responding to Chuck Noll and to the things that they wanted to get done on the football field. It was a great assembly of football talent—young and experienced. But Franco was the key."

Harris is paid $250,000 a year, a little more than half of what Walter Payton makes. It is less than the $300,000 Washington fullback John Riggins makes. Yet no one on the Steelers is paid more than Harris. There are a dozen who make more than $100,000, but none more than $250,000.

HARRIS IS AS much an enigma as a runner as he is as a person.

"I can't compare Franco to anyone," said Steeler Coach Chuck Noll. "He can be a power runner, but he also has the ability to make people miss him—an uncanny ability in the open field. In other words, he has a style all his own."

His style has been misunderstood, sometimes by his own teammates, frequently by fickle fans.

In his second year, when Preston Pearson was a teammate, Pearson criticized Harris' jitterbugging.

"That's all right for me," Pearson said. "But Franco weighs 230. He ought to blow."

In practice, Harris insists that no one tackle him or hit him unnecessarily.

"The other guys joke about that," he said. "But frankly, I feel that I take enough punishment during the season, and I don't want to get hurt when we're playing among ourselves. It makes no sense to me."

HARRIS STARTED this season slowly, as usual, gaining only 189 yards after playing in four of the first five games. His fumble at the goal line cost the Steelers a loss to Philadelphia. Fans were yelling for rookie Greg Hawthorne, figuring Franco was getting old at 29.

But he finished with his seventh 1,000-yard

Continued on page 4

Inside:

Art Rooney Jr. is the Steelers' vice president in charge of talent scouting. It is because he has done his job so well that Pittsburgh is looking for its fourth Super Bowl title. *Page 2.*

Jack Youngblood is the Rams' "Abominable Rushman," jokes teammate Fred Dryer. Youngblood will be playing with a broken leg in the Super Bowl, just as he did in the NFC title game, but he says it's no big deal. "Pain is something you can control," he says. *Page 3.*

Horrible! The Steelers once were just that—the laughingstock of the league, the butt of every joke. That has all changed now, but the "old" Steelers live on in memory and ignominy. *Page 8.*

Figure 28-1. A number of large and medium-sized daily newspapers have introduced special sports sections once a week in addition to the regular sports coverage. Several publish them on Monday to wrap up the weekend events. Others, such as the Chicago Tribune, publish the section late in the week to feature major weekend sports activities. Courtesy of the Chicago Tribune.

FRIDAY

Sports Weekend

DECEMBER 14, 1979

The Washington Star

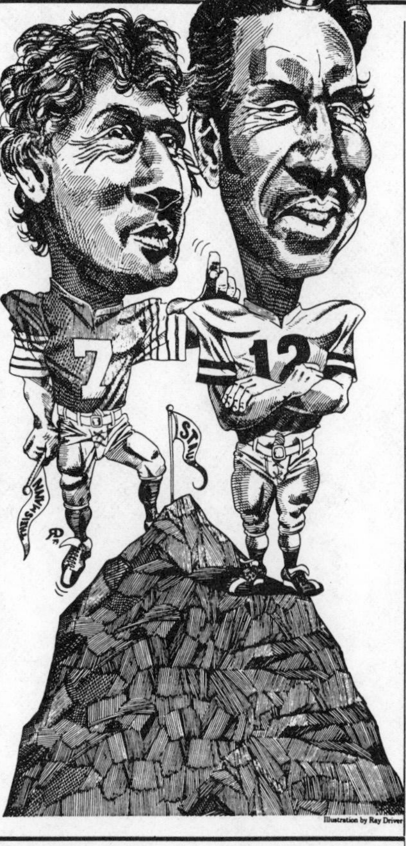

Illustration by Ray Driver

At 30, Joey T Has Received Team's Trust

By Steve Guback
Washington Star Staff Writer

The game has ended and now the microphones, the television cameras and a small army of reporters are clustered around the locker as Joe Theismann wraps himself in a towel and smiles, awaiting the first question.

"Isn't this exciting?" Theismann says, and nobody is quite sure whether he is referring to the game or the interviews.

"You love the pressure," a radio man says for openers.

"What pressure?" Theismann answers. "Geez, it's interesting. Everybody says, 'You guys just won a must football game.' There hasn't been one in the last four weeks that hasn't been a must football game for us."

Life in the National Football League has just begun for Joe Theismann at age 30.

But that's the way it always seems to be in this town. Redskins quarterbacks, like good wine, must be properly aged. Sonny Jurgensen didn't arrive in Washington until he was 30, and had his most dazzling season for the Redskins at age 33. Billy Kilmer strung enough of his wobbly passes together at age 33 to take the Redskins to the Super Bowl.

Nobody can be president of the United States until age 35, or a bona fide quarterback of the Redskins until he is at least 30. Those seem to be the hard-and-fast rules.

"I think I'm a quarterback who knows the system better now," said Theismann, trying to explain his dazzling year for the benefit of the corps of media out-of-towners, which grows in number each week. "I think I'm a guy who relies on the other players more, which I didn't do as much in the past. But other than that, my physical being and my mental capabilities have always been there, I think."

So now it's Dallas Week II. The Redskins vs. the Cowboys in Dallas. Theismann vs. Roger Staubach. With the NFC East title at stake.

Theismann had all the pluses in the last meeting at RFK Stadium four weeks ago. The Redskins won, 34-20, as Theismann completed 15 of 24 passes for 210 yards, three touchdowns and no interceptions. He got a game ball. Staubach was 23 for 38 with one touchdown pass and three interceptions.

"We wanted to mix things up and give them a lot to look at, and utilize the big plays if we could get them," said Theismann.

"It was Theismann's best game yet," Coach Jack Pardee said at the time. "He kept his poise. When you throw on first down, you can't come up second-and-10 and expect to win."

Theismann, who waited five seasons with the Redskins for this year, already has been picked by his teammates as the Redskins' most valuable player. That says enough. Yet he still has much to prove. He was shunted aside, seemingly a rank injustice, in the balloting by the players for the Pro Bowl, with Staubach and Archie Manning the NFC choices.

"Who has done any more than Joe for his team?" asked Pardee, not mentioning any other names. "Who has been more valuable or consistent? All you've got to do is look at the statistics. I'd sure vote for him."

"All-Pro? I think any guy who puts on the uniform thinks about that, but I don't worry about it," said Theismann, who asked that the matter be dropped and quickly steered the conversation to other topics. "Beating Dallas is the most important thing."

See THEISMANN, C-3

TODAY'S NEWS

Spingarn basketball sensation Earl Jones is ruled ineligible to play the rest of the semester. And Jack Mann comments on the hearing. C-2

Joe Theismann is overlooked in Pro Bowl voting, but four Redskins are honored. C-3

Dallas' All-Pro defensive back, Cliff Harris, is using his head more, his helmet less. Tom Callahan's column. C-3

THE SCORES

National Basketball Association	National Hockey League
Wash. 115, Cleveland 113 (OT)	Detroit 6, Boston 6
Utah 144, San Antonio 114	Philadelphia 6, Quebec 4
Phoenix 121, Houston 113	Buffalo 5, Chicago 4

The Bullets Win By 2 in Overtime

By Steve Hershey
Washington Star Staff Writer

RICHFIELD, Ohio — The struggling Bullets are pressing so hard for victories these days that when a game is handed to them, they don't know how to accept it.

Although they started this three-game road trip with a 115-113 overtime victory over the Cleveland Cavaliers last night, it was hardly a time for celebrating. In fact, as soon as all the players reached the dressing room, Coach Dick Motta gave a little clinic.

"The first thing we did was talk about working against the press," said Jim Cleamons, after the Bullets blew a 100-91 lead in the last 1:54 of the fourth quarter and a 111-105 advantage with 1:13 left in overtime and then needed two free throws from Elvin Hayes with three seconds remaining to escape with a victory.

Coach Jerry Sloan of Chicago was scouting last night's game and Bob Leonard of Indiana is aware of the Bullets' problems with defense, so Motta's men can expect more of the same tactics at Indiana tonight (8:05, WDCA-20) and Saturday in Chicago.

"If we had lost this game in overtime, and we very well could have, it would have been very discouraging," Motta said. "We just didn't protect the ball very well. We wanted to win so badly, we got too cautious.

"When we had a timeout and then Elvin made those two free throws to put us up (98-89 with 2:39 remaining), I told him to run some time off the clock, then go into our offense with 10 seconds left. Except for Elvin's breakaways, we didn't get another basket."

The hustling young Cavaliers came out pressing after the timeout and took advantage of four turnovers by Bobby Dandridge to get back in the game. Dandridge was forced to handle the ball in the backcourt because the guards were being overplayed.

After Hayes' breakaway dunk made it 100-91, Randy Smith scored on a breakaway and Campy Russell got a layup following an interception. Russell scored again after Cleamons missed the second of two free throws to make it 101-97 and then stole the ball from Dandridge for another layup with 21 seconds to play.

With the Bullets trying to run out the clock, Dandridge was double-teamed and swung an elbow at Foots Walker, giving Cleveland possession with 15 seconds remaining.

Walker took the ball, made a move on Kevin Porter and banked in a 14-footer with five seconds left to tie the game. Russell again stole the ball from Dandridge but didn't have time to shoot and the game went into overtime.

The Bullets quickly broke on top, 109-103, as the Cavaliers missed the first six shots. Kevin Grevey's two free throws gave the Bullets a 111-105 lead, but Smith made a three-point play on an offensive rebound, and Mike Mitchell's bank shot made it 111-110 with 27 seconds left.

Grevey, who scored 14 of his 22 points in the first quarter, swished a 12-footer with 12 seconds to go. But after a timeout, Smith made a three-pointer to tie with seven seconds left to play.

When the Bullets set up, Hayes called for the ball and when he went for Grevey's pass, he was fouled by Mitchell and cashed in on both attempts. Again, the Cavaliers tried to go to Smith for a three-pointer, but the All-Star guard slipped and the pass bounced away.

"Mitchell had been leaning on me all night," Hayes said. "I took a step to my right and tried to get enough body on him for a foul to be called.

"We really needed this one," he continued, after his 25-point performance. "We have lost so many close games here. They put pressure on us at the end and we didn't handle it very well. Bobby got in trouble a few times because we didn't give him any help."

Grevey, who played only 10 minutes after the first quarter, admitted the Bullets were fortunate to gain a rare victory on the road.

"We were lucky we got fouled at the end," he said. "We were standing around too much instead of cutting and getting ourselves open. When you have a nine-point lead late in the game, you should just spread out and make them foul."

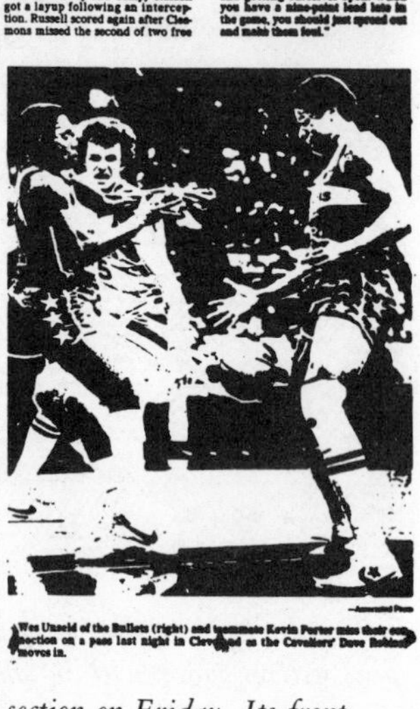

—Associated Press

Wes Unseld of the Bullets (right) and teammate Kevin Porter miss their connection on a pass last night in Cleveland as the Cavaliers' Dave Robinson moves in.

THIS WEEKEND

Things to Do

Rangers Visit Cap Centre
514

The New York Rangers come to Capital Centre tomorrow night as living proof of what is possible in the National Hockey League. After three consecutive losing seasons, the Rangers turned their program around last year under new coach Fred Shero and went all the way to the Stanley Cup finals. The Capitals, riding their own miserable five-year streak of losing seasons, now have a new coach of their own, Gary Green. The game may show the Caps how far they still have to go. Game time is 7:35.

Maryland Takes On CU

On one of the most demanding stops of a very demanding schedule, Catholic University visits Cole Field House tomorrow night at 8 p.m. to play Maryland in the first meeting between these schools since 1944. CU (2-3) is coming off an impressive victory over St. Joseph's, but Maryland (3-1) is the prohibitive favorite

Schools: Tip-Off Tournament

Area high school fans can get a look at some of the better players in the Interhigh League in the annual double-header Tip-Off Tournament tonight at McKinley High School. Cardozo plays Eastern in the first game at 6 p.m. and H.D. Woodson takes on McKinley in the 8 p.m. nightcap.

Pro Wrestling: Animal House

They'll all be there — Bulldog Brower, Dominic Denucci, Gorilla Monsoon and 17 more — for a 20-man battle royal in the wrestling extravaganza tonight at 8 p.m. at Capital Centre. The card includes 12 matches, with the winner of the battle royal earning a title shot at World Wrestling Federation heavyweight champion Bob Backlund. This will be the final D.C. wrestling event of the year.

Things to View

Pro Football: D-Day

The Redskins' season has come down to the final regular-season game, and who would have thought back in September that this game would mean so much? The winner will be the NFC East champion, and the Cowboys, despite their biggest injury problem in recent years, are favored by about nine points. Turn on the tube (4 p.m., Sunday, Ch. 9) to see how accurate the line turns out to be.

Pro Basketball: Bullets on Twice

These are dark times for the Washington Bullets, the once-mighty NBA champions of two years ago who now have the eighth worst record in the league. Management is confused, Coach Dick Motta is perplexed and the team is playing marginally at best. It's tough to turn a team around on the road, but area fans will get two chances to see how things progress tonight and tomorrow night. The Bullets play in Indianapolis against the Pacers tonight (8:05, Ch. 20) and in Chicago against the Bulls tomorrow (8:35 p.m., Ch. 20).

Gymnastics: Worlds Revisited

The World Gymnastics Championships, held in Houston last week, will be shown in highlight form on ABC's Wide World of Sports (5 p.m., tomorrow, Chs. 7 and 13). This is the nation's last real glimpse before the Olympics at how the U.S. team stacks up against the rest of the world. The Russians won the overall men's championship, the Japanese took second but the U.S. men's team won the bronze medal, exceeding many experts' forecasts.

Colleges: Basketball and Football

It's that bonus time of year. Depending on which station is on, there's the best of both college basketball and football. UCLA's basketball team, coming off a narrow loss at Notre Dame earlier this week, entertains DePaul (3:30 p.m., tomorrow, Ch. 4). In football, Temple and California meet in the Garden State Bowl (1 p.m., tomorrow, Ch. 20). And the NCAA Division I-AA title is at stake when Eastern Kentucky and Lehigh meet (1:30 p.m., tomorrow, Chs. 7 and 13).

Monday Night: Title Match

ABC's Monday night football season closes down with a dandy — Denver at San Diego for the AFC Western Division title (9 p.m., Chs. 7 and 13). This season, Dan Fouts has proven himself as one of the NFL's top quarterbacks. The Chargers have already clinched a playoff berth and the oddmakers have made Denver a 6½-point underdog.

Television Today

Pro Basketball:	8 p.m., 20. Washington at Indiana.
The Olympiad:	8 p.m., 5. "Jessie Owens Returns to Berlin."
Tennis:	10 p.m., 32. U.S.-Italy Davis Cup competition. 10:30 p.m., 26. U.S.-Italy Davis Cup competition.

Television Tomorrow

Wrestling:	11 a.m., 20. Professional matches. 4 p.m., 45. Professional matches.
Pro Football:	Noon. 4. NFL '79. 12:30 p.m., 4, 11. N.Y. Jets at Miami. 3 p.m., 2. NFL Game of the Week. 3:30 p.m., 9, 2 NFL Today. 4 p.m., 9, 2. Green Bay at Detroit.
College Football:	1 p.m., 20, 45. Garden State Bowl (California vs. Temple). 1:30 p.m., 7, 13. Eastern Kentucky vs. Lehigh, NCAA Div 1-AA championship.
College Basketball:	12:30 p.m., 45. Maryland Coach Lefty Driesell's Show. 3:30 p.m., 4, 11. DePaul at UCLA. 4:30 p.m., 7. Lefty Driesell Show.
Soccer:	7 p.m., 32. West German Soccer League matches.
Wide World of Sports:	5 p.m. 7, 13. World Gymnastics Championships.
Tennis:	5 p.m., 26, 32. U.S.-Italy Davis Cup competition.
Pro Basketball:	8 p.m., 20. Washington at Chicago.

Television Sunday

Pro Football:	Noon. 9. Redskins Coach Jack Pardee's Show. 12:30 p.m., 4. "NFL '79." 12:30 p.m., 9, 2. "NFL Today." 1 p.m., 9, 2. Minnesota at New England. 1 p.m., 4, 11. Baltimore at N.Y. Giants. 4 p.m., 9, 2. Washington at Dallas.
Tennis:	10 p.m., 32. U.S.-Italy Davis Cup competition 11 p.m., 26. U.S.-Italy Davis Cup competition
Olympiad:	4:30 p.m., 13. "Marathon."

Television Monday

Pro Football:	7:30 p.m., 9. Redskin Sidelines. 8 p.m., 20. "The Redskins Game." 9 p.m., 7, 13. Denver at San Diego.
College Football:	12 [illegible] a.m. 7. NCAA bowl preview. 12 [illegible] a.m. 13. NCAA bowl preview.

Figure 28-2. The Washington Star publishes its Sports Weekend section on Friday. Its front page is a combination of feature stories, art and a listing of sports events scheduled for the weekend. Courtesy of The Washington Star.

The body of the sports story must, of course, complete the development of the lead. If the lead is a summary, the body may proceed in the 1, 2, 3, 4 development of the various features. If the lead is an outstanding feature, it must be followed by a summary of the other features and by the subsequent development of each feature. These are the general principles of lead and body development that have been observed from the beginning as applying to all types of stories.

In many sports stories, however, two types of body development must be utilized: (a) the general interpretation; (b) the running story.

The general interpretation is essential. It is merely the development of the lead or lead block. The reporter must narrate and explain (interpret) the highlights (features) of the event. This is the logical body development which is used in other types of stories. The running (chronological) story (play-by-play, inning-by-inning, round-by-round) is sometimes given, appearing after the general interpretation or printed separately under its own headline. Play-by-play or blow-by-blow accounts of sports events are used only infrequently by some newspapers and not at all by others, particularly when radio or television covers the major events.

EXERCISES

1. Using any newspapers available to you, clip at least 10 stories on different sports and analyze them.
2. Attend a current sports event on your campus or in your community and write a straight sports story about it.
3. Using the same event you covered and any additional color material or after-the-game activities you can collect, write a second story using the optional lead approach.
4. Invite the coach of a major male or female athletic team at your college or university to the class for an interview. Write a story based on that interview.
5. Using any newspapers available to you, clip a syndicated sports column of a writer the stature of Jim Murray of the Los Angeles Times or Red Smith of the New York Times and compare the writing style to the best-known sports columnist in your area. Write a critical analysis of the syndicated column and the local one. Look for examples of vividness and of hackneyed expressions—if any are used—in both columns.
6. Sports pages generally use tabulations to summarize certain important facts and statistics (names of players, statistics on each player, and statistics on the entire team). The form varies from newspaper to newspaper. Study the newspapers in your area and draw up sample tabulations used in stories on (a) a football game, (b) a baseball game, (c) a basketball game, (d) a track meet, (e) any other popular sport in your community. Define all abbreviations used in these tabulations. (*Note:* Check back issues of the newspapers in the library for sample tabulations on seasonal sports.)
7. Write stories on the following notes:
   A. Green Mountain Marathon
      Qualifying race for
      The Boston Marathon
      Race over a 26.2-mile course
      In suburban Foxhills on Saturday
      Eighty-nine runners competed

Sixty-eight runners finished

Twenty-seven covered course in less than three hours

Tom Turner, 23, student at State University

Major in accounting

From Johnson City

Completed race in two hours, 20 minutes and nine seconds

He was 25 minutes ahead of next finisher

Kevin Anderson, 22, a senior at Bowling Green State University

Anderson's time was 2:45:48

The course was wet but no icy spots

B. Basketball game

George Washington High School vs.

Old Hickory High School

At Old Hickory High School gym last night

George Washington won

Score was 56–50

Washington down 28-17 at half

Fought back to 44-38 with 9:31 remaining

Pulled ahead in next three minutes

Never behind again

Points scored by George Washington players: Craig McCormick, center, 14; Bill Bryant, guard, 24; Bobby Laugherty, guard, 14; Robert Ruse, forward, 1; Scott Peavy, forward, 3.

Points scored by Old Hickory players: Barry Johnson, forward, 16; Gary Turner, forward, 15; Bob Chambers, center, 13; Martin King, guard, 3; Peter Whitehead, guard, 3.

George Washington now 11-1 for season. Old Hickory is 7-5

Approximately 1,610 attended

C. Crescent City Jaycees Indoor Track Meet

Held last Saturday at Memorial Coliseum

Gwen Dougherty of Greeneville Community College

Located in nearby Greeneville

Broke American indoor record

In women's 440-yard dash

Sprinted past Brenda Frazier

Of San Antonio Flyers

In 55.04, one-hundredth of a second

Faster than record set last year

By Roseann Aceto to Mid State University

D. City Interscholastic Swim League

Championship meet scheduled Saturday

At State School for the Deaf pool here

Preliminaries start at 9 a.m.

Finals start two hours after preliminaries are completed

No charge for admission

One-meter diving scheduled

For first time since league formed

Diving won't count toward team points

Each swimmer limited to three events

Two relays and one individual.

Or two individuals and one relay

George Willis, clerk of course

Said 18 teams entered
School for Deaf, Oak Ridge, Farragut, West,
Jefferson County, Heritage, Maryville, William Blount,
Sevier County, Bearden, Carter, Catholic, Central,
Doyle, Holston, Gibbs, Halls and Webb

8. Invite a member of your university's athletic board to class for an interview. Write a story based on the interview.

9. Write a story comparing the financing of the men's and women's athletic programs at your college or university.

CHAPTER 29

Entertainment, Literature, Fine Arts, Criticism

Pauline Kael, for many years the movie critic for *The New Yorker,* once wrote that in the arts "there are no absolute standards; there is no final authority. There is only fallible human judgment." Unfortunately, many reviewers and critics write as if their judgment is infallible. And when they move on, there are countless others waiting in line who feel their judgment is, indeed, the final authority.

Perhaps no job around a newspaper is as coveted as that of reviewer or critic. And while newspapers are devoting more and more space to the coverage of entertainment and cultural events, a job as a reviewer or critic is often hard to come by. Not everyone has the broad background in such areas as dramatic literature, films, music and fine arts to write with authority about these fields.

In writing about these areas the reporter has far more latitude than he has in any other area. Unlike the straight-news story, much of what is written about entertainment or fine arts requires more than just hard facts or interpretation.

While straight-news stories do come out of these areas daily and are written in the news style, the purpose of much writing about the world of entertainment, literature and fine arts is to appraise and evaluate. There is, of course, almost always a news peg on which to hang the story—a new book or play, a concert, art show or performance by a theatrical company. But the writer is no longer limited to writing just a news story. He is expected not only to describe the work of art or the performance but also to help his readers enjoy, understand and appreciate it.

29a   *Reviewing Versus Criticism.* The difference between reviewing and criticism may be mainly one of definition. In practice at most newspapers and magazines today, the terms are almost synonymous. Yet there is a distinction.

A reviewer should not pass critical judgment if he is not competent by way of background and knowledge to criticize the performance or work of another. A reviewer should confine himself to presenting the facts without editorializing. A reviewer assigned to cover a popular music performance, for example, should tell the reader who performed and where and when the concert took place, give a summary of its content and describe the reaction of the audience. He may tell the reader what the performance was like; but he generally does not engage in a critical evaluation of the performers' musicianship. Of course, as noted earlier, in a number of newspapers some reviewers do engage in various degrees of criticism in their reviews.

Pure criticism, on the other hand, requires expert judgment. Usually the newspaper will not engage in criticism unless it has a qualified staff member to handle the assignment. Many smaller newspapers buy columns by professional critics in such areas as theater and music from syndicates and feature services. At times, however, a newspaper may assign its most cultured reporter or employ an outside specialist (musician, artist, author) for special occasions. The critic, using his thorough understanding of the field, evaluates the performance or work of art. He knows the standards that should be achieved, and he measures the success and failure of the work or performance. He compares the given work with others of its class and judges the ability of artists or performers. But he must do this without allowing his particular bias against a composer or a style of art or writing to color his judgment. If his bias interferes, the critic then loses his usefulness to the reader.

Entertainment, literature and the fine arts that are the subject of reviews or criticism in newspapers include:

1. Books and articles.
2. Dramatic performances.
3. Concerts and other musical performances (classical and popular).
4. Recordings.
5. Films.
6. Radio and television programs.
7. Lectures.
8. Art—painting, sculpture.
9. Architecture.
10. Professional dancing.
11. Photography.
12. Nightclub performances.

Principles of Criticism. The person assigned to write a review or a critical **29b** piece should remember that the standards of good writing always apply. Far too many critics write more in the jargon of the particular field they are covering than in the language the typical reader of a mass publication can understand. This is particularly true in such a field as abstract art.

Following are important points anyone writing a review or critical article should consider:

1. It is important to give readers a view of the woods before pointing out the individual trees. The reader is interested in knowing what sort of experience he will encounter in the book, play or painting. What is the nature of the work? Is it sensational, intellectual, calm or boisterous? Is it worthwhile and in what way?

2. The work should be criticized in the light of its intentions and within its genre. A detective story or mystery play should not be compared with a classic drama. Amateurs have a right to compete with other amateurs and not to be judged by professional standards. However, amateurs should not be praised lavishly if they do not deserve it. It is generally wise to report amateur performances fairly, emphasizing the audience reaction.

3. The contents of books or plays should be outlined only to the extent needed for readers to determine whether they are interested, not so fully as to give away the plot. One purpose of the critic is to promote popular interest, not to discourage it.

4. The criticism should be interesting in itself. Readers will not read dull criticism any more readily than they will read dull news. Good criticism may rise to the heights of literature itself.

5. The critic is addressing lay readers who do not possess technical vocabularies. They probably cannot be expected to know the difference between *crisis* and *climax, protagonist* and *antagonist,* and they are not familiar with Aristotle's theory of the dramatic purge. The critic should write in simple language. He should not attempt to "show off" his literary prowess.

6. The significance of the work should be suggested. Is it extraordinary, distinguished, superior, mediocre, below standard? Does it have social or economic implications?

7. If the critic likes or dislikes what he is evaluating, he should explain why. It is not enough merely to praise or to condemn a literary or artistic production. Critical comment should be supported with examples.

8. The critic must stay within ethical and legal bounds (see Chapter 5). In using copyrighted material, he may quote a reasonable amount with no fear of violating the law. A reasonable amount may be interpreted as a taste (but not the full swallow) of the quality of the material. In other words, the critic cannot steal the full impact of this quality under the guise of a critical review.

9. Above all, the critic must keep in mind that his major responsibility is to the reader—not to authors, performers, painters. He must tell the readers whether the production is worth seeing or hearing, and he must be honest with them. He should not be too harsh or too lenient. By all means he should not permit himself to become so involved with a production that he is nothing more than a publicity agent.

29c *Writing Style of Criticism.* Some newspapers use a certain set form to give essential data at the beginning of a critical review. Following is an example from the New York Times:

AMERICAN GIGOLO, written and directed by Paul Schrader; director of photography, John Bailey; edited by Richard Halsey; music by Giorgio Moroder; produced by Jerry Bruckhelmer; released by Paramount Pictures. At Loews State 1, Loews Orpheum and 34th Street East. Running time: 117 minutes. This film is rated R.

Julian . . . . Richard Gere
Michaelle . . . . Lauren Hutton

Sunday .... Hector Elizando
Ann .... Nina Van Pallandt

Others set no particular pattern for critics to follow in writing their stories. If anything, these stories could be described as essays, a form that gives the writer all of the liberties in composition that they could expect. The first person is permitted and often used, because the critic is writing under his by-line.

The average small newspaper does not offer too many opportunities for a beginning reporter to develop his critical faculties. But a reporter interested in developing as a critic will benefit greatly by reading the works of other critics— especially good ones—and analyzing all of the devices and techniques they use. The beginning critic should strive for his own writing style, one that reflects his character. He should not try to copy the style of another critic.

SUBJECTS FOR CRITICISM

Books and Articles. Most metropolitan dailies have book-review columns or pages. They generally are a part of the Sunday or weekend edition. The public looks to the local critic not only to help mold its taste but also to enable it to guide its selection of books. The critic has an opportunity to promote the use of libraries and otherwise to stimulate cultural activities. The active critic will not confine his attention to new books coming to his desk.

29d

In judging a book, the critic must not lean too heavily upon the publisher's *blurb,* which is issued in publicizing the book. He should not write his review from the notes on the dust jacket, a practice many authors insist is commonplace. Blurbs or the dust jacket notes can be used as aids, and the critic may find that he agrees with some of their claims, but they should not influence the critic's own appraisal.

Here are several leads from book reviews:

Another Kind of Autumn by Loren Eiseley (Scribner's $8.95)

Harriet Van Horne said it best: A friend I never knew died last weekend. Let me paraphrase it: A friend I met only once died a few weeks ago. There is a large hole where he vanished. One can only hope that as with those problematical black holes in space, there is a compensating white hole in some far part of the universe where his energies are a source of never-ending wonder.

Loren Eiseley is the name of the friend met only once, a shy man, seemingly unaware of his genius. His new and last book of poetry is properly titled "Another Kind of Autumn." Autumn was always in his work, as was poetry. His earliest essays, 30 years ago in *Harper's,* struck an awe into me that never stopped, but went on from article to article, prose-poem to prose-poem and finally to his poetry itself, the poems with brightness in them, but with autumn marrowing the light . . .

[RAY BRADBURY, LOS ANGELES TIMES]

Chance Meetings, by William Saroyan. New York: W. W. Norton $8.95

William Saroyan once estimated he had met a million people. In New York City, in Paris. On buses, on shipboard, at work, at play. Family members, school friends, poets, wrestlers, used-book salesmen, phonies, bullies. And he seems to be saying, with Will Rogers, "I never met a man I didn't like."

At seventy, and still meeting, Saroyan remembers those he meets, because he tends "to react intensely to everything and everybody I reach."

His mother, Takoohi of Bitlis, daughter of Lucy and Mimas Saroyan, "had the greatest skill of mimicry, of impersonation, of caricature I ever saw in action: every person she met she nailed instantly to his mark; in appearance, stance, movement, speech, silence, gesture and quality."

In "Chance Meetings" Takoohi's son William does a pretty good job of nailing himself . . .

[VICTOR HAWES, THE CHRISTIAN SCIENCE MONITOR]

Movies. For the young writer, movies present one of the best opportunities to develop as a critic or reviewer. A student interested in this type writing would benefit greatly from some of the film courses now being offered at many colleges and universities. He should also study the works of a wide range of critics writing for major newspapers and magazines as well as the many excellent collections of movie reviews in book form. The collected reviews of James Agee, for example, are excellent for style, form and critical judgment. And the works of Pauline Kael, film critic for *The New Yorker,* should not be overlooked.

Too often newspaper writers who report on films content themselves with simple reviewing, but there is an opportunity for conscientious criticism in the manner of Agee and Kael. The critic has an opportunity to do more than promote audiences. He can exert much influence upon the medium, and can help bring about a higher type of entertainment. In the final analysis the moviegoer is the one who really determines the fare offered. However, an effective critic can do much to refine the moviegoer's taste.

A movie reviewer or critic should prepare for the job by studying the works of the great critics while making every effort to keep current on the economic as well as the artistic trends in the film industry.

Although the temptation might be great, a reviewer or critic should resist seeking to make a name for himself through snide and devastating comments. A review or critique should be an honest and fair evaluation of the work. Criticism is not synonymous with slurs. A fair critic—one who gains the respect and even the admiration of his readers—is not constantly negative and neither does he forever praise every film he sees. Few works are entirely good or entirely bad. A reader who has been misled by a reviewer or critic generally ceases to be a reader.

Here are the leads from several movie reviews:

If "The Black Hole" represents a step in the right direction for Disney, the silly and crass "Midnight Madness" does not.

It is yet another of those collegiate comedies made in the wake of "Animal House" that dubiously equates grossness with hilarity, thus overlooking the key ingredients of Animal House's success: inspiration and imagination . . .

[KEVIN THOMAS, LOS ANGELES TIMES]

"Manhattan" is a distillation of Woody Allen's art—a black and white Valentine to his hometown, a comic triumph and a sensitive look at the human inability to fill the gaps between our individual personalities.

This is "Annie Hall" grown complete and tough, "Interiors" on ground elevated by a sense of humor. Where some filmmakers have peaked and faded under the demands of vision and distance, Allen has made a career of evolving into higher forms . . .

[THOMAS FOX, THE COMMERCIAL APPEAL, MEMPHIS]

Television, Radio, Recordings. The wire services and most feature syndicates sell special columns and features on television, radio and popular recordings. However, many newspapers also have a staff television-radio columnist or writer. Often these columns are devoted to program announcement and information about local or regional personalities and programs. But a number of the columnists also write critical reviews, especially of new programs, major dramatic presentations and specials.

The same basic standards for all critical writing apply to television and radio as well. The criticism should be fair and just and the critical comments should be supported. It is never enough to say a program, an actor, a comedian is good or bad. The writer has to tell why and give examples.

Television plays a major role in the lives of millions of persons daily, and it should be written about as the serious social phenomeneon it is. A critic who contents himself with dashing off flippant reviews of his least favorite program is shirking his responsibilities.

When recordings became a growth industry, many newspapers began their own record column, using a staff writer with some musical training or purchasing columns for the feature services. In many cases the job was turned over to someone on the staff who also was the critic or reviewer of live musical performances. The stars of the music field—especially the popular music stars—are national and international heroes to their fans, and a reporter who attempts to write about them and their work must be knowledgeable or risk the wrath of legions of irate fans. A performer's work should not be dismissed or denigrated simply because it does not please the taste of the reviewer. In addition to evaluating the performance, the reporter writing about recordings also has a responsibility to keep the public informed on the best in new recordings. He should also report on the many fads, trends and other changes in the field. A thoughtful critic can do much to elevate the taste of his readers.

Here are several examples of reviews of television and recording reviews:

> Six hours are probably not excessive to commemorate 31 years of entertaining U.S. troops. But it does make for tortuous viewing. And so the first three hours of last Sunday's "Bob Hope's Overseas Christmas Tours: Around the World with the Troops (1941–1972)" on NBC was almost as unwieldy as its title . . .
>
> [HOWARD ROSENBERG, LOS ANGELES TIMES]

> Some musical marriages are made in heaven, but the pairing of violinist Arthur Grumiaux and pianist Claudio Arrau must have been hatched in purgatory. Their performances on Phillips of Beethoven's Sonata No. 1 and Sonata No. 5 (Spring) constantly find both men working at cross purposes . . .
>
> [LARRY KART, CHICAGO TRIBUNE]

Live Performances—Music, Drama, Dance, Lectures. The most sensitive job **29f** of the critic always is his appraisal of the work of performers when he sees them in person. In other forms of the fine arts he views their work at long range, so to speak; in live performances he must be a careful observer as well as a listener. And he must learn to translate such relative words as "good" and "bad," "adequate" and "inadequate" into visual words that re-create in the reader's mind what the critic saw on the stage or platform. While it may not be necessary to be quite as graphic as Alexander Wollcott, who once described an actress as being "as nervous as a pregnant fox in a forest fire," it is necessary to call up visual images for the reader.

What has been said about critical writing in regard to movies applies to live performances. But the critic of a live performance may have to make certain allowances for unpleasant conditions of the presentation that are the fault of local facilities (which he should point out). Certainly he should not pounce or dwell upon a minor defect if the performance as a whole is superior. Nor should he compare a star's live performance with his appearance in a film, which has been shorn of imperfections, it is to be hoped, by the film editor.

On the other hand, because a star should be expected to perform like a professional, the critic has full rights to give an honest appraisal of a local appearance. If the performance is shoddy, the critic certainly should say so. He owes it to the reader who attended and those who may be planning to attend.

If it is a stage play, especially a new one, the critic should evaluate how well the author achieved his purpose. If it is a performance of a widely known work, comparisons can be made with interpretations by other performers. The same applies to new music or a new dance.

As was pointed out earlier, performances of amateurs are not to be judged by professional standards. A critic should not praise every amateur production out of a sense of loyalty, nor should he attack it viciously. He can (and should) be as encouraging as he is critical.

Many critics or reviewers try to develop a personalized style in their writing. Since first-person writing is an acceptable form in reviewing, critics often write highly personal reactions to performances.

Here are several examples of leads from reviews of live performances:

Broadway virtuosity doesn't just run rampant on the wide-open stage of the Broadhurst Theater. It leaps and glides. It whirls, twirls, and swaggers. It tap-dances and boogies and turns cartwheels. Bob Fosse is the shaker and mover of this boundlessly energetic entertainment. "Dancin' " is its title. And at its best, "Dancin' " is entrancin'.

Sixteen sensationally gifted dancers are set in motion by Mr. Fosse for this choreographic spectacular . . .

[JOHN BEAUFORT, THE CHRISTIAN SCIENCE MONITOR]

The Act at last completed its broken-field run across the country, bouncing off bad reviews, to fling itself gasping across the goal line onto Broadway. Touchdown? No; someone forgot to give Lisa Minnelli the ball—a shot, that is. But Liza's run to daylight is unquestionably the trajectory of a star. At $25 top ticket, it had better be.

Like nature, a true star abhors a vacuum, and Liza hurls herself into her vacuous material with demonic cheerfulness, You've never seen anyone work so hard on a stage before . . .

[JACK KROLL, NEWSWEEK]

Art—Paintings, Sculptures, Photographs. The art critic must be versatile in his knowledge of the different forms and various interpretations of art. One who is prejudiced for or against any distinctive interpretation will obviously find it difficult to be a fair judge. Before the critic ventures to assess the worth of a production, he should understand not only what the artist sought to do but also how well the artist succeeded in his efforts.

Here are several examples of art and photography review leads:

> "Photography Rediscovered," the large show of American images currently at the Art Institute, is one of the best photography exhibitions to appear in town.
>
> It was organized last year for the Whitney Museum by the Institute's curator of photography, David Travis. And there are few better ways to acknowledge the decade's involvement with the medium than by viewing 241 prime examples . . .
>
> [ALAN G. ARTNER, CHICAGO TRIBUNE]

> The exhibition that Margit Rowell has organized at the Solomon R. Guggenheim Museum under the title "Ad Reinhardt and Color" is, in several respects, an unusual event. It is not the sort of retrospective that surveys an artist's entire oeuvre.
>
> Reinhardt, who died in 1967 at the age of 53, was one of the founding members of the New York School, and it was expected that sooner or later there would be another museum retrospective of his work. (The last one in New York was the exhibition at the Jewish Museum in the winter of 1966–67). But this is not what Miss Rowell has chosen to give us.
>
> She concentrates instead on 32 paintings—mainly the red, blue and black abstract paintings that Reinhardt produced in the years 1948–66 . . .
>
> [HILTON KRAMER, THE NEW YORK TIMES]

EXERCISES

1. Using any newspaper available to you, clip a review and a critical review of a movie, television show, book, play, popular or classical concert or art exhibit. Underline the phrases in the critical review that put it in that category. Evaluate the critical review from the standpoint of the "principles" given in this chapter.
2. Obtain a copy of the book *Agee on Film,* by James Agee, from a library. Compare the reviews of several movies he wrote when he was critic for *Time* magazine and *The Nation* at the same time. How do they differ in form and in writing style?
3. Compare three movie reviews appearing in a daily newspaper with three appearing in such magazines as *Time, Newsweek* and *The New Yorker.* Analyze them. How do they differ in form and in writing style?
4. Invite a director and an actor from the drama department or a theatrical company in your area to class for an interview on what they think of critics. Write a story on that interview.
5. Write a review or critical review, as assigned by your instructor, of the following:
   A. A motion picture
   B. A television program
   C. An art show
   D. A book
   E. A live musical performance
   F. A live dramatic performance

     G. The architecture of some building on campus

     H. A collection of photographs

     I. A new record album

6. Check the card catalog of your college or community library for books that are collections of criticism of movies, art, architecture, music and so forth. (Several collections of Pauline Kael's movie reviews have been issued.) Study each reviewer's writing style. Compare it to the style used in reviews that appear in newspapers in your area. Write an essay comparing the styles.

7. Locate a copy of *Book Review Digest* in your college or community library. Compare the reviews of several current books. Analyze the writing style of the reviewers.

Editorials and Columns

Although the editorial page has undergone a much-needed revival in recent years, it is still one of the most maligned parts of the American newspaper. It regularly draws the anger of readers who disagree with the editor's point of view. And it is usually held in contempt by media critics, who insist that at best it is timid and at worst useless.

There are almost as many opinions of what an editorial page should be as there are editors. Essentially the editorial page deals with news but it is written from a different viewpoint. Here the editor and his editorial writers, columnists, cartoonists and other specialists are commenting on the same subjects that appear on other pages of the newspaper—especially the front page. The reporter may be called upon to cooperate with the editorial page staff by providing background information, and if he is the best-informed staff member on a given subject he may be asked to write an occasional editorial.

The editorial page represents journalism as practiced in its early days, the days of "personal journalism" when the editor interpreted current events as he saw them, and when readers were about as familiar with the name of the editor as with the name of the newspaper. In that era, the policies and opinion of the editor for or against a public issue or candidate were known by the readers, recognizable through the editor's presentation of the news. Coverage of the Civil War is a classic example. And during the presidential campaign that followed there could be no doubt where the editor of the Chicago Times stood on Gen. Ulysses Grant's candidacy. Here is part of his comment after Grant received the Republican nomination:

> Hiram Ulysses Grant, did you resign your commission in the army in 1853, for fear that you would be court-martialed for conduct unbecoming an officer and a gentleman? Did you scandalously foul a soup tureen? Was it your habit frequently to get into a state of beastly intoxication when you were living on a farm of your father-

in-law, General Dent, near St. Louis? In Galena, were you supported by charity of your father and brother, although you were then in good health? Were you intoxicated on the day of the battle of Belmont? Were you intoxicated on the day of the battle of Shiloh? . . . Is it true as charged by . . . prominent members of the Republican party that you "cannot stand before a bottle of whisky without falling down?" . . . Did you get into a controversy with President Johnson in which was mixed a question of veracity and did you come out of that controversy branded a liar and as a man who was guilty of an act of inexpressible meanness and dishonor?

Perhaps it is because most editorial writers refrain from such direct, slashing attacks that they are branded as being timid by media critics. As modern journalism evolved from those early personalized newspapers, the news was presented in a more objective (and, presumably, more accurate) manner by reporters. The editor, however, retained his right to express his opinions and state his policies—on the editorial page. The by-lined opinion column developed early in the twentieth century as an adjunct to the editorial page.

A major criticism through the years has always been that the editorial page was a closed shop—that only the editor's opinion was expressed and that editors often printed only columnists who reflected their own point of view. To counteract this criticism, a number of newspapers began searching for ways to bring a more diverse set of opinions to the public. If a newspaper was politically liberal, it might run a conservative column regularly, for example. Others tried for liberal, conservative and middle-of-the-road comment from columnists. One of the most successful has been the New York Times, which introduced an Op-Ed page and deliberately sought views of persons who differed from the newspaper's stand on public issues. Political, social, religious and academic leaders are asked to write articles for the page. Often the newspaper presents side by side the views of two persons who differ on a particular issue. And in its editorials, on the opposite page, the newspaper's editorial writers may present still another point of view.

30a This is also an outgrowth of the concept that on the modern editorial page the readers have a right to express their opinions, and they may "talk back" to editors and columnists. They do this in "letters to the editor" which are used in increasing numbers for both daily and weekly editors. The National Observer, published by Dow Jones & Company, from time to time, urged its readers to express their views on controversial issues. And on several occasions the letters were used to cover the front page and then continued on several inside pages. Only bona fide, signed letters are generally used, and the editor reserves the right to reject a letter or to reduce its length in order to meet space limitations or to abide by the journalistic code of ethics or the laws of libel. In a sense, each of these letters is an editorial, but it is an expression of the opinions of a reader instead of the editor.

Although editorials' normally do not carry by-lines, they are understood to be statements of the editor—whose name usually appears in the newspaper's *masthead*. The editor may use contributions of special editorial writers or reprint editorials from other newspapers, but he still assumes responsibility for the views expressed in all editorials. The "editorial we" in the regular editorial section refers to the editor.

With by-line columns, however, the situation is different. While these often appear on the editorial page (but also appear on sports page, entertainment page and elsewhere), the editor does not necessarily agree with the views expressed by the writer. Statements in regular editorials are sometimes quite contrary to statements in by-line columns. As pointed out earlier, publishers today assume that a newspaper has a social responsibility to seek out and publish the opinions of writers who effectively represent all points of view which citizens of a democracy deserve to know. Usually the by-line writer uses the first-person "I," but if he uses the "editorial we" he is still referring to himself alone.

Both the editorial and the by-line column represent personal journalism and have some things in common (personal opinion), but other characteristics are different. Such differences are brought out in the sections that follow.

EDITORIALS

It is essential for the writer to recognize that there is no formula for writing editorials. They will vary widely, depending upon the writing style of the editor. But a good editorial is a carefully constructed analytical essay in which the writer explains, interprets and appraises an event or public issue. It should not be simply a restatement of an issue with a few lines of criticism or comment tacked on the end. Following are some generalized statements about the attributes, purposes, value and content of editorials that can serve as guidelines for editorial writers.

Attributes of Editorials. To comment on current events, editorials should be timely. Readers are more interested in news than in history, unless there is a historical tie-in to the day's news. What happened today affects them today, and they are open to suggestions and opinions on such matters. This factor dovetails with the second essential attribute—consequence. Minor news stories rarely make interesting editorials. The editorial writer usually may choose from a large selection of important events—events that attract and affect a large number of readers. The current issues and problems arising from events, rather than events themselves, form the subject matter for editorials.

Value of Editorials. The editorial is valuable to both the newspaper and the reader. It gives the newspaper a chance to present its policies and beliefs without coloring the regular news stories with biased statements. If the newspaper believes taxes are high, it can carry on a campaign to try to get them lowered, using every timely opportunity that arises to present its arguments. The newspaper's appraisal of local, state, national and international events can be offered effectively in this manner.

On the other hand, readers benefit by the expert interpretations and opinions on current events offered by the well-informed editorial writer. The key here is "expert." The editorial writer must be a trained thinker, a keen student of society and a skilled interpreter if he is to be believed and respected. His work requires knowledge in many fields as well as patience and aptitude for careful research. The average reader—who spends somewhere between 30 and 45 minutes a day reading his newspapers—does not have the time or the ability to unravel the complexities of day-by-day events. He does not have the general background and knowledge to know if the city really will benefit from a pro-

30b

ST. LOUIS POST-DISPATCH

Founded by JOSEPH PULITZER
December 12, 1878

THE POST-DISPATCH PLATFORM

I KNOW THAT MY RETIREMENT WILL MAKE NO DIFFERENCE IN ITS CARDINAL PRINCIPLES, THAT IT WILL ALWAYS FIGHT FOR PROGRESS AND REFORM, NEVER TOLERATE INJUSTICE OR CORRUPTION, ALWAYS FIGHT DEMAGOGUES OF ALL PARTIES, NEVER BELONG TO ANY PARTY, ALWAYS OPPOSE PRIVILEGED CLASSES AND PUBLIC PLUNDERERS, NEVER LACK SYMPATHY WITH THE POOR, ALWAYS REMAIN DEVOTED TO THE PUBLIC WELFARE, NEVER BE SATISFIED WITH MERELY PRINTING NEWS, ALWAYS BE DRASTICALLY INDEPENDENT, NEVER BE AFRAID TO ATTACK WRONG, WHETHER BY PREDATORY PLUTOCRACY OR PREDATORY POVERTY.

JOSEPH PULITZER

April 10, 1907

Friday October 26, 1979

letters

Rape Stand Praised

Gov. Teasdale has been receiving criticism, but there's one thing he's trying to do that I think he should be commended for — the plan to alter state laws on rape. The law says that a convicted rapist using a weapon can be sentenced to life in prison. A rapist not using a weapon can only be sentenced to 15 years in prison. The new thinking is to move the sentence to life imprisonment regardless of whether a weapon was used.

Many rapists are second offenders. I feel this is made possible because of the lax laws of this state. If the penalty was stiff enough, there would hardly be any second offenders. Also, a stiffer penalty would give a would-be rapist a lot more to think about.

I see this new rape proposal as a very good thing and hope that it is put into action very quickly.

Perez Eric Maxwell

Restoring A Railroad

The last great transcontinental railway built in this country was the Milwaukee Road. In 1906, it already had its rails built from Chicago to the Missouri River.

In the same year the railroad began the extension that finally took it to the Pacific Coast at Seattle. This gave it the distinction of being the only railroad that owned its own rails from Chicago to Seattle.

Now this great road is bankrupt. Why did the Interstate Commerce Commission permit this to happen?

Several years ago, I was one of the first engineers to propose that we create a Department of Transportation. The purpose of this agency was to regulate and coordinate all forms of transportation. To say the least, this department has done a sorry job.

It is now up to Congress to re-establish the Milwaukee Road in the interest of our national defense.

Vernon N. Pyle

Belleville

Diet Pill Article

The Oct. 21 front page article on diet pills by Roger Signor was barely newsworthy, much less front-page material.

If one read the entire article one would find that two women died who happened to be taking diet pills. However the cause of death was from choking and massive heart damage, possibly a congenital condition.

Surely the *Post-Dispatch* can present a better story on its front page in a more unbiased manner.

Jo Ann Berg

Time For Children

So much of the argument for Sunday sales seems to be based on the fact that Illinois does it, Kansas City does it, etc. Remember when your children came to you and said, "John is going to stay out until 3 o'clock in the morning, why can't I?" And you would say, "Just because John does it, doesn't make it right!"

Our society has become so money conscious that we are losing sight of some of our most important traditions. Parents have little enough time with their children these days.

As a volunteer in an elementary school in St. Louis County, I can tell you the children need more "family" time. My husband has had to work weekends for years, with his "weekend" during the week.

This has made a great difference in our family activities and I would not recommend it to anyone.

Let's stop and think a little beyond our pocketbooks. It is important for our children, for our families, and for our country.

Betty Heitzler

Manchester

Disappointed

I was surprised and disappointed that President Carter wasn't given the Nobel Peace Prize. If anyone ever earned it, he did.

I believe it was because of widespread prejudice against him in Europe that he was denied the honor. I think that Europeans don't have any idea of how difficult it is to be president of this country today. They especially blame the president because Americans use too much oil, which raises the price for Europeans too.

I think they are also influenced by the fact that he is criticized so much in this country. It may be that they presume from that that he is not a good president and therefore can't be deserving of any kind of prize.

Mother Teresa is well deserving of recognition for her nobility of spirit, but that should not preclude consideration of President Carter's significant contribution to peace in the Middle East, which is so important to all of us.

June Lund

[illegible]

2B

editorials

Ahead With The Alton Lock

A federal judge's ruling that a new Alton dam and lock system may be constructed has been met with relief in the St. Louis area and is equally good news for the vast Mississippi River basin economy.

The dam was first proposed 20 years ago. For five years it has been the target of a suit by railroads and environmental groups, which helped to delay congressional authorization until last year. During all that delay, construction costs once estimated at $493 million have escalated, and commercial traffic bottlenecks have grown at the outmoded Locks and Dam 26.

The importance of this lock is that it feeds barge and other river traffic into and out of both the Mississippi and Illinois rivers. Thus it carries a vast proportion of Midwestern grain from the farms and other commodities to the cities of the nation's largest inland river system and to its ocean and lake ports. It has been called "the gateway to America's breadbasket." Yet that gateway has become a kind of blockade. Commercial tows sometimes face 80-hour delays because of traffic jams. This naturally adds to shipping and consumer costs.

Hence Congress authorized a new dam about two miles downstream from the present one and a 1200-foot lock to replace the existing locks, the longest of which is 600 feet. The capacity of the new lock will be only 14 percent greater, and it might reach full capacity by the time it is finally completed. Moreover, railroads competing with the barges scored a point when the Carter administration won, as a price paid for the authorization, a logical requirement that barge lines pay modest fees for using the public waterways.

Still, 21 railroads plus the Sierra Club and Izaak Walton League persisted in their suit to halt the project. They contended that the Army Corps of Engineers had not made adequate environmental studies of the effects of the dam or of an expected increase in river traffic resulting from it.

Now U.S. District Judge Charles R. Richey, in Washington, has ruled that the Corps of Engineers did comply with the National Environmental Policy Act and that its impact statement permits an informed decision about the project. The judge said that the Corps had failed to heed its own regulations as to public hearings, and suggested that these be held, as they should be. But the effect of his decision is to permit construction to proceed.

The plaintiffs still insist that they will press their case on appeal "until we're convinced the Corps is obeying the law." They may never be convinced; their purpose was to halt the dam project. For the moment it is enough that the federal judge was convinced. The new Alton dam has been delayed far too long. The work should begin.

The Tilt Toward Peking

By sending the U.S.-China trade agreement to Congress for approval, the Carter administration formally has suspended its policy of evenhandedness toward the two communist superpowers. Given the existence of the agreement, which was signed in July and which governs a broad range of bilateral economic relations, and given the current shakiness in U.S.-Soviet ties, it probably was inevitable that Washington decided to tilt towards Peking on the issue of trade. Even so, the advantages of impartiality ought not to be lost sight of.

Although most-favored-nation (MFN) trading status is only a component of the agreement, it is the key to it. Under MFN, which would extend to China tariff advantages the U.S. offers its other trading partners, the 5,000 or so U.S. tariffs on Chinese imports will be reduced on an average from 34 percent to 7 percent of value. That should do much to increase the trade between the two countries, which last year reached $1.2 billion.

The trade laws require China, as a communist country, to make assurances of free emigration before it can receive trade concessions from the U.S. Mr. Carter, as he is authorized to, has waived that requirement and he could do the same for the Soviet Union, where Jewish emigration is running at near record levels. That would qualify the U.S.S.R., which refuses to give formal emigration assurances, for MFN. But with the strategic arms treaty still to be guided through the Senate, where anti-Soviet feelings are inflamed by disclosure of the Russian brigade in Cuba, Mr. Carter has decided against that course for now.

The circumstances at hand, however, are no brief for favoritism as a basis for foreign policy. And while there are important reasons for improving relations with China, there are even better ones for improving them with the U.S.S.R. — and not only because of its military potential. As a more developed country, it offers greater trading opportunities than does China. President Carter has veered out of necessity, but he ought to straighten out his course insofar as China and the U.S.S.R. are concerned as soon as possible.

Medical Ads

Some of the nation's medical associations and physicians who have expressed disapproval of a recent Federal Trade Commission order that allows doctors to advertise no doubt genuinely fear that the profession will never be the same. And they probably have some basis for expecting a certain amount of unflattering commercialism that they feel will tarnish the profession's image. But apart from a blow to the profession's image of itself, the FTC ruling is not likely to wreak the havoc predicted and could prove a boon for consumers. Doctors will still be judged on their competence, and the public now will have the advantage of price comparisons on routine services. In addition, the ruling ordered the American Medical Association not to interfere with doctors' ability to work for low-cost group health plans by branding such as "unethical."

The AMA, however, will still be allowed to regulate deceptive ads, and can impose ethical guidelines on the advertising. Certainly maintenance of high standards is vital for the sake of all concerned, but the standards that the AMA settles upon ought to be watched carefully to see that they do not encourage monopolistic practices and are not unduly restrictive.

Hot County Dirt

Several north St. Louis County communities are trying to decide what should be done about 20,000 tons of radioactive dirt at a site in Hazelwood. The owners of the land say they were not aware that it contained dangerous radioactive material. They have been working with the Nuclear Regulatory Commission for three years to devise a decontamination plan.

The NRC has approved trucking the dirt to an already radioactive landfill at Lambert Field and then covering the airport site with asphalt and using it for police driver training. The NRC says the plan is safe. But then the federal government had previously assured the owners of the Hazelwood tract that the firm which had used the site for radioactive materials had cleaned it up.

Environmental, health and citizen groups have expressed alarm about the both sites — and about the presence of radioactive dirt in yet another north county landfill — because the radioactive garbage they contain releases radon — a low-level radioactive gas that attaches itself to particles in air or water and can cause cancer when it lodges in lungs or other internal organs. It was only last year that the NRC acknowledged the dirt left over from uranium mining and processing is a potential hazard for thousands of years. Even if asphalt could be maintained that long, what would prevent the hot dirt from leaching into the area's water supply? It is shameful — but hardly surprising — that the NRC, whose laxity has helped create the current situation, should be pushing so strongly for a solution that really is not a solution. All three county sites ought to be cleaned up — at federal expense. And sooner rather than later.

'No' In 28 Counties

Voters in 28 Missouri counties, including virtually all those on the St. Louis area's fringe, will be asked Nov. 6 to adopt county sales taxes at levels ranging variously from a fourth to a half cent. The sales tax is a regressive way to raise public money, bearing as it does most heavily on those least able to pay, and so each of the proposals surely merits defeat.

The proposal, which will be on the ballot in St. Charles, Franklin, Jefferson, Lincoln, Warren and nine other counties in eastern Missouri, is frankly being sold as a way of shifting some of the burden of financing local government from property owners to consumers — and out-of-county consumers at that, which is an outrage. Proponents say that about 20 percent of the tax in counties in metropolitan or resort areas will be paid by outsiders.

The scheme grows out of an enabling act approved by the Missouri Legislature. It requires that at least half of any new sales tax revenue be dedicated to reduction of county property taxes. The remainder goes into the county treasuries. But schools are generally the largest users of property taxes (as, indeed, they deserve to be). A regressive tax employed for the wrong purpose is doubly objectionable.

City Hall Relents

A triumph over City Hall is a rare experience, but it occurred when the city street director decided to revoke Eugene P. Slay's special permit to park his tractor-trailers on the street in the 2000 block of South Broadway. For six years merchants and others nearby have been annoyed by Mr. Slay's special parking privilege and their failure to get the permit rescinded until now is testimony to his enduring popularity around City Hall.

However, trustees of the South Broadway Shopping Center saw their opportunity when the *Post-Dispatch* began calling public attention to Mr. Slay's extraordinary ability to penetrate the red tape and inertia that most citizens encounter at 12th and Market, citing the special parking privilege as an example. They presented a petition to the mayor's office asking that the privilege be terminated and, lo and behold, it was. Did Mr. Slay say it was okay to do so?

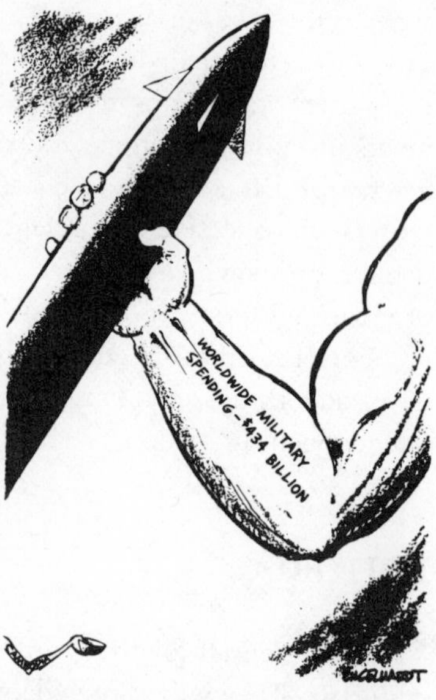

Arms

More Letters From Readers

Edward Teller's Views

At the very top of this page, the *Post-Dispatch* platform lies dormant, for on Oct. 16 the *Post* printed a personal opinion on page 8A instead of the editorial section, thus implying an actual article.

I'm referring to Dr. Edward Teller's plea for nuclear power and criticism of Ralph Nader and Jane Fonda. The headline reads as if it came out of the *National Inquirer*.

Craig Swartz

I am generally sympathetic to your newspaper and its publishing policies, but the recent printing of a pro-nuclear opinion with a two-page format disturbed and disappointed me a great deal.

Was it good editorial judgment to print such a statement, at least with its final conspicuous form? There appears to be a moral lassitude when large companies can afford to pay for a highly visible, biased "advertisement" in their interest, while the ordinary citizen finds himself or herself restricted to a scant few lines tucked away somewhere in the editorial section.

Dr. Teller cannot be faulted as a recognized authority on the technicalities of nuclear power. What he says, nonetheless, is not above debate.

Douglas E. Oakman

In referring to himself as "the only victim," Mr. Teller ignores the possibility of long-term increases in the incidence of cancer, leukemia and birth defects.

He forgets the thousands of people whose lives were interrupted, who left their homes as a precaution against harm to themselves and their children. Teller must believe this was unnecessary. Who called for that evacuation, anyway? Was it Jane Fonda, or the governor of Pennsylvania?

Andrew & Paula Ayers

Editor's note: The advertisement was identified as "sponsored by a group of companies and organizations concerned with the future of nuclear power."

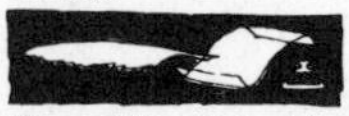

Hospital Costs Defended

I have just been provided a copy of the *Newsday* editorial reprinted Sept. 29 on hospital cost controls.

It is absolutely unbelievable to read in your newspaper that a government imposed artificial control on hospital expenditures has now been equated to "budgetary control" and to further indicate that the "measure is one familiar to people in every line of business except hospitals."

I hasten to point out to you that in recent years very few businesses with some notable exceptions such as the oil industry are at all familiar with the measure comparable to that proposed by the Carter administration.

This is not to say that business is not familiar with the sound management technique of careful budgeting and cost control, but the majority of business does not have artificial, federally imposed controls set on its finances.

To imply that hospital administrators "are free to spend as they wish regardless of cost" in the context in which the phrase is used is an illegitimate attempt to convince the public that there are no restraints on hospital spending or on the charges passed on to the public.

To make such a statement is to ignore facts which are readily determined by anyone who would care to be responsible about his or her role in the news media. The facts are that hospital rates are subject to substantial review across the country, utilizing a variety of mechanisms.

It is ironic that Blue Cross was cited as a source for making up the deficits which result from the profligate spending habits of hospital administrators.

It so happens that in Missouri Blue Cross plays a substantial role in reviewing and substantiating the necessity for increases in hospital rate structures.

Federal government reimbursement programs are based on cost reimbursement determined by eliminating all expenses not incurred on behalf of patients covered under Medicare and Medicaid and for those expenses that fall outside of benefits covered, such as patient telephones and patient television services.

I should point out the need for the *Post-Dispatch* to become acquainted with the organized statewide effort on the part of physicians and hospitals to reduce the rate of increase in hospital and health care expenses. This program is referred to as the "voluntary effort" and has made substantial strides.

The fact is that the health care related components of the Consumer Price Index over the last several months have increased at a rate substantially less than many other elements in the CPI.

A close examination of a longer term history will reflect that inflation in health care costs as reflected in the CPI over the past 20 years has increased at a lower rate than many other segments of the index.

James J. O'Connell
Executive Director
St. Mary's Hospital

Kansas City

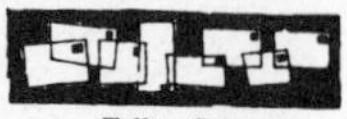

Tellico Dam

I am writing to express our appreciation for your fair and factual handling of the Tellico Dam dispute. As a result of your perceptive coverage, and that of a few other newspapers, I think many Americans realize that the battle was not fought over the snail darter alone.

Environmental groups opposed completion of the dam not only because it violates the Endangered Species Act (a finding confirmed by the U.S. Supreme Court) but because Tellico was, and is, a monstrous boondoggle.

A congressionally created Cabinet-level committee found that — apart from its environmental damage to the Little Tennessee River valley — Tellico's benefits would not equal the cost of completing it, much less its total cost.

We also opposed the Tellico exemption on grounds that it would set a terrible precedent, encouraging every congressman with a pet pork barrel project in his district to seek an exemption, regardless of environmental cost.

In capitulating to a Congress that was hoodwinked into approving the exemption, President Carter signed a Faustian pact. In exchange for his signature, he is supposed to get congressional support for a Water Resources Council (which could help stamp out worthless pork barrel projects) and a reauthorization of the Endangered Species Act without weakening amendments or further exemptions.

Thomas L. Kimball
National Wildlife Federation

Washington

A Simple Message

With the U.S. Senate apparently moving toward decisive action on the Alaska lands legislation I think a simple message should be given to Sens. Eagleton and Danforth.

It is, neither they nor we have the foresight to know how many acres should be retained for the future in their natural wild condition, uncut, uninhabited and undriven over by four wheel drive vehicles.

Therefore the next generation or two should have the right to apply their wisdom or lack of it to the disposal of the remainder of this last wild natural resource still in its original form.

Because this corner of our earth is unique and if developed can never be returned to its natural condition, let us for this generation give it the protection of the Durkin-Nelson-Roth Alaska lands bill.

The present generation has no right to claim for its own development, all but the token acreage proposed by the timber companies, the mining companies and the other developers.

W. F. Baggerman

ST. LOUIS POST-DISPATCH

[illegible]

JOSEPH PULITZER, EDITOR AND PUBLISHER 1878-1911
JOSEPH PULITZER, EDITOR AND PUBLISHER 1912-1955

JOSEPH PULITZER JR., EDITOR AND PUBLISHER
MICHAEL E. PULITZER, ASSOCIATE EDITOR
DAVID LIPMAN, MANAGING EDITOR
WILLIAM F. WOO, EDITOR OF THE EDITORIAL PAGE
G. A. CHRISTOPHER, VICE PRESIDENT AND GEN. MANAGER

Figure 30-1. The editorial page of the St. Louis Post-Dispatch is unusual because it places letters to the editor in the first column on the page. Most other major papers place the editorials in that position. Courtesy of the St. Louis Post-Dispatch.

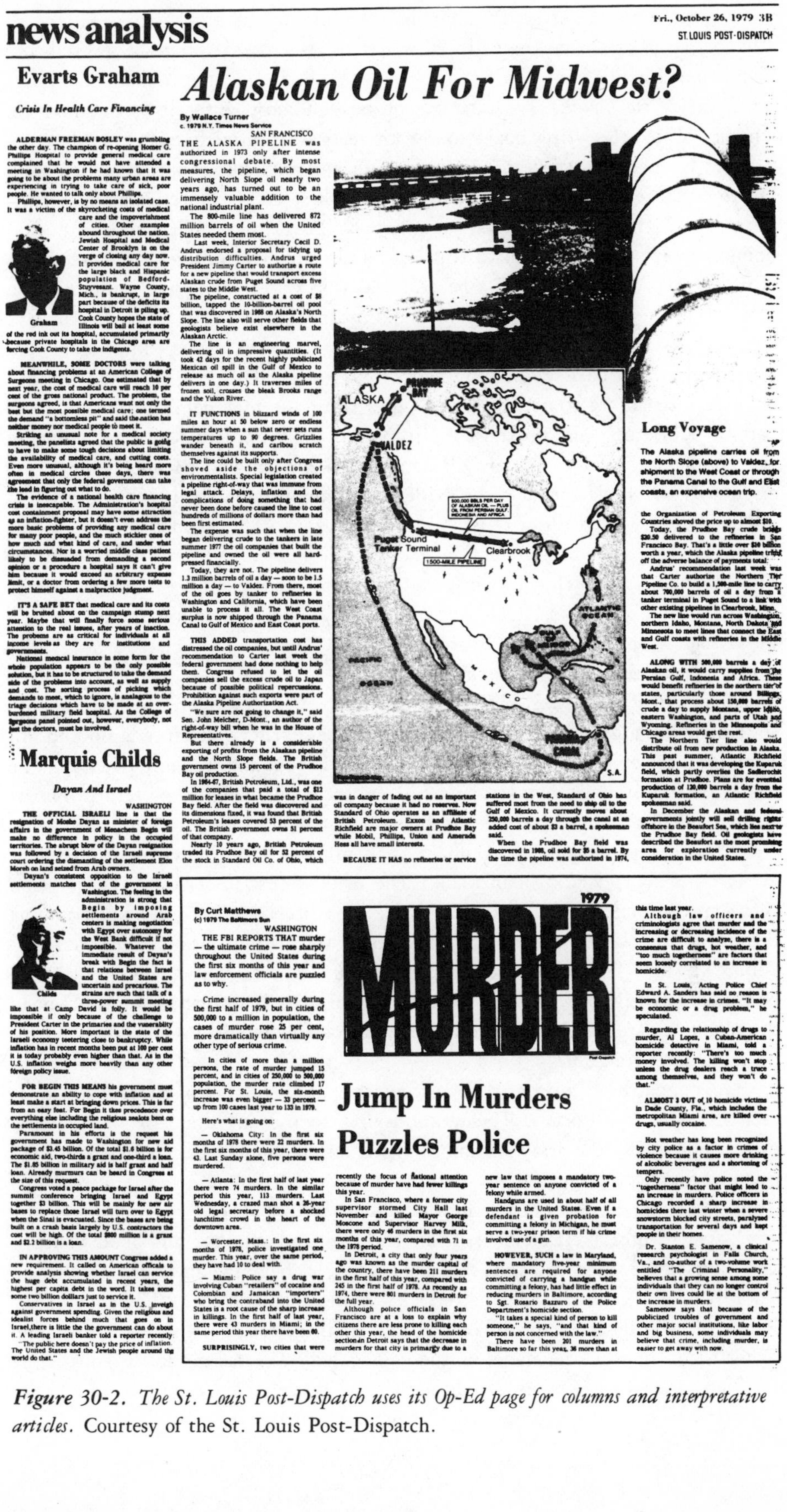

news analysis

Fri., October 26, 1979 3B
ST. LOUIS POST-DISPATCH

Evarts Graham

Crisis In Health Care Financing

ALDERMAN FREEMAN BOSLEY was grumbling the other day. The champion of re-opening Homer G. Phillips Hospital to provide general medical care complained that he would not have attended a meeting in Washington if he had known that it was going to be about the problems many urban areas are experiencing in trying to take care of sick, poor people. He wanted to talk only about Phillips.

Phillips, however, is by no means an isolated case. It was a victim of the skyrocketing costs of medical care and the impoverishment of cities. Other examples abound throughout the nation. Jewish Hospital and Medical Center of Brooklyn is on the verge of closing any day now. It provides medical care for the large black and Hispanic population of Bedford-Stuyvesant. Wayne County, Mich., is bankrupt, in large part because of the deficits its hospital in Detroit is piling up. Cook County hopes the state of Illinois will bail at least some of the red ink out its hospital, accumulated primarily because private hospitals in the Chicago area are forcing Cook County to take the indigents.

Graham

MEANWHILE, SOME DOCTORS were talking about financing problems at an American College of Surgeons meeting in Chicago. One estimated that by next year, the cost of medical care will reach 10 per cent of the gross national product. The problem, the surgeons agreed, is that Americans want not only the best but the most possible medical care; one termed the demand "a bottomless pit" and said the nation has neither money nor medical people to meet it.

Striking an unusual note for a medical society meeting, the panelists agreed that the public is going to have to make some tough decisions about limiting the availability of medical care, and cutting costs. Even more unusual, although it's being heard more often in medical circles these days, there was agreement that only the federal government can take the lead in figuring out what to do.

The evidence of a national health care financing crisis is inescapable. The Administration's hospital cost containment proposal may have some attraction as an inflation-fighter, but it doesn't even address the more basic problems of providing any medical care for many poor people, and the much stickier ones of how much and what kind of care, and under what circumstances. Nor is a worried middle class patient likely to be dissuaded from demanding a second opinion or a procedure a hospital says it can't give him because it would exceed an arbitrary expense limit, or a doctor from ordering a few more tests to protect himself against a malpractice judgment.

IT'S A SAFE BET that medical care and its costs will be bruited about on the campaign stump next year. Maybe that will finally force some serious attention to the real issues, after years of inaction. The probems are as critical for individuals at all income levels as they are for institutions and governments.

National medical insurance in some form for the whole population appears to be the only possible solution, but it has to be structured to take the demand side of the problems into account, as well as supply and cost. The sorting process of picking which demands to meet, which to ignore, is analagous to the triage decisions which have to be made at an over-burdened military field hospital. As the College of Surgeons panel pointed out, however, everybody, not just the doctors, must be involved.

Marquis Childs

Dayan And Israel

WASHINGTON

THE OFFICIAL ISRAELI line is that the resignation of Moshe Dayan as minister of foreign affairs in the government of Menachem Begin will make no difference in policy in the occupied territories. The abrupt blow of the Dayan resignation was followed by a decision of the Israeli supreme court ordering the dismantling of the settlement Elon Moreh on land seized from Arab owners.

Dayan's consistent opposition to the Israeli settlements matches that of the government in Washington. The feeling in the administration is strong that Begin by imposing settlements around Arab centers is making negotiation with Egypt over autonomy for the West Bank difficult if not impossible. Whatever the immediate result of Dayan's break with Begin the fact is that relations between Israel and the United States are uncertain and precarious. The strains are such that talk of a three-power summit meeting like that at Camp David is folly. It would be impossible if only because of the challenge to President Carter in the primaries and the vunerablity of his position. More important is the state of the Israeli economy teetering close to bankruptcy. While inflation has in recent months been put at 100 per cent it is today probably even higher than that. As in the U.S. inflation weighs more heavily than any other foreign policy issue.

Childs

FOR BEGIN THIS MEANS his government must demonstrate an ability to cope with inflation and at least make a start at bringing down prices. This is far from an easy feat. For Begin it tkes precedence over everything else including the religious zealots bent on the settlements in occupied land.

Paramount in his efforts is the request his government has made to Washington for new aid package of $3.45 billion. Of the total $1.6 billion is for economic aid, two-thirds a grant and one-third a loan. The $1.85 billion in military aid is half grant and half loan. Already murmurs can be heard in Congress at the size of this request.

Congress voted a peace package for Israel after the summit conference bringing Israel and Egypt together $3 billion. This will be mainly for new air bases to replace those Israel will turn over to Egypt when the Sinai is evacuated. Since the bases are being built on a crash basis largely by U.S. contractors the cost will be high. Of the total $800 million is a grant and $2.2 billion is a loan.

IN APPROVING THIS AMOUNT Congress added a new requirement. It called on American officals to provide analysis showing whether Israel can service the huge debt accumulated in recent years, the highest per capita debt in the word. It takes some some two billion dolllars just to service it.

Conservatives in Israel as in the U.S. inveigh against government spending. Given the religious and idealist forces behind much that goes on in Israel,there is little the the government can do about it. A leading Israeli banker told a reporter recently:

"The public here doesn't pay the price of inflation. The United States and the Jewish people around the world do that."

Alaskan Oil For Midwest?

By Wallace Turner
c. 1979 N.Y. Times News Service

SAN FRANCISCO

THE ALASKA PIPELINE was authorized in 1973 only after intense congressional debate. By most measures, the pipeline, which began delivering North Slope oil nearly two years ago, has turned out to be an immensely valuable addition to the national industrial plant.

The 800-mile line has delivered 872 million barrels of oil when the United States needed them most.

Last week, Interior Secretary Cecil D. Andrus endorsed a proposal for tidying up distribution difficulties. Andrus urged President Jimmy Carter to authorize a route for a new pipeline that would transport excess Alaskan crude from Puget Sound across five states to the Middle West.

The pipeline, constructed at a cost of $8 billion, tapped the 10-billion-barrel oil pool that was discovered in 1968 on Alaska's North Slope. The line also will serve other fields that geologists believe exist elsewhere in the Alaskan Arctic.

The line is an engineering marvel, delivering oil in impressive quantities. (It took 42 days for the recent highly publicized Mexican oil spill in the Gulf of Mexico to release as much oil as the Alaska pipeline delivers in one day.) It traverses miles of frozen soil, crosses the bleak Brooks range and the Yukon River.

IT FUNCTIONS in blizzard winds of 100 miles an hour at 50 below zero or endless summer days when a sun that never sets runs temperatures up to 90 degrees. Grizzlies wander beneath it, and caribou scratch themselves against its supports.

The line could be built only after Congress shoved aside the objections of environmentalists. Special legislation created a pipeline right-of-way that was immune from legal attack. Delays, inflation and the complications of doing something that had never been done before caused the line to cost hundreds of millions of dollars more than had been first estimated.

The expense was such that when the line began delivering crude to the tankers in late summer 1977 the oil companies that built the pipeline and owned the oil were all hard-pressed financially.

Today, they are not. The pipeline delivers 1.3 million barrels of oil a day — soon to be 1.5 million a day — to Valdez. From there, most of the oil goes by tanker to refineries in Washington and California, which have been unable to process it all. The West Coast surplus is now shipped through the Panama Canal to Gulf of Mexico and East Coast ports.

THIS ADDED transportation cost has distressed the oil companies, but until Andrus' recommendation to Carter last week the federal government had done nothing to help them. Congress refused to let the oil companies sell the excess crude oil to Japan because of possible political repercussions. Prohibition against such exports were part of the Alaska Pipeline Authorization Act.

"We sure are not going to change it," said Sen. John Melcher, D-Mont., an author of the right-of-way bill when he was in the House of Representatives.

But there already is a considerable exporting of profits from the Alaskan pipeline and the North Slope fields. The British government owns 15 percent of the Prudhoe Bay oil production.

In 1964-67, British Petroleum, Ltd., was one of the companies that paid a total of $12 million for leases in what became the Prudhoe Bay field. After the field was discovered and its dimensions fixed, it was found that British Petroleum's leases covered 53 percent of the oil. The British government owns 51 percent of that company.

Nearly 10 years ago, British Petroleum traded its Prudhoe Bay oil for 52 percent of the stock in Standard Oil Co. of Ohio, which was in danger of fading out as an important oil company because it had no reserves. Now Standard of Ohio operates as an affiliate of British Petroleum. Exxon and Atlantic Richfield are major owners at Prudhoe Bay while Mobil, Phillips, Union and Amerada Hess all have small interests.

BECAUSE IT HAS no refineries or service stations in the West, Standard of Ohio has suffered most from the need to ship oil to the Gulf of Mexico. It currently moves about 250,000 barrels a day through the canal at an added cost of about $3 a barrel, a spokesman said.

When the Prudhoe Bay field was discovered in 1968, oil sold for $5 a barrel. By the time the pipeline was authorized in 1974, the Organization of Petroleum Exporting Countries shoved the price up to almost $10.

Today, the Prudhoe Bay crude brings $20.50 delivered to the refineries in San Francisco Bay. That's a little over $10 billion worth a year, which the Alaska pipeline trims off the adverse balance of payments total.

Andrus' recommendation last week was that Carter authorize the Northern Tier Pipeline Co. to build a 1,500-mile line to carry about 700,000 barrels of oil a day from a tanker terminal in Puget Sound to a link with other existing pipelines in Clearbrook, Minn.

The new line would run across Washington, northern Idaho, Montana, North Dakota and Minnesota to meet lines that connect the East and Gulf coasts with refineries in the Middle West.

ALONG WITH 500,000 barrels a day of Alaskan oil, it would carry supplies from the Persian Gulf, Indonesia and Africa. These would benefit refineries in the northern tier of states, particularly those around Billings, Mont., that process about 150,000 barrels of crude a day to supply Montana, upper Idaho, eastern Washington, and parts of Utah and Wyoming. Refineries in the Minneapolis and Chicago areas would get the rest.

The Northern Tier line also would distribute oil from new production in Alaska. This past summer, Atlantic Richfield announced that it was developing the Kuparuk field, which partly overlies the Sadlerochit formation at Prudhoe. Plans are for eventual production of 120,000 barrels a day from the Kuparuk formation, an Atlantic Richfield spokesman said.

In December the Alaskan and federal governments jointly will sell drilling rights offshore in the Beaufort Sea, which lies next to the Prudhoe Bay field. Oil geologists have described the Beaufort as the most promising area for exploration currently under consideration in the United States.

Long Voyage

The Alaska pipeline carries oil from the North Slope (above) to Valdez, for shipment to the West Coast or through the Panama Canal to the Gulf and East coasts, an expensive ocean trip.

1979 MURDER

Jump In Murders Puzzles Police

By Curt Matthews
(c) 1979 The Baltimore Sun

WASHINGTON

THE FBI REPORTS THAT murder — the ultimate crime — rose sharply throughout the United States during the first six months of this year and law enforcement officials are puzzled as to why.

Crime increased generally during the first half of 1979, but in cities of 500,000 to a million in population, the cases of murder rose 25 per cent, more dramatically than virtually any other type of serious crime.

In cities of more than a million persons, the rate of murder jumped 15 percent, and in cities of 250,000 to 500,000 population, the murder rate climbed 17 percent. For St. Louis, the six-month increase was even bigger — 33 percent — up from 100 cases last year to 133 in 1979.

Here's what is going on:

— Oklahoma City: In the first six months of 1978 there were 22 murders. In the first six months of this year, there were 43. Last Sunday alone, five persons were murdered.

— Atlanta: In the first half of last year there were 74 murders. In the similar period this year, 113 murders. Last Wednesday, a crazed man shot a 26-year old legal secretary before a shocked lunchtime crowd in the heart of the downtown area.

— Worcester, Mass.: In the first six months of 1978, police investigated one murder. This year, over the same period, they have had 10 to deal with.

— Miami: Police say a drug war involving Cuban "retailers" of cocaine and Colombian and Jamaican "importers" who bring the contraband into the United States is a root cause of the sharp increase in killings. In the first half of last year, there were 43 murders in Miami; in the same period this year there have been 60.

SURPRISINGLY, two cities that were recently the focus of national attention because of murder have had fewer killings this year.

In San Francisco, where a former city supervisor stormed City Hall last November and killed Mayor George Moscone and Supervisor Harvey Milk, there were only 46 murders in the first six months of this year, compared with 71 in the 1978 period.

In Detroit, a city that only four years ago was known as the murder capital of the country, there have been 211 murders in the first half of this year, compared with 245 in the first half of 1978. As recently as 1974, there were 801 murders in Detroit for the full year.

Although police officials in San Francisco are at a loss to explain why citizens there are less prone to killing each other this year, the head of the homicide section in Detroit says that the decrease in murders for that city is primarily due to a new law that imposes a mandatory two-year sentence on anyone convicted of a felony while armed.

Handguns are used in about half of all murders in the United States. Even if a defendant is given probation for committing a felony in Michigan, he must serve a two-year prison term if his crime involved use of a gun.

HOWEVER, SUCH a law in Maryland, where mandatory five-year minimum sentences are required for anyone convicted of carrying a handgun while committing a felony, has had little effect in reducing murders in Baltimore, according to Sgt. Rosario Bazzuro of the Police Department's homicide section.

"It takes a special kind of person to kill someone," he says, "and that kind of person is not concerned with the law."

There have been 201 murders in Baltimore so far this year, 36 more than at this time last year.

Although law officers and criminologists agree that murder and the increasing or decreasing incidence of the crime are difficult to analyze, there is a consensus that drugs, hot weather, and "too much togetherness" are factors that seem loosely correlated to an increase in homicide.

In St. Louis, Acting Police Chief Edward A. Sanders has said no reason is known for the increase in crimes. "It may be economic or a drug problem," he speculated.

Regarding the relationship of drugs to murder, Al Lopez, a Cuban-American homicide detective in Miami, told a reporter recently: "There's too much money involved. The killing won't stop unless the drug dealers reach a truce among themselves, and they won't do that."

ALMOST 3 OUT of 10 homicide victims in Dade County, Fla., which includes the metropolitan Miami area, are killed over drugs, usually cocaine.

Hot weather has long been recognized by city police as a factor in crimes of violence because it causes more drinking of alcoholic beverages and a shortening of tempers.

Only recently have police noted the "togetherness" factor that might lead to an increase in murders. Police officers in Chicago recorded a sharp increase in homicides there last winter when a severe snowstorm blocked city streets, paralyzed transportation for several days and kept people in their homes.

Dr. Stanton E. Samenow, a clinical research psychologist in Falls Church, Va., and co-author of a two-volume work entitled "The Criminal Personality," believes that a growing sense among some individuals that they can no longer control their own lives could lie at the bottom of the increase in murders.

Samenow says that because of the publicized troubles of government and other major social institutions, like labor and big business, some individuals may believe that crime, including murder, is easier to get away with now.

Figure 30-2. The St. Louis Post-Dispatch uses its Op-Ed page for columns and interpretative articles. Courtesy of the St. Louis Post-Dispatch.

posed new eight-lane street through the heart of the business district. He has to rely to a large extent on the editorial writer to research the proposal and tell him if it is worthwhile.

30c   *Types of Editorials.* The ultimate purpose of most editorials is to convince, whether or not the writer hopes to stir his readers to immediate action. An analogy can be made between an editorial writer and an attorney speaking to a jury. "Here is the evidence," he declares. "With these facts before you, the verdict should be as I have indicated." Just how far he goes in his effort to influence opinion varies from editorial to editorial, and from his purpose arise three principal "types" of editorials. In one editorial the writer may merely interpret an event, offering no specific action. But he must do more than the interpretative reporter does. His editorial should add dimension to the reader's knowledge and understanding of an issue. In another, he may suggest (outright, or subtly) one or more satisfactory courses of action. In a third, he may demand action on the part of public officials or exhort his readers to take immediate action, pointing out the gravity of the matter. Of course, the writer who shouts "Wolf!" too often without sufficient cause or evidence to support his cry is soon unheeded. Still another type of editorial is a short, humorous one intended to lighten the seriousness of the editorial section and to inject an element of amusement or lightheartedness into the day's events, although it also can be a humorous jab at a serious subject. No matter what type editorial it is, the writer should keep in mind that it should be kept reasonably short. Some experts recommend 1,000 words as the outer limits of length.

30d   *Contents of Editorials.* Editorials usually have a news peg, an introductory statement explaining the subject followed by the writer's interpretation and appraisal of the topic. The two parts should be tied together in a unified essay. The writer should organize his facts and his arguments in a logical pattern in his attempt to bring the reader around to his point of view. (Courses in argumentation and debate or participation in college debating can give the writer an excellent background for preparing editorials.) The reader must understand the question

30e   before he can understand comments on it. The editorial writer often must assume that the reader knows little or nothing about the current event under consideration. He first serves as a reporter by briefly reporting the news which has prompted his editorial, and this part of the editorial is similar to the tie-back in the follow-up story. Then the editorial writer is free to add his own (the "editorial we") interpretation.

No standardized form or style, except that of effective newspaper English, is used in writing editorials. The writer is free to use any dramatic device if he prefers not to use the essay approach. Open letters, mock reviews of documents (such as the city budget), question-and-answer and even verse can be used effectively. In style, however, the editorial should be as polished as anything in the newspaper. Editorial effectiveness is a blend of sound thinking and good writing,

30f   and the two are often indistinguishable. A catchy headline and opening will be helpful for any editorial, no matter what subject is discussed. The concluding

30g   paragraph also deserves special care in the writing, for it is the last chance the writer has to impress the reader on the points that he is making in the editorial.

Here are two examples of editorials, one treating a local topic, the other dealing with a national subject with a local angle:

THE ONLY THREAT IN 911

They have to be kidding. Officials of the 18 St. Louis County fire districts who have called for a "boycott" of the 911 emergency telephone system are asking people to ignore a tool that might save their lives, their property or both. What could be more stupid?

The 911 number is the quickest, simplest way for anyone in St. Louis and St. Louis County to reach the police, a fire department or an ambulance in an emergency. The service will go into effect on Feb. 25, which will be none too soon. That one number will quickly summon help in an emergency regardless of where the person needing assistance may be calling from. More than 60 police departments, each with its own seven-digit telephone number, serve St. Louis, the county and the county's 91 municipalities; 25 independent fire districts and 20 or so municipal departments provide fire protection, and more than three dozen private and public ambulance services are operated by a mind-boggling array of agencies. What a mess! But what a relief that 911 will finally make sense out of it.

The fire district officials see all this as somehow threatening to their political empires, which may be reason enough to consider abolishing them. In fact, the only threat here is the threat to life and property created by the foolish advice to boycott 911.

[St. Louis Post-Dispatch]

DANGEROUS TURN FOR CONSTITUTION

Any time emotion sweeps reason aside, the consequences are to be feared.

Such happened yesterday when the Tennessee Legislature listened to the emotional pleadings of those calling for a constitutional convention to outlaw abortions. By an overwhelming vote, the legislators helped pave the way for exposing the precious rights and fundamental doctrines of our government to dangerous, intemperate tampering.

The point is not whether abortions are good or bad. The point is that there can be no way to guarantee against a full-scale onslaught on the Constitution, an attack which could undermine the rights of all of us, if a convention were held.

A dire mistake has been made in our state capital. We should vehemently hope that this ill-considered attempt can go not one state further.

[The Jackson Sun]

COLUMNS

The column is closely related to the editorial in a sense, yet considerably different. Many columnists do make editorial comments on public issues and their work could serve as editorials. The major difference is, of course, that the column carries the by-line of the writer. It is that by-line (and, of course, the writer's style) that attracts readers. Columnists seek to develop such rapport with readers that they will turn to the page on which the column regularly appears to see what their favorite columnist has to say. If a columnist cannot recruit a sufficient following to do just that, he will not remain for long as a columnist.

Essential Qualities of Columns. How does the column writer cultivate box-office appeal? First and foremost, he must have something to say. He must possess the knowledge and the resources that qualify him as a commentator on the subjects that he covers. Trying to write a political column, for example,

30h

30i

without a broad knowledge of politics and politicians and the resources needed to obtain information would be futile.

Next, the columnist must be interesting. The most erudite individual fails as a columnist if he cannot convey his knowledge in a readable, interesting style. Having something to say and saying it interestingly are absolute requirements for a successful columnist.

If, in addition, he can say it entertainingly, he has an even greater chance for success. Almost every major columnist writing on the national political scene frequently departs from a more serious tone to present a subject in a witty and entertaining manner.

The acid test of a columnist is his durability. If he can maintain high quality day after day and week after week, he has a chance. As soon as he runs out of something to say, or as soon as he falls into the trap of saying everything exactly the same way with no effort to entertain as well as inform his readers, he will run out of box-office appeal.

30j

Types of Columns. There are several broad types of by-line columns. The largest group, one that includes a wide variety of offshoots, is the public affairs (or straight editorial) type, which comments on current issues and events. This type dominates the editorial pages of most newspapers. James Reston, William F. Buckley, James J. Kilpatrick, and Mary McGrory are a few of the dozens whose columns are syndicated in American newspapers. A number of other columnists, however, have made a reputation for themselves and gathered legions of fans by their lighthearted approach to some of the more serious topics of the day. And most newspapers now try to include at least one such columnist on their editorial or Op-Ed pages. One of the more successful practitioners of the "art" is Russell Baker of the New York Times.

Among the other types of columns prominent in most newspapers are sports, humor, advice and social—there are columns covering almost every topic imaginable, from pets to stamp collecting. Most newspapers use their own staff members to write sports and social columns that deal with local personalities. Often they augment the local efforts with syndicated sports columns covering the national scene and columns devoted to the life and times of the famous and infamous. Most other columns are purchased from feature services and cover a broad spectrum. They are used in the section or on the page most closely related to their subject as a general rule. However, they can be used anywhere in the newspaper.

EXERCISES

1. Collect one week's editions of any newspaper available to you, then clip five editorials or editorial columns from them. Check the previous editions of the paper to find the news stories on which the editorials and columns were based. Paste the "pairs" on sheets of paper and analyze the difference between pairs.
2. Read editorials in any newspaper available to you. Clip one that interprets an issue, another that recommends a solution or course of action. Paste them on sheets of paper and analyze their content and style.
3. Invite the editor of your local newspaper to class for an interview. Discuss with him

the newspaper's editorial stand on an important local issue. Write a story based on that interview.

4. Read a number of syndicated columnists who write about public affairs such as William F. Buckley, Jr., James J. Kilpatrick, James Reston and Tom Wicker. Select three who obviously have different points of view on a particular current event. Clip and paste the three on sheets of paper and write your own opinion of the logic, form and style of each.

5. Using any newspaper available to you, select three news stories that you believe are subjects worthy of editorial comment. Paste the clippings on sheets of paper and write an editorial on each of them. Make one interpretative, the second, suggestive, the third, exhortative. Then write an editorial column in which you comment on all three of these news stories, using any form or style you desire.

6. Write a "Letter to the Editor," the length assigned by your instructor, on a subject of current interest. The instructor may assign the subject or he may permit you to write on any subject you choose. Submit the letter to a local newspaper for possible publication.

PART VIII

EDITING THE NEWS

Stories do not just spring into print when they leave a reporter's typewriter or video display terminal. So it is important that a reporter, early in his career, be aware of what happens to the story after it leaves his hands. He must know and understand the complete editing process. This section will deal with the editing of news.

After the news story is written and before it appears in print, it is handled by several persons. Generally, it moves through most or all of the following stages:

1. It may need rewriting.
2. It must be copy edited.
3. It must be headlined.
4. It must be set in type.
5. It must be proofread.
6. It must be assigned a place in the newspaper by the makeup editor.
7. It must be printed.
8. It must be circulated (delivered, mailed and sold on streets).

Only the first, second, third, and sixth steps are the responsibility of the editorial department. These will be discussed in detail.

It is essential that a reporter learn these steps, because he frequently may be called upon to perform them, especially at smaller newspapers. He should already understand the copy editing process because it is his duty to turn in clean copy requiring minimum alternations. In addition, a reporter may be asked to serve on editing desks from time to time. This type of duty, even for limited periods, invariably strengthens a reporter's grasp of his work as a writer.

Rewriting Faulty Stories

Three types of stories generally are called "rewrites" in most newspaper offices. Two of them—rewrites of stories appearing in competitive papers and stories written by a rewrite man in the office from facts given over the telephone by a beat reporter or a reporter on the scene of an event—were discussed in Chapter 11, "Rewrites and Follow-ups." The third type is the story that has to be rewritten because it has serious flaws in construction, organization or tone.

SERIOUS ERRORS

Try as they may, few reporters turn out completely errorless copy. Many errors in news stories—matters of grammar and style, spelling, punctuation, for example—can be corrected by the copy editor. However, some errors are so serious they require that the story be completely rewritten. In many instances, the original writer of the story is asked to do the job. In others, the story is turned over to a rewrite man, who is generally one of the newspaper's most experienced staff members.

What are those "serious" errors that would require a story to be completely rewritten?

The Main Feature May Not Be Stressed in the Lead. As pointed out, choice of the main feature may be a matter of opinion. The reporter's sense of values is usually an excellent guide in selecting the lead feature if there are several to choose from. However, the reporter sometimes does overlook what is undoubtedly the outstanding feature, burying it deep in the story. For example, suppose a reporter wrote his lead about a fire in a nursing home, using two or three paragraphs to describe the scene and mentioning for the first time in the third or fourth paragraph that 11 persons died in the fire. The story, or at least the lead, would have to be rewritten.

31a

421

31b   *The Story May Be Badly Organized.* In some stories the main feature may be handled properly in the lead, but the body of the story may be jumbled and confusing. Or the reporter may jump too quickly into a chronological account of events, forgetting to summarize all features before he relates details. Sometimes the rewrite man needs only to change a few paragraphs of the story (and this might be done by clipping the story apart and pasting it back together in a reorganized form or rearranging the paragraphs on the VDT screen). But other times he is fortunate to salvage one paragraph of the original.

31c   *The Story May Be the Wrong Type.* Deciding just how to handle a story properly can present a problem for some reporters. Sometimes a story cries out for the feature approach, but the reporter—especially if he is not accustomed to writing features—will ignore it and produce a lackluster hard-news story. And, at other times, the reporter may try to write a feature about an event that definitely is straight news; the results often appear strained, which will be obvious to the reader. When he converts a feature into a straight-news story or a straight-news story into a feature, the rewrite man usually must revise the entire story.

EXERCISES

1. The following story has, among other errors, a faulty lead that does not get into the "news" properly. Rewrite the story:

   The state law on marijuana gives a term of one to five years in the penitentiary and/or $3,000 fine for the felony; not more than 11 months and 29 days and/or $1,000 fine for the misdemeanor.

   William Charles Henry, 22, Route 2, Murphysboro, had his punishment fixed by a jury at 60 days in the county jail and received a fine of $500.

   David Lee George, 22, 1033 N. Seneca Rd., was sentenced to six months in the county jail.

   Both youths received lesser terms than recommended by Walter Fischer, assistant district attorney of the 19th judicial circuit.

   They are two more among the 29—mostly young people—indicted by the May 31 Grand Jury in the drug-roundup cases in which the defendants were indicted prior to their apprehension. Some of those indicted have not yet been arrested.

   As the procession of drug-related cases being heard in the current term of the Anderson County Criminal Court continues, two young men pled guilty to charges of selling marijuana on Wednesday morning.

   Today the cases of Paul Nipper and Dean Hallocx, both charged with selling marijuana are being tried.

   For the first time in these drug cases, two jurors (males) were not accepted for jury duty because, under questioning by Fischer, they stated that they did not feel that the law was fair.

   The trials did not take long. The selection of the two juries and the time both spent in deliberation took more than two hours, however.

   Henry, accused of selling two marijuana cigarettes for a dollar on Feb. 24 to Clyde B. Jackson, an undercover agent for the state Bureau of Criminal Investigation, was guilty of committing a felony, Fischer told the jury. He explained that sale of less than half an ounce is a misdeameanor; over half an ounce a felony. For Henry, he asked the jury for six months in prison.

   George was accused of selling 21.70 grams on Feb. 22 to Jackson for $20. An ounce of marijuana is 28.35 grams, Jackson told the court. For this charge the state had asked a prison term of 11 months, 29 days.

Since both men had pleaded guilty, the state did not exhaustively pursue the case.

2. The following story has flaws in its lead and in the organization of the story. Rewrite it.

Ralph Garrett, 22, a senior from Peoria, was not injured in the collision of his car and the University Police ambulance at the intersection of Harwood and Main Wednesday morning.

Garrett was turning north onto Main Street when the southbound ambulance struck his 1980 Thunderbird on the left rear side.

Sgt. Luther Dixon, of the University Police, driver of the ambulance, said he was returning to the main gym with Dr. Robert Garrett of the Health Service in answer to a call concerning an injured student, when Garrett's car pulled onto Main Street.

Garrett said that he neither saw the red light of the ambulance, nor heard its siren. A car parked on Main blocked his view and he was watching a student who was walking in his intended path.

City Patrolman S. L. Endicott said that further investigation would not be conducted until statements from witnesses Al Caskey, a student, and Jake T. Wells, associate professor of chemistry, could be obtained.

Damage to the vehicles included a smashed left fender to the ambulance and a smashed left side of Garrett's car. Dixon and Dr. Garrett were not injured.

A city police emergency squad was dispatched to handle the call at the gym after the accident. The student had suffered minor neck injuries.

3. Convert the following straight-news story into a human-interest story.

Michael Wilson, 30, 1314 Garcia St., was arrested on a hit-and-run traffic charge today after his pickup truck tore down a section of chain-link fence around a mobile home about a block away from where he lives.

He was booked briefly at city jail and scheduled for a preliminary hearing in traffic court next Thursday.

Patrolman Eugene Cassidy said he recognized a description of the truck after James Grant, who lives at 1200 Garcia St., reported that a pickup had ripped down his fence. Cassidy said he went to Wilson's home and found fresh scrape marks on the right front fender of Cassidy's truck.

Wilson told Cassidy that his dog, Booger, was driving the truck even though he had to push the gas pedal for her. Wilson said the dog should be arrested. He said the entire fence would have been pulled down if he had not jerked the wheel.

Wilson plans to bring Booger to court with him next Thursday.

4. Rewrite the following stories to make them more lively and interesting.

A. Efforts by zoo personnel to capture a boa constrictor that showed up in the basement apartment of Ann O'Hara today have failed.

The snake retreated to the heating system of the building at 4014 Northshore Dr., where it could survive for months, Milo Farnsworth, zoo director said.

Mrs. O'Hara, a 62-year-old widow, said she had returned from visiting her daughter on the east side of the city and went into her bathroom.

"When I opened the linen closet door, I got the scare of my life," she said. "There was this slimy-looking monster hanging down from the shelf."

She called the building manager, Bill Glenn, who brought wire cutters to cut off the snake's head.

"But it was too big. It just stayed there for about 30 minutes, poking its tongue out and staring at us," Mrs. O'Hara said. "So I slammed the closet door and decided to call the zoo."

423

Farnsworth and a reptile specialist tried to capture the snake but it slipped into a heating duct and disappeared. Farnsworth said the snake is not dangerous.

But that didn't satisfy Mrs. O'Hara. She said she would move in with her daughter until the snake is captured.

B. Jack Kubelsky, 31, 418 Woodlawn St., was arrested yesterday after his bicycle hit a curb as he was riding it near his home.

Patrolman Don Long said he had observed Kubelsky weaving back and forth in the street on the bicycle. He charged Kubelsky with drunken driving.

However, City Court Judge Don Webster agreed with Kubelsky's attorney, Ronald Shepard, that there is no law on the books against drunk peddling. He said he could find no evidence of there ever being such a case in state courts before.

He postponed Kubelsky's trial two weeks so he can think it over and decide how to dispose of the case.

C. John D. Ross, mayor of Halls Crossroads, a town with only 2,100 residents, announced today that he would not seek reelection to the unpaid post he has held for 22 years.

"I'm just fed up with the whole mess," Ross said. "I don't get paid but I get a lot of lip when something goes wrong."

Ross has repeatedly been reelected despite the fact that he always claimed he wasn't interested in the job. Several times he refused to have his named placed on the ballot but won anyway as a write-in candidate.

What will happen if he wins by write-in again this year?

"I'll just tell them to get another sucker," Ross said. "I want to sit back now and do some griping at whoever is foolish enough to take the job—just like they've been griping at me all these years."

The mayor and three city councilpersons all serve in nonpaying positions. The community has nine full-time city employees, including a police force of four.

Ross, 62, owns the town's only grocery store.

"I can't make up a grocery order without someone complaining about the high price of groceries and the lousy city trash collection or snow removal or something else I can't do a dad-blamed thing about.

"I've had it with all of them."

D. A man armed with a pistol attempted to rob the Bayside Bakery about 10 a.m. today, police said.

But the holdup attempt was foiled by Douglas Bradley, 36, owner of the bakery at 1117 Bayside Drive, who hit the holdup man over the head with a rolling pin.

"He wanted my money. I gave him a headache. That's all I had to give him," Bradley said.

Bradley told police the man pulled the pistol and ordered him to empty the cash register into a paper bag.

"I didn't say a word, I started to ring open the cash register but instead I grabbed my rolling pin next to it and hit him right between the eyes," Bradley said. "The guy went down like a stone. I weigh 230 and I hit him with everything I had."

He told police the man staggered out the front door and crawled into a waiting car, which sped from the scene.

"I don't think he'll bother any more bakers," Bradley said.

E. Forty football fans returned to where their bus had been parked yesterday and found the bus driver standing in the empty parking spot.

Driver Cal Kirland told police he had parked the bus after letting the passengers off at the main entrance to the stadium and got out to stretch his legs. He said he started talking to several other bus drivers and when he looked around about 10 minutes before the State University-Maryville College game was over, the bus he had been driving had disappeared.

A witness told police he had seen the bus being driven away at a high rate of speed. University police located the bus approximately 30 minutes later behind a student housing complex across campus from the stadium.

They arrested Frank Park, 21, and Frederick Division, 20, both of the Presidential Complex, on charges of grand theft auto. They were released on $5,000 bond.

The bus reportedly sideswiped four parked cars leaving the stadium area. The bus, however, was not damaged.

Kirland arranged with other drivers to take his passengers on their buses. He finally was able to reclaim his bus about 9 p.m.

5. Using any newspapers available to you, clip at least five examples of stories that should be rewritten because they have flaws in their organization. Rewrite the stories, handing in both the clippings and your version of each story.

6. Using any newspapers available to you, clip at least four examples of straight-news stories that can be made more lively by rewriting as human interest stories. Rewrite the stories, handing in both the clippings and your version of each story.

CHAPTER 32

Copy Editing

The copy desk, in the view of many editors, is the heart of a good newspaper. While some newspapers may retire over-the-hill reporters to the copy desk, most realize the tremendous contribution copy editors make and reward them financially.

A study by the Writing and Editing Committee of the Associated Press Managing Editors Association shows that many newspapers pay copy editors more than they pay reporters. Others give weekly or monthly cash awards.

Editor Al McCready of the Portland Oregonian told the committee: "We regard the copy desk as an elite group, with premium pay . . . they have a better chance of promotion to management positions than reporters have . . ."

This special attention to copy editors is essential because of the vital role they play at any newspaper. Comparatively few stories, when they have been completed by the reporter, are perfect. Most writers need some careful checking and expert editing, and the job falls to the copy editor, who reads the story carefully to eliminate mistakes, to improve the language and to write the headline.

The copy editor's main function is simply: to correct everything that is wrong with a reporter's story. He is the last person to check the story before it goes to the printer, so he must be the watchdog of the newspaper and the guardian of the reporters. Copy editing is one of the most important and painstaking jobs on a newspaper because the number of possible "wrongs" in a newspaper story is very great. Many of the most common errors that he might have to correct are violations of the "do's" and "do not's" of past chapters.

COPY EDITOR'S DUTIES

The copy editor

1. *Checks the story for accuracy.* A careful and well-informed reader of the newspaper, he should know the background of most news events or where to check them out in case he does not. He has the habit of automatically checking doubtful statements. He usually is familiar with the city—its streets, buildings, leading citizens, officials. He keeps the city directory, dictionary, atlas, encyclopedia, perhaps clippings and other reference material nearby. With his background and references, the copy editor is able to correct many errors, but he is helpless when the reporter makes an erroneous statement that can be verified only on the scene or at the source of the story. **32a**

2. *Makes corrections of grammar.* Haste and carelessness on the part of the writer often result in grammatical errors. The copy editor makes certain that standards of good English are observed in all newspaper stories. **32b**

3. *Eliminates verbosity in newspaper copy.* Newspaper writing style should be lean and crisp. The copy editor, by killing one word or even a complete paragraph, can often make a dull, wooden story come alive. **32c**

4. *Eliminates libelous statements.* He tones down "dangerous" statements and makes sure that defamatory reports are justified. He can catch some libelous statements but not those resulting from erroneous reporting. **32d**

5. *Simplifies the story.* He eliminates all confusing or ambiguous statements and all words that will not be understood by the layman. He replaces or defines all technical terms reporters may use in their stories. **32e**

6. *Eliminates editorialized matter in news stories.* If a story is by-lined, however, a certain amount of editorial expression is sometimes permitted when the writer is relating a first-hand account. **32f**

7. *Checks all stories for adequacy.* If the reporter evidently has omitted certain essential facts, the copy editor often returns the story to the city desk. The story may be given back to the reporter or to a rewrite man for completion. **32g**

8. *Sometimes trims or shortens a story.* If the story is longer than the news editor desires, the copy editor may be instructed to "cut it down" to a certain length. He eliminates the least essential paragraphs as he edits the story. **32h**

9. *Makes the story conform to the newspapers' style.* Each newspaper has certain rules covering optional forms of punctuation, abbreviations, capitalization and spelling, and the copy editor sees that every story observes those rules. **32i**

10. *Attempts to polish and improve the story.* He tries to transform every story into a smooth and lively account by inserting or deleting certain words and phrases, or by rearranging paragraphs or sentences. Yet he must restrain himself from attempting to completely rewrite every story he edits. He should preserve the reporter's original story as far as possible. **32j**

11. *Writes identifying labels and instructional notes.* He does this for each story or portion of a story to expedite processing in the mechanical department. These include: **32k**

a. Sluglines of one to three words, written at the top left of each page of copy. These slugs are set in type to accompany the story until it is matched with the proper headline, which may be set on a separate machine, depending upon the equipment used. Many newspapers use a system of slugging each story with the first word or two of the headline; others use a story label, such as "storm" or "fire," which may be the same as the one used by the reporter.

b. Identifications for materials to be combined with stories already sent to the composing room. These identifying terms are:

(1) *Add*—to be added at the end of a story.

(2) *Insert*—to be inserted with a story, as material or as a substitute for material deleted.

(3) *New lead*—to replace the lead.

(4) *Precede*—to precede the lead of the story.

(For electronic editing see page 430.)

COPYREADING SYMBOLS

321   Copy editors use a standard set of symbols that, in most instances, allow them to indicate changes without using words. The reporter has already studied some of the symbols in the exercise on "preparing copy." Following is a more complete list:

Symbol	Definition	Example
⊗ or ⊙	Period mark	He was there⊗ He was there⊙
∧	Comma	Therefore‸ he will . . .
⋎	Apostrophe	Ill let you know . . .
⋎	Quotation marks	I'll let you know . . .
≡ or ⟋	Make capital letter	later that monday . . .
/	Make lowercase letter	Later in The day . . .
◯	Abbreviate or spell out word or number	(Doctor) Smith said .. . Dr. (Wm.) Smith said . . . The (2) men were . . . The (twelve) men were . . .

Symbol	Definition	Example
⌞ or ⌟ or ¢	Start new paragraph	⌞The end of the . . . ⌟The end of the . . . ¢ The end of the . . .
no ¢	Do not make this a new paragraph	*no* ¢ The end of . . .
⌉ or ⌈ or	Indent on left or right	⌉ This symbol may be used ⌈ on either side of the page or on both sides. If used on both sides, it indicates that the ma- terial should be centered. ⌊
/	Separate letters	Some ofbur students . . .
⌢	Bring letters together or close space	So⌢me of the students . . . Some⌢ of the students . . .
Line from one word to the beginning of the following word.	Bring copy together or join paragraphs	Four·men who were found were found adrift near . . .
⊇	Delete letter, word, or phrase	Saailing on . . . Sailing on ⌢on toward . . .
∧ or ⌃	Insert letter, word, or phrase	Sa∧ling on . . . Sailing on the . . . ∧
∼	Transpose letters, words, or phrases	Sailing on . . . Sailing to on the . . .
Stet	Restore original text	stet Four of the men . . .
∼∼∼	Set in boldface text	New residents here . . .
—	Set in italics	The habeas corpus case

It should be pointed out that there is a difference between copy editing and proofreading. The copyreading symbols make changes at the points in the original copy at which the errors occur, as a general rule. In proofreading, the mark is generally placed in the margin after the story has been set in type.

At newspapers where reporters still produce stories on typewriters and copy editors polish and correct them by hand, it is not uncommon for whole words or phrases to be written in between the lines of copy. The copy editor, in such cases, generally uses a particular symbol to clarify those corrections. The handwritten *a* looks much like the *o,* the *u* like the *n* and the *m* like the *w*. To

429

call attention to this in the composing room where an operator may be setting the type on a composing machine such as a Compugraphic, the copy editor draws a short line beneath the handwritten *a, u* or *w* and above the *o, n* or *m* if there is a danger that a letter may be misread (for example, *bay* in handwriting may look like *boy*).

Copy editors who still correct stories by hand customarily use the paragraph symbol (illustrated in the preceding list) to indicate the beginning of every paragraph, whether or not the paragraph is indented. This prevents possible errors by making paragraph indentation readily apparent, and it offers an easy method of determining whether the story has been copy edited in part or in whole.

Electronic Editing. The advent of electronic equipment both in the newsroom and in the backshop introduced into copy editing a new set of codes and symbols needed to give proper instructions to the typesetting equipment used and the "program" specifically designed for that newspaper by the equipment manufacturer. Each paper will have its own set of printed instructors for copy editing. Most programs are similar, and it would require very little adjustment for a copy editor, once he has learned one set, to use a different set at another newspaper.

Of all the new equipment, the Video Display Terminal (VDT) is the most commonly used device in the newsroom. Although many newspapers have completely converted to them for reporters and copy editors, it was the copy desk at most newspapers where they were first installed. After the reporter has written his story and it has been stored in the computer memory bank, the copy editor, by using the correct code, can recall the story on his VDT screen and complete the editing process.

A copy editor can perform the following functions on a VDT:

1. Delete characters, words, lines and paragraphs as well as move entire blocks of copy in a single story.
2. Delete the total story.
3. Add new text into any location of the story being displayed on the screen.
4. Move a definable block of the story anywhere on the display screen.
5. Instruct the typesetting machine how wide to set the copy and what type size and type face to use on the particular story.
6. Write the headline for the story.

A wide range of electronic editing systems are available and they are being refined and made more sophisticated every year. What functions can be performed depends entirely on how sophisticated the equipment is. Some, for example, have split-screen capabilities on which two stories can be shown at the same time should a copy editor want to compare or possibly combine the stories. Others are part of a total electronic system that permits the movement of the story from one VDT unit to the next and onto the computer and finally into the typesetting machine. And some stand alone and contain their own minicomputer from which paper tape is punched, which is then fed into the typesetting machine.

It is important to remember that the VDT is the central device for the system. The codes a reporter and copy editor must learn will vary from newspaper to newspaper and the keyboard on the VDT may vary slightly. However, all systems are essentially the same.

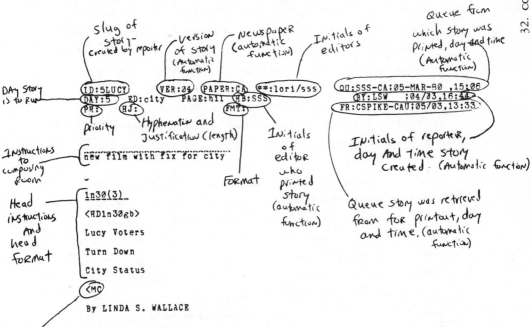

Figure 32-1. Here is an example of a story prepared on a VDT, with an explanation of the editing codes and symbols.

431

IO is printed on each page of printout automatically

The failure of incorporation in Lucy, according to many residents, probably can be attributed in part to the fact that residents are not ``afraid'' of immediate annexation by Memphis or a consolidated city-county government.

``We aren't scared of Memphis,'' said Dale Burkett, secretary-treasurer of the anti-incorporation group. ``When I moved out here some 20 years ago I knew sooner or later Memphis would get us. And I am not afraid. Of course, I would rather be annexed by Millington. But that's another issue.''

<UPLINE>   Incorporation has divided the community in recent weeks, but the atmosphere at polling places yesterday appeared to be friendly. Every now and then, a few people gathered outside the elementary school to discuss the weather, the latest local gossip and to kid each other about incorporation.

``It is like I always say, it is wonderful to disagree, but not to the point of being disagreeable,'' Burkett said. ``There are no hard feelings. There hasn't been since that meeting Thursday. I think the incorporation supporters realized then they had lost.''

One resident, Sandra Buchanan, said the incorporation drive had a positive side because it brought the community together. ``I have never seen so much togetherness,'' she said.

Burkett added, ``It got to the point that we really know each other and we work well together. Of course, we are all looking for a way to

(MORE)

keep our community together. Incorporation has drawn our community together. We (anti-incorporation group) are going to continue to function. We are going to set up a legal charter and everything after the election and become a community group. We are more or less concerned with the children and people as a whole.''

Jack Perry, election commission executive director, said it cost approximately $3,395 to hold the election. The entire cost was paid by the residents, he said.

(END)

Figure 32-2. *Second and third pages of a story prepared on a VDT, with explanations of the editing codes and symbols.*

Another electronic device that is used in the production of copy at some newspapers is the Optical Character Recognition (OCR), commonly called the scanner. It is used in the production department rather than in the newsroom. It "reads" typewritten copy into a computer or onto paper tape at rates of more than 1,200 words a minute (depending on the particular scanner) for setting either cold type or hot metal, if the latter is still used. It can be connected through a computer directly to the photocomposition machines, permitting the production of type in a matter of minutes.

Here is an example of scanner-ready copy with an explanation of the editing marks:

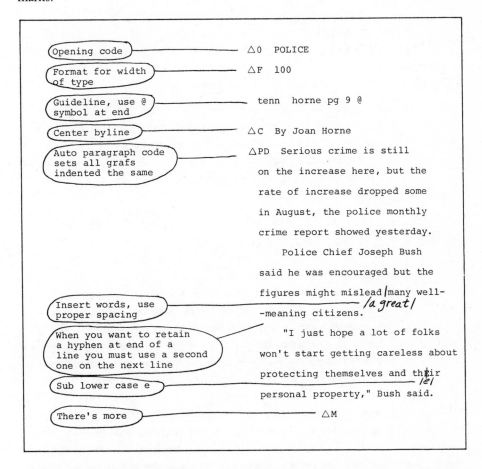

Wire News. Most of the copy coming into the newspaper office via teletype from the wire services requires different treatment from that given local copy. The introduction of electronic equipment in the newsroom and the backshop has changed dramatically how wire copy is handled.

At one time, wire services used to send copy on the teletype machines in all capital letters, as illustrated:

NEW YORK (AP)—A SOVIET PLANE DELAYED AT KENNEDY INTERNATIONAL AIRPORT FOR 27 HOURS FOR LACK OF A GROUND CREW TOOK OFF FOR HOME WITH THE AID OF A PRIVATE SERVICING COMPANY AND AN AGREEMENT WORKED OUT UNDER THE SUPERVISION OF THE STATE DEPARTMENT.

It was edited by hand by the copy editor and sent on to the backshop to be set in type in the normal capitals and lowercase used by newspapers. However, with the introduction of the teletypesetter, the copy was sent in capitals and lowercase because it was punched into a paper tape that was fed automatically into the typesetting machines at the newspaper to produce justified type. Many papers elected not to do much editing on the wire copy because added editing slowed down production.

An example of how wire copy looks now when it reaches a newspaper office follows:

005T
   RU
      PM-CULT SKED 12-28
      CHATTANOOGA, Tenn. (UPI)—Twin sisters who were "deprogrammed" after four years in a so-called religious cult charged the sect's leaders with beating children and refusing to let them see their parents . . .

Not all copy comes in capitals and lowercase letters. Some wire services, often those owned by individual newspapers, send copy in all capital letters. If the proper symbol were used to mark down all letters to be set in lowercase, the copy would be covered with pencil marks. As a result, the copy editor indicates only the letters to be capitalized, and all unmarked letters are set in lowercase. Here is an example:

CONCORD, N.H. -- SEVEN REPUBLICANS AND FIVE DEMOCRATS HAVE WON THE RIGHT TO SLUG IT OUT IN NEW HAMPSHIRE'S SHOWCASE PRIMARY. . .

With the advent of the computer in the electronic composing room, the handling of wire copy in newspapers that have modernized their printing operation has taken a completely new turn. As the hard copy is being printed on the teletype printer, the same stories are being fed directly into a computer in the composing room. Using the copy from the printer, copy editors can make all changes in the story they deem necessary. With this edited copy as a guide, the copy editor, sitting at the keyboard of a VDT, orders the original story from the computer's memory to the video display screen. He then makes all the corrections, additions and deletions on the copy by using the keyboard. The completed, corrected story is returned to the computer's memory and will be later fed directly into the photocomposition machine. Great care must be exercised by the copy editor to include the proper codes and signals to the computer; otherwise, the copy might come out as lines of jumbled letters, resulting in delays and costly corrections. Each newspaper will have its own set of codes and symbols depending upon the type equipment used.

EXERCISES

1. Copy edit the following stories. (*Note to instructor:* To avoid mutilating the text, these exercises can be duplicated for student use, or the student can be instructed to make a copy of the stories on a copying machine before copy editing them.)

A. Hopkins
   Cruiser

   Helipoter traff ic Sgt. Alan Charmichael, who daiily warns motor ists of ice and snow, accidents and traffic jams , got a little ground action xxxxx himself yesterday.

   Officer Cyarmichael's police cruiser sld into the rear of a stop ped car on Interstate 40 west, undre the Western avenue Bridge at 6:07 p.m. The driver of the other car, Claude M. Stiles, 47, 4550 Rutledge Pike, xxx told polcie he had stoped for traffic when struck.

   xxx Police said there was ice along the road way. no charges were pla ced.

B. Benton
   Volunteer

   a 24 year-old volunteer firman who set fire to his girldfriends c ar after learning that she had xxxxx married another man was snetenced Friday to 18 mont hs supervsied probation for destruction of Property.

   Terry James Granville of Potomac, a volun teer fighter at the Hamilton Volunteer fire Department, pleaded guilty and thne told xxxxxxxxxxxx district court Judge Stanley Klavan that he poured paint thiner on his former girlfriends Chebrolet corvette and set it a blaze after friends he had been drink ing with informed him of te mariage.

   Neighbooors who saw Granville set the fire put the blaze out before it caused exrensive dammage to the car, according to Granvilles attorney, Michael Budow.

   budow told the judge that the case was umusual because Granville west to the pol ice on his own. They did not go out xxxxx and arrets him. He also said the former girl friend had "no desire to proescute or press any charges.

   Granville told the Judge he was sorry for xxxxx the incident. He al so said he had paid $200 to repiar the damages to the car.

   As a condition of his provation, Granville whill have to under go alcohol abuse counselling, the judge rueled.

C. Flynn
   Drugs

   A new progrram to conbat drug abuse will focus no parents in the Einstein high School community in Kensington.

   The Parents of teen agers will be encoraged to fomr groups—paralel to existing friendships among there children-

—to support each other in prebenting drug abuse xxxx and copping with current drug users.

A circular has beeen sent to the par ents of elementary and high school students in the area advertising a metting tomorrow in the einstein cafeteria at 7:30 p.m.

tomorrow's meeting is not aimed at parenst of drug users alone, but too all parents, to prebent drug abuse.

parents will discus the pressures on youth to us drugs, ways to talk to a child about gurg abuse, how to tell a child not to use drugs in the home or elswhere, and the need for curfeus, superbision at parties and consistant discipline.

D. Hedling

Money

Two armed robbery suspect were apprehended by montgomery County po lice shortly after a Hill's store at 15531 New Hampshire avenue in Silver Spring xxxxx was robed monday night, polcie sa id.

According to police, off duty policeman Daniel Crumpler ovserbed a lat model BMW matching the description of the car usde by the rob bers on Ednor road.

crumpler followed the car alone Ednor xxxxx x xxxxx where he saw the occupents toss a shot gun and money out the cars window in an apparent attempt to get rid of them, police said. The money and shotgun was recovered by police.

Police stoped the car and arreste Richard W. Grant, 28, of nearby Boulevard Heights, and Ralph Allen Thomas, 28, of 910 Larch avenue, in Thompson Park. Both men were carged with armed rob bery, police said.

E. Ahlers

Burglaires

JEFFERSON CITY (Soecial)—The ar rest of a 17 year old Silver spring youth last Friday for the burglery of 2 houses has resluted in the sol ving of 75 other burglaries, police said.

Jim Bob Crawford, who had been living with foster parents for two years, was arrested near the scene of one of the burglaries in the west H ills subdivision Friday.

Det. Frank Mathers of the Montgomer county police said he spent Saturday and sunday driving around with the youth who pointed out other houses in suburban developments that xxxxxxx he had brokne into during the past 2 years.

All together , the youth pointed out aproximately 140 loc ations where he had comitted either burglaries or larcenies. Police were able to verify 75 of the burglaries thorough their records. Mathers siad an investigation into the others is con- tiniuing.

Mathers said Crawford tol d him that he would xxxxxx ca rry goods out o f the homes and into nearby woods. He said he would throw awya items he count not use or seel to his freinds, regardless of its value.

Crawford is being held in the Montgomery county Jenenile home, pending a hearing before Juvenile cout judge Bel Prado.

CHAPTER 33

Proofreading

Most reporters do not get an opportunity to proofread their own stories after they have been set in type. That important job most often is done by persons who work in the composing room. However, some newspapers do send proof copies back to the newsroom for checking to prevent possible errors.

33a   Proofreading is the final step in checking the news story after it has been set in type. The object is to eliminate any errors made during the typesetting process. While proofreading and copy editing are similar in that they are both designed to catch errors, the proofreader does not attempt to improve the story. His sole job is to see that the proof follows the original copy. However, the proofreader is free to correct misspelled words, incorrect English and other such blunders that have slipped past the reporters and copy editors.

USING PROOFREADING SYMBOLS

33b   Many of the proofreading symbols are similar to the copy editing symbols. But there is an important difference in the use of them. The copy editor uses his symbols within the body of the story, making changes at the point in the text at which the error occurs. The proofreader must place all of his symbols in the margin of the galley proof, indicating at what point changes are needed in the story. This speeds the process of correcting errors after the story is in type and he does not have to check the entire story word for word.

Two methods are used by proofreaders to indicate corrections are needed:

1. The correction is noted in the margin directly to the right or left of the line in which the error appears, with an additional symbol within the line

pointing out the error. The correction should appear in the margin closest to the error. For example:

```
A 77-year-old man apparently died of a heart attack  #
```

If a line contains several errors, the correction symbols in the sequence are placed as needed and are separated by slanting lines:

```
A 77-year-old man apparently died of a  heart attack  #/l.c./tr.
```

2. The correction is noted in the margin with a line drawn from the symbol to the error. This method is satisfactory if there are few errors. Example:

```
A 77-year-old man apparently died of a heart attack  tr.
```

Corrections requiring words and short phrases usually can be handled as marginal corrections by either of the two methods illustrated above. However, the second method is recommended when the correction is rather long. If a complete line of copy has been omitted, or jumbled, the proofreader may mark "See copy" in the margin, returning the original copy to the printer with the corrected proof. For all such corrections as those mentioned in this paragraph, the proofreader must indicate exactly where words or phrases must be changed or added. For example:

33c

```
A 77-year-old man apparently/of a heart attack  died
```

If the error is only a single letter, the correction can be made as follows:

33d

```
A 77-year-old man apparently died of a  heart attack  h
```

As an additional duty, the proofreader must check the method used of splitting words between lines. He must correct the words which are not split between syllables according to accepted usage. As dictionary is usually his guide for this purpose. Split-word corrections are made as follows:

33e

33f

```
            next door and had failed to rep-
  P    place rocks and gravel which were
```

The more common proofreader's symbols are shown on page 443.

EXERCISES

1. Following are newspaper stories in manuscript form, and below each story is a galley proof of that story. Proofread each galley proof. (*Note to instructor:* These galley proofs can be duplicated to avoid defacing the text. Or the student can be instructed to copy the lines containing errors and to indicate the proper method of correcting the errors.)

A.

The Department of Recreation and Parks will sponsor three 10-week dog obedience clas̃ses beginning next week. Sessions will be held on Tuesdays, Thursdays and Saturdays.

Tuesday sessions will be from 7:30 to 8:30 p.m. in the Twinbrook Community Center, 411 Twinbrook Parkway.

Thursday sessions will be from 7:30 to 8:30 p.m. in the West Hills Community Center, 5678 Dean Hill Drive.

Saturday sessions will be from 10 to 11 a.m. in the Montrose Recreation Center, 451 Congressional Lane.

Charles W. Jackson, director of recreation, said the classes will cost $20 for city residents and $22 for non-residents.

Registration for classes will be on a first-come, first served basis, Jackson said. No advanced registration by mail or by telephone will be accepted.

All dogs must be at least six-months old or they will not be accepted for the classes, Jackson added.

The Department of Recreation and Farks will sponser threee 10-week dog obedience clas ses beginning nextg week. Sessions will be held on Tuesdays, Thrusdays, and Saturdays.

Tuesday sessions wil be from 7;30 to 8:30 p.m in the Twinbrook Community Center, 411 Twinbrook Parkway.

Thursday sessions will be from 7;30 to 8;30 pm in the West Hills Community Center, 5678 Dean Hill Drive.

Saturday sessions will be from 10 to 11 a.m. in the Montrose Recreation Center, 451 Congressional Lanef.

Charles W. Jackson director of re-creation, said the classes will cost ×20 for city residents and $22 for non-residents.

Registration will be on a first-come, first served bases, Jackson said. No advanced registration by mail or by telephone will be excepted.

All dogs must be at least six-months old or they will not be acepted for the classes, Jakcson added.

B.

A former Jefferson County police department lawyer has filed as
a candidate in this year's Republican State Senate primary.

Warren G. Fabrizo, 39, who now practices law in nearby Madisonville,
filed papers of candidacy this week to oppose incumbent Sen. James Stuart
Emmett in the GOP primary.

Fabrizo, who served as police legal adviser here for five years
in the late 1970s, sought the Republican nomination for county executive
in 1978, losing in the primary to Maxwell Keen. Keen later lost to
Democrat Harvey Mathias.

"I think it is time for some new leadership," Fabrizo said. "I will
represent the people, not the special interest groups."

He described himself as pro-life, anti-busing and opposed to the
"power big business and industry have in the state legislature and the
state house."

Sen. Emmttt, who earlier announced he would seek re-election, has
served four consecutive terms in the State Senate.

A former Jefferson Country poliec
deparmtent lawyer has filled a as candidate in this years'Replublican State
Senate primary.

Warren G Fabrizo, 39, who now
practices law in nearbye Madisonvile,
filled papors of acndidacey this week to
oppose inclement Sen James Stuart Emmett in the GDP primaruy.

Fabrizo, who served as police legel
adivsor for five years in the late 1970,s'
sought the Republicain nomination for
county executive in 1978, loosing the
in primary to Maxwell Keen.. Keen
lator last to demcrat Harvey Mathias.

"I think it is time for some
newleadershi9p." Fabrizo said. 'I will
represent the peple, not the specail interest groups."
He descrived himself as pre-life, anti-
busting and oplopsed to the "power big
business and industry has in the state
legislature and the state house."

Sen. Memttt, who earlier announced he would seek re-election, has
served four ronsecutive terms in the
State Senate

C.

Two would-be burglars decided to drop in to the Do Drop Inn near Greeneville after hours today, but the owner got the drop of them, deputies said.

Greene County Sheriff's Distatcher Rick Coyle said he received a call from the tavern owner, Jerry Bodkin, about 12:30 a.m.

"He called me and said he had them spread-eagled on the floor in front of him. He said he had a .38 on them," Coyle said.

Deputies went to the tavern, off Highway 93, in the Walkertown area, and arrested Robert R. Goodlet, 20, and Arthur W. Goodman, 25, both of Route 4, Chicky, on burglary charges.

Bodkin told the deputies he had closed the tavern about midnight and went home. However, he couldn't remember locking the rear door so he returned and found the two men inside.

The two men are being held in the Greene County Jail pending a preliminary hearing on the charges.

Two would-be bunglers decided to drop in to the do Drop Inn near Greeneville after hours today, but th onwer got the drop of them, deputies said.

Greene county Sherif's Distacher Rick Coyle said he received a call from the tavern owner, Jerry Bodkin, about 1230 a.m.

"he called me and siad he had them spread-eagled on the floor in front of him. He said he had a .38 on them," Coyle said.

Deputies went to the tavern, off Higheway 93, in the Walkertown area, and arrested Robert r. Goodlet, 20, and Arthur W Goodman, 25, both of Route4, Chicky, on burlary chances.

Bodkin told the deputies he had closed the tavren about midnight and went home. However, he couldnt remember looking the rear door so eh returned and found the two man inside.

The two men are being held in the Greene County Jail bending a preliminary hearling on the charges.

2. Using any newspapers available to you, check stories for errors that have been overlooked by proofreaders. Clip at least five stories containing errors and paste each one on a blank sheet of paper. Make corrections as a proofreader would.

Symbol	Definition	Example of Use
X	A defective letter	Civil liberty is freedom from restraint by any law, save that which conduces in a greater or less degree to the general welfare.
℘	Delete material	To do what I will is natural liberty. To do what I will, consistently
℘	Letter is inverted	with equal rights of others, is civil liberty,
#	Insert space	the only liberty possible in a state of civilized society.
w.f.	Wrong font	
stet….	Do not make change. Let copy stand as it is.	If I wish to act, in accordance with my own unrestrained will, I am made to reflect that all
(;)	Insert semicolon	others may do the same, in which case I shall meet
⌒	Close up space	with so many checks and obstructions to my
tr. ∼	Transpose	own will, my liberty and happiness will be far less than if I, with the
⋏	Insert comma	rest of the community were subject to the restraints of reasonable
⊙	Insert period	laws applying to all
¶	New paragraph	So it is, that proper and adequate laws are essential to the well-being and good order of
cap ≡	Capital letter	civil society. but legal restraint, for no other Reason than mere restraint, is certainly unphilosophical, and inherently wrong, be-
l.c. /	Lowercase letter	

Symbol	Definition	Example of Use
Rom +++	Use Roman type	cause it amounts to a deprivation of natural liberty without any compensating benefits to the public at large.
Ital —	Use italics	James C. Carter, in his "Origin and Function of Law," says,
⊙ (colon)	Insert colon	"It is the function] of government to define the limits or sphere
] or [	Move to right or left, as indicated	in which the individual may act as a member of the social state, without
or	Move down or up, as indicated	at the same time encroaching upon the freedom of others.
eq # ⌄	Equalize spacing	It follows, therefore, that to live under
⟩	Insert quotation marks	
spell out ○	Spell out circled word	civil gov is to surrender a portion of our natural liberty for the public
⟩	Insert apostrophe	good, in order that that which remains to us may be the better safeguarded
⊔	Push down slug that prints	by the strong arm of the law. But liberty may be destroyed by law. The Romans furnish a concrete example. The prevailing ethos or national spirit of the Romans
! /	Insert exclamation mark	
b.f.	Use boldface type	was law. Did not law regulate everything. A citizen could not fix a price upon his own goods. It was the oppression of
? /	Insert question mark	law which cheapened the desire for life.
= /	Insert hyphen	

CHAPTER 34

Headlines

34a A copy editor's job is not complete once he has edited the story. Still facing him is the task of writing the headline. It can be the most demanding part of the job. Writing good headlines requires skill and a command of the language. What a reporter says in 30 words or more, the headline writer may have to say in five or six. Moreover, the reader appeal of the story itself depends upon the headline. Like the lead, the headline is the showcase of the story.

Modern headlines should

1. Draw the reader's attention to the story.
2. Summarize the story so that the hurried reader can get the gist of the story at a glance.
3. Help the reader evaluate the news.
4. Help make the newspaper attractive to the reader.

And all of this must be done in a maddeningly small amount of space, with additional restrictions placed by the size of the type used for the head.

Since the lead summarizes the whole story, the headline on most straight news stories should be drawn largely from the lead. It is, in fact, the lead translated into sharp, punchy, dramatic words. Material from the body of the story may be used if the newspaper's headline style permits the use of *decks* (secondary heads).

The headline writer will encounter problems similar to those of the reporter in packing a great deal of information into a few words. A good headline does not require translation. The reader understands it immediately, unlike this example of a headline that was actually used:

BN VP at BS

Translated, that means "Boys Nation Vice-president at Boys State." It is also good practice to read headlines aloud to make certain they say specifically what is intended. This is an excellent way to catch awkward and sometimes embarrassing word combinations. Here are several examples from *Columbia Journalism Review's* "The Lower Case" page:

Devine feels Packers behind last year

Skeleton Tied To Missing Diplomat

Stolen Painting Found by Tree

Although under considerable restrictions when writing a straight-news head, the copy editor will find he has considerably more freedom in writing feature heads. The feature head should reflect the tone of the story rather than summarize the facts in it. Feature heads should not divulge a surprise or unusual twist in a story.

Here are several examples of well-written headlines:

The Commercial Appeal, Memphis, used this head on a story about the new temperature settings that were part of the president's energy-saving program:

It's Patriotic to Perspire

The New York Times dressed up its story on the great red-white-and-blue-pickle hoax story with this headline:

A Dilly of a Story Turns Sour

And the Chicago Tribune used this headline on a story about fatigue:

Doing 'nothing' can give you an energy shortage

TRENDS IN HEADLINES

In modern typography the trend is for simplicity. This means shorter main **34b** heads and fewer, if any, secondary headlines. Some newspapers have eliminated the decks completely. Others have introduced a variety of headline techniques, often similar to those used in magazine makeup.

The flush-left headline is the most common in modern newspaper typography. Edmund G. Arnold, whose book, *Modern Newspaper Design,* is something of a bible in the field, says, "To the best of the knowledge that we have at this time, flush-left setting is the most effective for heads, for it is based on the instinctive pattern in which the reading eye moves." That pattern is, of course, from left to right. Arnold adds that any head with a ragged left margin is "non-functional" because it can be an "annoyance to the reader."

Here is an example of a flush-left head:

Governors
Can't Agree
On Energy

Nevertheless, some newspapers still hold fast to a variety of other heads. They include:

1. Inverted pyramid—two or three lines, each one shorter than the line above it, all centered:

Pacific Science Parley
Hears Appeal by
UN Official

2. Drop or stepped lines—two or three lines, each approximately the same length. The first one is flush left, the third one flush right, and the middle one (if any) centered.

City Granting Reduction
In Realty Tax at Fast Rate

3. Hanging indentation—two, three or four lines, the first line longer than other lines and flush left. Other lines are equal in length, and are indented an identical space at the left.

Lawyers Protesting
Efforts to Repeal
Bar Examinations

4. Crossline or barline—a single line, centered.

Waitress Bags Suspect

There are, of course, a variety of other techniques used by newspapers from time to time. Some put the entire headline in a box. Others put a box around the head, but leave a break in the top line of the box and insert a smaller, centered head in the space. And some use flush-right heads, usually on a feature story.

Most American newspapers keep their headlines to one, two or three lines. However, some four- and even five-line heads are being used from time to time. Arnold calls that "A Britishism that is beginning to creep into some American papers. They are not effective with readers used to U.S. newspaper style."

In recent years almost three-fourths of all American newspapers have eliminated the use of *decks* and *banks* (the latter term generally applies only to second and third decks, if used). Some, however, continue to use them on news stories.

The New York Times, for example, uses decks with its headlines, especially on page one. It does not use them in such special sections as the Sunday art and leisure pages.

Here are several examples of headlines with decks:

New Flight
Safety Rule
Sparks Row

Controllers Must
Warn Pilots of
Perilous Altitudes

* * * * * * * * * *

PHYSICIANS BEGIN
JOB ACTION HERE;
IMPACT IS SLIGHT

——

A Quiet Sunday, As Usual, Is
Marked by Most Hospitals
—Nassau an Exception

——

TEST MAY COME TODAY

——

Protest, Aimed at Insurance
Law, Expected to Have
a Spotty Effect in City

Although decks tend to give a newspaper an old-fashioned look to the modern typographer, there are several practical reasons for using them from time to time. When a newspaper uses a banner headline, a deck (also called a drop or readout) may serve the very functional purpose of guiding the reader's eye to the body type of the story, especially if there are other headlines right under the banner. A deck can also serve a visual function to help the reader's eye adjust from the large headline type size to the much smaller body type.

In recent years a number of headline techniques have been developed that not only add to a newspaper's attractiveness but also aid the headline writer in telling the story. The most popular of these is the kicker. It is a short head, sometimes underlined, above a larger main head. (This head is also called by a variety of other names, although "kicker" is the most generally accepted.) The kicker usually is about one-third the width of the main headline and should be approximately one-half the type size of the main head. A 60-point headline should have a 30-point kicker. Kickers, most often, are used on multicolumn headlines, although they can be used on one-column heads if they are kept short. With a kicker the main head should have no more than two lines, as a general rule, and a deck should not be used. The main head under a kicker should be indented several spaces but the kicker is set flush left or centered over the main head. The combination of the kicker and the indentation of the main head creates white space around the mass of type in the head, and white space tends to attract the reader's eye.

The use of the kicker has led to the introduction of a reverse kicker, also called a hammer. In this style, the headline writer simply reverses the size of the main headline and the kicker. The reverse kicker usually is twice the size of the main head and it is set flush left. It should be no wider than half the headline area, which means it should not be attempted too often in two columns of space and never in one. The main head under a reverse kicker also is indented to help balance the area of white space at the right created by the kicker.

Following are examples of kicker and a reverse kicker headlines:

Libel Suit Filed

Newspaper Fights Order
Prohibiting Editorials

BARGAIN SOURCE
. . . Postal Service auctions packages
that can't be delivered, returned

Kickers and reverse kickers allow the headline writer to expand the ideas he wants to convey in the headlines. However, they are difficult to write and unless done with care can be pointless or, worse yet, can lead to problems for the paper. Even when excellent kickers are written, the reader should be able to get an accurate message from the main headline alone. If a kicker, using a qualifying word or phrase for the main head, is accidently left off, the main head might end up more of an editorial comment.

Headlines can be either in all caps or in caps and lowercase. The choice will make a difference in the number of units. Tests have shown that all-cap headlines are more difficult to read than caps and lowercase headlines. However, some newspapers still use all-cap heads regularly, although the standard style is for just the first letter in each word to be capitalized. Some headline schedules require that prepositions, conjunctions of three or fewer letters and definite and indefinite articles in headlines be in lowercase, also. There is another head style that continues to gain popularity. It is called "down" style. Only the first letter of the first word in the head and any proper names are capitalized.

Here are some examples of headlines:

All caps:

ARGENTINA FIGHTS
80% INFLATION

Caps and lower case:

Dad Brings
Shotgun
To Wedding

Down style:

Sailor saves women in crash

The copy editor or headline writer does not have an unlimited choice of headlines at most newspapers. Generally every newspaper has specific limits on the number of headline combinations available. These combinations usually are illustrated in a headline schedule showing each head style and size of type available. The number of letters and spaces (units) that will fit in any given number of columns for a particular type size is shown, also.

34c

Counting Heads. Every line of type contains a definite number of letters and spaces depending upon the size of the type—the smaller the type, the more letters and spaces. Extra letters cannot be squeezed in very successfully. The head writer must compose a headline that will fit in that limited space. He does it by using a schedule for counting the units (or letters). Headline counts will vary from newspaper to newspaper depending upon the type used. However, here is a typical schedule:

For heads set in capital and small letters, use this unit count:

One-half Unit

Small i and l, capital I, numeral 1
Punctuation marks (except dash and question mark)
Spaces between words

One Unit

All small letters except i, l, m and w
All figures except 1
Dash and question mark

One and One-half Units

Small m and w
All capitals except M, W (and I which is ½)

449

Two Units

Capital M and W
For heads set in capitals, use this unit count:
For all-capital heads the following applies:

One-Half Unit

I, numeral 1
Punctuation marks (except dash and question mark)

One Unit

All letters except I, M and W
All figures except 1
Spaces between words
Dash and question mark

One and One-half Units

M and W

If, for example, a headline writer is told to write a three-column, one-line, 30 point head, caps and lower case, he would count it this way:

½ ½ 1 1 ½ 1½ ½ 1 1 ½ 1½ 1 1 1 1 ½ ½ 1½ 1 ½ 1 1 1 1 ½ 1½ 1 1 1 1 ½ 1 1 1 1
F i r e H i t s L a u r e l H e i g h t s A p a r t m e n t s

This is the accepted method of counting in headlines, but head writers on some staffs do not follow the system carefully. Writing heads on a typewriter, they count each letter and space as one unit, depending upon the compositors or pasteup men to space the lines correctly. In most cases such headlines will fit the space, but sometimes they must be rewritten because they are too long.

To become a good headline writer requires a mastery of the language, a love of words and a bag full of tricks. Every good copy editor has filed away—in his mind or on paper—a handy list of synonyms (short ones) that quickly become an important part of his headline vocabulary. For example: "bar" for prevent or "hike" for increase.

It is important, of course, that the headline writer not abuse the use of these words in an effort to make a headline fit. One must always be aware of the shades of meaning. One man's warning may be another man's threat. To select the wrong word would distort the story.

SELECTING THE HEADLINE

While the practice will vary from newspaper to newspaper, generally the responsibility for evaluating news stories and deciding what size headlines should be written on them is the job of the makeup editor or the news editor. They may be the same person. How does an editor determine which headline should go on each story?

In general, the importance or local interest of a news story dictates the size of the headline for the story. Since reader interest of a news event dictates the length of the story, one can conclude that the larger headlines are generally found on the longer stories. Generally, this is true, but there are exceptions. Just because a story is long does not automatically mean that it gets a large headline. In deciding the size of a headline, that long story must be weighed against all other stories available that day to determine the relative value of each to the readers. Stories compete with each other. A short story may be the most significant that given day and may end up with a large headline, prominently displayed on the page. News is inconsistent. A fairly good story may get a rather large headline on a day when good stories are scarce. On other days, several leading stories might be of equal importance but the editor cannot use the same type headline for all of them. In such a case, he will attempt to make all of them approximately equal but use a variety of type faces and headline combinations. The importance of the story should always dictate the approximate size of the headline. While planning is necessary, stories should not be greatly overplayed or underplayed to meet space requirements or a predetermined design of a page.

A few suggestions for selecting heads are: (1) nearly every page will need a few large heads, (2) double-column and other multicolumn heads improve the appearance of the pages and (3) both roman and italic typefaces are available. Italic type is generally used to break the monotony of straight heads or on change-of-pace heads.

PRINCIPLES OF HEADLINE WRITING

Good headline writing is an art that must be practiced under the pressure of deadlines. Each headline writer will develop his own techniques, but a study of headlines, good and bad, will show that there are a few general principles usually practiced at all newspapers:

1. The headline should tell the story's essentials and tell them accurately. **34e** It should be based on the lead, in the case of news stories, and given as many of the 5 W's as necessary—playing up the proper W. Each head should be a complete sentence, with unnecessary words omitted:

POOR

**Man Sustains
A Fatal Injury**

BETTER

**Guard Killed
In Gun Fight**

2. The symmetry of line length required by the style of a particular head- **34f** line should be achieved. The lines must not appear too crowded with type or too empty. They should not appear grossly unbalanced:

POOR

**McDonald to
Head FBI Office**

BETTER

**McDonald Named
FBI Agent Here**

451

POOR

**Mayor
Urges
Crackdown**

BETTER

**Mayor Urges
Crackdown**

34g

3. If a headline is made up of several different forms, each part should be a full statement and should stand alone:

POOR

**Huge Oil Slick
100 Miles Long**

**Reported by
Coast Guard**

BETTER

**Huge Oil Slick
Threat to Coast**

**Covers 100 Miles,
Reports Guard**

34h

4. A thought should not be repeated. Each deck or bank should advance the story with additional information:

POOR

**Heavy Truck
Bill Postponed**

**Truck Weight
Increase Sought**

BETTER

**Heavy Truck
Bill Postponed**

**Public Hearings
Planned for Fall**

34i

5. Involved, confusing or ambiguous heads should be avoided:

POOR

**Aged Fight Pension
Plans for Future**

BETTER

**Aged Group Fights
New Pension Plans**

34j

6. Feature stories should have feature headlines:

POOR

Dog Is Favorite White House Pet

BETTER

'Dogging' It at the White House

—

POOR

**Patrons Borrow Free
Umbrellas Permanently**

BETTER

**Free Umbrella Idea
Picked up Quickly**

7. Each headline should contain a verb in order not to appear as a mere label. The verb should be in the first line if possible, but the headline should not start with a verb:

34k

POOR	BETTER
College Mall	**College Mall Opens**
—	—
Urge Milk Fund For City's Needy	**Milk Fund Urged For City's Needy**

8. Headlines generally should be written in the active voice, not the passive, for impact:

34l

POOR	BETTER
Strikers Warned by Mayor	**Mayor Warns Rail Strikers**

9. Headlines should be written in the historical present tense (or future). However, some newspapers permit past tense in headlines:

34m

POOR	BETTER
Penal Farm Inmate Escaped Into Woods	**Penal Farm Inmate Escapes Into Woods**

10. The headline should use vivid, fresh language; avoid dull and trite words:

34n

POOR	BETTER
Congress Studies Gun Control Again	**Congress Takes Aim At Gun Control Again**

34o

11. Words should not be repeated in the headline:

POOR

Strike Conference Ends
Steelworkers Strike

BETTER

Mediation Session Ends
Steelworkers Strike

34p

12. Headlines should be specific. Try to find the exact word to convey a thought:

POOR

Youth Injured
In Knife Battle

BETTER

Youth Slashed
In Knife Fight

34q

13. Provincial slang expressions should be avoided:

POOR

Stockers Sales
Cut in Half

BETTER

Local Cattle Sales
Drop 50 Per Cent

34r

14. The headline writer cannot use simplified spelling (such as "tho") unless it is the style of the newspaper:

POOR

Rain to Continue
Thru Another Day

BETTER

Rain to Continue
Through Tomorrow

34s

15. Single quotation marks should be used in headlines. Divide thoughts with a semicolon:

POOR

Kidnaped Boy
"Buried Alive"

BETTER

Kidnaped Boy
'Buried Alive'

34t

16. Abbreviations should not be used unless standard, conventional and generally understood, such as U.S., FBI:

POOR

500 of ASE
At Meeting Here

BETTER

500 Engineers
Convene Here

17. Words, phrases consisting of nouns and adjective modifiers, prepositional phrases and verb phrases should not be split between lines:

POOR

Council Passes Sales Tax Despite Protest

BETTER

Sales Tax Passes Despite Protest

18. Opinion headlines should be attributed or qualified:

POOR

Taxes Too High On Businesses

BETTER

Taxes Too High Say Businessmen

19. Articles and other unnecessary words should not be used, except with names of books and other proper titles:

POOR

Fireman Saves A Little Puppy

BETTER

Fireman Saves Dog from Blaze

20. "Half truths" must be avoided. Sometimes such heads can be libelous or misleading.

POOR

Pastor Sought In Larceny Case

BETTER

Pastor Sought As Eyewitness

Subheads. Subheads are boldface lines of body type used in long news stories. They are a typographical device used to break up the long columns of grayness. As a general rule, they start after the first three paragraphs and are placed evenly three or four paragraphs apart throughout the story. The last one generally is placed three paragraphs before the story ends. They usually are set in all caps and are centered, but the practice will vary from newspaper to newspaper. The general principles of headline writing apply to subheads. They should not fill the entire line or allow too much white space.

In recent years, some newspapers have eliminated subheads in favor of other devices to break the monotony of large masses of solid body type. One is to boldface whole paragraphs, parts of paragraphs or even parts of sentences—the first four words of a sentence, for example. Others have gone to writing secondary heads (similar to decks) and putting them in a box (or a half box), with ample white space around the head, and placing the box into the body type to give some visual relief.

EXERCISES

1. Using any newspaper available to you, clip 10 headlines that violate one or more of the rules for headline writing. Rewrite them to correct the errors. Indicate the number of units in each line of the head.

2. Using newspapers available to you on the newsstands or in your college library, compare the stories covering the same news event in two competing daily newspapers. Compare the headlines on the stories for content, size and style.

3. Clip from any newspaper available to you a sample of each different type headline used. Arrange in order from the largest to smallest. Paste on 8½ x 11 sheets of paper, count the number of units in each head. Indicate the number of units in the margin opposite each line.

4. Using those same headlines and the headline schedule at the end of the following chapter, indicate the size of type used in each one.

5. Following is a list of local stories available for one edition of a newspaper. Estimate as nearly as the given facts permit the news value of each story. Clip from a newspaper an example of the size and type of headline you would recommend for the story.
   A. Police manpower down. Crime up in the city. Story is 15 column inches long.
   B. School board approves 10.8 per cent budget boost. Twenty inches.
   C. Temperatures to drop near 20 overnight. No rain expected. Six inches.
   D. Planners approve rezoning farm land for housing development. Eight inches.
   E. School official wounded by angry student. Eight and one-half inches.
   F. Former governor dies at his home near here. Twenty-one inches.
   G. Man sentenced to 43 years in prison for attempting to escape from courtroom during trial. Five inches.
   H. City hires first woman fire fighter. Ten inches.
   I. Coal miner struck by locomotive, killed at entrance to nearby mine. Six inches.
   J. Man gets life for slaying of honeymooners. Four inches.
   K. Panel charges housing agency neglects low-income people. Twelve inches.

6. Write each of the following leads as briefly as possible, using either the same words or synonyms, but select only the important words and ignore every word a headline writer might ignore.
   A. Gary Wayne Wilson, 34, indicted on a murder charge in the fatal shooting of Patrolman Danny Hayes, pleaded innocent yesterday in Criminal Court.
   B. A 24-year-old graduate student was critically injured about 7:30 p.m. yesterday when he was struck by a hit-and-run car on Cumberland Avenue at Sixteenth Street.
   C. A woman who admitted in City Court yesterday she lied when swearing out a warrant against her former boyfriend has been charged with perjury.
   D. Four officials of Statewide Paving Contractors Inc. waived indictment and submitted guilty pleas yesterday to charges they conspired to rig bids on state paving contracts.
   E. A 33-year-old man broke the window of a Cumberland Avenue restaurant with his fist last night and then placed a knife at his throat and held police at bay for about 30 minutes.

7. Write a one-column, two-line, flush-left headline for each of the stories in Exercise 6. Use capitals and lower case with 15 to 16 units in each line. Make use of the telegraphic sentences already prepared in completing this exercise.

Makeup

A newspaper has a personality that should be expressed in its design as well as its news columns and editorial pages. Some papers have always done this more effectively than others.

Readers of metropolitan tabloids in the 1920s and 1930s knew that the big, brassy headlines and large illustrations signaled sensational stories. Some metropolitan tabloids still use the same basic design, but often their content is far less sensational. But bold and brassy was not the exclusive property of tabloids. Numerous full-sized newspapers have used—and continue to use—the same techniques, especially when displaying a major story such as a devastating earthquake or an airplane crash in which hundreds have been killed.

In contrast, many newspapers reveal their basic conservative personality through the use of modest headlines, relatively small photographs and rather long stories creating masses of solid gray type. Their approach to news is less excitable, and it is reflected in their design.

For the most part, the appearance of a newspaper is a reflection of the owner and the men and women who run it. In fact, there was a day not too long ago when newspapers did not pay too much attention to their makeup and format. They picked a design that pleased them and stuck with it, giving little or no regard to reader response. At most newspapers that time has passed.

Spurred on by the visual competition from television and the results of numerous research studies, most newspapermen have come to realize that if they do not put out a product that is easy to read, the customers might turn to another medium. The world is becoming more and more visual. One study shows that the average person has about 10,000 eye fixations a day. Students, office workers and others have up to 15,000. So when the average reader gets home, his eyes are getting tired whether he is aware of it or not. If he is not greeted by the easiest-to-read newspaper that can be produced, he is going to flick on his television set and may not read the newspaper.

457

The job of the makeup editor is to give him that easy-to-read newspaper. On larger newspapers the makeup editor's job is often a full-time one, and several very large newspapers, following the long-time practice of magazines, have hired art directors to design their makeup. (An electronic makeup device similar to the video display terminal is being used at some newspapers.) However, on an average-size daily the makeup editor often is the news or managing editor. Usually every story sent to the composing room goes through his hands or he gets a "schedule" (or log) of stories handled by the various editors and the copy desk. Most makeup editors also keep their own "schedule" of major stories, noting the size of the headline, typeface and the approximate length of each story and any pictures or illustrations connected with it. Major stories are sometimes listed on a separate sheet earmarked especially for "page-one" placement.

The selection of stories for page one and other important display pages (the front page of the second section, for example) can be handled in several ways. Most larger newspapers have an editorial conference daily before home edition deadline at which all editors—city, state, wire and frequently departmental—meet with the makeup editor and the managing editor. Each one presents his list of important stories and as a group they decide what stories will go on page one and where the stories will be placed on the page. At smaller newspapers the makeup editor may make the decision after he confers with the various editors, seeking a consensus on the most important stories of the day.

Changes in Makeup. For years most newspapers were vertical in appearance. Stories started at the top of the page, were covered by a one-column headline for the most part and ran straight down the column. A few newspapers still follow that style; but most modern newspapers, building on findings of countless studies, have learned to take advantage of the reader's habit of reading from left to right. So today the modern newspaper is more horizontal than vertical in appearance. Stories run across the pages and not down them. Most headlines are multicolumn rather than one column. Pictures are often large and more horizontal than vertical. The page is not crowded with stories and pictures, and there is abundant white space.

Traditionally, newspapers placed the main story in the top right corner, and a number still follow this practice. This was partly because most newspapers used an eight-column banner (a page-wide headline in very large type) as their standard headline on the main story of the day and it was logical to place the story where the headline ended. However, in modern typography, the eight-column banner head is not used as frequently and some newspapers are placing their main story in the upper left-hand corner of the page where it catches the reader's eye immediately. Then, they display a story or photograph of almost equal importance in the upper right corner of the page.

Designer Edmund Arnold cites the following as the principles on which a newspaper should base its design philosophy:

1. Good typography should be the packaging of content, and content should determine what the package looks like. You must first know what you are packaging. A good layout of any kind must be organic, must grow from what it has to work with—the content, the day's news budget.

2. The newspaper design should present a lot of different news in a minimum of space.

3. A good newspaper page must be functional. Every element—every line of type—must communicate with the reader, must transmit information.
4. Good typographic layout of any kind must be invisible. It should not overpower the message.

Procedure for Makeup. In designing a standard-sized page—the front page or **35a** one on the inside—the first step in the most modern procedure (sometimes called "functional") should be to place a strong attention-getter in the upper left-hand corner of the page, because that is where the reader's eye instinctively goes. If there is nothing in that spot to stop the wandering eye, it is likely to sweep across the page and go on to something else, perhaps less important, and one of the functions of makeup is to attract the reader into the body of the story. (Others are to help the reader grade the news by its placement on the page and the size of its headline, and to present the news in an orderly fashion.)

The attention-getter should be a strong headline or a large picture, or perhaps an unusual story placed in a box. Whatever it is, it must help rivet the reader's attention on that part of the page and get his eyes moving from left to right, reading the stories as he gets to them. This means that something equally inviting should be in the upper right corner to keep his eyes moving in that direction.

In designing the front page (inside pages will be discussed later), after placing materials across the top of the page, the makeup editor then moves back and plans the center of the page to get the reader's eye to sweep across it again, and, finally, he goes back and does it all over again across the lower part of the page.

How the attention-getter—and the entire top third of the page—is displayed will be influenced, of course, by where the newspaper's flag (nameplate) is placed. If the flag is a standard eight-column one that goes across the page, its position often is automatic—at the very top of the page. However, if it is a size that can be "floated" from one spot to another, it can be used as a basic display element in the top one-third of the page but never below the fold.

It is important for the makeup editor to try to achieve a sense of balance on this page. The top should not totally dominate the bottom of the page. There should be some strong display elements in the center as well as on the bottom one-third of the page. Many editors try to anchor the corners (as well as the center) with strong display elements. It may be a picture or multicolumn heads or a box or half box in the center of the page. And in the bottom one-third it could be any of these elements or even a banner. (Of course, a banner in this position should be in smaller type than the head on the main story.) Some typographers suggest that the makeup editor lay a dollar bill horizontally on the page. He knows he has covered all bases if, no matter where he places the bill, it touches at least one display element—such as a headline or picture. They say that the area the size of a bill is about all the body type the reader will accept without some typographic relief. Others suggest putting the hand over the center of the page with fingers spread. Each finger should touch a display unit, they say.

One of the marks of a modern front page is the lack of crowding. (The same goes for inside pages as well.) The use of white space is a significant makeup tool. It is used around the flag, or art, above headlines, between the lines of heads, between the head and the by-line and the by-line and the credit line, between the credit line and the lead, between paragraphs, between the photo and the caption and between the ads and editorial matter.

35b Many modern typographers insist that headlines should be as widely separated as possible. Headlines, whenever possible, should not be tombstoned (placed side by side), nor should they be armpitted (placing a narrow head immediately under a wider one with no body type between them). The separation of heads by the lighter body type makes the page more attractive, much easier to read and it creates contrast. (See Fig. 35-1.)

35c Contrast is also important in the selection of headlines. All the headlines on a page should not be the same size. There should be variety in size, not only because the headline is supposed to help grade the value of news stories but also because the contrast in size of headlines makes a more attractive and easier-to-read page.

35d Ideally, the news on the front page should be organized into horizontal blocks, not unlike books. Research shows that type in horizontal blocks will appear to have a smaller mass. And readers are always more willing to dive into a shorter story. In some tests, a 15-inch story displayed horizontally attracted more attention and was considered easier to read than a 15-inch story displayed vertically. This indicates that makeup editors should be aware that readership problems may arise in long stories. If a story runs more than 15 inches, should it be jumped from page one to an inside page? The practice varies from newspaper to newspaper, but some guidelines might be helpful:

35e 1. Avoid jumping too many stories from page one. Some newspapers allow no more than three jump stories. And others allow none. When a story runs long, it often is rewritten and made into two or more stories.

2. Do not jump short stories. Make room on the page by careful editing. Short jumps not only look silly but also are often ignored or missed by the reader.

3. Avoid jumping a story within the first few paragraphs. Enough paragraphs should be placed beneath the headline to balance the size of the headline (preventing the story from appearing top heavy).

4. Do not jump stories from one inside page to another. Unless there is enough space on an inside page to accommodate the entire story, it should not be placed in that position.

35f *Related Stories.* Sometimes the makeup editor finds that he has several stories relating to a single event. He usually groups such stories. The most common method is to put one large headline on the most important story and smaller, separate headlinesones on the secondary stories, placed adjacent to the larger story.

460

Joan Little Acquitted

BULLETIN

RALEIGH, N.C. (AP) — A jury of six whites and six blacks acquitted Joan Little of all charges today in the ice-pick stabbing of her white jailer. (Earlier story on Page 1b.)

Bangladesh Leader Slain

Military Coup Topples Government

NEW DELHI, India (AP) — President Mujibur Rahman of...

MPC Telephone Vote Is Declared Illegal

Pay Balance Shows Surplus

6-Month Total Is First for U.S.

WASHINGTON (UPI) — The nation's balance of payments showed a $1.25 billion surplus in...

Jackson Ave., 'Underground'

Detailed Study Planned for Downtown Area

Action Set Later on 2 Subdivisions

By BOB BARRETT
News-Sentinel Staff Writer

Metropolitan Planning Commission acted in haste Thursday after one member left, leaving a problem of not having a quorum on two items, and getting a vote by telephone from an absent member.
The members found our Fri. ____

Guitarist Chet Atkins to appear at RSCC Sept. 6

Chet Atkins, perhaps the greatest of country music guitarists, will perform here at Roane State Community College gymnasium on Saturday September 6.

Arrangements for Atkins to appear here were announced today by Dr Don King, chairman of the Roane County Committee for the Tennessee Performing Arts.

It will be Atkins's first appearance in Roane County, although he began his career as a guitarist on the 'Mid-Day Merry-Go-Round of Radio Station WNOX in Knoxville...

Squire Banker wants court to continue meeting monthly

BY WALTER SCARBROUGH

Only eleven new resolutions have been filed for consideration at next Monday night's regular session of Roane County Quarterly Court, but three of these relate to the proposed new budget and tax rate, and these are...

Man, wife injured as travel van jack-knives

Littleton named Kingston manager

Larry W. Littleton, 35, a native of Kingston, has been named new City Manager for the City of Kingston, getting the position in a special...

Town store of Sears in Knoxville.
The council, in hiring Mr Littleton, who has lived in Kingston all his life, set the...

Astronauts, cosomonauts visit each other's capsules

By HOWARD BENEDICT
AP Aerospace Writer

SPACE CENTER, Houston (AP). In a spirit of good humored camaraderie, Apollo astronauts and Soyuz cosmonauts exchanged their own brand of shuttle diplomacy today in a series of visits between their linked orbital homes.
There was much back slapping and hand-shaking as spacemen moved through a tunnel connecting the two ships...

Capt. Edwards becomes Blue Ridge, Ga., chief

Detective Captain Lee...

Figure 35-1. Here are some examples of tombstoned and armpitted headlines. They are frequently difficult to read and give the page a cluttered, unattractive appearance.

New postmaster

Jim Flowers appointed to Owingsville position

Jimmie L. Flowers is the new postmaster at Owingsville.

A Morehead postal employee, Flowers served as officer in charge of the Owingsville post office from April 8 through July 31 of last year after the retirement of Mrs. John R. Jones as postmaster.

The appointment of Flowers was announced by William R. Cummings, district manager of the Kentuckiana District. It was effective last Saturday, March 25.

Postmasters are selected on merit, based on recommendations by a management selection board and appointed by the postmaster general. Appointments are not subject to senate confirmation.

Flowers has been serving at the Morehead post office since Aug. 23, 1969, in the capacities of carrier and clerk. On July 29 of last year he was promoted to the position of superintendent, postal operations.

He received his formal education in Wilmington, N.C., followed by two years in the U.S. Army. He is active in community affairs, in the Jaycees, Kiwanis Club and has served as a Little League coach.

Jim Gossard, who has served as officer in charge here since August, will return to the Morehead post office.

Jimmie L. Flowers (right) is sworn in by Bill Long, Postal Systems Examiner

THE NEWS Bath County OUTLOOK

National and state prize-winning newspaper — prized by its community

| 99th Year–Number 31 | Phone 674-2181 | Thursday, March 30, 1978 | Single Copy: 20c | Owingsville, Kentucky 40360 |

The candidates

First of a series picturing the 21 Bath County May Day Festival candidates

June Hunt Daughter of Mrs. Ollie Hunt and the late Mr. Hunt

Elaine Richardson Daughter of Judge and Mrs. James M. Richardson

Debby Thornsburg Daughter of Mr. and Mrs. Herschel Thornsburg

May Festival plans moving

10 floats entered

With six weeks still to go before target date of the Bath County May Festival on Saturday, May 13, six class "A" floats and four class "B" floats already have been entered for the parade.

Twenty-one May Day candidates will be riding on the class "A" floats, so at least twelve of these will be necessary in order that no more than two can appear on each float.

To date, the class "A" floats and their themes include: Owingsville PTA - McDonald Land; Owingsville Chamber of Commerce - Chiffon Margarine; Linear Radio Club - Fruit of the Loom; Owingsville Woman's Club - Chiquita Bananas; Bethel Community - Nestle Strawberry Quick; and Bath County Homemakers - Ethan Allen.

Class "B" floats that have been registered so far, include Girl Scout Troop no. 790 - Parkay Margarine; Brownie Troop no. 789 - Chiffon Margarine; Salt Lick Brownie Troop no. 609-Oscar Mayer Boloney and Girl Scout Troop no. 446 - Coca Cola.

Parade Marshalls, clowns and bicycles will also be a part of the parade, set to start at 1 p.m. Saturday, May 13. The parade will start from Owingsville Elementary School and turn at the locker plant. Parade chairman is Lonnie Vice, who may be contacted by anyone wishing to enter a unit.

Rhonda's room

Her teaching takes special talent, plus singing, prayer and love

By Mrs. Phyllis Byron
News-Outlook editor

"I think it just takes a lot of love," said Rhonda Cooper, in discussing her work with special Education (trainable) students at the Owingsville Elementary School. Rhonda has made great progress with her eight students, as anyone who had seen them a few years ago, would immediately recognize.

"They're all such fun to work with and they each have qualities and dispositions that make them uniquely themselves." And Rhonda feels that her work with them is most rewarding.

Holds Degree

In her college work at MSU, where she received an AB and MA, Rhonda majored in Phys Ed and Special Education and enjoyed them both. She also had another interest in college, which has aided in her work with the children she now teaches, and that interest was music. She and her brother, Chuck, now in Seminary at Asbury, formed a trio with another friend, Donna Clark and the three sing together nearly every weekend at church meetings and revivals, where Chuck often also does the preaching.

Children Respond to Music

Rhonda finds that the children she teaches respond well to music, so she makes it a part of the class program. "Children express themselves in music as they cannot do in other ways and they love it," she says.

Teachers Aid Also Holds Degree

She feels that she has several things going for her at the school, one of them being her excellent teacher's aid, Beth Moore, who also holds a degree in special ed. The other asset is having the same children to work with for two years in sequence.

The eight children in her class range in age from eight through seventeen years, which she explains is why a good teacher's aid is needed. "But the children relate well with each other," she says, "the older ones learn how to help the younger ones and the younger ones learn how to depend on them."

Wanted to Teach Since A 1st-Grader

Her lovely brown eyes sparkling with enthusiasm, Rhonda says, "I have wanted to work with exceptional children since I was in the first grade-and these children are very special indeed-they have so much to give."

"I wonder sometimes," she continues, "if I'm giving them all they need-sometimes I think I learn more than they do! They're so real, so honest. But you have to do the best you can, so a lot of prayer goes into the program."

Program is Varied

The program for the class is varied-they're all learning to read some of the functional words (so that they can get along when by themselves) four of them can write their names, one of the students can print and the other three are working on 'hand-eye' coordination (such as tying shoes, buttoning clothes, etc.)

"Of course they all work on coordination," their teacher explained, "They love gym and are preparing right now for the special Olympics. They're excited about this, but not anymore excited than Beth and I are."

Children Express Their View

The children who had behaved extremely well during the interview with their teacher, wanted to express some opinions of their own, during which they said that they liked school fine and were glad to get back to classes after the weekend.

They also said they liked both the school play and work; hot dogs, singing and being read to.

Installation of new officers

Commissioner to speak at annual C of C banquet

Members of the Owingsville Chamber of Commerce and their guests, will hear Ralph Ed Graves, Commissioner of the Department for Local Government during their annual banquet set for tonight, Thursday, March 30, at 7 p.m., in the fellowship Hall of the Owingsville Christian Church. Judge-executive Ray Bailey will introduce Commissioner Graves.

Owns two weekly papers

Born in 1927, in Bard, Mr. Graves went into the newspaper business in 1960 and is now the owner of two weekly newspapers in Western Kentucky.

During 1969, 1971 and 1973, he was a member of the State Legislature, but resigned in 1974, to join Governor Carrol's staff in Frankfort.

From 1971 to 1974, he served as a member of the Purchase Area Administration Board.

Other business during the meeting will be awarding of certificates to the 1977 Outstanding Citizen, the Teacher of the Year, the Farmer of the Year and

Ralph Ed Graves Local Government Commissioner

the Business person of the year. The naming of these outstanding persons is always a highlight of the Chamber of Commerce affair.

Also on the agenda will be the installation of new Chamber of Commerce officers for 1978.

The new officers include Donald Manuel, president, Majorie Boyd, vice president; Monterey Garner, secretary and Laura Manuel, treasurer.

Outgoing officers are Ray Ellis, president and Ken Curtis, second vice president. Ellis will officiate at the meeting.

Tickets for the 'old-ham' dinner will be available at 9¢ each from any Chamber of Commerce member.

Science Fair tomorrow at high school

The Bath County High School Science Fair will be held Friday, March 31. Science students will exhibit their projects Friday afternoon, with the judging taking place at 3:00 p.m.

Local teachers will serve as judges. Overall winners will be awarded 1st, 2nd, and 3rd place prizes. Projects judged to be excellent will go on to regional competion at Morehead State University on Saturday, April 8.

The Bath County Science Fair will be open to the public from 6:30 to 8:00 p.m. We encourage all parents and interested persons to visit the Science Fair.

In high school gymnasium

Band concert is set for 8 o'clock tonight

Tonight (Thursday) at 8 o'clock, the Bath County High School band will present its spring concert at the high school gym, with George Strellenberger directing.

Some of the numbers will be: New Spirit Fanfare and March by Nowak; Liebestram by F. Liszt; That's All Folks By Balent; Prelude to Act II of Lohengrin by R. Wagner; Lonesome Valley by Nestico; Billboard March by Klohr.

Dianetta Clemmons, senior trumpet, will play the solo trumpet part to Lonesome Valley. Assisting Mr. Strellenberger directing will be Bill Schumacker, a MSU student teacher. The concert is open to the public.

Following are the members of the concert band:

Flutes: Kim Becknel, Beverly Johnson, Cindy Carey, Teresa Carey, Donetta Johnson.

Clarinets: Jeanette Hawkins, Jennifer McGuire, Vicki Thomas, Jennifer Richards, Kim Cooch, Sandra Tuttle, Sandy Karrick, Molly Plymale, Jennifer Campbell.

Bass Clarinets: Kim Richie, Lee Ann Cline, Lisa Highley.

Bassoon: Kerry Jane Settles.

French Horn: Lannie Turner, and Vicki Carpenter.

Trumpets: Harvy Thompson, Timmy Utterback, Franklin Crouch, Dianetta Clemmons, Gerald McClain, Neal Oliver, Anita Hunt, Wesley Crouch.

Saxophones: Jennie Maze, Bess Byron, and Pam Barber.

Trombones: Cindy Bohn, Ronda Young and George Emmons.

Baritones: Dale Doyle and Dana Fraley.

Tuba: Eric Highley.

Percussion: Eddie Chapman, Roy Hodge and Leslie Hall.

Happiness is learning Students of the trainable special education class at the Owingsville Elementary School and their teacher, Rhonda Cooper, left, and Beth Moore, aid. (News-Outlook Staff Photo)

Figure 35-2. The News Outlook, Owingsville, Ky., has won more than 125 state and national awards, many of them for makeup and design. Courtesy of The News Outlook, Owingsville, Ky.

MONTGOMERY
THE **Journal**
Montgomery County's Community Newspaper

VOL. 7 N 2 sectio | ©1980 Journal Newspapers Inc | Member Audit Bureau of Circulations | FRIDAY, JANUARY 4, 1980 | EDITORIAL: (202)554-5650 CIRCULATION: (202)554-7500 | CLASSIFIED ADVERTISING: (202)554-7565 DISPLAY ADVERTISING: (202)554-7552 | 25 CENTS

Aquatic Center in New 'No- Frills' Building Budget

usan Hedling
nal Staff Writer

Except for a proposed $8.6 million aquatic center, complete with saunas and a wave-making machine, the latest six-year construction budget contains no frills and few new projects.

The annual update of the Capital Improvements Program (CIP) was released this week with little flourish by county officials who called it "a relatively austere or hold the line approach."

The construction budget is revised each year to provide an overview for the next six fiscal years of what the county is building and how much it is borrowing to pay for it.

This year's version, spanning 1981 to 1986, contains about 850 projects which will cost $1.4 billion. Last year's version of the CIP totalled about $1.2 billion.

Expenditures actually made in fiscal year 1981 will total $278 million. This is an increase over the $244.4 million spent this year.

Most of that increase, according to statements in the voluminous budget document, are caused by inflation and not by the addition of new projects. Within county departments alone, and not counting other agencies such as schools and bi-county commissions, the construction budget has increased 13.6%, largely due to higher costs of the new County Office Building under construction in Rockville and Metro road improvements and parking lots.

The only project in the county government section of the CIP which might require special voter approval is the aquatic center because it is estimated to cost almost twice the $4.5 million ceiling on construction projects imposed by a referendum passed in 1978 allowing voter approval of expensive projects.

If the aquatic center is built it would be a complex with year-round use to serve everyone in the county, and recreation planners say it would generate enough revenue to support its operating costs.

A location has not been chosen, but the CIP shows construction in 1984 through 1986.

If built the center would have indoor facilities with a 14,000 square foot water area, seating for 500 persons, health and exercise rooms, men and women's saunas and locker and shower rooms.

See CONSTRUCTION, Page A5

County May Sue On Assessments

By Susan Hedling
Journal Staff Writer

The County Council might file a class action suit, or at least support an individual test case against the new state-mandated system of assessments which council members claim will mean an additional average 7% property tax hike for one-third of the county's homeowners.

As assessment notices went out the end of last month under the first year of the triennial assessment system passed in the 1979 session of the General Assembly, council members said they were inundated with phone calls from homeowners in the third of the county being reassessed in 1980.

This so-called Beck Bill changed assessments from an annual to a triennial system. It imposed a state-wide *average* ceiling of 6% per year assessment increases, thus shutting off the automatic, assessment-generated increases in tax collections that local governments had received.

The Beck Bill forces local governments to raise their tax rates if they want higher revenues, thus shifting the apparent responsibility for higher taxes from the state's assessments to the local government's tax rates. It met with howls of protest from local government throughout the state.

The system created by the bill is extremely complex, and some County Council members say it is unconstitutional because, they say, it distributes the tax burden unequally.

The council agreed to ask the county attorney to consider a class action suit, and members said they would support an appeal from an individual taxpayer in court.

The council urged all homeowners who are due for an assessment this year to file an appeal immediately to preserve their rights in case a court decision is not retroactive.

The average reassessment notices for the 60,000 homeowners in the one-third of the county affected this year is averaging a 7% increase in the market value of their property, according to council member Neal Potter.

"We'll probably have to raise the tax rate by about 7% for everyone in the county this spring," said Potter. "This means that the one-third who have been reassessed by 7% will end up paying at least 14% more on their tax bill."

A property tax bill is determined by the assessed value of a house and the tax rate applied to that value. This means that if an assessment stays the same and the rate goes up slightly, the tax bill will go up slightly. But, if both the assessment and the tax rate go up the bill will be higher.

"We've never seen an increase as high as 14% before," Potter said. "Something must be done to obey the Maryland Constitution which requires equality in taxation for all residents."

Council President Scott Fosler said the Beck Bill is so complicated that the State Dept. of Taxation issued a 12-page paper to explain it to the public.

"The council should try to determine how we're going to translate this to the citizens," Fosler said.

"I spent 20 hours studying the Beck Bill and I'm not sure I can explain it," Potter quipped.

Potter suggested that the county's public advocate in tax matters, Frank Ecker, file an individual appeal on behalf of other taxpayers.

Paint Lie Costs Man $500 Fine

By Curtis Barton
Journal Staff Writer

A Wheaton man who lied to a traffic court judge last summer about a painted-over traffic sign was fined $500 for perjury by a county judge last week.

John Ray Marino Jr., 25, earlier had pleaded guilty in connection with painting over the sign the night before his appearance in traffic court on a ticket charging him with ignoring the sign.

Marino told the judge the sign had been obstructed when he got the ticket, and showed the judge a photograph of the painted-over sign he said he had taken right after he got the ticket, two months before.

The judge found Marino innocent of the traffic charge.

Ofc. Scott Loomis, who gave Marino the ticket, wasn't satisfied by Marino's explanation and went back to Veirs Mill and Gridley, where the sign is located. He encountered some children who remembered seeing men painting the sign with a spray can the night before.

See PERJURY, Page A8

New Paper Collector

By Susan Hedling
Journal Staff Writer

The firm that ran the troubled newspaper collection program and got into financial difficulty with bounced payroll checks lost its county contract this week.

National Recovery Industry of Columbia, a non-profit company that employs some handicapped persons in its resource recycling programs, was dismissed by the county because of poor contract performance, according to a statement issued Wednesday by the county's Department of Environmental Protection.

"We have lent every conceivable effort to help the contractor build his capabilities to provide the needed level of service," said DEP director James Baker. "Despite our efforts, however, streets continue to be missed on collection routes presenting us with a serious problem since citizen cooperation has been so great."

As a temporary step, according to DEP, another company will pick up the contract to continue newspaper collection without interruption until final arrangements are made.

The new firm is Mason-Dixon Recyling Corp., located in Tysons Corner. The company will operate under the same terms of the old contract, DEP officials said. Mason-Dixon is a subsidiary of Garden State Paper Company, the firm that has been buying newspaper from the county.

Officials of the new contractor said they will retain the handicapped workers. In the spring, the county will solicit bids for a long-term contractor.

The newpspaper collection program, started by the county last September and mandatory for all homeowners in the down-county districts in which garbage collection is provided by the county, has been a severe administrative headache for DEP.

More newspapers than anticipated were collected — latest estimates are about 1000 tons of paper per month — and residents were outraged when routes were missed and soggy

See PAPERS, Page A8

Journal Staff Photo by Linda White

Theresa O'Brien, at 82, is still making beautiful music for many of the same friends who listened to her piano around the time of the first World War. She is shown above playing for residents of Fernwood House in Bethesda. Below is a photo taken in 1919.

Theresa O'Brien Still Plays for Her Friends

By Angie Vignola

Spirited describes her, even at 82.

Sitting at the piano, straight-backed, hands poised, she begins to play and could go on forever. Theresa Inez Cecilia Matthews O'Brien's repertoire coincides with a lifetime of memories.

It's New Year's Eve at 2:00 in the afternoon. The atmosphere is bright and beautiful at Fernwood House, a Bethesda nursing home. Hats, horns, noisemakers, champagne and hors d'oeuvres add to the festivities.

Some patients are wheeled in. Most come on their own power. Today is special. Everyone looks and feels excited as if a celebrated movie star were about to enter. And she may well be. Theresa O'Brien's nimble fingers will transport her audience to an idyllic world of yesterday. Like them, she is aware of aging's limited joys.

Music is life's blood for Theresa O'Brien. It has been pumping through her veins as far back as she can remember. The caption in her Eastern High School yearbook states, "When she plays, everybody dances." That still happens. When Theresa entertains in nursing homes, the able-bodied impulsively get up and move around. Today's nursing home generation are in essence, one and the same, as her high school classmates. They applaud now as they did then.

"I lived during the dance craze that began about 1912. No one left the grounds at Eastern during lunch time. We went to the gym and danced. After school we stopped at one another's homes, rolled up the carpet and danced again. Social scientists of the day related this to the 'war fever' of World War I, a soon-to-be-reality."

I was recently asked if I knew 'Too Much Mustard.' This not-too-well-known oldie called for a one-step. We also did the one-step to marches by John Philip Sousa. I adored him. He reached me through music. He lived on Capitol Hill, and got into the Marines at 13 because he was a gifted musician. Years later someone wanted to know if he played the piano. Not finding the answer in his biography I wrote him. He answered, 'Yes I do, but don't tell Paderewski' (famous Polish pianist and statesman). His sense of humor delighted me."

On graduating from Normal School (later, Wilson Teachers College, in Washington, D.C.), Mrs. O'Brien was recommended to the Haskin News Service as a "born researcher." The Haskin Service consisted of a short, question and answer column running concurrently in The Evening Star, and in a hundred-odd newspapers throughout the country.

Its staff included ten women. Between 1917 and 1956 Mrs. O'Brien developed a following among Senators, House members and White House staff, who used the service when their sources failed to uncover needed information. "They felt they could depend on me," said Mrs. O'Brien.

"I earned eight dollars for a six-day week. I loved my work, and would have worked without pay had it been possible. There was no effort I wouldn't make to obtain the information wanted. In fact, Mr. Haskin often chided me, 'You dig too deep, Theresa, and bring out more than we need.' I couldn't help it. I enjoyed what I was doing. My working hours were not 9 to 5, and I never earned more than thirty dollars a week at any time."

When Frederic J. Haskin updated his book,

See SHE STILL, Page A8

INSIDE

Classified Ads	B8
Dining Out	B5
Entertainment Calendar	B4
Fashions	B8
Health	B8
Homes Sold	B12
Horoscope	B5
Letters to the Editor	A6
Lunch Menus	B3
Movies	B2
Music Review	B3
Police Beat	B12
Sports	A8
Tempo	B1
Theater Notes	B4

Planning Board Stays in Silver Spring

By Susan Hedling
Journal Staff Writer

The Park and Planning Commission will stay in Silver Spring, ending months of controversy over whether the prestigious agency's planned move to Rockville would undermine the revitalization of the down-county eastern corridor.

In a 4-0 vote the County Council agreed to keep the planning board in the headquarters of the bi-county Maryland National Capital Park and Planning Commission at its Georgia Avenue headquarters, a few blocks north of the retail center of Silver Spring.

Voting in favor of not moving the planning agency were Esther Gelman, Scott Fosler, Ruth Spector and Michael Gudis. The other three council members — Elizabeth Scull, Neal Potter and Rose Crenca — abstained.

Gelman and Gudis had opposed the move, siding with Silver Spring businessmen and civic activists who feared that moving the agency would be a blow to the renewal effort. Fosler and Spector had not opposed the move, but said they changed their minds after hearing the emotional arguments from Silver Spring factions and being pressured by a U.S. Senate committee which is considering locating the Nuclear Regulatory Commission in Silver Spring.

County Executive Charles W. Gilchrist changed his mind on the move also after meeting with the U.S. senators who accused the county of being hypocritical in pulling out its own agency while soliciting a federal department. Gilchrist told the council yesterday that he now wants to keep the planners in Silver Spring.

But one council member called the senators' letter "blackmail."

"I was appalled by Senator (Jennings) Randolph's letter," Crenca said. "It was originated by people in Silver Spring and it has a blackmail aura about it."

Council members who abstained said they did not think Silver Spring would suffer if the planning commission were moved, but they admitted to the emotional and psychological effect Silver Spring residents felt.

"I'll change my vote but I think that government efficiency is being diminished because of pressure," Potter said.

Original plans had called for moving Park and Planning to the new county office building under construction in Rockville. Council members who supported the move said it would mean increased efficiency through consolidation, but other council members said they feared the planners would lose their independence and be under the thumb of the executive branch.

Gelman said costs associated with moving the planning board would be several million dollars.

Figure 35-3. The Montgomery Journal, Chevy Chase, Md., makes effective use of functional design with its main story on the left and a strong feature with pictures on the right. The award-winning newspaper is published twice a week. Courtesy of The Montgomery Journal, Chevy Chase, Md.

THE COMMERCIAL APPEAL SECTION A

140th Year No. 249 Memphis, Tenn., Thursday Morning, September 6, 1979 Price 15 Cents

U.S. Stance Involving Cuba: Soviet Battle Unit Must Go

From Our Press Services

WASHINGTON — In a blunt warning that brought back memories of the nail-biting 1962 missile crisis, the United States said Wednesday it simply won't stand for the presence of a Soviet combat brigade in Cuba.

"We regard this as a very serious matter, affecting our relations with the Soviet Union," said Secretary of State Cyrus Vance. "The presence of this unit runs counter to long-held American policies."

Vance stopped short of issuing the Kremlin an ultimatum as President John Kennedy did during the missile crisis — but he left little doubt of the U.S. position: the Soviet combat force must go.

"Let me say very simply that I will not be satisfied with the maintenance of the status quo," the secretary told reporters at a news conference.

The presence of up to 3,000 Soviet combat troops just 90 miles from Key West, Fla., cast a shadow over administration efforts to win Senate ratification of the new Strategic Arms Limitation Talks treaty.

Senate Democratic leaders tried to seperate the two issues. But the GOP warned of a SALT backlash, and at least one influential conservative called for a halt to treaty ratification hearings.

Vance refused to specify what the United States might do if the Kremlin ignored his warning, saying, "discussions with the Soviets will affect the action which we will take."

He said he has asked vacationing Soviet Ambassador Anatoly Dobrynin "to return at the earliest moment" for crisis talks in Washington. "I will be pursuing this matter with the Soviets in the coming days," he said.

One possible response to the presence of Soviet combat troops off the coast of Florida could be a buildup of American forces at the U.S. Navy base on Cuba's Guantanamo Bay.

Vance tried to play down comparisons between the 1962 discovery of Soviet warheads in Cuba — which brought the superpowers to the brink of nuclear war — and the stationing of the first Russian combat troops on the island.

"There is a vast difference . . . because there are no nuclear offensive weapons involved," he said.

In a two-page situation report, Vance said the the brigade-sized combat unit has from 2,000 to 3,000 personnel, including tank, artillery and motorized rifle battalions.

The report said the recently disclosed combat troops are in addition to some 1,500 to 2,000 Soviet military advisers who have been in Cuba for many years.

"The specific mission of the combat unit is as yet unclear," Vance said. "There is no air or sealift capability associated with the brigade which would give it an assault capability."

In what appeared to be a U.S. intelligence lapse, Vance conceded the Soviet combat force had been in Cuba "since at least the mid-1970s" although the United States didn't identify it until recently.

Senate Republican leader Howard Baker of Tennessee predicted the presence of the Soviet brigade would hurt the chances of the treaty because "you can't consider SALT in isolation."

But Senate Democratic leader Robert Byrd of West Virginia said SALT should be judged on its merits and the developments in Cuba should "not have an impact."

Byrd also called for a U.S. military buildup whether the Senate ratifies or rejects SALT.

Byrd said the United States must spend more than in recent years on defense and added that Soviet military might, deployed or under development, causes "serious concern" for the future.

In a Senate speech, Byrd allied himself with the chamber's "hawks" who have been pressing the administration to increase defense spending or risk becoming militarily weaker than the Russians.

Many of these are opponents of SALT 2 and others are linking their support of the treaty to a commitment to larger defense spending.

Byrd, however, made it clear he has not decided whether to support the treaty and is undecided to the point of having asked his staff to prepare a speech for either position.

Byrd predicted the American public would accept more defense spending.

He added, "In the days and weeks ahead, the Congress and the executive face the challenge of identifying our defense priorities and in moving to support them in a realistic but decisive manner."

Informed sources, meanwhile, said President Carter may ask Congress next week for nearly $4 billion in supplemental military appropriations, in a step administration officials hope might be enough to help win approval of SALT.

However, it was not clear whether such an increase would be enough to satisfy advocates of a stronger military posture or whether the treaty can survive a crisis posed by the presence of Soviet combat troops in Cuba.

Two administration officials said Carter had not firmly decided what military appropriations recommendations to make to Congress. But one said there was a strong possibility that Carter would recommend an increase of $3.8 billion in Pentagon spending for the 1980 fiscal year.

Sen. Bob Dole (R-Kan.) called for a halt to the Foreign Relations Committee's SALT hearings "until the administration and the Soviet Union provide an adequate explanation concerning the presence of Soviet troops in Cuba."

Sen. Frank Church (D-Idaho), chairman of the committee, demanded withdrawal of the Soviet troops — but said the two issues shouldn't be linked.

(Additional Story on Page A3)

"We regard this as a very serious matter, affecting our relations with the Soviet Union. . . Let me say very simply that I will not be satisfied with the . . . status quo."

Secretary of State Cyrus Vance

Staff Graphics

UPI

Slower Transit

A labor tieup on the San Francisco Bay Area Rapid Transit District has put about 75,000 BART commuters in cars, buses, trucks and other vehicles. Traffic officials in the Bay area said the thousands of extra cars and buses were moving well, with extra lanes opened at the Bay Bridge toll gates, more workers riding in carpools and drivers helping ease peak traffic loads by leaving home earlier or later.

(Story on Page C24)

Senate Urges Nixon Pay For Estate Work

WASHINGTON (AP) — The Senate voted Wednesday to urge former President Richard M. Nixon to repay the government for improvements made at taxpayer expense to his estate in San Clemente, Calif.

Nixon has sold the residence and has agreed to purchase a 12-room condominium apartment in New York for a reported $1 million.

A "sense of the Senate" resolution covering the Nixon property was approved by voice vote as an amendment to an $8.8-billion Treasury Department appropriations bill.

The resolution, which does not have the force of law, urges that Nixon compensate the goernment for the amount that the renovations improved the value of the estate.

When Nixon was president, the General Services Administration contracted for $702,321 in improvements to the San Clemente estate.

Some of the money was spent on improvements clearly intended to improve security of the residence. But Sens. David Pryor (D-Ark.) and Gary Hart (D-Colo.) said other renovations had little to do with protecting the president.

Pryor cited $6,600 for improving a gazebo, installation of a 44-foot aluminum flagpole for $2,300, a heating system worth $13,500, an interior fire protection system worth $33,300, and a sewer line constructed for $3,800.

The GSA has also listed a lighting and electronic system worth $217,006, landscaping worth $137,623 and a chimney exhaust fan worth $389.

Other items include a fire hydrant and a railway safety signal installed at taxpayer expense.

In a Senate speech, Pryor said he was seeking to prevent "the unjust enrichment of a former president."

A 1976 law will require President Carter to compensate the government for any improvements made to his property in Plains, Ga., unless the improvements are removed.

But the law is not retroactive and Hart said it "should be applied to all federal employes and officials — past, present and future."

Hart said, however, that neither he nor Pryor are attempting to "single out or discriminate against Mr. Nixon."

Dayan Expected To Continue Meetings With PLO Backers

From Our Press Services

HAIFA, Israel — Moshe Dayan has held at least eight meetings with Palestinians in the occupied West Bank and an aide said Wednesday the controversial foreign minister would continue to use such meetings in pursuit of Mideast peace.

Leaders of hawkish factions in the coalition government said only the current state visit here by Egyptian President Anwar Sadat was preventing a drive to chastise Dayan for his meetings with West Bank leaders, most of whom support Yasser Arafat's Palestine Liberation Organization.

Meanwhile at the summit, Egypt and Israel agreed to set up joint military patrols to monitor their peace agreement in the Sinai, freeing the United States from a written commitment to establish a multinational force in the region.

Dayan's personal crusade was in apparent direct conflict with the policies of Prime Minister Menachem Begin, who has said Israel will never negotiate with the PLO. So far, Begin has had no comment on Dayan's meetings and no other cabinet member has spoken publicly against the foreign minister.

Dayan's aide, who asked not to be identified, said there had been a minimum of eight meetings with West Bank Arabs since Israel and Egypt signed their peace treaty in March. Before he underwent surgery in June to remove an intestinal tumor, the meetings were kept secret. Since then several have been held more openly, the aide said.

Dayan already has been criticized in editorials and by some politicians for appearing to contradict the government's firm refusal to deal with the PLO.

Some even grumble that Dayan's forays in search of Arab opinions make Israel look silly for having complained last month that United Nations Ambassador Andrew Young had met with a PLO official in New York. Young resigned his post after the meeting was revealed.

In a television interview Tuesday, Dayan defended his meetings with Palestinians and made a distinction between PLO members and supporters.

"If someone is specifically a representative of the PLO, we should not meet him," Dayan said. But he said refusal to talk to PLO supporters was a position with which "I don't believe we will be able to reach any kind of agreement with the Arabs."

The distinction is lost on some Israelis, however, and Dayan has no shortage of political enemies, having left the Labor Party after the 1977 election when Begin asked him to be foreign minister in the coalition cabinet.

"We cannot agree to a situation in which this man does as he pleases," said Yehuda Ben-Meir, parliamentary leader of the coalition's National Religious Party. Dayan's behavior has "gone beyond all bounds of the acceptable and the permissible."

At a joint news conference after two days of talks, Sadat and Begin announced agreement on several bilateral issues.

Sadat agreed to sell oil to Israel while Begin, in a gesture that summit sources said was tied to the oil deal, agreed to hand over the Mount Sinai region to Egypt two months ahead of their peace treaty schedule.

But two tougher issues — the future of the Palestinians and the status of Jerusalem — apparently eluded progress during the talks held at a mountaintop hotel in this northern port city of 230,000 persons, 30,000 of them Arabs.

Sadat said he agreed with Begin that Jerusalem is one city and "should not be divided." But he maintained his demand that some formula must be found for the Arab administration of east Jerusalem.

g a Comeb

— Page A13.

Staff Graphics

Inside Today—

Loss Is Final

CHICKS END season in a 5-2 Southern League playoff loss to Nashville as 6,182 look on. — Page D31.

SENATE VOTES to block move by IRS to deny tax breaks to private schools that it determines are deliberately screening out minority students. — Page A8.

EARL MOUNTBATTEN of Burma is buried just as he planned — with spectacular pageantry in London. — Page A2.

After 60	B22	Movies	D35
Births	B20	People	D44
Business	B16-18	Puzzles	B21
Careers	B22	S. Security	B22
Comics	B20-21	Sports	D31-34
Corporates	B16	TV	D36
Deaths	C25, D36	Today	B20
Landers	C29	Want Ads	D37-43
Living	C26-29		

PHONES

News, General ... 529-2345 Circulation ... 529-2666
Classified Ads ... 529-2700 Sports Scores ... 523-9191

EDITORIAL — Realignment, not nonalignment, seems to be high on host Fidel Castro's list for the international conference in Havana. — Page A4.

Man, 23, Charged In Death Of Girl

By JAN TAYLOR and PAM CAMPBELL
From The Commercial Appeal Dyersburg and Martin, Tenn., Bureau

DRESDEN, Tenn. — Robert Glenn Coe, 23, of Gleason, was charged Wednesday with the murder, kidnaping and sexual assault of Cary Medlin, an 8-year-old Greenfield girl.

Dist. Atty. Gen. David Hayes of Union City said Coe confessed to the murder almost immediately after he was picked up and taken to the Weakley County Jail in Dresden about 8:30 p.m. Tuesday.

"He has made a statement," Hayes said in a press conference Wednesday morning. "His oral confession has been recorded and we have other physical evidence linking him to the murder."

Hayes said that Coe, who dyed his hair in an attempt to change his appearance, was about to leave the state when he was picked up. "Another 45 minutes and we would have been too late," Hayes said.

Coe was apprehended by Huntingdon police officers at the Greyhound bus station in Huntingdon and held on a charge of possession of marijuana until Tennessee Bureau of Criminal Identification (TBI) officers arrived.

Mrs. Carolyn Hamilton, ticket agent at the bus station, said Coe came into the station with his wife and infant daughter about noon Tuesday and bought a ticket to Marietta, Ga. After buying the ticket they left the station, Mrs. Hamilton said.

About two hours later Coe came back alone and asked if he could sit outside on a bench to wait for his bus, which was scheduled to leave for Nashville at 6:33 p.m., the ticket agent said. Coe was using the name "Watson" and was carrying a guitar and a single piece of luggage.

"He was calm," Mrs. Hamilton said. "He didn't bother anyone or talk to anyone. That baby is what threw me. I had no reason to suspect him of anything."

The Huntingdon Police Department was first alerted by a TBI bulletin about 5 p.m. Tuesday that Coe was going to the Huntingdon bus station, bound for Florida, according to Officer Richard Sawyers.

About 5:20 p.m., Sawyers said, Tennessee Highway Patrolman Lester Waugh saw Coe sitting on a bench outside the bus station and notified Huntingdon police, after which Sawyers and Capt. T. R. Brown went to the station.

"Coe was still sitting on the bench and did not try to flee," Sawyers said.

When they searched Coe for weapons, Sawyer said, they found two bags of marijuana in his pocket and arrested him at 5:28 p.m. for possession of the drug, took him to the police station and booked him.

Sawyers said Coe put up a $65 forfeit bond but the officers held him until TBI agents arrived. The police officer marveled over Coe's quietness, saying, "It's scary that somebody that has done what he allegedly has could be as calm about it as he was."

Hayes said Coe's arrest was the result of

(Continued on Page A3)

The Weather

National Weather Service

FOR MEMPHIS And Vicinity — Partly cloudy today. Fair tonight. Slight chance of thundershowers tomorrow. Highs both days near 90. Low tonight near 70. Winds northwest at 5 to 10 mph today. Sunrise, 6:36; sunset, 7:20.

YESTERDAY'S REPORT
High, 90 degrees at 3 p.m.
Low, 74 degrees at 7 a.m.
Normal high, 87 degrees, low, 6?

(Map, Details on Page C30)

Assignment: Memphis—

Delta Dragonflies Bring Concern Of Airborne Woolly Bear

By LYDEL SIMS

"DEAR UNK: I have observed a biological phenomenon in the Delta area that requires just the keen observations the Sims Laboratory of Unusual Research Problems (SLURP) can make.

"What I have seen are large numbers of dragonflies, sometimes known among us country folks as 'snake doctors.' These insects are to be seen over rice fields, along highways and in yards, and there are more this year than I can remember seeing in many years.

"Are these increased numbers a sign of things to come? Or is this an occurrence which comes on us periodically? I have seen very few woolly bears this year, and it has occurred to me that maybe the woolly bears have begun flying. Please see what SLURP can find out about this." —George L. Berry

This sounds sinister, and our researchers should get busy on it right away and report their findings. The way the world has been going in general, I fear the worst. If more dragonflies are about, surely it can only mean still more dragons loom ahead. Or more snakes, or even more doctors, which could be just as bad. Field reports are invited. Meanwhile, be on the lookout for those woolly bears.

"DEAR UNK: I have a fine old brain-teaser just right for the September weather. Maybe you remember it.

"There is an encyclopedia set with one book for each letter of the alphabet. Each book has 1 inch of pages, with a ¼-inch cover on each side — making each book 1½ inches thick. The books sit on a shelf in the usual manner, that is, alphabetically.

"A bookworm gets into Book A and eats its way straight across from the first page of A to the last page of C. How many inches does it travel?

"In case you can't figure it out, turn this page over for the answer." —Jerry Baker

The puzzle is mere child's play, sir, as I realized the moment I read your answer. But in case anyone has trouble with it, I'll give it at the end of this column.

"DEAR UNK: I read with interest, tinged with nostalgia, about a hero of my childhood who has been legally restrained from wearing his mask and making appearances in supermarkets.

"If he goes to work for an Italian bank, couldn't he continue to be known as the Loan Arranger?"—Jean Luckett

Why seek out an Italian bank? Norma D. Hendrix tells me that shortly after she went to work for the Farmers Union Bank in Ripley, Tenn., some years ago, a fellow called and asked for the loan arranger. She thought he was joking, so she offered to turn him over to Tonto. Try explaining that to a bank president when you go for your first paycheck. Hi-yo.

"DEAR UNK: When a fly lights on the ceiling, does it do a half-loop or a half-roll?" — Ralph Tope Jr.

Now see here. Where were you during the turbulent '60s when we wrestled with this problem and solved it? Meanwhile, I've forgotten the answer, and you're the second person who has asked the question recently.

How can we engage in dragonfly research if people keep bringing up fly-landings? Well, maybe someone can help.

AND NOW FOR the solution to the bookworm problem. The worm traveled two inches, right?

Of course it did. When the books are arranged in the usual order on a shelf, page one of Book A is jam up against Book B, with only the covers intervening, and the last page of Book C is jam up against Book B. So you simply add the total width of Book B to the width of the front cover of Book A and the back cover of Book C, and you get two inches.

Well, I said it was child's play, didn't I?

Figure 35-4. *The Commercial Appeal, Memphis Tenn., uses graphic designs combining sketches, maps and drawings as well as photographs to create interesting and readable front pages.* Courtesy of The Commercial Appeal, Memphis.

Chicago Tribune

Saturday, May 26, 1979

5 Star Final ★★★★

6 Sections 15¢

Worst U.S. crash; 272 die at O'Hare

Pennants mark the location of victims of Friday's DC-10 crash near O'Hare International Airport as firefighters search for more bodies amid the huge jetliner's wreckage.

'There was rain of fire falling'

By Michael Hirsley

ABE MARMEL was tending his tomatoes, beets, and onions — his back to the airplane plunging to earth less than 100 yards away.

"I heard a loud explosion," Marmel said. "By the time I looked up, there was a rain of fire falling down on me.

"Parts of the airplane were flying around me. I got singed right here." He brushed a sooted right hand against a red blotch on his forehead.

The American Airlines DC-10 with 270 persons aboard crashed on Marmel's property at 320 W. Touhy Av., just east of Touhy Mobile Home Park.

No one in the plane survived. Abe Marmel, 73, and his wife, Shirley, 69, did.

But they went through a few moments of hell.

AS ABE stood beside his small frame office building, Shirley stood petrified with fear inside. The back of the office was engulfed in flames within seconds after the crash.

"I was working on the books when I heard the explosion," Shirley said. "By fire I couldn't move. If Abe hadn't come, I would have died. I saw the scene. I would have died. I say it by my garden on the side of the house," Abe said. "But there were clumps of fire all over. I got to the near

and saw Shirley standing there. 'Get out!' I shouted. She didn't move. I had to grab her and pull her out.

"We moved as fast as we could. The smoke was so black we couldn't see. We tried to go toward Touhy, but we weren't sure we were going in the right direction. We just kept moving until we got out of the smoke."

The Marmels regained their composure in the trailer camp office.

THEIR OFFICE—the one where they sold airplane parts—and five other buildings they leased to such businesses as an excavation company and a roofing firm were all burned to the ground.

An emergency door from the aircraft had been thrown completely over the burned buildings and onto the first of several unnamed streets in the trailer park.

"I saw the plane come in. It looked like it was perpendicular to the ground," a young man said, looking at the door. "It looked like it bounced."

"I didn't see the plane, but I heard two explosions, felt two pounding sensations in my chest, and I could feel two flashes of heat before I saw the ball of flame," said Rosemary Perdew, whose trailer is three streets west of the crash site.

SHE RUSHED to her mother's trailer adjacent to the field where the plane

Continued on page 2, col. 1

Inside
Full reports on O'Hare air disaster

● Chaplain describes scene of crash. "It was too hot to touch anybody." Page 2

● Playboy managing editor, his wife, and two other employes of the magazine feared to be victims of the crash. Page 2

● The "jumbo" three-engine DC-10 is considered one of the world's most advanced aircraft. Page 4.

● A full page of photos, including an aerial of the scene, is on page 3.

● Confusion at Los Angeles points to grief of those waiting for friends and relatives on Flight 191. Page 4.

● DC-10s have been involved in history's worst single-plane air disasters and in several incidents. Page 5.

● AMERICAN 191, do you want to come back? It is what runway do you want?

Emergency no answer.

The engine for the concrete and pointed at about the two-thirds mark of runway 32 flight—officials said it may have struck the left wing or bounced

---

'It went up in flame, swish, just like napalm'

By John O'Brien and David Axelrod

A WIDE BODY DC-10 jetliner plummeted to earth moments after takeoff from O'Hare International Airport Friday afternoon, killing all 270 persons aboard in the worst air disaster in U.S. aviation history.

Two persons not aboard the plane also were killed.

American Airlines Flight 191, bound nonstop for Los Angeles, had just taken off from Runway 32 Right, headed northwest, when, from an altitude of only 200 feet, it nosed down and burst into a pillar of flame and smoke that could be seen up to eight miles away.

"Immediately after takeoff, part of all of the left engine fell off," said Michael Laughlin, 24, of Toronto, an employe of British Petroleum and a licensed pilot who witnessed the crash.

An air traffic controller watching from the control tower saw the engine fall just as the big plane lifted off about halfway down the 10,600-foot runway. He immediately radioed

over it—then skidded until it stopped at about the 8,000-foot mark.

The plane, floundering with one of its three engines gone, banked and crashed half a mile away.

"As soon as it went down, it went up in flame, swish, just like napalm," said Michael Delany, a Chicago policeman who witnessed the crash. ". . . I saw a guy—his pants were on fire. I threw him on the ground and put the fire out."

THE MAN Delany aided did not come from the plane. All aboard—237 passengers and the crew of 13—were killed in the crash.

Rescue workers later reported finding two bodies on the site of the Courtney-Veto Excavating Co., believed to be employes of the firm.

And the death toll had risen to 272.

The downed plane slammed into an abandoned hangar near a trailer court, throwing burning debris for half a mile around. Two trailer homes were destroyed by the flaming shards.

At least two persons on the ground were injured during the crash. Richard Maskero, 26, of 1319 N. Valley Lake Dr., Schaumburg, was reported in good condition at Alexian Brothers Hospital, Elk Grove Village, with second-degree burns over his face, neck, and back.

ANDREW BELLAVIA, 18, of 557 S. Jeffery Lane, Wheeling, was transferred to the Loyola University Hospital burn

unit in Maywood and was reported in critical condition with second-degree burns over 50 per cent of his body.

Brian Pekovic, 18, a resident of the Touhy Mobile Homes, 400 W. Touhy Av., near where the plane nosed down, gave this account of the crash:

"It [the plane] was leaning over. I knew something was wrong. It was shaking and going up and down, up and down.

"Then it rose just went straight down and then we heard the crash. All the area was full of black smoke. And then the heat. It must have been over 100 degrees blowing across the trailer park.

"JUST BEFORE the nose of the plane dipped, I saw something fly off the plane. It was a big piece of something that looked about half the size of my

Continued on page 5, col. 1

Weather

CHICAGO AND VICINITY: Saturday. Mostly sunny, high 68 to 72 F [20 to 22 C], lower near the lake; east to southeast winds 8 to 15 miles [12 to 24 kilometers] an hour. Saturday night: Partly cloudy, chance of showers of a thundershower, low around 52 F [11 C]. Sunday: Partly sunny, high 70 to 75 F [21 to 24 C]. Map and other reports indexed on page 6.

Figure 35-5. When disaster strikes, newspapers use large headlines and large dramatic pictures such as the Chicago Tribune did to report the nation's worst air crash. Courtesy of the Chicago Tribune.

465

News-Democrat

A Growing Paper In A Growing Area

VOL. 29—NO. 9   2 PAGES   WAVERLY, TENNESSEE, WEDNESDAY, MARCH 1, 1978   15 CENTS

12 Dead And Scores Injured

By RICHARD McCOY
Editor

Crews cleaning up wreckage from the train crash in Waverly last week were more concern with the tank car that didn't explode than the one that did, according to E.R. Butler, an investigator with the National Transportation Board's Atlanta office.

Both car's were carrying liquid propane gas and were part of a 23 car wreck on L & N tracks in Waverly last Wednesday night.

One of the cars exploded Friday about 2:55 p.m. killing at least 12 persons and injuring over 50 others.

Butler said investigators are looking into the cause of the explosion but do not have any findings at this time.

Parts of the exploded car have been sent to Bruceton for study by Transportation Board investigators, he said.

Butler did say Tuesday afternoon that the cause of the wreck was thought to be known.

He said it appeared that the wheels on a gondola car carrying railroad tires overheated. One of the wheels apparently separated from the axle about seven miles east of the crash site.

"What happened is that a wheel cracked," Butler said.

"The axle was free to move," he said.

The gondola car was in front of the two tankers, he said. The train was west bound with 93 cars.

The investigation into the matter is being carried on in two parts, Butler said.

One part concerns the wreck and the other the explosion.

According to Butler investigator feels that the tank that exploded had suffered structural damage.

One reason for the explosion might have been that heat caused the pressure in the tanker to increase causing a failure of the tank's body, Butler said.

"That is one of the area's we are looking at," he said.

"The derailment happened on a cool night. Friday it was bright and sunny."

Temperatures reached the mid-50's Friday.

"Radiant heat caused the tank to heat up (above the air temperature,)" he said.

The tank had a safety value which was designed to release gas at 300 pounds of pressure per square inch, he said.

"We feel the pressure wasn't up to that level," he said.

Butler said it was almost necessary to have fire under the tank to reach the 300 psi limit.

A fire did break out under the second car following the explosion but was apparently immediately extinguished, he said.

Continued on page 15

AFTERWARDS—This aerial photo was made Saturday morning some 18 hours after a tank car filled with liquid propane gas exploded killing at least a dozen persons and injuring many others. The top of the photo is north. Highway 13 is shown on the left. The remains of the Tate Lumber Company are shown in the center. Number one shows the location of the tanker prior to the explosion. Number two is its position after the explosion. The two number threes show pieces of the tank car. Number four is the tank which did not explode. Waverly Police Chief Guy Barnett and Fire Chief Wilbur York were standing near number five when the explosion occured. Both are dead. Number six shows a crater caused by the banks of the small creek caving-in. Also shown are numerous houses which were destroyed as well as businesses destroyed and damaged by fire.   Photo by Richard McCoy

Special Edition

This special edition of the News-Democrat is dedicated to those who died or were injured in the explosion and fire Friday afternoon.

It is also dedicated to everyone who helped.

It is dedicated to the fire fighters, rescue workers and police-also to all of the people who opened their homes to take in the homeless and to the many people who worked day and night at the armory, high school, churches, and other places making a place for those who were forced from their homes.

It is dedicated to those in other places who kept Waverly in their prayers and who came in to help or sent food or clothing.

It is dedicated to all those who came to Waverly to help.

HELP — Chuck Webb, a New Johnsonville Volunteer Fireman, was driving back from Nashville Friday afternoon when a tank car filled with liquid propane gas exploded. Here Webb rushes to aid Waverly Fire Chief Wilbur York who was fatally burned in the explosion. Also shown is the car of Waverly Police Chief Guy Barnett, who also died as a result of the explosion. A piece of the exploded car is shown next to the car. This photo was made minutes after the explosion.

TRAGIC — This photograph was made minutes after the blast about 2:55 p.m. Friday. A railroad tank car carrying liquid propane gas exploded killing many and injuring scores of people. A severely burned person is shown running in the right side of the photo. Also shown is a man with the back of his shirt blown off. The rescue workers shown here had just arrived on the scene.   Photo by Richard McCoy

Acting Safety Heads Are Named

By LYNN WYATT

Waverly Mayor Jimmy Powers said Monday that he had appointed Ted Tarpley and Francis (Dutch) Geisenhoffer, as acting heads of the police and fire departments respectively.

The appointments came in the wake of the explosion Friday of a derailed propane tanker which claimed several lives including those of Police Chief Guy Barnett and Fire Chief Wilbur York.

Powers said Monday that he did not know when he would make permanent appointments to the positions, but that the city is "in good shape" with the acting heads.

Powers said that the appointment of Tarpley, who has served as the city's chief criminal investigator is crucial because Tarpley is familiar with all of the cases the department has pending.

"All of the knowledge of these cases that the chief had, Ted has in his files," Powers said.

He said that this was especially important because of recently solved major burglaries in the community.

Powers also announced the appointment of Howard Deck as assistant acting police chief.

Deck, a retired Metro Nashville policeman, is also a former Humphreys County sheriff.

Powers said that Deck has expressed interest in working full time with the department to "help out in any way he can during this disaster."

Powers also expressed his gratitude to the various agencies involved in disaster relief.

"We want to thank all of the federal agencies who helped us,"

Continued on page 15

Figure 35-6. The News-Democrat, a weekly in Waverly, Tenn., produced this dramatic front page for a special edition covering a derailment and explosion in the center of town. Courtesy of the News-Democrat, Waverly, Tenn.

TYPES OF FRONT-PAGE MAKEUP

Although the term "functional" has come into common use among modern typographers, it is not easy to define. Basically it means that every element on a page should perform an essential job in the most efficient manner. As a result, today's modern newspaper is clean and uncluttered. Column rules, headlines with multiple decks, cutoff rules and many other unnecessary elements have been eliminated.

A number of front-page makeup schemes have been established over the years more by custom than by rule. They are worth noting.

Balanced Makeup. The balanced makeup style, as the name implies, requires that the editor be seeking perfect or almost perfect symmetry by balancing one side of the page with the other. The same size and type of headline is used above stories on corresponding sides of the page. However, rarely is a page perfectly balanced. And, when that does happen, some of the basic functions of headlining and display are ignored because stories seldom are perfectly matched in their order of importance, so that matching them perfectly in headline will tend to distort their news value.

Contrast and Balance. The contrast and balance style often is called "informal balance." Here the makeup editor observes balance but not symmetry. The object is to balance the focal points on the page so one part does not completely dominate the other parts of the page. This is the most commonly used form in horizontal makeup. It permits the makeup editor to freely use all the concepts of functional design to produce an attractive front page.

Brace Makeup. In brace makeup style, the attention is focused in the upper right-hand corner of the page. A picture or large headline is displayed in that area with several headlines wedged in under it, bracing it like the bracket under a shelf. This style is not commonly used today.

Broken or Razzle-Dazzle. Often the broken or razzle-dazzle style is also called "circus makeup." It is a no-holds-barred style in which headlines, stories and pictures are placed on the page in no apparent pattern and with complete disregard for all knowledge of reading patterns. Many European newspapers follow this style, and several of the more sensational weekly tabloids circulated through supermarkets and on newsstands in the United States have adopted it.

Other variations have been tried from time to time, but as noted above, the most commonly used today incorporates the best elements of contrast and balance with the functional concept.

Every good makeup editor works with dummy sheets and designs his front page only after having carefully studied the day's news budget. While planning is essential, the day's news should really determine the appearance of the front page. A number of researchers have even recommended that the front page be turned into a "super" news summary (or index)—a one-page newspaper that capsulizes the day's news. However, for newspapers electing to continue in the more traditional manner, here is a list of helpful hints for making up page one:

1. Do not design a page first and then force the news to fit it. That will destroy or distort the news value of the stories and undermine one of the prime purposes of makeup—to help grade the news.

35g

2. To follow the most modern procedure, put the most important story or display items in the upper left side of the page at the point of first eye contact for the reader.

3. Do not place multicolumn large heads in adjoining columns at the top of the page. Use a picture to separate them.

4. Avoid tombstoning headlines. Use display devices such as pictures, boxes, even white space to separate heads, especially if they are the same size.

5. Place at least one strong (multicolumn) headline in each quarter of the page and in the center.

6. Use pictures generously. If a picture looks good as a two-column it will look even better as three, most of the time. Crop pictures artfully. Do not waste space.

7. Put big pictures toward the top of the page, but do not be afraid to use one at the bottom as well. Make certain the one at the top is heavier, however.

8. Use multicolumn headlines at the bottom of the page—even a banner. Just make certain its type size is not larger than the main head at the top of the page.

9. Float the "flag" to give some variety in makeup, but keep it in the upper one-third of the page.

10. Avoid letting subjects in photographs look off the page when the picture is based in an outside column. Unity is destroyed when the person is gazing off the page.

11. Run stories horizontally rather than vertically whenever possible. Attempt to keep major stories to 15 to 20 inches on page one. If they run longer, either jump them or make two stories out of the one.

12. Run related stories in the same area on the page.

13. Vary the size of body type and the width some stories are set but do not overdo it.

14. Limit the number of one-column headlines on the page.

15. Use a variety of headline sizes to give the page contrast.

16. Do not let the story run out from under the headline.

Format. A full-size newspaper's page traditionally has been approximately 15 x 22 inches. There have been some variations over the years. Those pages as a general rule were divided into eight columns of type slightly under two inches each. Many newspapers use this format today. Others began to experiment with fewer columns—five, six and seven. Six seemed to be the most generally accepted, and such newspapers as the Louisville Courier-Journal have produced extremely attractive and readable newspapers with this format for a number of years.

The economic crunch of the mid-1970s brought the introduction of the smaller roll of newsprint and introduced to many newspapers what is commonly called the six-column format. It is based on the fact that the size of the page is approximately 13½ x 22 inches. The same makeup principles apply in using this slightly smaller sheet.

TYPES OF INSIDE-PAGE MAKEUP

Unlike the front page, the inside pages carry advertising—that is, most of them do—and this factor presents some special problems for the makeup editor.

The makeup editor generally receives from the advertising department page dummies with the advertisements drawn in. Using these as a guide, his job is then to make each page as attractive as possible within the framework of the stories and display elements that are available. Some newspapers automatically leave certain inside pages exclusively for editorial matter. Others keep advertisements to a minimum on the first several pages. Some put no advertisements on the front pages of each section or some sections of the paper.

No matter what the custom of ad placement, the makeup editor planning an inside page should remember that the reader's habits do not change when he reaches the inside pages. The eye still moves from left to right. The upper left-hand corner of the page is still the first place the eye touches down. The same basic principles of display that apply on the front page should apply on the inside pages—depending, of course, upon how the advertisements are placed on the page. Advertisements can be pyramided from the right or from the left. They also can be placed up each side of the page, forming a well in the center.

Ideally, pyramiding to the right is the best because it opens the upper left-hand corner for a display of editorial matter and allows the makeup editor to take advantage of the reader's normal eye pattern on the page. Also, ideally, the ad pyramid should leave about 3 or 4 inches of space at the top of the page. This creates a more usable space across the top of the page for editorial matter.

Some inside-page layouts showing a variety of advertisement placements are illustrated on pages 470 and 471.

In making up inside pages some handy guidelines to follow include:

35h

1. Put strong (multicolumn) headline or reasonably large picture in the upper left-hand corner of the page at the point of initial eye contact.
2. Use a careful combination of multicolumn and single-column headlines on the page.
3. Restrict the use of banner heads on inside pages. If one is used, do not use another on the adjacent page.
4. Do not tombstone heads. Also avoid butting headlines, especially heads the exact same size.
5. Include a picture (or pictures), cartoon, chart, map or some other graphic device on each page, if possible, except on pages containing advertisements with large photographs.
6. Keep pictures toward the top of the page. Avoid putting a picture right on top of an advertisement or adjacent to an advertisement.
7. Whenever possible, try to make the headline wide enough to cover all the body type.
8. Do not run the headline for a story across the top of an advertisement. Make certain there are at least one to two inches of body type separating the headline from the advertisement.
9. Use a variety of headline type sizes and widths to give the page some contrast.

Term starts Monday

Boone Youth Center unsure of new site

By FRANK ASHLEY
Courier-Journal Staff Writer

COVINGTON, Ky.—With top officials of the program either on vacation or attending extended meetings this week, staff members of the long-troubled Daniel Boone Youth Center still don't know where they will be located when fall semester classes begin next Monday.

Officials have said the program would continue its rural setting unless a new home could be found in downtown Covington or Newport by the beginning of the new term.

"I'm not certain of anything except that we're here today," center director Bob Jenkins said in a telephone interview yesterday.

Jenkins said the staff is intact and knows that the program could be moved to a new location at the last minute. He added that materials are on hand to operate the program at its current location if new facilities aren't found.

State officials in charge of the center have been looking for an urban location for more than a year.

Program officials have said they want to relocate the center in an urban setting to cut transportation costs and to serve troubled youngsters in their natural city environment.

The center's residential services already have been phased out and are being handled by group foster homes in the three-county area.

The program, now located in Boone County about 30 miles from Covington, serves as an alternative school for up to 30 students at a time from three Northern Kentucky counties.

Last year then-Gov. Wendell Ford canceled plans to move the center into a remodeled warehouse basement in downtown Covington after a special legislative committee looked into the state's lease arrangement with friends of the Ford administration.

Recently, plans to move the program into a former Knights of Columbus hall in Covington were stymied after residents at a home for the elderly next door complained that the youths would be troublesome neighbors.

"It's still up in the air," Tom McEntee, assistant district manager of the state Bureau of Social Services in Northern Kentucky, said of the center's plans. "We've not been told anything definite except to have a program ready and to have our bags packed."

McEntee was reached in Lexington at a meeting expected to end Thursday.

McEntee's boss, Bill Neuroth, district manager and a former center superintendent, is on vacation and, according to his secretary, is not scheduled to return until Monday.

Neuroth's boss, Jack C. Lewis, director of residential services for the bureau, also is on vacation and is not expected to return until Monday, a secretary in his office said.

Lewis' boss, social services commissioner Jerry Hissong, is attending a meeting in Louisville until Thursday, according to his secretary. He was scheduled to man the state Department for Human Resources' booth at the Kentucky State Fair last night and was too busy yesterday to talk about the center, his secretary said.

Another program official, Max Jackson, regional social services director, reportedly was attending the Lexington meeting and could not be reached for comment.

Photo by Verona Kidd

Into his work

James Devore, 15, Munfordville, wasn't actually entering his car from the front. He just needed to get above the work he was doing on a '57 Chevy. His father gave the car to him for something to do until he turns 16 and can begin driving it.

Increase in LG&E rates averages $2.03 a month

The Courier-Journal Bureau

FRANKFORT, Ky. — Louisville Gas & Electric Co. (LG&E) rates will go up tomorrow by about $2.03 a month for an average residential user.

At a Kentucky Public Service Commission (PSC) hearing yesterday, the company announced that it will put a $17.04 million a year rate increase into effect, subject to later refund if any part is not approved.

LG&E filed its rate request with the PSC last February and proposed an effective date of March 20.

The PSC suspended the increase and scheduled a series of hearings at which consumer representatives have opposed the increase. The final hearing ended yesterday in Frankfort.

However, a PSC ruling appears several weeks away. After the hearing record is typed, both sides will have 30 days to submit written arguments. The PSC then will study the case and rule.

LG&E's rate action is allowed by state law when the PSC has not ruled within five months. However, if the full increase is not granted by the PSC and, in case of appeal, by the courts, LG&E must refund excess collections.

For an average residential user, electricity will go up by about $1.51 a month and gas aboug 52 cents. For all customers, the average increase is about 12.4 per cent for electricity and about 4.6 per cent for gas.

Yesterday's hearing was devoted to cross-examination of company witnesses. Assitaant Atty. Gen. Laura Murrell of the consumer protection division said later that the information brought out was "not particularly important" in the overall case.

TVA raising electric rates in the Tennessee Valley

KNOXVILLE (AP) — Home electric bills in the Tennessee Valley will go up an average of $1.22 per 1,000 kilowatt hours in September, the Tennessee Valley Authority (TVA) said yesterday.

This is the 10th rate rise TVA has announced since it tied its rates to fuel and other costs in August 1974.

TVA said the September increase is due largely to the unusually large amount of power purchased in July for its customers from other generating systems.

Study will ask increased funds for law schools

The Courier-Journal Bureau

FRANKFORT, Ky. — A group of attorneys and law school deans studying Kentucky's needs in legal education indicated yesterday that its final report undoubtedly will call for additional financing for the state's three law schools.

The study, being conducted for the state Council on Public Higher Education, has been under way for several months and is expected to be completed this fall.

The group agreed yesterday that the final report should include recommendations to overcome:

- Severe shortages of classroom, library and other educational space at the University of Kentucky, University of Louisville and Northern Kentucky State College's Chase College of Law.
- Faculty-student ratios for above levels recommended by accrediting groups. Deans of the three schools said later yesterday that the ratios last year ranged from about one professor to 27 students at UK to a ratio of 1 to 46 at Chase.
- Inadequate "support services" for legal educators, including secretarial help, office equipment, research services and travel funds.
- Needed additional library resources and salaries to adequately pay law library staffs.

Panel approves consumer bill allowing co-ops

Associated Press

FRANKFORT, Ky. — An interim legislative committee yesterday approved for prefiling a bill providing for consumer cooperatives in Kentucky.

Current state law allows co-ops only for producers. A group of citizens in Berea asked for the change to allow them to get federal funds to build a cooperative retirement home.

The Interim Committee on Business Organizations and Professions approved the bill with no expression as to whether it should pass in the 1976 General Assembly. It would not apply to banking, insurance, labor union, rural cooperative corporation or railroad operations.

The committee approved for prefiling with a favorable expression a bill prohibiting ex-convicts from being denied public employment or a license to practice a profession or occupation. The only exception would be if the crime involved were related to the position sought.

A federal court recently ruled that the Kentucky Board of Barbering could not deny a license to someone solely because he was an ex-convict.

Bowling Green to weigh transfers

The Courier-Journal Bureau

BOWLING GREEN, Ky. — Whether students from Louisville, approximately 120 miles from Bowling Green, would be allowed to enroll in this city's schools this fall will be discussed at tonight's meeting of the Bowling Green Board of Education.

The board's official agenda includes the topic "out-of-district students — Jefferson County."

In a telephone interview yesterday, Mrs. Randy Kimbrough, supervisor of instruction for the Bowling Green schools, said parents or relatives of seven students from Jefferson County have made inquires about enrolling this year.

The inquiries have been by telephone and no formal applications for enrollment have been made, she said.

All the callers have denied that court-ordered busing in Jefferson County is the basis for the potential transfers, Mrs. Kimbrough said.

Some of the callers say children have spent the summer in Bowling Green and want to remain because they have found jobs or new friends. Others list "family problems" as the basis for the change, she said.

Mrs. Kimbrough said that she informs the callers that state law requires a student to reside with his parents or legal guardian and attend school in that district.

"They could go through a procedure to have someone else declared legal guardian," she added.

The Jefferson County school system announced last Friday that it no longer would be permitted to transfer state-aid money to other school districts in which students from Jefferson County are enrolled for special reasons.

Owensboro hearing reset in murder-arson case

Special to The Courier-Journal

OWENSBORO, Ky.—The hearing for an Owensboro police officer accused of murder and arson in the deaths of his wife and three of his children will be held Aug. 28.

James Stallings has pleaded innocent to charges of murder and murder in the course of arson, in the shooting of his wife, and in the deaths of Michael, 21, Phillip, 20, and Kathryn, 16, in a fire that destroyed the Stallings home.

Stallings, 39, has been held in the Daviess County Jail without bond pending the hearing, which originally was scheduled for yesterday.

London bank, state file appeal notices

The Courier-Journal Bureau

FRANKFORT, Ky. — Attorneys for the new London Bank & Trust Co. and the Kentucky Department of Banking and Securities yesterday filed notices of appeal of a ruling that set aside the bank's charter.

The filing delays the effect of the ruling by Franklin Circuit Court and allows the bank to continue operating, pending action by the Kentucky Court of Appeals, a state news release said.

A state agency's appeal automatically delays such a circuit court ruling, an attorney for the bank said later.

Last week Franklin Circuit Judge Henry Meigs set aside former Banking and Securities Commissioner Howard Sallee's 1974 order approving the new bank. The bank opened June 3.

Meigs acted in a suit filed last year by London's two other banks.

Police arrest 4, confiscate heroin

Associated Press

LEXINGTON, Ky. — Four persons were arrested yesterday in Lexington and about $4,000 worth of drugs was confiscated by police in a raid.

Police said they confiscated about seven grams of heroin and 90 individual foil packets of heroin ready for street sale. Also taken in the raid was a small quantity of amphetamines and marijuana, police said.

Mary R. Bullington, 22; Robert S. Scott, 28; Denise Specker, 20, and John W. Lacey, 19, all of Lexington, were charged with trafficking in heroin, possession of amphetamine and possession of marijuana.

Eastern Kentucky TV programs

Johnson City

WJHL-TV (Channel 11)

Knoxville

WATE-TV (Channel 6)

WBIR-TV (Channel 10)

WTVK-TV (Channel 26)

Huntington

WSAZ-TV (Channel 3)

WOWK-TV (Channel 13)

First time ever seen on television

Kathryn Kuhlman Miracle Service

from Las Vegas

TONIGHT ON WDRB CH 41
9:30 PM-11:00 PM

today

wave tv3
wave radio970
at the kentucky
state fair

at the
wave country tent
in front of the
coliseum

live broadcasts:

12:00 noon
wave newswatch at
midday
1:30 pm
the morning show
with nbc star earl holliman of "police woman"

free at the
wave country tent:

shopping bags
bicentennial cookbook
pictures of wave stars
trip to opryland

mud wave

Figure 35-7. The Courier-Journal uses the six-column format throughout the newspaper. The advertisements, stacked from the right, leave ample space for an attractive news display. Courtesy of the Courier-Journal, Louisville, Ky.

Gap Indicated Between Job Hopes, Vocational Opportunities

By GEORGE ZEPP

If Metro high school juniors went to work today, most would look for jobs in the entertainment field — a vocation their teachers have ranked dead last.

The findings were among those of a comprehensive survey presented yesterday to the Metro Board of Education recommending some

drastic changes in what has been known as vocational education.

STUDENT WORK preferences, based on a poll of Metro 11th graders, were:

● Entertainment.
● Clerical.
● Human services.
● Publishing/printing.

● Medical.
● Health services.

Training for rock band musicians, ambulance drivers and "white collar" workers in such areas as mass communications should be developed for high school vocational offerings, the study indicates.

But job openings for 1976 in

the Nashville area are still forecast to favor the traditional fields of clerical work, 2,208; sales, 1,211, and "hospitality" (janitors, waiters-waitresses, housekeepers, etc.), 1,030. The fewest openings are shown in the publishing-printing category, 201, according to the report.

TEACHERS SURVEYED

rated the trades (mechanics, repair and installation, etc.) the most important, followed by the professions and finally entertainment.

"It's obvious that we need to open some new (vocational) directions and cut off some we've had in the past," said schools director Dr. Elbert Brooks of the study, which is due for discussion by the

board at its June 24 meeting.

Called a "needs assessment of employment demands/interests" in Metro public schools, the report was prepared under direction of Dr. Kenneth Gray, a research specialist from Ohio State University's Center for Vocational Education.

"ONE OF THE strongest needs is accurate and meaningful job information for students and parents," Gray told the board. "Parents are the most influential people in the students' choice of a career. Nine times out of 10, parents say they want the same as their children."

Gray said students are obviously listening to parents

more than to teachers in choosing careers.

Other suggestions in the report were establishment of a job placement program in Metro schools —which Gray said would aid in monitoring needs for program changes — and a review and improvement of vocational course offerings every three years.

Boys State Elects Local 'Officeholders'

COOKEVILLE, Tenn. — Approximately 600 Boys State delegates balloted here yesterday at the Tennessee Tech campus to place 16 of their group in mythical county and city offices prior to election today of a governor.

Today's new governor will replace Randall Dove, Old Hickory, elected governor last year.

ELECTED yesterday as county judges, along with their home towns and mythical counties they represent were:

Mark Thomas, Union City, Harville.

Stanley Savage, Bells, Looney.

David Rutherford, Knoxville, Moss.

Billy Burgess, Memphis, Waring.

The 12 mayors elected yesterday, their home towns and the names of the mythical cities they represent were:

Rick Hassard, Chattanooga, Carroll.

Leon Summers, Nashville, Clement.

Thomas Rudehorst, Chattanooga, Cooper City.

Kurt Humberger, McDonald, Crump.

Zachery Williamson, Harriman, Duncan.

Ken Bleck, Hixson, Friedman.

Kenny Buckner, Gatlinburg, Griffin.

Randall Merrick, Huntingdon, Jones.

Thomas Jenkins, East Ridge, Lafon.

Barry Jarnagan, Union City, Lewis.

Gene Hampton, Memphis, Todd.

Charles Mattison, Jackson, Maddux.

Metropolitan Nashville's Vice Mayor David Scobey will speak tonight on metro government.

Drug Charges Send Dying Man Back to Jail

TACOMA, Wash. (AP) — Harold T. King has one leg, diabetes, throat cancer and is said to have less than a year to live.

He is back in jail on drug charges.

KING, 59, was sentenced last month to 10 years in prison for possessing illegal drugs, and Pierce County Superior Court Judge Hardyn B. Soule permitted the defendant 10 days to attend to personal affairs before going to prison.

But before the 10-day grace period was up, the former cook had been jailed twice and charged with six additional felony drug offenses.

King's attorney, J. Benedict Zederic, has asked the State Court of Appeals to reverse the prison sentence and send King back to Superior Court for a sentence that is "in accordance with humane standards in civilized nations."

Tullahoma Cuts School Budget

TULLAHOMA — Despite the appearance of 100 teachers protesting a proposed $20,000 slash in the city school budget, the Board of Mayor and Aldermen here unanimously approved the cut.

Minutes after the close of a public hearing Monday, the city government approved a $3 million budget on the first of three readings. The action contained the $20,000 cut in a $115,000 allocation increase sought for city schools.

INSTEAD, the city government cut the allocation increase to $95,000 in line with the finance committee's recommendation, bringing the city's share of the school budget next fiscal year to $883,952.

The school system sought the additional money for additional benefits for school personnel, including $62,500 for salary increases and $20,000 for a hospitalization insurance policy for which the school system would pay 75% of the premiums.

Mayor George S. Vibbert Jr. and several aldermen told the teachers that the reduction need not affect the proposed new personnel benefits.

"WE CAN FIND the $20,000 in the budget somewhere, but it's going to hurt," said Dr. James Burns, school superintendent.

The budget is slated for second reading Monday and final reading June 23.

Charges Holiday Inns With Neglect
Father Sues Over Son's Pool Injury

A Louisiana man filed suit on behalf of his son yesterday against Holiday Inns Inc. alleging that the child was permanently injured

when he dived in a motel pool and struck his head.

Filed in federal court here, the suit charges that the Tennessee corporation's Holiday Inn at James Robertson Parkway and Eighth Avenue, North, was operating a defective pool with water "much more shallow" than the eight-foot depth indicated.

ALFRED Alphonso Sr., bringing the suit on behalf of his son Alfred Alphonso Jr. and himself, alleges that his son was "severely and per-

manently injured and disabled" after he dove from the diving board and "struck a protrusion near the bottom of the pool."

The pool "is defectively designed," the suit charges, so that anyone diving from the board "either to the right or left, and not straight off the end, will likely strike the protrusions."

The suit also alleges that "further" negligence was involved because no action was taken to correct the situation "after the hazard was discovered."

In addition to the $50,000 in damages, the suit also asks for a jury to try the case. The plaintiffs are both from New

Orleans and were staying at the Holiday Inn here on June 10, 1974, according to the suit.

Princeton Has First Women Class Heads

PRINCETON, N.J. (AP)— The valedictorian and salutatorian at Princeton University's commencement yesterday both were women, for the first time in the formerly all-male Ivy League school's history.

Reef Damages Soviet Ship

SPLIT, Yugoslavia (AP) — A Soviet passenger ship, the Latvija of Odessa, with West German, Italian, Hungarian and Soviet tourists aboard, was damaged when it ran onto a reef near Solta Island, Yugoslav port authorities said yesterday.

Asparagus Lovers 'Fine, But Cherry...

SHELBY, Mich. (AP) — Asparagus lovers are an honest group of people, but the same can't be said for cherry fans, or so Shirley Beachum says.

Mrs. Beachum, 37, operates a roadside asparagus stand in front of her 80-acre asparagus farm.

When she can't be out in front to personally tend the stand, Mrs. Beachum sells asparagus by the honor system. Bags of the vegetable are marked with prices and folks just leave the money on the stand.

IN FIVE years of depending on asparagus lovers' honesty, she says she has lost only about $5.

But Mrs. Beachum can't say very much about cherry customers.

"I tried the honor system with cherries once and it just didn't work. When I tried cherries, I got a different class of people. They took all my cherries and left no money. I'd even left some sitting behind the stand and they took them."

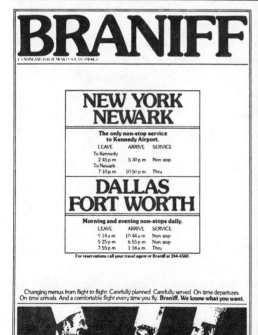
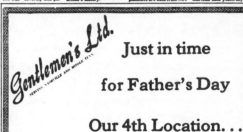

Figure 35-8. *Although different head sizes and type faces are used, the tombstoning of heads on this inside page creates a cluttered, unattractive news display.*

471

10. Avoid the cluttered look. Do not use too many stories, and leave generous white space.

35i   *Tabloid Makeup.* At one time in our modern history, tabloid-size newspapers were almost the exclusive property of metropolitan areas. And today several of the nation's largest newspapers—the New York Daily News, Newsday on Long Island, and the Chicago Sun Times—are tabloids. However, increasing numbers of newspapers are turning to this smaller format. A tabloid page is approximately one-half a full page turned horizontally. The page is approximately 10½ x 14 inches, but the dimensions can vary as much as two inches.

There are two basic kinds of makeup for the tabloid front page. The typical one used in most metropolitan tabloids is called "poster." It will consist of a large photo (or several photos) and several large headlines. There generally is no body type on the page. The headlines are keyed to the stories on the inside page. As a general rule, the lead story appears on page three along with the stories for the other front-page heads.

The poster technique, to be effective, requires excellent photos and stories with major impact. For that reason, and others, another format for tabloid-size pages has developed. It generally is referred to as "compact." Although the term has not been widely accepted, the style of makeup has. The compact makeup uses the same techniques used for a full-size page—only fewer stories, slightly smaller photos and smaller headlines.

Generally speaking, most of the same general rules of good page makeup for a full-size page apply to the tabloid page. However, special effort should be made to avoid overcrowding tabloid pages with large masses of body type and large headlines. Pages should be designed horizontally with a minimum number of vertical items (stories with one column heads and vertical photos).

Many tabloids leave four or more pages at the front of the issue free of advertisements to give the news department ample space to create attractively displayed news pages. Frequently several pages at the start of each special section such as editorial and sports also are left free of advertisements to allow for a more dramatic display of news.

In making up a tabloid page that does contain advertisements, the same general principles used in making up full-size pages should be followed.

EXERCISES

1. Using any newspapers available to you, clip and paste on separate sheets of paper examples of:
   A. Tombstoned heads
   B. A floating flag
   C. Effective example of "breaking up" long stories
   D. Effective example of placing several related stories on a page
2. From newspapers available to you, select several examples of different types of front-page and inside-page makeup. Bring them to class for a general class discussion on makeup. Be prepared to discuss their strong and weak points.

**Latest
markets**

Sun-Times

Chicago, Friday, January 25, 1980

Friday's
Red Streak

20¢ city and suburbs; 25¢ elsewhere

Walkout angering prisoners

Sheriff's police sent to keep order at County Jail.   Page 3

Iranians told to go to polls

In plaintive address, Khomeini urges the nation to choose a good leader carefully.
Page 4

Soviets down Carter speech

Tass calls address 'demagogical' attempt to extend U.S. interests to entire world. Page 5

Canteen exec is indicted

Walter Henely, owner of Airline Canteen Corp., faces federal income tax evasion charges.   Page 2

Bonuses to integration

An order to integrate Milwaukee's public schools, revitalized the system. Sixth in a series.   Page 7

Fuel choice: adapt or die

The U.S. has behaved like a sleepwalker in responding to its energy problem, says George Ball, a former undersecretary of state.
Page 43

Women may face draft registration

From Sun-Times Wires

WASHINGTON—President Carter's intention to resume peacetime registration of draft-age youths could involve women as well as men, a White House spokesman says.

Because of Soviet aggression in the vital Persian Gulf oil-producing area, Carter told Congress Wednesday night he will seek the resumption of peacetime registration but hopes it will not be necessary to reimpose the draft.

Carter noted he is at present only calling for registration—not a return to the actual draft. No

- *No 'selective' service: Royko; Page 2*
- *The U.S. gets tough; Page 5*

American has been drafted since 1973 and none registered since 1975.

The president has legal authority to order a resumption of draft registration, but would need legislation to authorize registering women and to induct young people into the armed services.

ADMINISTRATION officials said many details of the renewed draft registration and Selective Service System overhaul have yet to be worked out, indicating the plan may have been hastily put together to fit into the president's speech.

They said it is "an open question" whether young women will be subject to registration. But they stressed that there will be no physical examinations or classification for a possible draft, and procedures for deciding who would be exempt from a possible draft are "down the line."

Selective Service System officials said registration of 18 million young American men could be

Turn to Page 52

Truck cab tips on icy Kennedy

The cab of a trailer truck lies in the median strip of the Kennedy Expressway near Austin Thursday morning after the vehicle apparently went out of control on the ice-covered pavement. Snow and freezing drizzle that fell in the early hours made driving hazardous in the area during the morning rush hours, despite the efforts of salt truck crews. Story on Page 3. (Sun-Times Photo by Jim Frost)

School disgrace: editorial on P. 45

Byrne holding school summit

...ddles with Healey, Caruso: Page 3

Figure 35-9. *A modified poster format is frequently used by metropolitan tabloids such as the Sun-Times in Chicago.* Courtesy of the Sun-Times, Chicago.

THE CHRISTIAN SCIENCE MONITOR

COPYRIGHT © 198 THE CHRISTIAN SCIENCE PUBLISHING SOCIETY VOL. 72, NO. 28   Friday, January 4, 1980   25¢

Gold's soaring prospects

an ounce				
$600				
$500				
$400				14 K
$300				
$200				
$100	Dec. 1976 $134	Dec. 1977 $165	Dec. 1978 $226	Jan 3 1980 $634

By Gene Langley, staff artist

Can the price soon hit $1,000 an ounce?

'Gold rush' of 1980 sparked by turmoil in Iran, Afghanistan

By David R. Francis
Business and financial editor of
The Christian Science Monitor

Boston

Propelling the gold rush of 1980 is an international mood that has shifted from financial concern to political panic.

"The world anxiety level has just taken off," says Jeffrey A. Nichols, chief economist with Argus Research Corporation, a New York financial advisory firm.

The wealthy and well-to-do, particularly in the Middle East but also elsewhere, have been frightened by the events in Iran and Afghanistan. They have been buying gold as financial insurance, shoving up the price of the precious metal to $634 a troy ounce on the London gold market at the closing Jan. 3. That was up $74.50 from the Jan. 2 afternoon "fixing" – a record jump that smashed another record gain of $35.50 at the previous closing. Many

ordinary speculators have disappeared from the market, scared by its high risks.

After examining the international monetary reserve figures of Saudi Arabia, Kuwait, and the United Arab Emirates, Mr. Nichols "guesstimates" that as much as $10 billion to $20 billion has moved out of these countries to safer territory in the last several months. Some of this "flight capital" has been invested in gold.

There have been similar, but smaller, movements into gold in markets ranging from Paris to Hong Kong.

However, the motives of gold investors have altered. They used to worry mostly about the value of paper money, particularly the US dollar. They invested in gold coins or bullion as an economic hedge against the depreciation of currencies.

Now they are concerned about political stability. Those in more moderate Middle

★ Please turn to Page 14

A race to precious metals

By Harry B. Ellis
Staff correspondent of
The Christian Science Monitor

Washington

At home and abroad, deep concerns about peace and war and about the future supply and price of oil are distorting economic behavior.

Latest evidence is the skyrocketing price of gold, as a relative handful of moneyed investors – fleeing the uncertainty of paper currencies – push the precious metal above $600 an ounce.

"Panic," international economist Lawrence B. Krause said in a telephone interview, "appears first in precious metals, diamonds – everything movable."

The price of such tangible assets soars,

as speculators and investors – both governmental and private – liquidate holdings to which access might be lost through war, or whose value is shrinking.

The US dollar, for example, dropped sharply on European money markets – reaching a record low against the West German mark – as gold prices climbed.

Widespread unease over Soviet intentions in Afghanistan and elsewhere in the Middle East, coupled with the unresolved situation in Iran and the soaring price of oil – all fuel both the gold rush and, more important, worldwide inflation.

Another manifestation of investor uncertainty, sparked by the movement of Soviet troops through Central Asia, is an abrupt drop in the US stock market.

★ Please turn to Page 7

Soviets' Afghan attack perplexes Pentagon

Experts term invasion 'well oiled' (below), as an angry White House calls for delay of SALT treaty (Page 2). Soviets seem ready to dump better US relations for military gain (Page 4).

By John K. Cooley
Staff correspondent of The Christian Science Monitor

Washington

The Soviet Union's massive Christmas week invasion of Afghanistan was a swift, well-oiled operation, planned methodically with Moscow's Warsaw Pact allies.

This is the conclusion of senior US intelligence analysts who now seek to determine "where the Soviets go from here," as one Pentagon expert put it.

Urgency is added to their question by the realization here that not all of the Soviet moves were successfully tracked by Western intelligence. Some analysts are wondering whether present Soviet combat operations against the Afghan Muslim insurgents may not partly screen from view new Soviet preparations for further moves.

Such moves might include "hot pursuit" of Afghan rebel units to their bases inside Pakistan – which President Carter has said would trigger the 1959 US-Pakistani defense treaty – or even eventual moves across the border between Soviet and Iranian Azerbaidzhan, in Iran's northwest, where Turkish-speaking Azeri militants oppose Ayatollah Ruhollah Khomeini's Persian-speaking government.

US Defense Department experts, suspecting Soviet deception tactics, have been rereading passages like this one from a Soviet military commentator, Maj. M. A. Ziyeminsh, in Red Star, the Soviet army newspaper, published a year ago:

"It must be said how important it is to conceal one's true intentions, manpower and equipment, and combat resources from the enemy. Frequently, in order to achieve this and lead the enemy into a mistake, something more is required than just clever camouflage. . . . It is necessary, for example, to use military cunning, sometimes even on a very large scale."

Nearly 40,000 Soviet combat troops (including the original 3,500 Soviet military "advisers" assigned to the overthrown regime of the late President Hafizullah Amin) have crossed the northern frontier or have been airlifted to Bagrame air base, north of Kabul, or directly to Kabul, since Dec. 19.

By Jan. 3, fighting between the Soviets and the Afghans was in progress in mountains near Paghman, just west of Kabul and south of Herat, which is in western Iran. Eyewitnesses in Iran reported arrival of thousands of Afghan refugees from the fighting.

In the Hindu Kush mountain finger of northeast Afghanistan pointing at China, Soviet forces reportedly fought rebels along the single mountain road leading to the 50-mile-long border with China, near the junction of the Chinese, Pakistan, and Soviet frontiers.

Other Soviet units then fanned out to provincial capitals. Some were reported fighting Muslim rebels as well as some Afghan army units which apparently had refused Soviet orders to surrender their arms. Earlier, diplomatic reports from Kabul said the Soviets had disarmed the remnants of the first corps of the formerly 90,000-man Afghan army. In Konarha Province, bordering Pakistan, the Afghan commander has refused to obey Soviet orders and has halted operations against the rebels.

One Soviet motorized rifle division of 12,500 men has deployed along the main north-south road in Afghanistan's far west, between the Soviet border base of Kushka and

★ Please turn to Page 10

Iranians have odd view of US ... and vice versa

By Ned Temko
Staff correspondent of
The Christian Science Monitor

Tehran, Iran

"Blacks are still lynched there without trials, by ordinary people," contends the latest portrait of the United States in the English-language Tehran Times.

The picture of carefree hanging parties seems but one distortion on one side of a communications gap complicating the two-month-old hostage impasse at the US Embassy here.

UN Secretary-General Kurt Waldheim, in Tehran to try to bridge the gap and resolve the impasse, had a second "useful and constructive" meeting with Foreign Minister Sadeq Ghotbzadeh Jan. 3. But at the end of the day, it remained unclear whether Ayatollah Ruhollah Khomeini would meet the UN envoy.

Many Iranians, particularly younger ones like the militants holding the US mission, seem convinced that US history froze somewhere in the tumultuous 1960s. They sometimes portray an American society on the verge of collapse from within.

Blacks battle whites, women battle men, rich battle poor, as many Iranians see it. Atop a corrupt American power pyramid, they reason, sits a President soon to be toppled by an outraged, oppressed people sympathetic to Iran's grievances against Washington.

This vision, more than anything, may explain the release of 13 black and female hos-

★ Please turn to Page 9

Inside today...

'Sobering '70s' — fifth in series: sports and the money spiral   12

Business legislation for 1980s: What's in the works?   11

News — briefly	2	House/garden	16
Arts	15	Real estate	17, 18
Financial	11	Sports	6

Figure 35-10. *The Christian Science Monitor converted from full-size to tabloid and continued to follow the makeup style of a traditional newspaper rather than adopting a form of the poster style.* Courtesy of The Christian Science Monitor.

Laotians cloak their socialism with US T-shirts

Despite Vietnamese influence, Laos tries to go its own way

By Frederic A. Moritz
Staff correspondent of The Christian Science Monitor

Vientiane, Laos

Advisers from Vietnam, sneakers from Thailand, and young men still wearing T-shirts marked "US Coast Guard." These are just a few of the paradoxes a visiting correspondent quickly encounters in the "land of a million elephants."

Despite the continuing reports of rising Vietnamese influence, Laos today is a country of growing "liberalization," clearly intent on pursuing its own domestic line.

A quick path to orthodox communism has been decisively rejected. Any visitor can easily spot the signs.

Compared to a year and a half ago, Vientiane's free markets are bustling with sales of jeans, sneakers, electrical appliances, and cassette recorders from Thailand. Import restrictions on goods from across the Mekong River have been eased.

Agriculture authorities are no longer talking of pushing collectivization Vietnamese-style. That possibility was once a concern of some foreign aid officials here. But in December restrictions on free sales of animals and other farm goods were relaxed. Farm trade between provinces was permitted. And last summer a drastic slowdown in the rate of collectivization was announced.

Compared to a year and a half ago, more privately owned shops are open in Vientiane — another sign of greater tolerance for private enterprise.

There are changes, too, in the city's nightclubs, where singers croon socialist lyrics to the twang of electric guitars. Young men and women now sit together at the same table where once they sat segregated across the room from each other. And nonpolitical pantomimes and slapstick parodies now supplement the socialist lyrics.

Paradoxically much of this is happening amid reports of growing Laotian repressiveness circulating in the West. The underlying causes for most of these reports are the continuing flow of refugees to Thailand, the ongoing military campaign against Hmong hill tribes, and what is thought to be increased Vietnamese influence in the country.

Some of the refugees who have gone to Thailand describe what they see as Vietnam's growing influence in their country as one reason they have left. But conversations with refugees in Thailand and with Laotians contemplating leaving Laos indicate that a major motivation is often economic.

With relatively few consumer goods and a host of economic problems, Laos offers a bleak, uncertain future to those who stay. Many foreign observers believe an important factor behind recent liberalizations is to reduce the incentive for Laotians to join in the exodus which has already cost Laos many, if not most, of its skilled workers.

The campaign against the Hmong has produced its own straggling lines of refugees, as the defeated onetime CIA-supported army of Vang Pao retreats into Thailand. The Laotian government has sought to resettle many of these people in lowland or plateau areas — both for security reasons and to end the ecological damage to mountain tops caused by "slash and burn" agriculture.

Controversial charges by Hmong refugees that Vietnamese and Laotian forces have used poison gas against them have brought international attention, even though many experts say conclusive proof is lacking.

Most diplomats and foreign observers here say the degree of Vietnamese influence is extremely difficult to assess.

They generally agree it is greatest in defense, internal security, and transport, with at least a slight increase since the China-Vietnam war early last year. Still both Western and Vietnamese sources agree Vietnamese troop strength in Laos has stayed about the same — some 30,000 to 40,000 men.

Many observers agree that in spite of Vietnamese advisers, in most internal economic and social matters the Laotians run the show.

Reports that Laotian rice is being drained to feed Vietnam meet skepticism here from observers who say the fuel cost to the Vietnamese would make any such operation uneconomic.

Still many Laotian students are studying in Vietnam. Laotians say Vietnamese methods are carefully observed for usefulness in their own country. But the Soviet Union has more prestige, and many students would rather study there because it is more "modern," says one Laotian high school student.

Clearly Vietnam seeks to avoid offending the Laotians. At the one hotel this correspondent saw the chief of a visiting economic mission from Hanoi graciously shake hands with and thank the head waiter after their stay. "Laotians and Vietnamese get along better now than two years ago," said one storekeeper.

Still, Westerners who work in the countryside report strong anti-Vietnamese feeling there. This is partly because Vietnamese military teams sometimes patrol the rural areas and partly because country people are suspicious of all foreigners, one source concludes.

The Laotian government has also moved closer to Vietnam in its foreign policy pronouncements on everything from Iran and Afghanistan to the United States. Some observers see this as a sign of Vietnamese dominance. Others say it is simply a polite gesture to Vietnam that Laos can afford to make at no great cost.

By Gordon N. Converse, chief photographer
Luang Prabang marketplace before communist takeover: today free markets are bustling again

'Poor man's coal' — lignite — attracting new Gulf coast interest as fuel alternative

By Paul Van Slambrouck
Staff correspondent of The Christian Science Monitor

Houston

Lignite, long considered "poor man's coal" because of its low heating value, has become an important resource in America's search for energy alternatives to diminishing oil and natural gas supplies.

This low-quality coal is abundant along the Gulf of Mexico and in North Dakota, South Dakota, and Montana. Yet economics has historically favored other cleaner and more energy-efficient types of coal, leaving lignite largely unexploited.

That is changing. The use of lignite as a fuel for generating power now is rising dramatically — far faster than coal in general.

"We've known about lignite for a long time, but we didn't take it seriously until the early 1970s," when the price of oil and natural gas began rising rapidly, notes an official with Phillips Coal Company in Dallas. Phillips Coal has a contract to sell lignite to Cajun Electric Cooperative of Louisiana for generating electricity in 1984.

"Lignite has become very popular in the last two or three years. For the next decade it will continue to grow at a very high rate," predicts David M. White, a lignite expert with the Texas Energy and Natural Resources Council.

Federal energy policy now requires electric utilities and industries to use less oil and natural gas as boiler fuels in favor of more coal.

Nationally, conversion to coal will be greatest in the gulf coast region, where utilities and industrial users have grown heavily dependent on once-cheap local supplies of natural gas and, to a lesser extent, oil. Sizable lignite reserves stretching from Texas to Alabama offer power plants and industrial facilities in this part of the country an attractive new energy source right in their own back yards.

Two factors encourage the use of indigenous lignite over types of coal in gulf coast states as well as in North Dakota: rising railroad rates for "importing" out-of-state coal and new air-quality regulations that do not favor burning Western low-sulfur coal as they once did.

Federal standards for coal-fired power plants were tightened last year so that all new facilities will need "scrubbers" to clean plant emissions. Previously, the Environmental Protection Agency required only that coal plant emissions have no more than 1.2 pounds of sulfur dioxide per million Btus (British thermal units) of fuel burned. Because of the low heating value and high sulfur content of lignite, plants using this fuel needed expensive scrubbers, adding 20 to 50 percent to their cost of construction. Plants using low-sulfur Western coal did not.

Now, emission standards call for a reduction in sulfur dioxide regardless of the initial sulfur content. This effectively requires scrubbers on all new facilities, making lignite economically competitive with other types of coal in terms of capital investment.

Since lignite is surface-mined, stepped-up production in Texas has caused some environmental concern over its impact on the landscape. However, Mr. White asserts that the soil and climate of eastern Texas, where lignite is found, ensures that "the land can be effectively reclaimed" as required by state and federal law.

Total coal consumption in the United States is rising at a sluggish rate, despite President Carter's goal of doubling domestic production by 1985. The National Coal Association forecasts output will increase a modest 1 percent this year, from 770 million tons in 1979.

However, lignite use, confined principally to Texas and North Dakota, is skyrocketing. In North Dakota, annual production has tripled since the early 1970s — to an estimated 15 million tons last year. Texas lignite production has grown tenfold since 1970 — to more than 22 million tons in 1979.

Texas Utilities Company of Dallas accounts for most of the lignite production in this state, but other utilities are making plans to use it. Houston Lighting & Power Company will build two lignite power generating units in 1985 and 1986. Two more lignite units are planned but no timetable has been set.

City Public Service of San Antonio has tentative plans to build a lignite plant some time in the late 1980s.

Outside Texas, Arkansas Power & Light in Little Rock has announced it will build two new lignite-fired generating units in 1988 and 1989.

Figure 35-11. *A number of inside pages on most tabloid newspapers are left free of advertisements to permit adequate display of major news stories.* Courtesy of The Christian Science Monitor.

3. Using any newspaper available to you, redesign the front page on any issue. Use all the same stories, photographs and other display devices (cartoons or art work if any is used). It is permissible to change the type size or column width of headlines but do not add any additional stories. Use of a different size masthead is permissible.

4. Adding the following list of national and international stories to the ones in Exercise 5 of Chapter 34, select the stories you would place on the front page (use as many as needed for an attractive layout) and draw a front-page dummy of your layout. Briefly specify which story goes in each position on the page:

A. Washington, D.C.—Number of families headed by women has increased 32 per cent over the decade. Twelve inches.

B. Karachi, Pakistan—A Pakistani Airlines Boeing 707 jetliner carrying 157 passengers crashed in Saudi Arabia on a flight from Nigeria to Karachi. All aboard were killed. Five inches.

C. San Francisco—An earthquake measuring 5.2 on the Richter scale shook the San Francisco area today. No casualties but extensive damage reported. Twelve inches.

D. Madrid—Police arrested the director of the Soviet Airlines offices in Spain on espionage charges and ordered him deported immediately. Six inches.

E. New York—City firemen voted to go on strike. Ask all other union to stay off the job for one day in support of their pay demands. Ten inches.

F. Chicago—Burglars took an estimated $1 million in cash and valuables from a major bank over the weekened, police said. Largest bank burglary in city's history, police said. Four inches.

G. Atlanta—Allergy expert says joggers should never run alone because some people who exercise regularly are subject to severe, possibly fatal allergic reaction. Six inches.

H. Slidell, La.—Two sisters, upset that their mother refused to give them another piece of bread for dinner, tried to kill their parents by setting fire to the family trailer, and almost succeeded, police said. Five inches.

I. Honolulu—A rain and wind storm that raked the Hawaiian Islands for three days last week caused more than $13 million in damage. Four inches.

J. Washington—An epidemic of lung cancer, heart disease, stroke and other ailments is beginning to spread among middle-aged American women who smoke cigarettes, the Surgeon General says. Eleven inches.

GENERAL EXERCISES IN HEADLINING AND MAKEUP

On the following pages are two general exercises on editing, including selecting and writing headlines, and makeup. Each exercise contains all the stories and pictures available for use in making up one front page. Instructions for handling stories in each exercise are as follows.

1. Sort the stories in order of their importance to the reader. While doing this, try to visualize where you might place each story on your page. After the stories have been sorted, use the headline schedule (samples of different headlines) that follows to determine what size head each story deserves. This headline schedule includes all sizes and types of heads you may use. Each head has been given an arbitrary number (to expedite there assignments), and the maximum unit count per line is designated. Keep in mind that all of these (and only these) stories are available for the front page of your newspaper.

2. Write all headlines.

3. Make up a dummy front page using the headlines you have written, Page-size dummies, marked off in two-inch columns (or whatever size column width the newspaper uses), are usually available at nearby newspapers, or they can be made from a large art pad usually available at bookstores. (Or, if the instructor so chooses, it will be satisfactory to line off an unruled 8½ × 11 sheet of writing paper, which will be half-scale, every inch equal to two inches on the page-size dummy.) The page should be made up as follows.

A. Clip a flag, or nameplate, from a newspaper, and paste it in the proper place on the dummy. (Students may design their own if they choose.)

B. Determine the appropriate place on the page for each story and picture in accordance with the way you ranked them by their importance to the reader. Before the actual front-page dummy is completed, you may want to practice arranging the stories to determine the best display. An excellent way to do this is to clip headlines similar to those in the headline schedule of this exercise and lay them on the dummy page in various positions to give a clear picture of the appearance of the page.

C. When a final decision is reached on the position of a story, print the story's headline (which you have written) on the dummy and in the space reserved for the head. (Make certain to allow enough room for the heads on the dummy. To do this, measure the size of the type in headline schedule and then double or triple that amount, depending upon the number of lines in your headline. Allow at least one-eighth of an inch between lines and at the top and bottom of the head.) The size and style of the handprinted letters should resemble as much as possible the size and style of letters in the headline schedule for this exercise.

D. In the column or columns below each head (where the story would appear if printed), measure and mark the amount of space necessary to provide for the story. If a story is to be continued to another page, mark the length of the part jumped at the end of the story on page one (e.g., "5 inches jumped"). In the column space reserved for the story, write the story's slugline.

HEADLINE SCHEDULE

Note: The schedule offers the instructor and the student considerable flexibility not only in selection of head sizes but in style of headlines. It is flexible enough to permit the instructor to assign only one headline style if he chooses. On the other hand, it allows for considerable freedom on the part of the student who might want to experiment with various combinations of headlines such as the reverse kicker (page 448).

Designed for Six-Column Pages

Number of Head		Sample Letter and Description of Head	Size of Type	Maximum Count per Line in One Column (2¼ inches wide)
1	S	Streamer—one line deep. Roman type, caps and lower case. Six, seven, or eight columns wide.	96	4 units

Number of Head	Sample Letter and Description of Head	Size of Type	Maximum Count per Line in One Column (2¼ inches wide)
la	**V** Streamer—one line deep. Roman type, caps and lowercase. Five, six, seven or eight columns. Also can be scheduled two lines deep.	84	4½ units
1b	**C** Streamer—one line deep. Roman type, caps and lowercase. Five, six, seven or eight columns. Also can be scheduled two lines deep.	72	5½ units
2	**F** Streamer—one line deep. Roman type, caps and lowercase. Five, six, seven or eight columns. Also can be scheduled two lines deep.	60	6½ units
2a	*F* Streamer—one line deep. Italic type, caps and lowercase. Five, six, seven or eight columns.	60	7½ units
3	**D** Two-column head, three lines deep. Roman type, caps and lowercase.	48	8 units
3a	*D* Three-column head, two lines deep, Italic type, caps and lowercase.	48	9 units
4	**R** Two-column head, two lines deep. Roman type, caps and lowercase	48	8 units
4a	*R* Two-column head, two lines deep. Italic type, caps and lowercase.	48	9 units
5b	**M** One-column head, three lines deep. Roman type, caps and lowercase.	36	9½ units
5a	**R** Two-column head, two lines deep. Roman type, caps and lowercase.	36	9½ units

Number of Head		Sample Letter and Description of Head	Size of Type	Maximum Count per Line in One Column (2¼ inches wide)
5	**V**	Three-column head, one line deep. Roman type, caps and lowercase.	36	9½ units
6	**H**	Two-column head, two lines deep. Roman type, caps and lowercase.	30	11½ units
6a	**O**	One-column head, three lines deep. Roman type, caps and lowercase.	30	11½ units
7	**N**	Two-column head, two lines deep. Roman type, caps and lowercase.	24	13½ units
7a	**E**	One-column head, two lines deep. Roman type, caps, and lowercase. Also can be scheduled three lines deep.	24	13½ units
7b	*C*	One-column head, two lines deep. Italic type, caps and lowercase. Also can be scheduled three lines deep.	24	14½ units
8	**T**	One-column head, two lines deep. Roman type, caps and lowercase. Also can be scheduled three lines deep.	18	18 units
8a	*P*	One-column head, two lines deep, Italic type, caps and lowercase. Also can be scheduled three lines deep.	18	19 units
9	**H**	One-column, two lines deep. Roman type, caps and lowercase. Also can be scheduled three lines deep.	14	23 units
9a	*H*	One-column head, two lines deep. Italic type, caps and lowercase. Also can be scheduled three lines deep.	14	24 units

Note: Kickers may be ordered for any of the multiple-column headlines above. They should be in a type size approximately one-half the size of the main headline and should be more than half the width of the main head. (See page 448.) If kickers are ordered, write the main headline at least one count short to allow more white space around the head and to avoid a cluttered look.

EXERCISES

1. Story notes appearing at the end of each preceding chapter of *The Complete Reporter* will be considered as stories in this and the second exercise. Since copy editing and rewriting are not involved in these exercises, it is not necessary to have the stories written as they would appear in a newspaper. And since the student's study of previous chapters has familiarized him with these story notes, he should be able to select and write suitable headlines after a quick review of each set of notes. However, if the student has retained the stories he has written from these notes, he will find them helpful.

The stories listed below have been chosen as those "available" for the front page of one edition. (Obviously not all of the stories can be used.) They are listed by chapter and exercise number as well as page number. A slug (guideline) is designated for each story. The length of the story is also listed:

Chapter and Exercise Number	Page Number	Guideline	Length in Column Inches
Ch. 20, Ex. 4D	270	Rainstorms	17
Ch. 16, Ex. 6	231	Michael's testimony	12
Ch. 9l Ex. 7	151	Train wreck	25
Ch. 10, Ex. 6B	169	Chocolate chip	4
Ch. 17, Ex. 5	240	Consumer convention	6
Ch. 16, Ex. 5	230	Maxwell speech	8
Ch. 19, Ex. 2A	260	Car-truck accident	10
Ch. 26, Ex. 5	361	Methodist missionaries	8
Ch. 21, Ex. 4D	283	Intruder	3
Ch. 9, Ex. 9E	155	Court shootout	12
Ch. 22, Ex. 5C	300	Damage suit	6
Ch. 6, Ex. 6F	98	Stabbing	3
Ch. 23, Ex. 4B	322	Towing fees	6
Ch. 19, Ex. 2H	263	Plane crash	15
Ch. 24, Ex. 3C	334	Driving school	6

Pictures available for use, if desired, with stories above:
1. Two-column, 4 inches deep, Man with chocolate chip cookies
2. Four-column, 6 inches deep, Rainstorm
3. Three-column, 5 inches deep, Rainstorm
4. Two-column, 7 inches deep, Rainstorm
5. Three-column, 5 inches deep, Car-truck accident
6. Three-column, 6 inches deep, Plane crash
7. One-column, 3 inches deep, Michael's
8. One-column, 5 inches deep, Maxwell
9. One-column, 3 inches deep, Court shootout victim
10. One-column, 3 inches deep, Driving school owner

Instructions: Indicate placement of pictures on the dummy by shading the space covered by each picture or drawing in the representative size of the picture and making a large X through it. Make certain to indicate the exact picture size.

Note: It will be impossible to use all of these stories and pictures on one page. The least important ones should be discarded.

2. Follow the same instructions as for Exercise 1

Chapter and Exercise Number	Page Number	Guideline	Length in Column Inches
Ch. 10, Ex. 5	168	Hovercraft	4
Ch. 17, Ex. 6	241	Law meeting	8
Ch. 22, Ex. 6	301	Villalobo trial	16
Ch. 24, Ex. 3G	336	Egyptian visitors	4
Ch. 16, Ex. 12	233	Adams interview	12
Ch. 23, Ex. 5	323	Bond issue	7
Ch. 8, Ex. 9B	127	Sneed speech	8
Ch. 18, Ex. 4A	253	Judge Thompson	3
Ch. 6, Ex. 6L	100	Bradshear award	3
Ch. 19, Ex. 2G	262	Horse trailer accident	12
Ch. 25, Ex. 4	351	School Board	15
Ch. 24, Ex. 3D	335	Jackson layoffs	6
Ch. 20, Ex. 4E	272	Snowstorm	10
Ch. 19, Ex. 2E	261	Motorcycle crash	8
Ch. 21, Ex. 4H	284	Gino's robbery	17
Ch. 23, Ex. 6	324	Beer law	12

Pictures available for use, if desired:
1. Two-column, 5 inches deep, Hovercraft
2. Three-column, 6 inches deep, Villalobo after trial
3. Three-column, 5 inches deep, Egyptian visitors
4. Five-column, 6 inches deep, Snowstorm
5. Two-column, 5 inches deep, Gino's robbery
6. Four-column, 6 inches deep, Gino's robbery
7. Three-column, 5 inches deep, Wrecked horse trailer
8. One-column, 3 inches deep, Thompson
9. One-column, 3 inches deep, Sneed
10. Three-column, 5 inches deep, Motorcycle wreck

Journalistic Terms

Ad. Advertisement.

Add. Copy to be added to a story already written.

Advance. A preliminary concerning a future event.

Agate. Type 5½ points in depth (72 points to the inch).

A.M. Morning paper.

Angle. The aspect of or phase emphasized in a story.

A.P. or **AP.** The Associated Press, press service.

Art. All newspaper illustrations.

Assignment. Reporter's task.

Bank. (1) Part of headline (also called *deck*); (2) table upon which type is set.

Banner. A page-wide headline (also called *streamer*).

Barline. A one-line headline.

Beat. (1) The reporter's regular run; (2) an exclusive story.

Benday. Mechanical process used in shading engravings.

B.F. or **bf.** Boldface or black type.

Blind interview. Interview that does not give name of person interviewed.

Blurb. A short statement used to promote the sale of a new book or publication.

Body type. Small type in which most of paper is set.

Boil down. Reduce in size.

Border. Metal or paper strips of type used to box stories, ads, etc.

Box. An enclosure of line rules or borders.

Break. (1) The point at which a story is continued to another column or page; (2) as a verb, refers to the time a story is available for publication.

Bromide. A trite expression.

Bulletin. A brief, last-minute news item on an important event.

By-line. The author's name at the start of a story: "By John Smith."

C. and **L.C.** or **clc.** Capital and lowercase letters.

Canned copy. Publicity material.

Caps. Capital letters.

Caption. See Cutlines.

Clip. Newspaper clipping.

Col. Column.

Condensed type. Type that is narrower than regular width.

Copy. All typewritten material.

Copy editor. One who edits and headlines news stories.

Copypaper. Paper used by newspapermen in writing stories.

Correspondent. Out-of-town reporter.

Cover. To get the facts of a story.

Credit line. Line acknowledging source of a story or picture.

CRT. System of editing using a cathode-ray tube and computer or memory bank that produces paper or electronic tape used in composing machines to produce "type."

Crusade. Campaign of a newspaper for a certain reform.

Cub. A beginning reporter.

Cut. (1) A newspaper engraving; (2) to reduce the length of a story.

Cutlines. Explanatory lines with a picture or illustration, usually under the picture. Also called caption.

Dateline. Line at the beginning of a story that includes both date and place of origin of story: "NEW YORK, Jan. 1—."

Deadline. The time all copy must be completed in order to make an edition.

Deck. Part of a multibank headline.

Desk. The copy desk.

Double truck. Two adjoining pages made as one.

Down Style. A newspaper headline style calling for a minimum of capitalization.

Dummy. Diagram of a page for use in making up a page.

Ear. Small box in the upper corners of the name plate (flag).

Edition. Issue for one press run, as mail edition, home edition, extra edition.

Editorialize. To include opinion of the writer in copy.

Em. Unit of spacing. The pica em is approximately one-sixth of an inch.

Embargo. A restriction, such as the precise date and time, placed upon the release of news.

En. One-half em.

Filler. Short news or informational items used to fill small spaces in a page.

Flag. Name of paper appearing on first page.

Flash. A short message briefly summarizing a news event.

Fold. Place where paper is folded.

Follow or **Follow-up.** Story giving later developments of an event already written up.

Follow copy. Instructions on copy to set story or word exactly as written, used often to indicate that word is purposely misspelled or that spelling is unorthodox.

Folio. Page or page number.

Folo. Short for *follow*.

Font. Type face of one size and style.

Fotog. Short for photographer.

Future. Memo of future event.

FYI. For your information.

Galley. Metal tray for holding type. In offset, the columns of type to be pasted down also are called galleys.

Galley proof. Proof made of a galley of type.

Graf. Short for paragraph.

Green proof. Uncorrected proof.

Guideline. A slug line, giving title of the story for convenience of makeup editor and compositors.

Half stick. Type set a half-column in width.

Halftone. A cut made from a photograph.

Hammer. See *kicker*.

Head. Short for headline.

Headline schedule. All of the headline combinations used by a newspaper.

Hold for release. Instructions to hold copy until editor orders it printed.

HTK or HTC. Instructions on copy of a "head to come."

Insert. Copy that is to be inserted in a story already sent to the compositor.

Itals. Italics.

Jump. To continue a story from one page to another.

Jump head. Headline above a continued story.

Jump lines. Lines such as "Continued on page 6" or "Continued from page 1" to identify a continued story.

Kicker. A short one-line head, sometimes underlined, either centered above or slightly to the left of main head, usually in type about one-half type size of main head. Also called *hammer*.

Kill. To delete or exclude copy.

Layout. (1) Diagram of page (see dummy), showing where stories and ads are to be placed; (2) arrangement of pictures in order to make a cut.

L.C. or lc. Lowercase type.

Lead (*lĕd*). (1) As noun, metal pieces placed between lines of type for spacing; (2) as verb, to space out page with these metal pieces.

Lead (*leed*). The first paragraph of a news story.

Leg man. Reporter who gathers news, phoning it in instead of going in to write it.

Letterpress printing. Process of printing that uses metal type or other raised surfaces that make a direct impression on paper.

Library. Newspaper morgue or files of clippings, photographs, prepared obituaries, biographies, etc.

Localize. To emphasize the local angle in a story.

Log. City editor's assignment book.

Make-over. Rearrangement of stories on page to provide for new copy or to change the position of stories.

Makeup. Arranging stories, pictures, ads, etc., on a page.

Masthead. Editorial page heading, giving information about the newspaper.

Matrix or Mat. A matrix or papier-mâché impression of a cut or of type.

Minion. Seven-point type.

More. Used at end of a page of copy to indicate story is continued on another page.

Morgue. Files for depositing clippings, pictures, etc. (also called *library*).

Mug shot. Head-and-shoulders photograph of an individual.

Must. Instructions that story must be used on that day without fail.

Nameplate. Name of paper on page one (also called *flag*).

Newsprint. The grade of paper used in printing newspapers.

Nonpareil. Six-point type.

Obit. Obituary.

Offset printing. Process of printing that uses a rubber roller that takes the impression from a metal plate and transfers it to the paper.

Overline. Caption above a *cut*. Also another word for kicker.

Overset. Type in addition to that needed to fill a paper.

Op-Ed. Page opposite the editorial page featuring comment, cartoons and other editorial matter.

Pad. To make longer.

Pasteup. Method of making up a page for the camera in the offset process—pasting in proofs of headlines, body type, line drawings, etc.

Pi. Jumbled type.

Pica. Twelve-point type; also unit of measurement, one-sixth of an inch.

Pick up. Instructions to use material already set in type.

Pix. Picture.

Plate. A stereotyped page of type, ready to lock in the press.

Play up. To emphasize.

P.M. Afternoon paper.

Point. A depth measurement of type approximately $1/72$ inch.

Policy story. A story showing directly or indirectly the newspaper's stand on an issue.

Precede. Material to precede the copy already set in type.

Proof. An imprint of set type used in correcting errors.

Proofreader. Person who reads proof to correct errors.

Puff. Editorialized, complimentary statements in a news story.

Q and A. Question-and-answer copy, printed verbatim.

Quad. A type character or space equal in width and height.

Query. Question on an event sent by a correspondent to a paper or by a paper to a correspondent.

Quote. Quotation.

Railroad. To rush copy through to the compositor without careful editing.

Release. Instructions on the time to publish a story, as "Release after 3 p.m. Feb. 6."

Revise. Proof made after type is corrected.

Rewrite. (1) To write a story again to improve; (2) to write a story that already has been reported in a competing newspaper; (3) to write a story from facts given by another reporter (sometimes from a leg man over the telephone).

Rule. Metal strip used in separating columns, making borders, etc.

Run. A press run (edition).

Run in. Instructions to make a series of sentences, names, etc., into one paragraph, if each one of the series has been set up as a separate short paragraph or line.

Running story. Story sent to compositors in sections.

Runover. Part of a story that is continued on another page.

Sacred cow. News or promotional material that the publisher or editor demands printed in a special manner.

Scanner. Optical Character Reader (also known as OCR) which converts typewritten material to electronic impulses and transmits these to a tape punch or computer.

Schedule. List of assignments.

Scoop. An exclusive story.

Second front. The first page of a second section.

Sheet. Brief stories.

Sked. Schedule.

Slant. To emphasize a certain phase of a news event.

Slot. The place occupied by the head of the copy desk (on the inside of horsehoe-shaped desks). Slot man is also called copy desk chief.

Slug. (1) The guideline at the beginning of the story, to make it easy to identify (see "guideline"); (2) a strip of metal, less than type high and used to space between lines; (3) a line of type cast by the typesetting machine.

Soc. Society.

Squib. A brief story.

Stet. Restore text of copy which has been marked out. (This is a copyreader's and proofreader's sign.)

Stick. (1) A measuring unit for type—about two inches; (2) a small amount of type, about 100 words. Also short for "composing stick."

Streamer. Headline stretching completely across a page (also *banner*).

String. Newspaper clippings pasted together.

Subhead. Small, one-line headline used in the body of a story.

Take. A section of a running story.

Thirty. The end of a story (numeral usually used).

Tie-back or **Tie-in.** That part of the story which reiterates past events to remind the reader or to give background for the latest developments.

Time copy. Copy that might be held over and used when needed.

Top heads. Headline at top of a column.

Tr. Transpose or change the position of.

Trim. Reduce length of story.

U.C. and **L.C.** Uppercase and lowercase type.

U.P.I. or **UPI.** United Press International, press service.

VDT. Short for Video Display Terminal, which looks like a typewriter with a small television set sitting on top. Stories may be composed or corrected on these units and stored in a computer for later use or may be punched into paper tape for use in the photocomposition machines.

Wrong font or **W.F.** Wrong style or size of type.

Selected
Bibliography

GENERAL REFERENCES ON JOURNALISTIC WRITING

Anderson, David and Benjamin. *Investigative Reporting.* Bloomington, Ind.: Indiana University Press, 1976.

Bernstein, Theodore M. *Watch Your Language.* Manhasset, N.Y.: Channel Press, 1958.

Bulch, Judith and Kay Miller. *Investigate and In-Depth Reporting.* New York: Hastings House, 1978.

Callihan, E. R. *Grammar for Journalists.* Radnor, Pa.: Chilton Book Co., 1969.

Cutlip, Scott M. and Allen H. Center. *Effective Public Relations.* 4th ed. Englewood Cliffs, N.J.: Prentice-Hall, 1971.

Flesch, Rudolf. *The Art of Readable Writing.* 25th anniversary ed. New York: Harper & Row, 1974.

Hohenberg, John. *The Professional Journalist.* 3rd ed. New York: Holt, Rinehart and Winston, 1973.

Garst, Robert E. and Theodore M. Bernstein. *Headlines and Deadlines.* 3rd ed. New York: Columbia University Press, 1961.

MacDougall, Curtis D. *Interpretative Reporting.* 7th ed. New York: Macmillan, 1977.

Metzler, Ken. *Creative Interviewing.* Englewood Cliffs, N.J.: Prentice-Hall, Inc., 1977.

Mott, George F. (ed.). *New Survey of Journalism.* New York: Barnes & Noble, 1963.

Rivers, William L. *Mass Media: Reporting, Writing, Editing.* 2nd ed. New York: Harper & Row, 1974.

———. *Writing: Craft and Art.* Englewood Cliffs, N.J.: Prentice-Hall, 1975.

———. *Finding Facts.* Englewood Cliffs, N.J.: Prentice-Hall, 1975.

Stein, M. L. *Reporting Today: The Newswriter's Handbook.* New York: Cornerstone Library, 1971.

Strunk, William, Jr., and E. B. White. *The Elements of Style*. 3rd ed. New York: Macmillan, 1979.

Zinsser, William. *On Writing Well*. 2nd ed. New York: Harper & Row, 1980.

THE JOURNALISTIC PROFESSION ·

(History of Journalism, Biographies of Famous Journalists, Journalism as a Profession)

Berger, Meyer. *The Story of the New York Times*. New York: Simon and Schuster, 1951.

Brucker, Herbert. *Communication Is Power: Unchanging Ideas in Changing Journalism*. New York: Oxford University Press, 1973.

———. *Eyewitness to History*. New York: Macmillan, 1962.

Buranelli, V. (ed.). *The Trial of Peter Zenger*. New York: New York University Press, 1957.

Canham, E. D. *Commitment to Freedom: The Story of the Christian Science Monitor*. Boston: Houghton, 1958.

Carlson, O. *The Man Who Made News: James Gordon Bennett*. New York: Duell, Sloan & Pearce, 1942.

Dennis, Everette E. and William L. Rivers. *Other Voices: The New Journalism in America*. San Francisco: Canfield Press, 1974.

Emery, E. *The Press and America*. Englewood Cliffs, N.J.: Prentice-Hall, 1962.

Fowler, Gene. *Timber Line: A Story of Bonfils and Tammen*. Garden City, N.Y.: Halcyon House, 1943.

Gramling, O. *AP: The Story of News*. New York: Farrar, 1940.

Johnson, G. W. *An Honorable Titan: A Biographical Study of Adolph S. Ochs*. New York: Harper, 1946.

Johnson, Michael L. *The New Journalism*. Lawrence, Kan.: University of Kansas Press, 1971.

Kaltenborn, H. V. *Fifty Fabulous Years, 1900–1950*. New York: Putnam, 1950.

Knight, Oliver (ed.). *I Protest: Selected Disquisitions of E. W. Scripps*. Madison, Wis.: University of Wisconsin Press, 1969.

Liebling, A. J. *Mink and Red Herring: The Wayward Pressman's Casebook*. Garden City, N.Y.: Doubleday, 1949.

Luskin, John. *Lippman, Liberty, and the Press*. University, Ala.: University of Alabama Press, 1972.

Lyons, Louis M. *Newspaper Story: One Hundred Years of the Boston Globe*. Cambridge, Mass.: Belknap Press of Harvard University Press, 1971.

McNulty, John B. *Older Than the Nation: The Story of the Hartford Courant*. Stonington, Conn.: Pequot Press, 1964.

Miller, Lee. *The Story of Ernie Pyle*. New York: Viking Press, 1950.

Morris, J. A. *Deadline Every Minute*. Garden City, N.Y.: Doubleday, 1957.

Mott, F. L. *American Journalism: A History of Newspapers in the United States Through 270 Years, 1690–1960*. New York: Macmillan, 1962.

———. *Jefferson and the Press*. Baton Rouge, La.: Louisiana State University Press, 1943.

Nixon, R. B. *Henry W. Grady: Spokesman of the New South*. New York: Knopf, 1943.

Peterson, T. *Magazines in the Twentieth Century*. Evanston, Ill.: University of Illinois Press, 1956.

Pilat, Oliver. *Drew Pearson: An Unauthorized Biography*. New York: Harpers Magazine Press, 1973.

Ross, I. *Ladies of the Press*. New York: Harper, 1936.

Rucker, Bryce, W. *Twentieth Century Reporting at Its Best*. Ames, Ia.: Iowa State University Press, 1965.

Rutland, Robert A. *The Newsmongers: Journalism in the Life of the Nation—1690–1972*. New York: Dial Press, 1973.

Seitz, Don Carlos. *Horace Greeley: Founder of the New York Tribune*. New York: AMS Press, 1970.

Starr, L. M. *Bohemian Brigade: Civil War Newsmen in Action*. New York: Knopf, 1954.

Stone, C. *Dana and the Sun*. New York: Dodd, Mead, 1938.

Swanberg, W. A. *Citizen Hearst*. New York: Charles Scribner's Sons, 1961.

———. *Pulitzer*. Charles Scribner's Sons, 1967.

Talese, Gay. *The Kingdom and the Power*. New York: World Publishing Co., 1969.

Williamson, Samuel T. *Frank Gannett: A Biography*. New York: Duell, Sloan & Pearce, 1940.

Wolfe, Tom and E. W. Johnson (eds.). *The New Journalism*. New York: Harper & Row, 1973.

REFERENCES ON SPECIAL TYPES OF JOURNALISTIC WRITING

Baird, Russell N. and A. T. Turnbull. *Industrial and Business Journalism*. Philadelphia: Chilton Book Co., 1961.

Bird, George, L. *Modern Article Writing*. Dubuque, Ia.: Wm. C. Brown Co., 1967.

Burkett, David, W. *Writing Science News for the Mass Media*. Houston, Tex.: Gulf Publishing Co., 1968.

Bush, Chilton R. *Newswriting and Reporting Public Affairs*. 2nd ed. Philadelphia: Chilton Book Co., 1970.

Click, J. W. *Magazine Editing and Production*. Dubuque, Ia.: Wm. C. Brown Co., 1974.

Copple, Neale. *Depth Reporting*. Englewood Cliffs, N.J.: Prentice-Hall, 1964.

Fang, I. E. *Television News*. New York: Hasting House, 1972.

Field, Stanley. *Professional Broadcast Writer's Handbook*. Blue Ridge Summit, Pa.: TAB Books, 1974.

Foster, J. *Science Writer's Guide*. New York: Columbia University Press, 1963.

Gunther, Max. *Writing the Modern Magazine Article*. Boston: The Writer, Inc., 1968.

Heath, Harry and Louis I. Gelfand. *Modern Sportswriting*. Ames, Ia.: Iowa State University Press, 1969.

Hilliard, Robert. *Writing for Radio and Television*. 2nd ed. New York: Hasting House, 1972.

Hunt, Todd. *Reviewing for the Mass Media*. Philadelphia: Chilton Book Co., 1972.

MacDougall, Curtis D. *Principles of Editorial Writing.* Dubuque, Ia.: Wm. C. Brown Co., 1972.

Meyer, Philip. *Precision Journalism: A Reporter's Introduction to Social Science Methods.* Bloomington, Ind.: Indiana State University Press, 1975.

Reddick, DeWitt C. *Literary Style in Science Writing.* New York: Magazine Publishers Association, 1969.

Schapper, Beatrice (ed.). *Writing the Magazine Article from Idea to Printed Page.* Cincinnati: Writer's Digest, 1970.

Waldrop, Arthur G. *Editor and Editorial Writer.* Dubuque, Ia.: Wm. C. Brown Co., 1967.

JOURNALISM AND SOCIETY

(Freedom of the Press, Journalistic Ethics, Legal Aspects of Journalism, Public Opinion and Propaganda)

Bagdikain, Ben H. *The Effete Conspiracy and Other Crimes of the Press.* New York: Harper & Row, 1972.

Bettinghaus, Erwin Paul. *Persuasive Communication.* New York: Holt, Rinehart and Winston, 1968.

Bush, Chilton R (ed.). *Free Press and Fair Trial.* Athens, Ga.: University of Georgia Press, 1970.

Emery, Edwin. *The Press and America.* 3rd ed. Englewood Cliffs, N.J.: Prentice-Hall, 1972.

Emery, Michael C. and Ted Curtis Smythe. *Readings in Mass Communications: Concepts and Issues in the Mass Media.* Dubuque, Ia.: Wm. C. Brown Co., 1972.

Emery, Walter Bryon. *Broadcasting and Government: Responsibilities and Regulations.* Rev. ed. East Lansing, Mich.: Michigan State University Press, 1971.

Gross, Gerald (ed.). *The Responsibility of the Press.* New York: Simon and Schuster, 1966.

Hohenberg, John. *A Crisis for the American Press.* New York: Columbia University Press, 1978.

Knappman, Edward W. (ed.). *Government & the Media in Conflict/1970–74.* New York: Facts on File, 1974.

Krieghbaum, Hillier. *Pressures on the Press.* New York: Thomas Y. Crowell Co., 1972.

MacDougall, Curtis D. *Understanding Public Opinion.* Dubuque, Ia.: Wm. C. Brown Co., 1966.

Merril, John C. and Ralph L. Lowenstein. *Media Messages and Men.* New York: David McKay Co., 1971.

Pember, Don R. *Mass Media in America.* Chicago: Science Research Associates, 1974.

Phelan, John (ed.). *Communications Control: Readings in the Motives and Structure of Censorship.* New York: Sheed and Ward, 1969.

Nelson, Harold L. and DeWight L. Teeter, Jr. *Law of Mass Communications.* Mineola, N.Y.: The Foundation Press, 1973.

Rivers, William L., Theodore Peterson and Jay W. Jensen. *The Mass Media and Modern Society.* 2nd ed. San Francisco: Rinehart Press, 1971.

Rucker, Bryce W. *The First Freedom*. Carbondale, Ill.: Southern Illinois University Press, 1968.

Schramm, Wilbur Lang. *The Process and Effects of Mass Communication*. Rev. ed. Urbana, Ill.: University of Illinois Press, 1971.

Siebert, Frederick, Theodore Peterson, and Wilbur Schramm. *Four Theories of the Press*. Urbana, Ill.: University of Illinois Press, 1956.

Wicker, Tom. *On Press*. New York: The Viking Press, 1978.

REFERENCES ON EDITING THE NEWS

Arnold, Edmund G. *Modern Newspaper Design*. New York: Harper & Row, 1969.

Craig, James. *Designing with Type: A Basic Course in Typography*. New York: Watson-Guptill Publications, 1971.

Crowell, Alfred A. *Creative News Editing*. Dubuque, Ia.: Wm. C. Brown Co., 1969.

Baskette, Floyd K. and Jack Z. Sissors. *The Art of Editing*. 2nd ed. New York: Macmillan, 1977.

Nelson, Roy Paul. *Publications Design*. Dubuque, Ia.: Wm. C. Brown Co., 1972.

Riblet, Carl, Jr. *The Solid Gold Copy Editor*. Chicago: Aldine, 1972.

Westley, Bruce H. *News Editing*. 2nd ed. Boston: Houghton Mifflin, 1972.

A

Abbreviations, in headlines, 454; in
  stories, 54
Accident stories, 36, 256–263
Accuracy, copyreader's duties, 427; in
  headlines, 451; in reporting, 43, 44,
  67
Accuracy in Media (AIM), 11
Active voice, 45; in headlines, 453
Address, in identification, 46
Adds, to stories, 175–176
Adjectives, unnecessary, 43
Advertising, 6, 14, 15
Agee, James, 404
Agricultural news, 36, 322–326
Airlines, as news source, 22
American Society of Newspaper
  Editors, 66
Anniversaries as news, 264–265
Apostrophe, use of, 53
Art, critical reviews of, 407
Articles, avoiding in headlines, 455;
  unnecessary, 43
Artist, staff, 180
Associated Press, 5, 20, 482
Astronomical phenomena as news, 264
Attribution, 47–48, 90
Authority, statement of, 47–48, 90
Ayer's Directory of Publications, 6

B

Baker, Russell, 416
Balanced makeup, front page, 467; in-
  side page, 469
Banks, headlines, 447
Barron, John, 71
Beats, news, 21–22
Beg-your-pardon notices, 75
Bibliography, 488–492
Birth announcements, 376
Block paragraphs, 148
Body of the story, 135–157; chronolog-
  ical order, 144–147; developing sev-
  eral features, 137–144; developing
  single feature, 136–137; logical
  order, 135; multiple casualties,
143–144; quote-summary-quote,
  225–226; surprise climax, 165–167
Books, critical reviews, 400–403
Brace makeup, front page, 467
Briefs, 36, 215, 218
Broken makeup, front gage, 467–468
Bromides, 44
Buckley, William, 416
Bulletin, 176
Business department, 14–15
Business houses, as news sources, 21,
  37
Business manager, 14–15
Business news, 326–339
Byline writer, 5

C

Campaigns, political, 307, 317–321
Capitalization of letters, 53–54
Cartoons, 206–207
Censorship, 78–81
Chamber of commerce, as news source,
  21, 328
Charities (philanthropy), 353,
  357–359
Cherry sisters case, 73
Chicago Sun-Times, 473
Chicago Tribune, 382–384, 465
Chronological order, use of, 144–147
Churches, news of, 21, 353–357
Cincinnati Enquirer, 16
Circulation department, 14–15
Circus makeup, front page, 467
City editor, functions of, 18–20
City government, forms of, 309–310
City hall, as a news source, 21
Civic organizations, as news sources, 21
Clauses, unnecessary, 44
Clinton Courier-News, 14
Code of ethics, 66
College training for journalism, 7
Colleges, journalism in, 7–8
Colon, use of, 50
Columbia Journalism Review, 11, 445
Column writing, 409, 415–416; as a
  vocation, 5; editorial, 37
Columnist, 5

Comma, use of, 50
Community chest, 21
"Complete Reporting" (interpretative writing), 92, 124, 148–149, 210–211, 226–227, 219–321, 333
Complex lead, 102–106
Composing room, functions of, 14–18
Conciseness, in news writing, 43
Confidences, keeping, 64, 65, 67
Connectives, unnecessary, 43
Constitution of U.S., 10, 78, 80
Consumer News, 377
Contrast and balance makeup, front page, 467
Conventions, news of, 22, 238–239
Copy, correction of, 57–58; preparation of newspaper, 49, preparation of radio and television, 189–197
Copyediting marks (symbols), 428–429
Copyreading, 427–428
Copyrights, 80–81
Coroner, as news source, 278
Correspondents, 18
Counting in headlines, 449–450
County courthouse, as news source, 21
County government, forms of, 311–312
County jail, as news source, 21
Court procedure, civil cases, 297–298; criminal cases, 294–297
Court stories, 36, 289–305
Creative writing, 6
Crime, court procedure, 294–298; reporting of, 274–297
Criminal libel, 75
Critical reviews, 36; avoiding libel in, 73–74; principles of, 401
Crossline headline, 446
Crusading by newspaper, 204–214
Cutlines, 181

D

Dancing, critical reviews, 405–406
Dash, use of, 51
Dateline, 20

Death stories, 248
Decks, headline, 447
Dedications as news, 240
Defamatory statements, 68–69
Democracy and journalism, 9–10
Department editors, functions of, 19
Derogatory statements, 41, 68–69
Desk men, newspaper, 420
Developing stories, 175–176
Direct quotations, 147, use of, 52
Down style, in headlines, 449
Drama, critical reviews of, 405
Drop-line headlines, 446

E

Editing, copyediting, 426–434; electronic editing, 430–433; makeup, 457–477; proofreading, 438–439
Editing as a vocation, 5
Editing symbols, copyediting, 428–429; proofreading, 443
Editor, city, 15, 22, 23; departmental, 15, 19; functions of, 15–19; lifestyle, 18, 367–377; makeup, 15, 457–471; managing, 15; sports, 15, 19, 388–396; state news, 15, 19; Sunday, 15, 19; telegraph (or wire), 15–19
Editor and Publisher Yearbook, 6
Editorial columns, 409–415
Editorializing, in news, 45; in policy stories, 204–210; puffs, 45, 409–415
Editorials, 18–19, 37, 409–415
Editorials and policy, 204–208
Education editor, 6
Education for journalism, 7–8
Education news, 36, 340–342
Elections, reporting of, 317–319
Ellsberg, Daniel, 78
Engagements, stories of, 372
English and the news style, 42
Engravings, 19
Entertainment, 36, 400–406
Ethics, Code of, 11; newspaper, 66–67

F

Fair play in the news, 67
Fairs, news of, 240
Features and human-interest stories, 158–166
Federal buildings, as news sources, 21
Federal courts, 21, 290–295
Federal officers, as news sources, 21
Festivals, news of, 240
Figures, use of, 56
Fillers, 219
Finance in the news, 326–332
Fine arts, news of, 400–407
Fire departments, as news sources, 21, 256–258
Firestone, Mary Alice, 70
Fire stories, 256–258, 267–268
Five W's, playing up a W, 89–92
Flesch, Rudolph, 89
Flush headline, 446
Follow-ups, 171–173
Fourth estate, 10
Fractions, style for, 55
Fraternal organizations, as news sources, 21
Free advertising, business propaganda, 327
Free enterprise, newspapers in a, 9–10
Freedom of the press, 9–10, 62, 78–80
Front-page makeup, types of, 467
Funeral homes, as news sources, 21, 245–252
Funeral stories, 245–252

G

Gannett Co. v. De Pasquale, 79
Garbling news in policy stories, 207–208
Gatlinburg Press, 205
General manager, functions of, 14–15
Gertz, Elmer, 69–70
Government, forms of, news, 310–313
Greenville Sun, 17
Guideline, 49
Gunning, Robert, 89

H

Handouts, propaganda, 327
Hanging indentation headline, 446
Headlines, abbreviations in, 454; accuracy, 451; active voice in, 453; counting in, 450; crossline, 446; drop line, 446; editing symbols, 428–429; editorial, 414; editorializing in, 455; feature story, 452; flush, 446; hanging indentation, 446; inverted pyramid, 446; passive voice in, 453; phrases in, 455; punctuation, 454; rules in writing, 451–455; schedule of, 478–479; selecting the, 450–451; slang words, 454; spelling in, 454; split words, 455; stepped line, 446; streamer, 447; subheads, 455; tense in, 453; triteness in, 453; types of, 451; use of articles, 455; verb use in, 453; voice in, 453; word division in, 455
Headlining, rules for, 451–455
Health organizations, as news source, 21
Hearst, Patty, 32
Herbert, Col. Anthony, 70–71
Highway patrol, as news source, 21, 274
Hohenberg, John, 62
Holidays, as news, 264–266
Hospital news, 21, 245–246
Hotels, as news sources, 21, 235–238
Human interest, as news value, 32–33; stories, 158–166
Hutchinson, Ronald, 71
Hyphen, use of, 51

I

Identification of persons, 46–47, 89–90
Illness stories, 245–247
Industry in the news, 21, 36, 326–333
Inserts, in stories, 176
Inside page makeup, 469
Interpretative reporting. See "Complete Reporting"

Interview stories, 222, 228–230
Invasion of private rights, 75–77
Inverted pyramid headline, 446

J

Jail blotters, as news sources, 274–277
Journalism, as profession, 8–12; training for, 7–8; vocations in, 5–6
Journalist, definition of, 3–4; qualifications of, 7–8
Journalistic terms, 482–487
Jumping stories, 460

K

Kael, Pauline, 400
Kilpatrick, James J., 416
Kingsport Times-News, 27
Knoxville Journal, 206

L

Labor news, 326, 328, 332–333
Lando, Barry, 70–71
Lawsuits, 36
Lead, cartridge, 120; combination, 106–107; complex, 102; contrast, 121, crowding the, 91; descriptive, 122; direct address, 121; direct quotation, 121; features identifying, 109; features summarizing, 111; historical allusion, 123; how, 91; literary allusion, 123; localizing, 119; novelty, 120; outstanding feature, 103; parody, 122; prominence, 119; proximity, 119; punch, 120; question, 120; quotation, 121; rhetoric in, 118; several feature, 102; single feature, 87; speech story, 224–225; staccato, 123; summary, 103; tabulation in, 107; testing a, 93; timeliness, 119; what, 90; when, 90; where, 90; who, 90; why, 91
Legislative meetings, reporting of, 311–316
Letterpress printing, 15
Libel, avoiding, 67–75

Library (morgue), 19–20
Library of Congress, 80
Literature, news of, 400–401; criticism of, 403
Localizing stories, 119
Logical order in news writing, 88–89
Loh, Jules, 42
Louisville Courier-Journal, 12, 470

M

Makeup: balanced front page, 467; brace front page, 467; broken (razzle dazzle), 467; contrast and balance front page, 467; front page, 457–568; inside page, 469; jumping stories, 460; plugging inside page, 218; related stories, 468; tombstone, 468
Makeup editor, functions of, 15, 18, 457–472
Mass communications, 10
Matrix (mat), 15
McGrory, Mary, 416
Mechanical department, 14
Meetings, news of, 235–237
Mines and mining as news sources, 22
Minnelli, Liza, 74
Mitchell, John, 78
Montgomery Journal, 463
Morgue, 19–20
Motion pictures, critical reviews, 404–405; as news source, 21
Music, critical reviews of, 405–406
Must story, 23

N

Names, style in use, 55–56
National Observer, 410
Nationalities, capitalizing, 53
Newsday, 472
News Democrat, Lebanon, 466
News, definition of, 26–29; sources of, 21–22; story styles, 36–37
News editor, functions of, 15, 23
Newscasts, 191–197
News Outlook, 462

Newspaper English, 43–48
Newspaper organization, 13–20
Newspaper platform, 207
News values, 29–33; animals as, 33; conflict as, 29–30; consequence as, 30–31; disaster as, 30; eminence as, 31; human interest in, 32–33; novelty as, 31–32; progress as, 30; prominence as, 31; proximity as, 31; sex as, 33; timeliness as, 31
New York Daily News, 472
New York Times, 69, 78, 205, 402, 407, 410, 416
Nicknames, use of, 53
Novelty as news value, 31–32
Numbers, use of, 56

O

Obituaries, 245–252
Occasions, news of, 235–240
Offset printing, 15–16, 23
Ombudsmen, 12
Opportunities in journalism, 5–6
Optical Character Reader (scanner), 18

P

Paintings, critical reviews of, 407
Paragraphs in news story, 46
Parentheses, use of, 51–52
Period, use of, 50
Personal interviews, 228–230
Personals, 216
Persons, identification of, 46–47, 89–90
Pett, Saul, 85, 163–164
Philanthropy, news of, 353, 357–358
Photographers, function of, 179–186
Photographs, critical reviews of, 407
Pictures, in makeup, 179, 408–469
Place names, 53
Platform, newspaper, 207
Police records, as news sources, 21
Police station, as news source, 274
Policy in the news, 204
Post Office, as news source, 21
Political organizations, capitalizing, 53

Political reporter, 307–308
Politics, as news, 21, 306–320; newspaper policy in, 205
Precede to lead, 428
Prepositions, unnecessary, 43
Press and society, 9–10
Pressroom, functions of, 15, 24
Privacy, invasion of, 75–77
Privileged statements, 72–73
Probate court, 298
Professional organizations, as news sources, 21; status of journalism, 11–12
Programs of meetings, 235–237
Promotional stories, 21, 353–358
Proofreader, functions of, 438–439
Proofreader's symbols, 443
Proofreading, 438
Proxmire, William, 71
Public opinion, 10, 72
Public records, 308, 317
Public relations work, 6
Publications, reviews of, 403
Publisher, functions of, 6, 14–15
Punctuating, in headlines, 454; in stories, 50–56

Q

Q. and A. form, 230, 291–292
Qualifications of a reporter, 7–8
Quotation marks, in headlines, 454; in stories, 52–53
Quotations, direct, use of, 147

R

Radio, critical reviews of, 405; libel and slander on, 71–72; news writing, 191–197
Radio stations as news sources, 21
Recordings, critical reviews of, 405
Reader's Digest, 71
Reed, Rex, 228
Religion, news of, 253–256
Religious denominations, capitalizing of, 53; titles of ministers, 56
Research news, 343

Retraction of errors, 75
Rewrite men, functions of, 15, 421
Rewriting faulty stories, 421; stories in competitive newspaper, 171

S

Scanner, 18
Schools, as news source, 21, 340–343
Science editor, 343
Science news, 340–345
Sculptures, critical reviews of, 407
Seasons as news, 21, 264–265
Self-censorship, 209
Semicolon, use of in headlines, 454; in stories, 50–51
Sentences in news story, 46
Several feature story, body of, 138–144; lead, 137
Ships and shipping, as news source, 21
Simon, John, 73
Single feature story, lead, 136; writing, 135–149
Slander, 68, 71–72
Slanting the news, 207
Slug, 49
Society editor, 371
Society news, 371
Source, statement of, 41, 89–90
Speech stories, 222–226
Spelling, in headlines, 454; in stories, 49
Split words, in headlines, 455; in stories, 49
Sports editor, 15, 388
Sports news, 388–396
St. Petersburg Times, 205
Stage, critical reviews of, 405–406
State capitol, as news source, 21
State courts, 295
State government, 311–313
State news editor, functions of, 12, 20
Stepped line headline, 446
Streamer headline, 47
Style book (or style sheet), 48–58
Subheads, 455
Suicides, stories of, 280
Summary story, body of, 137–138

Sun Times, 473
Superlatives, 44
Suppressing news, 207–208
Surprise, climax story form, 165–166
Symbols, copyreading, 428–429; proofreading, 443
Syndicates, news, 20

T

Tabulation in leads, 107
Talese, Gay, 6, 42, 228
Telegraph editor, functions of, 15; news copyreading, 433–434
Television, critical reviews of, 405; libel and slander on, 71–72; newswriting, 189–196; stations as news sources, 21
Tennessee Press Association, 317
Tense, in headlines, 452; in stories, 45
Terms, journalistic, 482–487
Tieback or tie in, 174
Timeliness, as news value, 31, 34; in editorials, 411; in news leads, 119
Titles, as identification, 46; use of, 53, 55–56
Tombstone, in makeup, 460–461
Training for journalism, 8
Transitional phrases, 147
Triteness, in headlines, 453; in news stories, 45
Trivia, avoiding, 148–149
Typewriter, use of, 8

U

United Press International (UPI), 5, 20
"Up" style, 49

V

Verbosity, in stories, 42–43
Verbs, circuitous forms, 43; in headlines, 453
Video display terminal, 17, 18, 22, 23, 24, 430–431
Vocation, journalism as, 5–6
Voice, active and passive, in headlines, 443; in stories, 45

W

Wartime censorship, 78
Washington Post, 3, 12
Washington Star, 396
Weather Service, 21, 264–266
Weather as news, 21
Weddings, stories of, 372
Welfare agencies, as news sources, 21;
  see also Philanthropy
Who's Who, 19
Wicker, Tom, 27
White, E. B., 42

Wolfe, Tom, 6, 42, 228
Wolston, Ilya, 71
W's, the five; playing up, 88–92

Y

Youth organizations, as news sources,
  21

Z

Zinsser, William, 117

SIMPLE STORY TYPES

Note: in many cases "story" has been abbreviated as "Sy." on this page.)

Illness, Deaths, Funerals	18a Contents, Illness Sy.	18b Illness Features	18c Obituary	18d Death Story	18e Contents, Death Sy.	18f Objective-ness
	18g Contents, Funeral Sy.					
Fires, Accidents	19a Story Contents	19b Features F. & A.	19c Story Forms	19d Fact Reporting		
Seasons, Weather	20a Writing Seasonal Sy.	20b Contents Seasonal Sy.	20c Routine Weather Sy.	20d Special Weather Sy.	20e Contents Weather Sy.	
Crime	21a Stating Charges	21b Contents Crime Sy.	21c Features, Crime Sy.	21d Policies, Suicides	21e Contents Suicide Sy.	21f Suicide Features

COMPLEX STORY TYPES

Courts, Trials	22a Trial Features	22b Body of Trial Sy.	22c Q. & A. Forms	22d Interpreting Trials		
Government, Politics	23a Interpreting Government	23b Reporting Government	23c Covering Election	23d Interpreting Politics		
Business, Industry, Agriculture, Labor	24a Free Advertising	24b Story Forms	24c Simplifying Statistics	24d Technical Terms	24e Covering Business	24f Covering Industry
	24g Covering Agriculture	24h Covering Labor	24i Interpreting Economics			
Education, Research	25a Covering Education	25b Education Sy. Forms	25c Covering Research	25d Interpreting Research	25e Research Sy. Forms	
Religion, Philanthropy	26a Religion Section	26b Interpreting Religion	26c Promoting Philanthropy			

SPECIAL STORY TYPES

Lifestyle Section	27a Stereotyped Stories	27b Lead Features	27c Writing Style			
Sports	28a Interpreting Sports	28b Gambling in Sports	28c Sports Language	28d Sports Leads	28e Body of Sports Sy.	
Literature, Fine Arts, Criticism	29a Reviewing vs. Criticism	29b Criticism Principles	29c Writing Style	29d Books & Articles	29e Movies, Radio, TV	29f Live Performances
	29g Art					
Editorials and Columns	30a Letters to Editor	30b Timeliness of Editorials	30c Types of Editorials	30d Explaining Events	30e Appraising Events	30f Editorial Headlines
	30g Concluding Paragraph	30h Substance of Columns	30i Writing Interestingly	30j Style of Columnists		